The Changing World
of Mormonism

A drawing of Joseph Smith,
the founder of the Mormon Church.

The Changing World of Mormonism

"A condensation and revision of
Mormonism: Shadow or Reality?"

Jerald and Sandra Tanner

MOODY PRESS
CHICAGO

82-60

Second Printing, 1980

Library of Congress Cataloging in Publication Data

Tanner, Jerald, 1938-
  The changing world of Mormonism.

  Bibliography: p.
  1. Mormons and Mormonism—Doctrinal and contro-
versial works—Protestant authors. I. Tanner, Sandra, 1941—joint author. II. Title.
BX8645.T26   230'.9'33   79-18311
ISBN 0-8024-1234-3

Printed in the United States of America

Many italicized words that appear in quoted sections were added by the
authors of this book for emphasis.

Contents

A drawing of the Mormon Temple in Salt Lake City

FOREWORD

Those of us who have delved, over a period of many years, into the maze of Mormon doctrines and practices have looked with admiration and awe at the labors of Jerald and Sandra Tanner.

Probably no pseudo-Christian cult has accumulated such a volume of literature, in the creation and defense of its doctrines, as has the Church of Jesus Christ of Latter-day Saints. And no body of literature has drawn such a volume of rebuttal. Joseph Smith's writings are especially vulnerable to criticism because they were based on his dreams and visions. Smith's mother and others of Smith's associates were equally obsessed with dreams and omens, and those concepts entered quite freely into the early writings.

As Smith's successors viewed those early writings with more balanced viewpoints, they began to write defensive literature, correcting and interpreting, deleting and amending, usually without footnotes. All of that was done in such a way as to retain the integrity of the Prophet.

In the process of rewriting Joseph Smith's teachings, variant interpretations and even outright contradictions entered into the literature, all of which complicated the research of students like the Tanners. For instance, there are at least six versions of the famed First Vision of the Prophet, with his own final version, written about 1838, being the least credible. There are a dozen variations of the story of the finding and translating of the Book of Mormon's golden plates, and several versions of the experiences of the three witnesses who claimed to have seen the plates.

Jerald and Sandra Tanner were both sincere Mormons, descended from Mormon "first families." They believed the

Mormon writings and, in studying them, applied the same sincerity in examining the seeming contradictions. As they began to compare the Mormon scriptures with the Bible, they could come to only one conclusion—that the two did not agree. It was with deep conviction that they yielded to the claims of the Bible, left Mormonism, and became newborn Christians.

In this new volume of documentation, the Tanners have provided an encyclopaedia of Mormonism's lack of credibility. Their book contains no satire or spitefulness but rather a knowledgeable yearning and hoping that former Mormon friends will be converted to the Lord Jesus as a result of reading the Tanners' documented study. Certainly that has been the result in the lives of many of their readers.

With the publishing of this new volume, the authors are not finished with their task. Mormons are still making errors and are still trying to cover up the blunders of the past. The Tanners have come through many battles unflinchingly and have won the respect of their adversaries in the Mormon camp.

This volume is a must for anyone who would study the cult of Mormonism in depth.

GORDON H. FRASER

PREFACE

The Apostle Paul admonishes Christians to "Prove all things; hold fast that which is good." (1 Thessalonians 5:21) In our research on Mormonism, which has stretched out to a period of over twenty years, we have always tried to keep this statement in mind. Many writers have lifted their pens to warn the outside world against Mormonism, but very few books have been effective with the Mormons themselves. Since we were once Mormons and have a deep love and concern for our people, we have tried to produce a work that will be read and appreciated by Mormons who are seeking the truth.

As early as 1965, Wallace Turner, a correspondent for the *New York Times*, realized the effectiveness of such an approach:

> Dr. Thomas F. O'Dea, . . . insists that the church is in the midst of a crisis. . . . in keeping with Dr. O'Dea's theory of the sleeping crisis, one of the most influential apostates of the 1960s has been a young machinist, who with his wife, left the church and now makes a living printing books and documents which contradict official Mormon pronouncements.
>
> His name is Jerald Tanner. His wife, Sandra, is a great-great-granddaughter of Brigham Young. . . . They lived in the summer of 1965 in an old house at 1350 S. West Temple Street. . . . He and Nathan Eldon Tanner, the high LDS official, are both descended, he thought, from John Tanner, the man who helped Joseph Smith in the 1830s. Both the young man and his wife grew up in the LDS church. He drifted away first and she followed. . . . the three of us sat in the high-ceilinged living room of the old house and discussed the general question of how one feels on leaving the company of the Saints.
>
> "It was a long time before I could admit I didn't believe the Book of Mormon," said Sandra Tanner, dandling Brigham Young's

great-great-great grandchild on her knee. "It was weeks after that before I could say it out loud." . . .

'The Tanners operate as the Modern Microfilm Company. They specialize in copying books and documents that are out of print, or have been suppressed in one way or another, but that bear on the history and doctrine of the LDS church. When I talked with them, they had thirty-one titles for sale. . . . the Tanners have signed individual statements setting out their religious experience. Jerald Tanner wrote that he was born and reared in the Mormon church, but that he was nineteen years old before he heard the Word of Christ preached. . . . He considers himself a Protestant, a believer in Christ and in the doctrines of eternal salvation preached by Protestants. However, he now refuses to accept any of the doctrine that belongs exclusively to the LDS church. . . .

Sandra Tanner's statement shows that she had doubts about her religion, but was generally able to contain them—until "I met Jerald and we began studying the Bible and Mormonism together. As we studied I began to see the contradictions between the Bible and the teachings of the Mormon Church."

As a child she had been taught to admire her ancestor, Brigham Young. This was the point at which Jerald Tanner made his attack on her faith. He did it in Brigham's own words.

"Then Jerald had me read some of Brigham Young's sermons in the *Journal of Discourses* on Blood Atonement," Mrs. Tanner wrote. "I was shocked! I knew what Brigham Young was saying was wrong but I couldn't reconcile these sermons with the things I had always been taught concerning him. I knew these were not the words of a Prophet of God.

"As I studied I not only found errors in Mormonism, I also began to comprehend there was something wrong in my own life. As I studied God's word I realized I was a sinful hypocrite."

That day as she talked in the living room of the old house across from the ballpark in Salt Lake City, she remembered her first meeting with Jerald Tanner. She was visiting her grandmother.

"I fell in love with him," she said quite simply and without embarrassment. Then she used a typical Mormon analogy to explain what she thinks their present life purpose to be. "What we do is more of a mission, you might say," . . .

There also is the demonstration by the Tanners that an apostate from the Mormon church generally takes with him their techniques of indefatigable research and argument that he was taught while in the church's embrace. . . .

With the Tanners the church today finds itself faced by its own techniques of argument and its own words turned back against it. . . . The campaign is effective, too, and of this there is no doubt" (*The Mormon Establishment* by Wallace Turner, pages 153-160, 162. Copyright © 1966 by Wallace Turner. Reprinted by permission of Houghton Mifflin Company.)

The Mormon apologist Hugh Nibley once boasted that "of all churches in the world only this one has not found it necessary to readjust any part of its doctrine in the last hundred years" (*No Ma'am, That's Not History*, page 46). The very title of this book, *The Changing World of Mormonism*, makes it clear that we do not agree with Dr. Nibley on this matter. In this regard it is interesting to note that even while we were in the process of preparing this book, the Mormon Church made a major revision of its doctrine concerning Blacks (see Chapter 10).

ACKNOWLEDGMENTS

We are very grateful to many people and a number of libraries for their assistance. Both members and non-members of the Mormon Church have given books, pamphlets and photographs to us. A number of people have given us access to their own research. Others have helped in various ways. We are particularly indebted, however, to James Wardle, LaMar Petersen, Wesley P. Walters, Michael Marquardt, and Jerry Urban for their help. Dee Jay Nelson and Grant Heward have provided a great deal of help and valuable material on the Egyptian language and Joseph Smith's Egyptian Papyri. The University of Utah Library and the Utah State Historical Society have greatly assisted by allowing photographs to be made of many of their rare books. The Yale University Library, the Mormon Church Genealogical Library, the Brigham Young University Library and the Salt Lake Public Library have also provided help. The Reorganized Church of Jesus Christ of Latter Day Saints kindly allowed us to read microfilm copies of Joseph Smith's private diaries, correspondence, and other items. We would also like to thank the personnel at Moody Press for their patience and help. The amount of time they have spent on this project clearly demonstrates that they want an accurate and dependable book on Mormonism.

INTRODUCTION

"Oh, this stuff is dynamite!", exclaimed a prestigious director of a Mormon Institute of Religion. "I tell you, though you may not believe it, I have seen people get utterly crushed, almost devastated with some of the material that the Tanners have reproduced."

"I will tell you," he continues, "there was an Institute teacher here, not long ago . . . who lost his testimony and went out of the church on the basis of this stuff."

That description of the effects of Jerald and Sandra Tanner's publishing efforts to unmask Mormonism is hardly an overstatement.

The Church of Jesus Christ of Latter-day Saints, with its smooth public relations presentation and its well-veneered appearance, would hardly lead one to expect to find lurking beneath the surface teachings and actions that would shock the average Mormon if he knew them. Few Mormons or non-Mormons know that the founder-prophet, Joseph Smith, Jr., palmed off on the public an Egyptian funeral papyrus as the actual writings of the patriarch Abraham; or that early Mormons were encouraged to marry Indian women so that a Mormon prophecy would be fulfilled that the Indians would become a "white and delightsome people." These are but a few of the myriads of inner weaknesses, corruptions, contradictions, and suppressions of documents and information that the Tanners have uncovered and published in their twenty years of ministry to the Mormons.

Their major work, *Mormonism—Shadow or Reality?*, has sold more than thirty thousand copies without any advertising campaign, simply because it is the most definitive work in print on the fallacies of Mormonism. This condensed version of that earlier work, though still of necessity lengthy, sets forth the heart of their extensive research.

The Mormon authorities have usually answered the Tanners by the silent treatment, apparently feeling that the less exposure their work received the better it would be for the church. Recently, however, Mormon authorities have issued an anonymous reply that any reputable scholar and historian would be rightly ashamed to sign his name to. The Tanners' research has repeatedly held up under attack, especially during this most recent effort by the Mormon Church.

The difficulty with answering the Tanners, as one Mormon scholar has pointed out, is that it "would require certain admissions that Mormon history is not exactly as the Church has taught it was, that there were things taught and practiced in the nineteenth century of which the General Church membership is unaware."

It is into that startling area of the suppressed and censored, behind the facade of present respectability—to the real Mormonism that lurks in the shadows—that the Tanners lead us in their book *The Changing World of Mormonism.*

WESLEY P. WALTERS
Contributing editor
Journal of Pastoral Practice

A MARVELOUS WORK?

Chapter 1

In 1830 the Mormon Prophet Joseph Smith published the *Book of Mormon*—a book which purports to be a history of the "former inhabitants of this continent." The same year he organized a church in the state of New York.

Today, the two main groups which claim to base their teachings upon Joseph Smith's works are the Church of Jesus Christ of Latter-day Saints and the Reorganized Church of Jesus Christ of Latter Day Saints. The Church of Jesus Christ of Latter-day Saints is by far the largest of these two groups, claiming to have over four million members. Church leaders predict that if the church continues to grow at the same rate, it will have ten million members by 2000 A.D. (*Deseret News*, Church Section, October 21, 1967, p.1). At a Mormon conference meeting on March 31, 1979, it was reported that in 1978 the church had "27,669" full-time missionaries and that "152,000" converts were baptized into the church (*The Ensign*, May 1979, p.18).

Members of the Church of Jesus Christ of Latter-day Saints, headquartered in Salt Lake City, Utah, are commonly referred to as "Mormons." In this book we will deal primarily with this church.

Besides being one of the fastest growing churches in the world, the Mormon Church is one of the richest. Bill Beecham and David Briscoe comment in *Utah Holiday* Magazine:

> Today, the LDS church is a religious and financial empire with . . . assets in the billions of dollars and an income in contributions and in sales by church-controlled corporations estimated at more than $3 million a day. . . .

> There has never been an accounting of modern church income or wealth. The church's last disclosure of expenditures was made 17 years ago, when it was reported in a church General Conference that $72,794,306 was spent the previous year on the church's far-reaching religious and social programs.

A photograph of the 28-story Mormon church office building

Asked by two Associated Press reporters why this information is now withheld, President N. Eldon Tanner of the church's First Presidency said, "It was determined that continued publication of the expenditure was not desirable." He did not elaborate. Asked about church income, he replied, "I don't think the public needs to have that information." President Tanner acknowledges that one of his assignments in the church as First Counselor is to oversee the church's financial interests. . . .

Church holdings, as outlined in the Associated Press report, would rank the church among the nation's top 50 corporations in total assets—those with $2 billion or more. Church property includes more than 5,000 mostly-religious buildings throughout the world, a 36-story apartment house in New York City, a 260,000 acre ranch near Disney World in Florida, a village in Hawaii and an estimated 65 acres of business and religious property in downtown Salt Lake City, including a $33 million headquarters building (*Utah Holiday*, March 22, 1976, pp.4-6).

The *Salt Lake Tribune* for July 2, 1976, reported that Mormon President Spencer W. Kimball "was asked on the NBC 'Today' show about an Associated Press estimate last year that the church and corporations it controls bring in more than $3 million a day. . . .

"He neither disputed nor confirmed the AP estimate that would place the church among the nation's top 50 corporations in total assets."

Miraculous Claims

The validity of Mormonism rests upon the claims of Joseph Smith. When he was a young man, his family moved to the state of New York. Within a few miles of his home there was a hill, which Joseph Smith later called the Hill Cumorah. According to Joseph Smith, this was no ordinary hill, for on this hill two of the greatest battles in history were fought. Apostle Bruce R. McConkie says that "both the Nephite and Jaredite civilizations fought their final great wars of extinction at and near the *Hill Cumorah* (or *Ramah* as the Jaredites termed it), which hill is located between Palmyra and Manchester in the western part of the state of New York. It was here that Moroni hid up the gold plates from which the Book of Mormon was translated" (*Mormon Doctrine*, 1966, p.175).

Apostle McConkie further stated: "It is reported by President Brigham Young that there was in the Hill Cumorah a room containing many wagon loads of plates" (p.454).

An ordinary person would probably see nothing of importance about this hill, but to the Mormons this is one of the most important places on earth.

While Joseph Smith was digging a well for Clark Chase, he found "a chocolate-colored, somewhat egg-shaped stone" (*Comprehensive History of the Church*, by B.H. Roberts, vol. 1, p.129). This might have been just an ordinary stone (maybe a little unusual in appearance), but to Joseph Smith it became a "seer stone." This stone was supposed to have been prepared by God, and through it Joseph Smith received revelations.

Joseph Smith claimed that on the night of September 21, 1823, he had a visitor. But this was no ordinary visitor, it was an angel sent from God. The angel told Smith that gold plates were buried in the Hill Cumorah. The next day Joseph Smith found these plates, and, if his story is true, he made the greatest discovery in the history of archaeology. Archaeologists have searched for years trying to piece together the history of the ancient inhabitants of this land, but Joseph Smith turned over one stone and found all the answers. Underneath this stone he found a box which held the gold plates. The plates contained "an account of the former inhabitants of this continent, and the source from whence they sprang." More important than this, however, they contained "the fulness of the everlasting Gospel." According to the Mormon leaders, the *Book of Mormon* is far superior to the Bible because it contains the "pure" words of Christ. The Bible, they charge, has been altered by wicked priests. Mormon Apostle LeGrand Richards claims that "the 'everlasting gospel' could not be discovered through reading the Bible alone ... this is the only Christian church in the world that did not have to rely upon the Bible for its organization and government . . ." (A Marvelous Work And A Wonder, 1966, p.41).

After the Mormon church was organized, Joseph Smith gave a revelation which stated that the Saints were to gather at Jackson County, Missouri. To the Mormon leaders, this was no ordinary land; they taught that it was the place where the "Garden of Eden" was located. Apostle McConkie explains: "The early brethren of this dispensation taught that the Garden of Eden was located in what is known to us as the land of Zion, an area for which Jackson County, Missouri, is the center place" (Mormon Doctrine, p.20).

In Daviess County, Missouri, Joseph Smith found some rocks which he claimed were the remains of an altar built by Adam. McConkie continues: "At that great gathering Adam offered sacrifices on an altar built for the purpose. A remnant of that very altar remained on the spot down through the ages. On May 19, 1838, Joseph Smith and a number of his associates stood on the remainder of the pile of stones at a place called Spring Hill, Daviess County, Missouri" (Mormon Doctrine, p.21). Oliver B.

Huntington adds further details in an article published in the Mormon publication, *The Juvenile Instructor* (November 15, 1895, pp.700-701):

> Adam's Altar, . . . I have visited many times. . . . Joseph said, "That altar was built by our Father Adam and there he offered sacrifice." . . . according to the words of the Prophet Joseph, mankind in that age continued to emigrate eastwardly until they reached the country on or near the Atlantic coast; and that *in or near Carolina Noah built his remarkable ship*, in which he, his family, and all kinds of animals lived a few days over one year without coming out of it.

In the year 1835 a man came to Kirtland, Ohio, with some mummies and rolls of papyrus. Joseph Smith examined the rolls and stated that "one of the rolls contained the writings of Abraham, another the writings of Joseph of Egypt" (*History of the Church*, vol. 2, p.236). When Josiah Quincy visited Nauvoo in 1844, Joseph Smith showed him the papyrus rolls. Quincy later wrote:

> "And now come with me," said the prophet, "and I will show you the curiosities." . . . There were some pine presses. . . . These receptacles Smith opened, and disclosed four human bodies, shrunken and black with age. "These are mummies," said the exhibitor. "I want you to look at that little runt of a fellow over there. He was a great man in his day. Why, that was Pharaoh Necho, King of Egypt!" Some parchments inscribed with hieroglyphics were then offered us. . . . *"That is the handwriting of Abraham*, the Father of the Faithful," said the prophet. "This is the autograph of Moses, and these lines were written by his brother Aaron. Here we have the earliest account of the Creation, from which Moses composed the First Book of Genesis." . . . We were further assured that the prophet was the only mortal who could translate these mysterious writings, and that his power was given by direct inspiration (*Figures of the Past*, by Josiah Quincy, as cited in *Among the Mormons*, 1958, pp.136-37).

The Mormons claimed that Joseph Smith's power as a "seer" extended even beyond the earth. In February 1881 Oliver B. Huntington recorded the following in his journal:

> *Inhabitants of the Moon* are more of a uniform size than the inhabitants of the Earth, being about 6 feet in height.

> They dress very much like the quaker Style & are quite general in Style, or the one fashion of dress.

> They live to be very old; comeing [sic] generally, near a thousand years.

bad for your growing, impressionable girls. Comedies, farces, operas of the lighter sorts, dramas, concerts and negro shows are good to cheer and amuse all, even the dear innocent girls, so once a week, say, we will allow Our Girl to visit a theatre. Out of door sports in winter or summer are excellent if conducted by the proper people and in proper places. It is self-evident that reading and quiet games are beneficial to all. Yet, see to it that the book is elevating in tone and treatment, and full of such thoughts as you want impressed on the plastic young mind. The games will be interesting, if you will help to make them so. The point is, that you yourselves must enter into every one of these amusements and attend every one that you allow. your daughter to attend if that is at all possible. If you are kept at home, you will find your girls will be willing to get most of their innocent "fun" at home, if you will allow them to invite their young friends to share

their pleasure. Don't scowl and be cross when the young visitors come in, but welcome them with a smile, and do you take the lead of their fun and frolic; at least take the leading-strings in your own firm yet gentle hands, turning the current whenever it seeks to approach danger-spots, and with all the enthusiasm you can muster enter into the youthful sports and plays. I know one mother who goes down upon her knees in company with her young daughters just before the young visitors arrive and asks the blessings of God to rest within the portals of that house and upon the heart of every inmate and visitor while enjoying themselves together. I may add, the young people love to visit at that house and consider it an honor to be invited there. In one last word let me call your attention to the fact that you must insist upon one especial point in every sort and kind of amusement and that last word, that especial point, is *moderation*.

OUR SUNDAY CHAPTER.

THE INHABITANTS OF THE MOON.

O. B. HUNTINGTON.

ASTRONOMERS and philosophiers have, from time almost immemorial until very recently, asserted that the moon was uninhabited, that it had no atmosphere, etc. But recent discoveries, through the means of powerful telescopes, have given scientists a doubt or two upon the old theory.

Nearly all the great discoveries of men in the last half century have, in one way or another, either directly or indirectly, contributed to prove Joseph Smith to be a Prophet.

As far back as 1837, I know that he said that the moon was inhabited by men and women the same as this earth, and that they lived to a greater age than we do—that they live generally to near the age of a 1000 years.

He described the men as averaging near six feet in height, and dressing quite uniformly in something near the Quaker style.

In my Patriarchal blessing, given by the father of Joseph the Prophet, in Kirtland, 1837, I was told that I should preach the gospel before I was 21 years of age; that I should preach the gospel to the inhabitants upon the islands of the sea, and—to the inhabitants of the moon, even the planet you can now behold with your eyes. The first two promises have been fulfilled, and the latter may be verified.

From the verification of two promises we may reasonably expect the third to be fulfilled also.

ONE truth after another men are finding out by the wisdom and inspiration given of God to them.

The inspiration of God caused men to hunt for a new continent until Columbus discovered it. Men have lost millions of dollars, and hundreds of lives to find a country beyond the north pole; and they will yet find that country—a warm, fruitful country, in-

habited by the ten tribes of Israel, a country divided by a river, on one side of which lives the half tribe of Manasseh, which is more numerous than all the others. So said the Prophet. At the same time he described the shape of the earth at the poles as being a rounded elongation, and drew a diagram of it in this form:

which any one can readily see will allow the sun's rays to fall so near perpendicular to the center that that part of the earth may be warmed and made fruitful. He quoted scripture in proof of his theory which says that "the earth flieth upon its wings in the midst of the creations of God," and said that there was a semblance in the form of the earth that gave rise to the saying.

CEDAR FORT, Utah,
Feb. 6, 1892.

HOUSEHOLD DEPARTMENT.

DAINTY HOUSEKEEPING.

LUCY PAGE STELLE.

I HAVE in mind, as I write, one of those mirth-provoking cartoons that give one some suggestion of truth as well. It was two pictures of a kitchen that was prepared for the new servant. The first showed how tastily it was fixed with a flowering plant in the window, a pretty chintz ruffle on the mantle shelf with a comfortable rocking chair with a neat tidy upon it, and so on. The next picture showed the kitchen after Bridget had *unfixed* the place to suit herself. The flowering plant was reduced to a few dry stems. Some utensils were on the shelf, the tidy from the rocking chair was gone, and perfect havoc was wrought generally by the iconoclastic Bridget. To be sure, Bridget's early education was not conducive to elegance and refinement of surroundings, her only thought being the accomplishment of what she is paid to do.

It seems to me that a lady's sur-

A photograph of two pages from the *Young Woman's Journal*, vol. 3. This was published by the Young Ladies' Mutual Improvement Associations of Zion in 1892. Notice that O. B. Huntington claimed that Joseph Smith taught the moon was inhabited.

This is the description of them as given by Joseph the Seer, and he could "See" whatever he asked the Father in the name of Jesus to see ("Journal of Oliver B. Huntington," book 14, original at Huntington Library, San Marino, Calif.; also vol. 3, p.166 of typed copy at Utah State Historical Society).

For many years after Joseph Smith's death the Mormons continued to teach that the moon was inhabited. On July 24, 1870, Brigham Young, the second president of the Mormon church, stated: "Who can tell us of *the inhabitants* of this little planet that shines of an evening, called *the moon?* . . . when you inquire about the inhabitants of that sphere you find that the most learned are as ignorant in regard to them as the ignorant of their fellows. So it is in regard to the inhabitants of the sun. Do you think it is inhabited? I rather think it is. Do you think there is any life there? No question of it; it was not made in vain" (*Journal of Discourses*, vol. 13, p.271).

As late as 1892 the teaching that the moon was inhabited appeared in a church publication. In an article published in the *Young Woman's Journal*, O. B. Huntington stated:

> Nearly all the great discoveries of men in the last half century have, in one way or another, either directly or indirectly, contributed to prove Joseph Smith to be a Prophet.

> As far back as 1837, I know that he said the moon was inhabited by men and women the same as this earth, and that they lived to a greater age than we do, that they live generally to near the age of a 1000 years.

> He described the men as averaging near six feet in height, and dressing quite uniformly in something near the Quaker style.

> In my Patriarchal blessing, given by the father of Joseph the Prophet, in Kirtland, 1837, I was told that I should preach the gospel before I was 21 years of age; that I should preach the gospel to the inhabitants upon the islands of the sea, and—to the inhabitants of the moon, even the planet you can now behold with your eyes (*The Young Woman's Journal*, published by the Young Ladies' Mutual Improvement Associations of Zion, 1892, vol. 3, pp.263-64).

While very few Mormons today would try to defend Joseph Smith's ideas about the "inhabitants of the moon," the church still teaches that the *Book of Mormon* is Scripture, that Adam's altar is in Missouri, and that the Book of Abraham was translated from the Egyptian papyrus.

Although Joseph Smith lived to be only 38 years old, the Mormon leaders claim that he had numerous visits from "glorious personages" from heaven. Not only was he visited by God the Father and His Son Jesus Christ, but by John the Baptist, Peter, James, John, Moses, Elijah, Elias, Michael, Raphael, Nephi, Moroni, Mormon and possibly others.

It should be obvious that Joseph Smith was either one of the greatest prophets who ever walked the face of the earth, or the whole thing is a fraud from beginning to end. John Taylor, the third president of the church, set forth the issue in these terms: "... if God has not spoken, if the angel of God has not appeared to Joseph Smith, and if these things are not true of which we speak, then the whole thing is an imposture from beginning to end. There is no halfway house, no middle path about the matter; it is either one thing or the other" (*Journal of Discourses*, vol. 21, p.165).

Joseph Fielding Smith, the tenth president of the church, maintained that "Mormonism, as it is called, must stand or fall on the story of Joseph Smith. He was either a prophet of God, divinely called, properly appointed and commissioned, or he was one of the biggest frauds this world has ever seen. *There is no middle ground.*

"If Joseph Smith was a deceiver, who wilfully attempted to mislead the people, then he should be exposed; his claims should be refuted, and his doctrines shown to be false, . . . I maintain that Joseph Smith was all that he claimed to be" (*Doctrines of Salvation*, 1959, vol. 1, pp.188-89).

The Only True Church?

The Mormon church sends missionaries throughout the world with the message that God has spoken from heaven and restored the true church of Christ to the earth. These missionaries are instructed to teach that the Mormon church is the only true church and that Joseph Smith was a prophet of God. They are supposed to persuade the contact that his church is false and that he should join "the true church of Jesus Christ."

The Mormon church definitely teaches that all other churches are in a state of apostasy. More than fifty pages of the introduction to the *History of the Church of Jesus Christ of Latter-Day Saints* are devoted to proving that all churches except the Mormon church are in apostasy. The following, for example, is found on page XL: "Nothing less than a complete apostasy from the Christian religion would warrant the establishment of the Church of Jesus Christ of Latter-day Saints."

Mormons claim that in 1820 God the Father and His Son Jesus Christ visited Joseph Smith and told him that he "must join none" of the churches, "for *they were all wrong*; and the Personage who addressed me said that *all their creeds were an abomination in his sight*; that those professors were all corrupt; that: 'they draw near to me with their lips, but their hearts are far from me, they teach for doctrines the commandments of men, having a form of godliness, but they deny the power thereof' "(*Pearl of Great Price*, Joseph Smith 2:18-19).

Mormon Apostle Orson Pratt wrote: "The gates of hell have prevailed and will continue to prevail over the Catholic Mother of Harlots, and over *all* her Protestant Daughters; . . . the apostate Catholic church, with all her popes and bishops, together with all her harlot daughters shall be hurled down to hell . . ." (*Pamphlets by Orson Pratt*, p.112).

Although the present-day leaders of the Mormon church are becoming more subtle in their attacks on other churches, they still teach that the Mormon church is the only true church and that all others are in a state of apostasy.

The Mormon church makes claims that most other churches would not dare to make. Their third President John Taylor boasted: ". . . we are the only people that know how to save our progenitors, how to save ourselves, and how to save our posterity in the celestial kingdom of God; . . . we in fact are the saviours of the world . . ." (*Journal of Discoveries*, vol. 6, p.163).

Joseph Fielding Smith, tenth president, maintained that the Mormons "are, notwithstanding our weaknesses, the *best people* in the world. I do not say this boastingly, for I believe that this truth is evident to all who are willing to observe for themselves. We are morally clean, in every way equal, and in many ways *superior to any other people*" (*Doctrines of Salvation*, vol. 1, p.236).

In the *History of the Church* (vol. 7, p.287), Brigham Young even claimed that "Every spirit that confesses that Joseph Smith is a Prophet, that he lived and died a Prophet and that the *Book of Mormon* is true, is of God, and *every spirit that does not is of anti-Christ.*"

President Joseph Fielding Smith added that there is "*no salvation without accepting Joseph Smith*. If Joseph Smith was verily a prophet, and if he told the truth. . . . No man can reject that testimony without incurring the most dreadful consequences, for *he cannot enter the kingdom of God*" (*Doctrines of Salvation*, vol. 1, pp.189-90).

Thus we see that the claims of the Mormon church are of such a nature that it cannot be considered as just another church. It is either the only true church, or it is nothing but a shadow. The Mormon Apostle Orson Pratt said that if the Mormon religion had errors in it the members would be grateful if someone would point them out: "... convince us of our errors of doctrine, if we have any, by reason, by logical arguments, or by the word of God, and we will be ever grateful for the information, and you will ever have the pleasing reflection that you have been instruments in the hands of God of redeeming your fellow beings from the darkness which you may see enveloping their minds" (*The Seer*, pp.15-16). After making a long and careful study of the *Book of Mormon* and the history of the Mormon church, we have come to the conclusion that the claims made by the Mormon church leaders are false. In this book we will present some of the evidence which has led to this conclusion, in the hope that Mormons will be grateful for the information.

CHANGE, CENSORSHIP AND SUPPRESSION

Chapter 2

The fact that Mormonism is changing is very obvious to anyone who studies the history of the church. Things that were approved of when Mormonism first began are now condemned, and things that are now approved were once condemned. For instance, the Mormon church has made a major doctrinal change with regard to polygamy. John Taylor, third president, once declared: ". . . we are not ashamed . . . to declare that *we are polygamists*. . . . that we are firm, conscientious *believers in polygamy*, and that it is part and parcel of our religious creed' " (*Life of John Taylor*, p.255).

Brigham Young, the second president of the church, once stated: "The *only men who become Gods,* even the Sons of God, are those *who enter into polygamy*" (*Journal of Discourses*, vol. 11, p.269).

Today the Mormon leaders teach that "Plural marriage is *not essential* to salvation or exaltation" (*Mormon Doctrine*, 1958, p.523). Bruce R. McConkie also stated that "Any who pretend or assume to engage in plural marriage in this day, . . . are *living in adultery*, have already sold their souls to satan, and . . . will be damned in eternity" (*Ibid.*, pp.522-23).

There are a number of different doctrines—for example, rebaptism, the law of adoption and plural marriage—which were so important in the early Mormon church that God had to give special revelations concerning them, yet they were later repudiated by the Mormon leaders.

Censorship

Mormon leaders have made many important changes in the policies and doctrines of the church, but since they do not want their people to know that such changes take place, they have often altered the church records.

A prime example of a policy change that caused a number of changes in Mormon records is the attitude of the Mormon lead-

blessings which Abraham obtained, you will be polygamists at least in your faith, or you will come short of enjoying the salvation and the glory which Abraham has obtained. This is as true as that God lives. You who wish that there were no such thing in existence, if you have in your hearts to say: "We will pass along in the Church without obeying or submitting to it in our faith or believing this order, because, for aught that we know, this community may be broken up yet, and we may have lucrative offices offered to us; we will not, therefore, be polygamists lest we should fail in obtaining some earthly honor, character and office, etc,"—the man that has that in his heart, and will continue to persist in pursuing that policy, will come short of dwelling in the presence of the Father and the Son, in celestial glory. The only men who become Gods, even the Sons of God, are those who enter into polygamy. Others attain unto a glory and may even be permitted to come into the presence of the Father and the Son; but they cannot reign as kings in glory, because they had blessings offered unto them, and they refused to accept them.

The Lord gave a revelation through Joseph Smith, His servant; and we have believed and practiced it. Now, then, it is said that this must be done away before we are permitted to receive our place as a State in the Union. It may be, or it may not be. One of the twin relics—slavery—they say, is abolished. I do not, however, wish to speak about this; but if slavery and oppression and iron-handed cruelty are not more felt by the blacks to-day than before, I am glad of it. My heart is pained for that unfortunate race of men. One twin relic having been strangled, the other, they say, must next be destroyed. It is they and God for it,

and you will all find that out. It is not Brigham Young, Heber C. Kimball and Daniel H. Wells and the Elders of Israel they are fighting against; but it is the Lord Almighty. What is the Lord going to do? He is going to do just as he pleases, and the world cannot help themselves.

I heard the revelation on polygamy, and I believed it with all my heart, and I know it is from God— I know that he revealed it from heaven; I know that it is true, and understand the bearings of it and why it is. "Do you think that we shall ever be admitted as a State into the Union without denying the principle of polygamy?" If we are not admitted until then, we shall never be admitted. These things will be just as the Lord will. Let us live to take just what he sends to us, and when our enemies rise up against us, we will meet them as we can, and exercise faith and pray for wisdom and power more than they have, and contend continually for the right. Go along, my children, saith the Lord, do all you can, and remember that your blessings come through your faith. Be faithful and cut the corners of your enemies where you can—get the advantage of them by faith and good works, take care of yourselves, and they will destroy themselves. Be what you should be, live as you should, and all will be well.

Who knows but the time will come when the inquiry will be made in Washington, by the President, by the Congressmen: "Are things any worse in Utah than in Washington: than they are in New York? or in any State of the Union? are they more unvirtuous, are they more disloyal to the Government? But then there is polygamy." That has nothing in the least to do with our being loyal or disloyal, one way or the other. But is not the practice of

A photograph from the *Journal of Discourses*, vol. 11, page 269. Notice that President Brigham Young taught polygamy was essential for exaltation.

ers toward the "Word of Wisdom." The Word of Wisdom is a revelation given by Joseph Smith on February 27, 1833, forbidding the use of hot drinks, alcoholic beverages and tobacco. Mormon writer John J. Stewart wrote concerning the Word of Wisdom that "no one can hold high office in the Church, on even the stake or ward level, nor participate in temple work, who is a known user of tea, coffee, liquor or tobacco. . . .

"The Prophet himself carefully observed the Word of Wisdom, and insisted upon its observance by other men in high Church positions . . ." (*Joseph Smith the Mormon Prophet*, 1966, p.90).

In spite of this statement by John J. Stewart, the evidence shows that Joseph Smith did not keep the Word of Wisdom, and at times he would even advise others to disobey it. In a thesis written at the Mormon-operated Brigham Young University, Gary Dean Guthrie gives the following information:

"Joseph tested the Saints to make sure their testimonies were of his religion and not of him as a personable leader. Amasa Lyman, of the First Presidency, related: 'Joseph Smith tried the faith of the Saints many times by his peculiarities. At one time, he had preached a powerful sermon on the Word of Wisdom, and immediately thereafter, he rode through the streets of Nauvoo *smoking a cigar*. Some of the brethren were tried as was Abraham of old' " ("Joseph Smith As An Administrator," Master's Thesis, Brigham Young University, May 1969, p.161).

Because of the importance that is now placed upon the Word of Wisdom, most members of the Mormon church are thoroughly shocked when they find out that Joseph Smith, the man who introduced the Temple Ceremony into the Mormon church, would not be able to go through the Temple if he were living today because of his frequent use of alcoholic beverages. In his history, Joseph Smith admitted several times that he drank wine, and under the date of June 1, 1844, he stated that he had "a glass of beer at Moessers." The statement concerning the glass of beer was obviously very embarrassing to later Mormon leaders, for in recent editions of the *History of the Church* it has been deleted. When Joseph Smith's statement was first published in the *Latter-Day Saints' Millennial Star*, (vol. 23, p.720), it read as follows: "Then went to John P. Greene's, and paid him and another brother $200. *Drank a glass of beer at Moessers*. Called at William Clayton's . . . ."

When this statement was reprinted in the *History of the Church*, (vol. 6, p.424), seven words were deleted without any indication: "Then went to John P. Greene's, and paid him and another brother $200. Called at William Clayton's. . . . "

Other important changes concerning the Word of Wisdom

ment is based. That assumption may be true, but it is often false; and when neither logic nor the logician can determine which, then syllogising is mere building on the sand. Therefore it is well for us that the Lord does not arm the messenger of salvation with sophistry, but with truth, because those who have the truth and the ability to apply it can at once discern the specious falsehoods of dishonest claptrap, and send conviction and remorse into the hearts of those who thought to confound them. Witness the answers of Christ to the Scribes and Pharisees, and see also the admirable handling of Zeezrom, the lawyer, by Amulek (Book of Mormon, pars. 239-40).

Let no one suppose, however, that the mere profession of truth enables men to use this power. They must, as before stated, have the ability to apply it. Now, the Lord's mode of imparting this ability is through the gift of the Holy Ghost; and the Holy Ghost leads men into truth without the noise and clamour of debate, wherein men generally lose the very truths they are debating about, and get the spirit of the Devil, which causes them to hate and often to destroy each other. If the Saints would testify with power, or the Priesthood preach with effect, they must be earnest in their work, and so live that the good Spirit will dictate them continually.

HISTORY OF JOSEPH SMITH.

(Continued from page 706.)

A Presidential election was recently held on board the *Osprey*, and the result was as follows:—

Joseph Smith, 65 gentlemen, and 6 ladies·
Henry Clay,   27   ,,   ,,   3   ,,
Van Buren,   12   ,,   ,,   0   ,,

Friday, 31.—"State of Illinois, } ss.
     City of Nauvoo, } ss.
        May 31, 1844.

Then and there personally appeared before me, Joseph Smith, Mayor of the City of Nauvoo, the undersigned H. T. Hugins, of Burlington, Iowa Territory, and made solemn oath that Thomas B. Johnson did, on the 30th day of May, 1844, declare in his presence that he intended to bring dragoons and troops of the United States from Iowa Territory into this city, for the purpose of resisting the authority and power of the Municipal Court of said city, and that he should disregard entirely the authority of said court, and that he deemed the authority of said court of no effect. Deponent further states that said Johnson, in his said conversation, had reference to the case of Jeremiah Smith, which had been decided by said court.

              H. T. HUGINS.

Subscribed and sworn to before me, this 31st day of May, 1844,

    WM. W. PHELPS, Clerk M. C."

Upon the foregoing affidavit, I issued a *capias* to arrest T. B. Johnson for threatening the peace of the city with

United States dragoons. At 10 a.m., called at my office. At 1 p.m., called to see sister Richards, who was sick. I administered to her the laying on of hands, when she felt better. Afternoon, I attended General Council, when brother Emmett made his report. Rode out in the evening to Van Orden's, and paid him $100. Two or three Indians staid in the hall all night.

Saturday, June 1. At home. Some gentle showers.

At one, p.m., I rode out with Dr. Richards and O. P. Rockwell. Called on Davis at the Boat. Paid Manhard $90. Met George J. Adams, and paid him $50. Then went to John P. Greene's, and paid him and another brother $200. Drank a glass of beer at Moessers. Called at William Clayton's, while Dr. Richards and O. P. Rockwell called at the Doctor's new house. Returned home at 4½ p.m.

At 8 p.m., Peter Maughan, John Saunders, and Jacob Peart called at Dr. Richards' to consult about a coalbed on Rock River. I suggested that it would be profitable to employ the *Maid of Iowa* in the business of carrying the coal, &c.; and all approved of this plan.

President B. Young and Elder John E. Page held a Conference in Pittsburgh.

A photograph from *Latter-Day Saints' Millennial Star*, vol. 23, page 720. The words "Drank a Glass of Beer at Moessers" were deleted when this was reprinted in the *History of the Church*.

were made in Joseph Smith's *History*. At one time Joseph Smith encouraged some "brethren" to break the "Word of Wisdom": "It was reported to me that some of the brethren had been drinking whisky that day in violation of the Word of Wisdom.

"I called the brethren in and investigated the case, and was satisfied that no evil had been done, *and gave them a couple of dollars, with directions to replenish the bottle to stimulate them in the fatigues of their sleepless journey*" (Millennial Star, vol. 21, p.283).

When this was reprinted in the *History of the Church*, (vol. 5, p.450), the twenty-three italicized words were deleted without any indication.

Another important change was made in the *History of the Church* under the date of June 27, 1844—the day of Joseph Smith's death. In the version that was first published, Joseph Smith recommended that Apostle Willard Richards use a pipe and tobacco to settle his stomach: "Dr. Richards was taken sick, when Joseph said, 'Brother Markham, . . . go and get the Doctor *a pipe and some tobacco* to settle his stomach,' and Markham went out for *them*. When he had got *the pipe and tobacco*, and was returning to jail, . . ." (*Millennial Star*, vol. 24, p.471).

This has been changed to read as follows: "Dr. Richards was taken sick, when Joseph said, 'Brother Markham, . . . go and get the doctor *something he needs* to settle his stomach,' and Markham went out for *medicine*. When he had got the *remedies desired*, and was returning to jail, . . ." (*History of the Church*, vol. 6, p.614).

Notice that the Mormon historians tried to make it appear that Joseph Smith was recommending "medicine" rather than "a pipe and some tobacco." It would appear from the reference as it was first published that Apostle Richards was accustomed to the use of tobacco, for tobacco would certainly not settle the stomach unless a person was accustomed to its use.

At any rate, recent Mormon leaders have been very embarrassed about the early leaders' disregard for the Word of Wisdom and they have made several important changes in the *History of the Church* and other publications to cover up this change in policy.

In another chapter we will show that thousands of important changes were made in Joseph Smith's *History of the Church* and that over sixty percent of this history was compiled after Smith's death. This fact is very important because Mormon leaders have maintained that it was finished before Joseph Smith's death and that it has never been changed or tampered with. If any legal document had been changed in the same way that the *History of the Church* has, someone would be in serious trouble.

Suppression and Book-Burning

In the year 1855 the Mormon Apostle Parley P. Pratt published a book entitled *Key to the Science of Theology*. In 1965, the Mormon-owned Deseret Book Company printed the "Ninth Edition" of this book. We have compared the 1965 reprint with the original 1855 edition and find that many important changes have been made. Hundreds of words concerning the doctrine of polygamy have been deleted without any indication. Many of Apostle Pratt's statements concerning the Godhead were changed or deleted without any indication.

Joseph Smith's mother, Lucy Smith, wrote a book, *Biographical Sketches of Joseph Smith*, which was published by Apostle Orson Pratt in 1853. By the year 1865, however, Brigham Young began to frown upon this book. The first presidency of the church ordered that the book "should be gathered up and *destroyed*, so that no copies should be left" (*Latter-Day Saint's Millennial Star*, vol. 27, pp.657-58).

Later Brigham Young ordered a "committee of revision" to go through Lucy Smith's book and change it to meet with his approval. Subsequently, a new edition was published by the church. In comparing the first edition with the edition printed in 1954, we have found that 2,035 words were added, deleted or changed without any indication.

Censorship seems to be a very important thing in the Mormon church. It is apparently felt that more converts can be won to the church with a bogus history than with a factual one.

For many years the Mormon church has encouraged the destruction of publications that are critical of Joseph Smith or the church. The Mormon-owned *Deseret News* carried an article in 1953 in which tacit approval seems to be given to book burning:

> Good-natured Sven A. Wiman can manage a cautious grin when his married daughter relates . . . how when he returned home each evening from his part-time employment in various used book stores throughout Sweden he would produce an anti-Mormon book and then proceed *to burn it*. Sweden, you learn, has literally no end of anti-Church books, and Elder Wiman set himself up as a one-man cleanup committee *to destroy* as many of these diatribes against the Church as possible (*Deseret News*, Church Section, May 16, 1953, p.10).

In 1965 we were visited by a student from Brigham Young University who had recently completed a mission for the Mormon church in Texas. He related that while on his mission he was instructed to see that books critical of the Mormon church were removed from libraries. He said that he was told to take a set of new Mormon books—furnished by the church—to each library and offer them in exchange for their old books dealing with Mormonism. He said that the project was very effective in Texas, and that many of the critical books were removed from the libraries by this method. That such a project was actually carried out by some Mormon missionaries has now been verified by the Mormon writer Samuel W. Taylor. He stated:

> . . . I wonder how many good-will tours by the Tabernacle Choir would be required to repair the damage done to the Mormon image when *Playboy*, with its enormous circulation and impact on young people, published the fact that Mormon missionaries were engaged in a campaign of book-burning? The item was a letter from a librarian of Northampton, Mass., Lawrence Wikander, published first in the *American Library Association's Newsletter on Intellectual Freedom*, May, 1963, . . . Wikander told of two Elders arriving at his library to inspect the index of Mormon material. They offered a list of "more up-to-date material" and after delivering it made the following proposition:

> "Now that we had these books which told the truth about their religion, undoubtedly we would like to discard other books in the library which told lies about the Mormon Church. Other libraries, they said, had been glad to have this pointed out to them."

> Following the expose . . . a friend of mine tried to find out how extensive the missionary book-burning campaign had been. A number of returned missionaries from both domestic and foreign missions admitted that they had participated in it; but data as to when and how and by whom the project had been originated was, understandably, unavailable.

> Self-appointed Comstocks among us have for years been dedicated to the unholy quest of seeking out and destroying books considered unfavorable. . . . My brother Raymond was approached by a zealot offering a number of rare Mormon books bearing library stamps; the devout saint blandly admitted stealing them to protect the public, but said he was sure that Raymond, would not be harmed (*Dialogue: A Journal of Mormon Thought*, Summer 1967, p.26).

Because of the fact that many church policies and doctrines have changed, and since many changes were made in the vital records of the church before they were published, it became necessary for the Mormon leaders to hide these records from members of the church. In 1961 we were denied access to Joseph Smith's diaries and a number of other documents which were very important to our research. Even the most faithful Mormon scholars were often refused access to vital documents. Dr. Hugh Nibley, of Brigham Young University, was "refused" access to his great-grandfather's journal (see *Mormonism—Shadow or Reality?* pp.11-12). Ralph W. Hansen, formerly manuscript librarian for the Brigham Young University, also complained of "the relative inaccessibility to scholars of the files of the Church Historian's Office" (*Dialogue: A Journal of Mormon Thought*, Spring 1966, p.157).

After we were denied access to church records in 1961 we began a campaign to force the Mormon leaders to make these documents available. We felt that the documents belonged to the Mormon people and should be published so that all could read them. Many people criticized us saying that our efforts would only backfire and make the Mormon leaders even more determined in their policy of suppression. We hoped, however, that many members of the church would join with us in an effort to force the church historian's office to release the documents.

Although it has taken a long time, it now appears that this campaign has not been in vain. After *Dialogue: A Journal of Mormon Thought* began publication in 1966, a number of Mormon writers began openly to denounce their church's policy of suppressing the records. Joseph Fielding Smith, who was church historian at the time, had been responsible for suppressing the records for many years. When, in 1970, he became the tenth president of the church, he turned the church historian's office over to Apostle Howard W. Hunter. This did not satisfy some of the more open-minded Mormons, who by this time had become very aroused over the policy of suppression. Sometime after Howard's appointment, a group of Mormon scholars presented the Mormon leaders with a list of suggestions on how they should run the historian's office. They wanted a trained historian to be appointed as church historian. They also wanted the records to be made available to scholars and for the church itself to start printing the rare documents.

When we heard of these requests we could not see how the church leaders could possibly comply with them without undermining the entire foundation of the church. Take, for instance, the idea of appointing a qualified historian. A true historian, if he were honest with himself, could never approve of the methods used by Joseph Fielding Smith and other church historians in the past. Besides, it had become traditional for a member of the Quorum of the Twelve Apostles to fill this position. It seemed very unlikely that the church would appoint a trained historian. But on January 15, 1972 we were surprised to read the following in the *Salt Lake Tribune:* "Dr. Leonard J. Arrington, noted Utah educator and author, has been named historian of the Church of Jesus Christ of Latter-day Saints. . . ." The thing that made the appointment of Dr. Arrington most surprising, however, was that he had been critical of the church leader's policy of suppressing the documents. Writing in *Dialogue: A Journal of Mormon Thought* (Spring 1966, p.26), Dr. Arrington stated: "it is unfortunate for the cause of Mormon history that the Church Historian's Library, which is in the possession of virtually all of the diaries of leading Mormons, has not seen fit to publish these diaries or to permit qualified historians to use them without restriction."

Since Dr. Arrington's appointment, the church historical department has been more open to researchers. Nevertheless, the Mormon leaders are still not making all the documents available. For instance, a Mormon scholar told us that the journal of George Q. Cannon may never be made available because it contains so much revealing material concerning the secret Council of 50. Also, the church has still "not seen fit to publish" the diaries of Joseph Smith and other leading Mormons. We can only hope that the Mormon people will continue to exert pressure until the diaries are printed and all of the records made available to the public.

CHANGES IN THE REVELATIONS

Chapter 3

Mormon Apostle John A. Widtsoe dogmatically stated: "The *Doctrine and Covenants* is a compilation of the revelations received by Joseph Smith . . .

"The book itself is a witness for the truth of the Prophet's claims. . . . Enemies of the Church have rather carefully avoided the discussion of this book. They have been afraid of it" (*Joseph Smith–Seeker After Truth*, 1951, pp.251, 254).

Contrary to Apostle Widtsoe's statement, anti-Mormon writers have not been afraid to discuss the *Doctrine and Covenants*. In fact, they have made some rather serious charges concerning it. The most serious charge, we feel, is that the revelations found in the *Doctrine and Covenants* have been changed. Some Mormon writers have admitted that changes were made. For instance, the Mormon historian B. H. Roberts admitted that paragraphs were added to the revelations: ". . . some of the early revelations first published in the 'Book of Commandments,' in 1833, were revised by the Prophet himself in the way of correcting errors made by the scribes and publishers; and *some additional clauses were inserted . . . and paragraphs added* to make the principles or instructions apply to officers not in the Church at the time some of the earlier revelations were given" (*History of the Church*, vol. 1, p.173).

In a thesis written at Brigham Young University, John William Fitzgerald stated: "Differences in wording and differences in wording that change the meaning have occurred in certain sections that appeared first in *A Book of Commandments* published in 1833 and that appeared later in *The Doctrine and Covenants* published in 1835" ("A Study of the Doctrine and Covenants," Master's thesis, BYU, 1940, p.329).

In another thesis written at the Brigham Young University, Melvin J. Petersen acknowledged: "*Many words were added* to the revelations in order to more clearly state what Joseph Smith intended to write. . . . *Many times phrases were added* to increase the ability of the reader to get the meaning of the verse" ("A Study of the Nature of and Significance of the Changes in the

Revelations as Found in a Comparison of the Book of Commandments and Subsequent Editions of the Doctrine and Covenants," Master's thesis, BYU, 1955, typed copy, p.147).

On pages 162 and 163 of the same thesis, Mr. Petersen wrote: ". . . Joseph Smith's language, as found in the revelations credited to him, needed correcting. There were many grammatical errors in the revelations he first published. . . . Joseph Smith in revising the first published commandments, found many of them needed clarification; therefore he *enlarged upon them* in order that the meaning might be more easily discerned. . . . Certain omissions were made when unnecessary *material was deleted* from the revelations; also incidents that were past and of no significance except to a few."

On page 140 of the same thesis, Melvin J. Petersen said: "In the 1835 edition, Section thirty-two, verse three was added in the place of verses five and six. Why such a change? Joseph Smith, while reviewing the revelations, was dissatisfied with the wording of verses five and six in portraying the concept he had received, and therefore *he omitted verses five and six* of Chapter four and *rewrote in their place verse three* of the 1835 edition which is identical with Section five, verse nineteen of the present 1921 edition.

"In chapter forty-four of the *Book of Commandments* (Section forty-two, 1921 edition) *the last three verses were left off.*"

While there have been a few Mormon writers who have been willing to admit that Joseph Smith's revelations have been changed, many have not been that honest. Mormon Apostle John A. Widtsoe said that the revelations "have remained *unchanged.* There has been no tampering with God's word" (*Joseph Smith— Seeker After Truth*, p.119).

Joseph Fielding Smith, tenth president, said that "there was no need for eliminating, changing, or adjusting any part to make it fit; but each new revelation on doctrine and priesthood fitted in its place perfectly to complete the whole structure, as it had been prepared by the Master Builder" (*Doctrines of Salvation*, vol. 1, p.170).

Book of Commandments

To properly understand the changes that have been made in the revelations we must understand the history of the *Doctrine and Covenants*.

In 1833 the Mormon church published the revelations that had been given to the church by Joseph Smith in a book entitled *Book of Commandments*. The Mormon writer William E. Berrett explains: "In the latter part of 1831, it was decided by a

A photograph of the title page and President Wilford Woodruff's
Book of Commandments

council of Church leaders to compile the revelations concerning the origin of the Church and its organization. The collection was to be called the 'Book of Commandments.' . . . Joseph Smith received a revelation which was made the preface for the new volume and is now Section 1 of the Book of Doctrine and Covenants. In this preface we read: 'Search these commandments, for they are true and faithful. . . .

"After accepting the collection as scripture it was voted to print 10,000 copies" (*The Restored Church*, 1956, pp.138-39).

The church was unable to finish the printing of the *Book of Commandments* as they had planned because the printing press was destroyed by a mob. In 1835 the revelations were printed again, and the name of the book was changed to the *Doctrine and Covenants*. New revelations were added to this book and many of the previous revelations were revised. In modern editions of the *Doctrine and Covenants* we find the following on the page just after the title page:

"Certain parts were issued at Zion, Jackson County, Missouri, in 1833, under the title, Book of Commandments for the Government of the Church of Christ.

"An enlarged compilation was issued at Kirtland, Ohio, in 1835, under the title, Doctrine and Covenants of the Church of the Latter-day Saints."

The exact number of *Book of Commandments* salvaged before the mob destroyed the printing press is not known. RLDS* Church Historian Richard P. Howard thinks there may have been "several hundred at least":

> . . . the typesetting for the Book of Commandments had progressed through five large galley-proof sheets, each containing thirty-two pages (sixteen printed on either side of each sheet) or a total of 160 pages including the title page. . . . The typesetting on the Book of Commandments was interrupted, . . . by the mob depredations committed against the church . . .

> Church members managed to salvage a small number of sets of the five galley sheets already printed and later had them bound and distributed. It is impossible to determine the precise number of copies of the unfinished Book of Commandments distributed in this way, but there must have been several hundred at least, since a number of references to the Book of Commandments were made in the writings of church leaders of that period (*Restoration Scriptures*, Independence, Mo., 1969, p.200).

David Whitmer, one of the three witnesses to the *Book of Mormon*, said that the "revelations were printed in the Book of

---

*Reorganized Church of Jesus Christ of Latter Day Saints

Commandments correctly. . . . just exactly as they were arranged by Brother Joseph and the others. And when the Book of Commandments was printed, Joseph and the church received it as being printed correctly" (*An Address To All Believers In Christ*, p.56).

That the church approved of the *Book of Commandments* and used it from 1833 until 1835 can be seen from a letter written by the leaders of the Church in Missouri in July, 1834. In this letter it was stated: "It will be seen by reference to the Book of Commandments, page 135, that the Lord has said . . . 'Let no man break the laws of the land . . .' " (*History of the Church*, vol. 2, p.129).

In the same letter outsiders were advised to "examine the Bible, the Book of Mormon, and the Commandments . . ." (p.133).

David Whitmer says that "Joseph and the brethren" received the *Book of Commandments* "at first as being printed correctly, but they soon decided to print the Doctrine and Covenants" (*An Address to Believers in the Book of Mormon*, p.5). The *Doctrine and Covenants* was printed in the year 1835. Since the same revelations that were published in the *Book of Commandments* were put into the first edition of the *Doctrine and Covenants*, one would expect them to read exactly the same as when they were first published. This is not the case, however, and David Whitmer objected to what was done:

> Some of the revelations as they now appear in the Book of Doctrine and Covenants have been changed and added to. Some of the changes being of the greatest importance as the meaning is entirely changed on some very important matters; *as if the Lord had changed his mind* a few years after he give [*sic*] the revelations, and after having commanded his servants (as they claim) to print them in the "Book of Commandments;" and after giving his servants a revelation, being a preface unto His Book of Commandments, which says: "Behold this is mine authority, and the authority of my servants, and my preface unto the Book of Commandments, which I have given them to publish unto you, oh inhabitants of the earth." Also in this preface, "Behold I am God, and have spoken it; These commandments are of me." "Search these commandments, for they are true and faithful." The revelations were printed in the Book of Commandments correctly! This I know, . . . Joseph and the church received it as being printed correctly. This I know. But in the winter of 1834 they saw that some of the revelations in the Book of Commandments had to be changed, because the heads of the church had gone too far, and had done things in which they had already gone ahead of some of the former revelations. So the book of "Doctrine and Covenants"

was printed in 1835, and some of the revelations changed and added to (Letter written by David Whitmer, published in the *Saints Herald*, February 5, 1887).

For many years the Mormon leaders tried to suppress the *Book of Commandments*. They would not allow us to obtain photocopies of the book from Brigham Young University. Fortunately, however, we were able to obtain a microfilm of the copy at Yale University and had the *Book of Commandments* printed by photo-offset. Even though the newspapers in Salt Lake City would not allow us to advertize this book we were able to sell all of the copies in a short time.

Study of Changes

In order to show some of the important changes that were made in the revelations we obtained photographs of the original *Book of Commandments*. We have compared these pages with the revelations as published in the 1966 printing of the *Doctrine and Covenants* and have marked the changes on the photographs. Therefore, in the pages which follow the text is an exact photographic reproduction of the original pages of the *Book of Commandments*, and the handwriting shows the changes that would have to be made in the text to bring it into conformity with the 1966 printing of the *Doctrine and Covenants*. Although there have been many changes in the chapter headings, we have not bothered to mark them. Since we are very limited on space in this study we have selected only the pages which contain the most important changes. The reader will notice that we have assigned a letter to some of the changes that we want to discuss later in the study.

The *Book of Commandments* only had short chapters which consisted of 65 of Joseph's revelations. However, it can be shown that the changes made in these revelations did not constitute all of the changes made in the *Doctrine and Covenants*. Section 68 of the *Doctrines and Covenants* was not printed in the *Book of Commandments*, but it was printed in *The Evening and The Morning Star*. When it was reprinted in the *Doctrine and Covenants* it was changed. Commenting on that particular revelation in their book *The Book of Commandments Controversy Reviewed* (p.81), Clarence and Angela Wheaton state that "323 words were added and 21 left out." We have included a photograph of this revelation as it was first printed in *The Evening and The Morning Star* in this study. Below is a key to abbreviations for the study which follows.

Abbreviations we use are: W.A., words added; W.D., words deleted; T.C., textual change.

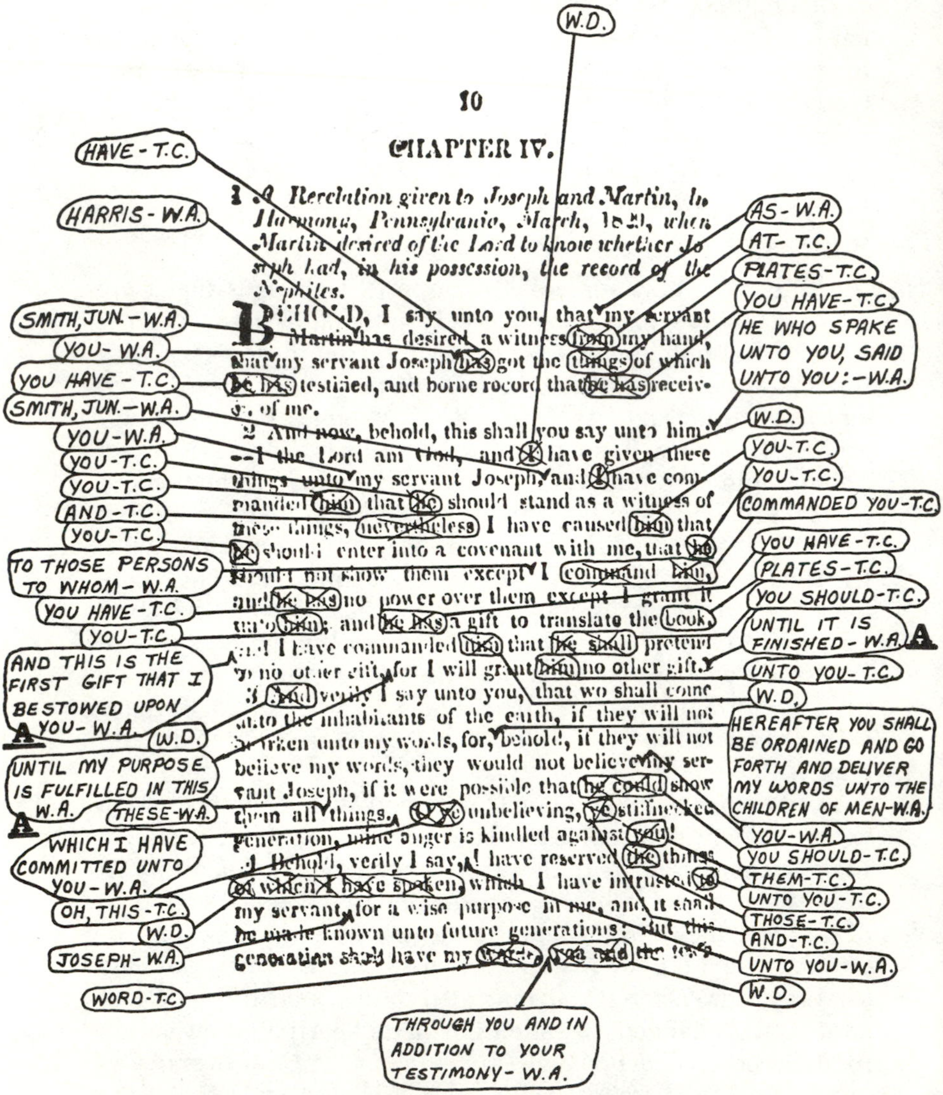

CHAPTER IV.

1. *A Revelation given to Joseph and Martin, in Harmony, Pennsylvania, March, 1829, when Martin desired of the Lord to know whether Joseph had, in his possession, the record of the Nephites.*

BEHOLD, I say unto you, that my servant Martin has desired a witness from my hand, that my servant Joseph has got the things of which he has testified, and borne record that he has received of me.

2 And now, behold, this shall you say unto him --I the Lord am God, and have given these things unto my servant Joseph, and have commanded him that he should stand as a witness of these things, nevertheless I have caused him that he should enter into a covenant with me, that he should not show them except I command him, and he has no power over them except I grant it unto him; and he has a gift to translate the book, and I have commanded him that he shall pretend to no other gift, for I will grant him no other gift.

3 And verily I say unto you, that wo shall come unto the inhabitants of the earth, if they will not hearken unto my words, for, behold, if they will not believe my words, they would not believe my servant Joseph, if it were possible that he could show them all things. And because of this unbelieving, and stiffnecked generation, mine anger is kindled against you! 4 Behold, verily I say, I have reserved the things of which I have spoken, which I have intrusted to my servant, for a wise purpose in me, and it shall be made known unto future generations: but this generation shall have my word...

Annotations (circled/boxed marginalia):

- W.D.
- HAVE - T.C.
- HARRIS - W.A.
- SMITH, JUN. - W.A.
- YOU - W.A.
- YOU HAVE - T.C.
- SMITH, JUN. - W.A.
- YOU - W.A.
- YOU - T.C.
- YOU - T.C.
- AND - T.C.
- YOU - T.C.
- TO THOSE PERSONS TO WHOM - W.A.
- YOU HAVE - T.C.
- YOU - T.C.
- AND THIS IS THE FIRST GIFT THAT I BESTOWED UPON YOU - W.A.
- W.D.
- UNTIL MY PURPOSE IS FULFILLED IN THIS - W.A.
- THESE - W.A.
- WHICH I HAVE COMMITTED UNTO YOU - W.A.
- OH, THIS - T.C.
- W.D.
- JOSEPH - W.A.
- WORD - T.C.
- AS - W.A.
- AT - T.C.
- PLATES - T.C.
- YOU HAVE - T.C.
- HE WHO SPAKE UNTO YOU, SAID UNTO YOU: - W.A.
- W.D.
- YOU - T.C.
- YOU - T.C.
- COMMANDED YOU - T.C.
- YOU HAVE - T.C.
- PLATES - T.C.
- YOU SHOULD - T.C.
- UNTIL IT IS FINISHED - W.A.
- UNTO YOU - T.C.
- W.D.
- HEREAFTER YOU SHALL BE ORDAINED AND GO FORTH AND DELIVER MY WORDS UNTO THE CHILDREN OF MEN - W.A.
- YOU - W.A.
- YOU SHOULD - T.C.
- THEM - T.C.
- UNTO YOU - T.C.
- THOSE - T.C.
- AND - T.C.
- UNTO YOU - W.A.
- W.D.
- THROUGH YOU AND IN ADDITION TO YOUR TESTIMONY - W.A.

Book of Commandments—Chapter 4
Compare Doctrine and Covenants—Sec. 5:1-11

Important Changes

As we indicated earlier, we have placed letters by some of the changes which we wish to discuss.

CHANGE A (see page 44). This is certainly one of the most significant changes in the *Doctrine and Covenants*. David Whitmer, one of the three witnesses to the *Book of Mormon*, gave this interesting information:

> After the translation of the *Book of Mormon* was finished, early in the spring of 1830, before April 6th, Joseph gave the stone to Oliver Cowdery and told me as well as the rest that he was through with it, and he did not use the stone anymore. He said he was through the work God had given him the gift to perform, except to preach the gospel. He told us that we would all have to depend on the Holy Ghost hereafter to be guided into truth and obtain the will of the Lord (*An Address To All Believers in Christ*, p.32).

The fact that Joseph Smith was not planning on doing any other work besides the *Book of Mormon* is verified by the revelation given in March of 1829. This revelation was printed in the *Book of Commandments* as chapter 4. Verse 2 reads as follows: ". . . and he has a gift to translate the book, and *I have commanded him that he shall pretend to no other gift, for I will grant him no other gift.*"

By the year 1835, when this revelation was reprinted in the *Doctrine and Covenants*, Joseph Smith had pretended to at least one other gift besides that of translating the *Book of Mormon*. He had pretended to the gift of correcting the Bible (his so-called *Inspired Version*), and a short time after this he brought forth the Book of Abraham. Certainly this revelation commanding Joseph Smith to pretend to no other gift but to translate the *Book of Mormon* could not remain in its original form. The church had decided to go beyond the *Book of Mormon* and accept Joseph Smith's other writings as Scripture. This change in church policy necessitated a change in the revelation. Therefore, it was changed to read as follows: "And you have a gift to translate the plates; and this is *the first gift that I bestowed* upon you; and I commanded that you should pretend to no other gift, *until my purpose is fulfilled in this*; for I will grant unto you no other gift until it is finished" (*Doctrine and Covenants*, 5:4).

The basic meaning of this revelation was changed by these insertions, making it appear that the Lord would grant Joseph other gifts besides that of translating the *Book of Mormon*. David Whitmer observed: "The way the revelation has been changed, twenty-two words being added to it, it would appear that God had broken His word after giving His word in plainness; com-

THAT ARE GIVEN THROUGH YOU — T.C.

WHOM I SHALL CALL AND ORDAIN, UNTO WHOM I WILL SHOW THESE THINGS, AND THEY — W.A.

IN THIS THE BEGINNING OF THE RISING UP AND THE COMING FORTH OF MY CHURCH OUT OF THE WILDERNESS—CLEAR AS THE MOON, AND FAIR AS THE SUN, AND TERRIBLE AS AN ARMY WITH BANNERS. W.A.

THEY — T.C.

FROM HEAVEN WILL I DECLARE IT UNTO THEM. W.A.

OF — T.C.

WORDS — T.C.

ON — T.C.

EVEN OF WATER AND OF THE SPIRIT—AND YOU MUST WAIT YET A LITTLE WHILE, FOR YE ARE NOT YET ORDAINED—W.A.

B

W.D. C

...y of grace of my servants shall go forth with my words to this generation; yea, they shall know of a surety that these things are true, for I will give them power, that they may behold and view these things as they are, and to none else will I grant this power, to receive this same testimony among this generation. And the testimony of three witnesses will I send forth of my word, and behold, whosoever believeth on my word, them will I visit with the manifestation of my spirit, and they shall be born of me, and their testimony shall also go forth.

5 And thus, if the people of this generation harden not their hearts, I will work a reformation among them, and I will put down all lyings, and deceivings, and priestcrafts, and envyings, and strifes, and idolatries, and sorceries, and all manner of iniquities, and I will establish my church, like unto the church which was taught by my disciples in the days of old.

6 And now if this generation do harden their hearts against my word, behold I will deliver them up unto satan, for he reigneth and hath much power at this time, for he hath got great hold upon the hearts of the people of this generation: and not far from the iniquities of Sodom and Gomorrah, do they come at this time: and behold the sword of justice hangeth over their heads, and if they persist in the hardness of their hearts, the time cometh that it must fall upon them. Behold I tell you these things even as I also told the people of the destruction of Jerusalem, and my word shall be verified at this time as it hath hitherto been verified.

7 And now I command my servant Joseph to repent, and walk more uprightly before me, and yield to the persuasions of men no more; and that he obey...

UNTO THE CONDEMNATION OF THIS GENERATION IF THEY HARDEN THEIR HEARTS AGAINST THEM; FOR A DESOLATING-SCOURGE SHALL GO FORTH AMONG THE INHABITANTS OF THE EARTH, AND SHALL CONTINUE TO BE POURED OUT FROM TIME TO TIME, IF THEY REPENT NOT, UNTIL THE EARTH IS EMPTY, AND THE INHABITANTS THEREOF ARE CONSUMED AWAY AND UTTERLY DESTROYED BY THE BRIGHTNESS OF MY COMING. W.A.

YOU — W.A.

TO — W.A.

YOU — T.C.

Book of Commandments—Chapter 4
Compare Doctrine and Covenants—Sec. 5:11-22

manding Brother Joseph to pretend to no other gift but to translate the Book of Mormon, and then the Lord had changed and concluded to grant Joseph the gift of a Seer to the Church. . . .

"May God have mercy on the heads of the church for their transgression is my prayer" (*An Address To All Believers in Christ*, pp.57-58).

CHANGE B (see page 46). Notice that the words "you must wait yet a little while, for ye are not yet ordained" have been added to this revelation. This revelation was supposed to have been given in March of 1829. Some Mormon writers have claimed that God has a right to add to His word after it is given. But, we ask, *why would the Lord wait more than five years to give them this information?* What good would it do to give them this information years later? In order for a warning to do any good it has to be given right at the time.

Many of the changes in the revelations appear to be equivalent to locking the barn door after the horse has gotten out.

CHANGE C (see page 46). Notice that 154 words have been deleted from verses 5 and 6 of this revelation. Melvin J. Petersen, a Mormon apologist, stated: "Joseph Smith . . . was dissatisfied with the wording of verses five and six in portraying the concept he had received, and therefore he omitted verses five and six of Chapter four and rewrote in their place verse three of the 1835 edition . . ." ("A Study of the Nature of and the Significance of the Changes in the Revelations . . ." typed copy, p.140). Mr. Petersen seems to feel that Joseph Smith had a perfect right to do this. Although we agree that Joseph Smith had a right to revise his own writings, we do not feel that he had a right to revise the revelations which he claimed to be the words of God. In the very first revelation that was published in the *Book of Commandments* we read:

> Behold, this is mine authority, and the authority of my servants, and my Preface unto the Book of my Commandments, . . .
>
> Search these commandments, for they are true and faithful, and the prophecies and promises which are in them, shall all be fulfilled. What I the Lord have spoken, I have spoken, and I excuse not myself, and though the heavens and the earth pass away, *my word shall not pass away* . . . (*Book of Commandments* 1:2, 7).

If these were really revelations from God, Joseph Smith could not revise them without discrediting the previous declaration.

CHANGE D (see page 48). This revelation is supposed to contain a translation of a parchment written by the apostle John. Mormons claim Smith translated this parchment by means of the Urim and Thummim. When this revelation was published in the

47

D

18

CHAPTER VI.

1 A. Revelation given to Joseph and Oliver, in Harmony, Pennsylvania, April, 1829, when they desired to know whether John, the beloved disciple, tarried on earth. Translated from parchment, written and hid up by himself.

AND the Lord said unto me, John my beloved, what desirest thou? and I said Lord, give unto me power, that I may bring souls unto thee.— And the Lord said unto me: Verily, verily I say unto thee, because thou desiredst this, thou shalt tarry till I come in my glory:

2 And for this cause, the Lord said unto Peter:— If I will that he tarry till I come, what is that to thee? for he desiredst of me that he might bring souls unto me: but thou desiredst that thou might speedily come unto me in my kingdom: I say unto thee, Peter, this was a good desire, but my beloved has undertaken a greater work.

3 Verily I say unto you, ye shall both have according to your desires, for ye both joy in that which ye have desired.

Annotations (handwritten):

- FOR IF YOU SHALL ASK WHAT YOU WILL, IT SHALL BE GRANTED UNTO YOU, W.A.
- OVER DEATH-W.A.
- UNTIL-T.C.
- DESIRED-T.C.
- DESIRED-T.C.
- THAT HE MIGHT DO MORE, OR-W.A.
- UNTO HIM-W.A.
- LIVE AND-W.A.
- AND SHALT PROPHESY BEFORE NATIONS, KINDREDS, TONGUES AND PEOPLE-W.A.
- MIGHTEST-T.C.

YET AMONG MEN THAN WHAT HE HAS BEFORE DONE. YEA, HE HAS UNDERTAKEN A GREATER WORK; THEREFORE I WILL MAKE HIM AS FLAMING FIRE AND A MINISTERING ANGEL; HE SHALL MINISTER FOR THOSE WHO SHALL BE HEIRS OF SALVATION WHO DWELL ON THE EARTH.
AND I WILL MAKE THEE TO MINISTER FOR HIM AND FOR THY BROTHER JAMES; AND UNTO YOU THREE I WILL GIVE THIS POWER AND THE KEYS OF THIS MINISTRY UNTIL I COME. —W.A.

E

Book of Commandments—Chapter 6
Compare Doctrine and Covenants—Sec. 7:1-8

Book of Commandments in 1833, it contained 143 words, but when it was reprinted in the *Doctrine and Covenants* in 1835, it contained 252 words. Thus we see that 109 words have been added.

Mormon writers are unable to explain why Joseph Smith changed this revelation. Melvin J. Petersen admitted that,

> When the 1835 edition of the Doctrine and Covenants was published this revelation had *many additions* and a few changes. . . . The additional words and sentences reveal more concerning John and his ministry. How Joseph Smith had this information revealed to him, by means of the Urim and Thummim, is not clear. . . . What part revelation played in receiving this information concerning John is not known, nor is it known as to how the translation was enacted. We do know that additions and changes were made by Joseph Smith. . . .
>
> Joseph Smith left nothing in his writings to indicate why he added to this translated version . . . and so any plausible answers will be merely conjecture ("A Study of the Nature of and the Significance of the Changes in the Revelations" typed copy pp.154-55).

Actually, there are only three logical explanations as to why this revelation does not read the same in the *Doctrine and Covenants* as it did in the *Book of Commandments*. First, before reprinting this revelation in the *Doctrine and Covenants*, Joseph Smith may have decided to falsely attribute words to the apostle John that he did not utter. This explanation would mean that Joseph Smith was guilty of deception.

Second, before the revelation was reprinted, the Lord may have shown Joseph Smith that he had not translated the parchment correctly with the Urim and Thummim and that he must add in 109 words to make it correct. This explanation would cast serious doubt upon Joseph Smith's ability as a translator. Any individual who left out 109 words in the translation of such a short document would be considered a very poor translator!

Third, Joseph Smith may have received the full text of the revelation to begin with but suppressed part of it when the *Book of Commandments* was printed. Melvin J. Petersen states: "Doctor Sidney B. Sperry, . . . has suggested that it is possible that Joseph Smith edited the translation in its first published form and then later wrote down the complete translation as it is found in our present text. Whether this suggested answer be right or wrong cannot be determined until further evidence is brought to light upon the problem" (p.155).

This explanation would also make Joseph Smith irresponsible, to say the least, because he did not put in "the little dots

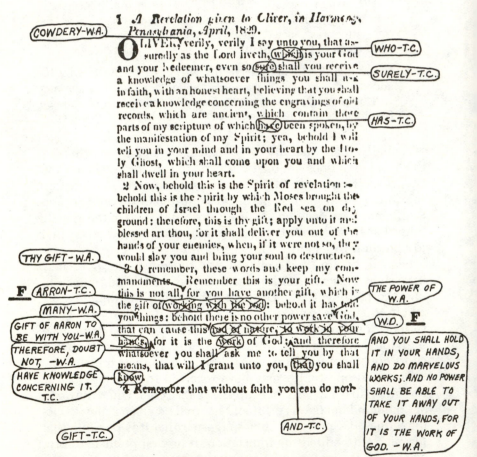

CHAPTER VII.

1 *A Revelation given to Oliver, in Harmony, Pennsylvania, April, 1829.*

OLIVER, verily, verily I say unto you, that assuredly as the Lord liveth, which is your God and your Redeemer, even so sure shall you receive a knowledge of whatsoever things you shall ask in faith, with an honest heart, believing that you shall receive a knowledge concerning the engravings of old records, which are ancient, which contain those parts of my scripture of which have been spoken, by the manifestation of my Spirit; yea, behold I will tell you in your mind and in your heart by the Holy Ghost, which shall come upon you and which shall dwell in your heart.

2 Now, behold this is the Spirit of revelation:—behold this is the spirit by which Moses brought the children of Israel through the Red sea on dry ground: therefore, this is thy gift; apply unto it and blessed art thou, for it shall deliver you out of the hands of your enemies, when, if it were not so, they would slay you and bring your soul to destruction.

3 O remember, these words and keep my commandments. Remember this is your gift. Now this is not all, for you have another gift, which is the gift of working with the rod: behold it has told you things: behold there is no other power save God, that can cause this rod of nature, to work in your hands, for it is the work of God; and therefore whatsoever you shall ask me to tell you by that means, that will I grant unto you, that you shall know.

4 Remember that without faith you can do noth-

Book of Commandments—Chapter 7
Compare Doctrine and Covenants—Sec. 8:1-10

Annotations:
- COWDERY–W.A.
- WHO–T.C.
- SURELY–T.C.
- HAS–T.C.
- THY GIFT–W.A.
- ARRON–T.C.
- MANY–W.A.
- THE POWER OF W.A.
- GIFT OF AARON TO BE WITH YOU–W.A.
- THEREFORE, DOUBT NOT, –W.A.
- HAVE KNOWLEDGE CONCERNING IT. T.C.
- W.D.
- GIFT–T.C.
- AND–T.C.
- AND YOU SHALL HOLD IT IN YOUR HANDS, AND DO MARVELOUS WORKS; AND NO POWER SHALL BE ABLE TO TAKE IT AWAY OUT OF YOUR HANDS, FOR IT IS THE WORK OF GOD. –W.A.

CHAPTER IX.

1 A Revelation given to Joseph, in Harmony, Pennsylvania, May, 1829, informing him of the alteration of the Manuscript of the fore part of the book of Mormon.

NOW, behold I say unto you, that because you delivered up so many writings, which you had power to translate, into the hands of a wicked man, you have lost them, and you also lost your gift at the same time, nevertheless it has been restored unto you again: therefore, see that you are faithful and go on unto the finishing of the remainder of the work as you have begun. Do not run faster than you have strength and means provided to translate, but be diligent unto the end, that you may come off conquerer; yea, that you may conquer satan, and those that do uphold his work.

2 Behold they have sought to destroy you; yea, even the man in whom you have trusted, and for this cause I said, that he is a wicked man, for he has sought to take away the things wherewith you have been intrusted; and he has also sought to destroy your gift, and because you have delivered the writings into his hands, behold they have taken them from you: therefore, you have delivered them up; yea, that which was sacred unto wickedness. And behold, satan has put it into their hearts to alter the words which you have caused to be written, or which you have translated, which have gone out of your hands; and behold I say unto you, that because they have altered the words, they read contrary from that which you translated and caused to be written; and so in this wise the devil has sought to lay a cunning

Handwritten annotations:
- GIVEN UNTO YOU — W.A.
- BY THE MEANS OF THE URIM AND THUMMIM, — W.A.
- AND YOUR MIND BECAME DARKENED — W.A.
- CONTINUE — T.C.
- PRAY ALWAYS — W.A.
- HAS SOUGHT TO DESTROY YOU — W.A.
- HATH — T.C.
- THOSE — T.C.
- IS NOW — T.C.
- OF TRANSLATION — W.A.
- OR LABOR MORE — W.A.
- ENABLE YOU TO — W.A.
- THAT YOU MAY ESCAPE THE HANDS OF THE SERVANTS OF SATAN — W.A.
- W.D.
- WICKED MEN — T.C.

Book of Commandments—Chapter 9
Compare Doctrine and Covenants—Sec. 10:1-12

which indicate that one is making deletions" (a failure for which Mormons have faulted anti-Mormon writers). Furthermore, there was no real reason to suppress 109 words from the revelation. This revelation is printed on page 18 of the *Book of Commandments*, and a careful examination of this page reveals that part of the page has been left blank and that there was enough room to include these words. Space-wise there would have been no reason to suppress part of the revelation. More important, in *Mormonism–Shadow or Reality?* (p.28), we have reproduced a photograph of a copy of this revelation in the handwriting of Joseph Smith's scribe Frederick G. Williams. This photograph proves beyond all doubt that the text of the revelation now published by the Mormon church in the *Doctrine and Covenants* has been doctored, for the manuscript agrees with the *Book of Commandments*.

CHANGES E and F (pp.48, 50). The first item relates to the priesthood and the second concerns one of the most important changes in the *Doctrine and Covenants*, both of which we will discuss at a more appropriate place.

CHANGE G (p.51). The reader will notice that this revelation speaks of the translation of the *Book of Mormon*. While the first printing of the *Book of Commandments* said nothing about the name of the instrument used in the translation of the *Book of Mormon*, in the *Doctrine and Covenants* the following clause has been interpolated: "By the means of the Urim and Thummim." This is obviously an attempt to tie into the "Urim and Thummim" mentioned in the Bible (see Exod. 28:30). This must have been an afterthought, for the *Book of Mormon* never uses the words "Urim and Thummim." In a document written in the early 1830's Joseph Smith did not use the words "Urim and Thummim," but instead he stated: ". . . the Lord had prepared *spectacles* for to read the Book . . ." ("An Analysis of the Accounts Relating Joseph Smith's Early Visions," Master's thesis, Brigham Young University, 1965, p.131).

CHANGE H (p. 53). David Whitmer made the following pointed comment about this change:

> The next important change I will speak of, is made in a revelation which was given to Brothers Joseph Smith, Oliver Cowdery, and myself in Fayette, New York, June, 1829. . . . In the Book of Commandments it reads thus.
>
> "Behold I give unto you a commandment, that you rely upon the things which are written; for in them are all things written, concerning my church, my gospel, and my rock. Wherefore if you shall build up my church, and my gospel, and my rock, the gates of hell shall not prevail against you."

Spirit in many instances, that the things which you have written are true:

3 Wherefore you know that they are true; and if you know that they are true, behold I give unto you a commandment, that you rely upon the things which are written; for in them are all things written, concerning my church, my gospel, and my rock.

THE FOUNDATION OF — W.A.   *H*

UPON THE FOUNDATION OF W.A.   *H*   W.D.

4 Wherefore if you shall build up my church, and my gospel, and my rock, the gates of hell shall not prevail against you.

5 Behold the world is ripening in iniquity, and it must needs be, that the children of men are stirred up unto repentance, both the Gentiles, and also the house of Israel:

HANDS—T.C.
JOSEPH SMITH, JUN. W.A.
W.D.

6 Wherefore as thou hast been baptized by the hand of my servant, according to that which I have commanded him:

7 Wherefore he hath fulfilled the thing which I commanded him.

8 And now marvel not that I have called him unto mine own purpose, which purpose is known in me:

9 Wherefore if he shall be diligent in keeping my commandments, he shall be blessed unto eternal life, and his name is Joseph.

WHITMER W.A.

COWDERY W.A.

10 And now Oliver, I speak unto you, and also unto David, by the way of commandment:

11 For behold I command all men every where to repent, and I speak unto you, even as unto Paul mine apostle, for you are called even with that same calling with which he was called.

12 Remember the worth of souls is great in the sight of God:

REDEEMER T.C.

13 For behold the Lord your God suffered death

Book of Commandments—Chapter 15
Compare Doctrine and Covenants—Sec. 18:2-11

and take the lead of meetings; but none of these
offices is he to do when there is an elder present, but
in all cases is to assist the elder.
38 The teacher's duty is to watch over the church
always, and be with them, and strengthen them,
and see that there is no iniquity in the church, neither hardness with each other, neither lying nor back-
biting, nor evil speaking;
39 And see that the church meet together often,
and also see that all the members do their duty;
40 And he is to take the lead of meetings in the
absence of the elder or priest, and is to be assisted
always, and in all his duties in the church by the
deacons;
41 But neither the teachers nor deacons have authority to baptize nor administer the sacrament, but
are to warn, expound, exhort and teach, and invite
all to come unto Christ.
42 Every elder, priest, teacher or deacon, is to be
ordained according to the gifts and callings of God
unto him, by the power of the Holy Ghost which is
in the one who ordains him.
43 The several elders composing this church of
Christ, are to meet in conference once in three
months, or from time to time as they shall direct or
appoint, to do church business whatsoever is necessary.
44 And each priest or teacher, who is ordained by
a priest, is to take a certificate from him at the time,
which when presented to an elder, he is to give him
a license, which shall authorize him to perform the
duty of his calling.
45 The duty of the members after they are received by baptism.
46 The elders or priests are to have a sufficient

I

WHEN THERE IS NO ELDER PRESENT; BUT WHEN THERE IS AN ELDER PRESENT, HE IS ONLY TO PREACH, TEACH, EXPOUND, EXHORT, AND BAPTIZE, AND VISIT THE HOUSE OF EACH MEMBER, EXHORTING THEM TO PRAY VOCALLY AND IN SECRET AND ATTEND TO ALL FAMILY DUTIES. IN ALL THESE DUTIES THE PRIEST -T.C.

HE IS TO -W.A.

W.D.

IF OCCASION REQUIRES - W.A.

W.D.

W.D.

IF OCCASION REQUIRES W.A.

W.D.

W.D.

OR LAY ON HANDS; THEY ARE, HOWEVER, T.C.

SAID CONFERENCES T.C.

AND HE IS TO BE ORDAINED -W.A.

W.D.

AND SAID CONFERENCES ARE -W.A.

TO BE DONE AT THE TIME. THE ELDERS ARE TO RECEIVE THEIR LICENSES FROM OTHER ELDERS, BY VOTE OF THE CHURCH TO WHICH THEY BELONG, OR FROM THE CONFERENCES W.A.

WHATEVER-W.A.

W.D.

MAY-T.C.

OR DEACON -W.A.

CERTIFICATE-W.A.

SHALL ENTITLE T.C.

TO-W.A.

DUTIES-T.C.

W.D.

OR HE MAY RECEIVE IT FROM A CONFERENCE. NO PERSON IS TO BE ORDAINED TO ANY OFFICE IN THIS CHURCH, WHERE THERE IS A REGULARLY ORGANIZED BRANCH OF THE SAME, WITHOUT THE VOTE OF THAT CHURCH; BUT THE PRESIDING ELDERS, TRAVELING BISHOPS, HIGH COUNCILORS, HIGH PRIESTS, AND ELDERS, MAY HAVE THE PRIVILEGE OF ORDAINING, WHERE THERE IS NO BRANCH OF THE CHURCH THAT A VOTE MAY BE CALLED. EVERY PRESIDENT OF THE HIGH PRIESTHOOD (OR PRESIDING ELDER), BISHOP, HIGH COUNCILOR, AND HIGH PRIEST, IS TO BE ORDAINED BY THE DIRECTION OF A HIGH COUNCIL OR GENERAL CONFERENCE. W.A.

Book of Commandments—Chapter 24
Compare Doctrine and Covenants–Sec. 20:49-68

But in the Book of Doctrine and Covenants it has been changed and reads thus: "Behold I give unto you a commandment, that you rely upon the things which are written; for in them are all things written, concerning '*the foundation of*' my church, my gospel, and my rock; wherefore, if you shall build up my church '*upon the foundation of*' my gospel and my rock, the gates of hell shall not prevail against you."

The change in this revelation is of great importance; the word "them" refers to the plates—the Book of Mormon: We were commanded to rely upon it in building up the church; that is, in establishing the doctrine, the order of offices, etc. "FOR IN THEM ARE ALL THINGS WRITTEN CONCERNING MY CHURCH, my gospel, and my rock." But this revelation has been changed by man to mean as follows: That therein is not all things written concerning the church, but only all things concerning "the foundation of" the church—or the beginning of the church: that you must build up the church, beginning according to the written word, and add new offices, new ordinances, and new doctrines as I (the Lord) reveal them to you from year to year: . . . I want to repeat that I was present when Brother Joseph received this revelation through the stone: . . . I know of a surety that it was changed when printed in the Doctrine and Covenants. . . .

These changes were made by the leaders of the church, who had drifted into error and spiritual blindness. Through the influence of Sydney Rigdon, Brother Joseph was led on and on into receiving revelations every year, to establish offices and doctrines which are not even mentioned in the teachings of Christ in the written word. In a few years they had gone away ahead of the written word, so that they had to change these revelations, as you will understand when I have finished (*An Address To All Believers In Christ*, pp.58-59).

CHANGE I (p. 54). Notice that 97 words have been added. David Whitmer made this statement concerning this interpolation:

The next change of importance is in a revelation given in Fayette, New York, June, 1830. . . .

The heading over it in the Book of Commandments is as follows: "The Articles and Covenants of the Church of Christ, given in Fayette, New York, June, 1830." Two paragraphs have been added to it, having been thrust into the middle of it. Paragraphs 16 and 17 is the part added, [vv. 65-67 in current Utah ed.] which part speaks of high priests and other high offices that the church never knew of until almost two years after its beginning: As if God had made a mistake in the first organization of the church, and left out these high important offices which are all above an elder; and as if God had made a mistake and left these high offices out of that revelation when it was first given. Oh the weakness and blindness of man! (*An Address To All Believers In Christ*, p.59).

HEARKEN UNTO THE VOICE OF THE LORD YOUR GOD, WHILE I SPEAK UNTO YOU, W.A.

W.D.

SMITH - W.A.

AND IF THOU ART FAITHFUL AND WALK IN THE PATHS OF VIRTUE BEFORE ME, I WILL PRESERVE THY LIFE, AND THOU SHALT RECEIVE AN INHERITANCE IN ZION. W.A.

SMITH, JUN., W.A.

FOR VERILY I SAY UNTO YOU, ALL THOSE WHO RECEIVE MY GOSPEL ARE SONS AND DAUGHTERS IN MY KINGDOM. — W.A.

WHILE THERE IS NO ONE TO BE A SCRIBE FOR HIM, — W.A.

COWDERY W.A.

MY SERVANT W.A.

IN - T.C.

CHAPTER XXVI.

1 *A Revelation to Emma, given in Harmony, Pennsylvania, July, 1830.*

EMMA, my daughter in Zion, a revelation I give unto you, concerning my will:

2 Behold thy sins are forgiven thee, and thou art an elect lady, whom I have called.

3 Murmur not because of the things which thou hast not seen, for they are withheld from thee, and from the world, which is wisdom in me in a time to come.

4 And the office of thy calling shall be for a comfort unto my servant Joseph, thy husband, in his afflictions, with consoling words, in the spirit of meekness.

5 And thou shalt go with him at the time of his going, and be unto him for a scribe, that I may send Oliver whithersoever I will.

6 And thou shalt be ordained under his hand to expound scriptures, and to exhort the church, according as it shall be given thee by my Spirit:

7 For he shall lay his hands upon thee, and thou shalt receive the Holy Ghost, and thy time shall be given to writing, and to learning much.

8 And thou needest not fear, for thy husband shall support thee in the church:

9 For unto them is his calling, that all things might be revealed unto them, whatsoever I will according to their faith.

10 And verily I say unto thee, that thou shalt lay aside the things of this world, and seek for the things of a better.

11 And it shall be given thee, also, to make a selection of sacred Hymns, as it shall be given thee;

Book of Commandments—Chapter 26
Compare Doctrine and Covenants—Sec. 25:1-11

K

CHAPTER XXVIII.

1 *A Commandment to the church of Christ, given in Harmony, Pennsylvania, September 4, 1830.*

LISTEN to the voice of Jesus Christ, your Lord, your God and your Redeemer, whose word is quick and powerful.

2 For behold I say unto you, that it mattereth not what ye shall eat, or what ye shall drink, when ye partake of the sacrament, if it so be that ye do it with an eye single to my glory;

3 Remembering unto the Father my body which was laid down for you, and my blood which was shed for the remission of your sins:

4 Wherefore a commandment I give unto you, that you shall not purchase wine, neither strong drink of your enemies:

5 Wherefore you shall partake of none, except it is made new among you, yea, in this my Father's kingdom which shall be built up on the earth.

6 Behold this is wisdom in me, wherefore marvel not, for the hour cometh that I will drink of the fruit of the vine with you, on the earth, and with all those whom my Father hath given me out of the world:

7 Wherefore lift up your hearts and rejoice, and gird up your loins and be faithful until I come: Even so. Amen.

W.D.

AND TAKE UPON YOU MY WHOLE ARMOR, THAT YE MAY BE ABLE TO WITHSTAND THE EVIL DAY, HAVING DONE ALL, THAT YE MAY BE ABLE TO STAND. STAND, THEREFORE, HAVING YOUR LOINS GIRT ABOUT WITH TRUTH, HAVING ON THE BREASTPLATE OF RIGHEOUSNESS, AND YOUR FEET SHOD WITH THE PREPARATION OF THE GOSPEL OF PEACE, WHICH I HAVE SENT MINE ANGELS TO COMMIT UNTO YOU; TAKING THE SHIELD OF FAITH WHEREWITH YE SHALL BE ABLE TO QUENCH ALL THE FIERY DARTS OF THE WICKED; AND TAKE THE HELMET OF SALVATION, AND THE SWORD OF MY SPIRIT, WHICH I WILL POUR OUT UPON YOU, AND MY WORD WHICH I REVEAL UNTO YOU, AND BE AGREED AS TOUCHING ALL THINGS WHATSOEVER YE ASK OF ME, —W.A.

AND YE SHALL BE CAUGHT UP, THAT WHERE I AM YE SHALL BE ALSO. —W.A.

MORONI, WHOM I HAVE SENT UNTO YOU TO REVEAL THE BOOK OF MORMON, CONTAINING THE FULNESS OF MY EVERLASTING GOSPEL, TO WHOM I HAVE COMMITTED THE KEYS OF THE RECORD OF THE STICK OF EPHRAIM; AND ALSO WITH ELIAS, TO WHOM I HAVE COMMITTED THE KEYS OF BRINGING TO PASS THE RESTORATION OF ALL THINGS SPOKEN BY THE MOUTH OF ALL THE HOLY PROPHETS SINCE THE WORLD BEGAN, CONCERNING THE LAST DAYS; AND ALSO JOHN THE SON OF ZACHARIAS, WHICH ZACHARIAS HE (ELIAS) VISITED AND GAVE PROMISE THAT HE SHOULD HAVE A SON, AND HIS NAME SHOULD BE JOHN, AND HE SHOULD BE FILLED WITH THE SPIRIT OF ELIAS; WHICH JOHN I HAVE SENT UNTO YOU, MY SERVANTS, JOSEPH SMITH, JUN., AND OLIVER COWDERY, TO ORDAIN YOU UNTO THE FIRST PRIESTHOOD WHICH YOU HAVE RECEIVED, THAT YOU MIGHT BE CALLED AND ORDAINED EVEN AS AARON; AND ALSO ELIJAH UNTO WHOM I HAVE COMMITTED THE KEYS OF THE POWER OF TURNING THE HEARTS OF THE FATHERS TO THE CHILDREN, AND THE HEARTS OF THE CHILDREN TO THE FATHERS, THAT THE WHOLE EARTH MAY NOT BE SMITTEN WITH A CURSE; AND ALSO WITH JOSEPH AND JACOB, AND ISAAC, AND ABRAHAM, YOUR FATHERS, BY WHOM THE PROMISES REMAIN; AND ALSO WITH MICHAEL, OR ADAM, THE FATHER OF ALL, THE PRINCE OF ALL, THE ANCIENT OF DAYS; AND ALSO WITH PETER, AND JAMES, AND JOHN, WHOM I HAVE SENT UNTO YOU, BY WHOM I HAVE ORDAINED YOU AND CONFIRMED YOU TO BE APOSTLES, AND ESPECIAL WITNESSES OF MY NAME, AND BEAR THE KEYS OF YOUR MINISTRY AND OF THE SAME THINGS WHICH I REVEALED UNTO THEM; UNTO WHOM I HAVE COMMITTED THE KEYS OF MY KINGDOM, AND A DISPENSATION OF THE GOSPEL FOR THE LAST TIMES; AND FOR THE FULNESS OF TIMES, IN THE WHICH I WILL GATHER TOGETHER IN ONE ALL THINGS, BOTH WHICH ARE IN HEAVEN, AND WHICH ARE ON EARTH; AND ALSO WITH —W.A.

Book of Commandments—Chapter 28
Compare Doctrine and Covenants–Sec. 27

committeth adultery and repenteth not, shall be cast out; and he that committeth adultery and repenteth with all his heart, and forsaketh, and doeth it no more, thou shalt forgive him; but if he doeth it again, he shall not be forgiven, but shall be cast out.

24 Thou shalt not speak evil of thy neighbor, or do him any harm.

25 Thou knowest my laws, they are given in my scriptures, he that sinneth and repenteth not, shall be cast out.

26 If thou lovest me, thou shalt serve me and keep all my commandments; and behold, thou shalt consecrate all thy properties, that which thou hast unto me, with a covenant and a deed which can not be broken; and they shall be laid before the bishop of my church, and two of the elders, such as he shall appoint and set apart for that purpose.

27 And it shall come to pass, that the bishop of my church, after that he has received the properties of my church, that it can not be taken from the church, he shall appoint every man a steward over his own property, or that which he has received, inasmuch as is sufficient for himself and family:

28 And the residue shall be kept to administer to him who has not, that every man may receive according as he stands in need:

29 And the residue shall be kept in my storehouse, to administer to the poor and needy, as shall be appointed by the elders of the church and the bishop; and for the purpose of purchasing lands, and building up of the New Jerusalem, which is hereafter to be revealed; that my covenant people may be gathered in one, in the day that I shall come to my temple:

Book of Commandments—Chapter 44
Compare Doctrine and Covenants—Sec. 42:24-36

Marginal annotations (left):
- BUT- T.C.
- REPENTS - T.C.
- W.D.
- FOR THEIR SUPPORT -W.A.
- L OF -T.C.
- THEM -T.C.
- AND INASMUCH AS YE IMPART OF YOUR SUBSTANCE UNTO THE POOR, YE WILL DO IT UNTO ME W.A.
- OR HAS APPOINTED -W.A.
- AND -W.A.
- AGAIN, IF THERE SHALL BE PROPERTIES IN THE HANDS OF THE CHURCH, OR ANY INDIVIDUALS OF IT, MORE THAN IS NECESSARY FOR THEIR SUPPORT AFTER THIS FIRST CONSECRATION, WHICH IS A RESIDUE TO BE CONSECRATED UNTO THE BISHOP, IT -W.A.
- THOSE -T.C.
- W.D.
- HAVE -T.C.
- THEREFORE -T.C.
- AND HIS COUNCIL -W.A.
- TO HIS WANTS -T.C.
- HIGH COUNCIL T.C.

Marginal annotations (right):
- HAS COMMITTED T.C.
- IT -W.A.
- W.D.
- NOR -T.C.
- CONCERNING THESE THINGS - W.A.
- WILT -T.C.
- REMEMBER THE POOR AND -W.A.
- TO IMPART -W.A.
- OR HIGH PRIESTS, -W.A.
- HIS COUNSELORS, W.A.
- AFTER THEY ARE LAID BEFORE - W.A.
- THESE TESTIMONIES CONCERNING THE CONSECRATION OF -W.A.
- THEY- T.C.
- SHALL BE MADE ACCOUNTABLE UNTO ME -W.A.
- W.D.
- BY CONSECRATION -W.A.
- AGREEABLE TO MY COMMANDMENTS -T.C.
- BE AMPLY SUPPLIED AND -W.A.
- WHO HAS NEED -W.A.
- FROM TIME TO TIME -W.A.
- THE -W.A.
- W.D.
- FOR THE PUBLIC BENEFIT OF THE CHURCH AND BUILDING HOUSES OF WORSHIP -W.A.
- WHEN -T.C.
- THAT -T.C.
- M
- N

CHANGE J (p. 56). Notice that in this revelation Emma Smith, Joseph's wife, is told that she would be supported *"from"* the church, but in the *Doctrine and Covenants* it has been changed to make it appear that Joseph Smith would support her *"in"* the church. Mormon leaders have condemned other churches for having a paid ministry. This change seems to have been made to cover up the fact that Joseph Smith was receiving money from the church.

CHANGE K (p. 57). Notice that over 400 words have been added to this revelation. Part of the interpolation concerns the visitation of Peter, James, and John to Joseph Smith. The Mormon leaders claim that they restored the Melchizedek priesthood. David Whitmer, however, said that the Melchizedek priesthood came into the church by a process of evolution rather than by revelation. The fact that these words concerning the visitation of Peter, James, and John had to be added to the revelation tends to confirm David Whitmer's charge. We will have more to say about this in the chapter on priesthood.

CHANGE L (p. 58). In the *Book of Commandments* the Mormons were told to "consecrate *all*" their properties to the church, but in the *Doctrine and Covenants* they were told only to "consecrate *of*" their properties.

The Mormons were accused of attempting "to establish communism." The change in the revelation was evidently made to cover up the truth concerning this matter. Fawn Brodie wrote that

> Joseph Smith set up an economic order in his church which followed with a certain fidelity the life history of the typical communistic society of his time. . . . Joseph issued a revelation setting up the United Order of Enoch. . . . Private property became church property, and private profit a community spoil. . . .
>
> Whatever surplus the steward exacted from the land, or whatever profit the mechanic derived from his shop, was contributed to the church storehouse and treasury, the convert keeping only what was "needful for the support and comfort" of himself and family. The spirit of true Marxian communism—"from each according to his ability, to each according to his need"—was implicit in the whole system (*No Man Knows My History*, 1957, p.106).

Sidney Rigdon may have been the one who influenced Joseph Smith to start the United Order. Fawn Brodie mentions that "Joseph's enthusiasm for the United Order was always tempered by the fact that it was Rigdon's conception" (*Ibid.*, p.108). Joseph Smith finally decided that the United Order would not work out,

you in my own due time where the New Jerusalem shall be built.

48 And behold, it shall come to pass, that my servants shall be sent forth to the east, and to the west, to the north, and to the south; and even now let him that goeth to the east, teach them that shall be converted to flee to the west; and this in consequence of that which is to come on the earth, and of secret combinations.

49 Behold, thou shalt observe all these things, and great shall be thy reward.

50 Thou shalt observe to keep the mysteries of the kingdom unto thyself, for it is not given to the world to know the mysteries.

51 The laws which ye have received, and shall hereafter receive, shall be sufficient for you both here, and in the New Jerusalem.

52 Therefore, he that lacketh knowledge, let him ask of me and I will give him liberally and upbraid him not.

53 Lift up your hearts and rejoice, for unto you the kingdom has been given; even so: Amen.

54 The priests and teachers, shall have their stewardships given them, even as the members; and the elders are to assist the bishop in all things, and he is to see that their families are supported out of the property which is consecrated to the Lord, either a stewardship, or otherwise, as may be thought best by the elders and bishop.

55 Thou shalt contract no debts with the world, except thou art commanded.

56 And again, the elders and bishop, shall counsel together, and they shall do by the direction of the Spirit as it must needs be necessary.

57 There shall be as many appointed as must

Marginal annotations:

FORTH-T.C.

COMING-T.C.

FOR UNTO YOU IT IS GIVEN TO KNOW-T.C.

BUT UNTO THE WORLD IT IS NOT GIVEN TO KNOW THEM -T.C.

AND BE FAITHFUL-W.A.

YE SHALL OBSERVE W.A.

YE-W.A.

CHURCH COVENANTS, SUCH AS - W.A.

TO -T.C.

ESTABLISH-W.A.

WISDOM-T.C.

OR IN OTHER WORDS, THE KEYS OF THE CHURCH - W.A.

HAVE-T.C.

W.D.

STEWARDSHIPS-T.C.

OR HIGH PRIESTS WHO- W.A.

AS COUNSELERS W.A.

O

P

APPOINTED-W.A.

ARE TO HAVE-T.C.

COUNSELORS -T.C.

W.D.

BISHOP, -T.C.

OR DECIDED-W.A.

FOR THE GOOD OF THE POOR, AND FOR OTHER PURPOSES, AS BEFORE MENTIONED; OR THEY ARE TO RECEIVE A JUST REMUNERATION FOR ALL THEIR SERVICES, - W.A.

W.D.

AND THE BISHOP, ALSO, SHALL RECEIVE HIS SUPPORT, OR A JUST REMUNERATION FOR ALL HIS SERVICES IN THE CHURCH. -W.A.

Book of Commandments—Chapter 44
Compare Doctrine and Covenants—Sec. 42:62-73

THE EVENING AND THE MORNING STAR.

Vol. I. Independence, Mo. October, 1832. No. 5.

A REVELATION, GIVEN NOVEMBER, 1831.

My servant, Orson, was called, by his ordinance, to proclaim the everlasting gospel, by the spirit of the living God, from people to people, and from land to land, in the congregations of the wicked, in their synagogues, reasoning with and expounding all scriptures unto them: And behold and lo, this is an ensample unto all those who were ordained unto this priesthood, whose mission is appointed unto them to go forth: And this is the ensample unto them, that they shall speak as they are moved upon by the Holy Ghost; and whatsoever they shall speak, when moved upon by the Holy Ghost, shall be scripture; shall be the will of the Lord; shall be the mind of the Lord; shall be the word of the Lord; shall be the voice of the Lord, and the power of God unto salvation; Behold this is the promise of the Lord unto you, O ye my servants: wherefore, be of good cheer, and do not fear, for I the Lord am with you, and will stand by you; and ye shall bear record of me even Jesus Christ, that I am the Son of the living God; that I was; that I am; and that I am to come. This is the word of the Lord unto you my servant, Orson; and also unto my servant, Luke; and unto my servant, Lyman; and unto my servant William; and unto all the faithful elders of my church: Go ye into all the world; preach the gospel to every creature; acting in the authority which I have given you; baptizing in the name of the Father, and of the Son, and of the Holy Ghost; and he that believeth, and is baptized, shall be saved, and he that believeth not shall be damned; and he that believeth shall be blessed with signs following, even as it is written: And unto you it shall be given to know the signs of the times, and the signs of the coming of the Son of man; and of as many as the Father shall bear record, to you it shall be given power to seal them up unto eternal life: Amen.

And now, concerning the items in addition to the Laws and commandments, they are these:— There remaineth hereafter in the due time of the Lord, other bishops to be set apart unto the church, to minister even according to the first; wherefore it shall be an high priest who is worthy; and he shall be appointed by a conference of high priests. And again, no bishop or judge, which shall be set apart for this ministry, shall be tried or condemned for any crime, save it be before a conference of high priests; and in as much as he is found guilty before a conference of high priests, by testimony that cannot be impeached, he shall be condemned or forgiven, according to the laws of the church. And again, in as much as parents have children in Zion, that teach them not to understand the doctrine of repentance; faith in Christ the Son of the living God; and of baptism and the gift of the Holy Ghost by the laying on of the hands, when eight years old: the sin be upon the head of the parents, for this shall be a law unto the inhabitants of Zion, and their children shall be baptized for the remission of their sins when eight years old, and receive the laying on of the hands: and they also shall teach their children to pray, and to walk uprightly before the Lord. And the inhabitants of Zion shall also observe the sabbath day to keep it holy. And the inhabitants of Zion, also, shall remember their labors, in as much as they are appointed to labor, in all faithfulness, for the idler shall be had in remembrance before the Lord. Now I the Lord am not well pleased with the inhabitants of Zion, for there are idlers among them; and their children are also growing up in wickedness: They also seek not earnestly the riches of eternity, but their eyes are full of greediness. These things ought not to be, and must be done away from among them: wherefore let my servant Oliver carry these sayings unto the land of Zion. And a commandment I give unto them, that he that observeth not his prayers before the Lord in the season thereof, let him be had in remembrance before the judge of my people. These sayings are true and faithful: wherefore transgress them not, neither take therefrom. Behold I am Alpha and Omega, and I come quickly: Amen.

HYDE-W.A.
ORDINATION-T.C.
JOHNSON-W.A.
JOHNSON-W.A.
HYDE-W.A.
E. M'LELLIN-W.A.
COVENANTS-T.C.
W.D.
THEY-T.C.
REMAIN-T.C.
ARE-T.C.
PRIESTS-T.C.
W.D.
THEY-T.C.
THE PRESIDENCY OF THE CHURCH-T.C.
THIS PRESIDENCY-T.C.
COVENANTS AND COMMANDMENTS-T.C.
OR IN ANY OF HER STAKES WHICH ARE OGANIZED - W.A.
HIGH PRIEST WHO T.C.
AND IF HE REPENT HE SHALL BE-T.C.
SHALL ALSO-T.C.
OR IN ANY OF HER STAKES WHICH ARE ORGANIZED-W.A.
HEADS-T.C.
COWDERY-W.A.

THE FIRST PRESIDENCY OF THE MELCHIZEDEK PRIESTOOD, EXCEPT THEY BE LITERAL DESCENDANTS OF AARON. AND IF THEY BE LITERAL DESCENDANTS OF AARON THEY HAVE A LEGAL RIGHT TO THE BISHOPRIC, IF THEY ARE THE FIRSTBORN AMONG THE SONS OF AARON; FOR THE FIRSTBORN HOLDS THE RIGHT OF THE PRESIDENCY OVER THIS PRIESTHOOD, AND THE KEYS OR AUTHORITY OF THE SAME. NO MAN HAS A LEGAL RIGHT TO THIS OFFICE, TO HOLD THE KEYS OF THIS PRIESTHOOD, EXCEPT HE BE A LITERAL DESCENDANT AND THE FIRSTBORN OF AARON. BUT, AS A HIGH PRIEST OF THE MELCHIZEDEK PRIESTHOOD HAS AUTHORITY TO OFFICIATE IN ALL THE LESSER OFFICES HE MAY OFFICIATE IN THE OFFICE OF BISHOP WHEN NO LITERAL DESCENDANT OF AARON CAN BE FOUND, PROVIDED HE IS CALLED AND SET APART AND ORDAINED UNTO THIS POWER, UNDER THE HANDS OF THE FIRST PRESIDENCY OF THE MELCHIZEDEK PRIESTOOD. AND A LITERAL DESCENDANT OF AARON, ALSO, MUST BE DESIGNATED BY THIS PRESIDENCY, AND FOUND WORTHY, AND ANOINTED, AND ORDAINED UNDER THE HANDS OF THIS PRESIDENCY, OTHERWISE THEY ARE NOT LEGALLY AUTHORIZED TO OFFICIATE IN THEIR PRIESTHOOD.

Q

BUT, BY VIRTUE OF THE DECREE CONCERNING THEIR RIGHT OF THE PRIESTHOOD DESCENDING FROM FATHER TO SON, THEY MAY CLAIM THEIR ANOINTING IF AT ANY TIME THEY CAN PROVE THEIR LINEAGE, OR DO ASCERTAIN IT BY REVELATION FROM THE LORD UNDER THE HANDS OF THE ABOVE NAMED PRESIDENCY. —T.C.

The Evening and the Morning Star—October 1832
Compare Doctrine and Covenants–Sec. 68

and therefore it became necessary to change the revelation to cover up the original plan.

CHANGES M,N,O,P and Q. These changes are concerning priesthood, a subject we shall deal with in a later chapter.

Besides the thousands of words which were added, deleted or changed in the revelations after they were published in the *Book of Commandments* and other early publications, one whole section on marriage has been removed. Also, the Lectures on Faith, which comprised seventy pages of the 1835 edition of the *Doctrine and Covenants*, have been completely removed from later editions. Mormon writers admit that the section on marriage and the Lecturers of Faith have been removed, but very few of them will admit that there have been actual meaning changes in the revelations which are still printed in the *Doctrine and Covenants*.

All of these alterations have been made within just a little over 140 years. Imagine what would have happened to the Bible if the churches that preserved it had altered it at the same rate the Mormons have altered the *Doctrine and Covenants*. We would be lucky to have anything the way it was originally written!

Important Change in Newly-Accepted Revelation

On April 3, 1976, the Church Section of the *Deseret News* reported: "Two revelations received by former Presidents of the Church, were accepted as scripture Saturday afternoon, April 3, by vote of Church membership. . . .

"The new scriptures, which will be arranged in verses as part of the Pearl of Great Price, include the account of the Prophet Joseph Smith's vision of the Celestial Kingdom received Jan. 21, 1836. . . ."

After these two revelations were canonized by the Mormon church, Michael Marquardt, a student of Mormon history, discovered that the one concerning Joseph Smith's vision of the Celestial Kingdom had been altered. Mr. Marquardt found that this revelation was recorded in Joseph Smith's own diary under the date of January 21, 1836. In Joseph Smith's diary the revelation read as follows:

"The heavens were opened upon us and I beheld the celestial Kingdom of God, . . . I saw father Adam, and Abraham *and Michael* and my father and mother, my brother Alvin . . ." (Joseph Smith's Diary, January 21, 1836, p.136; original in LDS historical department).

When the Mormon leaders printed this revelation they deleted the words "and Michael" without any indication. It reads as follows in the *Deseret News*, Church Section, April 3, 1976: "The

heavens were opened upon us and I beheld the celestial kingdom of God, . . . I saw Father Adam and Abraham, and my father
and my mother, my brother, Alvin, . . . "

At first glance the deletion of the words "and Michael" does
not appear too important. In Mormon theology, however, a serious problem is created by the statement "I saw father *Adam*, and
Abraham *and Michael.* . . ." According to Joseph Smith's other
revelations, *Adam is Michael.* In the *Doctrine and Covenants*
107:54 we read: "And the Lord appeared unto them, and they
rose up and blessed *Adam, and called him Michael,* the prince,
the archangel." In 27:11 we read: "And also with *Michael, or
Adam,* the father of all, the prince of all, the ancient of days."
Thus it is clear that if Adam is Michael, Joseph Smith could not
have seen "*Adam,* and Abraham *and Michael.*" The Mormon
leaders must have been aware that this would create a problem
in Mormon theology, and therefore they deleted the words "and
Michael" from the revelation.

This change was apparently made sometime while the church
was under Brigham Young's leadership. The fact that the change
was made after Joseph Smith's death is evident from Mr. Marquardt's research. He found that the revelation was copied into
the handwritten manuscript of the *History of the Church* (book
B-1, p.695), with the words "*and Michael*" still included. Mr.
Marquardt also found that the words were in the duplicate copy
of the "Manuscript History," (book B-2, p.618). This is significant because the Mormon leaders did not even start the duplicate copy until almost a year *after* Joseph Smith's death (see
Brigham Young University Studies, Summer 1971, p.469). This
would mean that the change had to have been made *after*
Smith's death. By the time the revelation was published in the
Deseret News, September 4, 1852, the words "and Michael" had
been deleted. Thus it appears that the change took place sometime between 1845 and 1852 and that current Mormon leaders
have canonized a falsified revelation.

Unthinkable?

Mormon leaders have been very free in accusing others of
making changes. Apostle Mark E. Petersen says that "deliberate
falsifications and fabrications were perpetrated" in the Bible (*As
Translated Correctly,* 1966, p.4). On page 27 of the same book,
the Apostle Petersen states: "It seems unthinkable to the honest
and devout mind that any man or set of men would deliberately
change the text of the Word of God to further their own peculiar
purposes."

We certainly agree that it would be dishonest to change the   **63**

"Word of God," but we wonder how the Mormon leaders can justify the changes in Joseph Smith's revelations, since they consider them also to be the "Word of God." Bruce R. McConkie stated: "As now constituted the Doctrine and Covenants contains 136 sections. . . . Most of these sections came to Joseph Smith by direct revelation, the recorded words being those of the Lord Jesus Christ himself" (*Mormon Doctrine*, 1966, p.206).

Now, certainly after we see the charges made against the Bible by the Mormon leaders, we would expect to find Mormon writings to be completely free of changes or alterations of any kind. Of all Mormon writings we would expect the *Doctrine and Covenants* to be the most pure and free from revision. The reason for this is that the *Doctrine and Covenants* purports to be the revelations given directly from God to Joseph Smith—not just a translation. We would expect these revelations to be completely free from alteration. Yet, upon careful examination, we find thousands of words added, deleted or changed. How can the Mormon leaders explain this?

Many Mormons deny that the revelations were changed. Those who have done more study admit that changes were made but try to justify them by saying that God has a right to change His word. Melvin J. Petersen wrote:

> Once a man has been recognized and accepted as a prophet and favored with communications from God, his great responsibility is to make sure, inasmuch as he has power to do so, that those to whom the communications are directed, understand what God has revealed for them. *The power is his to revise, correct, omit, or change any of his writings* in order that he might manifest more clearly what God revealed through him. . . .
>
> A prophet cannot be justly criticized when he rewrites the commandments he received from God, for he is only doing that which is part of his role as a prophet ("A Study of the Nature of and the Significance of the Changes in the Revelations," pp.164-165)

We cannot understand how Mr. Petersen can reason in this way. David Whitmer pointed out the absurdity of such an idea when he wrote:

> Is it possible that the minds of men can be so blinded as to believe that God would give these revelations—command them to print them in His Book of Commandments—and then afterwards command them to change and add to them some words which change the meaning entirely? As if God had changed his mind entirely after giving his word? Is it possible that a man who pretends to any spirituality would believe that God would work in any such manner? (*Saints' Herald*, February 5, 1887).

In the "Explanatory Introduction" to the *Doctrine and Covenants* (p. v) we find what purports to be the testimony of the Twelve Apostles to the *Doctrine and Covenants*. Among the names signed on this purported document we find that of Apostle William E. McLellin. In later years, however, McLellin claimed that this "testimony" was a "base forgery." McLellin also had a great deal to say about the changes in the revelations. The *Salt Lake Tribune* for October 6, 1875, printed the following statement regarding McLellin: "His faith was first shaken by the changes made in the revelations. He had been careful to keep copies of the originals, presented proof that all the early revelations were changed three times, and considerably amended before they appeared in their present form."

William E. McLellin was reported as saying:

> In 1835 in Kirtland another committee was appointed to fix up the revelations for print again. . . . I was often in Joseph's office, and know positively that some of the revelations were so altered, mutilated and changed that a good scholar would scarcely know them. In one revelation I counted 20 alterations! Hence, who can depend upon them? I cannot. I will not. . . . All your trouble arises from your taking that mutilated and altered Doctrine and Covenants (*Saints' Herald*, 17:556, 557, as quoted in *Changing of the Revelations*, by Daniel Macgregor, p.6).

Since William E. McLellin was an apostle in the Mormon Church, his statements are certainly important. Even more significant, however, is the fact that David Whitmer, one of the three special witnesses to the *Book of Mormon*, would write a book in which he criticized Joseph Smith for changing the revelations. He stated that

> . . . when the Book of Doctrine and Covenants was published . . . a very few of the brethren then knew about most of the important changes that had been put in the Book of Doctrine and Covenants. In time it was generally found out, and the result was that some of the members left the church on account of it. . . . When it became generally known that these important changes had been made in the Doctrine and Covenants, many of the brethren objected seriously to it, but they did not want to say much for the sake of peace, as it was Brother Joseph and the leaders who did it. The majority of the members—poor weak souls—thought that anything Brother Joseph would do, must be all right; so in their blindness of heart, trusting in an arm of flesh, they looked over it and were led into error . . . (*An Address To All Believers In Christ*, by David Whitmer, Richmond, Mo., 1887, p.61).

On page 49 of the same book, David Whitmer charged:

> You have changed the revelations from the way they were first

given and as they are to-day in the Book of Commandments, to support the error of Brother Joseph in taking upon himself the office of Seer to the church. You have changed the revelations to support the error of high priests. You have changed the revelations to support the error of a President of the high priesthood, high counselors, etc. You have altered the revelations to support you in going beyond the plain teachings of Christ in the new covenant part of the Book of Mormon. . . . You who are now living did not change them, but you who strive to defend these things, are as guilty in the sight of God as those who did change them (*An Address To All Believers In Christ*, p.49).

JOSEPH SMITH
AND MONEY-DIGGING

Chapter 4

In the *Salt Lake City Messenger* for August, 1971, we announced one of the most important discoveries since Joseph Smith founded the Mormon church in 1830. This is the discovery by Wesley P. Walters of an original document which is more than 140 years old. This document, found in Norwich, New York, proves that Joseph Smith was a "glass looker" and that he was arrested, tried and found guilty by a justice of the peace in Bainbridge, New York, in 1826. (See photograph of this document on p.68 of this book.) The importance of this document cannot be overstated, for it establishes the historicity of the account of the trial which was first published in *Frazer's Magazine* in 1873. We quote the following from that publication:

STATE OF NEW YORK v. JOSEPH SMITH.

Warrant issued upon written complaint upon oath of Peter G. Bridgeman, who informed that one Joseph Smith of Bainbridge was a disorderly person and an imposter.

Prisoner brought before Court March 20, 1826. Prisoner examined: says that he came from the town of Palmyra, and had been at the house of Josiah Stowel in Bainbridge most of time since; had small part of time been employed by said Stowel on his farm, and going to school. That he had a certain stone which he had occasionally looked at to determine where hidden treasures in the bowels of the earth were; that he professed to tell in this manner where gold mines were a distance under ground, and had looked for Mr. Stowel several times, and had informed him where he could find these treasures, and Mr. Stowel had been engaged in digging for them. That at Palmyra he pretended to tell by looking at this stone where coined money was buried in Pennsylvania, and while at Palmyra had frequently ascertained in that way where lost property was of various kinds; that he had occasionally been in the habit of looking through this stone to find lost property for three years, but of late had pretty much given it up on account of its injuring his health, especially

A photograph of Justice Albert Neely's bill showing the costs involved in several trials in 1826. The fifth item from the top mentions the trial of "Joseph Smith the Glass Looker." When the letter "S" was repeated in documents of Joseph Smith's time, as in in the word "Glass" the two letters appeared as a "P" (see the word "Assault" in items 1, 4, 7 and 9).

We have typed out the portion of the bill which mentions Joseph Smith. This bill proves that the published court record is authentic.

same
vs
Joseph Smith
The Glass looker
March 20, 1826

Misdemeanor

To my fees in examination
of the above cause   2.68

his eyes making them sore; that he did not solicit business of this kind, and had always rather declined having anything to do with this business.

Josiah Stowel sworn: says that prisoner had been at his house something like five months; had been employed by him to work on farm part of time; that he pretended to have skill of telling where hidden treasures in the earth were by means of looking through a certain stone; that prisoner had looked for him sometimes; once to tell him about money buried in Bend Mountain in Pennsylvania, once for gold on Monument Hill, and once for a salt spring; and that he positively knew that the prisoner could tell, and did possess the art of seeing those valuable treasures through the medium of said stone; that he found the (word illegible) at Bend and Monument Hill as prisoner represented it; that prisoner had looked through said stone for Deacon Attleton for a mine, did not exactly find it, but got a p--- (word unfinished) of ore which resembled gold, he thinks; that prisoner had told by means of this stone where a Mr. Bacon had buried money; that he and prisoner had been in search of it; that prisoner had said it was in a certain root of a stump five feet from surface of the earth, and with it would be found a tail feather; that said Stowel and prisoner thereupon commenced digging, found a tail feather, but money was gone; that he supposed the money moved down. That prisoner did offer his services; that he never deceived him; that prisoner looked through stone and described Josiah Stowel's house and outhouses, while at Palmyra at Simpson Stowel's, correctly; that he had told about a painted tree, with a man's head painted upon it, by means of said stone. That he had been in company with prisoner digging for gold, and had the most implicit faith in prisoner's skill.

Arad Stowel sworn: says that he went to see whether prisoner could convince him that he possessed the skill he professed to have, upon which prisoner laid a book upon a white cloth, and proposed looking through another stone which was white and transparent, hold the stone to the candle, turn his head to book, and read. The deception appeared so palpable that witness went off disgusted.

McMaster sworn: says he went with Arad Stowel, and likewise came away disgusted. Prisoner pretended to him that he could discover objects at a distance by holding this white stone to the sun or candle; that prisoner rather declined looking into a hat at his dark coloured stone, as he said that it hurt his eyes.

Jonathan Thompson says that prisoner was requested to look for chest of money; did look, and pretended to know where it was; and prisoner, Thompson, and Yeomans went in search of it; that Smith arrived at spot first; was at night; that Smith looked in hat while there, and when very dark, and told how the chest was situated. After digging several feet, struck upon something sounding like a board or plank. Prisoner would not look again, pretending that he was alarmed on account of the circumstances relating to the trunk being buried, [which], came all fresh to his mind. That the last time he looked he discovered distinctly the two Indians who buried the trunk, that a quarrel ensued between them, and that one of said Indians was killed by the other, and thrown into the hole beside the trunk, to guard it, as he supposed. Thompson says that he believes in the prisoner's professed skill; that the board which he struck his spade upon was probably the chest, but on account of an enchantment the trunk kept settling away from under them when digging; that notwithstanding they continued constantly removing the dirt, yet the trunk kept about the same distance from them. Says prisoner said that it appeared to him that salt might be found at Bainbridge, and that he is certain that prisoner can divine things by means of said stone. That as evidence of the fact prisoner looked into his hat to tell him about some money witness lost sixteen years ago, and that he described the man that witness supposed had taken it, and the disposition of the money:

And therefore the Court find[s] the Defendant guilty. Costs: Warrant, 19c. Complaint upon oath, 25½ c. Seven witnesses, 87½ c. Recongnisances, 25 c. Mittimus, 19 c. Recongnisances of witnesses, 75 c. Suboena, 18 c.—$2.68" (*Fraser's Magazine*, February, 1873, pp.229-30).

Although the Bainbridge court record was printed a few times it did not become too well known until Fawn Brodie printed it in her book *No Man Knows My History*. Immediately after her book appeared, Mormon leaders declared that the record was a forgery (see *Deseret News*, Church Section, May 11, 1946). Apostle John A. Widtsoe stated: "This alleged court record . . . seems to be a literary attempt of an enemy to ridicule Joseph Smith. . . . There is no existing proof that such a trial was ever held" (*Joseph Smith—Seeker After Truth*, Salt Lake City, 1951, p.78).

Mormon scholars continued to deny the authenticity of the court record until Mr. Walters made his discovery in 1971. The document which Walters found is Justice Albert Neely's bill showing the costs involved in several trials in 1826. The fifth item from the top mentions the trial of "Joseph Smith The Glass Looker" (see photograph on page 68 of this book).

The fact that the document says that Joseph Smith was a "Glass Looker" fits very well with the published version of the trial. In fact, this statement alone seems to show that the published account of the trial is authentic. Besides this, however, Neely's bill provides additional evidence. It states that the trial took place on "March 20, 1826," and this is precisely the date found in the published account of the trial: "Prisoner brought before Court March 20, 1826" (*Fraser's Magazine*, February, 1873, p.229). In Albert Neely's bill the fee for this trial is listed as "2.68," and this is the exact figure found in the printed record: "Costs: . . . $2.68." In the face of this evidence it is impossible to continue to deny the authenticity of the court record.

In addition to Justice Neely's bill for the trial of "Joseph Smith The Glass Looker," Mr. Walters discovered the bill of Constable Philip M. DeZeng, which tells of "Serving Warrant on Joseph Smith." We have included a photograph of this document in *Mormonism–Shadow or Reality?* (p.35). Mr. Walters has given an account of the discovery of these bills in an affidavit. We extract the following from that document:

> REVEREND WESLEY P. WALTERS, being first duly sworn upon his oath, deposes and states:
>
> On Saturday, May 22, 1971, while in Norwich, New York, I, . . . was shown by the County Historian, Mrs. Mae Smith, where Chenango County kept their dead storage, which was in a back, poorly-lit room in the basement of the County Jail. . . .
>
> On July 28, 1971, I was able to return to Norwich and in the late afternoon I went back to the County Jail accompanied by Mr. Fred Poffarl . . . Mr. Poffarl discovered two cardboard boxes in the darkest area of the room, containing more bundles of bills, all mixed up as to date, and some badly watersoaked and mildewed. . . . It was in Mr. Poffarl's box that the 1826 bills were soon found. . . . When I opened the 1826 bundle and got part way through the pile of Bainbridge bills, all of which were very damp and mildewed, I came upon, first, the J. P. bill of Albert Neeley and then upon the Constable's bill of Philip M. DeZeng. On Mr. Neely's bill was the item of the trial of "Joseph Smith The Glass Looker" . . . On the bill of Mr. DeZeng were the charges for arresting and keeping Joseph Smith, notifying two justices, subpoenaing 12 witnesses, as well as a mittimus charge for 10 miles travel "to take him," with no specification as to where he was taken on the Mittimus. . . .
>
> In my opinion, the bills are authentic, of the same paper quality and ink quality as the other 1826 and 1830 bills and appeared to me to have remained tied up and untouched since the day they were bound up and placed away in storage by the Board of Supervisors of Chenango County, New York . . . (Affidavit by Wesley P. Walters, dated Oct. 28, 1971).

Before Mr. Walters made his discovery of the bills, Mormon scholars were willing to admit that if the 1826 trial were authentic, it would disprove Mormonism. Dr. Francis W. Kirkham made these statements:

> A careful study of all facts regarding this alleged confession of Joseph Smith in a court of law that he had used a seer stone to find hidden treasure for purposes of fraud, must come to the conclusion that no such record was ever made, and therefore, is not in existence. . . . If any evidence had been in existence that Joseph Smith had used a seer stone for fraud and deception, and especially had he made this confession in a court of law as early as 1826, or four years before the Book of Mormon was printed, and this confession was in a court record, *it would have been impossible for him to have organized the restored Church* (*A New Witness For Christ In America*, vol. 1, pp.385-87).

> If a court record could be identified, and if it contained a confession by Joseph Smith which revealed him to be a poor, ignorant, deluded, and superstitious person—unable himself to write a book of any consequence, and whose church could not endure because it attracted only similar persons of low mentality—if such a court record confession could be identified and proved, then it follows that *his believers must deny his claimed divine guidance* which led them to follow him. . . . *How could he be a prophet of God*, the leader of the Restored Church to these tens of thousands, if he had been the superstitious fraud which 'the pages from a book' declared he confessed to be? (*Ibid.*, pp.486-87).

In his book *The Myth Makers*, Dr. Hugh Nibley has written almost twenty pages in an attempt to discredit the "Bainbridge court record." On page 142 of Dr. Nibley's book we find this statement: ". . . if this court record is authentic *it is the most damning evidence in existence against Joseph Smith*." Dr. Nibley's book also states that if the authenticity of the court record could be established it would be "*the most devastating blow to Smith ever delivered*" (*Ibid.*)

Since Wesley Walters' discovery verified the authenticity of the court record, Dr. Nibley has been strangely silent about the matter. The first Mormon scholar to attempt to deal with this issue since Walter's discovery is Marvin S. Hill, Assistant Professor of History at Brigham Young University. Dr. Hill differs with both Kirkham and Nibley by stating that even if Joseph Smith was guilty of "glass looking" this does not prove that he was a religious fraud:

> . . . Reverend Wesley P. Walters . . . discovered some records in the basement of the sheriff's office in Norwich, New York, which he maintains demonstrate the actuality of the 1826 trial and go far to substantiate that Joseph Smith spent part of his early

career in southern New York as a money digger and seer of hidden treasures. . . .

A preliminary investigation by the writer at the sheriff's office in Norwich, New York, confirmed that Walters had searched thoroughly the bills of local officials dated in the 1820s, many of which were similar to the two bills in question. The originals, however, were not at the sheriff's office but in Walter's possession. Presumably they will be available for study at a later date. Until then the final question of their authenticity must remain open. If a study of the handwriting and paper of the originals demonstrates their authenticity, it will confirm that there was a trial in 1826 and that glass looking was an issue at the trial. . . . if the bills should prove authentic and demonstrate that Joseph Smith was tried as a "Glass Looker," what shall we make of him? Nearly everybody seems to have conceded that if Joseph Smith was indeed a gold digger that he was also a religious fraud. This is a view, however, of our own generation, not Joseph Smith's. *Joseph himself never denied that he searched for buried treasure.* . . . In one place he admitted that he did such work but never made much money from it. . . . Hosea Stout, who believed in the Prophet, said that *the gold plates were found by means of a seer stone.*

If there was an element of mysticism in Joseph Smith and the other early Mormons which led them to search for treasures in the earth, *it does not disprove the genuineness of their religious convictions* (Brigham Young University Studies, Winter 1972, pp.224,225,231,232).

In another article published in *Dialogue: A Journal of Mormon Thought* (Winter 1972, pp.77,78), Marvin S. Hill wrote: "There may be little doubt now, as I have indicated elsewhere, that *Joseph Smith was brought to trial in 1826* on a charge, not exactly clear, associated with *money digging.* . . . For the historian interested in Joseph Smith the man, it does not seem incongruous for him to have hunted for treasure with a seer stone and then to use it with full faith to receive revelations from the Lord."*

In his *History of the Church*, Joseph Smith admitted that he

*In a new book entitled, *The Mormon Experience*, pages 10-11, Church Historian Leonard J. Arrington and his assistant Davis Bitton have now conceded that Joseph Smith was tried as a "glass looker": "Smith's self-admitted employment by Josiah Stoal resulted in the youth's being brought to trial in 1826, charged with either vagrancy or disorderly conduct. Bills drawn up by the local judge and constable refer to Smith as a 'glass looker' (one who, by peering through a glass stone, could see things not discernible by the natural eye). The bills class the offense as a misdemeanor and indicate that at least twelve witnesses were served with subpoenas."

worked for Josiah Stowel, but did not acknowledge the fact that he was arrested or that he used a "seer stone" to find treasures:

> In the month of October, 1825, I hired with an old gentleman by the name of Josiah Stowel, who lived in Chenango county, state of New York. He had heard something of a silver mine having been opened by the Spaniards . . . and had, previous to my hiring to him, been digging, in order, if possible, to discover the mine . . . he took me, with the rest of his hands, to dig for the silver mine, at which I continued to work for nearly a month, without success in our undertaking, and finally I prevailed with the old gentleman to cease digging after it. Hence arose the very prevalent story of my having been a money-digger (*History of the Church*, vol. 1, p.17).

Joseph Smith's mother did not mention the trial but admitted that Josiah Stowel came seeking Joseph Smith's help because of "having heard that he possessed certain keys, by which he could discern things invisible to the natural eye" (*Biographical Sketches of Joseph Smith the Prophet*, London, 1853, pp.91-92). The Mormon historian B. H. Roberts stated that Stowel came to Joseph Smith because he had "heard of Joseph Smith's gift of seership" (*Comprehensive History of the Church*, vol. 1, p.82).

Although Joseph Smith suppressed the 1826 trial in his *History of the Church*, Dale L. Morgan discovered that the trial was mentioned as early as 1831 in a letter published in the *Evangelical Magazine and Gospel Advocate*, printed in Utica, N.Y. We cite the following from that publication:

> Messrs. Editors— . . . thinking that a fuller history of their founder, Joseph Smith, jr., might be interesting . . . I will take the trouble to make a few remarks. . . . For several years preceding the appearance of his book, he was about the country *in the character of a glass-looker:* pretending, by means of a certain stone, or glass, which he put in a hat, to be able to discover lost goods, hidden treasures, mines of gold and silver, &c. . . . In this town, a wealthy farmer, named *Josiah Stowell*, together with others, *spent large sums of money in digging for hidden money, which this Smith pretended he could see, and told them where to dig;* but they never found their treasure. At length the public, becoming wearied with the base imposition which he was palming upon the credulity of the ignorant, for the purpose of sponging his living from their earnings, had him *arrested as a disorderly person, tried and condemned* before a court of Justice. . . . This was four or five years ago (*Evangelical Magazine and Gospel Adovcate*, April 9, 1831, p.120).

Now that the authenticity of the court record has been established, the Mormon church leaders are faced with a dilemma.

The court record plainly shows that Joseph Smith was deeply involved in magic practices at the very time he was supposed to be preparing himself to receive the plates for the *Book of Mormon*. The court record shows that Smith was searching for buried treasure in 1826, and according to his own story, the plates for the *Book of Mormon* were taken from the Hill Cumorah the following year. Joseph Smith claimed that he had known that the plates were buried in the Hill Cumorah since 1823. He made this statement concerning the discovery of the plates: "Having removed the earth, I obtained a lever, which I got fixed under the edge of the stone, and with a little exertion raised it up. I looked in, and there indeed did I behold the plates. . . .

"I made an attempt to take them out, but was forbidden by the messenger, and was again informed that the time for bringing them forth had not yet arrived, neither would it, until four years from that time . . ." (*Pearl of Great Price*, Joseph Smith 2:52-53).

Now, it is interesting to note that in the court record Joseph Smith confessed that "for three years" prior to 1826 he had used a stone placed in his hat to find treasures or lost property. According to Joseph Smith's own statement, then, he began his money-digging activities in about 1823. The reader will remember that the messenger was supposed to have informed Joseph Smith of the gold plates on September 21, 1823. From this it would appear that Joseph Smith became deeply involved in money-digging at the very time the messenger told him of the gold plates and that he was still involved in these practices for at least three of the four years when God was supposed to be preparing him to receive the gold plates for the *Book of Mormon*. These facts seem to undermine the whole foundation of Mormonism.

At the time the *Book of Mormon* was printed many people were engaged in searching for buried treasures. For instance, on February 16, 1825, the *Wayne Sentinel* (a newspaper published in Joseph Smith's neighborhood) reprinted the following from the *Windsor, (Vermont) Journal*:

> *Money digging.*—We are sorry to observe even in this enlightened age, so prevalent a disposition to credit the accounts of the Marvellous. Even the frightful stories of money being hid under the surface of the earth, and enchanted by the Devil or Robert Kidd, are received by many of our respectable fellow citizens as truths. . . .

A respectable gentleman in Tunbridge, was informed by means

are carefully watched. they can be removed from place to place according to the good pleasure of Him who made them and owns them. He has his messengers at his service, and it is just as easy for an angel to remove the minerals from any part of one of these mountains to another, as it is for you and me to walk up and down this hall. This, however, is not understood by the Christian world, nor by us as a people. There are certain circumstances that a number of my brethren and sisters have heard me relate, that will demonstrate this so positively, that none need doubt the truth of what I say.

I presume there are some present who have heard me narrate a circumstance with regard to the discovery of a gold mine in Little Cottonwood Cañon, and I will here say that the specimens taken from it, which I have in my possession to-day, are as fine specimens of gold as ever were found on this continent. A man whom some of you will well know, brought to me a most beautiful nugget. I told him to let the mine alone.

When General Conner came here, he did considerable prospecting; and in hunting through the Cottonwoods, he had an inkling that there was gold there. Porter, as we generally call him, came to me one day, saying, "They have struck within four inches of my lode, what shall I do?" He was carried away with the idea that he must do something. I therefore told him to go with the other brethren interested, and make his claim. When he got through talking, I said to him, "Porter, you ought to know better; you have seen and heard things which I have not, and are a man of long experience in this Church. I want to tell you one thing; they may strike within four inches of that lode as many times as they have a mind to, and they will not find it." They hunted and hunted, hundreds of them did; and I had the pleasure of laughing at him a little, for when he went there again, he could not find it himself." (Laughter.)

Sometimes I take the liberty of talking a little further with regard to such things. Orin P. Rockwell is an eye-witness to some powers of removing the treasures of the earth. He was with certain parties that lived near by where the plates were found that contain the records of the Book of Mormon. There were a great many treasures hid up by the Nephites. Porter was with them one night where there were treasures, and they could find them easy enough, but they could not obtain them.

I will tell you a story which will be marvelous to most of you. It was told me by Porter, whom I would believe just as quickly as any man that lives. When he tells a thing he understands, he will tell it just as he knows it; he is a man that does not lie. He said that on this night, when they were engaged hunting for this old treasure, they dug around the end of a chest for some twenty inches. The chest was about three feet square. One man who was determined to have the contents of that chest, took his pick and struck into the lid of it, and split through into the chest. The blow took off a piece of the lid, which a certain lady kept in her possession until she died. That chest of money went into the bank. Porter describes it so [making a rumbling sound]; he says this is just as true as the heavens are. I have heard others tell the same story. I relate this because it is of a dream, that a chest of money was buried on a small island. ... After having been directed by the mineral rod where to search for the money . . . he and his laborers came . . . upon a chest of gold . . . the chest moved off through the mud, and has not been seen or heard of since.

Many of the people who were digging for buried treasure were very superstitious. There were many strange stories connected with these treasure hunts. Martin Harris, one of the three witnesses to the *Book of Mormon*, related the following:

> Mr. Stowel was at this time at old Mr. Smith's digging for money. It was reported by these money-diggers, that they had found boxes, but before they could secure them, they would *sink into the earth.* . . . There were a great many strange sights. One time the old log school-house south of Palmyra, was suddenly lighted up, and frightened them away. Samuel Lawrence told me that while they were digging, a large man who appeared to be eight or nine feet high, came and sat on the ridge of the barn, and motioned to them that they must leave. . . . These things were real to them, I believe, because they were told to me in confidence, and told by different ones, and their stories agreed, and they seemed to be in earnest—I knew they were in earnest (An interview with Martin Harris, published in *Tiffany's Monthly,* 1859, p.165).

On another occasion Martin Harris admitted that he participated in some money-digging and that a stone box slipped back into the hill: "Martin Harris (speaking to a group of Saints at Clarkston, Utah in the 1870's): I will tell you a wonderful thing that happened after Joseph had found the plates. Three of us took some tools to go to the hill and hunt for some more boxes, or gold or something, and indeed we found a stone box. . . . but behold by some unseen power, it *slipped back into the hill*" (Testimony of Mrs. Comfort Godfrey Flinders, *Utah Pioneer Biographies*, vol. 10, p.65, Genealogical Society of Utah, as cited in an unpublished manuscript by LaMar Petersen).

It appears that even Brigham Young, the second president of the Mormon church, was influenced by the superstitions of his day. In a sermon delivered June 17, 1877, he stated:

> These treasures that are in the earth are carefully watched, they can be removed from place to place according to the good pleasure of Him who made them and owns them. . . . Orin P. Rockwell is an eye-witness to some powers of removing the treasures of the earth. He was with certain parties that lived near by where the plates were found that contain the records of the Book of Mormon. There were a great many treasures hid up by the Nephites. Porter was with them one night where there were

treasures, and they could find them easy enough, but they could not obtain them. ... He said that on this night, ... they dug around the end of a chest. ... One man who was determined to have the contents of that chest, took his pick and struck into the lid of it, and split through into the chest. The blow took off a piece of the lid, which a certain lady kept in her possession until she died. *That chest of money went into the bank.* Porter describes it so [making a rumbling sound]; he says this is just as true as the heavens are. ... to those who understand these things, it is not marvelous. ... I will take the liberty to tell you of another circumstance ... Oliver Cowdery went with the Prophet Joseph when he deposited these plates. ... the angel instructed him to carry them back to the hill Cumorah, which he did. Oliver says ... *the hill opened,* and they walked into a cave, in which there was a large and spacious room. ... They laid the plates on a table; it was a large table that stood in the room. Under this table there was *a pile of plates as much as two feet high*, and there were altogether in this room *more plates than probably many wagon loads*; ... there is a seal upon the treasures of earth; men are allowed to go so far and no farther. I have known places where there were treasures in abundance; but could men get them? No (*Journal of Discourses*, vol. 19, pp.36-39).

At the time the *Book of Mormon* came forth many people believed in "peep stones." These stones were sometimes placed in a hat and used to locate buried treasure. The following, taken from the *Orleans Advocate*, appeared in the *Wayne Sentinel* on December 27, 1825:

MR. STRONG—Please insert the following and oblige one of your readers.

Wonderful Discovery.—A few days since was discovered in this town, by the help of *a mineral stone*, (which *becomes transparent when placed in a hat* and the light excluded by the face of him who looks into it, provided he is fortune's favorite,) a monstrous potash kettle in the bowels of old mother Earth, filled with the purest bullion. ... His Satanic Majesty, or some other invisible agent, appears to keep it under marching orders; for no sooner is it dug on to in one place, than it moves off like "false delusive hope," to another still more remote.

In an affidavit dated December 11, 1833, Willard Chase claimed that Joseph Smith found his seer stone while he was helping dig a well. The Mormon historian B. H. Roberts accepted the story that the stone was found while digging a well: "The *Seer Stone* referred to here was a chocolate-colored, somewhat *egg-shaped stone which the Prophet found while digging a well* in company with his brother Hyrum, for a Mr.

Clark Chase, near Palmyra, N.Y. It possessed the qualities of Urim and Thummim, since *by means of it*—as described above—as well as by means of the Interpreters found with the Nephite record, *Joseph was able to translate the characters engraven on the plates*" (*Comprehensive History of the Church*, vol. 1, p.129).

Martin Harris, one of the three witnesses to the *Book of Mormon*, stated concerning Joseph Smith's "stone":

> These plates were found at the north point of a hill two miles north of Manchester village. *Joseph had a stone* which was dug from the well of Mason Chase, twenty-four feet from the surface. *In this stone he could see many things* to my certain knowledge. *It was by means of this stone he first discovered these plates.*
>
> In the first place, he told me of this stone, and proposed *to bind it on his eyes, and run a race with me in the woods.* A few days after this, I . . . was picking my teeth with a pin while sitting on the bars. The pin caught in my teeth, and dropped from my fingers into shavings and straw. . . . I then took Joseph on surprise, and said to him—I said, 'Take your stone.' I had never seen it, and did not know that he had it with him. He had it in his pocket. *He took it and placed it in his hat*—the old white hat—*and placed his face in his hat.* I watched him closely to see that he did not look one side; he reached out his hand beyond me on the right, and moved a little stick, and there I saw the pin, which he picked up and gave to me. . . . There was a company there in that neighborhood, who were digging for money supposed to have been hidden by the ancients. Of this company were old Mr. Stowel . . . also old Mr. Beman, also Samuel Lawrence, George Proper, *Joseph Smith, Jr.*, and his father, and his brother Hiram Smith. They dug for money in Palmyra, Manchester, also in Pennsylvania, and other places. *When Joseph found this stone,* there was a company digging in Harmony, Pa., and *they took Joseph to look in the stone* for them, and he did so for a while, and then he told them the enchantment was so strong that he could not see, and they gave it up. . . .
>
> The money-diggers claimed that they had as much right to the plates as Joseph had, as they were in company together. They claimed that Joseph had been a traitor, and had appropriated to himself that which belonged to them. For this reason Joseph was afraid of them, and continued concealing the plates. . . . *He found them by looking in the stone found in the well of Mason Chase.* The family had likewise told me the same thing.
>
> "Joseph said that the angel told him he must quit the company of the money-diggers. That there were wicked men among them. He must have no more to do with them. He must not lie, nor swear, nor steal" (*Tiffany's Monthly*, 1859, pp.163,164,167,169).

According to David Whitmer, one of the three witnesses to the *Book of Mormon*, Joseph gave the stone which he used to translate the *Book of Mormon* to Oliver Cowdery. Later this stone was brought to Utah. A newspaper reporter wrote the following in his account of an interview with David Whitmer: *"With this stone all of the present Book of Mormon was translated.* . . . For years Oliver Cowdery surrounded it with care and solicitude, but at his death old Phineas Young, . . . carried it in triumph to the apostles of Brigham Young's 'lion house' " (*Des Moines Daily News* October 16, 1886). We know that by 1856 Joseph Smith's "seer stone" had been brought to Utah, for Hosea Stout recorded the following in his diary under the date of February 25, 1856:"President Young exhibited *the Seer's stone with which The Prophet Joseph discovered the plates* of the Book of Mormon, to the Regents this evening . . . It was about the size but not the shape of a hen's egg" (*On The Mormon Frontier, The Diary of Hosea Stout*, vol. 2, page 593).

Book of Mormon from the Stone

In the *Book of Mormon* we read: "And the Lord said: I will prepare unto my servant Gazelem, *a stone, which shall shine forth in darkness unto light* . . ." (*Book of Mormon*, Alma 37:23). In the *Doctrine and Covenants* 78:9, Gazelam is identified as "Joseph Smith, Jun."

Joseph Smith claimed that his Urim and Thummim—which he also used to translate—consisted of "two stones in silver bows" (*History of the Church*, vol. 1, p.12). It would appear, then, that Joseph Smith fastened two of his "seer stones" together to make his "Urim and Thummim." The testimony given in the 1826 trial shows that as early as 1826 Joseph Smith was using two different stones.

At any rate, Joseph Smith's father-in-law, Isaac Hale, noticed a definite relationship between the method Joseph Smith used to translate the *Book of Mormon* and the way he searched for buried treasures. The following is taken from an affidavit by Mr. Hale:

> I first became acquainted with Joseph Smith, Jr. in November, 1825. He was at that time in the employ of a set of men who were called "money-diggers;" and *his occupation was that of seeing, or pretending to see by means of a stone placed in his hat,* and his hat closed over his face. In this way he pretended to discover minerals and hidden treasures. . . . Smith, and his father, with several other "money-diggers" boarded at my house. . . . Young Smith gave the "money-diggers" great encouragement, at first, but when they had arrived in digging, to near the place where he

had stated an immense treasure would be found—he said the enchantment was so powerful that he could not see. . . .

After these occurrences, young Smith made several visits at my house, . . . and while I was absent from home, carried off my daughter, into the state of New York, where they were married without my approbation or consent. . . . In a short time they returned . . .

Smith stated to me, that he had given up what he called "glass-looking," and that he expected to work hard for a living. . . . He also made arrangements with my son Alva Hale, to go up to Palmyra, and move his (Smith's) furniture &c. to this place. . . . Soon after this, I was informed they had brought a wonderful book of Plates down with them. . . . *The manner in which he pretended to read and interpret, was the same as when he looked for the money-diggers, with the stone in his hat, and his hat over his face*, while the Book of Plates were at the same time hid in the woods! (Affidavit of Isaac Hale, as printed in the Susquehanna Register, May 1, 1834).

David Whitmer frankly admitted that Joseph Smith placed the "seer stone" into a hat to translate the *Book of Mormon*: "I will now give you a description of the manner in which the Book of Mormon was translated. Joseph would put *the seer stone into a hat, and put his face in the hat*, drawing it closely around his face to exclude the light; and in the darkness the spiritual light would shine. A piece of something resembling parchment would appear, and on that appeared the writing" (*An Address To All Believers In Christ*, by David Whitmer, p.12).

Emma Smith, Joseph Smith's wife, related the following to her son: "In writing for your father I frequently wrote day after day, after sitting by the table close by him, he sitting with *his face buried in his hat, with the stone in it*, and dictating hour after hour with nothing between us" (*The Saints' Herald*, May 19, 1888, p.310).

Martin Harris, one of the three witnesses to the *Book of Mormon*, also said that a stone was used:

On Sunday, Sept. 4, 1870, Martin Harris addressed a congregation of Saints in Salt Lake City. He related an incident which occurred during the time that he wrote that portion of the translation of the Book of Mormon which he was favored to write direct from the mouth of the Prophet Joseph Smith, and said that the Prophet possessed *a seer stone*, by which he was enabled to translate as well as from the Urim and Thummim, and *for convenience he then used the seer stone*. . . . on one occasion, Martin Harris found a stone very much resembling the one used for translating, and on resuming their labor of translation, he put in place the stone he had found. He said that the Prophet remained silent, unusually and intently gazing in darkness, no traces of the usual sentences appearing. Much surprised, Joseph exclaimed, "Martin! What is the matter! All is as dark as Egypt!" Martin's countenance betrayed him, and the Prophet asked Martin why he had done so. Martin said, to stop the mouths of fools, who had told him that the Prophet had learned those sentences and was merely repeating them, etc. (*Historical Record*, by Andrew Jensen, p.216).

In a letter written March 27, 1876, Emma Smith said that the entire *Book of Mormon*, that we have today, was translated by the use of a stone. David Whitmer, one of the three witnesses, admitted that he never did see Joseph Smith use what was later known as the Urim and Thummim—i.e., the two stones set in silver bows. This information is found in an article by James E. Lancaster:

> According to the testimony of Emma Smith and David Whitmer, the angel took the Urim and Thummim from Joseph Smith at the time of the loss of the 116 pages. This was in June, 1828, one year before David became involved with the work of translation. David Whitmer could never have been present when the Urim and Thummim were used. All of this he clearly states in his testimony to Brother Traughber:

> "With the sanction of David Whitmer, and by his authority, I now state that he does not say that Joseph Smith ever translated in his presence by aid of Urim and Thummim, *but by means of one dark colored, opaque stone called a 'Seer Stone,' which was placed in the crown of a hat*, into which Joseph put his face, so as to exclude the external light" (*Saints' Herald*, November 15, 1962, p.16).

One thing that has caused confusion is the fact that the "seer stone" was sometimes called the Urim and Thummim. Bruce R. McConkie, who is now an Apostle in the Church, stated concerning the seer stone: "The Prophet also had *a seer stone* which was separate and distinct from the Urim and Thummim, and which (speaking loosely) *has been called by some a Urim and Thummim*" (*Mormon Doctrine*, 1966, p.818).

Joseph Fielding Smith, the tenth president of the Mormon church, admitted that the "seer stone" was sometimes called the Urim and Thummim: "The statement has been made that the Urim and Thummim was on the altar in the Manti Temple when that building was dedicated. The Urim and Thummim so spoken of, however, *was the seer stone* which was in the possession of the Prophet Joseph Smith in early days. *This seer stone is now in the possession of the Church*" (*Doctrines of Salvation*, vol. 3, p.225).

The fact that Joseph Smith used a stone, which he placed in a hat to translate the *Book of Mormon*, has caused a great deal of embarrassment because it so closely resembles crystal gazing. Bruce R. McConkie made this statement: "In imitation of the true order of heaven whereby seers receive revelations from God through a Urim and Thummim, the devil gives his own revelations to some of his followers through *peep stones* or *crystal balls*" (*Mormon Doctrine*, 1966, pp.565-66).

In early Utah the anti-Mormon paper *Valley Tan*, accused the Mormons of using peep stones to "see cattle beyond mountains twenty or a hundred miles, or even a greater distance off" (*Valley Tan*, October 5, 1859, p.2). The Mormon writer Arch S. Reynolds wrote a pamplet entitled, *The Urim and Thummim* in which he stated: "From the earliest days of the Church we have had many who have claimed to have had the power to see things in so-called peep-stones. There are stones among the Church members that are considered by some to be the means of their receiving communications from the unseen world."

Mormon apologists have a difficult time explaining the fact that Joseph Smith used a "seer stone." Mormon Apostle John A. Widtsoe asserted: "Some use was made also of *the seer stone* and occasional mention was made of it. This was a stone found while the Prophet assisted in digging a well for Clark Chase. By divine power *this stone was made serviceable* to Joseph Smith in the early part of his ministry. *There is no evidence that this stone was used in Joseph's sacred work*" (*Joseph Smith—Seeker After Truth*, 1951, p.267). Notice that Apostle Widtsoe states there is "no evidence that this stone was used in Joseph's sacred work," yet on page 260 of the same book Widtsoe states that Joseph did use the stone in his "spiritual work":

> Before Joseph received the Urim and Thummim *he had a stone*, obtained during the digging of a well for Clark Chase. This stone, through the blessing of the Lord, became *a seer stone which was used frequently by him in his spiritual work*.
>
> The use of the seer stone explains in part the charge against Joseph Smith that he was a "peep stone gazer." . . . The use of the seer stone and the Urim and Thummim was well-known to the people of his time and neighborhood.

Mormons, therefore, continue to remain uncertain about how to handle Joseph's "peeping" activities.

Money-Digging and the Book of Mormon

A careful examination of the whole story of the coming forth of the *Book of Mormon* and even the text of the book itself reveals that it originated in the mind of someone who was familiar with the practice of money-digging. To begin with, the "seer stone" used in "translating" the book seems to have been nothing but a common "peep stone." Many people in Joseph Smith's area were using these stones to search for buried treasures. Mormon scholars admit that Joseph Smith found the stone while digging a well, and the testimony given in the 1826 trial shows that he used his stone to search for treasures. Martin Harris, one of the three witnesses to the *Book of Mormon*, said that Joseph found the *Book of Mormon* plates by "looking in the stone found in the well of Mason Chase." Evidence also shows that in "translating" the *Book of Mormon*, Joseph Smith placed the stone in a hat in the same manner "as when he looked for the money-diggers."

According to witnesses, the plates didn't even have to be present when Joseph Smith was "translating." Mormon writer Arch S. Reynolds notes that "the plates were not always before Joseph during the translation. His wife and mother state that the plates were on the table wrapped in a cloth while Joseph translated with his eyes hid in a hat with the seer stone or the Urim and Thummim. David Whitmer, Martin Harris and others state that Joseph hid the plates in the woods and other places while he was translating" (*How Did Joseph Smith Translate?* p.21).

As we examine the *Book of Mormon* story in the light of the money-digging activities of the 1820s, we notice that the gold plates from which the *Book of Mormon* was "translated" were supposed to have been a very valuable treasure. Mormon author Paul R. Cheesman has brought to light a document prepared by Joseph Smith which the church suppressed for 130 years. In this manuscript Joseph Smith admitted that he wanted to obtain the *Book of Mormon* plates so that he would become rich and that the angel rebuked him:

> . . . I immediately went to the place and found where the plates was [sic] deposited . . . and straightway made three attempts to get them . . . I cried unto the Lord in the agony of my soul why can I not obtain them behold the the [sic] angel appeared unto me again and said unto me you *have not kept the commandments* of the Lord which I gave unto you therefore you cannot now obtain them for the time is not yet fulfilled . . . I had been tempted of the advisary [sic] and *sought the Plates to obtain*

riches and kept not the commandment that I should have an eye singled to the glory of God therefore I was chastened and sought diligently to obtain the plates and obtained them not until I was twenty one years of age . . . ("An Analysis of the Accounts Relating Joseph Smith's Early Visions," Master's thesis, Brigham Young University, 1965, pp.130-31).

The treasure-hunting fever, with its accompanying superstitions, even found its way into the *Book of Mormon* as the following extracts show:

And behold, if a man hide up a treasure in the earth, and the Lord shall say—Let it be accursed, because of the iniquity of him who hid it up—behold, it shall be accursed. And if the Lord shall say—Be thou accursed, that no man shall find thee from this time henceforth and forever—behold, no man getteth it henceforth and forever (*Book of Mormon*, Helaman 12:18-19).

For I will, saith the Lord, that they shall hide up their treasures unto me; and cursed be they who hide not up their treasures unto me; for none hideth up their treasures unto me save it be the righteous; and he that hideth not up his treasures unto me, cursed is he, and also the treasure, and none shall redeem it because of the curse of the land (Helaman 13:19).

The reader will remember that Brigham Young told of a "chest of money" that moved by itself "into the bank," and that Martin Harris told of a "stone box" that "slipped back into the hill." In Joseph Smith's 1826 trial, Jonathan Thompson testified that "on account of an enchantment the trunk kept settling away from under them when digging." This idea of treasures slipping into the earth can be found reflected in the *Book of Mormon*, Helaman 13:34-36:

Behold, we lay a tool here and on the morrow it is gone; and behold, our swords are taken from us in the day we have sought them for battle. Yea, *we have hid up our treasures and they have slipped away from us*, because of the curse of the land. O that we had repented in the day that the word of the Lord came unto us; for behold the land is cursed, and *all things are become slippery*, and we cannot hold them.

In Mormon 1:18 we read that the people "began to hide up their treasures in the earth; and they became slippery, because the Lord had cursed the land, that they could not hold them, nor retain them again."

From the available evidence it becomes clear that the *Book of Mormon* had its origin among a people who believed in "seer stones" and money-digging.

Working With the Rod

One important change Joseph Smith made in his revelations was an obvious attempt to cover up the endorsement of Oliver Cowdery's supposed gift from God to work with a divining rod. Below is a comparison of the way this revelation was first published in the *Book of Commandments* and the way it has been changed to read in recent editions of the *Doctrine and Covenants*.

Book of Commandments: "Now this is not all, for you have another gift, which is the gift of *working with the rod:* behold it has told you things: behold there is no other power save God, that can cause this *rod of nature, to work in your hands . . .*" (7:3).

Doctrine and Covenants: "Now this is not all thy gift, for you have another gift, which is the gift of *Aaron*; behold, it has told you many things;

"Behold, there is no other power, save the power of God, that can cause this *gift of Aaron to be with you*" (8:6-7).

The reader will notice that the words "working with the rod" and "rod of nature" have been entirely deleted from this revelation.

The money diggers used divining rods to find buried treasure. They were also used as "a medium of revelation." Those who used divining rods were at times referred to as "rodsmen." Richard P. Howard, RLDS church historian, makes some startling admissions in a book published by his church:

> Several writers have established that both in Vermont and in western New York in the early 1800's, one of the many forms which enthusiastic religion took was the adaptation of the witch hazel stick. . . . For example, the 'divining rod' was used effectively by one Nathaniel Wood in Rutland County, Vermont, in 1801. Wood, Winchell, William Cowdery, Jr., and his son, Oliver Cowdery, all had some knowledge of and associations with the various uses, both secular and sacred, of the forked witch hazel rod. Winchell and others used such a rod in seeking buried treasure; . . . when Joseph Smith met Oliver Cowdery in April, 1829, he found a man peculiarly adept in the use of the forked rod . . . and against the background of his own experiments with and uses of oracular media, Joseph Smith's April, 1829, affirmations about Cowdery's unnatural powers related to working with the rod are quite understandable. . . .
>
> By the time that Joseph Smith approached the reinterpretation and rewording of this document for the 1835 edition of the Doctrine and Covenants, he had had time and experience necessary

to place his 1829 assessment of the meaning of Cowdery's gift of working with the rod in a somewhat more accurate perspective. Both he and Cowdery had developed away from an emphasis on the religious or mystical meanings in such mechanical objects as the water witching rod. *Joseph's 1835 wording of this document ... left behind the apparent 1829 reliance upon external media,* which by 1835 had assumed in Joseph's mind overtones of superstition and speculative experimentation (*Restoration Scriptures*, Independence, Mo., 1969, pp.211-14).

We are not aware of any writer in the Utah Mormon church who has been this honest about the change concerning the gift of working with the rod in Joseph Smith's revelation, but Marvin S. Hill, assistant professor of history at BYU, has admitted that "when Oliver Cowdery took up his duties as a scribe for Joseph Smith in 1829 *he had a rod in his possession which Joseph Smith sanctioned ...*" (*Dialogue: A Journal of Mormon Thought*, Winter 1972, p.78). Marvin Hill goes on to state: "Some of the *rodsmen or money diggers* who moved into Mormonism were *Oliver Cowdrey, Martin Harris*, Orrin P. Rockwell, Joseph and Newel Knight, and Josiah Stowell." It is interesting to note that Marvin Hill includes two of the three witnesses to the *Book of Mormon* in his list of "rodsmen or money diggers."† (In *Mormonism—Shadow or Reality?* pp.47-49, we reproduced a number of affidavits and statements linking Joseph Smith to peep stones, divining rods and money-digging.)

Joseph Smith's interest in treasure hunting continued even after he published the *Book of Mormon*. Ebenezer Robinson, who was at one time the editor of the Mormon paper, *Times and Seasons*, gave the following information:

> A brother in the church, by the name of Burgess, had come to Kirtland and stated that a large amount of money had been secreted in a cellar of a certain house in Salem, Massachusetts. . . . We saw the brother Burgess, but Don Carlos Smith told us with

---

†Recently the Mormon writer D. Michael Quinn has admitted that "Oliver Cowdery was by revelation given the gift of working with a 'rod of nature . . .'" (*Brigham Young University Studies*, Fall 1978, p.82). Dr. Quinn further informs that "during the Nauvoo period Apostle Heber C. Kimball 'inquired by the rod' in prayer." In a footnote in the same article the following is cited from the Anthon H. Lund Journal for July 5, 1901: "In the revelation to Oliver Cowdery in May 1829, Bro. [B.H.] Roberts said that the gift which the Lord says he has in his hand meant a stick which was like Aaron's Rod. It is said Bro. Phineas Young [brother-in-law of Oliver Cowdery and brother of Brigham Young] got it from him [Cowdery] and gave it to President Young who had it with him when he arrived in this [Salt Lake] valley and that it was with that stick that he pointed out where the Temple should be built."

regard to the hidden treasure. His statement was credited by the brethren, and steps were taken to try and secure the treasure, of which we will speak more fully in another place" (*The Return*, vol. 1, p.105).

Ebenezer Robinson goes on to state: "We soon learned that four of the leading men of the church had been to Salem, Massachusetts, in search of the hidden treasure spoken of by Brother Burgess, viz: Joseph Smith, Hyrum Smith, Sidney Rigdon and Oliver Cowdery. They left home on the 25th of July, and returned in September."

Joseph Smith's *History* tells of this trip: "On Monday afternoon, July 25th, in company with Sidney Rigdon, Brother Hyrum Smith, and Oliver Cowdery, I left Kirtland, . . . and arrived in Salem, Massachusetts, early in August, where we hired a house, and occupied the same during the month . . ." (*History of the Church*, vol. 2, p.464).

On August 6, 1836, Joseph Smith received a revelation concerning this treasure hunt, which is still published in the *Doctrine and Covenants*. In this revelation we read the following:

> I, the Lord your God, am not displeased with your coming this journey, notwithstanding your follies.
>
> *I have much treasure in this city for you, . . . and its wealth pertaining to gold and silver shall be yours.*
>
> Concern not yourselves about your debts, for I will give you power to pay them. . . . inquire diligently concerning the more ancient inhabitants and founders of this city;
>
> For there are *more treasure than one* for you in this city (*Doctrine and Covenants*, (111:1,2,4,9,10).

Mr. Robinson informs us that the treasure was never found, and Joseph Smith was unable to pay his debts as the revelation had promised. The Mormon historian B. H. Roberts admitted that the Mormon leaders went to Salem seeking "an earthly treasure," but claims that the other treasures spoken of in the revelation were of a spiritual nature (see *Comprehensive History of the Church*, vol. 1, p.412).

Joseph Smith's Magic Talisman

In 1974 Dr. Reed Durham, who was director of the LDS Institute of Religion at the University of Utah and president of the Mormon History Association, made a discovery that was so startling that it caused great consternation among Mormon scholars and officials. Dr. Durham found that what had previously been identified as the "Masonic jewel of the Prophet Joseph Smith" was in reality a "Jupiter talisman." This is a medallion which contains material relating to astrology and magic. Dr. Durham, apparently not realizing the devastating implications of his discovery, announced this important find in his presidential address before the Mormon History Association on April 20, 1974:

> . . . I should like to initiate all of you into what is perhaps the strangest, the most mysterious, occult-like esoteric, and yet Masonically oriented practice ever adopted by Joseph Smith. . . . All available evidence suggests that Joseph Smith *the Prophet possessed a magical Masonic medallion, or talisman,* which he worked during his lifetime and which was evidently on his person when he was martyred. His talisman is in the shape of a silver dollar and is probably made of silver or tin. It is exactly one and nine-sixteenths in diameter, . . . the talisman, . . . originally purchased from the Emma Smith Bidamon family, fully notarized by that family to be authentic and to have belonged to Joseph Smith, can now be identified as *a Jupiter talisman.* It carries the sign and image of Jupiter and should more appropriately be referred to as the Table of Jupiter. And in some very real and quite mysterious sense, this particular Table of Jupiter was the most appropriate talisman for Joseph Smith to possess. Indeed, it seemed meant for him, because on all levels of interpretation: planetary, mythological, numerological, astrological, mystical cabalism, and talismatic magic, the Prophet was, in every case, appropriately described.

> The characters on the talisman are primarily in Hebrew, but there is one inscription in Latin. Every letter in the Hebrew alphabet has a numerical equivalent and those numerical equivalents make up *a magic square.* By adding the numbers in this Jupiter Table in any direction . . . the total will be the same. In this case, on the Jupiter Table, 34. . . .

> There is the one side of the talisman belonging to the Prophet Joseph Smith. You can see the Hebrew characters . . . you see on the margins, at the bottom is the Jupiter sign. . . . The cross at the top represents the spirit of Jupiter, and you will see the path of Jupiter in the orbit of the heavens, and then again the Jupiter sign.

> I wasn't able to find what this was, for—as I said—two months; and finally, in *a magic book* printed in England in 1801, published in America in 1804, and I traced it to Manchester, and to New York. It was a magic book by Francis Barrett and, lo and behold, how thrilled I was when *I saw in his list of magic seals the very talisman which Joseph Smith had in his possession at the time of his martyrdom.* . . . To the Egyptians, Jupiter was

known as Ammon, but to the Greeks he was Zeus: the ancient sky Father, or Father of the Gods. . . .

In *astrology*, Jupiter is always associated with high positions, getting one's own way, and all forms of status. And I quote: "Typically a person born under Jupiter will have the dignity of a natural ruler. . . . He will probably have an impressive manner. . . . In physical appearance, the highly developed Jupiterian is strong, personable, and often handsome. . . . the Jupiterian influence produces a cheerful winning personality, capable of great development." . . .

So closely is magic bound up with the stars and astrology that the term astrologer and magician were in ancient times almost synonymous. The purpose of the Table of Jupiter in talismanic magis [magic?] was *to be able to call upon the celestial intelligences, assigned to the particular talisman*, to assist one in all endeavors. The names of the deities which we gave to you, who could be invoked by the Table were always written on the talisman or represented by various numbers. Three such names were written on Joseph Smith's talisman: Abbah, Father; El Ob, Father is God or God the Father; and Josiphiel, Jehovah speaks for God, the Intelligence of Jupiter.

When properly invoked, with Jupiter being very powerful and ruling in the heavens, these intelligences—*by the power of ancient magic*—guaranteed to the possessor of this talisman *the gain of riches*, and favor, and power, and love and peace; and to confirm honors, and dignities, and councils. Talismatic magic further declared that any one who worked skillfully with this Jupiter Table would obtain the power of stimulating anyone to offer his love to the possessor of the talisman, whether from a friend, brother, relative, or even any female (*Mormon Miscellaneous*, published by David C. Martin, vol. 1, no. 1, October 1975, pp.14-15).

Reed Durham was severely criticized by Mormon scholars and officials for giving this speech. He was even called in by Mormon President Spencer W. Kimball, and finally found it necessary to issue a letter in which he reaffirmed his faith in Joseph Smith and said that he was sorry for the "concerns, and misunderstandings" that the speech had caused. We feel that Dr. Durham's identification of Joseph Smith's talisman is one of the most significant discoveries in Mormon history and that he should be commended for his research.

That Joseph Smith would own such a magic talisman fits very well with the evidence from his 1826 trial. W. D. Purple, who was an eye-witness to the trial, claimed it was reported that Smith said certain talismanic influences were needed to recover a box of treasure:

Mr. Thompson, an employee of Mr. Stowell, was the next witness. . . . Smith had told the Deacon that very many years before a band of robbers had buried on his flat a box of treasure, and as it was very valuable they had by a sacrifice placed a charm over it to protect it, so that it could not be obtained except by faith, accompanied by certain *talismanic influences*. . . . the box of treasure was struck by the shovel, on which they redoubled their energies, but it gradually receded from their grasp. One of the men placed his hand upon the box, but it gradually sunk from his reach. . . . Mr. Stowell went to his flock and selected a fine vigorous lamb, and resolved to sacrifice it to the demon spirit who guarded the coveted treasure . . . but the treasure still receded from their grasp, and it was never obtained (*The Chenango Union*, Norwich, N.Y., May 3, 1877, as cited in *A New Witness For Christ In America*, vol. 2, pp.366-67).

Dr. Durham was unable to determine just when Joseph Smith obtained his talisman, but the fact that he was recommending "certain talismanic influences" around the time of the 1826 trial is certainly interesting. The Jupiter talisman is probably the type of talisman a money digger would be interested in because it was supposed to bring its possessor "the gain of riches, and favor, and power." Regardless of when Joseph Smith obtained his talisman, we do know that he possessed it up to the time of his death. He must have felt that it was very important because the Mormon scholar LaMar C. Berrett reveals that *"This piece was in Joseph Smith's pocket when he was martyred at Carthage Jail"* (*The Wilford C. Wood Collection*, 1972, vol. 1, p.173). Wesley P. Walters says that "Charles E. Bidamon, who sold the talisman to the Wood collection, stated in his accompanying affidavit: 'Emma Smith Bidamon the prophet's widow was my foster mother. She prized this piece very highly on account of its being one of the prophet's intimate possessions (Charles E. Bidamon Affidavit. Wood Coll. #7-J-b-21)."

The discovery of evidence to prove Joseph Smith's 1826 trial was certainly a devastating blow to Mormonism, for it proved that Joseph Smith was a believer in magical practices. Reed Durham's new find that Joseph Smith possessed a magic talisman is also very significant because it shows that Smith continued to hold these ideas until the time of his death.

THE BOOK OF MORMON

Chapter 5

As we have already shown, Joseph Smith claimed that on the night of September 21, 1823, when he was seventeen years old, an angel appeared to him and stated that gold plates were buried in the Hill Cumorah. The angel explained that the plates contained "an account of the former inhabitants of this continent," and that they also contained "the fulness of the everlasting Gospel." Four years later, on September 22, 1827, he received the plates, and sometime later he began to translate them. The translation was published in 1830 under the title of the *Book of Mormon*.

Mormon Apostle Orson Pratt declared:

> The Book of Mormon claims to be a divinely inspired record.... If false, it is one of the most cunning, wicked, bold, deep-laid impositions ever palmed upon the world, *calculated to deceive and ruin millions . . . if true, no one can possibly be saved and reject it: if false, no one can possibly be saved and receive it. . . .*
>
> If, after a rigid examination, it be found an imposition, it should be extensively published to the world as such; the evidences and arguments on which the imposture was detected, should be clearly and logically stated. . . .
>
> But on the other hand, if investigation should prove the Book of Mormon true . . . the American and English nations . . . should utterly reject both the Popish and Protestant ministry, together with all the churches which have been built up by them or that have sprung from them, as being entirely destitute of authority . . . (*Orson Pratt's Works*, Divine Authenticity of the Book of Mormon," Liverpool, 1851, pp.1-2).

Our study has led us to the conclusion that the *Book of Mormon* is not an ancient or divinely-inspired record, but rather a product of the nineteenth century. In this chapter we hope to state "clearly and logically" the "evidences and arguments on which the imposture was detected."

DIVINE AUTHENTICITY

OF THE

BOOK OF MORMON.

BY ORSON PRATT,
ONE OF THE TWELVE APOSTLES OF THE CHURCH OF JESUS CHRIST OF LATTER-DAY SAINTS.

INTRODUCTION.—TO EXPECT MORE REVELATION IS NOT UNSCRIPTURAL.—TO
EXPECT MORE REVELATION IS NOT UNREASONABLE.

INTRODUCTION.

THE Book of Mormon claims to be a divinely inspired record, written by a succession of prophets who inhabited Ancient America. It professes to be revealed to the present generation for the salvation of all who will receive it, and for the overthrow and damnation of all nations who reject it.

This book must be either *true* or *false*. If true, it is one of the most important messages ever sent from God to man, affecting both the temporal and eternal interests of every people under heaven to the same extent and in the same degree that the message of Noah affected the inhabitants of the old world. If false, it is one of the most cunning, wicked, bold, deep-laid impositions ever palmed upon the world, calculated to deceive and ruin millions who will sincerely receive it as the word of God, and will suppose themselves securely built upon the rock of truth until they are plunged with their families into hopeless despair.

The nature of the message in the Book of Mormon is such, that if true, no one can possibly be saved and reject it; if false, no one can possibly be saved and receive it. Therefore, every soul in all the world is equally interested in ascertaining its truth or falsity. In a matter of such infinite importance no person should rest satisfied with the conjectures or opinions of others: he should use every exertion himself to become acquainted with the nature of the message: he should carefully examine the evidences on which it is offered to the world: he should, with all patience and perseverance, seek to acquire a certain knowledge as to whether it be of God or not. Without such an investigation in the most careful, candid, and impartial manner, he cannot safely judge without greatly hazarding his future and eternal welfare.

If, after a rigid examination, it be found an imposition, it should be extensively published to the world as such; the evidences and arguments on which the imposture was detected, should be clearly and logically stated: that those who have been sincerely yet unfortunately deceived, may perceive the nature of the deception, and be reclaimed, and that those who continue to publish the delusion, may be exposed and silenced, not by physical force, neither by persecutions, bare assertions, nor ridicule, but by strong and powerful arguments—by evidences adduced from scripture and reason. Such, and such only, should be the weapons employed to detect and overthrow false doctrines—to reclaim mankind from their errors—to expose religious enthusiasm—and to put to silence base and wicked impostors.

But on the other hand, if investigation should prove the Book of Mormon true and of divine origin, then the importance of the message is so great, and the consequences of receiving or rejecting it so overwhelming, that the American and English nations—to whom it is now sent, and in whose language it is now published, (being th

A photograph from *Orson Pratt's Works*, "Divine Authenticity of the Book of Mormon," page 1. Apostle Pratt says that if the Book of Mormon is found to be untrue the facts should be published to the world.

The Witnesses

Joseph Smith claimed that after the *Book of Mormon* was translated he returned the gold plates to the angel. Therefore, there is no way for us to know if there really were any gold plates or whether the translation was correct. Smith, however, did have eleven men sign statements claiming that they had seen the plates. The testimonies of these eleven men are recorded in the forepart of the *Book of Mormon* in two separate statements. In the first statement Oliver Cowdery, David Whitmer, and Martin Harris claimed that an angel of God showed the plates to them. The second statement is signed by eight men who claimed to see the plates, although they did not claim that an angel showed the plates to them. This statement is signed by Christian Whitmer, Jacob Whitmer, Peter Whitmer, Jun., John Whitmer, Hiram Page, Joseph Smith, Sen., Hyrum Smith and Samuel H. Smith.

The Mormon church claims that the witnesses to the *Book of Mormon* never denied their testimony. There are, however, at least two statements in Mormon publications which would seem to indicate that the witnesses had some doubts. Brigham Young, the second president, stated: *"Some of the witnesses of the Book of Mormon, who handled the plates and conversed with the angels of God, were afterwards left to doubt and to disbelieve that they had ever seen an angel."* (*Journal of Discourses*, vol. 7, p.164).

There is some evidence to indicate that Oliver Cowdery, one of the three witnesses, may have had doubts about his testimony. The following appeared in a poem that was published in the Mormon publication *Times and Seasons* in 1841 (vol. 2, p.482):

> Or does it prove there is no time,
>   Because some watches will not go?
>
> ....
>
> Or prove that Christ was not the Lord
>   Because that Peter cursed and swore?
> Or Book of Mormon not His word
>   *Because denied, by Oliver?*

Apostle John A. Widtsoe said that the eleven men who testified to the truthfulness of the *Book of Mormon* had "spotless reputations." Non-Mormons, on the other hand, have made many serious charges against the witnesses. Some of the most damaging statements against the *Book of Mormon* witnesses, however, came from the pen of Joseph Smith and other early

POETRY.

For the Times and Seasons.
BY J. H. JOHNSONS.

" The wise shall understand."—Daniel.

Amazed with wonder! I look round
  To see most people of our day,
Reject the glorious gospel sound,
  Because the simple turn away.
Or does it prove there is no time,
  Because some watches will not go?
But does it prove there is no crime
  Because not punished here below?
Or can it prove no gems remain,
  Because some fools, throw their's away?
Or can it prove no king can reign
  Because some subjects wont obey?
Or prove the gospel was not true
  Because old Paul the Saints could kill?
Because the Jews its author slew,
  And now reject their Saviour still?
Or prove that Christ was not the Lord
  Because that Peter cursed and swore?
Or Book of Mormon not his word
  Because denied, by Oliver?
Or prove, that Joseph Smith is false
  Because apostates say tis so?
Or prove that God, no man exalts
  Because from priests such doctrines flow?
O, no! the wise will surely say;
  No proof unto the man that's wise,
Then O! dig deep ye wise to-day;
  And soon the truth will be your prize.
Not like the fool who chane'd to see,
  The Saint forsake his heavenly course,
And turn to sin and vanity—
  Then cries your "scheme is all a farce."

For the Times and Seasons.
PSALM.
BY
MISS E. R. SNOW.

Praise the Lord O my soul: Praise him all
ye sons and daughters of Zion.

Let us sing unto him a new song: let us
sing of his marvellous doings in the last days.

He is the same yesterday, to-day and forever;
therefore I will praise him for what my eyes
have seen, and my ears have heard.

He hath opened the fountain of knowledge:
he hath unlock'd the treasures of wisdom and
understanding.

He hath brought to pass that which he spake
by the mouth of his ancient prophets: yea, he
hath caused truth to "spring up out of the
earth, and righteousness to look down from
heaven."

In ancient time he call'd his servant David
from the sheep-fold to preside over the nation of
Israel; yea, from a tender of flocks did he raise
him to the sovereignty of his covenant people.

He call'd Elijah from the occupation of hus-
bandry, even when "ploughing in the field with
twelve yoke of oxen;" to be a prophet in Israel:

Yea by the hand of Elijah, was he anointed
to the office of his calling, even to proclaim the
word of the Lord—to declare the counsels of the
Most High to the people.

In these last days the Lord hath call'd his
servant Joseph—the son of an husbandman; to
be a prophet and a teacher: yea, to be a mighty
instrument in rolling forward and establishing
that kingdom which "shall fill the whole earth."

The Lord hath spoken to him from the heavens—he hath instructed him thro' the ministra-
tion of angels—he hath taught him by the power of the holy spirit.

He hath opened the heavens, he hath rent
the veil thereof, before his face—he hath spread
the visions of eternity in his presence—he hath
drawn aside the curtain of futurity and showed
unto his servant things to come.

He hath anointed him with the oil of understanding, and instructed him in the great mysteries of the kingdom of heaven; even those
" mysteries which have been hid from ages and
from generations."

Rejoice all ye Saints of the Lord and listen
to the instructions of his prophet—be careful to
depart from evil—let your hearts be pure for
the great day of the Lord approaches.

He will perform a speedy work upon the
earth—he will cut it short in righteousness—he
will not suffer his word to perish.

Therefore, let the nations be wise—let the
great ones of the earth receive counsel; let the
honest in heart prepare and gather even unto
Zion:

For " the earth shall reel to and fro like a
drunken man," yea, she shall groan because of
iniquity which is already increasing heavily
upon her.

But " Zion shall be redeem'd with judgment,
and her converts with righteousness"—the nations of the earth will honor her—the glory of
the Lord will encompass her round about; and
his praises will be heard in her midst.

COMMUNICATIONS.

Manchester, April 17th **1841.**

DEAR BRO. JOSEPH:—

  Once more I take my pen
to write a few lines to you; most gladly
would I embrace the opportunity of a personal interview with you, did it offer; but
vain is the indulgence of such thoughts
at present.

A photograph of the Mormon publication *Times and Seasons*, vol. 2, page 482.
In the poem that appears on this page it is stated that *Book of Mormon* witness
Oliver Cowdery denied his testimony.

Mormon leaders. In fact, Joseph Smith gave a revelation in July of 1828 in which Martin Harris, one of the three witnesses, was called a "wicked man," who "has set at naught the counsels of God, and has broken the most sacred promises" (*Doctrine and Covenants* 3:12-13). In another revelation given sometime later, God was supposed to have told Joseph Smith that Harris "is a *wicked man*, for he has sought to take away the things wherewith you have been entrusted; and he has also sought to destroy your gift" (*Ibid.*, 10:7).

There is little doubt that the *Book of Mormon* witnesses were very gullible. For instance, Hiram Page had a peep stone which he used to obtain revelations. Joseph Smith himself admitted that Page gave false revelations through his stone and that the other witnesses to the *Book of Mormon* were influenced by his revelations:

> To our great grief, however, we soon found that Satan had been lying in wait to deceive, . . . Brother Hiram Page had in his possession *a certain stone*, by which *he obtained certain "revelations"* . . . all of which were entirely at variance with the order of God's house, . . . *the Whitmer family and Oliver Cowdery, were believing much in the things set forth by this stone*, we thought best to inquire of the Lord concerning so important a matter . . . (*History of the Church*, by Joseph Smith, vol. 1, pp.109-10).

The *Doctrine and Covenants* 28:11 instructs Joseph Smith to have Oliver Cowdery tell Hiram Page that "those things which he hath written from that stone are not of me, and that Satan deceiveth him."

Although Joseph Smith was able to prevail against the revelations from Hiram Page's peep stone, a more serious situation developed at Kirtland. Apostle George A. Smith related the following: "After the organization of the Twelve Apostles, . . . the spirit of apostasy became more general. . . . One of the First Presidency, several of the Twelve Apostles, High Council, Presidents of Seventies, *the witnesses of the Book of Mormon*, Presidents of Far West, and a number of others standing high in the Church were all carried away in this apostasy . . ." (*Journal of Discourses*, vol. 7, pp.114-15).

The three witnesses were finally excommunicated from the church. Martin Harris accused Joseph Smith of "lying and licentiousness." The Mormon leaders in turn published an attack on the character of Martin Harris. The *Elders' Journal*—a Mormon publication edited by Joseph Smith—said that Harris and others were guilty of "swearing, lying, cheating, swindling, drinking, with every species of debauchery . . ." (*Elders' Journal*, August, 1838, p.59).

In 1838 Oliver Cowdery had serious trouble with Joseph Smith. He accused Smith of adultery, lying and teaching false doctrines. Finally, in Far West, Missouri, the division became so great that the Mormons drove out the dissenters. David Whitmer, one of the three witnesses to the *Book of Mormon*, made this statement:

> *If you believe my testimony to the Book of Mormon;* if you believe that God spake to us three witnesses by his own voice, then I tell you that in June, 1838, *God spake to me again by his own voice from the heavens, and told me to* "separate myself from among the Latter Day Saints, for as they sought to do unto me, so should it be done unto them." In the spring of 1838, the heads of the church and many of the members had gone deep into error and blindness. . . . About the same time that I came out, the Spirit of God moved upon quite a number of the brethren who came out, with their families, all of the eight witnesses who were then living (except the three Smiths) came out; Peter and Christian Whitmer were dead. Oliver Cowdery came out also. Martin Harris was then in Ohio. The church went deeper and deeper into wickedness (*An Address to all Believers in Christ*, by David Whitmer, 1887, pp.27-28).

In a letter dated December 16, 1838, Joseph Smith said that "John Whitmer, David Whitmer, Oliver Cowdery, and Martin Harris are too mean to mention" (*History of the Church*, vol. 3, p.232). Smith was very upset with David Whitmer, one of the three witnesses: "God suffered such kind of beings to afflict Job. . . . This poor man who professes to be much of a prophet, has no other *dumb ass to ride but David Whitmer*, to forbid his madness when he goes up to curse Israel; and this ass not being of the same kind as Balaam's, . . . he brays out cursings instead of blessings. Poor ass!" (*History of the Church*, vol. 3, p.228).

Before driving the dissenters from Far West, Missouri, the Mormons wrote them a very threatening letter. In this letter the dissenters were accused of stealing, lying and counterfeiting:

> Whereas the citizens of Caldwell county have borne with the abuse received from you at different times, . . . until it is no longer to be endured; . . . out of the county you shall go, . . . depart, depart, or a more fatal calamity shall befall you.

> After Oliver Cowdery had been taken by a State warrant for stealing, and the stolen property found . . . in which nefarious transaction John Whitmer had also participated. Oliver Cowdery stole the property, conveyed it to John Whitmer . . . *Oliver Cowdery, David Whitmer*, and Lyman E. Johnson, united *with a gang of counterfeiters*, thieves, liars, and blacklegs of the deepest dye, to deceive, cheat, and defraud the saints out of their property. . . .

During the full career of *Oliver Cowdery and David Whitmer's bogus money business*, it got abroad into the world that they were engaged in it. . . . We have evidence of a very strong character that you are at this very time engaged with a gang of counterfeiters, coiners, and blacklegs, . . . we will put you from the county of Caldwell: so help us God (Letter quoted in *Senate Document 189*, February 15, 1841, pp.6-9).

The "Far West Record" contains some very important information concerning Oliver Cowdery and the bogus money business. The "Far West Record" is an unpublished "record book containing minutes of meetings in Kirtland and Far West, Missouri." It was suppressed for many years, but recently Leland Gentry, who was working on his thesis at Brigham Young University, was permitted access to it. On page 117 of the "Far West Record," Gentry found testimony given by Joseph Smith and Fredrick G. Williams that tended to link Cowdrey with the bogus money business. Leland Gentry states:

[Fredrick G.] Williams, . . . testified that Oliver had personally informed him of a man in the church by the name of Davis who could compound metal and make dies which could not be detected from the real thing. Oliver allegedly told Williams that there was no harm in accepting and passing around such money, provided it could not be determined to be unsound.

Joseph Smith's testimony was similar. He claimed that a nonmember of the Church by the name of Sapham had told him in Kirtland that *a warrant had been issued against Oliver "for being engaged in making a purchase of bogus money and dies to make the counterfeit money with."* According to the Prophet, he and Sidney Rigdon went to visit Oliver concerning the matter and told him that *if he were guilty, he had better leave town;* but if he was innocent, he should stand trial and thus be acquited. "That night or next," the Prophet said, *Oliver "left the country"* (*A History of the Latter-day Saints in Northern Missouri From 1836 to 1839*, p.146).

From this information it would appear that Joseph Smith was almost an accessory after the fact, since he warned Oliver Cowdery to flee from the law if he was guilty. At any rate, Joseph Smith's testimony was given at the time Oliver Cowdery was being tried for his membership in the church. The eighth charge against Cowdery read as follows: "Eighth—For disgracing the Church by being connected in the bogus business, as common report says" (*History of the Church*, vol. 3, p.16). According to Joseph Smith, the eighth charge against Cowdery was "sustained" (*Ibid.*, p.17). On page 147 of *A History of the Latter-day Saints in Northern Missouri From 1836 to 1839*, Leland Gentry states: "Joseph Smith, for example, testified that Cowdery had informed him that he had 'come to the conclusion to get property, and that if he could not get it one way, he would get it another, God or no God, Devil or no Devil, property he must and would have.' "

Since six of the nine charges against Cowdery were sustained, he was "considered no longer a member of the Church of Jesus Christ of Latter-day Saints" (*History of the Church*, vol. 3, p.17). After separating himself from the Mormons, Oliver Cowdery became a member of the "Methodist Protestant Church of Tiffin, Seneca County, Ohio." G. J. Keen gave an affidavit in which he stated:

> ... Mr. Cowdery expressed a desire to associate himself with a Methodist Protestant Church of this city. . . . he was unanimously admitted a member thereof.

> At that time he arose and addressed the audience present, admitted his error and implored forgiveness, and *said he was sorry and ashamed of his connection with Mormonism.*

> He continued his membership while he resided in Tiffin, and became superintendent of the Sabbath-School, and led an exemplary life while he resided with us (Affidavit of G. J. Keen, as quoted in *The True Origin of the Book of Mormon*, by Charles A. Shook, Cincinnati, Ohio, 1914, pp.58-59).

Mormon writer Richard L. Anderson admits that Cowdery joined the Methodists: "The cessation of his activity in the Church meant a suspension of his role as a witness of the Book of Mormon. Not that his conviction ceased, but he discontinued public testimony as he worked out a successful legal and political career in non-Mormon society . . . he logically affiliated himself with a Christian congregation for a time, the *Methodist Protestant Church at Tiffin, Ohio*" (*Improvement Era*, January 1969, p.56).

It is interesting to note that the poem about Oliver Cowdery denying his testimony to the *Book of Mormon* appeared in the Mormon publication *Times and Seasons* around the same time that Cowdery renounced Mormonism and joined the Methodist Protestant Church at Tiffin.

Some of the *Book of Mormon* witnesses were so credulous that they were influenced by a man named James Jesse Strang. Strang, like Joseph Smith, claimed that he found some plates that he translated with the Urim and Thummim. He had witnesses who claimed they saw the plates and their testimony is recorded in almost the same way that the testimony of the eleven witnesses is recorded in the *Book of Mormon*. Brigham

Young and the other Mormon leaders denounced Strang as an impostor, but some of the *Book of Mormon* witnesses became very interested in his claims. On January 20, 1848, James J. Strang wrote the following:

> ... early in 1846 the tract reprint of the first number of the *Voree Herald*, containing the evidence of my calling and authority, strayed into upper Missouri. Immediately I received a letter from Hiram Page, one of the witnesses of the Book of Mormon, and a neighbor and friend to the Whitmers' who lived near him, and that they rejoiced with exceeding joy that God had raised up one to stand in place of Joseph. ... He goes on to say that *all the witnesses of the Book of Mormon living in that region received the news with gladness*, and finally that they held a council in which David and John Whitmer and this Hiram Page were the principle actors; and being at a loss what they ought to do about coming to Voree, sent up to me as a prophet of God to tell them what to do. ... last April (1847) I received another letter from the same Hiram Page, acknowledging the receipt of mine . . . and giving me the acts of another council of himself at the Whitmers', . . . they invite me to come to their residence in Missouri and receive from them, David and John Whitmer, church records, and manuscript revelations, which they had kept in their possession from the time that they were active members of the church. These documents they speak of as great importance to the church, and offer them to me as the true shepherd who has a right to them . . ." (*Gospel Herald*, January 20, 1848).

In a letter to David Whitmer, dated December 2, 1846, William E. McLellin said that James J. Strang "told me that *all the witnesses to the book of Mormon yet alive were with him, except Oliver*" (*The Ensign of Liberty*, Kirtland, Ohio, April, 1847). Strang was probably telling the truth about the witnesses to the *Book of Mormon*.

John Whitmer, one of the eight witnesses, wrote the following in his history of the church which later, however, was crossed out: "*God* knowing all things *prepared a man* whom he visited by an angel of God and showed him where there were some ancient record hid, . . . whose name is *James J. Strang.* . . . and *Strang Reigns in the place of Smith* the author and proprietor of the Book of Mormon" (*John Whitmer's History*, p.23).

Martin Harris, one of the three witnesses to the *Book of Mormon*, joined the Strangite movement and even went on a mission to England for the Strangites. The Mormon church's own publication *Latter-Day Saints' Millennial Star* had a great deal to say about Martin Harris when he arrived in England:

One of the witnesses to the Book of Mormon, yielded to the spirit and temptation of the devil a number of years ago—turned against Joseph Smith and became his bitter enemy. He was filled with the rage and madness of a demon. One day he would be one thing, and another day another thing. He soon became *partially deranged* or shattered, as many believed, flying from one thing to another. . . . In one of his *fits of monomania, he went and joined the "Shakers"* or followers of Anna Lee. . . . but since *Strang* has made his entry . . . Martin leaves the "Shakers," whom he knows to be right, . . . and *joins Strang.* . . . We understand that he is appointed a mission to this country, . . . if the Saints wish to know what the Lord hath said to him they may turn to . . . the Book of Doctrine and Covenants, and *the person there called a "wicked man" is no other than Martin Harris* . . . Elder Wheelock will remember that evil men, like Harris, out of the evil treasure of their hearts bring forth evil things. . . .

Just as our paper was going to press, we learned that Martin Harris, about whom we have written in another article, had landed in Liverpool, . . . there was a strangeness about him, and about one or two who came with him . . . A *lying deceptive spirit* attends them, and has from the beginning. . . . they know that they are *of their father, the devil*, who was a liar from the beginning, and abode not in the truth (*Latter-Day Saints' Millennial Star*, vol. 8, pp.124-28).

Although the *Book of Mormon* witnesses were attracted to Strang for a short time, they soon became interested in a movement William E. McLellin (who had served as an Apostle under Joseph Smith) was trying to start. Five of the *Book of Mormon* witnesses definitely supported McLellin's movement and another gave some encouragement to it. Martin Harris was baptized and even joined with Leonard Rich and Calvin Beebe in a "Testimony of Three Witnesses" that Joseph Smith ordained David Whitmer to be his "Successor in office" (*The Ensign of Liberty*, December 1847, pp.43-44). The Mormons who went to Utah felt, of course, that Brigham Young was to be leader of the church. On July 28, 1847, Oliver Cowdery wrote a letter to David Whitmer in which he gave some support to McLellin's ideas and told Whitmer that "our right gives us the head." In a letter dated September 8, 1847, David Whitmer wrote to Oliver Cowdery and told him that "it is the will of God that you be one of my counsellors in the presidency of the Church. Jacob and Hiram have been ordained High Priests . . ." (*Ibid.*, May, 1848, p.93).

William E. McLellin tells how David Whitmer, one of the three witnesses to the *Book of Mormon*, gave revelations supporting his organization and condemning the Mormon Church: **101**

. . . after a few moments of solemn secret prayer, the following was delivered solely through and by David Whitmer, as the Re-velator, and written by me as scribe, viz:

"Verily, verily thus saith the Lord unto my servants David, and John, and William, and Jacob, and Hiram, . . . Behold I have looked upon you from the beginning, and have seen that in your hearts dwelt truth, and righteoness [sic]. . . . it must needs have been that ye were cast out from among those who had *poluted themselves and the holy authority of their priesthood.* . . . For verily, verily saith the Lord, even Jesus, your Redeemer, they have polluted my name, and have *done continually wickedness in my sight*, . . . Thou shalt write concerning the downfall of those who once composed my church . . ."

But here David [Whitmer] said a vision opened before him, and the spirit which was upon him bid him stop and talk to me concerning it. He said that *in the bright light before him he saw a small chest or box of very curious and fine workmanship*, which seemed to be locked, but he was told that it contained precious things, . . . I was told that it contained 'the treasure of wisdom, and knowledge from God.' . . . David and I turned aside, and called upon the Lord, and received direct instruction how we should further proceed. . . . I ordained H. Page to the office of High Priest, . . . we two ordained Jacob Whitmer to the same office. Then we all laid hands on John Whitmer and reordained him . . . we stepped forward and all laid hands upon David and re-ordained him . . . (*The Ensign of Liberty*, August 1849, pp.101-4).

McLellin's movement never really got off the ground, and later in his life David Whitmer was reluctant to talk about his association with McLellin.

Since a person who is investigating the *Book of Mormon* has only the testimony of eleven men to rely on, he should be certain that they were honorable men. If the *Book of Mormon* witnesses were honest, stable and not easily influenced by men, we would be impressed by their testimony. Unfortunately, however, we find that this is not the case. The evidence shows that they were gullible, credulous, and their word cannot always be relied upon.

Since the testimony of the three witnesses who claimed to see the angel is especially important, we want to summarize the information we have on their character.

Martin Harris: Martin Harris seems to have been very unstable in his religious life. G. W. Stodard, a resident of Palmyra, made this statement in an affidavit dated November 28, 1833: "I have been acquainted with Martin Harris, about thirty years. As a farmer, he was industrious and enterprising. . . . Although he possessed wealth, his moral and religious character was such, as not to entitle him to respect among his neighbors. . . . He was first an orthadox [sic] Quaker, then a Universalist, next a Restorationer, then a Baptist, next a Presbyterian, and then a Mormon" (*Mormonism Unveiled*, by E. D. Howe, 1834, pp.260-61).

Martin Harris' instability certainly did not cease when he joined the Mormon church. The Mormons themselves recorded that Harris "became partially deranged . . . flying from one thing to another" (*Millennial Star*, vol. 8, p.124). Mormon writer Richard L. Anderson admits that Martin Harris "changed his religious position eight times" during the period when he was in Kirtland, Ohio:

> The foregoing tendencies explain the spiritual wanderlust that afflicted the solitary witness at Kirtland. In this period of his life he changed his religious position eight times, including a rebaptism by a Nauvoo missionary in 1842. Every affiliation of Martin Harris was with some Mormon group, except when he was affiliated with the Shaker belief, a position not basically contrary to his *Book of Mormon* testimony because the foundation of that movement was acceptance of personal revelation from heavenly beings (*Improvement Era*, March 1969, p.63).

If we add the "eight times" that Martin Harris changed his religious position in Kirtland to the five changes he made before, we find that *he changed his mind thirteen times!* Richard Anderson is forced to acknowledge that Martin Harris' life shows evidence of "religious instability" (*Ibid.*). Mormon writer E. Cecil McGavin stated that "Martin Harris was an unaggressive, vacillating, easily influenced person who was no more pugnacious than a rabbit. . . . His conviction of one day might vanish and be replaced by doubt and fear before the setting of the sun. He was changeable, fickle, and puerile in his judgment and conduct" (*The Historical Background for the Doctrine and Covenants*, p.23, as cited in an unpublished manuscript by LaMar Petersen).

After changing his mind about religion many times, Martin Harris returned to the Mormon church. There is evidence to show, however, that he was still not satisfied (see *Mormonism—Shadow or Reality?* p.58). Joseph Smith's own revelations referred to Harris as a "wicked man," and the church's publication *Millennial Star* said that he was an "evil" man and that "a lying deceptive spirit" attended him and his friends. Dr. Storm Rosa said, "My acquaintance with him induces me to believe him a *monomaniac*. . . ."

This seems like a serious charge, but the Mormons themselves said that Harris had "fits of monomania." Harris' wife made some very serious charges against his character, but they are not actually much worse than those made by the Mormons. Mrs. Harris stated that Martin had "*mad-fits*." The Mormons said that when he left the church he "was filled with the rage and madness of a demon." She stated that Martin was a liar. The Mormons admitted that when he came to England "a lying deceptive spirit" attended him. She stated that Mormonism had made him "more cross, turbulent and abusive to me." Joseph Smith himself later classified Martin Harris as one of those who was "too mean to mention."

Oliver Cowdery: Oliver Cowdery was apparently rather credulous. According to Joseph Smith, Cowdery was led astray by Hiram Page's "peep-stone." He was excommunicated from the Mormon church and united with the "Methodist Protestant Church" at Tiffin, Ohio. In 1841 the Mormons published a poem which stated that the *Book of Mormon* was "denied" by Oliver. He accused Joseph Smith of adultery. The Mormons, on the other hand, claimed that Oliver "committed adultery." Joseph Smith listed Cowdery among those who were "too mean to mention." The Mormons claimed that he joined "a gang of counterfeiters, thieves, liars, and blacklegs." Joseph Smith testified that when a warrant was issued against Cowdery for "being engaged in making a purchase of bogus money and dies," he "left the country."

Cowdery seems to have returned to the Mormon church before his death, but David Whitmer claimed that Cowdery died believing Joseph Smith was a fallen prophet and that his revelations in the *Doctrine and Covenants* must be rejected:

> I did not say that Oliver Cowdery and John Whitmer had not endorsed the Doctrine and Covenants in 1836. They did endorse it in 1836; I stated that they "came out of their errors (discarded the Doctrine and Covenants), repented of them, and died believing as I do to-day," and I have the proof to verify my statement. If any one chooses to doubt my word, let them come to my home in Richmond and be satisfied. In the winter of 1848, after Oliver Cowdery had been baptized at Council Bluffs, he came back to Richmond to live. . . . Now, in 1849 the Lord saw fit to manifest unto John Whitmer, Oliver Cowdery and myself nearly all the errors in doctrine into which we had been led by the heads of the old church. We were shown that the Book of Doctrine and Covenants contained many doctrines of error, and that it must be laid aside. . . . They were led out of their errors, and are upon record to this effect, rejecting the Book of Doctrine and Covenants (*An Address to Believers in The Book of Mormon*, 1887, pp. 1-2).

David Whitmer: David Whitmer was also very gullible. He was influenced by Hiram Page's "peep-stone," and possibly by a woman with a "black stone," in Kirtland, Ohio. Joseph Smith identified David Whitmer with those who were "too mean to mention," and called him a "dumb ass." The Mormons also accused Whitmer of joining with a "gang of counterfeiters, thieves, liars, and blacklegs."

David Whitmer evidently supported James J. Strang for awhile, then changed his mind and supported the McLellin group. Whitmer was to be the prophet and head of the McLellin church. He gave a revelation in which the Lord was supposed to have told him the Mormons "polluted my name, and have done continually wickedness in my sight." David Whitmer also claimed that "in the bright light before him he saw a small chest or box of very curious and fine workmanship."

David Whitmer never returned to the Mormon church. Toward the end of his life he was a member of the "Church of Christ"—another small group which believed in the *Book of Mormon*. Just before his death, Whitmer published *An Address To All Believers In Christ* in which he stated:

> If you believe my testimony to the Book of Mormon; if you believe that God spake to us three witnesses by his own voice, then I tell you that in June, 1838, God spake to me again by His own voice from the heavens, and told me to 'separate myself from among the Latter Day Saints, for as they sought to do unto me, so should it be done unto them.' In the spring of 1838, the heads of the church and many of the members had gone deep into error and blindness (*An Address To All Believers In Christ*, by David Whitmer, 1887, p.27).

Apostle John A. Widtsoe said that the *Book of Mormon* plates were seen and handled "by eleven competent men, of independent minds and spotless reputations." We feel, however, we have demonstrated that these witnesses were easily influenced by men and therefore were not competent witnesses. Contrary to Apostle Widtsoe's statement, these witnesses were not men of "spotless reputation," but rather men whose word could not always be relied upon. Some of them even gave false revelations in the name of the Lord. Mormons ask us to accept David Whitmer's testimony to the *Book of Mormon*, but will they accept Whitmer's revelations which he gave when he was with the McLellin group? Certainly not. Neither will they accept his statement that "God spake to me again by His own voice from the heavens, and told me to 'separate myself from among the Latter Day Saints.' "

It would appear that some of the witnesses to the *Book of Mormon* would follow almost anyone who had a peep stone or claimed to have been visited by an angel. Take, for instance, their willingness to believe in the claims of the deceiver James J. Strang who claimed to translate ancient plates with the Urim and Thummim. The reader will remember that Martin Harris even served on a mission for the Strangites. This was not the only time that Harris endorsed a religion which claimed to have a sacred book given directly by the Lord. As we have already shown, in the *Millennial Star* the Mormons admitted that Martin Harris joined the Shakers: "In one of his fits of monomania, he went and joined the 'Shakers' or followers of Anne Lee." The Shakers felt that "Christ has made his second appearance on earth, in a chosen female known by the name of Ann Lee, and acknowledged by us as our Blessed Mother in the work of redemption" (*Sacred Roll and Book*, p.358). The Shakers, of course, did not believe the *Book of Mormon*, but they had a book entitled *A Holy, Sacred and Divine Roll and Book; From the Lord God of Heaven, to the Inhabitants of Earth*. More than sixty individuals gave testimony to the *Sacred Roll and Book*, which was published in 1843. Although not all of them mention angels appearing, some of them tell of many angels visiting them—one woman told of eight different visions. On page 304 of this book, we find the testimony of eight witnesses:

> We, the undersigned, hereby testify, that we saw the holy Angel standing upon the house-top, as mentioned in the foregoing declaration, holding the Roll and Book.

Betsey Boothe.	Sarah Maria Lewis.
Louisa Chamberlain.	Sarah Ann Spencer.
Caty De Witt.	Lucinda McDoniels.
Laura Ann Jacobs.	Maria Hedrick.

Joseph Smith only had three witnesses who claimed to see an angel. The Shakers, however, had a large number of witnesses who claimed they saw angels and the *Roll and Book*. There are over a hundred pages of testimony from "Living Witnesses." The evidence seems to show that Martin Harris accepted the *Sacred Roll and Book* as a divine revelation. Clark Braden stated: "*Harris declared repeatedly that he had as much evidence for a Shaker book he had as for the Book of Mormon*" (*The Braden and Kelly Debate*, p.173).

There is a Mormon source which indicates that Martin Harris claimed to have a greater testimony to the Shakers than to the *Book of Mormon*. In a thesis written at Brigham Young University, Wayne Cutler Gunnell stated that on December 31, 1844,

"Phineas H. Young [Brigham Young's brother] and other leaders of the Kirtland organization" wrote a letter to Brigham Young in which they stated: "There are in this place all kinds of teaching; *Martin Harris is a firm believer in Shakerism, says his testimony is greater than it was of the Book of Mormon*" ("Martin Harris—Witness and Benefactor to the Book of Mormon," 1955, p.52).

The fact that Martin Harris would even join with such a group shows that he was unstable and easily influenced by men. Therefore, we feel that his testimony that the *Book of Mormon* was of divine origin cannot be relied upon. How can we put our trust in men who were constantly following after movements like the Shakers, Strangites, and the McLellin group? We feel that the *Book of Mormon* witnesses have been "weighed in the balances" and found wanting.

The testimony of the three witnesses leaves a person with the impression that they all saw the angel and the gold plates at the same time. Such was not the case, however. In his *History of the Church* Joseph Smith admits that Martin Harris was not with Whitmer and Cowdery when he saw the plates. Joseph had the three witnesses pray continually in an effort to obtain a view of the plates, but to no avail. Finally:

> Upon this, our second failure, Martin Harris proposed that he should *withdraw himself* from us, believing, as he expressed himself, that his presence was the cause of our not obtaining what we wished for. He accordingly withdrew from us, and we knelt down again, . . . presently we beheld a light above us in the air, of exceeding brightness; and behold, an angel stood before us. In his hands he held the plates. . . .
>
> *I now left David and Oliver*, and went in pursuit of Martin Harris. . . . We accordingly joined in prayer, and ultimately obtained our desires, for before we had yet finished, the same vision was opened to our view . . . (*History of the Church*, vol. 1, pp.54-55).

There seems to be some question as to the time that elapsed between the two visions. Joseph Smith would have us believe that Martin Harris' vision occurred immediately after the other vision, but according to a reporter who interviewed David Whitmer, it was "a day or two after" (*The Myth of the Manuscript Found*, p.83). According to Anthony Metcalf, Martin Harris claimed that it was "about three days" later when he saw the plates (see *Mormonism—Shadow or Reality?* p.40).

Mormon writer Marvin S. Hill says:

> . . . there is a possibility that the witnesses saw the plates in vision only. . . . There is testimony from several independent

interviewers, all non-Mormon, that Martin Harris and David Whitmer said they *saw the plates with their "spiritual eyes" only*. . . . This is contradicted, however, by statements like that of David Whitmer in the *Saints Herald* in 1882, "these hands handled the plates, these eyes saw the angel." But Z. H. Gurley elicited from Whitmer a not so positive response to the question, "did you touch them?" His answer was, "We did not touch nor handle the plates." . . .

So far as the eight witnesses go, *William Smith said his father never saw the plates except under a frock*. And Stephen Burnett quotes Martin Harris that "*the eight witnesses never saw them. . . .*" Yet John Whitmer told Wilhelm Poulson . . . that he saw the plates when they were not covered, and he turned the leaves (*Dialogue: A Journal of Mormon Thought*, Winter, 1972, pp.83-84).

Marvin Hill refers to a letter written by Stephen Burnett. This document has been suppressed by the Mormon church until just recently. In this letter we find the following:

. . . when I came to hear *Martin Harris* state in public that *he never saw the plates with his natural eyes only in vision or imagination*, neither Oliver nor David & *also that the eight witnesses never saw them* & hesitated to sign that instrument for that reason, but were persuaded to do it, the last pedestal gave way, in my view our foundation was sapped & the entire superstructure fell in heap of ruins, I therefore three week since in the Stone Chapel . . . renounced the Book of Mormon . . . after we were done speaking M Harris arose & said he was sorry for any man who rejected the Book of Mormon for he knew it was true, he said he had hefted the plates repeatedly in a box with only a tablecloth or a handkerchief over them, but *he never saw them only as he saw a city throught [sic] a mountain*. And said that he never should have told that *the testimony of the eight was false*, if it had not been picked out of ———[him/me?] but should have let it passed as it was . . . (Letter from Stephen Burnett to "Br Johnson," dated April 15, 1838, Joseph Smith papers, Letter book, April 20, 1837—February 9, 1843, pp.64-66, typed copy).

Thomas Ford, who had been governor of Illinois, related a story which throws doubt upon the existence of the plates. Fawn Brodie quotes this story and then makes this statement: "Yet it is difficult to reconcile this explanation with the fact that these witnesses, and later Emma and William Smith, emphasized the size, weight, and metallic texture of the plates. Perhaps Joseph built some kind of makeshift deception" (*No Man Knows My History*, p.80).

While the testimony of the eight witnesses could be explained simply by admitting that Joseph Smith had some type of plates, the testimony of the three witnesses is more difficult to explain. They claimed that "an angel of God came down from heaven, and he brought and laid before our eyes, that we beheld and saw the plates, and the engravings thereon. . . ." When we consider, however, how credulous and visionary the three witnesses were, even this testimony is not impressive. As far as the claim for the visitation of angels is concerned, the Shakers had a much more impressive case with their *Sacred Roll and Book*.

Besides the angel that appeared to the three witnesses to the *Book of Mormon*, there were many other occasions in the history of Mormonism when angels were supposed to have appeared. Joseph Smith declared on March 27, 1836, that the Kirtland Temple was "filled with angels" (*History of the Church*, vol. 2, p.428). Under the date of March 30, 1836, the following appears in Joseph Smith's history: "The Savior made his appearance to some, while angels ministered to others, . . . the occurrences of this day shall be handed down upon the pages of sacred history, to all generations; as the day of Pentecost, so shall this day be numbered and celebrated as a year of jubilee . . ." (p.433).

Joseph Smith claimed that he and Oliver Cowdery saw Moses, Elias, Elijah and the Lord in the Kirtland Temple (see *Doctrine and Covenants*, sec. 110). If a person reads only Joseph Smith's account of this "endowment" he is apt to be very impressed. William E. McLellin, however, gives an entirely different story. He claims that *there was "no endowment"* (*Ensign of Liberty*, Kirtland, Ohio, March 1848, p.69). It should be remembered that McLellin was one of the Twelve Apostles at the time the endowment was supposed to have been given. On page 7 of the same publication, McLellin joined with five others in stating that "*the anticipated endowment*" was "*a failure!!*" It is interesting to note that David Whitmer, one of the three witnesses to the *Book of Mormon*, called the story of the endowment "a trumped up yarn." In fact, a reporter for the *Des Moines Daily News* stated that Whitmer absolutely denied the manifestations in the temple (in the article it reads "temple at Nauvoo," but it must refer to the Kirtland temple since Whitmer left the church before the Nauvoo temple was built):

> The great heavenly "visitation," which was alleged to have taken place in the temple at Nauvoo, *was a grand fizzle*. The elders were assembled on the appointed day, which was promised would be a veritable day of Pentecost, but *there was no visitation. No Peter, James and John; no Moses and Elias*, put in an appearance. "I was in my seat on that occasion," says Mr.

Whitmer, "and I know that the story sensationally circulated, and which is now on the records of the Utah Mormons as an actual happening, *was nothing but a trumped up yarn . . ."* (*The Des Moines Daily News*, October 16, 1886).

When we look at the testimony of the three witnesses to the *Book of Mormon* or the report of happenings in the Kirtland temple we must remember that some of the early Mormons were very gullible and could be worked up into a state of excitement in which they actually believed that they saw visions. Apostle George A. Smith made this statement concerning an incident in the Kirtland temple: "Sylvester Smith bore testimony of seeing the hosts of heaven and the horsemen. In his exertion and excitement it seemed as though he would jump through the ceiling" (*Journal of Discourses*, vol. 11, p.10).

John Whitmer, who was church historian in Joseph Smith's time, related the following concerning some of the visions that members of the church had:

> For a perpetual memory, to the shame and confusion of the Devil, permit me to say a few things respecting the proceedings of some of those who were disciples, and some remain among us, and will, and have come from under the error and enthusiasm which they had fallen.
>
> Some had visions and could not tell what they saw. Some would fancy to themselves that they had the sword of Laban, and would wield it as expert as a light dragon; some would act like an Indian in the act of scalping; some would slide or scoot on the floor with the rapidity of a serpent, which they termed sailing in the boat to the Lamanites, preaching the gospel. And many other vain and foolish maneuvers that are unseeming and unprofitable to mention. Thus the Devil blinded the eyes of some good and honest disciples (*John Whitmer's History*, chapter 6).

It seems that the early Mormons could see almost anything in vision. John Pulsipher recorded the following in his journal:

> One pleasant day in March, while I was at work in the woods, about one mile from the Temple, . . . there was a steamboat past [sic] over Kirtland in the air! . . . It passed right along and soon went out of our hearing. When it got down to the city it was seen by a number of persons. . . . Old Elder Beamon, who had died a few months before was seen standing in the bow of the Boat. . . . The boat went steady along over the city passed right over the Temple and went out of sight to the west! ("John Pulsipher Journal," as quoted in *Conflict at Kirtland*, p.331).

There is a great deal more that could be mentioned concerning the *Book of Mormon* witnesses, angels and gold plates.

Ancient or Modern?

In 1831 Alexander Campbell wrote concerning the *Book of Mormon*:

> This prophet Smith, through his stone spectacles, wrote on the plates of Nephi, in his book of Mormon, every error and almost every truth discussed in New York for the last ten years. He decides all the great controversies;—infant baptism, ordination, the trinity, regeneration, repentance, justification, the fall of man, the atonement, transubstantiation, fasting, penance, church government, religious experience, the call to the ministry, the general resurrection, eternal punishment, who may baptize, and even the question of free masonary [*sic*], republican government, and the rights of man (*Millennial Harbinger*, February 1831, p.93).

The Mormon writers George Reynolds and Janne M. Sjodahl admit that the *Book of Mormon* deals "with a number of modern theological controversies," but they claim that "Religious controversies must have been, to a large extent, the same anciently as they are today" (*Commentary on the Book of Mormon*, vol. 1, p.419). There is, of course, some truth in this statement, but there are just too many things in the *Book of Mormon* that are similar to Joseph Smith's environment to be explained away in this manner.

The *Book of Mormon* not only makes the mistake of trying to solve all the great religious controversies of the nineteenth century, but it also contains material from books that had not even been written at the time the Nephites were supposed to have existed. For instance, the author of the *Book of Mormon* seems acquainted with the Westminster Confession—a document adopted by the General Synod of the Presbyterian Church in 1729. The Westminster Confession and Catechisms were a vital part of the Presbyterian faith in the nineteenth century. Alexander Campbell claimed that it was "the 'text-book' for the religious instruction of the offspring and households of Presbyterians" (*The Christian Baptist*, vol. 3, p.42). According to Joseph Smith, his "father's family was proselyted to the Presbyterian faith" before he produced the *Book of Mormon*. Since the *Westminster Confession and Catechisms* were sold at the Wayne Bookstore in Palmyra (see *Wayne Sentinel*, January 26, 1825), it is very likely that the Smith family possessed them. Joseph Smith may have heard his brothers learning the catechisms at various times or he could have read the "Confession and Catechisms."

Although the *Book of Mormon* theology is not Calvinistic, certain portions of it resemble the Westminster Confession and

Catechisms. For instance, the Westminster Confession, chapter 32, is probably the source for Alma, chapter 40. Following is a comparison of the two:

Book of Mormon	**Westminster Confession and Catechism**

1. Both claim to give information concerning the state of man after death:

"... *the state of* the soul between *death and the resurrection* ... " (*Book of Mormon,* Alma 40:11)	"... *the State of* Men after *Death, and of the Resurrection* ... " (The Westminster Confession, chap. 32, as printed in *The Confession of Faith: The Larger and Shorter Catechisms,* Philadelphia, 1813)

2. Both state that the souls of men return to God after death:

"... the spirits ... are taken home *to* that *God who gave them* life" (Alma 40:11)	"... their souls ... return *to* God who gave them" (Westminster Confession 32:1)

3. Both claim that the righteous are received into a state of peace:

"... *the* spirits *of* those who are *righteous are received into* a state of happiness, ..." (Alma 40:12)	"*The* souls *of the righteous,* ... *are received into* the highest heavens, ... " (Westminster Confession 32:1)

4. Both state that the wicked are cast out into darkness:

"... *the spirits of the wicked,* ... shall be *cast* out *into* outer *darkness;* ..." (Alma 40:13)	"... *the souls of the wicked* are *cast into* hell, ... and utter *darkness,* ... ." (Westminster Confession 32:1)

5. Both state that the souls of the wicked remain in darkness until the judgment:

"... *the souls of the wicked,* yea, in *darkness, remain in* this state, ... *until the time of their resurrection*" (Alma 40:14)	"... *the souls of the wicked.* ... *remain in.* ... *darkness,* reserved to the judgment of the great day" (Westminster Confession 32:2)

Book of Mormon	Westminster Confession and Catechism

6. Both state that the soul will be united again with the body at the time of the resurrection:

"... the *souls* and the *bodies* are re-*united*, . . ." (Alma 40:20)	"... *bodies* ... shall be *united* again to their *souls* ..." (Westminster Confession 32:2)

There are other parallels between the *Book of Mormon* and the Westminster Confession which we do not have room to include here.

One book which we feel may have had an influence on the *Book of Mormon* is Josiah Priest's *The Wonders of Nature and Providence Displayed*, published in 1825 at Albany, New York. This book was available in Joseph Smith's neighborhood prior to the time the *Book of Mormon* was "translated." In *Mormonism—Shadow or Reality?* pages 84-85, we present evidence suggesting that the author of the *Book of Mormon* was familiar with Josiah Priest's book.

The *Wayne Sentinel*, a newspaper published in Joseph Smith's neighborhood, and a dream which his father had in 1811 may have also furnished structural work for the *Book of Mormon*.

The King James Version of the Bible, which was not published until A.D. 1611, probably had more influence on the *Book of Mormon* than any other book. Apostle Orson Pratt maintained that Joseph Smith was "unacquainted with the contents of the Bible," but we feel that the evidence shows that Smith was very familiar with the Bible. In a manuscript which the Mormon church suppressed for about 130 years, Joseph Smith himself stated:

> At about the age of twelve years my mind became Seriously imprest with regard to the all important concerns for the wellfare [sic] of my immortal Soul which led me to *Searching the Scriptures* believing as I was taught, that they contained the word of God . . . thus from the age twelve years to fifteen I pondered many things . . . and by *Searching the Scriptures* I found that . . . there was no society or denomination that built upon the gospel of Jesus Christ as recorded in the new testament . . . ("An Analysis of the Accounts Relating Joseph Smith's Early Visions," by Paul R. Cheesman, Master's thesis, Brigham Young University, 1965, pp.127-28).

Joseph Smith began his "translation" of the *Book of Mormon*   **113** at the time when there was a controversy over the Apocrypha. Apostle Bruce R. McConkie explains:

> Scholars and Biblical students have grouped certain apparently scriptural Old Testament writings, which they deem to be of doubtful authenticity or of a spurious nature, under the title of the Apocrypha. . . .
>
> The Apocrypha was included in the King James Version of 1611, but by 1629 some English Bibles began to appear without it, and since the early part of the 19th century it has been excluded from almost all protestant Bibles. . . . the British and Foreign Bible Society has excluded it from all but some pulpit Bibles since 1827.
>
> From these dates it is apparent that controversy was still raging as to the value of the Apocrypha at the time the Prophet began his ministry (*Mormon Doctrine*, 1966, p.41).

When Joseph Smith purchased a Bible in the late 1820's he picked one which contained "the Apocrypha," and evidence seems to show that he had a real interest in it (see *Mormonism—Shadow or Reality?* p.72). The Apocrypha seems to solve the mystery of the origin of the name "Nephi." While the name "Nephi" is not found in either the Old or New Testament of the Bible, it is one of the most important names in the *Book of Mormon*. At least four men in the *Book of Mormon* are named "Nephi." It is also the name of several books in the *Book of Mormon*, a city, a land, and a people. Mormon scholars have never been able to find the source of this name. Dr. Wells Jakeman admitted that "there does not seem to be any acceptable Hebrew meaning or derivation for this name." He states, however, that Nephi's name might have been derived from "the name of the young Egyptian grain god Nepri or Nepi," Dr. Nibley, on the other hand, feels that the name was derived from another Egyptian source. Other Mormon writers suggest entirely different sources for this name.

While Mormon writers seem to be in a state of confusion with regard to this name, the King James translation of the Apocrypha seems to settle the matter. In 2 Maccabees 1:36 we read: "And Neemias called this thing Naphthar, which is as much as to say, a cleansing; but many men call it Nephi."

It is obvious, then, that Joseph Smith must have borrowed the name "Nephi" from the Apocrypha. The name "Ezias" (Heleman 8:20) also seems to have been taken from the Apocrypha, 1 Esdras 8:2. There are many other parallels between the Apocrypha and the *Book of Mormon* which we do not have room to include here. Since the apocryphal books were written hundreds of years after the Nephites were supposed to have left Jerusalem, the parallels tend to demonstrate that the *Book of Mormon* is not the ancient record it claims to be.

There can be no doubt that the first books of the Bible furnished a great deal of source material for the writing of the *Book of Mormon*. The book of Genesis, for instance, seems to have had a real influence upon the first few chapters of the *Book of Mormon*. Two of Nephi's brothers, Joseph and Jacob, have names taken from the book of Genesis. His mother's name is Sariah, which reminds us of Abraham's wife Sarah—also called Sarai (Gen. 17:15). Ishmael—a friend of the family—is also a name taken from Genesis (see Gen. 17:18). The name Laban is likewise found in Genesis (see Gen. 24:29).

The story of Nephi in some ways parallels the story of Joseph found in Genesis, and the story of Moses leading the children of Israel out of bondage seems to have been the source for a good deal of the material found in the first book of Nephi and the book of Ether.

The Mormon leaders claim that the Nephites had the Old Testament books which were written prior to the time they left Jerusalem—i.e., about 600 B.C. More than eighteen chapters of Isaiah are found in the *Book of Mormon*. The Ten Commandments and many other portions of the Old Testament are also found in the *Book of Mormon*. In this book we cannot even begin to list all of the verses that are taken from the Old Testament. Since it is claimed that the Nephites had the books written before 600 B.C., we are not too concerned about quotations taken from them. The *Book of Mormon*, however, borrows from books written after 600 B.C. For instance, the book of Daniel seems to have had some influence on the *Book of Mormon*.

One of the most serious mistakes the author of the *Book of Mormon* made was that of quoting from the book of Malachi many years before it was written. Below is a comparison of some verses which were supposed to have been written by Nephi sometime between 588 and 545 B.C., and some verses which were written by Malachi about 400 B.C. In Malachi 4:1 we read: "For behold, the day cometh, that shall burn as an oven; and all the proud, yea, and all that do wickedly, shall be stubble: and the day that cometh shall burn them up. . . ."

In the *Book of Mormon*, 1 Nephi 22:15, Malachi's words have been borrowed: "For behold, *saith the prophet*, . . . the day soon cometh that all the proud and they who do wickedly shall be as stubble; and the day cometh that they must be burned."

There are also portions of 2 Nephi, chapters 25 and 26, which are taken from Malachi.

About 600 years after Nephi was supposed to have written these words, Jesus appeared to the Nephites and said: ". . . Behold other scriptures I would that ye should write, *that ye have not*" (*Book of Mormon*, 3 Nephi 23:6). Jesus then told the Nephites to "*write the words which the Father had given unto Malachi*, which he should tell unto them. . . . And these are the words which he did tell unto them, saying: Thus said the Father unto Malachi—Behold, I will send my messenger, and he shall prepare the way before me . . ." (3 Nephi 24:1).

"For behold, the day cometh that shall burn as an oven; and all the proud, yea, and all that do wickedly, shall be stubble; and the day that cometh shall burn them up . . ." (3 Nephi 25:1).

These words, attributed to Jesus, very plainly show that the Nephites could not have had the words of Malachi until Christ came among them. The Mormon writer George Reynolds acknowledged: "As Malachi lived between two and three hundred years after Lehi left Jerusalem, the Nephites knew nothing of the glorious things that the Father had revealed to him until Jesus repeated them" (*Complete Concordance of the Book of Mormon*, p.442). Now, if Nephi knew nothing concerning these words until the coming of Christ, how did Nephi quote them 600 years before?

Mark Twain said that the *Book of Mormon* "seems to be merely a prosy detail of imaginary history, with the Old Testament for a model; followed by a tedious plagiarism of the New Testament" (*Roughing It*, p.110). The ministry of Christ seems to have been the source for a good deal of the *Book of Mormon*. For instance, the story of Christ raising Lazarus from the dead seems to have had a definite influence upon the story of Ammon in the *Book of Mormon*. (The story of Ammon was supposed to have taken place in "about B.C. 90," or about 120 years before Christ began his public ministry.) Following are a few parallels between the two stories.

Book of Mormon	New Testament
In both stories a man seems to die and a period of time passes:	
"And it came to pass that after two days and two nights they were about to take his body and lay it in a sepulchre . . . " (Alma 19:1)	"Then when Jesus came, he found that he had lain in the grave four days already" (John 11:17)

Book of Mormon

New Testament

Both Martha and the queen use the word "stinketh":

". . . others say that he is dead and that *he stinketh* . . ." (Alma 19:5).

". . . by this time *he stinketh* . . ." (John 11:39).

Both Ammon and Jesus use the word "sleepeth" with regard to the man:

". . . *he sleepeth* . . ." (Alma 19:8)

". . . *Lazarus sleepeth* . . ." (John 11:11)

Both Ammon and Jesus say that the man will rise again:

". . . *he shall rise again* . . ." (Alma 19:8)

". . . *Thy brother shall rise again*" (John 11:23)

The conversation between Ammon and the queen contains other phrases that are similar to those used by Jesus and Martha:

"*And Ammon said unto her: Believest thou this? And she said unto him: . . . I believe* . . ." (Alma 19:9)

"*Jesus said unto her . . . Believest thou this? She saith unto him*, Yea, Lord: *I believe* . . ." (John 11:25-27)

In both cases the man arose:

". . . *he arose* . . ." (Alma 19:12)

". . . he that was dead came forth . . ." (John 11:44)

In the *Book of Mormon* we read the story of a great storm which the Nephites encountered on their way to the "promised land" (see 1 Nephi 18:6-21). This story bears a remarkable resemblance to a story concerning Jesus in Mark 4:3-39.

Book of Mormon

New Testament

The two stories use identical language when speaking of the storm:

". . . *there arose a great storm* . . ." (1 Nephi 18:13)

". . . *there arose a great storm* . . ." (Mark 4:37)

In both stories the storm becomes so severe that the people are about to "perish," and they seek help from their spiritual leader:

". . . my brethren began to see that . . . they must *perish* . . . wherefore, they . . . loosed the bands . . . " (1 Nephi 18:15)

". . . They awake him, and say unto him, Master, carest thou not that we *perish*?" (Mark 4:38)

117

Book of Mormon	New Testament

In both cases, after the leader comes forth, the storm ceases. Almost identical wording appears in both accounts concerning the calming of the sea:

"...the winds did cease ... and there was a great calm" (1 Nephi 18:21)	"...the wind ceased, and there was a great calm" (Mark 4:39)

It is very obvious that the author of the *Book of Mormon* has borrowed from Mark, yet the book of Nephi is supposed to be about 600 years older than the book of Mark. Therefore, the appearance of this story in the *Book of Mormon* proves beyond all doubt that it is not an ancient book.

One of the most striking parallels is the beheading of John the Baptist in the New Testament and the attempted beheading of Omer in the *Book of Mormon*. In Matthew 14:6-11 we read how "*the daughter of* Herodias *danced before*" and "*pleased*" Herod. When Herod promised to give her "whatsoever she would ask," she wanted "John Baptist's *head* in a charger." Now, in the *Book of Mormon* we read the following:

> And ... let my father send for Akish, ... and I will *dance before* him, ... wherefore if he shall desire of thee that ye shall give unto him me to wife, then shall ye say: I will give her if ye will bring unto me the *head* of my father ... the *daughter of* Jared *danced before* him that she *pleased* him, insomuch that he desired her to wife. ... And Jared said unto him: I will give her unto you, if ye will bring unto me the *head* of my father, the king (Ether 8:10-12).

While the incident in the Bible happened during Christ's lifetime, the incident in the *Book of Mormon* was supposed to have occurred many hundreds of years before Christ.

Wesley M. Jones points out that "the ministry of St. Paul is duplicated almost exactly in the ministry of Alma, one of Joseph's characters—even in manner of speech and travels" (*A Critical Study of Book of Mormon Sources*, pp.14-15). The reader will no doubt remember that when Paul was on the way to Damascus to persecute the church, the Lord appeared to him and said: "... Saul, *why persecutest thou me?*" (Acts 9:4). In the *Book of Mormon*, Alma also persecuted the church and, like Paul, he received a vision. The "angel of the Lord" spoke to him and said: "... Alma, ... *why persecutest thou* the church of God?" (Mosiah 27:11,13). We have found seventeen interesting parallels between Alma and the apostle Paul.

As we have already shown, the Nephites were not supposed to have had the books of the New Testament because they were written hundreds of years after they left Jerusalem. Nevertheless, we find many New Testament verses and parts of verses throughout the *Book of Mormon*. In the following list of parallels between the *Book of Mormon* and the New Testament we have tried to eliminate verses that also appear in the Old Testament. All of the verses from the *Book of Mormon* were supposed to have been written between 600 B.C. and A.D. 33. (In the following *BM* refers to the *Book of Mormon* and *KJV* refers to the King James Version of the Bible.)

> KJV: That which we have seen and heard declare we unto you (1 John 1:3)
>
> BM: to declare unto them concerning the things which he had both seen and heard (1 Nephi 1:18)

> KJV: that one man should die for the people, and that the whole nation perish not (John 11:50)
>
> BM: that one man should perish than that a nation should . . . perish in unbelief (1 Nephi 4:13)

> KJV: the love of God is shed abroad in our hearts (Rom. 5:5)
>
> BM: the love of God, which sheddeth itself abroad in the hearts (1 Nephi 11:22)

> KJV: made them white in the blood of the Lamb (Rev. 7:14)
>
> BM: made white in the blood of the Lamb (1 Nephi 12:11)

> KJV: shall be saved; yet so as by fire (1 Cor. 3:15)
>
> BM: shall be saved, even if it so be as by fire (1 Nephi 22:17)

> KJV: O wretched man that I am (Rom. 7:24)
>
> BM: O wretched man that I am (2 Nephi 4:17)

> KJV: death and hell delivered up the dead (Rev. 20:13)
>
> BM: death and hell must deliver up their dead (2 Nephi 9:12)

> KJV: he which is filthy, let him be filthy still: and he that is righteous, let him be righteous still (Rev. 22:11)
>
> BM: they who are righteous shall be righteous still, and they who are filthy shall be filthy still (2 Nephi 9:16)

> KJV: endured the cross, despising the shame (Heb. 12:2)
>
> BM: endured the crosses of the world, and despised the shame (2 Nephi 9:18)

> KJV: to be carnally minded is death; but to be spiritually minded is life (Rom. 8:6)
>
> BM: to be carnally-minded is death, and to be spiritually-minded is life (2 Nephi 9:39)

> KJV: Jew nor Greek, there is neither bond nor free, there is neither male nor female (Gal. 3:28)
>
> BM: Jew and Gentile, both bond and free, both male and female (2 Nephi 10:16)

KJV: there is none other name under heaven given among men, whereby we must be saved (Acts 4:12)

BM: there is none other name given under heaven save it be this Jesus Christ, . . . whereby man can be saved (2 Nephi 25:20)

KJV: the Lamb of God, which taketh away the sin of the world (John 1:29)

BM: the Lamb of God, who should take away the sins of the world (1 Nephi 10:10); the Lamb of God, which should take away the sins of the world (2 Nephi 31:4)

KJV: stedfast, unmoveable, always abounding in the work (1 Cor. 15:58)

BM: steadfast and immovable, always abounding in good works (Mosiah 5:15)

KJV: O death, where is thy sting? O grave, where is thy victory (1 Cor. 15:55)

BM: the grave should have no victory, and that death should have no sting (Mosiah 16:7)

KJV: they that have done good, unto the resurrection of life; and they that have done evil, unto the resurrection of damnation (John 5:29)

BM: If they be good, to the resurrection of endless life and happiness; and if they be evil, to the resurrection of endless damnation (Mosiah 16:11)

KJV: Stand fast therefore in the liberty wherewith Christ hath made us free (Gal. 5:1)

BM: stand fast in this liberty wherewith ye have been made free (Mosiah 23:13) stand fast in that liberty wherewith God has made them free (Alma 58:40)

KJV: Marvel not that . . . Ye must be born again (John 3:7)

BM: Marvel not that all mankind . . . must be born again (Mosiah 27:25)

KJV: come out from among them, and be ye separate, . . . and touch not the unclean thing (2 Cor. 6:17)

BM: come ye out from the wicked, and be ye separate, and touch not their unclean things (Alma 5:57)

KJV: lay aside every weight, and the sin which doth so easily beset us (Heb. 12:1).

BM: lay aside every sin, which easily doth beset you (Alma 7:15)

KJV: I say unto you, I have not found so great faith, no, not in Israel (Luke 7:9)

BM: I say unto thee, woman, there has not been such great faith among all the people of the Nephites (Alma 19:10)

KJV: And as Moses lifted up the serpent in the wilderness, even so must the Son of man be lifted up (John 3:14)

BM: And as he lifted up the brazen serpent in the wilderness, even so shall he be lifted up who should come (Helaman 8:14)

The verses or parts of verses from the *Book of Mormon* which we have presented above were all supposed to have been written between 600 B.C. and A.D. 33. Those which follow were supposed to have been written between A.D. 34 and A.D. 421. In A.D. 34 Jesus was supposed to have appeared to the Nephites and given them the Sermon on the Mount (see 3 Nephi, chapters 12-14). Since it is possible that Jesus could have given the same sermon to the Nephites we will not bother to list any of those verses. There are many other verses which Jesus was supposed to have given to the Nephites which are parallel to verses found in the four Gospels. We will not deal with any of these quotations in this study.

KJV: and heard unspeakable words, which it is not lawful for a man to utter (2 Cor. 12:4)

BM: and heard unspeakable things, which are not lawful to be written (3 Nephi 26:18)

KJV: whether in the body, or out of the body, I cannot tell (2 Cor. 12:3)

BM: whether they were in the body or out of the body, they could not tell (3 Nephi 28:15)

KJV: he said unto me, My grace is sufficient for thee: for my strength is made perfect in weakness (2 Cor. 12:9)

BM: the Lord spake unto me, saying: . . . my grace is sufficient for the meek, that they shall take no advantage of your weakness (Ether 12:26)

KJV: Charity suffereth long, and is kind; charity envieth not; . . . is not puffed up, . . . seeketh not her own, is not easily provoked, thinketh no evil; Rejoiceth not in iniquity, but rejoiceth in the truth; Beareth all things, believeth all things, hopeth all things, endureth all things (1 Cor. 13:4-7)

BM: charity suffereth long, and is kind, and envieth not, . . . is not puffed up, seeketh not her own, is not easily provoked, thinketh no evil, and rejoiceth not in iniquity but rejoiceth in the truth, beareth all things, believeth all things, hopeth all things, endureth all things (Moroni 7:45)

KJV: For to one is given by the Spirit the word of wisdom (1 Cor. 12:8)

BM: For behold, to one is given by the Spirit of God, that he may teach the word of wisdom (Moroni 10:9)

121

KJV: to another the word of knowledge by the same Spirit (1 Cor. 12:8)

BM: to another, that he may teach the word of knowledge by the same Spirit (Moroni 10:10)

KJV: to another the gifts of healing by the same Spirit (1 Cor. 12:9)

BM: to another, the gifts of healing by the same Spirit (Moroni 10:11)

These are only a small number of the parallels between the New Testament and the *Book of Mormon.* In *Mormonism—Shadow or Reality?* we listed over 200 parallels, and in another study we had a list of 400. We have found over a hundred quotations from the New Testament in the first two books of Nephi alone, and these books were supposed to have been written between 600 and 545 B.C.

One of the most serious mistakes in the *Book of Mormon* occurred when Christ appeared to the Nephites after His crucifixion and told them He was going to quote the words of Moses. The words which He should have quoted are found in Deuteronomy 18:15,18 and 19:

> The Lord thy God will raise up unto thee a Prophet from the midst of thee, of thy brethren, like unto me; unto him ye shall hearken; . . . I will raise them up a Prophet from among their brethren, like unto thee, and will put my words in his mouth; and he shall speak unto them all that I shall command him. And it shall come to pass, that whosoever will not harken unto my words which he shall speak in my name, I will require it of him.

Instead of quoting these words from Deuteronomy, however, Jesus quoted from Peter's paraphrase of Moses' words found in Acts 3:22-26. This is very obvious when we compare Peter's paraphrase of Moses' words and the words Christ was supposed to have quoted to the Nephites. Below is Peter's paraphrase as found in the book of Acts:

> For Moses truly said unto the fathers, A prophet shall the Lord your God raise up unto you of your brethren, like unto me; him shall ye hear in all things whatsoever he shall say unto you. And it shall come to pass, that every soul, which will not hear that prophet, shall be destroyed from among the people. *Yea, and all the prophets from Samuel and those that follow after, as many as have spoken,* have likewise foretold of these days. Ye are the children of the prophets, and of the covenant which God made with our fathers, saying unto Abraham, And in thy seed shall all the kindreds of the earth be blessed. Unto you first God, having raised up his Son Jesus, sent him to bless you, in turning away every one of you from his iniquities (Acts 3:22-26).

In the *Book of Mormon* we read:

> Behold, I am he of whom Moses spake, saying: A prophet shall
> the Lord your God raise up unto you of your brethren, like unto
> me; him shall ye hear in all things whatsoever he shall say unto
> you. And it shall come to pass that every soul who will not hear
> that prophet shall be cut off from among the people. Verily I say
> unto you, *yea, and all the prophets from Samuel and those that
> follow after, as many as have spoken,* have testified of me. And
> behold, ye are the children of the prophets; and ye are of the
> house of Israel; and ye are of the covenant which the Father
> made with your fathers, saying unto Abraham: And in thy seed
> shall all the kindreds of the earth be blessed. The Father having
> raised me up unto you first, and sent me to bless you in turning
> away every one of you from his iniquities . . . (3 Nephi 20:23-26).

It is obvious, then, that the *Book of Mormon* follows Peter's
paraphrase rather than the actual words of Moses recorded in
Deuteronomy. Verses 24 through 26 of the third chapter of Acts,
though slightly rewritten, are quoted in the *Book of Mormon.*
These words have nothing to do with Moses, but are in reality
the words of Peter. Peter spoke these words at the temple in
Jerusalem some time after the day of Pentecost. While it is
possible that these words could have been recorded at the time,
the book of Acts was probably not written until twenty or thirty
years later. George B. Arbaugh made the following statement
concerning this matter:

" '*Christ*' *in Book of Mormon Quotes Material Not Yet Written*
. . .

"Simon Peter here paraphrases and condenses Moses'
lengthy statement. . . . The wording is quite different from that
in Deuteronomy, but the writer of the Book of Mormon failed to
check on the original statement and assumed that Peter's report
of it was a verbatim quotation. Therefore the Book of Mormon
quotes Acts" (*Gods, Sex, and Saints,* p.36).

It is interesting to note that Nephi—who was supposed to
have written between 600 and 545 B.C.—also quoted this portion
of the book of Acts (see I Nephi 22:20).

Another serious mistake made by the author of the *Book of
Mormon* was that of having Jesus quote part of Revelation 21:6
to the Nephites. Following is a comparison of the way the
words appear in the book of Revelation and the way they are
found in the *Book of Mormon.*

"I am Alpha and Omega, the beginning and the end" (Rev.
21:6).

"I am Alpha and Omega, the beginning and the end" (3
Nephi 9:18).

The words *Alpha* and *Omega* are the first and last letters of the Greek alphabet. Apostle Bruce R. McConkie acknowledges this fact: "These words, the first and last letters of the Greek alphabet, are used figuratively . . ." (*Mormon Doctrine*, 1966, p.31).

The Greek language was used throughout the Roman Empire at the time of Christ; therefore, the New Testament was written in Greek and the words *Alpha* and *Omega* were well understood. The Nephites, however, were supposed to have left Jerusalem 600 years before the time of Christ, and therefore they would not have been familiar with these words. If Jesus had told the Nephites that He was "Alpha and Omega," it would have had absolutely no meaning to them. When the author of the *Book of Mormon* lifted these words from the book of Revelation he evidently did not realize that they were from the Greek language. Mormon writers maintain that the *Book of Mormon* "does not contain any of the numerous words in the New Testament that are of Greek origin" (*Contents, Structure, And Authorship of the Book of Mormon*, By J. N. Washburn, p.161). This idea is certainly incorrect. The words *Alpha* and *Omega* are definitely of Greek origin.

The *Book of Mormon* also contains the name Timothy (3 Nephi 19:4). Timothy is a Greek name and never appears in the Old Testament. In the same verse that we find the name Timothy we also find the name Jonas. Jonas is the New Testament name for Jonah and is found in Matthew 12:39. Joseph Smith seems to have been oblivious to the fact that the *Book of Mormon* contains Greek words. When it was suggested that the word Mormon came from the Greek, he stated: "This is not the case. There was *no Greek* or Latin upon the plates from which I, . . . translated the Book of Mormon" (*Times and Seasons*, vol. 4, p.194). The appearance of Greek words in the *Book of Mormon*—especially the words *Alpha* and *Omega*—is another evidence that it is not an ancient record, but rather a modern composition.

Mormon writers have tried to explain why so much of the New Testament is found in the *Book of Mormon*, but we feel that their explanations are only wishful thinking. The only reasonable explanation is that the author of the *Book of Mormon* had the King James Version of the Bible. And since this version did not appear until A.D. 1611, the *Book of Mormon* could not have been written prior to that time. The *Book of Mormon*, therefore, is a modern composition and not a "record of ancient religious history."

Origin of the Indians

Joseph Smith's mother tells that he had a great interest in the "ancient inhabitants" of this continent and that before he "translated" the *Book of Mormon* he used to entertain the family with stories about them: "He would describe . . . their dress, mode of traveling, and the animals upon which they rode; their cities, their buildings, with every particular; their mode of warfare; and also their religious worship. This he would do with ease, seemingly, as if he had spent his whole life among them" (*History of Joseph Smith by His Mother*, 1954 ed., p.83).

It is not surprising that Joseph Smith would take an interest in the ancient inhabitants of this continent, for many people were discussing the question at that time. The *Palmyra Register* for May 26, 1819, reported that one writer "believes (and we think with good reason) that this country was once inhabited by a race of people, at least, partially civilized, & that this race has been exterminated by the forefathers of the present and late tribes of Indians in this country."

The *Wayne Sentinel*, published at Palmyra, contained similar statements on July 24, 1829:

> The Aborigines. . . . are fast dwindling away, and will soon be buried in the depths of that oblivion which conceals the history and fate of a people who (judging from the traces discovered of the progress which they had made in civilization, and the arts and sciences, as developed by the western antiquities) must have been but a little behind the present generation in many respects. When we look at the straggling Indians who . . . reveal the ravages of intemperance and almost every other loathsome vice, we can hardly persuade ourselves that they are remnants of *the powerful race of people* who, as it were but yesterday, stretched from the Atlantic to the Pacific . . . we may picture them in our minds as a flourishing and mighty nation . . . powerful in wealth and natural resources; combining moral and political excellence . . . and we may suppose that some dreadful plague, some national calamity swept them from the face of the earth; or perhaps that like Sodom and Gomorrah of old, their national sins became so heinous, that the Almighty in his wrath utterly annihilated them. . . .

It is interesting to note that the *Book of Mormon* states that the Nephites were a civilized people who were destroyed by the Lamanites—a wicked people—for their sins.

An article published in the *Palmyra Herald* on February 19, 1823, said that one group of people might have "crossed the Pacific Ocean, and made settlements in North America" and that the "descendants of Japheth might afterwards cross the

Atlantic, and subjugate" the first group. The article goes on to state: "What wonderful catastrophe destroyed at once the first inhabitants, with the species of the mammoth, is beyond the researches of the best scholar and greatest antiquarian." There are some very interesting parallels between this article and the *Book of Mormon* which are discussed in *Mormonism–Shadow or Reality?* p.82.

During and even before Joseph Smith's time it was believed by many people that the Indians were the Lost Ten Tribes of Israel. Although the *Book of Mormon* does not claim that the Indians are the Lost Ten Tribes, it does claim that they are descendants of Joseph, thus making them Israelites. Because of this similarity anti-Mormon writers have suggested that Joseph Smith borrowed his idea concerning the origin of the Indians from the thinking of his time. Several books had been published prior to the coming forth of the *Book of Mormon* which contained the idea that the Indians were of Israelite origin. In 1816, at Trenton, New Jersey, Elias Boudinot published a book entitled, *A Star in the West; or, a Humble Attempt to Discover the Long Lost Tribes of Israel. . . ."* On pages 279-80 of this book we find the following rhetorical question: "What could possibly bring greater declarative glory to God, or tend more essentially to affect and rouse the nations of the earth, . . . and thus call their attention to the truth of divine revelation, than a full discovery, that these wandering nations of Indians are the long lost tribes of Israel. . . ."

Furthermore, the following was published in the *Wayne Sentinel* (the paper to which the family of Joseph Smith apparently subscribed) on October 11, 1825: "Those who are most conversant with the public and private economy of the Indians, are strongly of opinion that they are the *lineal descendants of the Israelites*, and my own researches go far to confirm me in the same belief" (*Wayne Sentinel*, October 11, 1825, as photographically reprinted in Larry Jonas, *Mormon Claims Examined*, p.45).

One of the most interesting books on this subject which was published prior to the *Book of Mormon* was Ethan Smith's *View of the Hebrews.* The first edition was printed in 1823; it was soon sold out and an enlarged edition appeared in 1825. The Mormon historian B. H. Roberts read *View of the Hebrews* and evidently became concerned because of the many parallels between it and the *Book of Mormon.* He prepared a manuscript in which these parallels are listed. Mimeographed copies of Roberts' list of parallels were "privately distributed among a restricted group of Mormon scholars," and in January 1956 Mervin B. Hogan had them published in *The Rocky Mountain Mason*. A careful reading of B. H. Roberts' work leads one to believe that he had serious doubts about the *Book of Mormon*. Notice some of his comments:

"Query: Could all this have supplied structural work for the Book of Mormon"? (p.20)

"Was this sufficient to suggest the strange manner of writing the book of Mormon in the learning of the Jews, and the language of the Egyptians, but in an altered Egyptian"? (p.22)

"Query: Would this treatise of the destruction of Jerusalem suggest the theme to the Book of Mormon author, is the legitimate query, since the View of the Hebrews was published seven to five years before the Book of Mormon"? (pp.24-25)

"Query: Did the author of the Book of Mormon follow too closely the course of Ethan Smith in this use of Isaiah, would be the legitimate query"? (p.25)

B. H. Roberts lists eighteen parallels between *View of the Hebrews* and the *Book of Mormon*. In his fourth parallel Roberts states: ". . . It is often represented by Mormon speakers and writers, that the Book of Mormon was the first to represent the American Indians as the descendants of the Hebrews; holding that the Book of Mormon is unique in this. The claim is sometimes still ignorantly made" (p.18).

In parallel number 5, B. H. Roberts points out that the idea of the Indians having a lost book may have been suggested by Ethan Smith's book. In parallel number 9, Roberts shows that the idea of the Lamanites destroying the Nephites and their culture could have been derived from *View of the Hebrews*. We cannot take the space here to discuss Roberts' parallels, but Hal Hougey of Pacific Publishing Company, Concord, California, has reprinted them in a pamphlet entitled *"A Parallel"—The Basis of the Book of Mormon*.

Some new evidence concerning B. H. Roberts' interest in *View of the Hebrews* has recently come to light. It has been discovered that Roberts wrote a manuscript of 291 pages entitled, "A Book of Mormon Study." In this manuscript 176 pages were devoted to the relationship of *View of the Hebrews* to the *Book of Mormon*. The manuscript was never published and remained in the family after his death. Only a few scholars have been allowed access to it. Michael Marquardt was given the privilege of reading the manuscript and has told us of its contents. It now appears that the eighteen "parallels" were a mere

127

sampling from the longer manuscript.*

Like the *Book of Mormon*, the *View of the Hebrews* has statements concerning the color of the Indians: "Mr. Adair expresses the same opinion; and the Indians have their tradition, that in the nation from which they originally came, all were of one color" (*View of the Hebrews*, 1825, p.88). "The Indians in other regions have brought down a tradition, that their former ancestors, away in a distant region from which they came, were white" (p.206).

The *Book of Mormon* states that the descendants of Lehi were white, but that the Lamanites were cursed with a dark skin: "And he had caused the cursing to come upon them, . . . as they were white, and exceeding fair and delightsome, that they might not be enticing unto my people the Lord God did cause a skin of blackness to come upon them" (2 Nephi 5:21).

We have previously mentioned that Josiah Priest's book, *The Wonders of Nature*, may have provided source material for the *Book of Mormon*. It is interesting to note that this book quotes extensively from Ethan Smith's *View of the Hebrews*. Over thirty pages are devoted to "Proofs that the Indians of North America are lineally descended from the ancient Hebrews." Priest's book was in the Manchester rental library and was circulated constantly in 1827 by members of the library.

Changes in the Book of Mormon

In 1965 we published a photographic reproduction of the first edition of the *Book of Mormon* showing that thousands of changes were made in the text since it was first published. We printed this study under the title *3,913 Changes in the Book of*

---

*A false rumor concerning this suppressed manuscript has recently been circulated—i.e., that B. H. Roberts tried to answer the objections which he himself had raised in his shorter work of eighteen parallels. This idea is certainly far from the truth. We have recently had the privilege of studying Roberts' work and have found that it not only fails to answer the objections to the Book of Mormon mentioned in the shorter work, but that it raises many new problems as well. In Part 1, chapter 14, Roberts summarizes: "In the light of this evidence, there can be no doubt as to the possession of a vividly strong, creative imagination by Joseph Smith, the Prophet. An imagination, it could with reason be urged, which, given the suggestions that are to be found in the 'common knowledge' of accepted American Antiquities of the times, supplimented [sic] by such a work as Ethan Smith's 'View of the Hebrews', would make it possible for him to create a book such as the Book of Mormon is." In Part 2, chapter 1, Roberts freely admits that "there is a certain lack of perspective in the things the book relates as history that points quite clearly to an undeveloped mind as their origin. The narrative proceeds in characteristic disregard of conditions necessary to its reasonableness, as if it were a tale told by a child, with utter disregard for consistency."

Mormon. Most of the changes are related to the correction of grammatical and spelling errors, but there are some that alter the meaning of the text. According to Joseph Smith's own testimony, there should not have been any reason to make changes in the *Book of Mormon*. He stated that when he and the witnesses went out to pray concerning it, "We heard a voice from out of the bright light above us, saying, 'These plates . . . have been translated by the power of God. The translation of them which you have seen is correct . . .'" (*History of the Church*, vol. 1, pp.54-55). On another occasion Joseph Smith stated that he "told the brethren that the Book of Mormon was the most correct of any book on earth . . ." (vol. 4, p.461).

The four most important changes in the *Book of Mormon* are related to the doctrine of a plurality of Gods, and therefore we will deal with them in chapter 7.

Another important change was made in Mosiah 21:28. In this verse the name of the king has been changed from Benjamin to Mosiah. In the 1830 edition of the *Book of Mormon* we read: ". . . king *Benjamin* had a gift from God, whereby he could interpret such engravings . . ." (*Book of Mormon*, 1830 ed., p.200).

In modern editions of the *Book of Mormon*, this verse has been changed to read: ". . . king *Mosiah* had a gift from God, whereby he could interpret such engravings . . ." (*Book of Mormon*, 1964 ed., p.176, v.28).

From chronology found in the *Book of Mormon* (see Mosiah 6:3-7 and 7:1) it would appear that king Benjamin should have been dead at this time, and therefore the Mormon church leaders evidently felt that it was best to change the king's name to Mosiah. Another change involving the names of Benjamin and Mosiah is found in the book of Ether. On page 546 of the first edition of the *Book of Mormon* we read: ". . . for this cause did king *Benjamin* keep them. . . ." In the 1964 edition (p.485, v. 1) this was changed to read: " . . . for this cause did king *Mosiah* keep them. . . ."

It is interesting to note that even the signed statement by the eight witnesses to the *Book of Mormon* has been altered. In the 1830 edition the last page read: ". . . Joseph Smith, Jr. the *Author and Proprietor* of this work, has shewn unto us the plates. . . ." In modern editions it has been changed to read: ". . . Joseph Smith, Jun., the *translator* of this work, has shown unto us the plates. . . ."

In the first edition of the *Book of Mormon*, page 87, this statement appears: ". . . the mean man boweth down. . . ." In modern editions (p.74, v. 9) this has been changed to read: ". . .

the mean man boweth *not* down. . . ."

The first edition of the *Book of Mormon* plainly shows that it was written by a man who did not have a great deal of education, although we must admit that the writer had ability and imagination. On page 31 of the first edition we read: ". . . neither will the Lord God suffer that the Gentiles shall forever remain in that *state of awful woundedness*. . . ." In modern editions (p.24, v. 32) this was changed to read: "Neither will the Lord God suffer that the Gentiles shall forever remain in that *awful state of blindness*. . . ."

On page 214 of the first edition we read: "My soul was *wrecked* with eternal torment. . . ." This was changed to read as follows in modern editions (p.188, v. 29): "My soul was *racked* with eternal torment. . . ."

One of the most frequent mistakes in the first edition of the *Book of Mormon* is the use of "was" instead of "were." The following are extracts from the first edition of the *Book of Mormon* in which "was" has been changed in later editions to "were":

". . . Adam and Eve, which *was* our first parents . . ." (p.15).

". . . the bands which *was* upon my wrists . . . " (p.49).

"And great *was* the covenants of the Lord . . ." (p.66).

". . . the arms of mercy *was* extended towards them; for the arms of mercy *was* extended . . . " (p.189).

". . . the priests *was* not to depend . . . " (p.193).

". . . those that *was* with him" (p.195).

". . . there *was* seven churches . . ." (p.209).

". . . there *was* many . . . " (p.209).

". . . I had much desire that ye *was* not in the state of dilemma . . . " (p.241).

". . . they *was* angry with me, . . . " (p.248).

". . . there *was* no wild beasts . . . " (p.460).

There are also many places where the word "were" has been changed to "was." The following are extracts from the first edition:

". . . it *were* easy to guard them . . ." (p.375).

"Behold I *were* about to write them . . ." (p.506).

". . . and I *were* forbidden that I should preach unto them . . ." (p.519).

Another common mistake in the first edition of the *Book of Mormon* is the use of the word "is" when it should read "are." The following are extracts from the first edition in which the word "is" has been changed to "are":

". . . there *is* save it be, two churches . . . " (p.33).

". . . the words which *is* expedient . . . " (p.67).

"But great *is* the promises of the Lord . . ." (p.85).

"And whoredoms *is* an abomination . . ." (p.127).

" . . . things which *is* not seen . . . " (p.315).

" . . . here *is* our weapons of war . . ." (p.346).

Another common mistake in the first edition is the use of the word "a" where it was not necessary. In the following extracts "a" has been deleted in later editions:

"As I was *a* journeying . . . " (p.249).

" . . . as Ammon and Lamoni was *a* journeying thither . . . " (p.280).

" . . . he found Muloki *a* preaching . . ." (p.284).

" . . . had been *a* preparing the minds . . . " (p.358).

" . . . Moroni was *a* coming against them . . ." (p.403).

On page 260 of the first edition the following statement appears: "Behold, the Scriptures are before you; if ye will *arrest* them, it shall be to your own destruction." In modern editions (p.229, v. 20) this has been changed to read: "Behold, the scriptures are before you; if ye will *wrest* them it shall be to your own destruction." A similar mistake is found on page 336 of the first edition: " . . . some have *arrested* the Scriptures. . . ." In modern printings (p.297, v. 1) this has been changed to read: " . . . some have *wrested* the scriptures. . . ."

The extracts that follow are from the first edition; the word "no" has been changed to "any" in later editions:

" . . . have not sought gold nor silver, nor *no* manner of riches . . ." (p.157).

" . . . they did not fight against God *no* more . . ." (p.290).

" . . . neither were there Lamanites, nor *no* manner of Ites . . ." (p.515).

On page 289 of the first edition this statement appears: " . . . or Omner, or Himni, nor *neither* of their brethren . . . " In the modern edition (p.255, v. 1) this has been changed to read: " . . . or Omner, or Himni, nor *either* of their brethren . . . "

In *Mormonism—Shadow or Reality?* pages 90-93, we included a much longer list of changes, but the examples we have cited here should give the reader an idea of some of the more interesting changes in the *Book of Mormon*. Many Mormons have claimed that there have never been any changes in the *Book of Mormon*. Although this is certainly incorrect, some anti-Mormons have gone to the other extreme and tried to make it appear that the *Book of Mormon* has been completely rewritten. As we stated earlier, most of the 3,913 changes which we found were related to the correction of grammatical and spelling errors and do not really change the basic meaning of the text.

Actually, the changes in the *Book of Mormon* do not even begin to compare with the serious changes found in Joseph Smith's revelations and in the *History of the Church*. Although we must not overemphasize the changes in the *Book of Mormon*, even changes in spelling and grammar are important when we consider the claims concerning the translation which were made by Joseph Smith and the witnesses to the book. Smith claimed that the *Book of Mormon* was "the most correct of any book on earth," and Martin Harris said that the words which appeared on the seer stone would not disappear until they were correctly written. Oliver B. Huntington recorded in his journal that in 1881 Joseph F. Smith, who later became the sixth president of the Mormon church, taught that the Lord gave Joseph Smith the exact English wording and spelling that he should use in the *Book of Mormon*:

> Saturday Feb. 25, 1881, I went to Provo to a quarterly Stake Conference. Heard Joseph F. Smith describe the manner of translating the Book of Mormon . . . Joseph did not render the writing on the gold plates into the English language in his own style of language as many people believe, but every word and every letter was given to him by the gift and power of God. . . . The Lord *caused each word spelled as it is in the book to appear on the stones in short sentences or words*, and when Joseph had uttered the sentence or word before him and the scribe had written it properly, that sentence would disappear and another appear. And if there was *a word wrongly written or even a letter incorrect the writing on the stones would remain there.* . . . and when corrected the sentence would disappear as usual ("Journal of Oliver B. Huntington," p.168 of typed copy at Utah State Historical Society).

Anti-Mormon writers criticized the grammar of the *Book of Mormon* stating that God could not make the many grammatical mistakes found in the *Book of Mormon*. Finally, the Mormon church leaders became so embarrassed about the grammar that they decided to abandon the idea that God gave Joseph Smith the English that is found in the *Book of Mormon*; their new idea was that God just gave Joseph Smith the idea and that he expressed it in his own words. This new theory makes it easier to explain why grammatical and spelling changes were made, but it does not explain changes such as the one where "Benjamin" was changed to "Mosiah."

Most of the more important changes in the *Book of Mormon* were made by Joseph Smith in the second edition, but the Mormon scholar Sidney B. Sperry admits that Apostle Talmage made many of the changes in 1920: "The writer happens to know that Dr. Talmage was a stickler for good English. . . . He knew as well as anyone the imperfections of the literary dress of the First Edition of the Nephite record and took a prominent part in correcting many of them in a later edition of the work (1920)" (*The Problems of the Book of Mormon*, p.190).

When a person examines the unchanged text of the 1830 edition of the *Book of Mormon* it becomes very obvious that it was written by someone without a great deal of education. The style and the type of mistakes which are found in the first edition of the *Book of Mormon* are similar to those found in a document written by Joseph Smith in the early 1830's (see *Mormonism—Shadow or Reality?* pp.88-89).

Archaeology and the Book of Mormon

Some members of the Mormon church have made fantastic claims about archaeologists using the *Book of Mormon*. For instance, we are informed that a letter which was written to Earnest L. English on May 3, 1936, was duplicated and "distributed to LDS church members by leaders (local) in Cleveland, Ohio in 1959." We quote the following from that letter:

> The inquiry you made regarding the Book of Mormon is a commendable one and I will be pleased to mention *the part which it has played in helping the government to unravel the problem of the aborigines. . . . it was 1920 before the Smithsonian Institute officially recognized the Book of Mormon as a record* of any value. All discoveries up to this time were found to fit the *Book of Mormon* accounts and so the heads of the Archaeological Department decided to make an effort to discover some of the larger cities described in the Book of Mormon records.
>
> *All members of the department were required to study the account* and make rough-maps of the various populated centers. . . . During the past fifteen years the Institute has made remarkable study of its investigations of the Mexican Indians and it is true that *the Book of Mormon has been the guide to almost all of the major discoveries.*
>
> When Col. Lindbergh flew to South America five years ago, he was able to sight heretofore undiscovered cities which the archaeologists at the Institute had mapped out according to the locations described in the *Book of Mormon. This record is now quoted by the members of the Institute as an authority and is recognized by all advanced students in the field.*

Because of many false statements, such as the one cited above, the Smithsonian Institution has been forced to publish a statement concerning these matters (see photograph of this statement in *Mormonism—Shadow or Reality?* p.97). In this statement we find the following: "The Smithsonian Institution *has never used the Book of Mormon* in any way as a scientific guide. Smithsonian archeologists see *no connection* between the archeology of the New World and the subject matter of the Book."

Frank H. H. Roberts, Jr., of the Smithsonian Institution, elaborated further on the subject in a letter dated February 16, 1951:

> In reply to your letter of February 11, 1951, permit me to say that the *mistaken idea* that the Book of Mormon has been used by scientific organizations in conducting archeological explorations has become quite current in recent years. It can be stated definitely that *there is no connection between the archeology of the New World and the subject matter of the Book of Mormon.*
>
> There is no correspondence whatever between archeological sites and cultures as revealed by scientific investigations and as recorded in the Book of Mormon, hence *the book cannot be regarded as having any historical value* from the standpoint of the aboriginal peoples of the New World.
>
> The Smithsonian Institution has *never officially recognized the Book of Mormon as a record of value on scientific matters*, and the Book has never been used as a guide or source of information for discovering ruined cities (Letter dated February 16, 1951, photographically reproduced in *The Book of Mormon Examined*, by Arthur Budvarson, La Mesa, California, 1959, p.37).

In 1973 Michael Coe, one of the best known authorities on archaeology of the New World, wrote an article for *Dialogue: A Journal of Mormon Thought.* In this article he stated:

> Mormon archaeologists over the years have almost unanimously accepted the Book of Mormon as an accurate, historical account of the New World peoples. . . . They believe that Smith could translate heiroglyphs. . . . Likewise, they accept the Kinderhook Plates as a bona fide archaeological discovery, and the reading of them as correct. Let me now state uncategorically that as far as I know *there is not one professionally trained archaeologist, who is not a Mormon, who sees any scientific justification* for believing the foregoing to be true, and I would like to state that there are quite a few Mormon archaeologists who join this group. . . .
>
> The bare facts of the matter are that nothing, absolutely nothing, has ever shown up in any New World excavation which would suggest to a dispassionate observer that the Book of Mormon, as claimed by Joseph Smith, is a historical document relating to the history of early migrants to our hemisphere (Dialogue: A Journal of Mormon Thought, Summer 1973, pp.41,42,46).

134   In his pamphlet *Archeology and the Book of Mormon*, Hal

Hougey gives us the following information:

> Latter-day Saints have only recently entered seriously into the field of anthropology, though they have "long evidenced an avid, though amateur, interest in the subject" since the earliest days of the Mormon Church. . . .
>
> While there are today only a few Latter-day Saints with a doctor's degree in anthropology, these few have served to curtail the extravagant claims which have been made by Mormon missionaries and by the lavish picture books published by Mormons. . . .

When Mormon missionaries and writers make extravagant claims about American archeology proving the *Book of Mormon*, we need only to refer them to the following statements by their own anthropologists:

> "The statement that the Book of Mormon has already been proved by archaeology *is misleading*. The truth of the matter is that we are only now beginning to see even the outlines of the archaeological time-periods which could compare with those of the Book of Mormon. How, then, can the matter have been settled once and for all? That such an idea could exist indicates *the ignorance of many of our people with regard to what is going on in the historical and anthropological sciences*." (Christensen in *U.A.S. Newsletter*, no. 64, January 30, 1960, p.3).
>
> "Many times, Mormon missionaries have told their investigators that such late-period ruins as Monte Alban (periods III-V), Yagul, and Mitla were built by the Nephites and that the archaeologists would confirm this. Both claims are untrue. However, the earliest periods of the area, Monte Alban I and II, although as yet little known, are of Preclassic (i.e. Book of Mormon period) date. One may think of these earlier peoples as Jaredites or Nephites, but if so *it must be on the basis of faith, not archaeology*, for so far there is no explicit evidence that Book of Mormon peoples occupied this area [Oaxaca, in the Isthmus of Tehuantepec area of Mexico]" (Joseph E. Vincent in *U.A.S. Newsletter*, no. 66, May 7, 1960, p.2).

Christensen chides his brethren with the following comment:

> "As for the notion that the Book of Mormon has already been proved by archaeology, I must say with Shakespeare, 'Lay not that flattering unction to your soul!' (Hamlet III:4)" (*U.A.S. Newsletter*, no. 64, January 30, 1960, p.3).

What about the Mormon claim that non-Mormons have found the Book of Mormon helpful as a guide in locating ruins of cities in Central America? M. Wells Jakeman, Mormon anthropologist, answers this question:

> "It must be confessed that some members of the 'Mormon' or Latter-day Saint Church are prone, in their enthusiasm for the

Book of Mormon, *to make claims for it that cannot be supported. So far as is known to the writer, no non-Mormon archaeologist at the present time is using the Book of Mormon as a guide in archaeological research.* Nor does he know of any non-Mormon archaeologist who holds that the American Indians are descendants of the Jews, or that Christianity was known in America in the first century of our era" . . . (*Ibid.*, no. 57, March 25, 1959, p.4).

"With the exception of Latter-day Saint archaeologists, members of the archaeological profession do not, and never have, espoused the Book of Mormon in any sense of which I am aware. Non-Mormon archaeologists do not allow the Book of Mormon any place whatever in their reconstruction of the early history of the New World" (Christensen in *U.A.S. Newsletter*, no. 64, January 30, 1960, p.3).

. . . We conclude, therefore, that the *Book of Mormon* remains completely unverified by archaeology. The claims Mormon missionaries have made are fallacious and misleading (Archeology and the Book of Mormon, by Hal Hougey, rev. ed., 1976, pp.4-6,8,9,14).

John L. Sorenson, a Mormon archaeologist who was assistant professor of Anthropology and Sociology at BYU, added his comments concerning some of the popular Mormon books on archaeology and the *Book of Mormon*:

Various individuals unconnected with these institutionalized activities have also wrestled with the archaeological problem. Few of the writings they have produced are of genuine consequence in archaeological terms. Some are clearly on the oddball fringe; others have credible qualifications. Two of the most prolific are Professor Hugh Nibley and Milton R. Hunter; however, they are not qualified to handle the archaeological materials their works often involve. . . . As long as Mormons generally are willing to be fooled by (and pay for) the uninformed, uncritical drivel about archaeology and the scriptures which predominates, the few L.D.S. experts are reluctant even to be identified with the topic (Dialogue: A Journal of Mormon Thought, Spring 1966, pp.145,149).

M. T. Lamb, a writer critical of the *Book of Mormon*, observed concerning archaeology and the *Book of Mormon*:

We shall find a great many other representations of the Book of Mormon equally at fault, squarely and flatly contradicted by the facts of ancient American history.

For instance, what can be more clearly stated than the religious condition of this country, especially Central America, for a period of over two hundred years after Christ? A *Christian* civilization prevailed all over both continents.

It is not necessary here to repeat the passages in the Book of Mormon which describe such civilization. . . . It is only needful now to show that nothing could be wider from the truth, unless all ancient American history is a lie, and its ten thousand relics tell false tales.

It may be stated in a general way that there never has been a time upon this western hemisphere within the historic period, or within three thousand years past when a uniform civilization of ANY KIND prevailed over both continents.

But this will be considered hereafter. We are to learn now—

1st. That a Christian civilization has never existed in Central America, not even for a day.

2d. The people of Central America, as far back as their record has been traced (and that is centuries earlier than the alleged beginning of Nephite history), *have always been an idolatrous people*, as thoroughly heathen as any which the history of the world has described, worshiping idols the most hideous in form and feature that have ever been found upon earth, and accompanying that worship by human sacrifices as barbarous as the annals of history have recorded. . . . A sad fatality, is it not, dear reader, that in the very region of country where the Book of Mormon fixes magnificent temples and sanctuaries erected by a Christian people for the worship of the true God, there should be dug up out of the ruins of old temples and palaces such relics of the real religion of these ancient peoples? All the records that have come down to us make it certain that these horrid idols instead of the Lord Jesus were worshipped throughout Central America 2000 years ago. It would indeed be a bright page in Central American history if the assertions of the Book of Mormon were true. But no such bright spot can be discovered either in the Nahuan or the Mayan records. For more than three thousand years it was one unbroken record of superstition and human slaughter. . . . The entire civilization of the Book of Mormon, its whole record from beginning to end is flatly contradicted by the civilization and the history of Central America (*The Golden Bible; or, The Book of Mormon. Is It From God?*, New York, 1887, pp.284-289).

Dr. Hugh Nibley, the most well-known Mormon apologist of the present time, tries to explain away the fact that archaeologists have not found any evidence that the Nephites or Jaredites ever existed:

Book of Mormon archaeologists have often been disappointed in the past because they have consistently looked for the wrong things. . . . People underestimate the capacity of things to disappear, and do not realize that the ancients almost never built of stone. . . .

Proceed with Caution!: There is certainly no shortage of ruins on this continent, but until some one object has been definitely identified as either Nephite or Jaredite it is dangerous to start drawing any conclusions. . . . The search must go on, but conclusions should wait. We are asking for trouble when we describe any object as Nephite or Jaredite. . . . Aside from the danger of building faith on the 'highly ambiguous materials' of archaeology and the 'unavoidable subjective' and personal interpretations of the same, we should remember that archaeology at its best is a game of surprises.

A Disappointing Picture: People often ask, if the Book of Mormon is true, why do we not find this continent littered with mighty ruins? . . . Where are your Jaredite and Nephite splendors of the past? . . . In the Nephites we have a small and mobile population dispersed over a great land area, living in quickly-built wooden cities. . . . Their far more numerous and enduring contemporaries, the Lamanites and their associates including Jaredite remnants (which we believe were quite extensive) had a type of culture that leaves little if anything behind it. . . . We have no description of any Book of Mormon city to compare with Homer's description of Troy. How shall we recognize a Nephite city when we find it? (*An Approach to the Book of Mormon,* 1957, pp.366, 370, 373).

In his book *Since Cumorah*, Dr. Nibley admits that there is no real archaeological evidence to prove that the Nephites ever existed:

From the first both Mormons and their opponents recognized the possibility of testing the Book of Mormon in a scientific way. The book described certain aspects of civilizations purporting to have existed in the New World in ancient times. Very well, where were the remains? A vast amount of time, energy, and patience has been expended in arguing about the interpretations of the scanty evidence that is available, but very little has been devoted to the systematic search for more. Of course, almost any object could conceivably have some connection with the Book of Mormon, but nothing short of an inscription which could be read and roughly dated could bridge the gap between what might be called a pre-actualistic archaeology and contact with the realities of Nephite civilization.

The possibility that a great nation or empire that once dominated vast areas of land and flourished for centuries could actually get lost and stay lost in spite of every effort of men to discover its traces, has been demonstrated many times since Schliemann found the real world of the Mycenaeans. . . .

So it is with the Nephites. All that we have to go on to date is a written history. That does not mean that our Nephites are necessarily mythical. . . . But as things stand we are still in the pre-archaeological and pre-anthropological stages of Book of Mormon study. Which means that there is nothing whatever that an anthropologist or archaeologist as such can say about the Book of Mormon. Nephite civilization was urban in nature. . . . It could just as easily and completely vanish from sight as the worlds of Ugarit, Ur, or Cnossos; and until some physical remnant of it, no matter how trivial, has been identified beyond question, what can any student of physical remains possibly have to say about it? Everything written so far by anthropologists or archaeologists—even real archaeologists—about the Book of Mormon must be discounted, for the same reason that we must discount studies of the lost Atlantis: not because it did not exist, but because it has not yet been found (*Since Cumorah*, Salt Lake City, 1967, pp.243-44).

Fortunately, some Mormon scholars are beginning to face the truth with regard to *Book of Mormon* archaeology. Dee Green, assistant professor of Anthropology at Weber State College, has written an article for *Dialogue*. This article is very critical of "Book of Mormon archaeology," and this is very significant because Mr. Green was at one time deeply involved in archaeological work at the Mormon church's Brigham Young University. In 1953-54 he served as assistant editor of the *University Archaeological Society Newsletter*, and in 1958-61 he served as editor. In his article for *Dialogue: A Journal of Mormon Thought*, Dee F. Green stated:

Having spent a considerable portion of the past ten years functioning as a scientist dealing with New World archaeology, I find that nothing in so-called Book of Mormon archaeology materially affects my religious commitment one way or the other, and I do not see that *the archaeological myths so common in our proselytizing program* enhance the process of true conversion. . . .

The first myth we need to eliminate is that Book of Mormon archaeology exists. Titles on books full of archaeological half-truths, dilettanti on the peripheries of American archaeology calling themselves Book of Mormon archaeologists regardless of their education, and a Department of Archaeology at BYU devoted to the production of Book of Mormon archaeologists do not insure that Book of Mormon archaeology really exists. If one is to study Book of Mormon archaeology, then one must have a corpus of data with which to deal. We do not. The Book of Mormon is really there so one can have Book of Mormon studies, and archaeology is really there so one can study archaeology, but the two are not wed. At least they are not wed in reality since *no Book of Mormon location is known with reference to modern topography.* Biblical archaeology can be studied because we do know where Jerusalem and Jericho were and are, but *we do not know where Zarahemla and Bountiful (nor any other location for that matter) were or are.* It would seem then that a concentration on geography should be the first order of business, but we have already seen that twenty years of such an approach has *left us empty-handed (Dialogue: A Journal of Mormon Thought,* Summer 1969, pp.76-78).

While we found Dee F. Green's admissions rather startling, they cannot begin to compare with the surprise we received on December 2, 1970, when we received a visit from Thomas Stuart Ferguson.

Mr. Ferguson has devoted a great deal of his life trying to prove the *Book of Mormon* by archaeology and is recognized by the Mormon people as a great defender of the faith. He has written at least three books on the subject—one of them in collaboration with Milton R. Hunter of the First Council of the Seventy. On the jacket to his book, *One Fold and One Shepherd,* we find the following:

> Thomas Stuart Ferguson, 47, President of the New World Archaeological Foundation, is a distinguished student of the earliest high civilizations of the New World. He, with Dr. A. V. Kidder, dean of Central American archaeologists, first planned the New World Archaeological Foundation in 1952. . . . He raised $225,000 for the field work, incorporated the Foundation (being an attorney), assisted in the initial explorations in Central America and Mexico and has actively directed the affairs of the Foundation since its inception.

Thomas Stuart Ferguson really believed that archaeology would prove the *Book of Mormon.* In his book *One Fold And One Shepherd,* page 263, he stated: "The important thing now is to continue the digging at an accelerated pace in order to find more inscriptions dating to Book-of-Mormon times. Eventually we should find decipherable inscriptions . . . referring to some unique person, place or event in the Book of Mormon." In 1962 Mr. Ferguson said that "Powerful evidences sustaining the book are accumlating."

The first indication we had that Mr. Ferguson was losing his faith in Mormonism was just after Joseph Smith's Egyptian Papyri were rediscovered. In 1968 he wrote us a letter saying that we were "doing a great thing—getting out some truth on the Book of Abraham." Later we heard a rumor that he had given up Joseph Smith's Book of Abraham, but this hardly prepared us for his visit on December 2, 1970. At that time, Mr. Ferguson told us frankly that he had not only given up the Book of Abraham, but that he had come to the conclusion that Joseph

140

Smith was not a prophet and that Mormonism was not true. He told us that he had spent twenty-five years trying to prove Mormonism, but had finally come to the conclusion that all his work in this regard had been in vain. He said that his training in law had taught him how to weigh evidence and that the case against Joseph Smith was absolutely devastating and could not be explained away. Mr. Ferguson found himself faced with a dilemma, for the Mormon church had just given him a large grant ($100,000 or more) to carry on the archaeological research of the New World Archaeological Foundation. He felt, however, that the New World Archaeological Foundation was doing legitimate archaeological work, and therefore he intended to continue this work.

From 1948 to 1961 the Department of Archaeology at Brigham Young University sent "five archaeological expeditions to Middle America," but no evidence for the Nephites was discovered. After these expeditions had failed, the church leaders gave "large appropriations" to support Mr. Ferguson's New World Archaeological Foundation. This organization also failed to find evidence to prove the *Book of Mormon*, and the man who organized it, hoping that it would prove Mormonism, ended up losing his faith in the church.

The Anthon Transcript

In the *Book of Mormon*, Mormon 9:32-33, we read as follows:

> And now, behold, we have written this record according to our knowledge, in the characters which are called among us the reformed Egyptian, being handed down and altered by us, according to our manner of speech. And if our plates had been sufficiently large we should have written in Hebrew; but the Hebrew hath been altered by us also; and if we could have written in Hebrew, behold, ye would have had no imperfection in our record.

The anti-Mormon writer M. T. Lamb makes some observations concerning the idea of Hebrews writing in Egyptian:

> The Book of Mormon sets out with four very improbable and really absurd statements.
>
> 1. The first is that Lehi and his family used the Egyptian language. . . .
>
> There are a multitude of reasons that make such a statement altogether improbable. In the first place, Lehi had lived all his lifetime, . . . in the city of Jerusalem, surrounded constantly by those who spoke only the Hebrew language. . . . In the second place, the Jews hated the Egyptians with a bitter hatred, and it is

therefore inconceivable that a true-born Jew a real lover of his own people, loyal and patriotic as he professes to have been, would have been willing thus to insult his people, or that the Jews around him would have endured the insult. In the third place, the ancient Jew had an unusual veneration for his mother tongue, the sacred Hebrew.... Now that such a man with such a venerated language could have accepted instead the Egyptian tongue, which was associated only with ignomiy and dishonor, [is] the height of absurdity....

2. The second statement is still more objectionable—that there were found in the possession of a man by the name of Laban, a relative of Lehi's, and also a resident of the city of Jerusalem, certain brass plates upon which were engraven, in the Egyptian language, the five books of Moses, containing the law, the entire history of the Jews from the first down to Laban's time, ... all of the Old Testament as we have it, that had been written up to that time, six hundred years before Christ.... All this engraven in the Egyptian language.... This is more improbable and absurd than the first statement (*The Golden Bible*, pp.89-91).

Mormon writer J. N. Washburn admits that this is a real problem:

The point at issue is not that Father Lehi, the Jew, could read and understand Egyptian, though this is surprising enough.... No, the big question is how the scripture of the Jews (official or otherwise) came to be written in Egyptian.... If I were to suggest what I think to be the most insistent problem for Book-of-Mormon scholarship, I should unquestionably name this one: account for the Egyptian language on the Plates of Brass, and the Brass Plates themselves! (*The Contents, Structure and Authorship of the Book of Mormon*, p.81).

Joseph Smith claimed that he made a copy of some of the characters on the gold plates and that Martin Harris showed them to Professor Charles Anthon, in New York. According to Joseph Smith's *History of the Church*, (vol. 1, p.20), Martin Harris claimed that "Professor Anthon stated that the translation was correct, more so than any he had before seen from the Egyptian." Since Professor Anthon was not an Egyptologist, and since the science of Egyptology was just in its infancy at the time, even Mormon scholars have questioned this statement about Anthon's endorsement of the translation of the *Book of Mormon* (see *Mormonism—Shadow or Reality?* p.105). In a letter dated February 17, 1834, Professor Anthon denied that he had endorsed the translation: " 'The whole story about my pronouncing the Mormon inscription to be reformed Egyptian hieroglyphics is perfectly false.... the paper contained anything else but Egyptian hieroglyphics" (Letter by Charles Anthon, as quoted in *A Comprehensive History of the Church*, vol. 1, p.103).

According to Mormon historians, "a fragment of the transcript of the Book of Mormon characters" which was submitted to Professor Anthon is still in existence (see *A Comprehensive History of the Church*, vol. 1, p.100). Egyptologists who have recently examined the Anthon Transcript are unable to make any kind of a translation. Although Dee Jay Nelson thinks that the characters look like abbreviated hieratic, Klaus Baer, of the University of Chicago, thinks they are nothing but "doodlings."

Whether Joseph Smith copied the characters or made them up, the Anthon Transcript provides no evidence for the authenticity of the *Book of Mormon* because no one is able to read it. The Mormon scholar Sidney B. Sperry frankly stated that "no one, the prophet Joseph Smith excepted, has yet translated the Anthon Transcript. If modern students of Egyptians can't do it—at least they haven't—it is too much to believe that Professor Anthon could" (*The Problems of the Book of Mormon*, p.60).

Actually, the Anthon Transcript provides a great deal of evidence against the authenticity of the *Book of Mormon*. M. T. Lamb stated:

> The point we here wish to make is this: throughout North America, according to the Book of Mormon, this reformed Egyptian was the universal language of the people fifteen hundred years ago, when the Book of Mormon was compiled.
>
> Now fortunately or unfortunately Joseph Smith has preserved for us and for the inspection of the world, a specimen of the characters found upon the plates from which he claims to have translated the Book of Mormon. He transcribed a few of the characters from the plates as specimens. . . .
>
> Well, now, unfortunately for the claims of the Book of Mormon, we are able to learn precisely what kind of characters were used in Central America by its ancient inhabitants. They have been preserved in imperishable marble. Engraven upon stone in such a way as to retain to the end of time a silent though solemn rebuke to the false and foolish pretensions of the author of this book.
>
> In the ruins of the two oldest cities in Central America, Copan and Palenque, are found in abundance the strange hieroglyphics, the written language of the people who once inhabited those old cities. Thousands of these mysterious characters are scattered about, engraven over ruined doorways and arches, upon the sides and backs of hideous-looking idols carved in stone, upon

marble slabs, on the sides of immense pillars, here and there through the ruins of magnificent palaces and monster heathen temples. . . .

These same hieroglyphics have been preserved in other forms—for the ancient Mayas had books. . . . An examination of the three that are now known to be preserved, shows the same characters that are found upon the stone tablets, idols, etc., . . . and represent the actual written language of the ancient Mayas—a people who are known to have occupied Central America, and been the sole occupants of a portion of that country at the very time, and covering the whole period, when, according to the Book of Mormon, the Nephites lived and flourished there. . . . A woeful fatality, is it not? that there should not be even one of Mr. Smith's characters that bears a family likeness, or the least particle of resemblance to the characters actually used by the ancient inhabitants of Central America! . . . we should find, in thousands of places, these reformed Egyptian characters engraved upon marble blocks and granite pillars. . . . But need we say that just the contrary of all this is found to be true. . . . It would therefore be sheer nonsense to imagine that the assertions of the Book of Mormon may after all have been true, but that through the lapse of time all traces of such a written language may have disappeared. Stone and marble, and gold and silver, and copper and brass are not liable to disappear in the brief period of 1500 years (*The Golden Bible*, pp.259-72).

In 1959 the Mormon archaeologist Ross T. Christensen frankly admitted that " 'reformed' Egyptian" is a "form of writing which we have not yet identified in the archaeological material available to us" (*Book of Mormon Institute*, December 5, 1959, BYU, 1964 ed., p.10).

John A. Wilson, who was professor of Egyptology at the University of Chicago, summarized the situation in a letter to Marvin Cowan: "From time to time there are allegations that picture writing has been found in America. . . . In no case has a professional Egyptologist been able to recognize these characters as Egyptian hieroglyphs. From our standpoint there is no such language as 'reformed Egyptian' " (Letter from John A. Wilson dated March 16, 1966).

Richard A. Parker, department of Egyptology at Brown University, added his corroboration that, "No Egyptian writing has been found in this hemisphere to my knowledge" (Letter to Marvin Cowan, dated March 22, 1966). In the same letter Richard A. Parker stated: "I do not know of any language such as Reformed Egyptian."

In *Mormonism–Shadow or Reality?* (pp.108-16), we show

that there have been a number of discoveries in the New World which have been used to try to support the *Book of Mormon*. We demonstrate, however, that these finds do not support the claims of the *Book of Mormon* and a number of them have turned out to be forgeries.

Compared with Bible Archaeology

Apostle Orson Pratt once stated: "This generation have [*sic*] more than one thousand times the amount of evidence to demonstrate and forever establish the divine Authenticity of the Book of Mormon than they have in favor of the Bible!" (*Orson Pratt's Works,* "Evidences of the Book of Mormon and Bible Compared," p.64).

We feel that this statement is far from the truth. The only evidence for the existence of the gold plates is the testimony of eleven witnesses, and as we have already shown, this testimony cannot be relied upon. A comparison of the archaeological evidence for the *Book of Mormon* with the evidence for the Bible clearly shows the weakness of the Mormon position. This, of course, is not to imply that there are no problems connected with biblical archaeology, or that archaeological evidence alone can prove the Bible to be divinely inspired. Frank H. H. Roberts, Jr., of the Smithsonian Institute, commented in a letter written to Marvin Cowan on January 24, 1963: "Archaeological discoveries in the Near East have verified some statements in the Bible referring to certain tribes, places, etc. On the other hand there is no way in which they could verify the narrative parts of the Bible such as the actions, words, deeds, etc. of particular individuals." In the same letter he continues: "There is no evidence whatever of any migration from Israel to America, and likewise no evidence that pre-Columbian Indians had any knowledge of Christianity or the Bible."

The reader will remember that Dr. Nibley frankly admitted that no ancient inscription mentioning the Nephites has ever been found, and that "nothing short of an inscription which could be read and roughly dated would bridge the gap between what might be called a pre-actualistic archaeology and contact with the realities of Nephite civilization" (*Since Cumorah,* p.243).

While the Nephites are never mentioned in any ancient inscription, the existence of the Israelites is verified by many inscriptions dating back hundreds of years before the time of Christ. The "earliest archaeological reference to the people of Israel" is a stele of the Egyptian ruler Merneptah which is now in the Egyptian Museum in Cairo. In *The Biblical World* (pp.380-81), we find this information about the stele:

Merneptah, son and successor of Ramesses II, ruled Egypt from ca.1224 to ca.1214 B.C. . . . His campaign in Palestine, waged during the fifth year of his reign (ca.1220 B.C.) is commemorated on a large black granite stele which was found in Merneptah's mortuary temple in Thebes. At the top is a representation of Merneptah and the god Amun, . . . Merneptah states:

Israel is laid waste, his seed is not;

Hurru (i.e. Syria) is become a widow for Egypt.

The stele provides the first mention of Israel on ancient monuments, and provides proof that Israel was in western Palestine by 1220 B.C.

John A. Wilson, the noted Egyptologist, said that "an Egyptian scribe was conscious of a people known as Israel somewhere in Palestine or Transjordan" (*The Culture of Ancient Egypt*, University of Chicago Press, 1965, p.255. Copyright © 1951 by The University of Chicago. Used by permission.).

Many ancient inscriptions mentioning the Israelites have been found, and some inscriptions even give the names of kings mentioned in the Bible. The New Testament mentions a number of rulers that are known to have lived around the time of Christ. For instance, the Bible tells us that Jesus was crucified under Pontius Pilate. That Pilate was an actual historical person was proved beyond all doubt in 1961 when "an inscription with the name of Pontius Pilate was found in the theater excavations" at Caesarea (*The Biblical Archaeologist*, September 1964, p.71).

The fact that the Jews were in Palestine at the time the Bible indicates is proven by hundreds of ancient Hebrew inscriptions that have been found on rocks, pieces of pottery and coins. Portions of every book of the Old Testament, except for the book of Esther, have also been found. These manuscripts are known as the Dead Sea Scrolls. In addition many inscriptions from other countries verify the fact that the Jews were present in Palestine.

When we turn to the *Book of Mormon*, however, we are unable to find any evidence at all that the Nephites ever existed. We must agree with the Mormon archaeologist Dee F. Green when he states: "The first myth we need to eliminate is that Book of Mormon archaeology exists. . . . Biblical archaeology can be studied because we do know where Jersualem and Jericho were and are, but we do not know where Zarahemla and Bountiful (nor any other location for that matter) were or are" (*Dialogue: A Journal of Mormon Thought*, Summer 1969, pp.77-78).

Beyond the Book of Mormon

Although Joseph Smith once said that "the Book of Mormon was the most correct of any book on earth, and a man would get nearer to God by abiding its precepts, than by any other book," he departed from many of its teachings and proclaimed doctrines that were in direct contradiction to it. Although the *Book of Mormon* is still the primary tool used to bring converts into the Church, the *Doctrine and Covenants* and *Pearl of Great Price* have taken its place as far as doctrine is concerned. President Joseph Fielding Smith said that "the book of Doctrine and Covenants to us stands in a peculiar position *above them all*" (*Doctrines of Salvation*, vol. 3, p.198). In the chapters which follow we will show that many of the doctrines the Mormon leaders now teach are in direct contradiction to the *Book of Mormon*.

THE FIRST VISION

Chapter 6

Mormon Apostle LeGrand Richards proclaims: "On the morning of a beautiful spring day in 1820 there occurred one of the most important and momentous events in this world's history. God, the Eternal Father and His Son, Jesus Christ, appeared to Joseph Smith and gave instructions concerning the establishment of the kingdom of God upon the earth in these latter days" (*A Marvelous Work and a Wonder*, 1966, p.7).

Joseph Smith published his story in the Mormon publication *Times and Seasons* in 1842. The following is his description of the vision:

> So in accordance with my determination, to ask of God, I retired to the woods to make the attempt. It was on the morning of a beautiful clear day, early in the spring of eighteen hundred and twenty . . . I saw a pillar of light exactly over my head. . . . When the light rested upon me I saw two personages (whose brightness and glory defy all description) standing above me in the air. One os them spoke unto me, calling me by name, and said, (pointing to the other.) "This is my beloved Son, hear him." . . . I asked the personages who stood above me in the light, which of all the sects was right, . . . I was answered that I must join none of them, for they were all wrong, and the personage who addressed me said that all their creeds were an abomination in his sight; that those professors were all corrupt. . . . He again forbade me to join with any of them: and many other things did he say unto me which I cannot write at this time (*Times and Seasons*, vol. 3, pp.728,748).

This story is now published in the *Pearl of Great Price* and is accepted as Scripture by the Mormon people. Apostle John A. Widtsoe said that "the First Vision of 1820 is of first importance in the history of Joseph Smith. Upon its reality rest the truth and value of his subsequent work" (*Joseph Smith—Seeker After Truth*, p.19).

James B. Allen, who is now assistant church historian, stated that "belief in the vision is one of the fundamentals to which faithful members give assent. Its importance is second only to belief in the divinity of Jesus of Nazareth. The story is an essential part of the first lesson given by Mormon missionaries to prospective converts, and its acceptance is necessary before baptism" (*Dialogue: A Journal of Mormon Thought*, Autumn, 1966, p.29).

Fawn M. Brodie was one of the first to cast serious doubt upon the authenticity of Joseph Smith's story of the first vision:

> The description of the vision was first published by Orson Pratt in his *Remarkable Visions* in 1840, twenty years after it was supposed to have occurred. Between 1820 and 1840 Joseph's friends were writing long panegyrics; his enemies were defaming him in an unceasing stream of affidavits and pamphlets, and Joseph himself was dictating several volumes of Bible-flavored prose. But no one in this long period even intimated that he had heard the story of the two gods. At least, no such intimation has survived in print or manuscript. . . . The first published Mormon history, begun with Joseph's collaboration in 1834 by Oliver Cowdery, ignored it altogether . . . Joseph's own description of the first vision was not published until 1842, twenty-two years after the memorable event. . . .
>
> If something happened that spring morning in 1820, it passed totally unnoticed in Joseph's home town, and apparently did not even fix itself in the minds of members of his own family. The awesome vision he described in later years may have been the elaboration of some half-remembered dream stimulated by the early revival excitement and reinforced by the rich folklore of visions circulating in his neighborhood. Or it may have been sheer invention, created some time after 1834 when the need arose for a magnificent tradition to cancel out the stories of his fortune-telling and money-digging (*No Man Knows My History*, New York, 1957, pp.24-25).

Dr. Hugh Nibley, of Brigham Young University, was very disturbed by Mrs. Brodie's statements, but he admitted that Joseph Smith did not publish the story until 1842: "Joseph Smith's 'official' account of his first vision and the visits of the angel Moroni was written in 1838 and first published in the *Times and Seasons* in 1842" (*Improvement Era*, July 1961, p.490).

Perhaps one of the most damaging evidences that Joseph Smith did not see the Father and the Son in 1820, to those who believe in the restoration of the Priesthood, is the fact that in the year 1832 Joseph Smith claimed to have a revelation which stated that a man could not see God without the Priesthood. This revelation is published as Section 84 of the *Doctrine and Covenants*. In verses 21-22 we read:

"And without the ordinances thereof, and the authority of the priesthood, the power of godliness is not manifest unto men in the flesh;

"For without this no man can see the face of God, even the Father, and live."

Now, it is claimed that "The Father and the Son appeared to the Prophet Joseph Smith *before* the Church was organized and *the priesthood* restored to the earth" (*Doctrines of Salvation*, by Joseph Fielding Smith, vol. 1, p.4).

The revelation given in 1832 suggests that Joseph Smith's story of the first vision was made up years after it was supposed to have occurred. Smith did not even claim to have the Priesthood in 1820, and the *Doctrine and Covenants* clearly says that without the Priesthood no man can see God and live.

James B. Allen, who now serves as assistant church historian, frankly admitted that the story of the first vision "was *not* given general circulation in the 1830's." (*Dialogue: A Journal of Mormon Thought*, Autumn 1966, p.33). Dr. Allen makes some startling concessions in this article. He admits, for instance, that "none of the available contempory writings about Joseph Smith in the 1830's, none of the publications of the Church in that decade, and no contemporary journal or correspondence yet discovered mentions the story of the first vision. . . ." Dr. Allen goes on to state that in the 1830's "the general membership of the Church knew little, if anything, about it."

In the past Mormon apologists have argued that Joseph Smith's first vision was well known from the first time it was announced in 1820. It is refreshing to read James B. Allen's attempt to set the record straight. We were planning to extract a lengthy quotation from Dr. Allen's article, but he refused to give us permission. Those who are interested, however, can read his entire article in *Dialogue: A Journal of Mormon Thought*, Autumn 1966, pages 29-45.

"Strange" Accounts

Mormon leaders have maintained that Joseph Smith told only one story concerning his first vision. Preston Nibley asserted that "Joseph Smith lived a little more than twenty-four years after this first vision. During this time *he told but one story* . . ." (*Joseph Smith the Prophet*, 1944, p.30).

At the very time that Preston Nibley made this statement the Mormon leaders were suppressing at least three accounts of the first vision by Joseph Smith which were written prior to the account he published in the *Times and Seasons*. Levi Edgar Young, who was the head of the Seven Presidents of Seventies in the Mormon church, told LaMar Petersen that he had examined a "strange" account of the first vision and was told not to reveal what it contained. The following, from notes by LaMar Petersen, recounts the interview with Levi Edgar Young which was held on February 3, 1953: "His curiosity was excited when reading in Roberts' Doc. History reference to 'documents from which these writings were compiled.' Asked to see them. Told to get higher permission. Obtained that permission. Examined the documents. Was told *not to copy or tell what they contained*. Said it was *a 'strange' account of the First Vision*. Was put back in vault. Remains unused, unknown."

We became interested in the "strange" account and wrote to the church historian for a copy. Our letter was never answered, and we had almost given up hope of ever seeing this document. To our great surprise, however, three "strange" accounts of the first vision have now come to light. The first appeared in the thesis, "An Analysis of the Accounts Relating Joseph Smith's Early Visions," by Paul R. Cheesman. Mr. Cheesman was a student at Brigham Young University who was trying to gather information to support the first vision story. In his zeal, however, Mr. Cheesman brought to light a document which delivers a fatal blow to the official account of the first vision. Not realizing the serious implications of this document, Mr. Cheesman reproduced it as Appendix D of his thesis. This document, written by Joseph Smith himself, not only makes it evident that he did not see both the Father and the Son in 1820, but also casts a shadow of doubt upon his entire story of the origin of the church. Mr. Cheesman states that it "appears to be the earliest written account" of the first vision. He says that it "was never published or referred to by any of the authorities of the church as far as the writer has been able to determine. . . . Instead of going back over and revising, Joseph Smith evidently dictated the story later as we have it in Appendix A" ("An Analysis of the Accounts Relating Joseph Smith's Early Visions," M. A. thesis, Brigham Young University, 1965, p.64).

In 1965 we published this early account of the first vision under the title, *Joseph Smith's Strange Account of the First Vision*. Because the document was so unusual, some members of the Mormon church doubted its authenticity. Although the Mormon leaders would make no public statement concerning the document, James B. Allen, who was at the time associate professor of History at Brigham Young University, admitted that the document was genuine. In an article published in 1966, he stated:

One of the most significant documents of that period yet discovered was brought to light in 1965 by Paul R. Cheesman. . . . This is a handwritten manuscript apparently composed about 1833 and either written or dictated by Joseph Smith. It . . . includes the story of the first vision. . . . the story varies in some details from the version presently accepted. . . . The manuscript has apparently lain in the L.D.S. Church Historian's office for many years, and yet few if any who saw it realized its profound historical significance (*Dialogue: A Journal of Mormon Thought*, Autumn 1966, p.35).

The Mormon leaders suppressed this account of the first vision for over 130 years. But after we printed it thousands of copies were distributed throughout the world. Finally, four years *after* we published the document, the church historical department made a public statement confirming the authenticity of the manuscript. Dean C. Jessee, who is "a member of the staff at the LDS Church Historian's Office in Salt Lake City," claims that the document was written by Joseph Smith in 1831 or 1832:

On at least three occasions prior to 1839 Joseph Smith began writing his history. The earliest of these is a six-page account recorded on three leaves of a ledger book, written between the summer of 1831 and November 1832. . . .

The 1831-32 history transliterated here contains the earliest known account of Joseph Smith's First Vision (*Brigham Young University Studies*, Spring 1969, pp.277-78).

At first Dean Jessee felt that the document was penned by Frederick G. Williams, but on more careful examination he found that it was actually written by Joseph Smith himself:

A closer look at the original document has shown that while Williams wrote the beginning and end of the narrative, Joseph Smith wrote the remainder, including the portion containing the details of his First Vision. This is *the only known account of the Vision in his own hand*. Most of his writings were dictated, which is not to say that other accounts are less authentic (*Dialogue: A Journal of Mormon Thought*, Spring 1971, p.86).

Now that *Brigham Young University Studies* has published a photograph of this document in the Spring 1969 issue, page 281, we no longer have to depend upon Cheesman's typed copy. Below is the important part of this document taken directly from the photograph of the original document:

. . . the Lord heard my cry in the wilderness and while in the attitude of calling upon the Lord in the *16th year* of my age a piller [sic] of light above the brightness of the sun at noon day marvilous even in the likeness of him who created them and when i considered upon these things my heart exclaimed well hath the wise man said the fool saith in his heart there is no God my heart exclaimed all all these bear testimony and bespeak an omnipotant and omnipreasant power a being who maketh Laws and decreeth and bindeth all things in their bounds who filleth Eternity who was and is and will be from all Eternity to Eternity and when i considered all these things and that being seeketh such to worship him as worship him in spirit and in truth therefore i cried unto the Lord for mercy for there was none else to whom i could go and to obtain mercy and the Lord heard my cry in the wilderness and while in the attitude of calling upon the Lord a pillar of fire light above the brightness of the sun at noon day come down from above and rested upon me and i was filled with the spirit of god and the Lord opened the heavens upon me and i saw the Lord and he spake unto me saying Joseph my son thy sins are forgiven thee go thy way walk in my statutes and keep my commandments behold i am the Lord of glory i was crucifyed for the world that all those who believe on my name may have Eternal life behold the world lieth in sin and at this time and none doeth good no not one they have turned asside from the gospel and keep not my commandments they draw near to me with their lips while their hearts are far from me and mine anger is kindling against the inhabitants of the earth to visit them according to this ungodliness and to bring to pass that which hath been spoken by the mouth of the prophets and Apostles behold and lo i come quickly as it was written of me in the cloud clothed in the glory of my Father and my soul was filled with love and for many days i could rejoice with great joy and the Lord was with me but could find none that would believe the heavenly vision nevertheless i pondered these things in my heart about that time my mother but after many days

A photograph of Joseph Smith's first handwritten account of the first vision. This is the only account in Smith's own handwriting.

come down from above and rested upon me and I was filled with the spirit of god and the Lord opened the heavens upon me and *I saw the Lord* and he spake unto me saying *Joseph my son thy sins are forgiven thee*, go [*sic*] thy way walk in my statutes and keep my commandments   behold I am the Lord of glory   I was crucifyed [*sic*] for the world that all those who believe on my name may have Eternal life behold the world lieth in sin at this time and none doeth good no not one   they have turned asside [*sic*] from the gospel and keep not my commandments   they draw near to me with their lips while their hearts are far from me   and mine anger is kindling against the inhabitants of the earth to visit them according to this ungodliness and to bring to pass that which hath been spoken by the mouth of the prophets and Apostles   behold and lo I come quickly as it was w[r]itten of me in the cloud clothed in the glory of my Father. . . .

A careful examination of this document reveals that the reason church leaders have "never published or referred" to it is that it contains irreconcilable differences with the official account. These differences concern Joseph Smith's age, his reason for seeking the Lord, the question of a revival, and the presence of an evil power (see *Mormonism—Shadow or Reality?* p.146). The most serious contradiction between the accounts is the number of personages in the vision. In the first account Joseph Smith only mentions one personage: ". . . I saw *the Lord.* . . ." In the version published today in the *Pearl of Great Price*, Joseph Smith said: ". . . I saw *two personages.*" In the account that was suppressed by Mormon leaders, Joseph Smith related that the Lord said he was "crucifyed for the world." This, of course, would mean that the personage had to be Jesus Christ. Therefore, it is plain to see that Joseph Smith did *not* include God the Father in his first account of the vision. James B. Allen stated: "In this story, *only one personage was mentioned,* and this was obviously the Son, for he spoke of having been crucified" (*Dialogue: A Journal of Mormon Thought*, Autumn 1966, p.40).

Paul R. Cheesman tries to excuse the fact that the account which was suppressed only mentions one personage by stating: "As he writes *briefly* of the vision, he does not mention the Father as being present; however, this does not indicate that he was not present" ("An Analysis of the Accounts Relating Joseph Smith's Early Visions," p.63).

This explanation by Paul Cheesman does not seem reasonable. Actually, in this first account, Joseph Smith quotes the Lord as saying more words than in his later printed version.

Speaking of the "account of 1832," the Mormon writer Milton V. Backman says: "It is possible that after dictating the account, Joseph recognized the desirability of modifying certain statements. . . . Often when people record biographical sketches or historical incidents, they write and rewrite until their ideas are clearly expressed" (*Joseph Smith's First Vision*, 1971, p.124).

While it is true that many people have to "write and rewrite until their ideas are clearly expressed," we do not feel that Joseph Smith could have left out the most important part of the story by accident. If God the Father had actually appeared in this vision, Joseph Smith certainly would have included this information in his first account. It is absolutely impossible for us to believe that Joseph Smith would not have mentioned the Father if He had actually appeared.

The reader will notice how the wording is changed to support the idea of two personages. In the first account Joseph Smith says that "the Lord . . . spake unto me saying *Joseph my son* thy sins are forgiven thee." The later version also uses the word son, but this time it no longer refers to Joseph Smith but rather to another personage in the vision: "One of them spoke unto me, calling me by name, and said, (pointing to the other.) *'This is my beloved Son*, hear him.' "

We feel that the only reasonable explanation for the Father not being mentioned in the account which was suppressed is that Joseph Smith did not see God the Father, and that he made up this part of the story after the writing of the first manuscript. This, of course, throws a shadow of doubt upon the whole story.

After this "strange" account came to light, a Mormon seminary teacher told us that there was still another account of the first vision which the Mormon leaders were suppressing. To our great surprise, this second account was published in the Autumn, 1966, issue of *Dialogue: A Journal of Mormon Thought*. It appeared in the article by James B. Allen. We do not have room to deal with this account here. Although it is a very important account, it was overshadowed by still another account which was published by Dean C. Jessee of the church historical department in the Spring 1971 issue of *Dialogue: A Journal of Mormon Thought*. Mr. Jessee informs us that this account was recorded "in the Prophet's 1835-36 Diary by his scribe, Warren Parrish." The important part of this account reads as follows:

> . . . I called on the Lord in mighty prayer, a pillar of fire appeared above my head, it presently rested down upon me head, and filled me with joy unspeakable, a personage appeared in the midst of this pillar of flame which was spread all around, and yet nothing

consumed, another personage soon appeared like unto the first, he said unto me thy sins are forgiven thee, he testifyed [sic] unto me that Jesus Christ is the Son of God; and I saw many angels in this vision   I was about 14 years old when I received this first communication . . . (Joseph Smith's Diary, 1835-36, p.24, as quoted in *Dialogue: A Journal of Mormon Thought*, Spring 1971, p.87).

The reader will notice that in this account of the first vision there is absolutely nothing to show that the personages were God and Christ. The statement, "He testifyed unto me that Jesus Christ is the Son of God," would seem to show that the personages were *not* the Father and the Son. If Joseph Smith had intended to show that the personage who spoke was Jesus, he should have said something like this: "He testified also unto me that He was the Son of God." On the other hand, if he intended to show that the personage who spoke was the Father, he would probably have said something like this: "He testified also unto me that Jesus Christ was His son."

Adding to the confusion, Joseph Smith states that there were "many angels in this vision." Neither of the other versions indicate that there were "many angels."

It is also interesting to note that Joseph Smith's 1835-36 diary was used as a basis for much of his *History of the Church* for that period, but the portion containing this confusing account of the first vision was omitted.

We have now examined three different handwritten manuscripts of the first vision. They were all written by Joseph Smith or his scribes and yet every one of them is different. The first account says there was only one personage. The second account says there were many, and the third says there were two. The church, of course, accepts the version which contains two personages. If we had to accept any of the versions, we would chose the first account. It was written six or seven years closer to the event, and therefore it should give a more accurate picture of what really took place. Also, this account, which mentions only one personage, is the only account in Joseph Smith's own handwriting.

At any rate, when one becomes aware of the fact that there are conflicting versions of the story, it becomes very difficult to believe that Joseph Smith ever had a vision in the grove.

On top of all this, there is irrefutable evidence that an important reference to the first vision in the *History of the Church* has been falsified by Mormon historians after Joseph Smith's death. Over thirty years ago, Fawn M. Brodie suggested that there might be a problem with this reference:

Under the date of November 15, 1835 in the *History of the Church* appears the following statement by Joseph Smith: "I gave him [Erastus Holmes] a brief relation of my experience while in my juvenile years, say from six years old up to the time I received my first vision, which was when I was about fourteen years old . . . " (Vol. II, p.312). But Joseph admittedly did not begin writing his history until 1838, and the editors of this history do not state from which manuscript source in the Utah Church library this journal entry came. Access to all these important manuscripts is denied everyone save authorities of the Mormon Church (*No Man Knows My History*, p.24, footnote).

Apostle John A. Widtsoe tried to defend this reference from the *History of the Church* by stating:

> In 1835 he told one Erastus Holmes of his "First Vision which was when I was fourteen years old." . . . The proponents of the theory that the Prophet invented the First Vision in 1838 doubt the accuracy of the Holmes and similar references, because they hold that the Church History, the journal of Joseph Smith, has been tampered with by later workers. It is sad when a drowning man does not even have a straw to which he may cling!" (*Joseph Smith—Seeker After Truth*, pp.24-25).

In spite of John A. Widtsoe's statement, a woman who was doing research at the Utah State Historical Society searched through a microfilm of the early *Deseret News* and found information which proves that the Mormon historians deliberately altered Joseph Smith's statement. In the 1850's the *Deseret News* (the Mormon church's newspaper) was publishing Joseph Smith's *History of the Church*. In the issue for May 29, 1852, the following statement by Joseph Smith appeared:

> This afternoon, Erastus Holmes, of Newbury, Ohio, called on me to inquire about the establishment of the church, and to be instructed in doctrine more perfectly. I gave him a brief relation of my experience while in my juvenile years, say from six years old up to the time I received *the first visitation of angels*, which was when I was about *fourteen years old*; also the revelations that I received afterwards concerning the Book of Mormon, and a short account of the rise and progress of the church up to this date (*Deseret News*, vol. 2, no. 15, May 29, 1852).

Because this statement by Joseph Smith contradicted the teaching that the Father and the Son appeared to him in the first vision of 1820, the Mormon church historians altered the words when they reprinted it in later editions of the *History of the Church*. They changed the wording so that the word "angels" was completely left out. The following is a comparison of the way this reference was originally published in the *Deseret News*   **157**

DESERET NEWS.

"Truth and Liberty."

VOL. 2.] GREAT SALT LAKE CITY, U. T., SATURDAY, MAY 29, 1852. [NO. 15.

Which I would not exchange for all
That ever on the ear may fall.

[Copyright Secured.]

LIFE OF JOSEPH SMITH.

Saturday morning, 14th. Thus came the word of the Lord unto me, saying, Verily thus saith the Lord unto my servant Joseph, concerning my servant Warren, behold his sins are forgiven him, because of his desires to do the works of righteousness. Therefore, inasmuch as he will continue to hearken unto my voice, he shall be blessed with wisdom, and with a sound mind, even above his fellows. Behold it shall come to pass in his day, that he shall see great things shew forth themselves unto my people; he shall see much of my ancient records, and shall know of hidden things, and shall be endowed with a knowledge of hidden languages; and if he desires and shall seek it at my hands, he shall be privileged with writing much of my word, as a scribe unto me for the benefit of my people; therefore this shall be his calling until I shall order it otherwise in my wisdom; and it shall be said of him in time to come, behold Warren, the Lord's scribe, for the Lord's seer, whom he hath appointed in Israel. Therefore, if he will keep my commandments, he shall be lifted up at the last day; even so, amen.

This afternoon, Erastus Holmes, of Newbury, Ohio, called on me to inquire about the establishment of the church, and to be instructed in doctrine more perfectly. I gave him a brief relation of my experience while in my juvenile years, say from six years old up to the time I received the first visitation of angels, which was when I was about fourteen years old; also the revelations that I received afterwards concerning the Book of Mormon, and a short account of the rise and progress of the church up to this date. He listened very attentively, and seemed highly gratified, and intends to unite with the church.

On Sabbath morning, 16th, he went with me to meeting, which was held in the school house, as the chapel was not finished plastering.— President Rigdon preached on the subject of

A photograph of the *Deseret News*, May 29, 1852. Notice that Joseph Smith stated that "angels" appeared to him in the first vision. The word "angels" has been removed in recent editions of the *History of the Church*.

and the way it has been changed to read in recent printings of the *History of the Church*:

Deseret News	*History of the Church*
"... I received *the first visitation of angels*, which was when I was about fourteen years old ..." (May 29, 1852).	"... I received *my first vision*, which was when I was about fourteen years old ..." (vol. 2, p.312).

The original handwritten manuscript for this part of Joseph Smith's History reads exactly like the *Deseret News*: "... I received *the first visitation of angels* ..." (Manuscript History, Book B-1, p.642). In addition to this, Joseph Smith's 1835-36 diary, page 37, provides supporting evidence for the word "angels": "... I received *the first visitation of angels. . . .*"

The fact that Mormon historians had to make such a serious change in Joseph Smith's *History* after his death tends further to weaken the case for the first vision.

Not Unique

The Mormon writer Paul R. Cheesman says that "Joseph Smith's account is unique in that the Father and the Son appeared together and they both spoke. To those who accept the Bible and the Book of Mormon as authentic, nowhere in these histories do we have another example that parallels this experience in this respect" ("An Analysis of the Accounts Relating Joseph Smith's Early Visions," p.18).

Now that we have Joseph Smith's first account of his vision, which only mentions Christ as appearing, we know that his claim was not unique. Many people were making similar claims. For instance, in 1816 a minister by the name of Elias Smith published a book in which he told of his conversion. Notice how similar it is to Joseph Smith's first account: "... I went into the woods ... a light appeared from heaven. ... My mind seemed to rise in that light to the throne of God and the Lamb. ... The Lamb once slain appeared to my understanding, and while viewing him, I felt such love to him as I never felt to any thing earthly. ... It is not possible for me to tell how long I remained in that situation ... " (*The Life, Conversion, Preaching, Travels, and Sufferings of Elias Smith*, Portsmouth, N.H., 1816, pp.58-59).

Alexander Campbell wrote the following on March 1, 1824, concerning a "revival in the state of New York": "Enthusiasm flourishes. .... This man was regenerated when asleep, by a vision of the night. That man heard *a voice in the woods*, saying,

'*Thy sins be forgiven thee.*' A third *saw his Savior* descending to the tops of the trees at noon day" (*The Christian Baptist*, vol. 1, pp.148-49).

Asa Wild claimed to have a revelation which is very similar to the story Joseph Smith published. It was published in the *Wayne Sentinel* (the paper to which the family of Joseph Smith apparently subscribed) on October 22, 1823: "It seemed as if my mind ... was struck motionless, as well as into nothing, before the awful and glorious majesty of the Great Jehovah. He then spake ... He also told me, that every denomination of professing christians had become extremely corrupt. . . ."

It is plain to see, then, that the story Joseph Smith penned in the early 1830s is not much different than the visions related by others. It was only when he added the part about the Father appearing with the Son that the story began to sound unique.

First History

In the early years of the Mormon church the members were taught that the first vision Joseph Smith had was in 1823 when he was seventeen years of age, and that the personage who appeared was an angel (not God the Father and His Son Jesus Christ) who told him about the *Book of Mormon*. Oliver Cowdery, one of the three witnesses to the *Book of Mormon* and the first church historian, wrote a history of Mormonism which was published in the *Messenger and Advocate*—the official church organ at that time. This history shows that the story of the visit of the Father and the Son was not taught to the Mormon people. Francis W. Kirkham, in his book *A New Witness For Christ In America*, (vol. 1, p.17), says:

> The first published consecutive account of the origin of the Church began in the October, 1834, issue of the *Messenger and Advocate*. It consists of eight letters written by Oliver Cowdery to W. W. Phelps. This account is very important as Oliver Cowdery claims in a letter published in the October, 1834, issue, but dated September 7, 1834, that *Joseph Smith assisted him* in the writing of the letters.

The *Messenger and Advocate*, (vol. 1, p.13), said that it would be a "full history of the rise of the ch rch," and on page 42 of the same volume we read that it would contain "a correct statement of events." In the February, 1835, issue of the *Messenger and Advocate*, Oliver Cowdery told how Joseph Smith made his first contact with God:

> You will recollect that I mentioned the time of a religious excitement, in Palmyra and vicinity to have been in the 15th year of our

brother J. Smith Jr's age—that was an error in the type—it should have been in the 17th.—You will please remember this correction, as it will be necessary for the full understanding of what will follow in time. This would bring the date down to the year 1823... . while this excitement continued, he continued to call upon the Lord in secret for a full manifestation of divine approbation, and for, to him, the all important information, *if a Supreme being did exist*, to have an assurance that he was accepted of him. . . .

On the evening of the 21st of September, 1823, previous to retiring to rest, our brother's mind was unusually wrought up on the subject which had so long agitated his mind—his heart was drawn out in fervent prayer. . . . While continuing in prayer for a manifestation . . . on a sudden a light like that of day, . . . burst into the room.—. . . and in a moment a personage stood before him . . . he heard him declare himself to be *a messenger* sent by commandment of the Lord, to deliver a special message, and to witness to him that his sins were forgiven . . . (*Messenger and Advocate*, vol. 1, pp.78-79).

Several things should be noted concerning this history: first, that it was supposed to be a "correct" account; second, that Joseph Smith assisted in the writing; third, that the date of the religious excitement in Palmyra was 1823; fourth, that Joseph Smith desired to know at this time "if a Supreme being did exist"; fifth, that a "messenger sent by commandment of the Lord" appeared to him and told him that his sins were forgiven. If the reader examines this account carefully, he will see that it is absolutely impossible to reconcile it with Joseph Smith's later story that he saw the Father and the Son in 1820.

A Doctrinal Change

Prior to the time Paul Cheesman wrote his thesis at Brigham Young University, Mormon writers were emphatically proclaiming that Joseph Smith "told but one story" of the first vision. Now that the "strange" accounts of the first vision have been printed and widely circulated, Mormon apologists are forced to admit their existence and authenticity. They will not, however, face the serious implications of the differences in the accounts. Dr. Truman G. Madsen, of Brigham Young University, even goes so far as to say that "we are impressed with their harmony considering the very different circumstances of their writing . . ." (*Brigham Young University Studies*, Spring 1969, p.240).

When Lauritz G. Petersen, research supervisor at the church historian's office, was asked concerning the different accounts of the first vision, he wrote a letter in which he stated: "We are not concerned really with which of the two Versions of the First Vision is right. . . . Personally I would take the version which the Prophet Joseph gave himself when he stated that he saw two personages. Regardless *whether he saw one or two* the fact remains that Jesus Christ is mentioned in both of them."

It is obvious from this statement that some Mormon apologists are beginning to retreat from the idea that God the Father appeared to Joseph Smith. This is actually a very important matter, because Mormon leaders have used this vision as evidence for their doctrine of a plurality of gods. They have stated that this vision proves that God and Christ are two distinct personages and that they both have a body. They use the first vision to prove that God Himself is only an exalted man. George Q. Cannon, who was a member of the First Presidency of the Mormon church, declared in 1883:

> There was no man scarcely upon the earth that had a true conception of God. . . . But all this was swept away in one moment by the appearance of . . . God, the Father, and His Son Jesus Christ, to the boy Joseph. . . . The Father came accompanied by the Son, thus showing that there were two personages of the God-head . . . Joseph saw that the Father had a form; that He had a head; that He had arms; that He had limbs; that he had feet; that He tad a face and a tongue . . ." (*Journal of Discourses*, vol. 24, pp.371-72).

Apostle LeGrand Richards states: "This was the prophet's first vision. From this we learn among other truths, that God the Father and his Son, Jesus Christ, are *separate and distinct personages*, and that man is literally created in the image of God" (*A Marvelous Work And A Wonder*, 1966, p.12). Tenth president, Joseph Fielding Smith said that "there is *no account* in history or revelation extant, where ever before both the Father and the Son appeared in the presence of mortal man in glory" (*Essentials in Church History*, pp.46-47). Apostle John A. Widtsoe stated: "It was an extraordinary experience. *Never before* had God the Father and God the Son appeared to mortal man" (*Joseph Smith—Seeker After Truth*, p.4).

Actually, the fact that the first written account of the first vision only mentioned one personage is consistent with what Joseph Smith believed about God when he wrote the *Book of Mormon*. The *Book of Mormon*, which was first published in 1830, taught that there was but one God:

> And now Abinadi said unto them: I would that ye should understand that *God himself* shall come down among the children of men, and shall redeem his people. And because he dwelleth in flesh he shall be called the Son of God, and having subjected the

flesh to the will of the Father, being *the Father and the Son.* . . .
And thus the *flesh* becoming subject to the *Spirit,* or the *Son* to the
Father, being one God . . . (*Book of Mormon,* Mosiah 15:1,2,5).

The *Book of Mormon* tells of a visitation of the Father and the
Son to the "brother of Jared." The Father and the Son mentioned,
however, are *not two separate personages.* Only *one* personage
appears, and this personage says: "Behold, I am he who was
prepared from the foundation of the world to redeem my people.
Behold I am Jesus Christ. *I am the Father and the Son.* In me shall
all mankind have light . . ." (Ether 3:14).

The *Book of Mormon* clearly teaches that God the Father is a
Spirit, and the first edition of the *Doctrine and Covenants* also
contained a reference which stated that God is a Spirit.

It would appear, then, that Joseph Smith did not believe that
God the Father had a body at the time he wrote his first account
of the vision in the "wilderness." Towards the end of his life,
however, he changed his mind and decided that God was just an
exalted man. Consequently, he revised his story of the vision to
include the Father after he had changed his mind about the
Godhead. Marvin S. Hill, of the BYU history department, seems
willing to admit this, although he is still unwilling to concede
that this shows fraud on Joseph Smith's part:

> Brodie's assumption of a deceitful prophet was supported by her
> discovery that early Mormons did not relate the first vision story
> consistently, and, as she maintained in 1945, the earliest version
> by the prophet was not written until 1838. She has had to revise
> the argument somewhat since it is now known that the earliest
> account extant was written in 1832. But there are, undeniably,
> *differences in the several accounts, not all of them minor* from the
> standpoint of Mormon theology. . . . To focus upon the discrepan-
> cies touching the personages of the Godhead in the first vision
> story, *whether one or two* personages, is to concentrate on a
> theological question and to miss its historical significance. . . .
> Brodie and others have been preoccupied with the first vision's
> theological implications as to the social and religious origins of
> Mormonism which may be the essential point. If over the years
> *Joseph's conception of the Godhead changed,* this is not evidence
> of fraud any more than the adaptation of other aspects of his
> theology in later years proves to be (*Dialogue: A Journal of Mor-
> mon Thought,* Winter 1972, pp.78-79).

While we feel that Marvin Hill has still not faced the real
implications of this matter, it is refreshing to see a noted Mormon writer admit that "Joseph's conception of the Godhead"
might have changed.

Anti-Mormon writers have pointed out that after Joseph Smith's death the Mormon leaders made some very confusing statements concerning the first vision. Now that we have Joseph Smith's first written accounts of the vision we are able to understand why they were in such a state of confusion. Wesley P. Walters states: "... the shift from an angel to Christ, then to angels, and finally to two personages introduced such haziness that even the Mormon leaders appeared confused as to the nature of the story itself" (*Dialogue: A Journal of Mormon Thought*, Spring 1969, p.73).

In 1855 Brigham Young preached a sermon in which he denied that the Lord came to Joseph Smith in the first vision:

> But as it was in the days of our Savior, so was it in the advent of this new dispensation. It was not in accordance with the notions, traditions, and pre-conceived ideas of the American people. *The messenger* did not come to an eminent divine of any of the so-called orthodoxy, he did not adopt their interpretations of the Holy Scriptures. *The Lord did not come* with the armies of heaven, in power and great glory, nor send *His messengers* panoplied with aught else than the truth of heaven, to communicate to the meek, the lowly, and the youth of humble origin, the sincere enquirer after the knoweldge of God. But He did send His *angel* to this same obscure person, Joseph Smith jun., who afterwards became a Prophet, Seer, and Revelator, and informed him that he should not join any of the religious sects of the day, for they were all wrong ... (*Journal of Discourses*, vol. 2, p.171).

John Taylor, the third president of the church, made the following statement on March 2, 1879: "... just as it was when the Prophet Joseph asked *the angel* which of the sects was right that he might join it. The answer was that none of them are right. What, none of them? No. We will not stop to argue that question; *the angel* merely told him to join none of them that none of them were right" (*Journal of Discourses*, vol. 20, p.167).

George A. Smith, who was sustained as first counselor in the First Presidency in 1868, made this statement in November of the same year:

> When Joseph Smith was about fourteen or fifteen years old, ... there was a revival of religion ... He had read the Bible and had found that passage in James. ... he went humbly before the Lord and inquired of Him, and the Lord answered his prayer, and revealed to Joseph, *by the ministration of angels*, the true condition of the religious world. When *the holy angel* appeared, Joseph inquired which of all these denominations was right and which he should join, and was told they were all wrong ... (*Journal of Discourses*, vol. 12, pp.333-34).

that the Lord sent forth His angel to reveal the truths of heaven as in times past, even as in ancient days. This should have been hailed as the greatest blessing which could have been bestowed upon any nation, kindred, tongue, or people. It should have been received with hearts of gratitude and gladness, praise and thanksgiving.

But as it was in the days of our Savior, so was it in the advent of this new dispensation. It was not in accordance with the notions, traditions, and pre-conceived ideas of the American people. The messenger did not come to an eminent divine of any of the so-called *orthodoxy*, he did not adopt their interpretation of the Holy Scriptures. The Lord did not come with the armies of heaven, in power and great glory, nor send His messengers panoplied with aught else than the truth of heaven, to communicate to the meek, the lowly, the youth of humble origin, the sincere enquirer after the knowlege of God. But He did send His angel to this same obscure person, Joseph Smith jun., who afterwards became a Prophet, Seer, and Revelator, and informed him that he should not join any of the religious sects of the day, for they were all wrong; that they were following the precepts of men instead of the Lord Jesus; that He had a work for him to perform, inasmuch as he should prove faithful before Him.

No sooner was this made known, and published abroad, and people began to listen and obey the heavenly summons, than opposition began to rage, and the people, even in this favored land, began to persecute their neighbors and friends for entertaining religious opinions differing from their own.

I pause now to ask, had not Joseph Smith a right to promulgate and establish a different, a new religion and form of worship in this government?

Every one must admit he had. This right was always held sacred, for upon it was based the religious liberty of every citizen of the Republic. It was a privilege held sacred in the bosom of every class of people; no Judge dared invade its holy precincts? No Legislator nor Governor ventured to obstruct the free exercise thereof. How then should it be esteemed an object worthy of persecution that Joseph Smith, the man called of God to perform a work in restoring the Gospel of salvation unto the children of men, and his followers, true believers in his divine mission, should attempt to exercise the same privilege held sacred by all others, of every name, nature, and description, and equally so by them? Why should he and his followers be debarred the privilege of worshipping God according to the dictates of their consciences? Legally they cannot, and I will further state, that legally they have not. No! whenever the iron hand of oppression and persecution has fallen upon this people, our opposers have broken their own laws, set at defiance and trampled under foot every principle of equal rights, justice, and liberty found written in that rich legacy of our fathers, THE CONSTITUTION OF THE UNITED STATES.

Whenever popular fury has been directed against us, no power in the government has been found potent enough to afford protection, and what is still more astonishing, honorable enough to yield redress, nor has any effort succeeded in bringing to justice those individuals who had perpetrated such fearful crimes. No! The *murderer*, the *assassin*, the *midday plunderer*, and *highway robber* roam unmolested, and mingle unquestioned in the society of the rulers of the land; they pass and re-pass as current coin, producing no jar in the sensibilities of refinement, no odium in the atmosphere in which they move.

A photograph of the *Journal of Discourses*, vol. 2, page 171. Brigham Young says that "the Lord did not come" to Joseph Smith in the first vision, but instead He sent "His angel."

Many other confusing statements about the first vision were made by Mormon leaders after Joseph Smith's death.

Today the first vision has become of such importance that a person must believe it to be considered a good Mormon. David O. McKay, the ninth president of the church, stated that the first vision is the very *"foundation of this Church"* (*Gospel Ideals*, p.85). In his thesis (p.75), Paul R. Cheesman stated that the Mormon church "must *stand or fall* on the authenticity of the First Vision and the appearance of the Angel Moroni." Apostle Widtsoe stated: "The story of the First Vision need only be studied from original sources to assure the seeker not only of its truth, but also of the time of its occurrence" (*Joseph Smith— Seeker After Truth*, p.26). When we examine the original sources, especially the sources suppressed by the Mormon leaders for over 130 years, we find that the first vision story rests on a very sandy foundation.

Dr. Hugh Nibley once criticized anti-Mormon writers for omitting the "all-important" words, "This is my beloved Son," when giving Joseph Smith's story. If Dr. Nibley had read Joseph Smith's first handwritten account of the vision, perhaps he would not have been so eager to criticize, for Joseph Smith not only omitted the "all-important" words, but he also left God the Father completely out of the vision!

The second account by Joseph Smith also did *not* contain the "all-important" words; in fact, it contained words which seem to show that it was *not* the Father and the Son.

An examination of the first published history of the church makes matters even worse, for it does not even mention the first vision. Moreover, Oliver Cowdery claimed that in 1823 Joseph Smith did not even know "if a Supreme being did exist." Certainly, if Joseph Smith had seen the Father and the Son in 1820, as the official account proclaims, he would know in 1823 that a Supreme Being did exist!

Besides all this, falsification has been found in the *History of the Church*. Joseph Smith told Erastus Holmes about his "first visitation of angels," but later Mormon historians altered this to read: "my first vision." It is very difficult to believe in the authenticity of Joseph Smith's first vision story when there is so much evidence against it.

No Revival in 1820

Joseph Smith claimed that just before he received his first vision there was a great revival in his neighborhood:

> Some time in the second year after our removal to Manchester, there was *in the place where we lived* an unusual excitement on

the subject of religion. It commenced with the Methodists, but soon became general among all sects in that region of country, indeed the whole district of country seemed affected by it, and *great multitudes* united themselves to the different religious parties, which created no small stir and division amongst the people . . .

I was at this time in my fifteenth year. My father's family was proselyted to the Presbyterian faith, and four of them joined that church, namely, my mother Lucy, my brothers Hyrum, Samuel, Harrison, and my sister Sophronia.

During this time of great excitement my mind was called up to serious reflection. . . . So in accordance with this my determination, to ask of God, I retired to the woods to make the attempt. It was on the morning of a beautiful clear day, early in the spring of *eighteen hundred and twenty* (*Times and Seasons*, vol. 3, pp.727-28).

In 1967 the Utah Christian Tract Society published Wesley P. Walters's study, *New Light on Mormon Origins From The Palmyra (N.Y.) Revival.* In the foreword to this work, Mr. Walters states:

Mormons account for the origin of their movement by quoting from a narrative written by their prophet Joseph Smith, Jr. in 1838. In this account he claims that a revival broke out in the Palmyra, New York area in 1820. . . .

Information which we have recently uncovered conclusively proves that the revival *did not occur until the fall of 1824* and that *no revival* occurred between 1819 and 1823 in the Palmyra vicinity.

On pages 5,8,11 and 12 of the same pamphlet we find these statements by Mr. Walters:

Such a revival does not pass from the scene without leaving some traces in the records and publications of the period. In this study we wish to show by the contemporary records that the revival, which Smith claimed occurred in 1820, did not occur until the fall of 1824. We also show that *in 1820 there was no revival* in any of the churches in Palmyra or its vicinity. In short, our investigation shows that the statement of Joseph Smith, Jr. can not be true when he claims that he was stirred up by an 1820 revival to make his inquiry in the grove near his home. . . .

An even more surprising confirmation that this revival occurred in 1824 and not in 1820 has just recently come to light. While searching through some dusty volumes of early Methodist literature at a near-by Methodist college, imagine our surprise and elation when we stumbled upon Rev. George Lane's own personal account of the Palmyra revival. It was written, not at some years distance from the event as the Mormon accounts all were, but while the revival was still in progress and was printed a few months later. Lane's account gives us not only the year, 1824, but even the month and date. . . .

By September 1825 the results of the revival for Palmyra had become a matter of record. The Presbyterian church reported 99 admitted on examination and the Baptist had received 94 by baptism, while the Methodist circuit showed an increase of 208. . . .

When we turn to the year 1820, however, the 'great multitudes' are conspicuously missing. The Presbyterian Church in Palmyra certainly experienced no awakening that year. Rev. James Hotchkin's history records revivals for that church as occurring in the years 1817, 1824, 1829, etc., but nothing for the year 1820. The records of Presbytery and Synod give the same picture. . . . Since these reports always rejoice at any sign of a revival in the churches, it is inconceivable that a great awakening had occurred in their Palmyra congregation and gone completely unnoticed.

The Baptist Church records also show clearly that they had no revival in 1820, for the Palmyra congregation gained only 5 by baptism, while the neighboring Baptist churches of Lyons, Canandaigua and Farmington showed net losses of 4, 5 and 9 respectively. . . .

The Methodist figures, though referring to the entire circuit, give the same results, for they show net losses of 23 for 1819, 6 for 1820 and 40 for 1821. This hardly fits Joseph Smith's description of 'great multitudes' being added to the churches of the area. In fact, the Mormon Prophet could hardly have picked a poorer year in which to place his revival, so far as the Methodists were concerned.

Mormon scholars became very concerned when they saw Mr. Walters' study. They were so disturbed, in fact, that a team was sent back east to do research concerning the first vision and other matters dealing with the history of the Mormon church in New York. Although the scholars "scoured libraries, studied newspapers, and sought to find private individuals who might uncover hitherto unknown source materials" (*BYU Studies*, Spring 1969, p.242), they were unable to find evidence of a revival in Palmyra in 1820. In their article, "Mormon Origins in New York," James B. Allen and Leonard J. Arrington (now church historian) report:

What evidence do we have, other than the word of Joseph Smith, that there was 'an unusual excitement on the subject of religion' in the vicinity of Palmyra in 1820? Up to this point *little such evidence has been uncovered*, and Walters challenged the story in the article referred to above. Milton Backman, however, has discovered interesting new material which he presents in his important article on the historical setting of the First Vision (*Brigham Young University Studies*, Spring 1969, p.272).

In his article, "Awakenings in the Burned-over District: New Light on the Historical Setting of the First Vision," Milton V. Backman, Jr., seems unable to provide evidence that there was a revival in Palmyra. He indicates, however, that Joseph Smith may have heard or read of revivals in other portions of the state. Mormon writer Richard L. Bushman makes these comments concerning Walters' work:

> Mr. Walters' main argument is that no revival occurred in Palmyra itself. But even that fact cannot be established absolutely. It is a negative claim and depends on negative evidence, which is always tenuous. Mr. Walters relies on the absence of revival reports, but *just because someone failed to write a report of an event does not mean it did not occur.* . . . lots of things happen that are never recorded. . . . The news included in the Palmyra paper depended on the taste and inclinations of the editor. . . . The point is that *although we think a revival should have been recorded*, there are many reasons why it could have been missed. We cannot know for sure that an event did not occur unless reliable witnesses on the scene say no, and thus far Mr. Walters has found none such to testify (*Dialogue: A Journal of Mormon Thought*, Spring 1969, p.87).

Richard L. Bushman goes on to say that "Mr. Walters relies on the absence of reports in newspapers and general histories to reach his conclusion of no revivals" (pp.89-90). In reply, however, Mr. Walters shows that the denominational magazines would have mentioned a revival if one had actually occurred:

> Another significant lack of information concerning an 1820 revival lies in the area of the religious press. The denominational magazines of that day were full of reports of revivals, some even devoting sections to them. These publications carried more than a dozen glowing reports of the revival that occurred at Palmyra in the winter of 1816-17. Likewise, the 1824-25 revival is covered in a number of reports. These magazines, however, while busily engaged in reporting revivals during the 1819 to 1821 period, contain *not a single mention of any revival taking place in the Palmyra area* during this time. It is unbelievable that every one of the denominations which Joseph Smith depicts as affected by an 1820 revival could have completely overlooked the event. Even the Palmyra newspaper, while reporting revivals at several places in the state, has no mention whatever of any revival in Palmyra or vicinity either in 1819 or 1820. The only reasonable explanation

for this massive silence is that no revival occurred in the Palmyra area in 1820 (*Dialogue*, Spring 1969, p.67).

Before Mr. Walters's study appeared, Mormon writers taught that the revival occurred right in Palmyra, but since the Mormon research team has been unable to find evidence of a revival in Palmyra, Mormon apologists are now beginning to forsake Palmyra and search elsewhere for a revival. Lauritz G. Petersen, of the church historical department, made these statements in a letter dated November 1, 1968:

> Now let me ask you a question. Where was the revival? In Palmyra? He doesn't mention a revival at all. He mentions an unusual excietment [sic] in the "Whole district of country." Could an excietment [sic] be caused by a revival somewhere near the area? He doesn't mention being to a revival. If there was a revival somewhere outside of Palmyra and the news of it had already excited the village, would or could it be possible that the Smith family have travelled there to sell root beer and cakes? (Letter from Lauritz G. Petersen, dated November 1, 1968).

Although it is true that Joseph Smith does not use the word "Palmyra," his description makes it very clear that he was referring to this area. He states that there "was *in the place where we lived* an unusual excitement on the subject of religion" (*History of the Church*, vol. 1, p.2). In 1843 Joseph Smith told a reporter that this excitement occurred right "*in the neighborhood* where I lived . . ." (*New York Spectator*, Sept. 23, 1843, as cited in *Joseph Smith the Prophet*, by Preston Nibley, pp.30-31). The Mormon historian B. H. Roberts definitely stated that the revival was in "Palmyra" (*Comprehensive History of the Church*, vol. 1, p.35). On page 51 of the same volume Mr. Roberts claims that the "churches *in and about Palmyra* decided upon a 'union revival,' in order to 'convert the unconverted.' "

Since Mormon apologists have been unable to prove that the revival took place in Palmyra, they have tried to find reasons why Joseph Smith would have been in another city. Milton V. Backman, Jr., and other Mormon writers have suggested that Joseph Smith might have been present at conference meetings held in Vienna (now known as Phelps). Wesley Walters, however, answered this argument in *Dialogue: A Journal of Mormon Thought*, Spring 1969, page 69.

Before Walter's work appeared, Mormon writers claimed to have a great deal of evidence to prove that the revival occurred in Palmyra in 1820. Preston Nibley, who later became assistant church historian, stated that there are "several accounts of the religious revival which took place at Palmyra in the spring of

1820" (*Joseph Smith the Prophet*, p.21). We have checked the references which Preston Nibley gives and find them to be spurious (see *Mormonism—Shadow or Reality?* p.160). Mr. Nibley gives two references from a publication that are supposed to refer to the 1820 revival. We have found, however, that these references do not refer to a revival in 1820, but rather to one in the years 1824-25. These references have been found in the *Wayne Sentinel* under the date of March 2, 1825. Apostle Gordon B. Hinckley continues to use these spurious references in his book *Truth Restored*. He seems to be oblivious to the fact that the church's own research team has failed to verify them.

It would appear, then, that all evidence for a revival in Palmyra and vicinity has fallen, and that Wesley P. Walters's work has been vindicated. All that the Mormon research team has been able to do is to confirm his original findings. Mr. Walters made this interesting observation: "Joseph made his great mistake when he tried to alter the course of history by moving a whole revival back some 4 years. This defect places his entire movement upon a crumbling foundation."

THE GODHEAD

Chapter 7

In the book of Isaiah 44:8 we read: ". . . Is there a God beside me? yea, there is no God; I know not any." Joseph Smith's first published work, the *Book of Mormon*, seems to be in harmony with the teachings of the Bible on this point, for it states that there is only one God. In Alma 11:26-31 we read as follows:

"And Zeezrom said unto him: Thou sayest there is a true and living God? And Amulek said: Yea, there is a true and living God. Now, Zeezrom said: Is there more than one God? And he answered, No. Now Zeezrom said unto him again: How knowest thou these things? And he said: An angel hath made them known unto me."

The Bible teaches that God is a Spirit. In John 4:24, Jesus himself said: "God is a Spirit: and they that worship him must worship him in spirit and truth." In Jeremiah 23:24 we read: "Can any hide himself in secret places that I shall not see him? saith the Lord. Do not I fill heaven and earth? saith the Lord." The *Book of Mormon* also teaches that God is a Spirit. In Alma 18:26-28, we read as follows: "And then Ammon said: Believest thou that there is a Great Spirit? And he said, Yea, And Ammon said: This is God."

As we have already shown, the *Book of Mormon* teaches that Christ was God Himself manifest in the flesh. In Mosiah 15:1,2 and 5 we read: ". . . God himself shall come down among the children of men, and shall redeem his people. And because he dwelleth in flesh he shall be called the Son of God, and having subjected the flesh to the will of the Father, being the *Father and the Son*. . . . And thus the *flesh* becoming subject to the *Spirit*, or the *Son* to the *Father*, being one God. . . . "

This is also similar to the biblical teaching, for in 2 Corinthians 5:19 we read as follows: "To wit, that God was in Christ, reconciling the world unto himself. . . . "

It is interesting to note that the three witnesses to the *Book of Mormon* finished their testimony with the following statement: "And the honor be to the Father, and to the Son, and to the Holy

Ghost, which is *one God*. Amen" (*Book of Mormon*, Preface).

From One to Many

By the year 1844 Joseph Smith had completely disregarded the teachings of the *Book of Mormon*, for he declared that God was just an exalted man and that men could become Gods. He stated as follows:

> First, *God himself*, who sits enthroned in yonder heavens, *is a man* like unto one of yourselves, that is the great secret. . . . I am going to tell you *how God came to be God*. We have imagined that God was God from all eternity. . . . God himself; the Father of us all dwelt on an earth the same as Jesus Christ himself did. . . . You have got to learn *how to be Gods yourselves*. . . . No man can learn you more than what I have told you (*Times and Seasons*, vol. 5, pp.613-14).

The best way to illustrate Joseph Smith's change of mind concerning the Godhead is to compare the Book of Moses with the Book of Abraham. Both of these books are printed in the *Pearl of Great Price*—one of the four standard works of the Mormon church. The Book of Abraham was supposed to have been given some years after the Book of Moses. Both books are supposed to contain a direct revelation concerning the creation of the world. While the Book of Moses states that "I, God" created the heavens and the earth, the Book of Abraham states that "they (the Gods)" created them.

Book of Moses	Book of Abraham
". . . the Lord spake unto Moses saying: Behold I reveal unto you concerning this heaven, and this earth; write the works which I speak. . . .	"And the Lord said unto me: Abraham, I show these things unto thee before ye go into Egypt, that ye may declare all these words . . .
"And *I God*, said: Let there be light; and there was light. . . .	"And *they (the Gods,* said: Let there be light; and there was light. . . .
"And *I, God*, called the dry land Earth. . . .	"And *the Gods* pronounced the dry land, earth. . . .
"And *I, God*, made the beasts of the earth after their kind. . . .	"And *the Gods* organized the earth to bring forth the beasts after their kind. . . .
"And *I, the Lord God*, planted a garden eastward in Eden. . . ." (Moses 2:1,3, 10,25; 3:8)	"And *the Gods* planted a garden in Eden. . . . " (Abraham 3:15; 4:3,10,25; 5:8)

173

in a well, I have been requested to speak by his friends and relatives, and inasmuch as there are a great many in this congregation who live in this city, as well as elsewhere, and who have lost friends, I feel disposed to speak on the subject in general, and offer you my ideas so far as I have ability, and so far as I shall be inspired by the Holy Spirit to dwell on this subject. I want your prayers and faith, the instruction of Almighty God and the gift of the Holy Ghost, that I may set forth things that are true, that can easily be comprehended, and shall carry the testimony to your hearts; pray that the Lord may strengthen my lungs, stay the winds and let the prayers of the saints to heaven appear, that it may enter into the ear of the Lord of Sabaoth; for the effectual prayers of righteous men availeth much, and I verily believe that your prayers shall be heard before I enter into the investigation fully of the subject that is laying before me. Before entering fully into the investigation, I wish to pave the way: I will make a few preliminaries, in order that you may understand the subject when I come to it. I do not calculate to please your ears with superfluity of words or oratory, or with much learning; but I calculate to edify you with the simple truths from heaven. In the first place, I wish to go back to the beginning of creation; there is the starting point, in order to be fully acquainted with the mind, purposes, decrees, &c. of the great Eloheim, that sits in yonder heavens, it is necessary for us to have an understanding of God himself in the beginning. If we start right, it is easy to go right all the time; but if we start wrong, it is a hard matter to get right. There are a very few beings in the world who understand rightly the character of God. They do not comprehend any thing, that which is past, or that which is to come; and consequently, but little above the brute beast. If a man learns nothing more than to eat, drink, sleep, and does not comprehend any of the designs of God, the beast comprehends the same thing; it eats, drinks, sleeps, knows nothing more; yet knows as much as we, unless WE are able to comprehend by the inspiration of Almighty God. I want to go back to the beginning, and so lift your minds into a more lofty sphere, a more exalted understanding; that what the human mind generally understands. I want to ask this congregation, every man, woman and child, to answer the question in their own heart, what kind of a being is God? ask yourselves. I again repeat the question, what kind of a being is God? Does any man or woman know? have any of you seen him, heard him, communed with

him? Here is the question that will peradventure from this time henceforth, occupy your attention. The apostle says this is eternal life, to know God and Jesus Christ, whom he has sent. If any man enquire what kind of a being is God, if he will search diligently his own heart, if the declaration of the apostle be true, he will realize that he has not eternal life, there can be eternal life on no other principle. My first object is, to find out the character of the only wise and true God, and if I should be the man to comprehend God, and explain or convey the principles to your hearts so that the spirit seals it upon you, let every man and woman henceforth put their hand on their mouth and never say any thing against the man of God again; but if I fail, it becomes my duty to renounce all my pretensions to revelations, inspirations, &c., and if all are pretentious to God, they will all be as bad off as I am at any rate. There is not a man but would breathe out an anathema, if they knew I was a false prophet; and some would feel authorized to take away my life. If any man is authorized to take away my life, who says I am a false teacher; then upon the same principle am I authorized to take away the life of every false teacher, and where would be the end of blood, and who would not be the sufferer. But no man is authorized to take away life in consequence of their religion; which all laws and governments ought to tolerate, right or wrong. If I show verily, that I have the truth of God, and show that ninety-nine out of a hundred are false teachers, while they pretend to hold the keys of God, and to kill them because they are false teachers, it would deluge the whole world with blood. I want you all to know God, to be familiar with him, and if I can bring you to him, all persecutions against me will cease; you will know that I am his servant, for I speak as one having authority — What sort of a being was God in the beginning Open your ears and hear all ye ends of the earth; for I am going to prove it to you by the Bible, and I am going to tell you the designs of God to the human race, and why he interferes with the affairs of man.

First, God himself, who sits enthroned in yonder heavens, is a man like unto one of yourselves, that is the great secret. If the vail was rent to-day, and the great God, who holds this world in its orbit, and upholds all things by his power; if you were to see him to-day, you would see him in all the person, image and very form as a man; for Adam was created in the very fashion and image of God; Adam received instruction, walked, talked and

A photograph of the *Times and Seasons*, vol. 5, page 613. Joseph Smith says that God is just an exalted man.

Apostle Orson Pratt expounded concerning the Mormon doctrine of a plurality of Gods: "If we should take a million of worlds like this and number their particles, we should find that *there are more Gods than there are particles of matter in those worlds*" (*Journal of Discourses*, vol. 2, p.345).

The Mormon church teaches that God the Father had a Father, and that God's Father also had a Father, and so on. President Brigham Young claimed: "He [God] is our Father—the Father of our spirits, and was once *a man in mortal flesh* as we are, and is now an exalted being. How many Gods there are, I do not know. But there never was a time when there were not Gods . . . *God has once been a finite being* . . . " (*Journal of Discourses*, vol. 7, p.333).

Heber C. Kimball, who was a member of the First Presidency, made these similar comments: " . . . then we shall go back to our Father and God, who is connected with *one who is still farther back*; and this Father is connected with *one still further back*, and so on . . . " (*Journal of Discourses*, vol. 5, p.19).

" . . . for our *God is a natural man,* . . . the first of all mechanics. Where did he get his knowledge from? From his Father, just as we get knowledge from our earthly parents" (*Ibid.*, vol. 8, p.211).

Orson Pratt explains further: "*The Gods* who dwell in the Heaven . . . *have been redeemed* from the grave in a world which existed before the foundations of this earth were laid. They and the Heavenly body which they now inhabit were once *in a fallen state* . . . they were exalted also, *from fallen men to Celestial Gods* to inhabit their Heaven forever and ever" (*The Seer*, p.23).

"We were begotten by our Father in Heaven; the person of *our Father in Heaven was begotten on a previous heavenly world by His Father;* and again, He was begotten *by a still more ancient Father;* and so on, from generation to generation, . . . we wonder in our minds, how far back the genealogy extends, and how the first world was formed, and the first father was begotten" (*The Seer*, p.132).

Brigham Young added further statements about men becoming Gods: "The Lord created you and me for the purpose of becoming Gods like himself. . . . We are created . . . *to become Gods like unto our Father in heaven*" (*Journal of Discourses*, vol. 3, p.93). ". . . man is the king of kings and lord of lords in embryo." (vol. 10, p.223).

Milton R. Hunter, who was a member of the First Council of Seventy, had a great deal to say about the doctrine of a plurality of Gods:

in the spirit, in the other departments of the house of God, passing on from truth to truth, from intelligence to intelligence, until he is prepared to again receive his body and to enter into the presence of the Father and the Son. We cannot enter into celestial glory in our present state of ignorance and mental darkness.

I know that we have been taught from our infancy, and it is now a popular doctrine with all the denominations of the Christians of the nineteenth century, that, when the mortal tenement is committed to the grave, there is an end of all further progress in intelligence and learning with regard to this probation. In support of this idea, they advance the scripture, " If the tree fall toward the south, or toward the north, in the place where the tree falleth, there it shall be." Again, " Whatsoever thy hand findeth to do, do it with thy might ; for there is no work, nor device, nor knowledge, nor wisdom in the grave whither thou goest."

The worms have work to do in the grave until the body is reduced to mother earth. But the active, intelligent, divine organization that inhabited the body does not descend with it into the grave to work with the worms ; but it goes to the spirit-world, and is much more busily engaged there than when it was a tenant in a mortal tabernacle.

Suppose, then, that a man is evil in his heart—wholly given up to wickedness, and in that condition dies, his spirit will enter the spirit-world intent upon evil. On the other hand, if we are striving with all the powers and faculties God has given us to improve upon our talents, to prepare ourselves to dwell in eternal life, and the grave receives our bodies while we are thus engaged, with what disposition will our spirits enter their next state ? They will be still striving to do the things of God, only in a much greater degree—learning, increasing, growing in grace and in the knowledge of the truth.

The people called Christians are shrouded in ignorance, and read the Scriptures with darkened understandings.

Do you read the Scriptures, my brethren and sisters, as though you were writing them a thousand, two thousand, or five thousand years ago? Do you read them as though you stood in the place of the men who wrote them? If you do not feel thus, it is your privilege to do so, that you may be as familiar with the spirit and meaning of the written word of God as you are with your daily walk and conversation, or as you are with your workmen or with your households. You may understand what the Prophets understood and thought—what they designed and planned to bring forth to their brethren for their good.

When you can thus feel, then you may begin to think that you can find out something about God, and begin to learn who he is. He is our Father—the Father of our spirits, and was once a man in mortal flesh as we are, and is now an exalted Being.

How many Gods there are, I do not know. But there never was a time when there were not Gods and worlds, and when men were not passing through the same ordeals that we are now passing through. That course has been from all eternity, and it is and will be to all eternity. You cannot comprehend this ; but when you can, it will be to you a matter of great consolation.

It appears ridiculous to the world, under their darkened and erroneous traditions, that God has once been a finite being ; and yet we are not in such close communion with him as many have supposed. He has passed on, and is exalted far beyond what we

A photograph of the *Journal of Discourses*, vol. 7, page 333. Brigham Young teaches that there are many Gods and that God the Father was once a finite being.

Mormon prophets have continuously taught the sublime truth that *God the Eternal Father was once a mortal man* who passed through a school of earth life similar to that through which we are now passing. *He became God*—an exalted being—through obedience to the same eternal Gospel truths that we are given opportunity today to obey (*The Gospel Through the Ages*, Salt Lake City, 1958, p.104).

... we must accept the fact that there was a time when *Deity was much less powerful than He is today.* Then how did He become glorified and exalted and attain His present status of Godhead? In the first place, aeons ago God undoubtedly took advantage of every opportunity to learn the laws of truth.... From day to day He exerted His will vigorously, ... he gained more knowledge.... Thus *he grew in experience and continued to grow until He attained the status of Godhood.* In other words, He became God by absolute obedience to all the eternal laws of the Gospel. ...

No prophet of record gave more complete and forceful explanations of the doctrine that *men may become Gods* than did the American Prophet ... (*Ibid.*, pp.114-15).

Bruce R. McConkie, who is now an Apostle, has also written on this subject: "... *God* ... is a personal Being, a holy and *exalted man, a glorified, resurrected Personage having a tangible body of flesh and bones,* an anthropomorphic Entity ..." (*Mormon Doctrine*, 1966, p.250). " ... as the Prophet also taught, there is '*a God above the Father of our Lord Jesus Christ* ...' " (p.322).

Joseph Fielding Smith explains:

Some people are troubled over the statements of the Prophet Joseph Smith. ... The matter that seems such a mystery is the statement that *our Father in heaven at one time passed through a life and death and is an exalted man.* This is one of the mysteries. ... The Prophet taught that *our Father had a Father and so on.* Is not this a reasonable thought, especially when we remember that the promises are made to us that we may become like him? (*Doctrines of Salvation*, vol. 1, pp.10,12).

Apostle LeGrand Richards wrote a letter to Morris L. Reynolds on July 14, 1966, in which he stated: "There is a statement often repeated in the Church, and while it is not in one of the Standard Church Works, it is accepted as Church doctrine, and this is: '*As man is, God once was; as God is, man may become.*' "

The Heavenly Mother

Because of their belief that God is just an exalted man, Mormon leaders teach that He had a mother as well as a wife. Brigham Young stated: "Brother Kimball quoted a saying of Joseph the Prophet, that he would not worship a God who had not a Father; and I do not know that he would if he had not a mother; the one would be as absurd as the other" (*Journal of Discourses*, vol. 9, p.286).

Although the Mormon leaders do not worship God's wife, they teach that she is our "Eternal Mother." Apostle Bruce R. McConkie made these interesting comments:

> Implicit in the Christian verity that all men are the spirit children of an *Eternal Father* is the usually unspoken truth that they are also the offspring of an *Eternal Mother*. An exalted and glorified Man of Holiness (Moses 6:57) could not be a Father unless a *Woman of like glory, perfection, and holiness was associated with him as a Mother*. The begetting of children makes a man a father and a woman a mother whether we are dealing with man in his mortal or immortal state.

> This *doctrine* that there is a *Mother in Heaven* was affirmed in plainness by the First Presidency of the Church (Joseph F. Smith, John R. Winder, and Anthon H. Lund) . . . they said that "man, as a spirit, was begotten and born of heavenly parents . . ." (*Mormon Doctrine*, 1966, p.516).

Milton R. Hunter, who served in the First Council of the Seventy, affirmed the same teaching: "The stupendous truth of the existence of a *Heavenly Mother*, as well as a Heavenly Father, became established facts in Mormon theology" (*The Gospel Through the Ages*, 1958, p.98).

On April 8, 1973, the *Salt Lake Tribune* reported:

> Outburst after outburst of delighted laughter filled the Tabernacle Saturday. . . . The speaker was Elder LeGrand Richards of the Council of Twelve Apostles, . . . Elder Richards told of speaking to a large gathering of clergymen. " . . . when I finished my remarks, one of them stood up and said, 'Mr. Richards, we've been told *you believe God had a wife*. Would you please explain this.' "

> "I think he thought he had me," said Elder Richards. The audience in the Tabernacle began to chuckle. "I retorted that *I didn't see how God could have a Son if He didn't have a wife*."

The Apostle Abraham H. Cannon recorded in his journal on August 25, 1890, that it was claimed that Joseph Smith saw the Eternal Mother in a vision. President Joseph Fielding Smith defended the idea of an Eternal Mother although he had to admit it was not found in the Scriptures: "The fact that there is no reference to *a mother in heaven* either in the Bible, Book of

Mormon or Doctrine and Covenants, is not sufficient proof that no such thing as a mother did exist there. . . . does not common sense tell us that we must have had a mother there also?'' (*Answers to Gospel Questions*, vol. 3, p.142).

The Virgin Birth

The idea that God is just an exalted man has led Mormon leaders to proclaim a doctrine about the birth of Christ which is very shocking to orthodox Christians.

Brigham Young once stated: "Now remember from this time forth, and for ever, that Jesus Christ was not begotten by the Holy Ghost" (*Journal of Discourses*, vol. 1, p.51).

This statement is in conflict with both the Bible and the *Book of Mormon*. In Matthew 1:18 and 20 we read: "Now the birth of Jesus Christ was on this wise: When as his mother Mary was espoused to Joseph, before they came together, *she was found with child of the Holy Ghost*. . . . for that which is conceived in her *is of the Holy Ghost*." The *Book of Mormon* agrees with the Bible on this point, for in Alma 7:10 we read: "And behold, he shall be born of Mary, . . . she being a virgin, a precious and chosen vessel, who shall be overshadowed and *conceive by the power of the Holy Ghost*, and bring forth a son, yea, even the Son of God."

In spite of these plain statements, Joseph Fielding Smith denied that the *Book of Mormon* and the Bible teach that Christ was begotten by the Holy Ghost: "They tell us the Book of Mormon states that Jesus was begotten of the Holy Ghost. I challenge that statement. The Book of Mormon teaches no such thing! Neither does the Bible" (*Doctrines of Salvation*, vol. 1, p.19).

The reason that Joseph Fielding Smith objects to the teaching that Jesus was begotten by the Holy Ghost is that, according to Mormon theology, this would make Jesus the son of the Holy Ghost rather than the Son of God the Father. This idea arises from an improper understanding of the term Holy Ghost. The term Holy Ghost means exactly the same as the term Holy Spirit. The *American College Dictionary* defines the term "Holy Spirit" as 'the Holy Ghost." Now, since the Bible tells us that God is a Spirit and that He is holy, it is apparent that God Himself must be the Holy Spirit. So we see that there is no contradiction in saying that Jesus was begotten by the Holy Ghost and also is the Son of God.

Since Christians believe that God is a Spirit, they view the conception of Christ as a miraculous event having nothing to do with sex or any physical act. Mormon theology, on the other hand, teaches that God is a man and that Christ was conceived through a sexual act between Mary and God the Father. In other words, the birth of Christ is considered a natural, rather than a miraculous occurrence. Joseph Fielding Smith, Jr., said: "The birth of the Savior was a *natural occurrence* unattended with any degree of mysticism, and the *Father God was the literal parent of Jesus in the flesh* as well as in the spirit" (*Religious Truths Defined*, p.44). The late President Joseph Fielding Smith declared: "Christ was begotten of God. He was not born without the aid of Man, and *that Man was God!*" (*Doctrines of Salvation*, vol. 1, p.18).

Apostle Bruce R. McConkie further explains:

"These name-titles all signify that our Lord is the only Son of the Father in the flesh. Each of the words is to be understood literally. Only means only; Begotten means begotten; and Son means son. Christ was begotten by an Immortal Father *in the same way that mortal men are begotten by mortal fathers*" (*Mormon Doctrine*, 1966, pp.546-47).

"And Christ was born into the world as the literal Son of this Holy Being; he was born in the same personal, real, *and literal sense that any son is born to a mortal father*. There is nothing figurative about his paternity; *he was begotten, conceived and born in the normal and natural course of events*, . . . Christ is the Son of Man, meaning that his Father (the Eternal God!) is a Holy Man" (p.742).

The Mormon writer Carlfred B. Broderick made these comments:

> There are two basic elements in the Gospel view of sexuality as I interpret it from the scriptures. The first is that sex is good—that *sexuality*, far from being the antithesis of spirituality, is *actually an attribute of God*. . . .
>
> In the light of their understanding that *God is a procreating personage of flesh and bone*, latter-day prophets have made it clear that despite what it says in Matthew 1:20, *the Holy Ghost was not the father of Jesus*. . . . The Savior was *fathered by a personage of flesh and bone*, and was *literally* what Nephi said he was, "Son of the Eternal Father" (*Dialogue: A Journal of Mormon Thought*, Autumn, 1967, pp.100-101).

President Brigham Young had this to say concerning the birth of Christ: "The man Joseph, the husband of Mary, did not, that we know of, have more than one wife, but *Mary the wife of Joseph had another husband*" (*Deseret News*, October 10, 1866).

This same type of reasoning led Apostle Orson Pratt to say:

pure, and sublime attributes which are perfected in all their fulness in themselves.

If none but Gods will be permitted to multiply immortal children, it follows that each God must have one or more wives. God, the Father of our spirits, became the Father of our Lord Jesus Christ according to the flesh. Hence, the Father saith concerning him, "Thou art my Son, this day have I begotten thee." We are informed in the first chapter of Luke, that Mary was chosen by the Father as a choice virgin, through whom He begat Jesus. The angel said unto the Virgin Mary, "The Holy Ghost shall come upon thee, and the power of the Highest shall overshadow thee: therefore, also, that holy thing which shall be born of thee shall be called the Son of God." After the power of the Highest had overshadowed Mary, and she had by that means conceived, she related the circumstance to her cousin Elizabeth in the following words: "He that is Mighty hath done to me great things; and holy is His name." It seems from this relation that the Holy Ghost accompanied "the Highest" when He overshadowed the Virgin Mary and begat Jesus; and from this circumstance some have supposed that the body of Jesus was begotten of the Holy Ghost without the instrumentality of the immediate presence of the Father. There is no doubt that the Holy Ghost came upon Mary to sanctify her, and make her holy, and prepare her to endure the glorious presence of "the Highest," that when "He" should "overshadow" her she might conceive, being filled with the Holy Ghost; hence the angel said, as recorded in Matthew, "That which is conceived in her is of the Holy Ghost;" that is, the Holy Ghost gave her strength to abide the presence of the Father without being consumed; but it was the personage of the Father who begat the body of Jesus; and for this reason Jesus is called "the *Only* Begotten of the Father;" that is, the only one in this world whose fleshly body was begotten by the Father. There were millions of sons and daughters whom He begat before the foundation of this world, but they were spirits, and not bodies of flesh and bones; whereas, both the spirit and body of Jesus were begotten by the Father—the spirit having been begotten in heaven many ages before the tabernacle was begotten upon the earth.

The fleshly body of Jesus required a Mother as well as a Father. Therefore, the Father and Mother of Jesus, according to the flesh, must have been associated together in the capacity of Husband and Wife; hence the Virgin Mary must have been, for the time being, the *lawful* wife of God the Father: we use the term *lawful* Wife, because it would be blasphemous in the highest degree to say that He overshadowed her or begat the Saviour unlawfully. It would have been unlawful for any *man* to have interfered with Mary, who was already espoused to Joseph; for such a heinous crime would have subjected both the guilty parties to death, according to the law of Moses. But God having created all men and women, had the most perfect right to do with His own creation, according to His holy will and pleasure: He had a lawful right to overshadow the Virgin Mary in the capacity of a husband, and beget a Son, although she was espoused to another; for the law which He gave to govern men and women was not intended to govern Himself, or to prescribe rules for his own conduct. It was also lawful in Him, after having thus dealt with Mary, to give her to Joseph her espoused husband. Whether God the Father gave Mary to Joseph for time only, or for time and eternity, we are not informed. Inasmuch as God was the first husband to her, it may be that He only gave her to be the wife of Joseph while in this mortal state, and that He intended after the resurrection to again take her as one of his own wives to raise up immortal spirits in eternity.

As God the Father begat the fleshly body of Jesus, so He, before the world began, begat his spirit. As the body required an earthly Mother, so his

The fleshly body of Jesus required a Mother as well as a Father. Therefore, *the Father and Mother of Jesus*, according to the flesh, must have been associated together *in the capacity of Husband and Wife*; hence the Virgin Mary must have been, for the time being, *the lawful wife of God the Father*: we use the term lawful Wife, because it would be blasphemous in the highest degree to say that He overshadowed her or begat the Saviour unlawfully. It would have been unlawful for any man to have interfered with Mary, who was already espoused to Joseph; for such a heinous crime would have subjected both the guilty parties to death, according to the law of Moses. But God having created all men and women, had the most perfect right to do with His own creation, according to His holy will and pleasure: He had a lawful right to overshadow the Virgin Mary in the capacity of a husband, and beget a Son, although she was espoused to another; for the law which He gave to govern men and women was not intended to govern Himself, or to prescribe rules for his own conduct. It was also lawful in Him, after having thus dealt with Mary, to give her to Joseph her espoused husband. Whether God the Father gave Mary to Joseph for time only, or for time and eternity, we are not informed. Inasmuch as *God was the first husband to her*, it may be that He only gave her to be the wife of Joseph while in this mortal state, and that He intended after the resurrection to again take her as one of his own wives to raise up immortal spirits in eternity (*The Seer*, p.158).

Brigham Young added that "The birth of the Saviour was as natural as are the births of our children; it was the result of natural action. He partook of flesh and blood—was begotten of his Father, as we were of our fathers" (*Journal of Discourses*, vol. 8, p.115).

In a sermon delivered in the tabernacle on April 9, 1852, Brigham Young climaxed his teaching with the following explanation:

I have given you a few leading items upon this subject, but a great deal more remains to be told. Now remember from this time forth, and for ever, that *Jesus Christ was not begotten by the Holy Ghost*. I will repeat a little anecdote. I was in conversation with a certain learned professor upon the subject, when I replied, to this idea—"*if the Son was begotten by the Holy Ghost, it would be very dangerous to baptize and confirm females*, and give the Holy Ghost to them, *lest he should beget children*, to be palmed upon the Elders by the people, bringing the Elders into great difficulties" (*Journal of Discourses*, vol. 1, p.51).

A careful examination of the Mormon teaching concerning the conception of Christ reveals that it is far closer to paganism than it is to Christianity!

Serious Changes

As we pointed out in another chapter, the Mormons claim that a voice from heaven told the witnesses to the *Book of Mormon* that the translation was correct. In spite of this Joseph Smith tried to change the *Book of Mormon* to support his concept of a plurality of Gods. Four important changes were made in the second edition of the *Book of Mormon* concerning the Godhead. One of the most significant changes was made in 1 Nephi 13:40. In the 1830 edition it was stated that the very purpose of the Nephite records was to make known that Christ is the Eternal Father: ". . . These last records, . . . shall make known to all kindreds, tongues, and people, that the Lamb of God is the Eternal Father and the Savior of the world . . ." (*Book of Mormon*, 1830 ed., p.32).

In the current Utah edition, page 25, verse 40, three words have been interpolated: ". . . These last records, . . . shall mkeknown to all kindreds, tongues, and people, that the Lamb of God is the *Son of the* Eternal Father, and the Savior of the world. . . ."

A second important change was made in 1 Nephi 11:18; this is page 25 of the 1830 edition. In the first edition it read: ". . . Behold, the virgin which thou seest, is the mother of God, after the manner of the flesh." In modern editions it has been changed to read: ". . . Behold, the virgin whom thou seest is the mother of *the Son of* God, after the manner of the flesh." Notice that the words "the Son of" have been inserted in the middle of the sentence. Verse 21 of the same chapter originally read: "And the angel said unto me, behold the Lamb of God, yea, even the Eternal Father!" It was changed to read: "And the angel said unto me: Behold the Lamb of God, yea, even the *Son of the* Eternal Father!" Verse 32 of the same chapter, which is on page 26 of the original edition, was also changed. In the 1830 edition it read: ". . . the Everlasting God, was judged of the world; and I saw and bear record." It was changed to read: ". . . the *Son of the* everlasting God was judged of the world: and I saw and bear record." These additions begin to distinguish the Son from the Father and are part of the process that ultimately led Joseph Smith to declare the Father and the Son as two separate gods.

Removing the Lectures

In 1835 the "Lectures on Faith," which were originally delivered before a class of the elders, in Kirtland, Ohio, were printed in the *Doctrine and Covenants*. In these lectures it was definitely stated that God the Father was a personage of spirit.

unto me, Knowest thou the condescention of God? And I said unto him, I know that he loveth his children; nevertheless, I do not know the meaning of all things. And he said unto me, Behold, the virgin which thou seest, is <u>the mother of God</u>, after the manner of the flesh.

And it came to pass that I beheld that she was carried away in the spirit; and after that she had been carried away in the spirit for the space of a time, the angel spake unto me, saying, look! And I looked and beheld the virgin again, bearing a chid in her arms. And the angel said unto me, behold the Lamb of God, yea, <u>even the Eternal Father</u>! Knowest thou the meaning of the tree which thy father saw? And I answered him, saying: Yea, it is the love of God, which sheddeth itself abroad in the hearts of the children of men; wherefore, it is the most desirable above all things. And he spake unto me, saying, Yea, and the most joyous to the soul. And after that he had said these words, he said unto me, look! And I looked, and I beheld the Son of God going forth among the children of men; and I saw many fall down at his feet and worship him.

And it came to pass that I beheld that the rod of iron which my father had seen, was the word of God, which led to the fountain of living waters, or to the tree of life; which waters are a representation of the love of God; and I also beheld that the tree of life was a representation of the love of God. And the angel said unto me again, Look and behold the condescention of God! And I looked and beheld the Redeemer of the world, of which my father had spoken; and I also beheld the prophet, which should prepare the way before him. And the Lamb of God went forth, and was baptised of him; and after that he was baptised, I beheld the Heavens open, and the Holy Ghost come down out of Heaven and abode upon him in the form of a dove. And I beheld that he went forth ministering unto the people, in power and great glory; and the multitudes were gathered together to hear him; and I beheld that they cast him out from among them. And I also beheld twelve others following him.

And it came to pass that they were carried away in the spirit, from before my face, that I saw them not. And it came to pass that the angel spake unto me again, saying, look! And I looked, and I beheld the Heavens open again, and I saw angels descending upon the children of men; and they did minister unto them. And he spake unto me again, saying, look! And I looked, and I beheld the Lamb of God going forth among

A photograph of page 25 of the original 1830 *Book of Mormon*. At the two places where the arrow points the words "The Son Of" have been added in later editions.

In the fifth lecture we find this statement about the Godhead: ". . . *the Father being a personage of spirit,* glory, and power, possessing all perfection and fullness, the Son, who was in the bosom of the Father, a personage of tabernacle . . . " (*Doctrine and Covenants,* 1835 ed., p.53).

The Lectures on Faith not only taught that God the Father is a "personage of Spirit," but also that God is "omnipresent"—i.e., present everywhere at the same time (*Ibid.,* pp.12,26).

Joseph Fielding Smith admitted that Joseph Smith helped prepare these lectures: "Now the Prophet did know something about these Lectures on Faith, because he helped to prepare them, and he helped also to revise these lectures before they were published . . ." (*Doctrines of Salvation,* vol. 3, p.195).

These Lectures on Faith were printed in all of the early editions of the *Doctrine and Covenants,* but in 1921 they were completely removed and have not appeared in subsequent editions. John William Fitzgerald, who wrote his thesis at BYU, asked Joseph Fielding Smith why they were removed from the *Doctrine and Covenants.* One of the reasons given was that they were not complete as to their teachings regarding the Godhead. Actually, these lectures were considered complete with regard to their teachings concerning the Godhead at the time they were given. On page 58 of the 1835 edition of the *Doctrine and Covenants* the following question and answer appear: "Q. Does the foregoing account of the Godhead lay a sure foundation for the exercise of faith in him unto life and salvation? A. *It does.*"

Now that the Mormon church teaches a plurality of Gods and that men become Gods, these lectures are considered "not complete" as to their teachings on the Godhead. The truth of the matter is that they contradict what is presently taught by church leaders with regard to this subject.

To avoid "confusion and contention" over the Godhead the Mormon leaders slyly removed the Lectures on Faith from the *Doctrine and Covenants.* This was done in spite of the fact that Joseph Smith himself had considered them important enough to include. Since these lectures were about seventy pages long, this amounted to a major deletion. On page 345 of his thesis, "A Study of the Doctrine & Covenants," Mr. Fitzgerald supplies this information: "The 'Lectures on Faith' were voted on unanimously by the conference assembled August 17, 1835 to be included in the forthcomng book of doctrine and covenants. The writer could find no documentary evidence that they were voted on by a general conference of the Church to be omitted in the 1921 and all subsequent editions o *The Doctrine* [*and*] *Covenants.*"

all things—by whom all things were created and
made, that are created and made, whether visible or
invisible: whether in heaven, on earth, or in the earth,
under the earth, or throughout the immensity of space
—They are the Father and the Son: The Father being a personage of spirit, glory and power: possessing all perfection and fulness: The Son, who was
in the bosom of the Father, a personage of tabernacle,
made, or fashioned like unto man, or being in the
form and likeness of man, or, rather, man was formed after his likeness, and in his image;—he is also
the express image and likeness of the personage of
the Father: possessing all the fulness of the Father,
or, the same fulness with the Fathe; being begotten
of him, and was ordained from before the foundation
of the world to be a propitiation for the sins of all
those who should believe on his name, and is called
the Son because of the flesh—and descended in suffering below that which man can suffer, or, in other
words, suffered greater sufferings, and was exposed
to more powerful contradictions than any man can be.
But notwithstanding all this, he kept the law of God,
and remained without sin: Showing thereby that it is
in the power of man to keep the law and remain also
without sin. And also, that by him a righteous judgment might come upon all flesh, and that all who walk
not in the law of God, may justly be condemned by
the law, and have no excuse for their sins. And he
being the only begotten of the Father, full of grace
and truth, and having overcome, received a fulness of
the glory of the Father—possessing the same mind
with the Father, which mind is the Holy Spirit, that
bears record of the Father and the Son, and these
three are one, or in other words, these three constitute
the great, matchless, governing and supreme power
over all things: by whom all things were created and
made, that were created and made: and these three

A photograph of page 53 of the 1835 edition of the *Doctrine and Covenants*.
Notice this lecture teaches the Father is a personage of spirit. Today the Mormon Church maintains the Father has a body of flesh and bones. Consequently,
these lectures on faith have been removed from recent editions of the *Doctrine
and Covenants*.

A Changeable God

The idea of a progressive God was a natural outgrowth of the Mormon teaching of a plurality of Gods. Apostle Orson Hyde commented: "Remember that *God*, our heavenly Father, was perhaps *once a child*, and *mortal* like we ourselves, and rose step by step in the scale of progress, in the school of advancement; has moved forward and overcome, until He has arrived at the point where He now is" (*Journal of Discourses*, vol. 1, p.123).

Brigham Young declared: "We are now, or may be, as perfect in our sphere as God and Angels are in theirs, but the greatest intelligence in existence can continually ascend to greater heights of perfection" (*Journal of Discourses*, vol. 1, p.93).

Wilford Woodruff, who became the fourth president of the church, said that "*God himself is increasing and progressing* in knowledge, power, and dominion, and will do so, worlds without end" (*Ibid.*, vol. 6, p.120).

This idea of a progressive and changeable God is very different from the concept of God taught in the Bible and *Book of Mormon*. In Malachi 3:6 we read: "For I am the Lord, I change not. . . ." In the *Book of Mormon*, page 517, verse 18, we find this statement: "For I know that God is not a partial God, neither a changeable being; but he is unchangeable from all eternity to all eternity."

While Brigham Young and other leaders of the Mormon church openly rejected the *Book of Mormon* teaching that God is "unchangeable," Apostle Orson Pratt had a difficult time accepting the new ideas about God. Although he accepted the idea of a plurality of Gods, he did not seem to believe that they progressed in knowledge. In a sermon delivered in the tabernacle on January 13, 1867, Brigham Young chided: ". . . Brother Orson Pratt, has in theory, bounded the capacity of God. According to his theory, God can progress no further in knowledge and power; *but the God that I serve is progressing eternally*, and so are his children: they will increase to all eternity, if they are faithful" (*Journal of Discourses*, vol. 11, p.286).

It is interesting to note that the Mormon church is still divided over this issue. Joseph Fielding Smith sided with Orson Pratt. He stated: "It seems very strange to me that members of the Church will hold to the doctrine, 'God increases in knowledge as time goes on.' . . . I think this kind of doctrine is very dangerous" (*Doctrines of Salvation*, vol. 1, pp.7-8).

Though there seems to be a division over whether God is continuing to increase in knowledge, Mormon leaders agree that there was a time when He was only a man. Marion G. Romney, a member of the First Presidency, recently made this vivid statement: "*God* is a perfected, *saved soul* enjoying eternal life. He is both immortal and exalted to the highest glory. He is enjoying that blessed condition which men may attain to by obedience to the laws and ordinances of the gospel" (*Salt Lake Tribune*, October 6, 1974, p.1).

Spencer W. Kimball, currently president of the church, still maintains that "in each of us is the potentiality *to become a God*" (*Salt Lake Tribune*, October 7, 1974). Speaking to "priesthood holders," President Kimball made these comments: "Brethren 225,000 of you are here tonight. I suppose *225,000 of you may become gods*. There seems to be plenty of space out there in the universe. And the Lord has proved that he knows how to do it. I think he could make, or probably have us help make, worlds for all of us, for every one of us 225,000" (*Ensign*, November 1975, p.80).

The Holy Ghost

One of the most confusing areas of Mormon theology is that area dealing with the Holy Ghost. In the Lectures on Faith, published in the first edition of the *Doctrine and Covenants* in 1835, it was declared that there were only two personages in the Godhead—the Father and the Son—and that the Holy Spirit is the mind of the Father and the Son:

> There are *two personages* . . . the Father and the Son: The *Father being a personage of spirit*, glory and power: possessing all perfection and fulness: The Son, who was in the bosom of the Father a personage of tabernacle, . . . called the Son because of the flesh . . . possessing the same mind with the Father, *which mind is the Holy Spirit*, . . .
> Q. How many personages are there in the Godhead?
> A. *Two*: the Father and the Son.
> Q. How do you prove that there are *two personages* in the Godhead?
> A. By the Scriptures. . . .
> Q. Do the Father and the Son possess the same mind?
> A. They do. . . .
> Q. *What is this mind?*
> A. *The Holy Spirit*. . . .
> Q. Do the Father, Son and Holy Spirit constitute the Godhead?
> A. They do. . . .
> Q. Does the foregoing account of the Godhead lay a sure foundation for the exercise of faith in him unto life and salvation?
> A. It does (*Doctrine and Covenants*, 1835 ed., pp.52,53,55,57,58; removed from modern editions).

The Mormon leaders now teach that there are *three person-ages* in the Godhead—the Father and the Son both being personages of tabernacle and the Holy Ghost being a personage of spirit. It is interesting to note, however, that in 1855 Orson Pratt was still not certain whether there was a personal Holy Ghost: "I am inclined to think from some things in the revelations, that there is such a being as a personal Holy Ghost, but it is not set forth as a positive fact, and the Lord has never given me any revelation upon the subject, and consequently *I cannot fully make up my mind* one way or the other" (*Journal of Discourses*, vol. 2, p.338). On another occasion Pratt stated: "In the Book of Covenants, page 45, we are informed that there are two person-ages besides the Holy Spirit, which constitute the Godhead; but *we are not there informed whether the third, called the Holy Spirit is a personage or not*" (*Millennial Star*, vol. 12, p.308).

Today, of course, the Mormons teach that the Holy Ghost is an actual personage. William E. Berrett quoted Joseph F. Smith as saying: "The Holy Ghost is a personage of Spirit, he constitutes the third person in the Godhead" (*The Restored Church*, 1956, p.541).

Since Mormon leaders teach that God has a wife, some people have speculated that the Holy Ghost might be the wife of God the Father. Joseph Fielding Smith, however, vigorously opposed such an idea: "The Holy Ghost is not a personage with a body of flesh and bones, and in this respect differs from the Father and the Son. The Holy Ghost is not a woman, as some have declared, and therefore is not the mother of Jesus Christ" (*Doctrines of Salvation*, vol. 1, p.39).

Apostle LeGrand Richards says that "the Holy Ghost is a male personage. . . . He is a male personage of spirit . . ." (*A Marvelous Work And A Wonder*, p.118).

Heber C. Kimball, who was a member of the First Presidency, said that "*the Holy Ghost is a man*; he is one of the sons of our Father and our God . . ." (*Journal of Discourses*, vol. 5, p.179).

William E. Berrett gives this information concerning the Holy Ghost: "The Holy Ghost is a person. Unlike the Father and the Son who have bodies of flesh and bone, the Holy Ghost has no body of flesh and bone (that is, of the elements as we know them) but is a personage of spirit" (*The Restored Church*, p.540).

While the Mormon church leaders teach that the Holy Ghost does not have a body of flesh and bones, they also teach that it is absolutely essential to have one. In fact, they claim that the devils were denied bodies of flesh and bone as a punishment for their sins. Joseph Fielding Smith said: "The punishment of

Satan and the third of the hosts of heaven who followed him, was that they were denied the privilege of being born into this world and receiving mortal bodies. They did not keep their first estate and were denied the opportunity of eternal progression" (*Doctrines of Salvation*, vol. 1, p.65).

Brigham Young related that Joseph B. Nobles once told a Methodist priest that the devil was "a being without a body, whereas our God has a body, parts, and passions. The Devil was cursed and sent down from heaven. He has no body of his own . . ." (*Journal of Discourses*, vol. 5, p.331).

Mormon leaders are unable to explain why God the Father should have a body and yet the Holy Ghost be without one. It is claimed that a body is necessary for eternal progression, yet the Mormon church teaches that the Holy Ghost became a God without one. Milton R. Hunter said that the "crowning Gospel ordinance requisite for Godhood is celestial marriage . . . obedience to this law is absolutely necessary in order to obtain the highest exaltation in the Kingdom of God" (*The Gospel Through the Ages*, pp.118-19).

According to Mormon theology, then, it would have been impossible for the Holy Ghost to have obtained Godhood, since he had no body with which to obey the law of "celestial marriage." In a revelation given by Joseph Smith we read: "Broad is the gate, and wide the way that leadeth to the deaths; and many there are that go in thereat . . ."(*Doctrine and Covenants* 132:25).

Mormon writers explain that these are the ones who have not obeyed the law of "celestial marriage" and who cannot have children in the resurrection. Bruce R. McConkie comments: "The opposite of eternal lives is eternal deaths. Those who come up separately and singly in the resurrection and who therefore do not have spirit children eternally are said to inherit 'the deaths.' (D. & C. 132:16-17,25.)" (*Mormon Doctrine*, 1958, p.220). According to this reasoning, the Holy Ghost seems to be on the path that "leadeth to the deaths."

Some members of the Mormon church have been concerned as to whether the Holy Ghost will get a body at some future time. Joseph Fielding Smith, however, claimed that he was not concerned about the matter: "I have never troubled myself about the Holy Ghost whether he will sometime have a body or not because it is not in any way essential to my salvation" (*Doctrines of Salvation*, vol. 1, p.39). Apostle McConkie calls the Holy Ghost "a Spirit Man" and then goes on to state: "In this dispensation, at least, nothing has been revealed as to his origin or destiny; expressions on these matters are both speculative and fruitless" (*Mormon Doctrine*, p.329).

No Real Answers

In this chapter we have seen how the Mormon concept of God has changed from one God to a plurality of gods. Mormon leaders claim that all Christians are in a state of apostasy and have lost the true knowledge of the Godhead, yet a careful examination of Mormon teachings concerning the Godhead reveals a serious state of confusion. Mormon missionaries go throughout the world using Joseph Smith's story of the first vision as evidence that Christians are in error about the Godhead. In the new missionary manual we read the following: "*Missionary*: Mr. Brown, we learn another beautiful principle from Joseph Smith's visit from the Father and the Son. When he saw and talked with them, he learned that the Father and his Son, Jesus Christ, *are separate and distinct individuals* and not just different manifestations of the same person. He also learned that *they each have a body of flesh and bones*" (*The Uniform System For Teaching Families*, Deseret Press, 1973, p.C-31). The missionaries, however, fail to inform their contacts that in the first handwritten account of the first vision Joseph Smith never even mentions that God the Father was present.

While Mormonism claims to give all the answers about the Godhead, the honest investigator soon finds that these answers do not solve the real problems and that many of them are built upon the sandy foundation of change or falsification.

In the next chapter we will deal with Brigham Young's Adam-God doctrine, which is certainly one of the low points in Mormon theology.

THE ADAM-GOD DOCTRINE

Chapter 8

The Adam-God doctrine was a natural outgrowth of the doctrine of a plurality of Gods. Although this doctrine was not publicly taught until 1852, Adam was held in high esteem at the very beginning of the Mormon church. Apostle John A. Widtsoe said that "In Joseph Smith's philosophy of existence Adam and Eve were raised to a foremost place among the children of men, *second only to the Savior*. Their act was to be acclaimed. They were the greatest figures of the ages. *The so-called 'fall' became a necessary, honorable act* in carrying out the plan of the Almighty" (*Joseph Smith–Seeker After Truth*, p.160).

Joseph Fielding Smith also said that "the fall of man came as a blessing in disguise, . . . *I never speak of the part Eve took in this fall as a sin, nor do I accuse Adam of a sin*. . . . it is not *always a sin to transgress a law*" (*Doctrines of Salvation*, vol. 1, pp.114-15).

Sterling W. Sill, a member of the First Quorum of Seventy, made the same point in colorful language:

> This old sectarian doctrine, built around the idea of man's natural depravity and weakness inherited from Adam, is at the root of innumerable problems among us. Adam was one of the greatest men who has ever lived upon the earth. . . .
>
> Under Christ Adam yet stands at our head. . . . Adam fell, *but he fell in the right direction*. He fell toward the goal. . . .
>
> Adam fell, *but he fell upward*. Jesus says to us, "Come up higher" (*Deseret News*, Church Section, July 31, 1965, p.7).

In his thesis, Owen Kendall White, Jr., makes some further observations:

> Mormonism rejects the notion that man's condition is best described as "depravity." Nowhere within Mormon theology is its optimism concerning man's natural condition more clearly ap-

parent than in this denial of the Christian doctrine of original sin. . . . In contrast with the orthodox Christian notion that the fall resulted in a condition of human depravity, the Mormon view asserts that the fall was a necessary condition for man to realize his ultimate potential. . . . to the Mormon the fall is a fall upward rather than downward. . . . Rather than the view of literalistic Christian orthodoxy where Adam is conceived as the cause of human suffering, . . . Mormonism holds Adam in very high esteem. . . .

Within Mormon angelology Adam is Michael the Archangel, the Ancient of Days. He assisted in the creation process and will assist in the resurrecting of the dead. He holds positions of importance next to the members of the Godhead. Indeed, Adam was so highly regarded within early Mormonism that Brigham Young elevated him to the status of God ("The Social Psychological Basis of Mormon New-Orthodoxy," Master's thesis, by Owen Kendall White, Jr., University of Utah, June 1967, pp.101-4).

On April 9, 1852, Brigham Young publicly preached the Adam-God doctrine. In this sermon he declared:

Now hear it, O inhabitants of the earth, Jew and Gentile, Saint and sinner! When our father Adam came into the garden of Eden, he came into it with a celestial body, and brought Eve, one of his wives, with him. He helped to make and organize this world. He is Michael, the Arch-angel, the Ancient of Days! about whom holy men have written and spoken—*He is our Father and our God, and the only God with whom we have to do*. Every man upon the earth, professing Christians or non-professing, must hear it, and will know it sooner or later . . . the earth was organized by three distinct characters, namely, Eloheim, Yahovah, and Michael, these three forming a quorum, as in all heavenly bodies, and in organizing element, perfectly represented in the Deity, as Father, Son, and Holy Ghost (*Journal of Discourses*, vol. 1, pp.50-51).

This sermon was reprinted in *The Latter-Day Saints' Millennial Star* on November 26, 1853 (vol. 15, pp.769-70). The fact that the Mormon people understood Brigham Young to mean just what he said concerning Adam being God is verified by other articles which appeared in the church's own *Millennial Star*. On December 10, 1853, an article entitled, "Adam, the Father and God of the Human Family" appeared in the *Millennial Star*. In this article the following statements are found:

"The above sentiment appeared in Star No. 48, a little to the surprise of some of its readers: and while the sentiment may have appeared blasphemous to the Ignorant; it has no doubt

lead me." I was trying to think of the place where God is not, but it is impossible, unless you can find *empty* space; and *there* I believe He is not. If you can find such a place, it will become useful for a hiding place to those who wish to hide themselves from the presence of the Lord, in the great day of accounts. I will close this sermon, as I intend to preach another before I present the subject I more particularly wish to speak upon.

My next sermon will be to both Saint and sinner. One thing has remained a mystery in this kingdom up to this day. It is in regard to the character of the well-beloved Son of God, upon which subject the Elders of Israel have conflicting views. Our God and Father in heaven, is a being of tabernacle, or, in other words, He has a body, with parts the same as you and I have; and is capable of showing forth His works to organized beings, as, for instance, in the world in which we live, it is the result of the knowledge and infinite wisdom that dwell in His organized body. His son Jesus Christ has become a personage of tabernacle, and has a body like his father. The Holy Ghost is the Spirit of the Lord, and issues forth from Himself, and may properly be called God's minister to execute His will in immensity; being called to govern by His influence and power; but *He* is not a person of tabernacle as we are, and as our Father in Heaven and Jesus Christ are. The question has been, and is often, asked, who it was that begat the Son of the Virgin Mary. The infidel world have concluded that if what the Apostles wrote about his father and mother be true, and the present marriage discipline acknowledged by Christendom be correct, then Christians must believe that God, is the father of an illegitimate son, in the person of Jesus Christ! The infidel fraternity teach *that* to their disciples. I will tell you how it is. Our Father in Heaven begat all the spirits that ever were, or ever will be, upon this earth; and they were born spirits in the eternal world. Then the Lord by His power and wisdom organized the mortal tabernacle of man. We were made first spiritual, and afterwards temporal.

Now hear it, O inhabitants of the earth, Jew and Gentile, Saint and sinner! When our father Adam came into the garden of Eden, he came into it with a *celestial body*, and brought Eve, *one of his wives*, with him. He helped to make and organize this world. He is MICHAEL, *the Archangel*, the ANCIENT OF DAYS! about whom holy men have written and spoken — HE *is* our FATHER *and our* GOD, *and the only God with whom* WE *have to do*. Every man upon the earth, professing Christians or non-professing, must hear it, and *will know it sooner or later*. They came here, organized the raw material, and arranged in their order the herbs of the field, the trees, the apple, the peach, the plum, the pear, and every other fruit that is desirable and good for man; the seed was brought from another sphere, and planted in this earth. The thistle, the thorn, the brier, and the obnoxious weed did *not* appear until after the earth was cursed. When Adam and Eve had eaten of the forbidden fruit, their bodies became mortal from *its effects*, and therefore their offspring were mortal. When the Virgin Mary conceived the child Jesus, the Father had begotten him in his own likeness. He was *not* begotten by the Holy Ghost. And who is the Father? He is the first of the human family; and when he took a tabernacle, it was begotten by *his Father* in heaven, after the same manner as the tabernacles of Cain, Abel, and the rest of the sons and daughters of Adam and Eve; from the fruits of the earth, the first earthly tabernacles were originated by the Father, and so

given rise to some serious reflections with the more candid and comprehensive mind . . . *Adam is really God!* And why not?" (*Millennial Star*, vol. 15, p.801).

On page 825 of the same volume the following appeared: "It has been said that *Adam is the God and Father of the human family*, and persons are perhaps in fear and great trouble of mind, lest they have to acknowledge him as such in some future day. For our part we would much rather acknowledge Adam to be our Father, than hunt for another, and take up with the devil."

In volume 17, page 195, of the *Millennial Star* this statement was made: ". . . every Knee shall bow, and every tongue confess that he is the God of the whole earth. Then will the words of the Prophet Brigham, when speaking of *Adam*, be fully realized—'He is our Father and our God, and the only God with whom we have to do.' "

Elder James A. Little confessed: "I believe in the principle of obedience; and if I am told that *Adam is our Father and our God*, I just believe it" (*Millennial Star*, vol. 16, p.530).

Brigham Young's Adam-God doctrine met with opposition both within and without the church. In October 1857 he stated: "Some have grumbled because I believe *our God to be so near to us as Father Adam*. There are many who know that doctrine to be true" (*Journal of Discourses*, vol. 5, p.331).

That the Adam-God doctrine was causing dissension in the Mormon church is evident from the articles that appeared in the *Millennial Star*. One article admitted that some of the officers had not met in council for three years because of the Adam-God doctrine:

> . . . some of the officers have not met in council for three years. They are lacking faith on one principle—the last "cat that was let out of the bag." Polygamy has been got over pretty well, that cloud has vanished away, but they are *troubled about Adam being our Father and God*. There is a very intelligent person investigating our principles, . . . and can get along very well with everything else but the last "cat," and as soon as he can see that clearly, he will become a "Mormon." I instructed him to write to Liverpool upon it (*Millennial Star*, vol. 16, p.482).

An answer to this problem appeared on page 534 of the same volume: "Concerning the item of doctrine alluded to by Elder Caffall and others, viz., that *Adam is our Father and God*, I have to say do not trouble yourselves, neither let the Saints be troubled about this matter. . . . If, as Elder Caffall remarked, there are those who are waiting at the door of the Church for the objection to be removed, tell such, the Prophet and Apostle Brigham

Young has declared it, and that *it is the word of the Lord"* (*Millennial Star*, vol. 16, p.534).

In his journal and autobiography, Joseph Lee Robinson commented that he feared Apostle Orson Pratt would apostatize because of his opposition to the Adam-God doctrine:

> "Oct. 6th attend Conference, a very interesting Conference, for at this meeting President Brigham Young said thus, that Adam and Eve, ware [sic] the names of the first man and woman, of every Earth that was ever organized, and that Adam and Eve were the natural father and mother of every spirit that comes to this planet, or that receives, tabernacles on this plannet [sic], concequently [sic] we are brothers and sisters, and that *Adam was, God our Eternal Father*, this as Brother Heber remarked was letting the cat out of the Bag, and it came to pass, I believed every word . . . our Beloved Brother *Orson Prat*[t] *told me he did not believe it* He said he could prove by the Scriptures it was not correct. I felt very sorry to hear professor, Orson Prat[t] say that, I feared lest he should apostetize [sic] . . . (Journal of Joseph Lee Robinson, microfilm copy in LDS Genealogical Library).

According to the "Minutes of the School of the Prophets," held in Provo, Utah, the Apostle Lyman as well as Orson Pratt opposed Brigham Young's Adam-God doctrine. Under the date of June 8, 1868, we read:

> The doctrine preached by Prest Young for a few years back wherein he says that *Adam is our God–the God we worship—* that most of the people believe this . . . Amasa Lyman stumbled on this he did not believe it—he did not believe in the atonement of Jesus—Orson Pratt has also told the Prest that he does not believe it—this is not the way to act—we should not suffer ourselves to entertain one doubt—we are not accountable on points of Doctrine if the President makes a statement it is not our prerogative to dispute it ("Minutes of the School of the Prophets," Provo, Utah, 1868-71, p.38 of typed copy at Utah State Historical Society).

In spite of the opposition, Brigham Young continued to teach the Adam-God doctrine. In 1873, just a few years before his death, he declared:

> How much unbelief exists in the minds of the Latter-day Saints in regard to one particular doctrine which I revealed to them, and which God revealed to me—namely that *Adam is our Father and God*. . . . Our Father Adam helped to make this earth, . . . he and his companions came here. He brought one of his wives with him. . . . Our Father Adam is the man who stands at the gate and

---

A photograph of the *Deseret News*, June 18, 1873. Brigham Young claimed that "God revealed" to him that "Adam is our Father and God." ➤

hard to take their measurement as Saints. I carry in my pocket a rule on which the inches are divided into a hundred parts. Such a rule would be necessary, in my opinion, to measure the standing of those professing to be Saints who would refuse to sign a petition to stop drunkenness. You may differ from me in your opinion, and you have a perfect right to, and I have the same right to differ from you; but it is my opinion that the man or woman whose name is upon our records as a Latter-day Saint, who would fellowship what we see and have to endure here all the time, is a very poor Saint. I have some notion to ask you whether you like these things, and who among you will sign a petition to the City Council to stop them. I must explain here that the evils we see in our city are the result of the acts of men who, though administrators of the law in various capacities, instead of sustaining the laws, say, "Sell liquor as much as you please, pay no attention to the City Council, disregard the laws of this city and Territory, ride over and trample them under your feet, and break whatever law the City Council may make." This is what our administrators of the law say, and to this cause only can be attributed whatever of crime and defiance of law we see manifested here.

It has been said that Brother Brigham has proffered his services to help stop the liquor traffic in this city. I will say, that is true, and I do it upon the principle of justice and truth, and within the bounds of our local laws, and in no other way; and if the inhabitants of this city are disposed to raise their voices and influence against the conduct we see here, and the City Council passes a law to stop the drunkenness and gambling, they will find us—the citizens—ready to sustain them by our faith and works. "For lo, the wicked bend their bow, they make ready their arrow upon the string, that they may privately shoot at the upright in heart."

I leave it to the people of the United States, to all good citizens from the Atlantic to the Pacific, if it is not better to live without gambling and drunkenness than to have them in our midst? What would they say if they were to express an opinion on the subject? The leading portion of them would say, "Let us have sober, civil communities," and they would rejoice to see the time when our Presidents, law-makers, and executors of the law would live continually with a sober, steady brain, able to judge between right and wrong, and with willing hearts and steady hands administer the laws to this great nation in righteousness. Will we Latter-day Saints sign a petition to the Mayor and City Council to stop these evils entirely? (Congregation said, "Yes.") I will invite all, whether citizens or strangers, who are in favor of a people living a sober, steady life, to vote on this question, if they desire to do so. (The congregation voted unanimously in favor, by showing their right hands.) Does anybody want to vote against it? Is there a

ing honestly. I want the bishops to go to and find out how many in their wards will sign a paper to the City Council, asking its members to pass a law for the suppression of liquor selling and enforce the present law against gambling. I am thankful that I have the privilege and am willing to put my name at the head of such a paper, for I am opposed to these things. At the present time it seems to be impossible for the City Council to license people to keep bars for the accommodation of strangers. They would be glad to do so, and would be reasonable with those who wanted them, but owing to circumstances it does seem that our citizens will be bound to stop the whole of it, or else let a few ride over every law enacted for the preservation of the peace and good order of the city.

I wanted to make a few remarks upon the subject touched upon by my brother, but I shall not have the time. I frequently think, in my meditations, how glad we should be to instruct the world with regard to the things of God, if they would hear, and receive our teachings in good and honest hearts and profit by them. I have been found fault with a great many times for casting reflections upon men of science, and especially upon theologians, because of the little knowledge they possess about man being on the earth, about the earth itself, about our Father in heaven, his Son Jesus Christ, the order of heavenly things, the laws by which angels exist, by which the worlds were created and are held in existence, &c. How pleased we would be to place these things before the people if they would receive them! How much unbelief exists in the minds of the Latter-day Saints in regard to one particular doctrine which is revealed to them, and which God revealed to me—namely that Adam is our father and God—I do not know, I do not inquire, I care nothing about it. Our Father Adam helped to make this earth, it was created expressly for him, and after it was made he and his companions came here. He brought one of his wives with him, and she was called Eve, because she was the first woman upon the earth. Our Father Adam is the man who stands at the gate and holds the keys of everlasting life and salvation to all his children who have or who ever will come upon the earth. I have been found fault with by the ministers of religion because I have said that they were ignorant. But I could not find any man on the earth who could tell me this, although it is one of the simplest things in the world, until I met and talked with Joseph Smith. Is it a great mystery that the earth exists? Is it a great mystery, that the world can not solve, that man is on the earth? Yes, it is; but to whom? To the ignorant—those who know nothing about it. It is no mystery to those who understand. Is it a mystery to the Christian world that Jesus is the Son of God, and still the son of man? Yes it is, it is hidden from them, and this fulfils the Scripture —"If our gospel be hid, it is hid to

priests and people—would follow after. Where did I declare this? In the cities of New York, Albany, Boston, throughout the United States and in England. Have I seen this fulfilled? I have. I told the people that as true as God lived, if they would not have truth they would have error sent unto them, and they would believe it. What is the mystery of it?

The Christian world read of, and think much about, St. Paul, also St. Peter, the chief of the Apostles. These men were faithful to and magnified the priesthood while on the earth. Now, where will be the mystery, after they have passed through all the ordeals, and have been crowned and exalted, and received their inheritances in the eternal worlds of glory, for them to be sent forth, as the Gods have been for ever and ever, with the command—"Make yourselves an earth, and people it with your own children?" Do you think the starry heavens are going to fall? Do the Christian world or the heathen world think that all things are going to be wrapped up, consumed, and annihilated in eternal flames? Oh fools, and slow of heart to believe the great things that God has purposed in his own mind?

My brother said that God is as we are. He did not mean those words to be literally understood. He meant simply, that in our organization we have all the properties in embryo in our bodies that our Father has in his, and that literally, morally, socially, by the spirit and by the flesh we are his children. Do you think that God, who holds the eternities in his hands and can do all things at his pleasure, is not capable of sending forth his own children, and forming this flesh for his own offspring? Where is the mystery in this? We say that Father Adam came here and helped to make the earth. Who is he? He is Michael, a great prince, and it was said to him by Eloheim, "Go ye and make an earth." What is the great mystery about it? He came and formed the earth. Geologists tell us that it was here millions of years ago. How do they know? They know nothing about it. But suppose it was here, what of it? Adam found it in a state of chaos, unorganized and incomplete. Philosophers, again, in talking of the development of the products of the earth, for instance, in the vegetable kingdom, say the little fibres grew first, then the larger vegetation. When this preparatory stage was completed then came the various orders of the animal creation; and finally man appeared. No matter whether these notions are true or not, they are more or less speculative. Adam came here and got it up in a shape that would suit him to commence business. What is the great mystery about it? None, that I have seen. The mystery in this, as with miracles, or anything else, is only to those who are ignorant. Father Adam came here, and then they brought his wife. "Well," says one, "Why was Adam called Adam"? He was the first man on the earth, and its framer and maker. he, with the help of his brethren, brought it into existence. Then he said, "I want my children who are in the spirit world to come and live here. I once dwelt upon an earth something like this, in a mortal state, I was faithful, I received my crown and exaltation. I have the privilege of extending my work, and to its increase there will be no end. I want my children that were born to me in the spirit world to come here and take tabernacles of flesh that their spirits may have a house, a tabernacle or a dwelling place as mine has, and where is the mystery?

Now for mother Eve. The evil principle always has and always will exist. Well, a

holds the keys of everlasting life and salvation to all his children who have or who ever will come upon the earth. . . . We say that Father Adam came here and helped to made the earth. Who is he? He is Michael. . . . He was the first man on the earth, and its framer and maker. He, with the help of his brethren, brought it into existence. Then he said, "I want my children who are in the spirit world to come and live here. I once dwelt upon an earth something like this, in a mortal state. I was faithful, I received my crown and exaltation. I have the privilege of extending my work, and to its increase there will be no end. I want my children that were born to me in the spirit world to come here and take tabernacles of flesh, that their spirits may have a house, a tabernacle or a dwelling place as mine has, and where is the mystery?" (*Deseret News*, June 18, 1873).

There are four important points that should be noted concerning the Adam-God doctrine.

Not Created of the Dust of This Earth

In a sermon delivered in 1852, Brigham Young stated: "When our father Adam came into the garden of Eden, he came into it with a celestial body. . . . He helped to make and organize this world" (*Journal of Discourses*, vol. 1, p.50). Brigham Young also taught: "You believe Adam was made of the dust of this earth. *This I do not believe*, though it is supposed that it is so written in the Bible; . . . I have publicly declared that *I do not believe that portion of the Bible as the Christian world do* [sic]," (vol. 2, p.6). "Adam was made from the dust of an earth, but not from the dust of this earth. He was made as you and I are made, and no person was ever made upon any other principle" (vol. 3, p.319).

Rodney Turner, of Brigham Young University, adds the following comment concerning this matter: "Apparently President Young means that Adam was provided with a physical body through the normal pattern of conception, embryonic development, and birth, since that is [the] method by which 'you and I are made' " (The Position of Adam in Latter-day Saint Scripture and Theology," M.A. thesis, BYU, August 1953, p.20).

The Only God with Whom We Have to Do

Brigham Young stated: "He is our Father and our God, and *the only God with whom we have to do*" (*Journal of Discourses*, vol. 1, p.50). In the book *Women of Mormondom*, page 196, we read: "When Brigham Young proclaimed to the nations that Adam was our Father and God, and Eve, his partner, the Mother of a world—both in a mortal and celestial sense—he made the most important revelation ever oracled to the race since the days of Adam himself." The reader will also remember that we quoted this statement from the "Minutes of the School of the Prophets": ". . . Prest Young . . . says that Adam is *our God—the God we worship—*that most of the people believe this. . . ."

The Father of Our Spirits

Brigham Young also taught that Adam was the Father of our spirits. In 1873 he stated: ". . . Father Adam came here and helped make the earth. . . . Then he said, 'I want *my children who are in the spirit world to come and live here. . . .* I want my children that were *born to me in the spirit world* to come here and take tabernacles of flesh . . ." (*Deseret News*, June 18, 1873). Joseph Lee Robinson explained that Brigham Young taught that "Adam and Eve were the natural father and mother of every spirit that comes to this plannet [sic], or that receives, tabernacles on this planet, . . . and that Adam was God our Eternal Father. . . ." On page 180 of *Women of Mormondom* we are told that "Adam and Eve are the names of the fathers and mothers of worlds. . . . These were father and mother of a world of spirits who had been born to them in heaven."

The Father of Jesus Christ

Since Brigham Young was teaching that Adam was the father of our spirits, it was very easy to teach that Adam was also the father of Jesus. In a discourse delivered April 9, 1852, Brigham Young declared:

> When the Virgin Mary conceived the child Jesus, the Father had begotten him in his own likeness. He was not begotten by the Holy Ghost. And *who is the Father? He is the first of the human family* . . . I could tell you much more about this; but were I to tell you the whole truth, blasphemy would be nothing to it, in the estimation of the superstitious and over-righteous of mankind. However, I have told you the truth as far as I have gone. . . . Jesus, our elder brother, was begotten in the flesh by the same character that was in the garden of Eden, and who is our Father in Heaven. Now, let all who may hear these doctrines, pause before they make light of them, or treat them with indifference, for they will prove their salvation or damnation (*Journal of Discourses*, vol. 1, pp.50-51).

John A. Widtsoe, who recently served as an Apostle, denied that Brigham Young taught Adam was the Father of Christ. He claimed that only "Enemies of the Church or stupid people" could reach such a conclusion. It is very easy to show that

199

Apostle Widtsoe's statement is false, for the evidence shows that many good Mormons in Utah held to this belief. For instance, Hosea Stout, who was a prominent Mormon, recorded the following in his diary under the date of April 9, 1852: "Another meeting this evening. President B. Young taught that *Adam was the father of Jesus* and the only God to us. That he came to this world in a resureted [*sic*] body &c more hereafter" (*On the Mormon Frontier, The Diary of Hosea Stout*, University of Utah Press, 1964, vol. 2, p.435).

In the *Women of Mormondom* we read: "Adam is our Father and God. He is the God of the earth. So says Brigham Young. . . . He is *the father of our elder brother, Jesus Christ*—the father of him who shall also come as Messiah to reign. He is the father of the spirits as well as the tabernacles of the sons and daughters of man. Adam!" (*Women of Mormondom*, p.179).

Heber C. Kimball, first counselor to Brigham Young, claimed that "there is but one God that pertains to this people, and he is the God that pertains to this earth—the first man. *That first man sent his own Son* to redeem the world . . ." (*Journal of Discourses*, vol. 4, p.1).

In 1856 the Mormons published a hymnal which contained a hymn entitled, "We Believe In Our God." This hymn plainly taught that Adam was the father of Christ:

> We believe in our God the great Prince of His race,
> The Archangel Michael, the Ancient of Days,
> Our own *Father Adam*, earth's Lord, as is plain,
> Who'll counsel and fight for his children again.
>
> We believe in *His Son, Jesus Christ*, who, in love
> To his brethren and sisters, came down from above
> To die to redeem them from death, and to teach
> To mortals and spirits the Gospel we preach.

(*Sacred Hymns and Spiritual Songs for the Church of Jesus Christ of Latter-day Saints*, Liverpool, 1856, p.375, as quoted in "The Position of Adam in Latter-day Saint Scripture and Theology," p.16.)

George Q. Cannon, a member of the First Presidency, seemed to believe that Adam was the father of Christ. His son recorded the following in his journal:

> . . . Father [George Q. Cannon] . . . asked me what I understood concerning Mary conceiving the Savior; and as I found no answer, he asked what was to prevent *Father Adam from visiting and overshadowing the mother of Jesus*. "Then," said I, "He must have been a resurrected Being." "Yes," said he, "and

though Christ is said to have been the first fruits of them that slept, yet the Savior said he did nothing but what He had seen His Father do, for He had power to lay down His life and take it up again. Adam, though made of dust, was made, as Pres. Young said, of the dust of another planet than this." I was very much instructed by the conversation and this day's services ("Daily Journal of Abraham H. Cannon," March 10, 1888, vol. 10, pp.178-79; original at Brigham Young University).

Under the date of June 23, 1889, Abraham Cannon recorded that George Q. Cannon taught that *"Jesus Christ is Jehovah"* and *"Adam is His Father and our God"* (vol. 11, p.39).

The information given above certainly shows that Brigham Young did teach that Jesus was the son of Adam, and it was not just "Enemies of the Church, or stupid people" who believed that he taught this doctrine. The most devastating evidence, however, comes from the "Journal of L. John Nuttall," who was "a special secretary to President Young." On Wednesday, February 7, 1877, L. John Nuttall recorded in his journal that Brigham Young taught that Jesus was the son of Adam:

Wed 7 . . . Prest Young was filled with the spirit of God & revelation & said, . . . This is life eternal that they might know thee the only true God and Jesus Christ whom thou hast sent . . . Adam was an immortal being when he came on this earth . . . and had begotten all the spirit that was to come to this earth and Eve our common Mother who is the mother of all living bore those spirits in the celestial world. . . .

Father Adam's oldest son (Jesus the Savior) who is the heir of the family is Father Adams first begotten in the spirit World, who according to the flesh is the only begotten as it is written. (In his divinity he having gone back into the spirit world, and come in the spirit to Mary and she conceived . . . ("Journal of L. John Nuttall," vol. 1, pp.18-21, taken from a typed copy at Brigham Young University).

When the Mormon church was accused of teaching that "Adam is God . . . and that Jesus is his son," the Mormon historian B. H. Roberts replied: "As a matter of fact, the 'Mormon' Church does not teach that doctrine. A few men in the 'Mormon' Church have held such views: and several of them quite prominent in the councils of the Church, . . . *Brigham Young and others may have taught that doctrine* . . ." (*Deseret News*, July 23, 1921).

Brigham Young's Adam-God doctrine has brought much confusion into the Mormon church. Wilford Woodruff, the fourth president of the church, once stated:

> Cease troubling yourselves about who God is; who Adam is, who Christ is, who Jehovah is. For heaven's sake, let these things alone . . . God is God. Christ is Christ. The Holy Ghost is the Holy Ghost. That should be enough for you and me to know . . . I say this because we are troubled every little while with inquiries from Elders anxious to know who God is, who Christ is, and who Adam is. I say to the Elders of Israel, stop this (*Millennial Star*, vol. 57, pp.355-56).

In all fairness to the Mormon leaders it should be stated that they no longer teach the Adam-God doctrine, even though some members of the church still believe it. Anyone who is caught teaching this doctrine is liable to be excommunicated. This, however, shows the inconsistency of the Mormon church, for they say that Brigham Young was a prophet, and at the same time they will excommunicate a person for believing in his teachings.

Even before the turn of the century the Mormon leaders seemed to be ashamed of the Adam-God doctrine. On November 28, 1898, George Q. Cannon, a member of the First Presidency, stated that Brigham Young had taught some things concerning Adam and Jesus, but they felt it was not "wise to advocate these matters":

> I was stopped yesterday afternoon by a young man, who wanted to know whether Adam was the Father of our Lord and Savior—whether he was the being we worshipped, etc. Now, we can get ourselves very easily puzzled, if we choose to do so, by speculating upon doctrines and principles of this character. The Lord has said through His Prophet that there are two personages in the Godhead. That ought to be sufficient for us at the present time. . . . Concerning the doctrine in regard to Adam and the Savior, the Prophet Brigham Young taught some things concerning that; but the First Presidency and the twelve do not think it wise to advocate these matters (*Proceedings of the First Sunday School Convention of the Church of Jesus Christ of Latter-day Saints*, Salt Lake City, 1899, as quoted in "The Position of Adam in Latter-day Saint Scripture and Theology," pp.69-70).

Even though the Mormon leaders were trying to put down Brigham Young's Adam-God doctrine many Mormons continued to believe it. Rodney Turner cites Charles W. Penrose, a member of the First Presidency, as making this statement in 1916: "There still remains, I can tell by the letters I have alluded to, an idea among some of the people that Adam was and is the Almighty and Eternal God" ("The Position of Adam in Latter-day Saint Scripture and Theology," p.81). On the same page of his thesis, Rodney Turner cites Penrose as saying:

".... the notion has taken hold of some of our brethren that Adam is the being that we should worship."

In a letter dated May 11, 1966, Apostle LeGrand Richards wrote: "Your third question: 'Is the Adam God Doctrine, as taught in the Journal of Discourses, true?' Answer: No." Some of the Mormon leaders now claim that Brigham Young was misquoted. This claim is completely untrue. Rodney Turner, who now teaches religion at Brigham Young University, feels that it is impossible to maintain such a position:

> *Was Brigham Young Misquoted?* It is the writer's opinion that the answer to this question is a categorical *no.* There is not the slightest evidence from Brigham Young, or any other source, that either his original remarks on April 9, 1852, or any of his subsequent statements were ever misquoted in the official publications of the Church. . . .
>
> In the light of Brigham Young's attitude toward the errors of others, and in view of the division created by his remarks concerning Adam, it would be stretching one's credulity to the breaking point to believe that he would have remained silent had he been misquoted. . . . The complete absence of any real evidence to the contrary obliges the writer to conclude that *Brigham Young has not been misquoted* in the official publications of the Church ("The Position of Adam in Latter-day Saint Scripture and Theology," M.A. thesis, BYU, pp.45-47).

On page 58 of the same thesis, Rodney Turner declares: "A careful, detached study of his available statements, as found in the official publications of the Church, will admit of no other conclusion than that the identification of Adam with God the Father by President Brigham Young *is an irrefutable fact.*"

PLURAL MARRIAGE

Chapter 9

Mormon apologist John J. Stewart admits that "there are at least two points of doctrine and history of the Church about which many LDS themselves—to say nothing of non-members—feel apologetic or critical. One of these is its doctrine and history regarding plural marriage. There is probably no other Church subject on which there is so much ignorance and misunderstanding and so many conflicting views" (*Brigham Young and His Wives*, p.8).

On pages 21 and 22 of the same book, Mr. Stewart states:

> So gross have been the falsehoods circulated against it, and so strong the feelings created over it, that it may be an under-statement rather than an over-statement to say that within the Church itself misunderstanding and lack of understanding about it are more nearly universal than a correct understanding of it. This despite the fact that seven of our nine Church presidents have lived plural marriage, and that this principle still is and always will be a doctrine of the Church.

The revelation sanctioning the practice of plural marriage was given by the Prophet Joseph Smith on July 12, 1843. This revelation is still printed in the *Doctrine and Covenants*—one of the four standard works of the Mormon church. The following is taken from this revelation:

> Verily, thus saith the Lord unto you my servant Joseph, that inasmuch as you have inquired of my hand to know and understand wherein I, the Lord, justified my servants Abraham, Isaac, and Jacob, as also Moses, David and Solomon, my servants, as touching the principle and doctrine of their having many wives and concubines—
>
> Behold, and lo, I am the Lord thy God, and will answer thee as touching this matter.
>
> Therefore, prepare thy heart to receive and obey the instructions which I am about to give unto you; for all those who have this law revealed unto them must obey the same.

For behold, I reveal unto you a new and an everlasting covenant; and if ye abide not that covenant, then are ye damned; for no one can reject this covenant and be permitted to enter into my glory. . . .

And again, verily I say unto you, if a man marry a wife by my word, which is my law, and by the new and everlasting covenant, . . . they shall pass by the angels, and the gods, which are set there, to their exaltation. . . .

Then shall *they be gods*, because they have no end. . . .

God commanded Abraham, and Sarah gave Hagar to Abraham to wife. . . .

Was Abraham, therefore, under condemnation? Verily I say unto you, Nay; for I, the Lord, commanded it. . . .

Abraham received *concubines*, and they bore him children; and it was accounted unto him for righteousness. . . .

David also received *many wives and concubines*, and also Solomon and Moses my servants, . . . and in nothing did they sin save in those things which they received not of me.

David's *wives and concubines* were given unto him of me. . . .

And let mine handmaid, Emma Smith, *receive all those that have been given unto my servant Joseph*, and who are virtuous and pure before me; and those who are not pure, and have said they were pure, shall be destroyed, saith the Lord God. . . .

Let no one, therefore, set on my servant Joseph; for I will justify him. . . .

And again, as pertaining to the law of the Priesthood—if any man espouse a virgin, and desire to espouse another, and the first give her consent, and if he espouse the second, and they are virgins, and have vowed to no other man, then is he justified; *he cannot commit adultery* for they are given unto him; for he cannot commit adultery with that that belongeth unto him and to no one else.

And if he have ten virgins given unto him by this law, he cannot commit adultery, for they belong to him, and they are given unto him; therefore is he justified (*The Doctrine and Covenants*, published by the Church of Jesus Christ of Latter-day Saints, 1966, 132: 1-4, 19, 20, 34, 35, 38, 39, 52, 60-62).

    In the beginning Mormon church leaders claimed they did not believe in the practice of plural marriage. In the first edition of the *Doctrine and Covenants*, printed in 1835, there was a section which absolutely denounced the practice of polygamy.

SECTION CI.

MARRIAGE.

1 According to the custom of all civilized nations, marriage is regulated by laws and ceremonies: therefore we believe, that all marriages in this church of Christ of Latter Day Saints, should be solemnized in a public meeting, or feast, prepared for that purpose: and that the solemnization should be performed by a presiding high priest, high priest, bishop, elder, or priest, not even prohibiting those persons who are desirous to get married, of being married by other authority. We believe that it is not right to prohibit members of this church from marrying out of the church, if it be their determination so to do, but such persons will be considered weak in the faith of our Lord and Savior Jesus Christ.

2 Marriage should be celebrated with prayer and thanksgiving; and at the solemnization, the persons to be married, standing together, the man on the right, and the woman on the left, shall be addressed, by the person officiating, as he shall be directed by the holy Spirit; and if there be no legal objections, he shall say, calling each by their names: "You both mutually agree to be each other's companion, husband and wife, observing the legal rights belonging to this condition; that is, keeping yourselves wholly for each other, and from all others, during your lives." And when they have answered "Yes," he shall pronounce them "husband and wife" in the name of the Lord Jesus Christ, and by virtue of the laws of the country and authority vested in him: "may God add his blessings and keep you to fulfill your covenants from henceforth and forever. Amen."

3 The clerk of every church should keep a record of all marriages, solemnized in his branch.

4 All legal contracts of marriage made before a person is baptized into this church, should be held sacred and fulfilled. Inasmuch as this church of Christ has been reproached with the crime of fornication, and polygamy: we declare that we believe, that one man should have one wife; and one woman, but one husband, except in case of death, when either is at liberty to marry again. It is not right to persuade a woman to be baptized contrary to the will of her husband, neither is it, lawful to influence her to leave her husband. All children are bound by law to obey their parents; and to influence them to embrace any religious faith, or be baptized, or leave their parents without their consent, is unlawful and unjust. We believe that all persons who exercise control over their fellow

A photograph of Section 101 of the 1835 edition of the *Doctrine and Covenants*. This section, which condemns the practice of plural marriage, was deleted from the *Doctrine and Covenants* in 1876.

In section 101:4 it was stated: "Inasmuch as this church of Christ has been reproached with the crime of fornication, and polygamy: we declare that we believe, that one man should have one wife; and one woman, but one husband, except in the case of death, when either is at liberty to marry again."

This section was printed in every edition of the *Doctrine and Covenants* until the year 1876. At that time the Mormon leaders inserted section 132, which permits a plurality of wives. Obviously, it would have been too contradictory to have one section condemning polygamy and another approving of it in the same book! Therefore, the section condemning polygamy was completely removed from the *Doctrine and Covenants*.

Just when and how the practice of plural marriage started in the Mormon church has caused much controversy. There is evidence, however, to show that it was secretly practiced when the church was in Kirtland, Ohio. In the introduction to volume 5 of Joseph Smith's *History of the Church*, the Mormon historian B. H. Roberts stated that the "date in the heading of the Revelation on the Eternity of the Marriage Covenant, including the Plurality of Wives, notes the time at which the revelation was committed to writing, not the time at which the principles set forth in the revelation were first made known to the Prophet."

Suppressed 1831 Revelation

Joseph Fielding Smith, who was LDS church historian and later became the tenth president of the church, made this statement in a letter written to J. W. A. Bailey in 1935:

> The exact date I cannot give you when this principle of plural marriage was first revealed to Joseph Smith, but I do know that there was *a revelation given in July 1831*, in the presence of Oliver Cowdery, W. W. Phelps and others in Missouri, in which the Lord made this principle known through the Prophet Joseph Smith. Whether the revelation as it appears in the Doctrine and Covenants as [*sic*] first given July 12, 1843, or earlier, I care not. It is a fact, nevertheless, that this principle was revealed at an earlier date (Letter dated September 5, 1935, typed copy).

In 1943 Joseph Fielding Smith told Fawn Brodie about this revelation, but he would not allow her to see it: "Joseph F. Smith, Jr., the present historian of the Utah Church, asserted to me in 1943 that a revelation foreshadowing polygamy had been written in 1831, but that it had never been published. In conformity with the church policy, however, he would not permit the manuscript, which he acknowledged to be in possession of the church library, to be examined" (*No Man Knows My History*, 1971, p.184, footnote).

Michael Marquardt, a student of Mormon history who became very disturbed with the church's policy of suppressing important records, became interested in this revelation. He found that some Mormon scholars had copies of the revelation, but had to promise not to make any additional copies. Finally, however, Mr. Marquardt learned what appears to be the real reason why the revelation was suppressed: because the revelation commanded the Mormons to *marry the Indians to make them a "white" and "delightsome" people!*

Now, to a Christian who is familiar with the teachings of the Bible, the color of a man's skin makes no difference. In Mormon theology, however, a dark skin is a sign of God's displeasure. In the Mormon publication *Juvenile Instructor* (vol. 3, p.157), the following statement appeared: "We will first inquire into the results of the approbation or *displeasure of God* upon a people, starting with the belief that *a black skin is a mark of the curse of heaven* placed upon some portions of mankind. . . . We understand that when God made man in his own image and pronounced him very good, that he made him white."

The teaching that a dark skin is the result of God's displeasure comes directly from Joseph Smith's *Book of Mormon*. The *Book of Mormon* teaches that about 600 B.C. a prophet named Lehi brought his family to America. Those who were righteous (the Nephites) had a white skin, but those who rebelled against God (the Lamanites) were cursed with a dark skin. The Lamanites eventually destroyed the Nephites; therefore, the Indians living today are referred to as Lamanites. The following verses are found in the *Book of Mormon* and explain the curse on the Lamanites:

> And it came to pass that I beheld, after they had dwindled in unbelief they became a *dark*, and loathsome, and a filthy people, full of idleness and all manner of abominations (*Book of Mormon*, I Nephi 12:23).

> And he had caused the cursing to come upon them, yea, even a sore *cursing*, because of their iniquity . . . wherefore, as they were white, and exceeding fair and delightsome, that they might not be enticing unto my people the Lord God did cause *a skin of blackness* to come upon them (2 Nephi 5:21).

> And the skins of the Lamanites were *dark*, according to the mark which was set upon their fathers, which was *a curse* upon them because of their transgression . . . (Alma 3:6).

The *Book of Mormon* stated that when the Lamanites repented of their sins "their curse was taken from them, and their skin became white like unto the Nephites" (3 Nephi 2:15). The

Book of Mormon also promised that in the last days the Lamanites—i.e., the Indians—will repent and "many generations shall not pass away among them, save they shall be a *white and delightsome* people" (2 Nephi 30:6).

These teachings have caused the Mormon church some embarrassment. The anti-Mormon writer Gordon H. Fraser claims that the "skin color" of the Indians converted to Mormonism "has not been altered in the least because of their adherence to the Mormon doctrines" (*What Does The Book of Mormon Teach?* p.46).

Spencer W. Kimball, who on December 30, 1973, became the twelfth president of the church, feels that the Indians are actually becoming a "white and delightsome people." In the LDS General Conference, October 1960, Mr. Kimball stated:

> I saw a striking contrast in the progress of the Indian people today . . . they are fast becoming *a white and delightsome people*. . . . For years they have been growing delightsome, and they are *now becoming white* and delightsome, as they were promised. . . . The children in the home placement program in Utah are often *lighter* than their brothers and sisters in the hogans on the reservation.
>
> At one meeting a father and mother and their sixteen-year-old daughter were present, the little member girl—sixteen—sitting between the dark father and mother, and it was evident *she was several shades lighter* than her parents—on the same reservation, in the same hogan, subject to the same sun and wind and weather. . . . These young members of the Church are *changing to whiteness* and to delightsomeness. One white elder jokingly said that he and his companion were donating blood regularly to the hospital in the hope that the process might be accelerated (*Improvement Era*, December 1960, pp.922-23).

While Spencer W. Kimball seems to feel that the Indians are to be made white by the power of God, Michael Marquardt, a student of Mormon history, learned that Joseph Smith's 1831 revelation says they are to be made "white" through intermarriage with the Mormons. Because of this fact Mormon leaders seemed to feel that it was necessary to suppress this revelation. Only the most trusted men, such as Dr. Hyrum Andrus, were allowed a copy of it. It was only after a great deal of research that Mr. Marquardt was able to obtain a typed copy of it. We printed this revelation in its entirety in *Mormonism Like Watergate?* (pp.7-8). The important part of the revelation reads as follows:

> Verily, I say unto you, that the wisdom of man, in his fallen state, knoweth not the purposes and the privileges of my holy priest-

hood, but ye shall know when ye receive a fulness by reason of the anointing: For it is my will, that in time, ye should take unto you wives of the Lamanites and Nephites, that their posterity may become white, delightsome and just, for even now their females are more virtuous than the gentiles.

After the contents of the revelation are given, the following appears:

Reported by W. W. P.
About three years after this was given, I asked brother Joseph, privately, how "we," that were mentioned in the revelation could take wives from the "natives" as we were all married men? He replied, instantly 'In the same manner that Abraham took Hagar and Keturah; and Jacob took Rachel, Bilhah Zilpah; by revelation—the saints of the Lord are always directed by revelation.

According to what Mr. Marquardt could learn, the original revelation is preserved in a vault in the LDS church historical department. The paper on which it is written has the appearance of being very old. There is also a second copy of the revelation in the church historical department. This appears in a letter from W. W. Phelps to Brigham Young. The letter is dated August 12, 1861. Dr. Hyrum Andrus, of Brigham Young University, actually quoted part of this revelation as it appears in the letter, but he was very careful to suppress the fact that the wives to be taken were Lamanites:

The Prophet understood the principle of plural marriage as early as 1831. William W. Phelps stated that on Sunday morning, July 17, 1831, he and others were with Joseph Smith over the border west of Jackson County, Missouri, when the latter-day Seer received a revelation, the substance of which said in part: "Verily I say unto you, that the wisdom of man in his fallen state knoweth not the purposes and the privileges of my Holy Priesthood, but ye shall know when ye receive a fulness." According to Elder Phelps, the revelation then indicated that in due time the brethren would be required to take plural wives (*Doctrines of the Kingdom*, by Hyrum L. Andrus, Salt Lake City, 1973, p.450).

The reader will notice that in his quotation from the revelation, Dr. Andrus suppressed the important portion concerning marriage to the Indians.

In 1976 we were able to examine a microfilm of the original revelation, but we found it difficult to determine when it was actually recorded. From Phelps' letter to Brigham Young we know that the revelation had to have been recorded by 1861. As we understand it, the first document—containing only the revelation and Phelps' comment—appears to be older than the letter dated August 12, 1861. It is possible that the revelation could have been recorded any time between 1831 and 1861. W. W. Phelps served as scribe on a number of occasions during Joseph Smith's lifetime. If the revelation and the note at the bottom were written at the same time, then obviously the revelation could not have been written until sometime after 1834. It could be, however, that Phelps added the note at a later time. It will not be possible to decide this vital question unless Mormon leaders allow scholars to closely examine the document itself and any other material relating to it.

Regardless of when the revelation was actually written on paper, we have found definite historical proof that such a revelation was given in 1831. The proof is derived from a letter written by Ezra Booth and published in the *Ohio Star* only five months after the revelation was given! In this letter, Ezra Booth stated:

> In addition to this, and to co-operate with it, it has been made known *by revelation*, that it will be pleasing to the Lord, should they form *a matrimonial alliance with the Natives*; and by this means the Elders, who comply with the thing so pleasing to the Lord, and for which the Lord has promised to bless those who do it abundantly, gain a residence in the Indian territory, independent of the agent. It has been made known to one, who has left his wife in the state of N.Y. that he is entirely *free from his wife*, and he is at liberty to take him *a wife from among the Lamanites*. It was easily perceived that this permission, was perfectly suited to his desires. I have frequently heard him state, that the Lord had made it known to him, that he is as free from his wife as from any other woman; and the only crime that I have ever heard alleged against her is, she is violently opposed to Mormonism (*Ohio Star*, December 8, 1831).

This letter furnishes irrefutable proof that Joseph Smith gave the revelation commanding the Mormons to marry the Lamanite women. On March 6, 1885, S. F. Whitney, Newel K. Whitney's brother, made an affidavit which furnishes additional evidence that there was a revelation on this subject:

> Martin Harris . . . claimed he had *a revelation* when he first came to Kirtland for him to go to Missouri, and *obtain an Lamanite squaw* for a wife to aid them in propagating Mormonism. Martin told me soon after Joseph, the prophet, left Kirtland, that, two years before, he had told him that as his wife had left him he needed a woman as other men (*Naked Truths About Mormonism*, Oakland, California, January, 1888, p.3).

It is interesting to note that Martin Harris, one of the three   211 witnesses to the *Book of Mormon*, was one of "seven Elders" present when the 1831 revelation was given.

Like Joseph Smith, Brigham Young taught that the Indians would "become 'a white and delightsome people' " (*Journal of Discourses*, vol. 2, p.143). While Brigham Young never released the 1831 revelation, there is evidence that he was familiar with its teaching that the Indians should be made white through intermarriage. In a book published in 1852, William Hall commented:

> About the time of the breaking up of the camp at Sugar Creek, the people were called together and several speeches delivered to them by Brigham Young, and others. The speech of Young was in substance as follows:
>
> ". . . We are now going to the Lamanites, to whom we intend to be messengers of instruction. . . . We will show them that in consequence of their transgressions *a curse* has been inflicted upon them—in the *darkness of their skins*. We will have *intermarriages* with them, they marrying our young women, and we taking their young squaws to wife. *By these means* it is the will of the Lord that *the curse of their color shall be removed* and they restored to their pristine beauty . . ." (*The Abominations of Mormonism Exposed*, Cincinnati, 1852, pp.58-59).

Juanita Brooks gives the following information concerning the marriage of Mormons to Indians at the Salmon River Mission:

> Very early, some of the Mormon leaders recommended that the missionaries marry Indian women as a means of cementing the friendship between the races. . . .
>
> The Elders who were sent to the Salmon River Mission were given similar instructions by Brigham Young and his party, who visited them in May, 1857. At least three different missionaries tell of them, all under date of Sunday, May 10, 1857. Milton G. Hammond says simply, "The president and members of the Twelve all spoke. Pres. Young spoke of Elders marrying natives."
> . . .
>
> As a result of these teachings, at least three of the brethren married Indian women. . . . As to the Indian women whom they had taken as wives the "L.D.S. Journal History" of April 9, 1858, records: "Two squaws who had married the brethren refused to come, fearing the soldiers would kill all the Mormons" (*Utah Historical Quarterly*, vol. 12, pp.28-30).

T. B. H. Stenhouse provides further information concerning the Salmon River Mission:

Before any of the married brethren could make love to a maiden with the view of making her a second, third, or tenth wife, he was expected to go and obtain Brigham's permission. . . . He sent at one time a mission to Fort Limhi, Salmon River. . . . When Brigham and Heber afterwards visited the missionaries to see how they were succeeding, Heber, in his quaint way, told them that he did not see how the modern predictions could well be fulfilled about the Indians becoming *"a white and delightsome people"* without extending polygamy to the natives. The approach of the United States army, in 1857, contributed to break up that mission, but not before Heber's hint had been clearly understood, and the prophecy half fulfilled! Heber was very practical, and believed that the people should never ask "the Lord" to do for them what they could do themselves, and, as all "Israel" had long prayed that the Indians might speedily become a "white and delightsome people," he thought it was the duty of the missionaries to assist "the Lord" in fulfilling his promises. This was not the first time that a Mormon prophet attempted to aid in bringing to pass the prophecies of "the Lord." More than one missionary appears to have thoroughly understood him! (*The Rocky Mountain Saints*, 1873, pp.657-59).

In 1857 John Hyde, Jr., made the following comments: ". . . Brigham now teaches that 'the way God has revealed for the purification of the Indians, and making them "a white and delightsome people," as Joseph prophesied, is by us taking the Indian squaws for wives!!' Accordingly several of these tawny beauties have been already 'sealed' to some of the Mormon authorities" (*Mormonism: Its Leaders And Designs*, pp.109-10).

William Hall claimed that "Brigham Young was married to two young squaws, . . . near Council Bluffs." So far we have been unable to find any additional documentation for his statement. If Hall's statement is correct, Brigham Young must have left these Indian women behind, because we do not find them mentioned as Young's wives in Utah. According to John D. Lee, on May 12, 1849, Brigham Young said that he did not want to take the Indians "in his arms until the curse is removed."

Pres. B. Y. Said that he did not aprehend [sic] any danger from the Indians. Neither did he feel, as Some of the Brethren do, he does not want to live amoung [sic] them & take them in his arms until the curse is removed from of [sic] them. . . . But we will take their children & shool [sic] them & teach them to be clenly [sic] & to love morality & then raise up seed amoung [sic] them & in this way they will be brought back into the presance [sic] & knowlege [sic] of God . . . (*A Mormon Chronicle, The Diaries of John D. Lee*, vol. 1, p.108).

213

It would appear, then, that Brigham Young would not follow Joseph Smith's revelation to take "wives of the Lamanites and Nephites, that their posterity may become white, delightsome and just." Even though the revelation said that "their females are more virtuous than the gentiles," Brigham Young built up his "kingdom" with women who were already "white" and "delightsome." If Brigham Young did not follow the 1831 revelation to marry the Lamanites, we must remember that he was only following Joseph Smith's example, for Smith also married "white" women. Even though Brigham Young suppressed Joseph Smith's 1831 revelation and chose "white" women in preference to the Lamanites, he did at least encourage others to marry them "that the curse of their color shall be removed and they restored to their pristine beauty."

Since Brigham Young's time the church has tended to frown upon interracial marriage with the Indians, even though there is no written rule against the practice. Apostle Mark E. Petersen has been especially vocal against interracial marriage. Apostle Petersen and other Mormon leaders who are opposed to intermarriage are probably very disturbed now that the 1831 revelation has come to light. The fact that they have suppressed this revelation could well mean that they do not really believe that it came from God. They have been involved in a cover-up to protect the image of Joseph Smith.*

At any rate, we know from many sources that plural marriage was being considered by the Mormon leaders in the early 1830s. Joseph F. Smith, the sixth president of the church, once stated: "The great and glorious principle of plural marriage was first revealed to Joseph Smith in 1831, but being forbidden to make it public, or to teach it as a doctrine of the Gospel, at that time, he confided the facts to only a very few of his intimate associates. Among them were Oliver Cowdery and Lyman E. Johnson . . ." (As quoted in *Historical Record*, 1887, vol. 6, p.219).

Mormon Apostle John A. Widtsoe said that "The evidence seems clear that the revelation on plural marriage was received by the Prophet as early as 1831" (*Joseph Smith—Seeker After Truth*, p.236).

---

*In their new book, *The Mormon Experience*, page 195, Church Historian Leonard J. Arrington and his assistant Davis Bitton, finally come to grips with the reality of the 1831 revelation: "A recently discovered document is a copy of a purported revelation of 1831 that instructed seven missionaries in Missouri as follows: 'For it is my will, that in time, ye should take unto you wives of the Lamanites and Nephites that their posterity may become white, delightsome and just, for even now their females are more virtuous than the gentiles.' "

The Mormon writer John J. Stewart claims that Joseph Smith may have entered into plural marriage "in the early or mid-1830's." On page 31 of his book *Brigham Young and His Wives,* he states that "Nancy Johnson" may have been Joseph Smith's first plural wife. Eli Johnson felt that Joseph Smith was "too intimate" with his sister Nancy. This may help explain why Smith was mobbed in March, 1832. In any event, less than a year after Joseph Smith gave the revelation to marry Lamanites his name was linked with Nancy Johnson.

While Joseph Smith was still living in Ohio his name was also linked with Fanny Alger. The Mormon writer Max Parkin commented about this matter: "The charge of adulterous relations 'with a certain girl' was leveled against Smith by Cowdery in Missouri in 1837; this accusation became one of the complaints the Church had against Cowdery in his excommunication trial in Far West, April 12, 1838. In rationalizing Cowdery's accusation, the Prophet testified 'that Oliver Cowdery had been his bosom friend, therefore he entrusted him with many things' " (*Conflict at Kirtland,* 1966, p.166).

The reader will remember that Oliver Cowdery was one of the three witnesses to the *Book of Mormon.* In a letter dated January 21, 1838, Cowdery plainly stated that Joseph Smith had an "affair" with Fanny Alger:

> When he [Joseph Smith] was there we had some conversation in which in every instance I did not fail to affirm that what I had said was strictly true. *A dirty, nasty, filthy affair of his and Fanny Alger's* was talked over in which I strictly declared that I had never deviated from the truth in the matter, and as I supposed was admitted by himself (Letter written by Oliver Cowdery and recorded by his brother Warren Cowdery; see photograph in *The Mormon Kingdom,* vol. 1, p.27).

Mormon writers admit that there was a connection between Joseph Smith and Fanny Alger. However, they claim that Fanny Alger was Joseph Smith's plural wife and that he was commanded by God to enter into polygamy. Andrew Jenson, who was the assistant L.D.S. church historian, made a list of 27 women who were sealed to Joseph Smith. In this list he said the following concerning Fanny Alger: "Fanny Alger, one of the first plural wives sealed to the Prophet" (*Historical Record,* p.233). John A. Widtsoe stated: "It seems that Fannie Alger was one of Joseph's first plural wives" (*Joseph Smith—Seeker After Truth,* p.237).

The Mormon writer John J. Stewart provides further information:

Benjamin F. Johnson, another close friend to Joseph . . . says, "In 1835, at Kirtland, I learned from my sister's husband, . . . 'that the ancient order of Plural Marriage was again to be practiced by the Church,' This, at the time, did not impress my mind deeply, although there lived then with his family [the Prophet's] a neighbor's daughter, Fannie Alger, a very nice and comely young woman . . . it was whispered even then that Joseph loved her." Johnson, a Church patriarch at the time of writing, put his finger on the beginning of Oliver Cowdery's and Warren Parrish's downfall—Parrish was the Prophet's secretary: "There was some trouble with Oliver Cowdery, and whisper said it was relating to a girl then living in his (the Prophet's) family; and I was afterwards told by Warren Parrish, that he himself and Oliver Cowdery did know that Joseph had Fannie Alger as wife, for they were spied upon and found together." . . . "Without doubt in my mind," says Johnson, "Fannie Alger was, at Kirtland, *the Prophet's first plural wife*, in which, by right of his calling, he was justified of the Lord, . . ." One of the charges against Cowdery when he was excommunicated was that he had insinuated that Joseph was guilty of adultery (*Joseph Smith the Mormon Prophet*, pp.103-4).

In his history of the church, John Whitmer, one of the witnesses to the *Book of Mormon*, also told that "plurality of wives" came into the church in the 1830s.

In 1842 Joseph Smith wanted to marry Newel K. Whitney's daughter Sarah Ann Whitney. At that time he gave a special revelation concerning polygamy. Orson F. Whitney stated:

This girl was but seventeen years of age, but she had implicit faith in the doctrine of plural marriage. . . . The revelation commanding and consecrating this union, is in existence, though it has never been published. It bears the date of July 27, 1842, and was given through the Prophet to the writer's grandfather, Newel K. Whitney, whose daughter Sarah, on that day, became the wedded wife of Joseph Smith for time and all eternity (*The Contributor*, vol. 6, no. 4, January 1885, p.131, as cited by H. Michael Marquardt in *The Strange Marriages of Sarah Ann Whitney to Joseph Smith the Mormon Prophet, Joseph C. Kingsbury and Heber C. Kimball*, p.1).

This revelation was suppressed by Mormon leaders, but in 1973 Michael Marquardt obtained a typed copy and published it in his pamphlet *The Strange Marriages of Sarah Ann Whitney . . .* , page 23. In this revelation we find the following:

Verily, thus saith the Lord unto my servant N. K. Whitney, the thing that my servant Joseph Smith has made known unto you and your family and which you have agreed upon is right in mine eyes. . . . These are the words which you shall pronounce

before, was fulfilled soon after they moved up from Quincy, in the spring of 1840. They at first resided in a very unhealthy neighborhood, and all fell sick with ague, chills and fever, a disease at that time very prevalent there. Joseph, on visiting them and witnessing their condition, was touched with compassion. He remembered how kindly they once received him and his family, when they were without a home, and at once urged them to come and occupy a comfortable cottage on his own premises, in a much healthier locality. His kind and generous offer was gladly accepted, and the change soon restored them to wonted health. Joseph had said to Sister Whitney, on his arrival at Kirtland in February, 1831, that even as she had opened her house to him when he was homeless and in need, he would do a similar act in her behalf and that of her family in a day when their circumstances would require it.

We have before spoken of the friendship and intimacy existing between the Prophet and Bishop Whitney. This bond of affection was strengthened and intensified by the giving in marriage to the former of the Bishop's eldest daughter, Sarah, in obedience to a revelation from God. This girl was but seventeen years of age, but she had implicit faith that the doctrine of plural marriage, as revealed to and practised by the Prophet, was of celestial origin. She was the first woman, in this dispensation, who was given in plural marriage by and with the consent of both parents. Her father himself officiated in the ceremony. The revelation commanding and consecrating this union, is in existence, though it has never been published. It bears the date of July 27, 1842, and was given through the Prophet to the writer's grandfather, Newel K. Whitney, whose daughter Sarah, on that day, became the wedded wife of Joseph Smith for time and all eternity.

The ceremony preceded by nearly a year the written document of the revelation on celestial marriage, which was first committed to paper on July 12, 1843. But the principle itself was made known to Joseph several years earlier. Among the secrets confided by him to Bishop Whitney while they were in Kirtland, was a knowledge of this self-same principle, which he declared would yet have to be received and practised as a doctrine of the Church; a doctrine so far in advance then of the ideas and traditions of the Saints themselves, to say nothing of the Gentile world, that he was obliged to use the utmost caution lest some of his best and dearest friends should impute to him improper motives. No wonder he should smite himself upon the breast which treasured up his mighty secrets, and exclaim, as we are told he often did: "Would to God, brethren, I could tell you who I am, and what I know!"

The original manuscript of the revelation on plural marriage, as taken down by William Clayton, the Prophet's scribe, was given by Joseph to Bishop Whitney for safe keeping. He retained possession of it until the Prophet's wife Emma, having persuaded her husband to let her see it, on receiving it from his hands, in a fit of jealous rage threw it into the fire and destroyed it. She triumphed in the wicked thought that she had thus put an end to the doctrine she so feared and hated—as though the parchment upon which it was written, the ink with which it was inscribed was all that made it valid or binding. But she was doubly deceived. She had not even destroyed the words of the revelation. Bishop Whitney, foreseeing the probable fate of the manuscript, had taken the precaution before delivering it up, to have it copied by his clerk, Joseph C. Kingsbury, who is a living witness that he executed the task under the Bishop's personal supervision. It was this same copy of the original that Bishop Whitney surrendered to President Brigham Young at Winter Quarters in 1846-7, and from which "polygamy" was published to the world in the year 1852.

Passing by the horrible tragedy which deprived the Church of its Prophet and its Patriarch, and the almost incessant

A photograph of *The Contributor*, Jan. 1885, page 131. Orson F. Whitney tells of a special revelation Joseph Smith received when he wanted to marry Newel K. Whitney's daughter.

upon my servant Joseph and your daughter S. A. Whitney. They shall take each other by the hand and you shall say, You both mutually agree, calling them by name, to be each other's companion so long as you both shall live. . . . If you both agree to covenant and do this, I then give you, S. A. Whitney, my daughter, to Joseph Smith, to be his wife. . . . Let immortality and eternal life hereafter be sealed upon your heads forever and ever.

The reader will notice that this revelation on polygamy is dated a year earlier than the one published in the *Doctrine and Covenants*.

The 1843 Revelation Examined

The 1843 revelation (now published in the *Doctrine and Covenants*) was apparently given to convince Emma Smith (Joseph's wife) that polygamy was right. William Clayton, who wrote the revelation as Smith dictated it, provides this intimate information:

On the morning of the 12th of July, 1843; Joseph and Hyrum Smith came into the office. . . . They were talking on the subject of plural marriage. Hyrum said to Joseph, "If you will write the revelation on celestial marriage, I will take it and read it to Emma, and I believe I can convince her of its truth, and you will hereafter have peace." Joseph smiled and remarked, "You do not know Emma as well as I do." . . . Joseph then said, "Well, I will write the revelation and we shall see." . . . Hyrum then took the revelation to read to Emma. Joseph remained with me in the office until Hyrum returned. When he came back, Joseph asked how he had succeeded. Hyrum replied that *he had never received a more severe talking to in his life*. . . .

Joseph quietly remarked, "I told you you did not know Emma as well as I did." Joseph then put the revelation in his pocket. . . . Two or three days after the revelation was written Joseph related to me and several others that Emma had so teased, and urgently entreated him for the privilege of destroying it, that he became so weary of her teasing, and to get rid of her annoyance, he told her she might destroy it and she had done so, but he had consented to her wish in this matter to pacify her, realizing that he . . . could rewrite it at any time if necessary (*History of the Church*, by Joseph Smith, Introduction to vol. 5).

Brigham Young said that,

Emma took that revelation, supposing she had all there was; but Joseph had wisdom enough to take care of it, and he had handed the revelation to Bishop Whitney, and he wrote it all off. . . . She went to the fireplace and put it in, and put the candle under it and burnt it, and she thought that was the end of it, and she will be damned as sure as she is a living woman. Joseph used to say that he would have her hereafter, if he had to go to hell for her, and he will have to go to hell for her as sure as he ever gets her (*Journal of Discourses*, vol. 17, p.159).

The revelation was not printed until 1852 and did not appear in the *Doctrine and Convenants* until 1876. As we have shown, the revelation on polygamy is now printed as section 132 of the *Doctrine and Covenants*. Upon careful examination it can be seen that this revelation is filled with inconsistencies. The first problem is the date it was given. The date on the revelation reads July 12, 1843, yet Lorenzo Snow, who became the fifth president of the church, testified that anyone who lived in plural marriage prior to the time the revelation was given was living in "adultery under the laws of the church and under the laws of the State, too" (*Temple Lot Case*, p.320).

We find that Joseph Smith was married to at least twelve women prior to July 12, 1843. According to Lorenzo Snow's statement, this would make Joseph Smith an adulterer. In an article published in the church's own *Millennial Star* on July 25, 1857, we read as follows: "The Latter-day Saints, from the rise of the Church in 1830, till the year 1843, had no authority to marry any more than one wife each. To have done otherwise, would have been a great transgression" (*Millennial Star*, vol. 19, p.475). In order to get out of this dilemma Mormon leaders now claim that Joseph Smith received the revelation prior to the time he wrote it down and that the date on the revelation is the date the revelation was written down, not the date it was actually received. Joseph Smith's *History of the Church*, however, says that the revelation was actually given on July 12, 1843: "Wednesday, 12.—I *received* the following revelation. . . . Revelation on the Eternity of the Marriage Covenant, including the Plurality of Wives. *Given* through Joseph, the Seer, in Nauvoo, Hancock County, Illinois, July 12th, 1843" (*History of the Church*, vol.5, pp.500-501).

The revelation on polygamy contradicts section 58, verse 21 of the *Doctrine and Covenants*, which reads as follows: "Let no man break the laws of the land, for he that keepeth the laws of God hath no need to break the laws of the land."

In order to practice polygamy in Nauvoo the Mormons had to break the law of the land, for the State of Illinois had laws against both adultery and bigamy (or "the crime of marrying while one has a wife or husband still living from whom no valid divorce has been effected"). The Mormon church leaders understood that polygamy was a crime. In an article published in the church's own *Times and Seasons* on November 15, 1844,   **219** the following appeared: "The law of the land and the rules of the church *do not allow one man to have more than one wife alive at once . . ."* (*Times and Seasons*, vol. 5, p.715).

After the Mormons came to Utah, Brigham Young commented: "If I had forty wives in the United States, they did not know it, and could not substantiate it, neither did I ask any lawyer, judge, or magistrate for them. *I live above the law*, and so do this people" (*Journal of Discourses*, vol. 1, p.361).

Just before he was murdered Joseph Smith was indicted because of his practice of polygamy. The following is found in the *Church Chronology* under the date of May 25, 1844: "Sat. 25.—Joseph Smith learned that the grand jury at Carthage had found two indictments against him, one of them for polygamy" (*Church Chronology*, p.25). According to Wesley Walters, the actual charge in the county records was "adultery."Joseph Smith was murdered shortly after this, but had he lived, it is very possible that he would have gone to prison for being a polygamist.

In his revelation Joseph Smith used the polygamous practices of David and Solomon as justification for polygamy. In the *Doctrine and Covenants* we read: "Verily, thus saith the Lord . . . you have inquired of my hand to know and understand wherein I, the Lord, *justified* my servants . . . David and Solomon, . . . as touching the principle and doctrine of having many wives and concubines . . . David's wives and concubines were given unto him of me . . ." (132:1, 39).

This is in direct contradiction to the teachings of the *Book of Mormon*. In the *Book of Mormon*, page 111, verses 23 and 24, we read:

> For behold, thus saith the Lord: This people begin to wax in iniquity; they understand not the scriptures, for they seek to excuse themselves in committing *whoredoms*, because of the things which were written concerning *David, and Solomon* his son.

> Behold, David and Solomon truly had many wives and concubines, which thing was *abominable before me*, saith the Lord.

Notice that the revelation states that David and Solomon were justified in their polygamous practices, whereas the *Book of Mormon* states that it was an abominable practice. In a letter to Morris Reynolds, dated July 14, 1966, Apostle LeGrand Richards admitted that he was unable to reconcile this contradiction (see *Mormonism—Shadow or Reality?* p.205).

Joseph F. Smith, the sixth president of the church, gave the following testimony in the "Reed Smoot Case":

THE CHAIRMAN. That is the Book of Mormon?
MR. SMITH. Yes, sir; that is the Book of Mormon.

. . . .

THE CHAIRMAN. Is the doctrine of polygamy taught in that revelation?
MR. SMITH. Taught in it?
THE CHAIRMAN. Yes.
MR. SMITH. *It is emphatically forbidden in that book.*
THE CHAIRMAN. In that book it is emphatically forbidden?
MR. SMITH. It is. (*Reed Smoot Case*, vol. 1, p.480.)

Orson Pratt once admitted that "The Book of Mormon, therefore, is the only record (professing to be divine) which condemns the plurality of wives as being a practice exceeding abominable before God" (*Journal of Discourses*, vol. 6, p.351).

The *Doctrine and Covenants* contains this statement: ". . . I, the Lord his God . . . commanded Abraham to take Hagar to wife" (132:65). This is in direct contradiction to the account given in the Bible, for the Bible says nothing about God commanding this but rather that "Abram hearkened to the voice of Sarai" (Gen. 16:2). Why, then, did Sarai give Hagar to Abram? Simply because she did not believe that she could have a child in her old age. It is obvious that God was not involved in this transaction, for Genesis 16:5 makes it clear that Sarai had sinned in this matter: "And Sarai said unto Abram, my wrong be upon thee. . . ."

Although some of the kings mentioned in the Old Testament had many wives, Deuteronomy 17:17 condemned this practice: "Neither shall he multiply wives to himself, that his heart turn not away. . . ."

There is no mention in the New Testament of any of the apostles practicing polygamy. In fact, in 1 Timothy the bishops and deacons were instructed to have only one wife: "A bishop then must be blameless, the husband of one wife. . . . Let the deacons be the husbands of one wife . . ." (I Timothy 3:2, 12).

The Mormon church uses the Old Testament to justify the practice of plural marriage. While it is true that it was practiced by the people of the Old Testament, that does not mean that it was right in the sight of God. These people also committed many other sins which God will not allow us to commit now that Christ has revealed the perfect way. The people in the Old Testament also had slaves, and cursed their enemies. To say that plural marriage is right because it was practiced in the Old Testament makes no more sense than to say that God approves of slavery since it was also practiced in the Old Testament.

Christ came to set us free from these Old Testament practices. For instance, divorce was common in the Old Testament, but Jesus said ". . . Moses because of the hardness of your hearts suffered you to put away your wives; but from the beginning it was not so" (Matt. 19:8). Polygamy, as well as divorce, was instituted by man, not God. Jesus said that the perfect pattern for marriage was that the "twain shall be one flesh" (Matt. 19:5).

In the revelation on polygamy (*Doctrine and Covenants* 132:54) Emma Smith, Joseph's wife, is threatened with destruction: " . . . I am the Lord thy God, and *will destroy her* if she abide not my law." It is interesting to note, however, that it was Joseph who was destroyed. He was killed less than a year after this revelation was written, while Emma lived until 1879 and was a bitter enemy to polygamy.

The *Doctrine and Covenants* 132:64 reads: "And again, verily, verily, I say unto you, if any man have a wife, holds the keys of this power, and he teaches unto her the law of my priesthood, as pertaining to these things, then shall she believe and administer unto him, or *she shall be destroyed*, saith the Lord your God; for *I will destroy her*; for I will magnify my name upon all those who receive and abide in my law."

Apostle John Henry Smith testified as follows in the case concerning "the application of John Moore, for naturalization":

"Q. Do you understand that revelation to be to this effect— that if the first wife refuses to consent to her husband taking a second wife, she shall be damned? A. I understand that principle; and a good many women have taken that chance. Under the Mormon theory *they shall be damned*." (*Reminiscences of Early Utah*, by R. N. Baskin, 1914, p.95).

In section 132 of the *Doctrine and Covenants* it is plainly stated that a man must obtain the consent of the first wife in order to be justified in taking more wives: " . . . if any man espouse a virgin, and desire to espouse another, and the first give her consent, and if he espouse the second, and they are virgins, and have vowed to no other man, then is he justified . . ." (*Doctrine and Covenants* 132:61).

Joseph Smith certainly did not follow the rules of his own revelation, for he took plural wives without his first wife's consent. Emily Dow Partridge claimed that she was married to Joseph before Emma gave her consent:

> . . . the Prophet Joseph and his wife Emma offered us a home in their family, and they treated us with great kindness. . . . I was married to Joseph Smith on the 4th of March 1843. . . . My sister Eliza was also married to Joseph a few days later. This was done

without the knowledge of Emma Smith. Two months afterward she consented to give her husband two wives, providing he would give her the privilege of choosing them. She accordingly chose my sister Eliza and myself, and to save family trouble Brother Joseph thought it best to have another ceremony performed. Accordingly on the 11th of May, 1843, we were sealed to Joseph Smith a second time, in Emma's presence. . . . From that very hour, however, Emma was our bitter enemy. We remained in the family several months after this, but things went from bad to worse until we were obligated to leave the house and find another home (*Historical Record*, vol. 6, p.240).

Joseph F. Smith, the sixth president of the church, was questioned as follows:

SENATOR PETTUS. Have there been in the past plural marriages without the consent of the first wife?

MR. SMITH. I do not know of any, unless it may have been *Joseph Smith himself.*

SENATOR PETTUS. Is the language that you have read construed to mean that she is bound to consent?

MR. SMITH. The condition is that *if she does not consent the Lord will destroy her,* but I do not know how He will do it.

SENATOR BAILEY. Is it not true that in the very next verse, if she refuses her consent her husband is exempt from the law which requires her consent?

MR. SMITH. Yes; he is exempt from the law which requires her consent.

SENATOR BAILEY. She is commanded to consent, but if she does not, then he is exempt from the requirement?

MR. SMITH. Then he is at liberty to proceed without her consent, under the law.

SENATOR BEVERIDGE. In other words, her consent amounts to nothing?

MR. SMITH. *It amounts to nothing but her consent* (*Reed Smoot Case*, vol. 1, p.201).

Many other Mormons married without obtaining the consent of the first wife. Joseph Smith told Heber C. Kimball to take a second wife and not to let his first wife know anything about it. Heber C. Kimball's daughter related:

. . . my father, . . . was taught the plural wife doctrine, and was told by Joseph, the Prophet, three times, to go and take a certain woman as his wife; but not till he commanded him in the name of the Lord did he obey. At the same time Joseph told him *not to divulge this secret, not even to my mother,* for fear that she would not receive it. . . . This was one of the greatest tests of his faith he had ever experienced. The thought of deceiving the kind and faithful wife of his youth . . .was more than he felt able to bear . . . his sorrow and misery were increased by the thought of my mother hearing of it from some other source, which would no doubt separate them, and he shrank from the thought of such a thing, or of causing her any unhappiness. Finally he was so tried that he went to Joseph and told him how he felt—that he was fearful if he took such a step he could not stand, but would be overcome. The Prophet . . . inquired of the Lord; His answer was "Tell him to go and do as he has been commanded, and if I see that there is any danger of his apostatizing, I will take him to myself" (*Life of Heber C. Kimball*, by Orson F. Whitney, pp.335-36).

In *Mormonism—Shadow or Reality?* page 207, we show that Apostle Orson Pratt published certain rules governing the practice of polygamy. One of those rules was that a man must obtain the consent of the first wife before entering into the practice of plural marriage, yet Pratt himself married two of his wives without the knowledge or consent of any of his other wives.

One thing that is very obvious when reading section 132 of the *Doctrine and Covenants* is the fact that Joseph Smith was already in the practice of plural marriage before he ever inquired of the Lord to see if it was right. The first verse of section 132 tells that Joseph Smith inquired of the Lord to see if plural marriage was right, but verse 52 shows that he had already taken wives before the revelation was given, for it commands Emma (his first wife) to receive the other women that had already been given to Joseph: "And let mine handmaid, Emma Smith, *receive all those that have been given unto my servant Joseph* . . ." (*Doctrine and Covenants* 132:52).

Some people have tried to excuse this by saying that the date on the revelation was only the date it was written down and not the date it was actually given, but anyone who honestly examines this argument must admit that it doesn't make any difference when the revelation was given. Whether it was given in 1843 or years before isn't important. Regardless of the date it was given, verse 52 plainly states that Joseph had already entered into the practice of polygamy.

It is interesting to note that section 132 not only says that plural marriage is justifiable in God's sight, but also concubinage: "Abraham received *concubines*, and they bore him children; and it was accounted unto him for righteousness . . ." (*Doctrine and Covenants* 132:37).

The Mormon leaders seem to be puzzled as to why the Lord gave the revelation on polygamy to Joseph Smith. Apostle John A. Widtsoe stated: "We *do not understand* why the Lord commanded the practice of plural marriage." (*Evidences and Rec-*

onciliations, 1960, p.393). One of the most popular explanations is that the church practiced polygamy because there was a surplus of women. The truth is, however, that there were less women than men.

Apostle Widtsoe admitted that there was no surplus of women:

> The implied assumption in this theory, that there have been more female than male members in the Church, is *not* supported by existing evidence. On the contrary, there seems always to have been more males than females in the Church. . . .

> The United States census records from 1850 to 1940, and all available Church records, uniformly show a preponderance of males in Utah, and in the Church. Indeed, the excess in Utah has usually been larger than for the whole United States, . . . there was no surplus of women (*Evidences and Reconciliations*, 1960, pp.390-92).

The sociologist Kimball Young says that "under polygamy some men would have to remain unwed. . . . it was not uncommon for a man to select a plural mate from among recent arrivals of converts in Salt Lake City" (*Isn't One Wife Enough?* 1954, p.124).

The Mormon leaders were evidently worried that the missionaries would take the best women. Heber C. Kimball, a member of the First Presidency, admonished: "I say to those who are elected to go on missions, . . . remember they are not your sheep: they belong to Him that sends you. Then do not make a choice of any of those sheep; do not make selections before they are brought home and put into the fold. You understand that. Amen" (*Journal of Discourses*, vol. 6, p.256).

Stanley P. Hirshon adds this instructive information:

> Kimball always kept an eye out for romance. "Brethren," he instructed some departing missionaries, "I want you to understand that it is not to be as it has been heretofore. The brother missionaries have been in the habit of picking out the prettiest women for themselves before they get here, and bringing on the ugly ones for us; hereafter you have to bring them all here before taking any of them, and let us all have a fair shake" (*The Lion of the Lord*, New York, 1969, pp.129-30).

The shortage of women was so great that some of the men were marrying girls who were very young. Fanny Stenhouse stated: "That same year, a bill was brought into the Territorial Legislature, providing that boys of fifteen years of age and girls of twelve might legally contract marriage, with the consent of their parents or guardians!" (*Tell It All*, 1875, p.607).

225

The early Mormon leaders certainly did allow their young people to marry at an early age. Mosiah Hancock was only 11 years old when he was "sealed" to a "young girl." According to his journal, he was "born in Kirtland, Ohio, on April the 9th, 1834." ("The Mosiah Hancock Journal," typed copy, p.1). On pages 20 and 21 of the same journal, he recorded:

> On about January 10, 1846, I was privileged to go in the temple and receive my washings and annointings. I was sealed to a lovely young girl named Mary, who was about my age, but it was with the understanding that we were not to live together as man and wife until we were 16 years of age. The reason that some were sealed so young was because we knew that we would have to go West and wait many a long time for another temple.

Stanley P. Hirshon provides this additional information:

> "Make haste and get married," Remy heard Young preach. "Let me see no boys above sixteen and girls above fourteen unmarried." . . . In 1857 *The New York Times*, reporting the sealings to old men of two girls aged ten and eleven, estimated that most girls married before they were fourteen. . . . Troskolawsski knew one bishop who was sealed to four of his nieces, the youngest thirteen years old. . . . On August 1, 1856, he put on the stagecoach for Ohio twelve-year-old Emma Wheat, who was being forced into a marriage she detested (*The Lion of the Lord*, pp.126-27).

Sorrows of Polygamy

The fact that plural marriage brought great sorrow to many of the women involved can hardly be denied. Heber C. Kimball once remarked: "There is a great deal of quarrelling in the houses, and contending for power and authority; and the second wife is against the first wife, perhaps, in some instances" (*Journal of Discourses*, vol. 4, p.178).

Brigham Young also spoke of the problems: "A few years ago one of my wives, when talking about wives leaving their husbands said, 'I wish my husband's wives would leave him, every soul of them except myself.' That is the way they all feel, more or less, at times, both old and young" (*Journal of Discourses*, vol. 9, p.195).

"Sisters, do you wish to make yourselves happy? Then what is your duty? It is for you to bear children, . . . are you tormenting yourselves by thinking that your husbands do not love you? I would not care whether they loved a particle or not; but I would cry out, like one of old, in the joy of my heart, 'I have got a man from the Lord!' 'Hallelujah! I am a mother . . .' " (p.37).

Zina Huntington, a wife of Brigham Young and a defender of

the doctrine of polygamy, counseled:

> It is the duty of a first wife to regard her husband not with a selfish devotion . . . she must *regard her husband with indifference,* and with no other feeling than that of reverence, for *love we regard as a false sentiment;* a feeling which should have no existence in polygamy . . . we believe in the good old custom by which marriages should be arranged by the parents of the young people (*New York World,* November 17, 1869, as cited in *The Lion of the Lord,* pp.229-30).

It is almost impossible to conceive of the sorrow that the Mormon women went through. Joseph Lee Robinson, who was himself a polygamist and a faithful member of the church, frankly admitted: "Plural marriage . . . is calculated in its nature to severely try the women even to nearly *tear their heart strings out of them* . . ." (Journal and Autobiography of Joseph Lee Robinson, p.60, microfilm in LDS Genealogical Library).

Kimball Young relates some of the heartaches of polygamy:

> When James Hunter took his second wife, the first who had accompanied the couple to the Endowment House for the ceremony could not sleep and walked the floor all night as she thought of her husband lying in the arms of his new bride. . . .

> A person brought up in a polygamous household . . . told this story: "There is one real tragedy in polygamy that I can remember. One evening a man brought home a second wife. It was in the winter and the first wife was very upset. That night she climbed onto the roof and froze to death" (*Isn't One Wife Enough?* pp.147-48).

At one time conditions became so bad in Brigham Young's family that he offered to set all his wives free:

> Now for my proposition; it is more particularly for my sisters, as it is frequently happening that women say they are unhappy. Men will say, "My wife, though a most excellent woman, has *not seen a happy day* since I took my second wife," "No, not a happy day for a year," says one; and another has not seen a happy day for five years. . . .

> I wish my own women to understand that what I am going to say is for them as well as others, and I want those who are here to tell their sisters, yes, all the women of this community, . . . I am going to give you from this time to the 6th day of October next, for reflection, that you may determine whether you wish to stay with your husbands or not, and then I am going to *set every woman at liberty* and say to them, Now go your way, my women with the rest, go your way. And my wives have got to do one of two things; either round up their shoulders to endure the afflictions of this world, and live their religion, or *they may leave, for*

I will not have them about me. I will go into heaven alone, rather than have scratching and fighting around me. I will set all at liberty. "What, first wife too?" Yes, I will liberate you all. . . .

I wish my women, and brother Kimball's and brother Grant's to leave, and every woman in this Territory, or else say in their hearts that they will embrace the Gospel—the whole of it . . . say to your wives, "Take all that I have and be set at liberty; but if you stay with me you shall comply with the law of God, and that too without any murmuring and whining. You must fulfil the law of God in every respect, and round up your shoulders to walk up to the mark without any grunting."

Now recollect that two weeks from to morrow I am going to set you at liberty. But the first wife will say, "It is hard, for I have lived with my husband twenty years, or thirty, and have raised a family of children for him, and it is a great trial to me for him to have more women;" then I say it is time that you gave him up to other women who will bear children. If my wife had borne me all the children that she ever would bare, the celestial law would teach me to take young women that would have children. . . .

Sisters, *I am not joking,* I do not throw out my proposition to banter your feelings, to see whether you will leave your husbands, all or any of you. But I know that there is *no cessation to the everlasting whining* of many of the women in this Territory; . . . if the women will turn from the commandments of God and continue to despise the order of heaven, I will pray that the curse of the Almighty may be close to their heels. . . .

Prepare yourselves for two weeks from to morrow; and I will tell you now, that if you will tarry with your husbands, after I have set you free, you must bow down to it, and submit yourselves to the Celestial law. You may go where you please, after two weeks from tomorrow; but, remember, that I will not hear any more of this whining (Sermon by Brigham Young, *Journal of Discourses,* vol. 4, pp.55-57; also printed in *Deseret News,* vol. 6, pp.235-36).

Jedediah M. Grant, second counselor to Brigham Young, depicted the tragic situation in similar terms: "And we have women here who like any thing but the celestial law of God; and if they could break asunder the cable of the Church of Christ, there is scarcely a mother in Israel but would do it this day. And they talk it to their husbands, to their daughters, and to their neighbors, and say they have not seen a week's happiness since their husbands took a second wife" (*Deseret News,* vol. 6, p.235; also *Journal of Discourses,* vol. 4, p.51).

Even Joseph Smith's home was not exempt from the problems caused by plural marriage. The Mormon writer John J. Stewart said: "Thus did Satan sow the seeds of discord in the

Father, you will see a being with whom you have long been acquainted, and He will receive you into His arms, and you will be ready to fall into His embrace and kiss Him, as you would your fathers and friends that have been dead for a score of years, you will be so glad and joyful. Would you not rejoice? When you are qualified and purified, so that you can endure the glory of eternity, so that you can see your Father, and your friends who have gone behind the vail, you will fall upon their necks and kiss them, as we do an earthly friend that has been long absent from us, and that we have been anxiously desiring to see. This is the people that are and will be permitted to enjoy the society of those happy and exalted beings.

Now for my proposition; it is more particularly for my sisters, as it is frequently happening that women say they are unhappy. Men will say, "My wife, though a most excellent woman, has not seen a happy day since I took my second wife;" "No, not a happy day for a year," says one; and another has not seen a happy day for five years. It is said that women are tied down and abused: that they are misused and have not the liberty they ought to have; that many of them are wading through a perfect flood of tears, because of the conduct of some men, together with their own folly.

I wish my own women to understand that what I am going to say is for them as well as others, and I want those who are here to tell their sisters, yes, all the women of this community, and then write it back to the States, and do as you please with it. I am going to give you from this time to the 6th day of October next, for reflection, that you may determine whether you wish to stay with your husbands or not, and then I am going to set every woman at liberty and say to them,

Now go your way, my women with the rest, go your way. And my wives have got to do one of two things; either round up their shoulders to endure the afflictions of this world, and live their religion, or they may leave, for I will not have them about me. I will go into heaven alone, rather than have scratching and fighting around me. I will set all at liberty. "What, first wife too?" Yes, I will liberate you all.

I know what my women will say; they will say, "You can have as many women as you please, Brigham." But I want to go somewhere and do something to get rid of the whiners; I do not want them to receive a part of the truth and spurn the rest out of doors.

I wish my women, and brother Kimball's and brother Grant's to leave, and every woman in this Territory, or else say in their hearts that they will embrace the Gospel—the whole of it. Tell the Gentiles that I will free every woman in this Territory at our next Conference. "What, the first wife too?" Yes, there shall not be one held in bondage, all shall be set free. And then let the father be the head of the family, the master of his own household; and let him treat them as an angel would treat them; and let the wives and the children say amen to what he says, and be subject to his dictates, instead of their dictating the man, instead of their trying to govern him.

No doubt some are thinking, "I wish brother Brigham would say what would become of the children." I will tell you what my feelings are; I will let my wives take the children, and I have property enough to support them, and can educate them, and then give them a good fortune, and I can take a fresh start.

I do not desire to keep a particle of my property, except enough to protect me from a state of nudity. And

A photograph of the *Journal of Discourses*, vol. 4, page 55. Brigham Young offered to set all his wives free.

Prophet's own home, cause a torment of mind to Emma, distress to Joseph, and lay the groundwork of the apostate Reorganized Church, eventually taking Emma and their sons outside the true Church" (*Brigham Young and His wives*, p.33).

In his thesis "Emma Hale—Wife of the Prophet Joseph Smith" (p.104 of typed copy), Raymond T. Bailey admitted that it was "public knowledge that there were quarrels between Emma and Joseph especially during the Illinois period of their lives." On April 17, 1844, the *Warsaw Signal* reported that Joseph Smith had "turned his wife out of doors. 'Sister Emma's' offence was, that she was in conversation with Mr. E. Robinson, and refused, or hesitated to tell the Prophet on what subject they were engaged. The man of God, thereupon, flew into a holy passion, and turned the partner of his bosom, and the said Robinson, into the street—all of which was done in broad daylight, and no doubt in the most approved style."

In his journal and autobiography, Joseph Lee Robinson (the brother of "E. Robinson" who is mentioned above) frankly admitted that Joseph and Emma had a fight over the doctrine of polygamy:

> . . . Angeline Ebenezers wife had some time before this had watched Brother Joseph the Prophet had seen him go into some house that she had reported to sister Emma the wife of the Prophet it was at a time when she [Emma] was very suspisous [sic] and jealous of him for fear he would get another wife . . . she was determined he should not get another if he did she was determined to leave and when she heard this she Emma became very angry and said she would leave . . . it came close to breaking up his family . . . the Prophet felt dreadful bad over it, he went to my brothers and talked with Angelene on the matter, and she would not give him any satesfaction [sic], and her husband did not reprove his wife, and it came to pass, *the Prophet cursed her severely* . . . I thought that I would not have a wife of mine do a thing of that kind for a world, but if she had done it she should get upon her nees [sic] at his feet and beg his pardon. . . .

The book *Mormon Portraits* provides further insight into Joseph's family troubles:

> Mr. W.: "Joseph kept eight girls in his house, calling them his 'daughters.' Emma threatened that she would leave the house, and Joseph told her, "All right, you can go." She went, but when Joseph reflected that such a scandal would hurt his prophetic dignity, he followed his wife and brought her back. But the eight 'daughters' had to leave the house."

> "Miss" Eliza R. Snow, . . . was one of the first (willing) victims of Joseph in Nauvoo. She used to be much at the prophet's house

... he made her one of his celestial brides. ... Feeling outraged as a wife and betrayed as a friend, Emma is currently reported as having had recourse to a vulgar broomstick as an instrument of revenge: and the harsh treatment received at Emma's hands is said to have destroyed Eliza's hopes of becoming the mother of a prophet's son (*Mormon Portraits*, by Dr. W. Wyl, 1886, pp.57-58).

The Mormon writer Claire Noall acknowledged: "Willard realized that Emma had refused to believe that any of the young women boarding at the Mansion when it was first used as a hotel had been married to Joseph. She had struck Eliza Snow at the head of the stairs, and Eliza, it was whispered, had lost her unborn child" (*Intimate Disciple, a Portrait of Willard Richards*, 1957, p.407).

There are some members of the Mormon church who maintain that Joseph Smith did not actually live with his wives here on earth. There is an abundance of evidence, however, to show that he did. For instance, Benjamin F. Johnson made the following statement in an affidavit dated March 4, 1870: "After a short period, President Smith . . . came again to Macedonia (Ramus), where he remained two days, lodging at my house with my sister as man and wife (and to my certain knowledge he occupied the same bed with her)" (*Historical Record*, vol. 6, p.222).

Number of Wives

Andrew Jensen, who was an assistant Mormon church historian, listed 27 women who were married to Joseph Smith (see the *Historical Record*, pp.233, 234). The Mormon author John J. Stewart, however, credits Joseph Smith with even more wives: ". . . he married many other women, perhaps *three or four dozen or more* . . ." (*Brigham Young and His Wives*, p.31). Fawn M. Brodie includes a list of forty-eight women who may have been married to Joseph Smith (see *No Man Knows My History*, pp.434-65). Stanley S. Ivins, who was considered "one of the great authorities on Mormon polygamy," said that the number of Joseph Smith's wives "can only be guessed at, but it might have gone as high as *sixty or more*" (*Western Humanities Review*, vol. 10, pp.232-33).

Before his death Stanley S. Ivins prepared a list of eighty-four women who may have been married to Joseph Smith during his lifetime. We published this information in the book *Joseph Smith and Polygamy* (pp.41-47). While Mr. Ivins was not certain that every woman listed was actually married to Smith, he pointed out that there may have been others who were married to Joseph Smith whose names did not appear on the list. In preparing this list Mr. Ivins did a great deal of research in the Nauvoo temple records, the Endowment House records and other genealogical records. After Mr. Ivins' study was completed, some of the temple records in the L.D.S. genealogical library were restricted and are no longer available to the general public.

Before listing the last eleven names on his list, Stanley S. Ivins stated:

> On April 4, 1899, eleven of the wives of Joseph Smith, all long since dead, were sealed to him by proxy. A not[e] accompanying the record of the sealing said: "The sealings of those named below were performed during the life of the Prophet Joseph but there is no record thereof. President Lorenzo Snow decided that they be repeated in order that a record might exist; and that this explanation be made." This incident suggests that others of the many dead women to whom Smith was sealed, by proxy, may have been married to him during his life. . . .

At the end of his paper Mr. Ivins remarked: "In addition to these dead women, Joseph Smith was sealed to *at least 229 others*, up to March 18, 1881. (Additional note: Sealed to *246 Dead Women*.)" (*Joseph Smith and Polygamy*, p.47).

In the Preface to the second edition of her book *No Man Knows My History*, Fawn Brodie states: ". . .over two hundred women, apparently at their own request, were sealed as wives to Joseph Smith after his death in special temple ceremonies. Moreover, a great many distinguished women in history, including several Catholic saints, were also sealed to Joseph Smith in Utah. I saw these astonishing lists in the Latter-day Saint Genealogical Archives in Salt Lake City in 1944."

The Apostle John A. Widtsoe admitted that women were sealed to Joseph Smith after his death and without his approval: "After the death of the Prophet, women applied for the privilege of being sealed to him for eternity. . . . To these requests, assent was often given. . . . *Women no longer living, whether in Joseph's day or later, have also been sealed to the Prophet for eternity*" (*Evidences and Reconciliations*, Single Volume Edition, 1960, pp.342-43).

If the Mormon doctrine concerning plural marriage were true, Joseph Smith would have hundreds of wives in the resurrection. Some of the women Brigham Young and Heber C. Kimball married, who were previously married to Joseph Smith, would have to be surrendered to Joseph in the hereafter. Lucy W. Kimball testified:

The contract when I married Mr. Kimball was that I should be his wife for time, and time only, and the contract on the part of Mr. Kimball was that he would take care of me during my lifetime, and in the resurrection would surrender me, with my children, to Joseph Smith. . . .

I decline to answer whether I had any children while I was sealed to Joseph Smith. I have nine children since I was married to Heber C. Kimball (*The Temple Lot Case*, 1893, p.379).

In an article published in *Western Humanities Review* (vol. 10, pp.232-33), Stanley S. Ivins observed that "Brigham Young is usually credited with only twenty-seven wives, but he was sealed to more than twice that many living women, and to at least 150 more who had died."

The Mormon writer John J. Stewart lists the names of *fifty-three women* who were sealed to Brigham Young, and then he adds: "There were perhaps one or two others, plus the some 150 women whom he had sealed to him; also a few women who were sealed to him after his death" (*Brigham Young and His Wives*, p.96).

In a speech delivered January 24, 1858, Apostle Ezra T. Benson indicated that Young had about "fifty or sixty" wives (see *Journal of Discourses*, vol. 6, pp.180-81).

Stanley P. Hirshon lists seventy women who may have been married to Brigham Young (see *Lion of the Lord*, pp.190-221). On pages 188 and 189 of the same book, he relates:

> . . . Young often joked about his wives. "Tell the Gentiles," he once observed, "I do not know half of them when I see them." Later, asked the usual question by a Gentile governor of Utah, Young answered: "I don't know myself! I never refuse to marry any respectable woman who asks me, and it is often the case that I separate from a woman at the marriage altar, never to meet her again to know her. My children I keep track of, however. I have fifty-seven now living, and have lost three"

Brigham Young boasted of his ability to obtain many wives: "Brother Cannon remarked that people wondered how many wives and children I had. He may inform them, that I shall have wives and children by the million, and glory, and riches and power and dominion, and kingdom after kingdom, and reign triumphantly" (*Journal of Discourses*, vol. 8, p.178). "I could prove to this congregation that I am young; for I could find more girls who would choose me for a husband than can any of the young men" (vol. 5, p.210).

Although Brigham Young was constantly marrying new wives, he claimed that "there are probably but few men in the world who care about the private society of women *less* than I do" (*Journal of Discourses*, vol. 5, p.99).

Heber C Kimball, a member of the First Presidency, had forty-five wives, but he claimed that in the resurrection he would be able to have thousands:

> Supposing that I have a wife or a dozen of them, and she should say, "You cannot be exalted without me," and suppose they all should say so, what of that? . . . Suppose that I lose the whole of them before I go into the spirit world, but that I have been a good, faithful man . . . do you think I will be destitute there. No, the Lord says there are more there than there are here . . . there are millions of them, . . . we will go to brother Joseph and say, "Here we are brother Joseph; we are here ourselves are we not, with none of the property we possessed in our probationary state, not even the rings on our fingers?" He will say to us, "Come along, my boys, we will give you a good suit of clothes. Where are your wives?" "They are back yonder; they would not follow us." "Never mind," says Joseph, "Here are thousands, have all you want" (*Journal of Discourses*, vol. 4, p.209).

The Mormon men certainly believed that they could have all the wives they wanted. Kimball Young stated: "One of the informants for this study said that her uncle had 'some hundreds of wives sealed to him for eternity only' " (*Isn't One Wife Enough?* p.146).

According to Stanley S. Ivins, the Endowment House Records reveal that on November 22, 1870, Mormon Apostle Orson Pratt had himself sealed to *101 dead women*. On November 29, 1870, he was sealed to *109 dead women*.

The same day (November 29, 1870) *91 dead women* were sealed to his brother, Parley P. Pratt, who had died in 1857.

Mr. Ivins found that the St. George Temple records show that Wilford Woodruff—who later became the fourth president of the church—was sealed to *189 dead women* in a period of slightly over two years (January 29, 1879 to March 14, 1881).

Moses Franklin Farnsworth was sealed to *345 dead women* in a two-year period. At one time we thought that Mr. Farnsworth held the record for the largest number of dead women sealed to him. New evidence, however, has forced us to revise that conclusion. On April 5, 1894, the Apostle Abraham Cannon recorded the following in his diary:

> THURSDAY, APRIL 5th, 1894. . . . I met with the Quorum and Presidency in the temple. . . . President Woodruff then spoke . . . "In searching out my genealogy I found about *four hundred* of my femal[e] kindred who were never married. I asked Pres. Young what I should do with them. He said for me to have them *sealed to me* unless there were more that [than?] 999 of them. the doc-

That day has come, and the other day has past. I have known men from Nauvoo, men who were there worth $150 or $200,000, come here with nothing but a handkerchief, containing a change of shirts, under their arms. They left their property there; and what we did not leave in hell's kitchen we left at Devil's Gate. The devil has a gate where he may catch everything that is not to do us good, but that is calculated to create a craving appetite for that which is not here.

There are some of this people who have been kept as long as they have, only upon the principle of their being fondled and pampered. If they could not have the privilege of nursing at the breast and have a full supply, or the use of a sugar teat to keep them alive, they would dwindle and die; they must have something to suck, in order to keep them alive and in existence, for they are nothing but pets; pets they are, and pets they will go to hell, but will find no sugar teats there.

Probably a few will leave next spring; they are all fair weather while they are in our midst, but when it comes spring they will leave. Thank the Lord for that; and while I feel as I do now, I shall be thankful for everything that transpires from this time henceforth, that is, if I live my religion.

Supposing that I have a wife or a dozen of them, and she should say, "You cannot be exalted without me," and suppose they all should say so, what of that? They never will affect my salvation one particle. Whose salvation will they affect? Their own. They have got to live their religion, serve their God, and do right, as well as myself. Suppose that I lose the whole of them before I go into the spirit world, but that I have been a good, faithful man all the days of my life, and lived my religion, and

had favour with God, and was kind to them, do you think I will be destitute there. No, the Lord says there are more there than there are here. They have been increasing there; they increase there a great deal faster than we do here, because there is no obstruction. They do not call upon the doctors to kill their offspring; there are no doctors there, that is, if they are there, their occupation is changed, which proves that they are not there, because they have ceased to be doctors. In this world very many of the doctors are studying to diminish the human family.

In the spirit world there is an increase of males and females, there are millions of them, and if I am faithful all the time, and continue right along with brother Brigham, we will go to brother Joseph and say, "Here we are brother Joseph; we are here ourselves are we not, with none of the property we possessed in our probationary state, not even the rings on our fingers?" He will say to us, "Come along, my boys, we will give you a good suit of clothes. Where are your wives?" "They are back yonder; they would not follow us." "Never mind," says Joseph, "here are thousands, have all you want." Perhaps some do not believe that, but I am just simple enough to believe it.

Help brother Brigham along, help brother Heber, brother Daniel, the Twelve, and every other good person. I am looking for the day, and it is close at hand, when we will have a most heavenly time, one that will be romantic, one with all kinds of ups and downs, which is what I call romantic, for it will occupy in full all the time, so that we may never become idle, nor sleepy, nor cease being active in the things of God, which will prevent dotage.

Am I thankful now? I never was more thankful in my life than I am to-day, to see this people. I know

A photograph of the *Journal of Discourses*, vol. 4, page 209. Herber C. Kimball, a member of The First Presidency, maintained that there will be thousands of women in heaven to choose from.

trine startled me, but I had it done . . ." ("Daily Journal of Abraham H. Cannon," April 5, 1894, vol. 18, pp.66-67, Brigham Young University Library).

Taking Other Men's Wives

The fact that Joseph Smith asked for other men's wives was made very plain in a sermon delivered in the tabernacle by Jedediah M. Grant, second counselor to Brigham Young. In this sermon, delivered February 19, 1854, Jedediah M. Grant stated:

> When the family organization was revealed from heaven—the patriarchal order of God, and Joseph began, on the right and on the left, to add to his family, what a quaking there was in Israel. Says one brother to another, "Joseph says all covenants are done away, and none are binding but the new covenants; now suppose Joseph should come and say *he wanted your wife*, what would you say to that?" "I would tell him to go to hell." This was the spirit of many in the early days of this Church. . . .
>
> What would a man of God say, who felt aright, when *Joseph* asked him for his money? He would say, "Yes, and I wish I had more to help to build up the kingdom of God." Or if he came and said, *"I want your wife?"* "O Yes," he would say, "here she is, *there are plenty more."* . . . Did the Prophet Joseph want *every* man's *wife he asked for?* He did not. . . . If such a man of God should come to me and say, "I want your gold and silver, or your wives," I should say, "Here they are, I wish I had more to give you, take all I have got" (*Journal of Discourses*, vol. 2, pp.13-14).

In his book *Mormon Portraits* (pp.70-72), Dr. Wyl presents some revealing information:

> Joseph Smith finally *demanded the wives of all the twelve* Apostles that were at home then in Nauvoo. . . . Vilate Kimball, the first wife of Heber C. Kimball, . . . loved her husband, and he, . . . loved her, hence a reluctance to comply with the Lord's demand that Vilate should be consecrated. . . . They thought the command of the Lord must be obeyed in some way, and a "proxy" way suggested itself to their minds. They had a young daughter only getting out of girlhood; and the father apologizing to the prophet for his wife's reluctance to comply with his desires, stating, however, that the act must be right or it would not be counselled . . . asked Joe if his daughter wouldn't do as well as his wife. Joe replied that she would do just as well, and the Lord would accept her instead. The half-ripe bud of womanhood was delivered over to the Prophet.

The fact that Joseph Smith asked for Heber C. Kimball's wife but actually married his daughter is verified in the book *The Life of Heber C. Kimball*, written by Apostle Orson F. Whitney:

Before he would trust even Heber with the full secret, however, he put him to a test which few men would have been able to bear.

It was no less than a requirement for him to surrender his wife, his beloved Vilate, and give her to Joseph in marriage!

The astounding revelation well-nigh paraly[z]ed him. He could hardly believe he had heard aright. Yet Joseph was solemnly in earnest. . . . He knew Joseph too well . . . to doubt his truth or the divine origin of the behest he had made. . . .

Three days he fasted and wept and prayed. Then, with a broken and a bleeding heart, but with soul self-mastered for the sacrifice, he led his darling wife to the Prophet's house and presented her to Joseph.

It was enough—the heavens accepted the sacrifice. The will for the deed was taken, and 'accounted unto him for righteousness.' Joseph wept at this proof of devotion, and embracing Heber told him that was all the Lord required. . . .

The Prophet joined the hands of the heroic and devoted pair, and then and there, . . . Heber and Vilate Kimball were made husband and wife for all eternity (*Life of Heber C. Kimball*, pp.333-35).

Helen Mar, the eldest daughter of Heber Chase and Vilate Kimball, was given to the Prophet in the holy bonds of Celestial Marriage (p.339).

Joseph Smith was apparently worried concerning adultery. Joseph Lee Robinson recorded the following in his journal and autobiography:

> . . . God had revealed unto him [Joseph Smith] that any man that ever committed adultery in either of his probations that that man could never be raised to the highest exaltation in the celestial glory, and that he felt anxious with regard to himself that he enquired of the Lord that the Lord told him that he Joseph had never committed adultery.

John D. Lee tells that Joseph Smith took H. B. Jacob's wife while Mr. Jacobs was absent: ". . . in his absence, she was sealed to the Prophet Joseph and was his wife" (*Confessions of John D. Lee*, p.132).

Juanita Brooks states that "Zina Diantha Huntington" was the woman who was married to Henry B. Jacobs and later sealed to Joseph Smith. She states that after she was sealed to Joseph Smith she continued to live with Jacobs, and that later she "renounced Jacobs and joined the family of Brigham Young" (*On The Mormon Frontier, The Diary of Hosea Stout*, vol. 1, p.141, footnote 18).

In the *Historical Record* (vol. 6, p.233), assistant church his-

Smith, and has been handed down to his successors.

I do not care how many devils rap, it is no trouble to me. I say, rap away, and give as many revelations as you please, whether you are good spirits or bad ones, it does not trouble my cranium. Rap away, for I trust in the anchor of my soul that is sure and steadfast, in the Priesthood of God upon the earth.

What would a man of God say, who felt aright, when Joseph asked him for his money? He would say, " Yes, and I wish I had more to help to build up the kingdom of God." Or if he came and said, " I want your wife?" " O yes," he would say, " here she is, there are plenty more."

There is another main thread connected with this, that I have not brought out. You know in fishing with the hook and line, if you draw out suddenly on the line when you have got a large trout, you may break your line; you must therefore angle a little, and manage your prize carefully. I would ask you if Jehovah has not in all ages tried His people by the power of Lucifer and his associates; and on the other hand, has He not tried them and proved them by His Prophets? Did the Lord actually want Abraham to kill Isaac? Did the Prophet Joseph want every man's wife he asked for? He did not, but in that thing was the grand thread of the Priesthood developed. The grand object in view was to try the people of God, to see what was in them. If such a man of God should come to me and say, " I want your gold and silver, or your wives," I should say, " Here they are, I wish I had more to give you, take all I have got." A man who has got the Spirit of God, and the light of eternity in him, has no trouble about such matters.

I am talking now of the present day. There was a time when we could be tried pretty severely upon these points, but I now could pick you out hundreds of men that cannot be tried in this way, but they will hand over every thing they possess. They understand the nature of such doctrines, and the object of such requirements. They know it is to prove the people, both men and women, and to develop what they will do. How can the Priesthood judge the people, if it does not prove them.

If ever you are brought into the presence of God, and exalted to a seat in His celestial kingdom, it will be by virtue of the Holy Priesthood; therefore you have got to be proved, not only by being tempted by the devil, but the Priesthood will try you—it will try you to the core. If one thing won't try you, something else will be adopted, until you are like the passive clay in the hands of the Potter. If the Lord our God does not see fit to let the devil loose upon you, and mob you, He will employ some other means to try you as in a crucible, to prove you as gold is tried seven times in the furnace.

The world philosophizes about the " Mormons," about their leaders, and the life they are living. There are a thousand conjectures among them in relation to the " Mormons." The grand secret is told in a few words; the fact is, the Almighty God has spoken from the heavens, sent heavenly messengers, and organized His Church, restored the Holy Priesthood, established His government on the earth, and exerted his power to extend it, and send forth His word. And that Priesthood understands the principles and motives by which men are actuated, and it understands the workings of the devil on the earth; that Priesthood knows how to govern, when to strike, and when not to strike.

Some things in this Church start up at times, that you would think the whole Church would be rent asunder, like the clans of Scotland. Clanism,

A photograph of *Journal of Discourses*, vol. 2, page 14. Jedediah M. Grant, second counselor to Brigham Young, frankly admits that Joseph Smith asked for some men's wives.

torian Andrew Jensen confirmed the fact that Zina D. Huntington married Joseph Smith and later became the wife of Brigham Young: "Zina D. Huntington, afterwards the wife of Pres. Brigham Young, *sealed to the Prophet* Oct. 27, 1841, Dimick B. Huntington officiating."

Zina Diantha Huntington Jacobs is listed as wife number five in Stanley Ivin's list: "5.—ZINA DIANTHA HUNTINGTON JACOBS. . . . wife of Henry B. Jacobs. . . . Married Jacobs March 7, 1841. Married Joseph Smith, October 27, 1841. On February 2, 1846, she was sealed to Smith for eternity and to Brigham Young for time. She lived with Young as his wife, and died August 29, 1901" (*Joseph Smith and Polygamy*, p.42).

Fawn M. Brodie relates:

> Zina left Jacobs in 1846 to marry Brigham Young. William Hall asserted that he had heard Young say publicly to Jacobs: "The woman you claim for a wife does not belong to you. She is the spiritual wife of brother Joseph, sealed to him. I am his proxy, and she, in this behalf, with her children, are my property. You can go where you please, and get another, but be sure to get one of your own kindred spirits." Jacobs apparently accepted Young's decision as the word of the Lord, for he stood as witness in the Nauvoo temple in January 1846 when Zina was sealed to Brigham Young "for time" and to Joseph Smith "for eternity" (*No Man Knows My History*, p.443).

Juanita Brooks further explains: ". . . Zina had been moved to Winter Quarters. She now renounced Jacobs and joined the family of Brigham Young, traveling west in 1848 in a wagon provided by him and driven by her brother Oliver" (*On The Mormon Frontier* . . ., vol. 1, p.141, footnote 18).

Ann Eliza Young, who had been married to Brigham Young, charged that Joseph Smith was guilty of adultery:

> Joseph not only paid his addresses to the young and unmarried women, but he sought "spiritual alliance" with many married ladies. . . . He taught them that all former marriages were null and void, and that they were at perfect liberty to make another choice of a husband. The marriage covenants were not binding, because they were ratified only by Gentile laws. These laws the Lord did not recognize; consequently all the women were free.
>
> . . .
>
> One woman said to me not very long since, while giving me some of her experiences in polygamy: "The greatest trial I ever endured in my life was living with my husband and deceiving him, by receiving Joseph's attentions whenever he chose to come to me." . . .

Some of these women have since said they did not know who was the father of their children; this is not to be wondered at, for after Joseph's declaration annulling all Gentile marriages, the greatest promiscuity was practiced; and, indeed, all sense of morality seemed to have been lost by a portion at least of the church (*Wife No. 19*, 1876, pp.70-71).

John A. Widtsoe admitted that Joseph Smith was sealed to married women, but he claimed that they were not to be his wives until after death:

Another kind of celestial marriage seems to have been practiced in the early days of plural marriage. It has not been practised since Nauvoo days, for it is under Church prohibition. Zealous women, *married* or unmarried, loving the cause of the restored gospel, considered their condition in the hereafter. Some of them asked that they might be *sealed to the Prophet* for eternity. They were not to be his wives on earth, in mortality, but only after death in the eternities. . . . Such marriages led to misunderstandings by those not of the Church. . . . Therefore any ceremony *uniting a married woman, for example to Joseph Smith* for eternity seemed adulterous to such people. Yet, in any day, in our day, there may be women who prefer to spend eternity with another than their husband on earth.

Such cases, if any, and they must have been few in number, gave enemies of the Church occasion to fan the flaming hatred against the Latter-day Saints (*Evidences and Reconciliations*, 1960, p.343).

John A. Widtsoe's statement that Joseph Smith did not live with the married women to whom he was sealed is certainly false. Patty Bartlett Sessions, the wife of David Sessions, made it very clear in her private journal that she was married to Joseph Smith for both "time" and "eternity": "I was sealed to Joseph Smith by Willard Richards Mar 9, 1842, in Newel K. Whitney's chamber, Nauvoo, *for time* and all eternity, . . . Sylvia my daughter was present when I was sealed to Joseph Smith. I was after Mr. Sessions' death sealed to John Parry for time on the 27th, March, 1852, GSL City" (Journal of Patty Sessions, as quoted in *Intimate Disciple, Portrait of Willard Richards*, 1957, p.611).

The following information concerning Patty Sessions is found in Stanley S. Ivins' list of 84 women who may have been married to Joseph Smith: "34.—PATTY BARTLETT SESSIONS. *Wife of David Sessions.* . . . Married Sessions, June 28, 1812. Married Joseph Smith on March 9, 1842. Her husband Sessions died about 1850. . . . On July 9, 1867, she was sealed to Joseph Smith in the Endowment House . . ." (*Joseph Smith and Polygamy*, p.44).

Mary Elizabeth Rollins Lightner, the wife of Adam Lightner, stated: "Joseph said I was his before I came here and he said all the Devils in Hell should never get me from him. I was sealed to him in the Masonic Hall, over the old brick store by Brigham Young in February 1842 and then again in the Nauvoo Temple by Heber C. Kimball . . ." (Affidavit of Mary Elizabeth Rollins Lightner, as quoted in *No Man Knows My History*, p.444).

In a speech given at Brigham Young University, Mrs. Lightner related:

> He [Joseph] preached polygamy. . . . It was given to him before he gave it to the Church. An angel came to him and the last time he came with a drawn sword in his hand and told Joseph if he did not go into that principle he would slay him. . . .
>
> I asked him if Emma knew about me and he said, "Emma thinks the world of you." I was not sealed to him until I had a witness. I had been dreaming for a number of years I was his wife. I thought I was a great sinner. I prayed to God to take it from me for I felt it was a sin, but when Joseph sent for me he told me all of these things. . . .
>
> Joseph came up the next Sabbath. . . . *My husband was far away from me at the time,* . . . I went forward and was sealed to him. Brigham Young performed the sealing and Heber C. Kimball the blessing.
>
> I knew he had six wives and I have known some of them from childhood up. I know he had three children. They told me. I think two of them are living today, they are not known as his children as they go by other names (Speech by Mary E. Lightner, Brigham Young University, April 14, 1905, typed copy).

Andrew Jenson admits that Mary Elizabeth Rollins was sealed to Joseph Smith (see *Historical Record*, vol. 6, p.234). In Stanley Ivins' list we find the following: "22.—MARY ELIZABETH ROLLINS LIGHTNER. . . . *wife of Adam Lightner.* . . . Married Lightner on August 11, 1835. . . . On January 17, 1846, she was sealed to Joseph Smith for eternity and to Brigham Young for time. However she remained with her legal husband and came to Utah with him in 1863. Her death was on December 17, 1913." It would appear, then, that Mary E. Lightner had two different husbands for "time" and a third for "eternity." The Mormon writer John J. Stewart confirms this in his book *Brigham Young and His Wives*: "17. Mary Elizabeth Rollins. . . . The *wife of a non-Mormon,* Adam Lightner. Sealed to the Prophet Joseph in February, 1842, at the age of 23, and again January 17, 1846, at which time she was sealed to Brigham for time" (p.89).

Stanley P. Hirshon tells of another married woman entering polygamy:

> ... Augusta Adams Cobb, ... married Henry Cobb, a prosperous Boston merchant, about 1822 and bore seven children.
>
> Augusta lived quietly until Young came east to preach in the summer of 1843. She heard him, converted to Mormonism, and with her two smallest children headed for Nauvoo. ... Augusta continued on to Nauvoo and on November 2, 1843, without divorcing her first husband married Young. A few months later she briefly returned to Boston, where she saw her other children and told Henry she was leaving him forever. ...
>
> Augusta returned to Nauvoo and on February 2, 1846, was sealed to Young for eternity. The following year Henry Cobb, still in Massachusetts, divorced her (*The Lion of the Lord*, pp.192-94).

The Mormon writer John J. Stewart confirms the fact that Mrs. Cobb was married to Brigham Young in 1843: "5. AUGUSTA ADAMS. ... Married to Brigham November 2, 1843, at the age of 40, and sealed to him February 2, 1846. She had several children by a previous marriage" (*Brigham Young and His Wives*, p.86).

From these facts it is hard to escape the conclusion that Joseph Smith and Brigham Young were living in adultery. John D. Lee stated: "Some have mutually agreed to *exchange wives* and have been sealed to each other as husband and wife by virtue and authority of the holy priesthood. One of Brigham's brothers, Lorenzo Young, now a bishop, made an exchange of wives with Mr. Decker, the father of the Mr. Decker who now has an interest in the cars running to York" (*Confessions of John D. Lee*, p.165).

A recent study by Michael Marquardt has brought to light the total disregard that Joseph Smith had for the sacred vows of marriage. As we have previously brought out, on July 27, 1842, Joseph Smith gave a special revelation that Sarah Ann Whitney was to become his plural wife. According to the assistant church historian Andrew Jenson, Sarah Ann Whitney was married to Joseph Smith by her father, Newel K. Whitney: "Sarah Ann Whitney, afterwards the wife of Pres. Heber C. Kimball, married to Joseph July 27, 1842, her father Newel K. Whitney officiating" (*Historical Record*, vol. 6, pp.233-34).

In *Mormonism—Shadow or Reality?* page 581, we pointed out that Michael Marquardt discovered photographs of a letter written by Joseph Smith himself and addressed to Bishop Newel K. Whitney and his wife. The letter is very interesting because Smith asks the "three" of them—presumably Mr. and Mrs. Whitney and their young daughter Sarah Ann, to whom Joseph Smith was secretly married—to come see him by night. In the letter, Joseph Smith makes it very clear that he does not want them to come when Emma, his first wife, would be present: ". . . all three of you can come and see me in the fore part of the night, . . . the only thing to be careful of, is to *find out when Emma comes then you cannot be safe*, but when she is not here, there is the most perfect safety: . . . *I think Emma wont come tonight if she dont dont fail to come tonight*, I subscribe myself your obedient and affectionate, companion, and friend. Joseph Smith"

Since finding photographs of this important letter in the George Albert Smith Collection at the University of Utah Library, Michael Marquardt has completed some very important research concerning this whole affair. He has published his findings under the title, *The Strange Marriages of Sarah Ann Whitney to Joseph Smith the Mormon Prophet, Joseph C. Kingsbury and Heber C. Kimball.* Among other things that Mr. Marquardt discovered is the fact that Joseph Smith actually performed a "pretended" marriage ceremony between Sarah Ann Whitney and Joseph C. Kingsbury so that his own relationship with her would not be noticed. Mr. Marquardt cites the following from "The History of Joseph C. Kingsbury," a document that is now in the Western Americana section of the University of Utah Library:

> . . . on 29th of April 1843 I according to President Joseph Smith Couscil [sic] & others agreed to Stand by Sarah Ann Whitny [sic] *as supposed to be her husband & had a prete [n]ded marriage* for the purpose of Bringing about the purposes of God in these last days as spoken by the mouth of the Prophets Isiah [sic] Jeremiah Ezekiel and also Joseph Smith, & Sarah Ann Should Recd a Great Glory Honor, & eternal lives and I Also Should Recd a Great Glory, Honor & eternal lives to the full desire of my heart in having my Companion Caroline in the first Resurection [sic] to claim her & no one have power to take her from me & we both shall be Crowned & enthroned together in the Celestial Kingdom of God. . . .

Mr. Marquardt has also found that Joseph Smith signed a document in which he stated: "I hereby certify, that I have upon this the 29th day of April 1843, joined together in Marriage Joseph C. Kingsbury and Sarah Ann Whitney, in the City of Nauvoo, Illinois." That a man professing to be a prophet of God would perform a "pretended" marriage to cover up his own iniquity is almost beyond belief.

243

In his pamphlet, Mr. Marquardt goes on to show that after Joseph Smith's death, Sarah Ann Whitney continued to live with Joseph C. Kingsbury in this "pretended" marriage—he referred to her as "Sarah my Supposed wife." While living with Kingsbury she became pregnant with Apostle Heber C. Kimball's child. Seven months later (January 12, 1846), she was married to Kimball for time and sealed to Joseph Smith for eternity in the Nauvoo Temple, but she continued to live with Kingsbury until after the child was born. All these facts are well documented in Michael Marquardt's pamphlet.

Some people have wondered how Joseph Smith could convince his people that polygamy was right in the sight of God. The answer is that the Mormon people were taught to follow their leaders in all things. When Smith announced that plural marriage was revealed by God, the Mormons were forced to accept it. Also the fact that Smith was very appealing to women must have helped him establish the doctrine. Mormon doctrine concerning women probably played an important role in preparing them to enter into plural marriage. Mormon leaders taught that a woman was inferior and that her salvation depended on a man. Brigham Young once stated: "The man is the head and *God of the woman*, but let him act like a God in virtuous principles . . ." (Sermon of Brigham Young, as quoted in *Journal of John D. Lee, 1846-47 and 1859*, edited by Charles Kelly, 1938, p.81). On page 114 of the same journal, John D. Lee related:

> Just in time I received a letter from Nancy the 1st stating that she had not forgotten that in the moment of passion that I was the man to whom she was to look for salvation spiritually or temporally . . . I read the letter to Pres. B. Young. His counsel was to tell her that inasmuch as she claimed salvation at my hands that she must come to me and place herself under my guidance and control and protection and respect the priesthood and my standing *as a saviour* but on no other consideration whatever.

Kimball Young further documents this attitude:

> . . . Daisy Barclay, herself brought up in a plural family, remarks: "Polygamy is predicated on the assumption that a man is superior to a woman . . . Mormon tradition . . . teaches woman to honor and obey her husband and look upon him as her lord and master." As a daughter of the second wife of Isaac Lambert once complained, "Mother figures you are supposed to spend your life taking care of a man, and *he is God*" (*Isn't One Wife Enough?* p.280).

Strange Marriages

On July 25, 1857, the following appeared in an article in the *Latter-Day Saints Millennial Star*:

> Among ancient Israel, marriage was forbidden within certain degrees of consanguinity. . . . The Polygamist was not only laid under the sme restraints as the Monogamist, but placed under additional restraints in regard to the persons whom he should select as additional wives. He was not permitted by the law of Moses to marry the sister of his wife. (See Leviticus xviii.18.) Neither was he permitted to marry a mother and daughter. "And if a man take a wife and her mother, it is wickedness; they shall be burnt with fire both he and they; that there be no wickedness among you." (See Leviticus xx.14.) . . . the Polygamist Israelite was under a law restricting him within certain limits. Though he had a right to marry many wives, yet he had no right to marry a mother and daughter or two sisters (*Millennial Star*, vol. 19, pp.473-74).

It is strange that the Mormon leaders would print these Old Testament rules because they certainly did not follow them. The Mormon writer T. Edgar Lyon admits that Apostle Orson Pratt was inconsistent in this regard:

> This controversy also illustrates one of the inconsistencies of the Mormon contention that their polygamy was Biblical. They did not abide by the rules of plural marriage as set forth in the Bible. Pratt himself had married two sisters. Others had done the same thing and even married mothers and daughters ("Orson Pratt—Early Mormon Leader," M.A. thesis, University of Chicago, 1932, p.104).

Although the early Mormon leaders wanted to return to the Old Testament practice of putting adulterers to death, they did not want to accept Leviticus 20:14, which said that when a man married "a wife and her mother" they should be put to death. If they had accepted this, Joseph Smith would have been one of the first to die, for he had married a woman and her mother. Fawn Brodie stated: "The prophet married *five pairs of sisters*: Delcena and Almera Johnson, Eliza and Emily Partridge, Sarah and Maria Lawrence, Mary Ann and Olive Grey Frost, and Prescinda and Zina Huntington. Patty and Sylvia Sessions were *mother and daughter*" (*No Man Knows My History*, p.336).

The fact that Patty and Sylvia Sessions were mother and daughter is verified by the Mormon writer Claire Noall: "Sylvia Lyon, Patty's daughter and the wife of Windsor J. Lyon, *was already sealed to Joseph.* This afternoon *she was to put her mother's hand in the Prophet's*" (*Intimate Disciple*, p.317).

245

The sociologist Kimball Young stated:

> Of our family records, 19 per cent of them report that the men *married sisters*. . . . Of these 30 cases all but one marriage were to full sisters; in this one it was to a half-sister. In one family a man married four sisters; in another he took twins as numbers one and two and a half-sister as wife number three. In still another a man married *two sisters and their widowed mother!* (*Isn't One Wife Enough*, p.111).

> Joseph Carey wanted to marry a certain widow, but she only consented if he would agree to *also marry her two daughters* when they grew up. They were then in their early teens. A few years after he wed the widow, she accompanied him to the temple where *he married his two stepdaughters* on the same day (p.142).

Fanny Stenhouse, a former polygamist wife, wrote:

> It would be quite impossible, with any regard to propriety, to relate all the horrible results of this disgraceful system. . . . Marriages have been contracted between the nearest of relatives; and old men tottering on the brink of the grave have been united to little girls scarcely in their teens; while unnatural alliances of every description, which in any other community would be regarded with disgust and abhorrence, are here entered into in the name of God. . . .

> It is quite a common thing in Utah for a man to marry two and even three sisters. . . . I know also another man who married a widow with several children; and when one of the girls had grown into her teens he insisted on marrying her also, having first by some means won her affections. The mother, however, was much opposed to this marriage, and finally gave up her husband entirely to her daughter; and to this very day the daughter bears children to her stepfather, living as wife in the same house with her mother! (*Tell It All*, 1874, pp.468-69).

Stanley P. Hirshon states: "Some Utah matches were even more startling. A man named Winchester married his mother, and Young himself sealed a mother and daughter to their cousin, Luman A. Shurtliff. . . . He also sealed an elderly man to a fifty-seven-year-old woman and her fourteen-year-old granddaughter" (*The Lion of the Lord*, p.126).

The anti-Mormon writer Joseph H. Jackson charged that Joseph Smith "feigned a revelation to have Mrs. Milligan, *his own sister, married to him spiritually*" (*The Adventures and Experience of Joseph H. Jackson . . .* , 1846, p.29). That Joseph Smith believed that a man could be married for eternity to his own sister has been confirmed by an entry added to Joseph

Smith's private diary after his death. It appears under the date of October 26, 1843, and reads as follows:

> The following named deceased persons were sealed to me (John M. Bernhisel) on Oct. 26th, 1843, by Pres. Joseph Smith—
>
> Maria Bernhisel, *Sister*—
> Brother Samuel's wife, Catherine Kremer
> Mary Shatto (Aunt)
> . . . .
> Recorded by Robt. L. Cambell
> July 29, 1868 (Joseph Smith's Diary, October 26, 1843, church historical dept.).

The reader will notice that Bernhisel claims that he was *sealed to his own sister by Joseph Smith*. Now, if the doctrine of Celestial Marriage were true, in the resurrection John Bernhisel would find himself married to his own sister, Maria Bernhisel! Stanley P. Hirshon claims:

> . . . Catherine, who lived with Kimball's family for twelve weeks, found plural marriage revolting. After the Twelve began taking Smith's wives, she heard Kimball might be *sealed to his own daughter*, Helen, the prophet's youngest widow. But in Catherine's presence Helen, . . . boldly told her mother: "I will never be sealed to my Father, . . . I will never be sealed to my Father; no, I will sooner be damned and go to hell, if I must. Neither will I be sealed to Brigham Young" (*The Lion of the Lord*, p.67).

There is evidence that John Taylor, who became the third president of the church, promised his sister that she could be sealed to him in the event that she could not be reconciled to continue with any of her husbands. L. John Nuttall recorded the following:

> Monday Feb 25/89. . . . Agnes Schwartz & her daughter Mary called this morning to see Prest. Woodruff, on her family matters. which he promised to write to her about. She said that *her brother John* the late *President John Taylor* had told her some 30 years ago that if She could not be reconciled to continue with any of her husbands *she might be sealed to his brother William or himself*. and she now wanted to be *sealed to him*. This is a very curious proceeding & which I dont understand (Journal of L. John Nuttall, vol. 2, pp.362-63 of typed copy at the Brigham Young University Library).

God and Christ Polygamists?

At the time the Mormon church was practicing polygamy the leaders of the church became very bitter against the one-wife system. Heber C. Kimball, first counselor to Brigham Young, was reported by the *Deseret News* as saying:

> I have noticed that a man who has but one wife, and is inclined to that doctrine, soon begins to wither and dry up, while a man who goes into plurality looks fresh, young and sprightly. Why is this? Because God loves that man, and because he honors his word. Some of you may not believe this, but I not only believe it but I also know it. For a man of God to be confined *to one woman is small business* . . . I do not know what we should do if we had only one wife apiece (*Deseret News*, April 22, 1857).

In a sermon reported in the church's *Deseret News* on August 6, 1862, Brigham Young stated:

> *Monogamy*, or restrictions by law to one wife, *is no part of the economy of heaven* among men. Such a system was commenced by the founders of the Roman empire. . . . Rome became the mistress of the world, and introduced this order of monogamy wherever her sway was acknowledged. Thus this monogamic order of marriage, so esteemed by modern Christians as a holy sacrament and divine institution, is nothing but a *system established by a set of robbers*. . . .

> Why do we believe in and practice polygamy? Because the Lord introduced it to his servants in a revelation given to Joseph Smith, and the Lord's servants have always practised it. "And is that religion popular in heaven?" It is the only popular religion there . . . (*Deseret News*, August 6, 1862).

Apostle George A. Smith boasted:

> We breathe the free air, we have the best looking men and hand-somest women, and if they envy us our position, well they may, for they are a poor, narrow minded, pinch-backed race of men, who chain themselves down to the law of monogamy and live all their days under the dominion of one wife. They ought to be ashamed of such conduct, and the still fouler channel which flows from their practices . . . (*Deseret News*, April 16, 1856).

Brigham Young said that the "monogamic system" had been a "fruitful source of prostitution and whoredom throughout all the Christian monogamic cities of the Old and New World . . ." (*Journal of Discourses*, vol. 11, p.128).

The following appeared in the church's *Millennial Star*: ". . . the *one-wife system not only degenerates the human family*, both physically and intellectually, but it is entirely incompatible with philosophical notions of immortality; it is a lure to temptation, and has always *proved a curse to a people*" (vol. 15, p.227).

George Q. Cannon claimed that the children of polygamists,

"besides being equally as bright and brighter intellectually, are much more healthy and strong (*Journal of Discourses*, vol. 13, p.207).

Brigham Young also believed that polygamy "is far superior to monogamy for the raising of healthy, robust children!" (p.317).

Brigham Young taught that Adam was a polygamist: "When our father Adam came into the garden of Eden, he came into it with a celestial body, and brought Eve, *one of his wives* with him" (vol. 1, p.50).

Some of the Mormon people believed "that Joseph Smith the Prophet taught that Adam had two wives" (vol. 26, p.115).

Some of the leading authorities of the church went so far as to proclaim that both the Father and the Son were polygamists. Jedediah M. Grant, second counselor to Brigham Young, made these comments:

> Celsus was a heathen philosopher; and what does he say upon the subject of Christ and his Apostles. . . . He says, "The grand reason why the Gentiles and philosophers of his school persecuted *Jesus Christ*, was, because *he had so many wives*; there were Elizabeth, and Mary, and a host of others that followed him." . . .
>
> The grand reason of the burst of public sentiment in anathemas upon Christ and his disciples, causing his crucifixion, was evidently based on polygamy. . . . A belief in the doctrine of a plurality of wives caused the persecution of Jesus, and his followers. We might almost think they were "Mormons" (*Journal of Discourses*, vol. 1, pp.345-46).

Apostle Orson Hyde asserted:

> It will be borne in mind that once on a time, there was a marriage in Cana of Galilee; . . . no less a person than *Jesus Christ was married* on that occasion. If he was never married, *his intimacy with Mary and Martha*, and the other Mary also whom Jesus loved, must have been highly unbecoming and improper to say the least of it.
>
> I will venture to say that if Jesus Christ were now to pass through the most pious countries in Christendom with a train of women, such as used to follow him, . . . he would be mobbed, tarred, and feathered, and rode not on an ass, but on a rail. . . .
>
> At this doctrine the long-faced hypocrite and the sanctimonious bigot will probably cry, blasphemy! . . . Object not, therefore, too strongly against the marriage of Christ . . . (*Journal of Discourses*, vol. 4, pp.259-60).

I discover that some of the Eastern papers represent me as a great

DESERET NEWS.

TRUTH AND LIBERTY.

GREAT SALT LAKE CITY, WEDNESDAY, AUGUST 6, 1862.

VOL. XII.

polygamist. And Paul says, "and if ye be Christ's then are ye Abraham's seed, and heirs according to the promise." D'd Abraham believe in Presbyterianism? Not much. Did he believe in Quakerism? Not much if ... ..., ... in sects of religion have some truth, and so are as they have the truth so far did Abraham believe. But 'is the religion of any one of the sects, as a whole, the religion of heaven? It is not. We all desire to join the popular party. Light, truth and intelligence are the side that is popular with the heavens, and the side that will rule, govern, and control the nations. If we join that society, we then all become popular with the popular party. Some people will render themselves ridiculous by topic out, on purpose to become popular. Their desire for popularity or notoriety is so great that they will not hesitate to do a mean act to gain it. The great majority want to be on the safe, wealthiest, and most popular side, and to be connected with that family which is possessed of immense wealth, influence, and power. Many of my brethren of the Elders of Israel rise up here to speak to the people, and they cannot give utterance to their ideas. What is the matter? They are fearful of making a slight mistake in their language, which they think would make them unpopular. I wish they were as I am, in this respect, and did not care what people may think or say, but pour out what the Holy Ghost shall give them to say, regardless of consequences. We all want to be on the side that will produce the most safety, the most joy, and the most interesting happiness. I can say, without fear of successful contradiction, that the man or woman who believes that the religion of Jesus has a thorny path, does not understand nor enjoy the true religion of heaven. We can say to all the world that the perse-

journey doing everything he can to restore the sick to sound health, and giving them all possible comfort and aid. Is there the same care and tender feeling manifested in the midst of emigration who are passing over the country in search of gold? Each person is seeking to better his condition, and they have no interest that extends further than self. It is with them as with the man that prayed, "O Lord, bless me, my wife, my son John and his wife, we four, no more. Amen." They are for themselves, and not for the kingdom of God. They know that the world is going to destruction. They see the whole world in confusion—one party seeking to destroy another in the vain hope of building themselves up. The present government of the United States is self-destroying, as they are now proving.

If there is one class of persons on earth who need comfort more than another, it is both the poor and rich who will not serve God. Those who serve him are comforted all the day long; they walk in the light of his salvation, even under the smiles of his countenance, and the works of their hands are abundantly prosperous. Still some apostatize from all this light—from this great salvation—to get gold. The reason of this is not because they have to offer so much for their religion, but because they have not enough good common sense. What is the grace of God? Who can define it? You say it is the favor of God. If you had good common sense, you never would be out of his favor. He is the Father of our spirits—the great ruler of the universe. If we had enough common sense to understand things as they are, we certainly would choose to serve him, and be on the strongest side.

Do we intend to make our all abode in hell, or in heaven? If we mean it to be in heaven, we must become faithful Latter Day

David, and the prophets down to the days of the Apostles.

Monogamy, or restrictions by law to one wife, is no part of the economy of heaven among men. Such a system was commenced by the founders of the Roman empire. That empire was founded on the ranks of the Tiber by wandering brigands. When these robbers founded the city of Rome, it was evident to them that their success in attaining a balance of power with their neighbors, depended upon introducing females into their body politic, so they stole them from the Sabines, who were near neighbors. The scarcity of women gave existence to laws restricting one wife to one man. Rome became the mistress of the world, and introduced this order of monogamy wherever her sway was acknowledged. This monogamic order of marriage, so esteemed by modern Christians, as a holy sacrament and divine institution, is nothing but a system established by a set of robbers.

The Congress of the United States have lately passed a law to punish polygamy in the Territories of the United States and in other places over which they have exclusive jurisdiction. In doing this, they have undertaken to dictate the Almighty in his revelations to his people, and those who handle edged tools, unless they are skillful, are apt to cut their fingers; and those who band out insult to the great I Am, in the end, are apt to get more than they have spoken for.

Why do we believe in and practice polygamy? Because the Lord introduced it to his servants in a revelation given to Joseph Smith, and the Lord's servants have always practiced it. "And is that religion popular in heaven?" It is the only popular religion there, for this is the religion of Abraham, and, unless we do the works of Abraham, we are not Abraham's seed and heirs according

A photograph of the *Deseret News*, August 6, 1862. Brigham Young claimed that Monogamy is a system "established by a set of robbers."

blasphemer, because I said, in my lecture on Marriage, at our last Conference, that *Jesus Christ was married* at Cana of Galilee, that *Mary, Martha, and others were his wives,* and that he begat children.

All that I have to say in reply to that charge is this—they worship a Savior that is too pure and holy to fulfill the commands of his Father. I worship one that is just pure and holy enough "to fulfill all righteousness;" not only the righteous law of baptism, but the still more righteous and important law "to multiply and replenish the earth" (vol. 2, p.210).

When the "Gentiles" stated that polygamy was one of the "relics of barbarism," Brigham Young replied: "Yes, one of the relics of Adam, of Enoch, of Noah, of Abraham, of Isaac, of Jacob, of Moses, David, Solomon, the Prophets, of *Jesus*, and his Apostles" (vol. 11, p.328).

On another occasion Young said: "The Scripture says that He, the LORD, came walking in the Temple, with His train; I do not know who they were, unless *His wives* and children . . ." (vol. 13, p.309).

Orson Pratt commented:

> . . . it will be seen that the great Messiah who was the founder of the Christian religion, *was a polygamist,* . . . the Messiah chose to . . . by marrying many honorable wives himself, show to all future generations that he approbated the plurality of wives under the Christian dispensation. . . .

> We have now clearly shown that *God the Father had a plurality of wives,* one or more being in eternity, by whom He begat our spirits as well as the spirit of Jesus His first Born, and another being upon the earth by whom He begat the tabernacle of Jesus, as his only begotten in this world. We have also proved most clearly that the Son followed the example of his Father, and became the great Bridegroom to whom kings' daughters and many honorable wives were to be married. We have also proved that *both God the Father and our Lord Jesus Christ inherit their wives in eternity* as well as in time; . . . it would be so shocking to the modesty of the very pious ladies of Christendom to see Abraham and his wives, Jacob and his wives, *Jesus and his honorable wives,* all eating occasionally at the same table, . . . If you do not want your morals corrupted, and your delicate ears shocked and your pious modesty put to the blush by the society of polygamists and their wives, do not venture near the New Earth; for polygamists will be honored there, and will be among the chief rulers in that Kingdom (*The Seer,* p.172).

> If none but Gods will be permitted to multiply immortal children, it follows that each God must have one or more wives (p.158).

and reputation here that it has in London, New York, Boston, Philadelphia, or Washington, then we might be comparatively silent while such vices carried the popular sway. But anything unusual, and of a corrupting character in our midst, excites in us an indignation that often finds vent in maledictions upon the heads of the demons that attempt to introduce it.

If there were none but Latter-day Saints living in Utah, we should have no occasion to speak upon this subject as we do; but being infested by those "*who profess the pure morality of the religion of Jesus*," such as the *Charleston Mercury* endorses and eulogizes, we are constrained to speak in great plainness. I will now leave this subject, knowing that he or she that is righteous will be righteous still; and they who are filthy will be filthy still.

I discover that some of the Eastern papers represent me as a great blasphemer, because I said, in my lecture on Marriage, at our last Conference, that Jesus Christ was married at Cana of Galilee, that Mary, Martha, and others were his wives, and that he begat children.

All that I have to say in reply to that charge is this—they worship a Savior that is too pure and holy to fulfil the commands of his Father. I worship one that is just pure and holy enough " to fulfil all righteousness;" not only the righteous law of baptism, but the still more righteous and important law " to multiply and replenish the earth." Startle not at this! for even the Father himself honored that law by coming down to Mary, without a natural body, and begetting a son; and if Jesus begat children, he only " did that which he had seen his Father do."

But to return to our subject—the fellowship of the world. Unite with them just as far as you require them to unite with you, and upon the same principle. If they are hungry, feed them when in your power. If they are in distress, trouble, or difficulty, relieve them. Take them in when strangers, if they ask you. Be kind unto them and courteous; yet remember that God has given to you His Holy Spirit as a standard, to which the world should come. It is your duty to honor that standard, and to keep it erect. If the world have fellowship and union with you, let it be in the Spirit of the Lord. But if you allow that standard to fall in your own hearts, or to become recumbent, and you slide back into the spirit of the world and unite with them, you have virtually struck your colors to the enemy, and gone over to his side! The salt has lost its savor, and is become powerless to save. It is only fit to be cast out and trodden under foot of men.

If you love and respect the welfare of the world, never allow yourselves to imbibe their spirit, or to become one with them. For if you do, you cannot be a savior, but need one as well as they; for you both stand upon one and the same level. The world hated the Savior before they hated us, and they killed him because he would never unite in heart and spirit with them. They will kill some of us for the same cause. But blessed are the man and the woman that are hated by the world because they will not be one with them. " Do them all the good you can, and as little harm as possible."

In conclusion, the present is an important era, an era in which the nations are becoming angry. They thirst for each other's blood; and who knows but that all nations will, respectively, file off under the heads of Greek and Roman, or " Gog and Magog," to fight the terrible battles spoken of in sacred writ?

Ye Saints of Latter-days, keep your lamps trimmed and burning, that you walk not in darkness. Ye virgins, wise and foolish, awake, for, behold, the

A photograph of the *Journal of Discourses*, vol. 2, page 210. Apostle Orson Hyde claimed that Jesus was a polygamist.

the five virgins are actually virgins or females who are to be married to the Bridegroom, then all the rest of the saints would constitute the guests. Are not these five wise virgins the "honorable Wives" which the Psalmist represents the Son of God as having taken from among king's daughters?

From the passage in the forty-fifth Psalm, it will be seen that the great Messiah who was the founder of the Christian religion, was a Polygamist, as well as the Patriarch Jacob and the prophet David from whom He descended according to the flesh. Paul says concerning Jesus, "Verily he took not on him the nature of angels; but he took on him the seed of Abraham." (Heb. 2: 16.) Abraham the Polygamist, being a friend of God, the Messiah chose to take upon himself his seed; and by marrying many honorable wives himself, show to all future generations that he approbated the plurality of Wives under the Christian dispensation, as well as under the dispensations in which His Polygamist ancestors lived.

We have now clearly shown that God the Father had a plurality of wives, one or more being in eternity, by whom He begat our spirits as well as the spirit of Jesus His First Born, and another being upon the earth by whom He begat the tabernacle of Jesus, as His Only Begotten in this world. We have also proved most clearly that the Son followed the example of his Father, and became the great Bridegroom to whom kings' daughters and many honorable Wives were to be married. We have also proved that both God the Father and our Lord Jesus Christ inherit their wives in eternity as well as in time; and that God the Father has already begotten many thousand millions of sons and daughters and sent them into this world to take tabernacles; and that God the Son has the promise that "of the increase of his government there shall be no end;" it being expressly declared that the children of one of His Queens should be made Princes in all the earth. (See Psalm 45: 16.)

Jesus says there shall be weeping and gnashing of teeth, when ye shall see Abraham, and Isaac, and Jacob, and all the prophets in the kingdom of God, and you yourselves thrust out." (Luke 13: 28.) There are many in this generation so pious that they would consider themselves greatly disgraced to be obliged to associate with a man having a plurality of wives; would it not be well for such to desire a place separate from the kingdom of God, that they may not be contaminated with the society of these old Polygamists? And then it would be so shocking to the modesty of the very pious ladies of Christendom to see Abraham and his wives, Jacob and his wives, Jesus and his honorable wives, all eating occasionally at the same table, and visiting one another, and conversing about their numerous children and their kingdoms. Oh, ye delicate ladies of Christendom, how can you endure such a scene as this? Oh, what will you do, when you behold on the very gates of the holy Jerusalem the names of the Twelve sons of the four wives of the Polygamist Jacob? If you do not want your morals corrupted, and your delicate ears shocked, and your pious modesty put to the blush by the society of polygamists and their wives, do not venture near the holy Jerusalem, nor come near the New Earth; for Polygamists will be honored there, and will be among the chief rulers in that Kingdom.

Peter says, Likewise ye wives be in subjection to your own husbands, * * * * even as Sarah obeyed Abraham, calling him Lord: whose daughters ye are, as long as ye do well." (1 Peter 3: 1, 6.) The females in the first age of Christianity considered it a great honor to become the daughters of Abraham, but now they have become so righteous that they think it a disgrace to be found in the society of a Polygamist; and no doubt they would think their characters ruined for ever, if any one should be so immodest as to call them the daughters of the Polygamist Abraham. But we will tell them how to avoid this deep disgrace; they can cease to do well; for Peter says that it is only on

A photograph of *The Seer*, page 172. Apostle Orson Pratt claimed that both God the Father and Jesus were polygamists.

Fanny Stenhouse told of a woman who wanted to be sealed to Jesus Christ:

> One of the wives of Brigham Young—Mrs. Augusta Cobb Young
> . . . requested of her Prophet husband a favor of a most extraordi-
> nary description. She had forsaken her lawful husband and fam-
> ily . . . to join the Saints, . . . when the lady of whom I speak
> asked him to place her at the head of his household, he refused:
> . . . finding that she could not be Brigham's "queen," and having
> been taught by the highest Mormon authorities that our Savior
> had, and has, many wives, she requested to be "sealed" to him!
> Brigham Young told her (for what reason I do not know) that it
> really was out of his power to do that, but that he would do "the
> next best thing" for her—he would "seal" her to Joseph Smith.
> So she was sealed to Joseph Smith, . . . in the resurrection she
> will leave him [Young] and go over to the original Prophet (*Tell It
> All,* p.255).

Stanley S. Ivins found evidence to show that Augusta Cobb Young was sealed to Joseph Smith as Mrs. Stenhouse indicated (see *Joseph Smith and Polygamy,* p.46).

It is interesting to note that some members of the Mormon church still maintain that God and Christ are polygamists. John J. Stewart, writing in 1961, explained:

> Now, briefly, the reason that the Lord, through the Prophet
> Joseph, introduced the doctrine of plural marriage, and the rea-
> son that the Church . . . has never and will never relinquish the
> doctrine of plural marriage, is simply this: The major purpose of
> the Church is to help man attain the great eternal destiny
> suggested in that couplet . . . *plural marriage* is the patriarchal
> order of marriage *lived by God* and others who reign in the
> Celestial Kingdom. As well might the Church relinquish its
> claim to the Priesthood as the doctrine of plural marriage
> (*Brigham Young and His Wives,* p.41).

> Plural marriage was a common practice among God's chosen
> people. . . . Mary, Martha, Mary Magdalene and many other
> women were beloved of Jesus. For a person to say that he believes
> the Bible but does not believe the doctrine of plural marriage is
> something akin to saying that he accepts the Constitution but
> not the Bill of Rights (p.26).

Writing in 1966, John J. Stewart continued to maintain that plural marriage "is the patriarchal order of marriage lived by God and others who reign in the Celestial Kingdom . . ." (*Joseph Smith the Mormon Prophet,* p.69).

Apostle LeGrand Richards, however, does not seem to agree with this idea (see his letter in *Mormonism—Shadow or Reality?* p.228).

Essential to Salvation

After a special conference held in 1852, the Mormon church leaders began to devote much of their time to the preaching of polygamy. During the period that the Mormon church was openly practicing polygamy, the leaders of the church were declaring that it was absolutely necessary and essential for exaltation. One woman testified as follows in the Temple Lot Case: "Yes, sir, President Woodruff, President Young, and President John Taylor, taught me and all the rest of the ladies here in Salt Lake that a man *in order to be exalted in the Celestial Kingdom must have more than one wife*, that having more than one wife was a means of exaltation" (*Temple Lot Case*, p.362).

Sixth president Joseph F. Smith spoke with clarity on the issue:

> Some people have supposed that the doctrine of plural marriage was a sort of superfluity, or non-essential to the salvation of mankind. In other words, some of the Saints have said, and believe that a man with one wife, sealed to him by the authority of the Priesthood for time and eternity, will receive an exaltation as great and glorious, if he is faithful, as he possibly could with more than one. I want here to *enter my protest against this idea, for I know it is false*. . . . Therefore, whoever has imagined that he could obtain the fullness of the blessings pertaining to this celestial law, by complying with only a portion of its conditions, has deceived himself. He cannot do it. When that principle was revealed to the Prophet Joseph Smith . . . an angel of God, with a drawn sword, stood before him and commanded that he should enter into the practice of that principle, or he should be utterly destroyed. . . .
>
> If then, this principle was of such great importance that the Prophet himself was threatened with destruction, and the best men in the Church with being excluded from the favor of the Almighty, if they did not enter into and establish the practice of it on earth, it is useless to tell me that there is no blessing attached to obedience to the law, or that a man with only one wife can obtain as great a reward, glory or kingdom as he can with more than one. . . .
>
> I understand the law of celestial marriage to mean that every man in this Church, who has the ability to obey and practice it in righteousness and will not, *shall be damned*. I say I understand it to mean this and nothing less, and I testify in the name of Jesus that it does mean that (*Journal of Discourses*, vol. 20, pp.28-31).

In 1891 the president and apostles of the Mormon church made the following statement in a petition to the President of the United States:

> We, the first presidency and apostles of the Church of Jesus Christ of Latter-Day Saints, beg to respectfully represent to Your Excellency the following facts:

> We formerly taught to our people that polygamy or Celestial Marriage as commanded by God through Joseph Smith was right; that it *was a necessity to man's highest exaltation* in the life to come.

> That doctrine was publicly promulgated by our president, the late Brigham Young, forty years ago, and was steadily taught and impressed upon the Latter-Day Saints up to September, 1890 (*Reed Smoot Case*, vol. 1, p.18).

In addition, the *Latter-Day Saints' Millennial Star* carried the following comments:

> And we, . . . are believers in the principles of plural marriage or polygamy, . . . as a principle revealed by God, *underlying our every hope of eternal salvation* and happiness in heaven . . . we cannot view plural marriage in any other light than as *a vital principle* of our religion (*Millennial Star*, vol. 40, pp.226-27).

> Upwards of forty years ago the Lord revealed to His Church the principle of celestial marriage. . . . the command of God was before them in language which no faithful soul dare disobey.

> "For, behold, I reveal unto you a new and an everlasting covenant and if ye abide not that covenant, then are ye damned; for no one can reject this covenant, and be permitted to enter into my glory. . . ."

> *Damnation was the awful penalty affixed* to a refusal to obey this law. It became an acknowledged doctrine of the Church; it was *indissolubly interwoven* in the minds of its members *with their hopes of eternal salvation* and exaltation in the presence of God. . . . Who could suppose that . . . Congress would enact a law which would present the alternative to religious believers of being consigned to a penitentiary if they should attempt to obey a law of God which would deliver them from damnation! (vol. 47, p.711).

William Clayton claimed that he learned from Joseph Smith that "the doctrine of plural and celestial marriage is the most holy and important doctrine ever revealed to man on the earth, and that without obedience to that principle no man can ever attain to the fulness of exaltation in the celestial glory" (*Historical Record*, vol. 6, p.226).

George Q. Cannon said that if he "had not obeyed that command of God, concerning plural marriage, I believe that I would have been damned" (*Journal of Discourses*, vol. 23, p.278).

they are traceable directly to some cause. I want to impress upon the minds of my hearers that the cause of such evils it not traceable to the practice of any principle which God has revealed touching these matters, but to the non-observance of them; and this is true in relation to every principle of the Gospel. Sometimes it is the fault of the man, sometimes of the woman, and oftener of both, but never the fault of the principle. The principle is correct, great, ennobling and calculated to bring joy, satisfaction and peace, if we would but observe and practice it as we should. But in order to do this we must get wisdom and understanding. These, by many, are acquired only through long experience. We begin as children, we have to learn precept by precept, line after line, here a little and there a little, which is good, provided we profit by that which we learn. Men must be just, so also must women, in relation to these matters. All must be just one towards another; also forbearing and patient, cultivating largely that Christian attribute called Charity, in order to get along peaceably with our neighbors, our brethren and sisters, as well as with our wives, husbands and children. We are all imperfect, we have to learn by littles as we pass along, profiting ofttimes by that which we suffer, yet often repeating the same errors. When we find ourselves overcome in a fault, that should be set down as an example for future time, if possible, never allowing ourselves to be caught in the same predicament again. Thus profiting by the experience we gain. Some people have supposed that the doctrine of plural marriage was a sort of superfluity, or non-essential to the salvation or exaltation of mankind. In other words, some of the Saints have said, and believe, that a man with one wife, sealed to him by the authority of the Priesthood for time and eternity, will receive an exaltation as great and glorious, if he is faithful, as he possibly could with more than one. I want here to enter my solemn protest against this idea, for I know it is false. There is no blessing promised except upon conditions, and no blessing can be obtained by mankind except by faithful compliance with the conditions, or law, upon which the same is promised. The marriage of one woman to a man for time and eternity by the sealing power, according to the law of God, is a fulfillment of the celestial law of marriage in part—and is good so far as it goes—and so far as a man abides these conditions of the law, he will receive his reward therefor, and this reward, or blessing, he could not obtain on any other grounds or conditions. But this is only the beginning of the law, not the whole of it. Therefore, whoever has imagined that he could obtain the fullness of the blessings pertaining to this celestial law, by complying with only a portion of its conditions, has deceived himself. He cannot do it. When that principle was revealed to the Prophet Joseph Smith, he very naturally shrank, in his feelings, from the responsibilities thereby imposed upon him; foreseeing, as he did in part, the apparently insurmountable difficulties in the way of establishing it, in the face of popular opinion, the traditions and customs of many generations, the frowns, ridicule, slander, opposition and persecution of the world. Yes, this man of God, who dared to meet the opposition of the whole world with bold and fearless front, who dared to dispute the religious authority and accumulated learning and wisdom of the age—who dared everything for the truth, and shrank not even from

A photograph of the *Journal of Discourses*, vol. 20, page 28. Joseph F. Smith, who became the sixth president of the church, stated that a man with one wife could not receive as great an exaltation as a man with more than one.

Brigham Young declared on August 19, 1866: *"The only men who become Gods, even the Sons of God, are those who enter into polygamy"* (*Journal of Discourses*, vol. 11, p.269).

At one time Joseph Smith told Heber C. Kimball that if he didn't enter into polygamy *"he would lose his apostleship and be damned"* (*Life of Heber C. Kimball*, p.336).

Kimball Young stated: "One man recalled a Stake conference in Southern Utah where the brethren were bluntly told to marry in polygamy or 'resign their church offices' " (*Isn't One Wife Enough?* p.108).

The Mormon writer John J. Stewart, writing in 1961, still upheld the teaching that plural marriage leads to exaltation: "Plural marriage is a pattern of marriage designed by God as part of His plan of eternal progress to further His kingdom and exalt His children" (*Brigham Young and His Wives*, p.71).

Lying About Polygamy

Apostle John A. Widtsoe boldly asserted: "The Church ever operates in full light. There is no secrecy about its doctrine, aim, or work" (*Evidences and Reconciliations*, Single-Volume Edition, p.282). On page 226 of the same book, Apostle Widtsoe said: "From the beginning of its history the Church has opposed unsupported beliefs. It has fought half-truth and untruth."

John A. Widtsoe's claim that the Mormon church operates in full light and has from the beginning fought half truth and untruth can hardly be supported by existing facts. Actually, untruth and secrecy were used by the church leaders to cover up the doctrine of polygamy. Mormon writer William E. Berrett acknowledged: "In 1840 the doctrine was taught to a few leading brethren who, with the Prophet, secretly married additional wives in the following year. . . . Only the secrecy surrounding its practice prevented a wholesale apostasy from the Church in 1844" (*The Restored Church*, pp.247, 249).

As we have already shown, the early editions of the *Doctrine and Covenants* contained an article which condemned the practice of polygamy. Joseph Smith and other Mormon leaders used this article as a shield to hide behind. Mormon writer John J. Stewart agrees that "the marriage article, in Oliver Cowdery's handwriting, sustains monogamous marriage and denies any LDS practice of plural marriage. Joseph was not yet ready to publicly acknowledge this doctrine, even though he had spoken of it in confidence to a few close friends" (*Joseph Smith the Mormon Prophet*, p.103).

An example of how the "marriage article" was used to counteract the report that polygamy was being practiced is found in the Mormon publication *Times and Seasons* for September 1, 1842:

> Inasmuch as the public mind has been unjustly abused through the fallacy of Dr. Bennett's letters, we make an extract on the subject of marriage, showing the rule of the church on this important matter. The extract is from the *Book of Doctrine and Covenants*, and is the only rule allowed by the church.

> " . . . Inasmuch as this church of Christ has been reproached with the *crime of fornication, and polygamy*; we declare that we believe, that *one man should have one wife*; and one woman, but one husband, except in case of death, when either is at liberty to marry again" (*Times and Seasons*, vol. 3, p.909).

Joseph Smith emphatically denied accusations linking him to polygamy. In 1838 he answered some questions for the *Elder's Journal*. Question number seven was: "Do the Mormons believe in having more wives than one?" The answer was: "*No, not at the same time*" (*Elder's Journal*, as cited in *History of the Church*, vol. 3, p.28).

At one time Joseph Smith was accused of "drinking, swearing, carousing, dancing all night, &c., and that he keeps six or seven young females as wives. . . ." (Letter by Parley P. Pratt concerning Augustine Spencer's accusations, in *History of the Church*, vol. 6, pp.354-55.)

According to the *History of the Church*, on May 26, 1844, Joseph Smith absolutely denied the accusation that he was living in polygamy: "What a thing it is for a man to be accused of committing adultery, *and having seven wives, when I can only find one*. I am the same man, and as *innocent* as I was fourteen years ago; and I can *prove them all perjurers*" (vol. 6, p.411).

Mormon writer John J. Stewart admits that "due to the extreme prejudice existing against the doctrine, it had to be kept as confidential as possible, and even *public denials* of it made" (*Joseph Smith the Mormon Prophet*, pp.67, 68). The following notice was published in the *Times and Seasons*, volume 5, page 423:

THURSDAY, FEBRUARY 1, 1844.

NOTICE.

As we have lately been credibly informed, that an Elder of the Church of Jesus Christ, of Latter-day Saints, by the name of Hiram Brown, has been preaching *polygamy*, and other false and corrupt doctrines, in the county of Lapeer, state of Michigan.

This is to notify him and the Church in general, that he has been *cut off* from the church, *for his iniquity*; and he is further notified to appear at the Special Conference, on the 6th of April next, to make answer to these charges.

> JOSEPH SMITH,
> HYRUM SMITH,
> Presidents of said Church.

Joseph Smith's brother Hyrum, who was a member of the First Presidency of the church, also secretly practiced plural marriage while denying it openly. Besides the statement quoted above, on March 15, 1844, Hyrum Smith stated:

> . . . brother Richard Hewitt . . . states to me that some of your elders say, that a man having a certain priesthood, may have *as many wives as he pleases*, and that doctrine is taught here: I say unto you that *that man teaches false doctrines*, for there is *no such doctrine taught: neither is there any such thing practised here.* And any man that is found teaching privately or publicly any such doctrine, is culpable, and will stand a chance to be brought before the High Council, and lose his license and membership also: therefore he had better beware what he is about (*Times and Seasons*, March 15, 1844, vol. 5, p.474).

The *Times and Seasons* records a further denial: "We are charged with advocating a *plurality of wives*, and common property. Now this is as *false* as the many other ridiculous charges which are brought against us. . . . we do what others do not, practice what we preach" (vol. 4, p.143).

In the *Latter-Day Saints' Millennial Star* there appeared another repudiation of polygamy: "But, for the information of those who may be assailed by those *foolish tales about two wives*, we would say that *no such principle ever existed* among the Latter-day Saints, and never will: . . . the Book of Mormon, Doctrine and Covenants; and also all our periodicals are very strict on that subject, indeed far more so than the bible" (vol. 3, p.74).

In the June 19, 1844, issue of the *Nauvoo Neighbor*, a Mormon publication, Joseph Smith and his brother Hyrum set forth a number of falsehoods with regard to polygamy. When this material was reprinted in the *History of the Church*, it was altered to cover up the fact that Joseph and Hyrum had not told the truth (see *Mormonism–Shadow or Reality?* p.247).

After Joseph Smith's death, the Mormon leaders still tried to keep the doctrine of plural marriage secret. John J. Stewart stated: ". . . the doctrine had to be kept confidential until after the Saints reached Utah" (*Brigham Young and His Wives*, p.31).

He comes to tell your honorable body, that the temple your fathers erected to freedom, whither their sons assembled to hear her precepts and cherish her doctrines in their hearts, has been desecrated; its portals closed, so that those that go up hither, are forbidden to enter.

He comes to tell your honorable body, that the blood of the heroes and patriots of the revolution, who have been slain by wicked hands for enjoying their religious rights, the boon of heaven to man, has cried, and is crying in the ears of the Lord of Sabaoth, saying,'redress,redress our wrongs, O Lord God of the whole earth.

He comes to tell your honorable body, that the dying groans of infant innocence, and the shrieks of insulted and abused females—and many of them widows of revolutionary patriots have ascended up into the ears of Omnipotence, and are registered in the archives of eternity, to be had in the day of retribution, as a testimony against the whole nation, unless their cries and groans are heard by the representatives of the people, and ample redress made, as far as the nation can make it, or else the wrath of the Almighty will come down in fury against the whole nation.

Under all these circumstances, your memorialist prays to be heard by your honorable body, touching all the matters of his memorial;and as a memorial will be presented to congress this session, for redress of our grievances, he prays your honorable body will instruct the whole delegation of Pennsylvania, in both houses, to use all their influence in the national councils, to have redress granted.

And, as in duty bound, your memorialist will ever pray.

SIDNEY RIGDON, P. M.

TIMES AND SEASONS,

CITY OF NAUVOO,

THURSDAY, FEBRUARY 1, 1844.

NOTICE.

As we have lately been credibly informed, that an Elder of the Church of Jesus Christ, of Latter-day Saints, by the name of Hiram Brown, has been preaching Polygamy, and other false and corrupt doctrines, in the county of Lapeer, state of Michigan.

This is to notify him and the Church in general, that he has been cut off from the church, for his iniquity ; and he is further notified to appear at the Special Conference, on the 6th of April next, to make answer to these charges.

JOSEPH SMITH.
HYRUM SMITH.
Presidents of said Church.

THE GATHERING.
(Continued.)

Jared and his brother, together with the families that were with them, and their several offsprings, were greatly blessed of God, for a length of time upon this continent ; they prospered exceedingly. They were blessed with communion with the Lord, with revelations, visions, faith wisdom, and in all temporal blessings they became a great people. But when they transgressed the laws of God, the curse of Jehovah fell upon them, and they were swept from the face of the earth, according to the word of the Lord.

Abraham was made use of, he was selected and chosen as a peculiar personage, to whom God would commit his laws and ordinances, and to his seed after him, and in order that he might accomplish his purposes, he gave unto him, the land of Canaan as his inheritance, that he might be selected and set apart from all other nations; and this was the only principle upon which God could teach him his law, and establish the priesthood. It is true, that Abraham obtained it by faith, but then if he had not possessed faith, he would not have been a fit personage for the Lord to select, through whom he could communicate his will, and preserve a chosen seed upon the earth. Abraham, through a long train of afflictions, and in many trials, had proven his unflinching integrity and faithfulness to God, for many years, and when the Lord saw that he was a proper person to exalt, he said unto him, 'get thee out of thy country, and from thy kindred, and from thy father's house, unto a land that I will shew thee, and I will make of thee a great nation, and I will bless thee, and curse them that curse thee, and in thee shall all families of the earth be blessed.' And when Abraham had journeyed to the place appointed, 'the Lord appeared unto him and said, unto thy seed will I give this land,' and he afterwards entered into a covenant with Abraham, saying , 'unto thy seed have I given this land, from the river of Egypt unto the great river, the river Euphrates. The Kenites, and the Kennizites, and the Kadmonites, and the Hittites, and the Perrizites, and the Rophaines, and the Ammorites, and the Canaanites, and the Girgashites, and the Jebusites.'

That land was given unto Abraham, and unto his seed, for an everlasting inheritance, and 'Isaac, and Jacob were heirs with him, of the same promise.' The land was allotted unto the

A photograph of the *Times and Seasons*, vol. 5, page 423. Joseph Smith orders a man cut off from the church for preaching polygamy.

On May 1, 1845, the following statement appeared in the *Times and Seasons* (vol. 6, p.894):

> Sidney Rigdon, I see by the papers, has made an exposition of Mormonism, charging Joseph Smith and the Mormons with *polygamy*, &c. . . .

> As to the charge of polygamy, I will quote from the Book of Doctrine and Covenants, which is the subscribed faith of the church and is strictly enforced. . . . "Inasmuch as this church of Christ has been reproached with the crime of fornication and *polygamy*, we declare that we believe that *one man should have but one wife*, and one woman but one husband. . . ."

Again, another article published in the *Times and Seasons*, November 15, 1844 proclaimed: "The law of the land and the *rules of the church* do not allow one man to have more than one wife alive at once . . ." (vol. 5, p.715).

When someone stated that Joseph Smith taught polygamy, the *Latter-Day Saints' Millennial Star*, volume 12, pages 29-30, called it a lie:

"12th *Lie—Joseph Smith taught a system of polygamy.*

"12th *Refutation.*—The Revelations given through Joseph Smith, state the following . . . 'We believe that *one man should have one wife.' Doctrine and Covenants*, page 331."

As late as 1850 John Taylor, who became the third president of the church, denied that the church believed in the practice of plural marriage, when he himself at the time had six living wives. In a public discussion in Boulogne-Sur-Mer, France, he stated:

> We are accused here of polygamy, and actions the most indelicate, obscene, and disgusting, such that none but a corrupt and depraved heart could have contrived. These things are too outrageous to admit of belief: . . . I shall content myself by reading our views of chastity and marriage, from a work published by us, containing some of the articles of our Faith. "Doctrine and Covenants," page 330 . . . Inasmuch as this Church of Jesus Christ has been reproached with the crime of fornication and polygamy, we declare that we believe that one man should have one wife, and one woman but one husband, except in case of death, when either is at liberty to marry again (A tract published by John Taylor in 1850, p.8; found in *Orson Pratt's Works*, 1851 edition).

Finally, in 1852, after years of deception, the Mormons publicly admitted that they were practicing polygamy.

The Manifesto

President John Taylor said that he believed in keeping all the laws of the United States except "The law in relation to polygamy" (*Journal of Discourses*, vol. 20, p.317).

Thomas G. Alexander, assistant professor of history at Brigham Young University, admitted that members of the Mormon church defied the law:

> Some maintain that because Mormons were law abiding they gave up plural marriage after the Supreme Court declared the anti-polygamy acts constitutional. But long after the 1879 Reynolds decision, Church members brought to bar for sentencing told federal judges that the law of God was higher than the law of the land and deserved prior obedience. The Manifesto officially ending polygamy as Church practice was not issued until 1890, and excommunication for practicing plural marriage did not come until 1904 (*Dialogue: A Journal of Mormon Thought*, Summer 1966, p.128).

The Mormons continued openly to preach polygamy until the year 1890. During this time the leaders taught that plural marriage was going to be a permanent part of the church and that it would never be stopped. Heber C. Kimball, first counselor to Brigham Young, commented:

> The principle of *plurality of wives never will be done away,* although some sisters have had revelations that, when this time passes away and they go through the veil, every woman will have a husband to herself (*Deseret News*, November 7, 1855).

> Some quietly listen to those who speak against the Lord's servants, against his anointed, against the plurality of wives, and against every principle that God has revealed. Such persons have half-a-dozen devils with them all the time. *You might as well deny "Mormonism," and turn away from it, as to oppose the plurality of wives.* Let the Presidency of this Church, and the Twelve Apostles, and all the authorities unite and say with one voice that they will oppose the doctrine, *and the whole of them will be damned* (*Journal of Discourses*, vol. 5, p.203).

> I speak of plurality of wives as one of the most holy principles that God ever revealed to man, and all those who exercise an influence against it, unto whom it is taught, man or woman, *will be damned,* . . . the curse of God will be upon them . . . (*Journal of Discourses*, vol. 11, p.211).

> It would be as easy for the United States *to build a tower to remove the sun, as to remove polygamy,* or the Church and kingdom of God (*Millennial Star*, vol. 28, p.190).

President John Taylor boldly asserted:

> God has given us a revelation in regard to celestial marriage. I did not make it. He has told us certain things pertaining to this

matter, and they would like us to tone that principle down and change it and make it applicable to the views of the day. This we cannot do; nor can we interfere with any of the commands of God to meet the persuasions or behests of men. I cannot do it, and will not do it.

I find some men try to twist around the principle in any way and every way they can. They want to sneak out of it in some way. Now God don't want any kind of sycophany like that. . . . If God has introduced something for our glory and exaltation, we are *not going to have that kicked over* by any improper influence, either *inside* or outside of the Church of the living God (*Journal of Discourses*, vol. 25, pp.309-10).

Apostle Orson Pratt added these resolute comments about polygamy:

God has told us Latter-day Saints that we shall be condemned if we do not enter into that principle; and yet I have heard now and then . . . a brother or sister say, "I am a Latter-day Saint, but I do not believe in polygamy." Oh, what an absurd expression! *What an absurd idea!* A person might as well say, "I am a follower of the Lord Jesus Christ, but I do not believe in him." One is just as consistent as the other. . . . *If the doctrine of polygamy*, as revealed to the Latter-day Saints, *is not true, I would not give a fig for all your other revelations* that came through Joseph Smith the Prophet; I would renounce the whole of them, because it is utterly impossible, according to the revelations that are contained in these books, to believe a part of them to be divine—from God—and a part of them to be from the devil . . . I did hope there was more intelligence among the Latter-day Saints, and a greater understanding of principle than to suppose that any one can be a member of this Church in good standing, and yet reject polygamy. The Lord has said, that those who reject this principle *reject their salvation, they shall be damned*, saith the Lord . . .

Now I want to prophecy a little. . . . I want to prophecy that all men and women who oppose the revelation which God has given in relation to polygamy will find themselves in darkness; the Spirit of God will withdraw from them the very moment of their opposition to that principle, until they will finally go down to hell and be damned, if they do not repent . . . if you want to get into darkness, brethren and sisters, begin to oppose this revelation. Sisters, you begin to say before your husbands, or husbands you begin to say before your wives, "I do not believe in the principle of polygamy, and I intend to instruct my children against it." Oppose it in this way, and teach your children to do the same, and *if you do not become as dark as midnight there is no truth in Mormonism* (*Journal of Discourses*, vol. 17, pp.224-25).

God requires. When that is done, the sins of the people will be remitted. I speak of this, that you may understand that your re-baptisms must be agreeable to the order laid down. It is not simply a man's saying, "Having been commissioned by Jesus Christ, I baptise you for the renewal of your covenant and remission of your sins," but you must be subject to your brethren and fulfil the law of God.

Supposing you have sinned against your brethren, or in some way offended them, will your sins be remitted, unless you go and make the proper acknowledgments? No, they will not. You have got to pay the debt; and sin cannot be remitted until you confess it and make satisfaction to the party aggrieved. You may try another course as much as you please, but you will find it to be just as I have told you.

If I have offended brother Brigham in any way whatever—rebelled against him, lied about him, or sought to abuse him, what is the use of my going to the water to renew my covenant, until I have made satisfaction to him? The proper way would be to go to him and say, "Brother Brigham, I lied against you wilfully, under the influence of an evil spirit;" or, "I have ill-treated and wronged you, and know that I must make satisfaction, and I am ready to do anything that you say." Satisfaction must be made to the one injured, or baptism will be of no benefit: the Holy Ghost will not ratify that act until I have paid the debt. Then brother Brigham would say, "I forgive you, and pray my Father, in the name of Jesus, to forgive you also." Then our Father in heaven would forgive you, and the Son, and the Holy Ghost would forgive you. And if you get pardon of those you have injured, and of the Father, Son, and Holy Ghost, you are free and ready to begin a new life.

You have heard brother Brigham say that if we sin against the Father, we must confess our sins to him, and get pardon from him; and if we sin against the Son, we must ask pardon of him, for he will not pardon you without you do ask him; and if you sin against the Holy Ghost you cannot get pardon, for that is a sin which cannot be forgiven. You must do that which is right, and get the forgiveness of the Father and the Son; then they and the Holy Ghost will take up their abode with you. That is my faith, and that is a part of "Mormonism," as I understand it.

If men and women make a practice of lying, stealing, and doing other things forbidden in the law of God, they need not go into the water until they have sincerely repented and will covenant and promise that they will not do those things again. Some of you make a practice of telling little lies, of deceiving and be rating each other, of disputing with each other, and with the servants of God. Is that right? You all know that it is not, and that God will punish you for it. Does the Son know when you do these things? Does the Holy Ghost know? Do the angels know? I answer, they do know, and they are displeased with such acts, and will not associate with you in consequence of them.

Some quietly listen to those who speak against the Lord's servants, against his anointed, against the plurality of wives, and against almost every principle that God has revealed. Such persons have half-a-dozen devils with them all the time. You might as well deny "Mormonism," and turn away from it, as to oppose the plurality of wives. Let the Presidency of this Church, and the Twelve Apostles, and all the authorities unite and say with one voice that they will oppose that doctrine, and the whole of them would be damned. What are you opposing

A photograph of the *Journal of Discourses, vol. 5, page 203.* Heber C. Kimball stated that a person might just as well deny Mormonism as to oppose polygamy.

President Brigham Young was very emphatic in proclaiming that the church could never give up polygamy:

> Now if any of you will *deny the plurality of wives* and continue to do so, *I promise that you will be damned;* . . . take this revelation, . . . and deny it in your feelings, and I promise that you will be damned (*Deseret News*, November 14, 1855).

> I heard the revelation on polygamy, and I believed it with all my heart, and I know it is from God . . . "Do you think that we shall ever be admitted as a State into the Union without denying the principle of polygamy?" *If we are not admitted until then, we shall never be admitted* (*Deseret News*, October 10, 1866).

George Q. Cannon, who was a member of the First Presidency, unabashedly preached:

> There has been some agitation . . . respecting plural marriage, and some people, calling themselves Latter-day Saints, have been almost ready to go into the open market, and bid for a State government, at the price of conceding this principle of our religion. . . . They are ready *to sell out their belief* as Latter-day Saints . . . for the sake of obtaining a little recognition of their rights as citizens. . . . Can such persons retain the Spirit of God, and take such a course as this? *No. they cannot* (*Journal of Discourses*, vol. 26, pp.7-8).

> *If plural marriage be divine, as the Latter-day Saints say it is, no power on earth can suppress it,* unless you crush and destroy the entire people. . . . If you are sentenced to prison for marrying more wives than one, round up your shoulders and bear it; prepare yourselves to take the consequences (*Journal of Discourses*, vol. 20, p.276).

> As the principle of patriarchal marriage is the one now so savagely attacked, this is the one such persons are preparing themselves to yield. I view such men as *apostates* already in heart. They are *more dangerous than our open enemies.* . . . If there are any in the Church who cannot stand the pressure instead of talking compromise, *let them withdraw* quietly from the Church (*Juvenile Instructor*, vol. 20, p.156).

Apostle George Teasdale bore this testimony concerning plural marriage:

> I believe in plural marriage as a part of the Gospel, just as much as I believe in baptism by immersion for the remission of sins. The same being who taught me baptism for the remission of sins, taught me plural marriage, and its necessity and glory. Can I afford to give up a single principle? I can not. If I had to give up one principle I would have to give up my religion. . . . I bear my solemn testimony that plural marriage is as true as any principle

that has been revealed from the heavens. I bear my testimony
that it is a necessity, and that the Church of Christ in its fulness
*never existed without it. Where you have the eternity of marriage
you are bound to have plural marriage; bound to;* and it is one of
the marks of the Church of Jesus Christ in its sealing ordinances
(*Journal of Discourses*, vol. 25, p.21).

Wilford Woodruff, who later became the fourth president of
the church and issued the manifesto in 1890 which was supposed to stop the practice of polygamy, openly declared in
1869: "*If we were to do away with polygamy,* it would only be
one feather in the bird. . . . Do away with that, then *we must do
away with prophets and Apostles,* with revelation and the gifts
and graces of the Gospel, . . . and finally give up our religion
altogether. . . . We just can't do that . . ." (*Journal of Discourses*,
vol. 13, p.166).

The *Latter Day Saints Millennial Star* summarized the issue
sharply:

> . . . the God of Israel . . . commanded Joseph Smith, . . . and the
> Latter-day Saints, to obey this law, "or you shall be damned,"
> saith the Lord. Now, . . . the Congress of the United States, and
> the supreme judges of the nation, stand forth and say, "You shall
> be damned if you do obey it." . . . God says, "We shall be damned
> if we do not obey the law." Congress says, "We shall be damned
> if we do." It places us precisely in the . . . position that it did the
> Hebrews in the fiery furnace, and Daniel in the den of lions. . . .
> Now who shall we obey? God or man? My voice is that we obey
> God. . . . The Congress of 1862, and the supreme judges of 1879,
> in their acts and decisions, have taken a dangerous and fearful
> step; their acts will sap the very foundation of our government,
> and it will be rent asunder . . . (vol. 41, pp.242-43).

The Mormons did everything they could to escape the fed-
eral deputies. Kimball Young describes their tactics in the
book, *Isn't One Wife Enough:*

> In addition to false names, disguises, and ruses, a whole system
> of information gathering, signaling, and spotting informers was
> developed. For example, the church authorities would pass the
> word down to the smaller communities of movements of federal
> deputies out of Salt Lake City in the direction of any particular
> town" (p.396).

> At very early ages children were introduced into conspiratorial
> operations. Not talking to strangers, being part of a warning
> system, and being taught outright falsification were all elements
> in their training during those years which would certainly not
> be considered normal today (p.402).

267

Wilford Woodruff had an armed guard to protect him. In a letter written in 1887, Woodruff wrote: "I have a large stout man who goes with me every _____[where?] night and day *carries 2 pistols & a double barrel shot gun and sayes [sic] he will shoot the marshals if they come to take me* (Don't tell anybody this) so I am _____ well garded [sic]..." (Letter from Wilford Woodruff to Miss Nellie Atkin, dated September 3, 1887, microfilm copy of the original in our possession).

Mormon Leaders Yield

The U.S. Government continued to increase the pressure against polygamy, but the Mormons were determined to continue the practice. In an article published in the *Millennial Star* in 1865, the Mormon people were told that they could not give up polygamy and that there would not be a revelation to suppress the practice:

It is time that members of the Government and the public at large should understand the true state of the question, and the the real issues involved in these propositions. The doctrine of polygamy with the "Mormons," is not one of that kind that in the religious world is classed with "nonessentials." *It is not an item of doctrine that can be yielded, and faith in the system remain.* "Mormonism" is that kind of religion *the entire divinity of which is invalidated, and its truth utterly rejected, the moment that any one of its leading principles is acknowledged to be false.* . . .

The whole question, therefore, narrows itself to this in the "Mormon" mind. *Polygamy was revealed by God, or the entire fabric of their faith is false.* To ask them to give up such an item of belief, is to ask them to relinquish the whole, to acknowledge their Priesthood a lie, their ordinances a deception, and all that they have toiled for, lived for, bled for, prayed for, or hoped for, a miserable failure and a waste of life.

All this Congress demands of the people of Utah. It asks the repudiation of their entire religious practice to-day; and inasmuch as *polygamy* is, in "Mormon" belief, the basis of the condition of a future life, it asks them to *give up their hopes of salvation hereafter* . . . in requiring the relinquishment of polygamy, they ask the renunciation of the entire faith of this people. . . .

There is no half way house. The *childish babble about another revelation* is only an evidence *how half informed men can talk* . . . those who so unwisely seek to stir up the Government to wrath, will yet learn there is but one solution of the "Mormon" problem—"Mormonism" allowed in its entirety, or "Mormonism" wiped out in blood (*Millennial Star*, October 28, 1865).

Under the date of April 6, 1884, Abraham H. Cannon recorded in his journal: "At a Priesthood meeting . . . the strongest language in regard to Plural Marriage was used that I ever heard, and among other things it was stated that all men in position who would not observe and fulfill that law should be *removed from their places.*"

Shortly before the revelation known as the Manifesto (which put a stop to the practice of polygamy) was given, Lorenzo Snow, who later became president of the Mormon church, was declaring that no such revelation would come. When Lorenzo Snow was on trial for practicing polygamy, Mr. Bierbower, the prosecuting attorney, predicted that if he was convicted, "a new revelation would soon follow, changing the divine law of celestial marriage." To this Mr. Snow replied:

> Whatever fame Mr. Bierbower may have secured as a lawyer, *he certainly will fail as a prophet.* The severest prosecutions have *never been followed by revelations changing a divine law,* obedience to which brought imprisonment or martyrdom.

> Though I go to prison, *God will not change His law* of Celestial Marriage. But the man, the people, the nation, that oppose and fight against this doctrine and the Church of God, will be overthrown (*Historical Record*, p.144).

Although Lorenzo Snow said that the "severest prosecutions have never been followed by revelations changing a divine law," Mormon church President Wilford Woodruff issued the Manifesto in 1890. He claimed that it was given to stop the persecution the church would have to go through if they continued to practice polygamy. He stated: "The Lord showed me by vision and revelation exactly what would happen if we did not stop this practice . . . all ordinances would be stopped . . . many men would be made prisoners . . . I went before the Lord, and I wrote what the Lord told me to write . . ." (*Evidences and Reconciliations*, 1 vol. ed., pp.105-6).

Mormon writer John J. Stewart says that "President Wilford Woodruff issued the manifesto . . . suspending the general practice of it in the Church, while still retaining it as a doctrine" (*Brigham Young and His Wives*, pp.29-30).

Before Wilford Woodruff became president of the Mormon church he stated that the church could not give up polygamy (see *Journal of Discourses*, vol. 13, p.166). After he became president he even claimed to receive a revelation that he should not yield to the pressure of the government. Under the date of December 19, 1889, Apostle Abraham H. Cannon recorded in his journal:

During our meeting a revelation was read which Pres. Woodruff received Sunday evening, Nov'r 24th. Propositions had been made for the Church to make some concessions to the Courts in regard to its principles. Both of Pres. Woodruff's counselors refused to advise him as to the course he should pursue, and he therefore laid the matter before the Lord. The answer came quick and strong. *The word of the Lord was for us not to yield one particle* of that which he had revealed and established. He had done and would continue to care for His work and those of the Saints who were faithful, and we need have no fear of our enemies when we were in the line of duty. We are promised redemption and deliverance if we will trust in God and not in the arm of flesh . . . my heart was filled with joy and peace during the entire reading. It sets all doubts at rest concerning the course to pursue.

Because Wilford Woodruff had previously taught that polygamy could not be discontinued and had even claimed to receive revelation to that effect, the other leaders of the Mormon church were confused by his Manifesto.

After the Manifesto

Russell R. Rich commented:

When the statement called "The Manifesto," which was signed by President Wilford Woodruff, was voted upon for acceptance by the membership of the LDS Church . . . it appeared that there was a unanimous vote of support for abandonment of the practice of plural marriage. As time passed, however, it became apparent that not even among the general authorities of the church was there unanimous support for abolishing the practice (*Brigham Young University Leadership Week: Those Who Would Be Leaders*, by Russell R. Rich, p.71).

In October, 1891, Wilford Woodruff testified that the Manifesto not only prohibited any more plural marriages, but that it also forbade the unlawful cohabitation of those who were already married in polygamy:

Q. Your attention was called to the fact that nothing was said in that manifesto about the dissolution of existing polygamous relations. I want to ask you, President Woodruff, whether in your advice to the church officials, and the people of the church, you have advised them that your intention was, and that the requirement of the church was, that the polygamous relations already formed before that should not be continued; that is, there should be no association with plural wives; in other words, that unlawful cohabitation as it is named and spoken of should also stop, as well as future polygamous marriages? A. Yes, sir; that has been the intention (Testimony of Wilford Woodruff, as quoted in *Reminiscences of Early Utah*, p.246).

While Wilford Woodruff and other Mormon leaders were publicly stating that members of the church should observe the law, they were secretly teaching that it was alright to break the law concerning unlawful cohabitation. This is evident from a number of entries in the journal of the Apostle Abraham H. Cannon. For instance, on October 2, 1890, he wrote: "It was, however, resolved that 'we use our private influence at present to prevent our brethren from going into Court and promising to obey the law; and as soon as possible we take steps to get some favors from the government for those who already have more wives than one.'"

Under the date of October 7, 1890, Apostle Cannon records some of the statements by Mormon church leaders:

> Geo. Q. Cannon [a member of the First Presidency]: "I feel like saying 'Damn the law.' We can expect neither justice nor mercy in the administration of the law with the present corrupt administrators. . . . my family understand [sic] that my liberty depends on refraining from visiting them in their homes, and they are contented." W. Woodruff [President of the Church]: "This manifesto only refers to future marriages, and does not affect past conditions. I did not, could not and would not promise that you desert your wives and children. This you cannot do in honor." . . . Angus M. Cannon: "Because of the manifesto many will feel justified in promising to obey the law when brought into Court. I would not feel justified in such a course, but many may" ("Daily Journal of Abraham H. Cannon," October 7, 1890, BYU Library).

Under the dates of October 17 and 18, 1890, Apostle Cannon recorded the following in his journal:

> Uncle David . . . told me that he had a conversation with Lindsey Sprague, a deputy marshal, who told him that there were papers out for my arrest . . . I got Chas H Wilcken to investigate the matter for me and he learned that it was a fact that a warrant was issued and in Doyle's hands for my arrest. . . . Saturday, Oct. 18th, 1890. . . . Bro. Wilcken came and informed me that *he had bought Doyle off*, and had got his promise that I should not be molested, nor should any other person without *sufficient notice being given for them to escape*, and to get witnesses out of the way. He gave Bro. Wilcken the names of some 51 persons whose arrest he intended to try and effect. . . . A messenger was therefore despatched to give these people warning. Thus *with a little money a channel of communication is kept open between the government offices* and the suffering and persecuted Church members."

Although the leaders of the Mormon church had promised to obey the law of the land, many of them broke their promises. Few people, however, realized to what extent until the leaders were called to testify in the "Proceedings Before the Committee on Privileges and Elections of the United States Senate in the Matter of the Protests Against the Right of Hon. Reed Smoot, a Senator From the State of Utah, to Hold His Seat." Frank J. Cannon reported:

> The first oracular disclosure made by the Prophets, on the witness stand, came as a shock even to Utah. They testified that they had resumed polygamous cohabitation to an extent unsuspected by either Gentiles or Mormons. President Joseph F. Smith admitted that he had had eleven children borne to him by his five wives, since pledging himself to obey the "revealed" manifesto of 1890 . . . Apostle Francis Marion Lyman, . . . made a similar admission of guilt, though to a lesser degree. So did John Henry Smith and Charles W. Penrose, apostles. . . . So did a score of others. . . . And they confessed that they were living in polygamy in violation of their pledges to the nation and the terms of their amnesty, against the laws and the constitution of the state, and contrary to the "revelation of God" by which the doctrine of polygamy had been withdrawn from practice in the Church! . . . Bishop Chas. E. Merill, *the son of an apostle*, testified that *his father had married him to a plural wife in 1891* . . . Mrs. Clara Kennedy testified that she had been married to a polygamist *in 1896*, in Juarez, Mexico, by *Apostle Brigham Young, Jr.* . . . There was testimony to show that *Apostle George Teasdale* had taken a plural wife *six years after the 'manifesto'* . . . It was testified that *Apostle John W. Taylor had taken two plural wives within four years*, and that *Apostle M. F. Cowley had taken one*; and both these men *fled from the country* in order to escape a summons to appear before the Senate committee (*Under the Prophet in Utah*, pp.268-70).

Joseph F. Smith, sixth president of the church, testified as follows in the *Reed Smoot Case*:

> THE CHAIRMAN. Do you obey the law in having five wives at this time, and having them bear to you eleven children since the manifesto of 1890?
> MR. SMITH. Mr. Chairman, *I have not claimed that in that case I have obeyed the law of the land.*
> THE CHAIRMAN. That is all.
> MR. SMITH. I do not claim so, and I have said before that *I prefer to stand my chances against the law*" (*Reed Smoot Case*, vol. 1, p.197).

> MR. TAYLER. You say there is a State law forbidding unlawful cohabitation?

MR. SMITH. That is my understanding.
MR. TAYLER. And ever since that law was passed you have been
violating it?
MR. SMITH. I think likely I have been practicing the same thing
even before the law was passed" (Ibid., p.130).

THE CHAIRMAN. . . . you are violating the law?
MR. SMITH. The law of my State?
THE CHAIRMAN. Yes.
MR. SMITH. Yes, sir.
SENATOR OVERMAN. Is there not a revelation published in the Book
of Covenants here that you shall abide by the law of the State?
MR. SMITH. It includes both unlawful cohabitation and polygamy.
SENATOR OVERMAN. Is there not a revelation that you shall abide by
the laws of the State and of the land?
MR. SMITH. Yes, sir.
SENATOR OVERMAN. If that is a revelation, *are you not violating the
laws of God?*
MR. SMITH. *I have admitted that, Mr. Senator, a great many times
here.* (Ibid., pp.334-35).

The Apostle Francis M. Lyman testified as follows:

SENATOR HOAR. . . . You have said more than once that in living in
polygamous relations with your wives, which you do and intend
to do, you knew that you were *disobeying this revelation?*
MR. LYMAN. *Yes. sir*
SENATOR HOAR. And that in disobeying this revelation you were
disobeying the law of God?
MR. LYMAN. *Yes. sir.*
SENATOR HOAR. Very well. So that you say that you, an apostle of
your church, expecting to succeed, if you survive Mr. Smith, to
the office in which you will be the person to be the medium of
Divine revelations, are living and are known to your people to
live in *disobedience of the law of the land and of the law of God?*
MR. LYMAN. *Yes, sir* (Reed Smoot Case, vol. 1, p.430).

Charles E. Merrill, the son of Apostle Marriner W. Merrill,
testified that he took a plural wife after the Manifesto and that
his father performed the ceremony:

MR. TAYLER. And the next marriage took place in 1891?
MR. MERRILL. *Yes, sir.*
MR. TAYLER. Who married you in 1891?
MR. MERRILL. My father.
. . . .
MR. TAYLER. Was your father then an apostle?
MR. MERRILL. *Yes, sir* (Reed Smoot Case, vol. 1, p.409).

Walter M. Wolfe, who was at one time professor of geology at
Brigham Young College, claimed that Apostle John Henry

Smith made this statement to him: "Brother Wolfe, don't you know that the Manifesto is only a trick to beat the devil at his own game?" (*Reed Smoot Case*, vol. 4, p.13).

Anthony W. Ivins, who later became a member of the First Presidency of the Mormon church, was appointed by the church leaders to perform plural marriages in Mexico after the Manifesto. Stanley S. Ivins, the son of Anthony W. Ivins, told us that his father received instructions after the Manifesto to perform marriages for time and all eternity outside the Mormon temples. He received a ceremony for these marriages, which Stanley S. Ivins had in his possession. He was sent to Mexico and was told that when the First Presidency wanted a plural marriage performed they would send a letter with the couple who were to be married. Whenever he received these letters from the First Presidency, he knew that it was alright to perform the ceremony. He performed regular marriages as well as plural marriages and kept a record of each marriage in a book. After his father's death Stanley S. Ivins copied the names of those who had been married in polygamy into another book and then gave the original book to the Mormon leaders.

Wallace Turner relates the following:

> In Salt Lake City I talked to . . . Stanley S. Ivins, one of the great authorities on Mormon polygamy. His father was Anthony W. Ivins, who was an apostle and first counselor to President Heber J. Grant.
>
> Anthony Ivins was an elder in the church in the mid-1890s when he was called in and told to go to Mexico to be president of the stake there. He was told that he was to have authority to perform plural marriages for those who were sent to him for that purpose. He would be able to identify them from the letters of introduction they would present, he was told.
>
> After Anthony Ivins died in 1934 . . . his family found the records of these marriages among his papers. They were turned over to the LDS church. *More than fifty polygamous marriages were easily identifiable*, beginning in June, 1897, when three men from Utah were married at Juarez, just across from El Paso. They had crossed over into Mexico just for the marriage ceremony, then went back into the United States. However, Ivins refused to perform marriages for the regular population of the Mormon colonies because the men lacked the letters from Salt Lake City which he considered to be his authority for the ceremony. However, by 1898 polygamous marriages were being performed routinely in Mexico by other Mormon leaders (*The Mormon Establishment*, by Wallace Turner, 1966, p.187).

Stanley Ivins claimed that his father continued to perform

plural marriages for the church until the year 1904, some four-teen years after the Manifesto.

In the *Reed Smoot Case*, Walter M. Wolfe testified:

> MR. WOLFE. In the summer of 1897 I was in Colorado. On my return, at the beginning of the school year, I found that Ovena Jorgensen was not in attendance. She returned to school some time during the month of October. Shortly after her return, she came to my house and asked to see me privately. She said: "Brother Wolfe, I have something that I must tell you, the reason why I have been late in coming back to school. I have been married." I said, "Not in polygamy." She said: "Yes, sir; in polygamy. I have married Brother Okey."
>
> . . . .
>
> MR. WORTHINGTON. I say, it was in October, 1897, that she told you?
> MR. WOLFE. Yes, sir . . . she said that some years before she had gone into service at the house of this man Okey; that he had loved her and she loved him. He had asked her to marry him and she had declined, saying that it was impossible on account of the manifesto. . . . In August, 1897, Okey and the girl went together to see President Wilford Woodruff, and they laid the case before him. He brushed them aside with a wave of his hand and said he would have nothing to do with the matter, but referred them to President George Q. Cannon. George Q. Cannon asked if the girl had been through the Temple and received her endowments. They told him no. He said that that must be done first and then he would see as to the rest of it. They went through the Temple and the girl received her endowments. Then they were given a letter by President George Q. Cannon to President Ivins, of the Juarez Stake, and they went to Mexico.
> THE CHAIRMAN. Who was this letter to?
> MR. WOLFE. President A. W. Ivins, of the Juarez Stake.
> THE CHAIRMAN. Mexico?
> MR. WOLFE. Mexico; yes, sir. They went to Mexico, and there the girl told me the marriage ceremony was performed, and they returned to Utah (*The Reed Smoot Case*, vol. 4, pp.10-11).

Stanley S. Ivins confirmed the fact that his father, Anthony W. Ivins, performed the marriage ceremony and recorded it in his record book. Stanley Ivins claimed that Walter Wolfe's testimony concerning this marriage hurt the church's image so much that the First Presidency of the church sent Anthony Ivins a letter requesting him to go back to Washington, D.C. and give false testimony before the Committee on Privileges and Elections of the United States Senate. The First Presidency of the Mormon church actually wanted him to lie under oath and state that he did not perform the ceremony. Mr. Ivins stated that his father refused to go back to Washington and lie about the

275

marriage, even if Wolfe's testimony did damage the image of the church.

Frank J. Cannon, the son of George Q. Cannon and formerly the senator from Utah, gives this important information:

> Late in July, 1896, when I was in New York on business for the Presidency, I received a telegram announcing the death of my brother, Apostle Abraham H. Cannon. . . . I realized that my father would have a greater stroke of sorrow to bear than I. . . .
>
> I found him and Joseph F. Smith in the office of the Presidency . . . "I know how you feel his loss," he said hoarsely, "but when I think what he would have had to pass through if he had lived—I cannot regret his death." . . .
>
> With a sweep of his hand toward Smith at his desk—a gesture and a look the most unkind I ever saw him use—he answered: "A few weeks ago, Abraham took a plural wife, Lillian Hamlin. It became known. He would have had to face a prosecution in Court. His death has saved us from a calamity that would have been dreadful for the Church—and for the state."
>
> "Father!" I cried. "Has this thing come back again! And the ink hardly dry on the bill that restored your church property on the pledge of honor that there would never be another case—" I had caught the look of Smith's face, and it was a look of sullen defiance. "How did it happen?"
>
> My father replied: . . . "I was asked for my consent, and I refused it. President Smith obtained the acquiescence of President Woodruff, on the plea that it wasn't an ordinary case of polygamy but merely a fulfillment of the biblical instruction that a man should take his dead brother's wife. Lillian was betrothed to David, and had been sealed to him in eternity after his death. I understand that President Woodruff told Abraham he would leave the matter with them if he wished to take the responsibility—and President Smith performed the ceremony."
> . . . here was the beginning of a policy of treachery which the present church leaders, under Joseph F. Smith, have since consistently practised, in defiance of the laws of the state and the "revelation of God," with lies and evasions, with perjury and its subornation, in violation of the most solemn pledges to the country, and through the agency of a political tyranny that makes serious prosecution impossible and immunity a public boast (*Under the Prophet in Utah*, pp.176,177,179).

John Henry Hamlin, the brother of Lillian Hamlin, testified as follows in the "Reed Smoot Case":

> MR. TAYLER. What relation are you to Lillian Hamlin?
> MR. HAMLIN. Brother.

. . . .

Mr. Tayler. And whom did she marry?

Mr. Hamlin. I only know what I heard.

Mr. Tayler. What was your family conviction and understanding about that?

Mr. Hamlin. That she was married to a Mr. Cannon.

. . . .

Mr. Tayler. An apostle of the church?

Mr. Hamlin. I believe so. I understand so.

Mr. Tayler. That was in the summer of 1896, was it not?

Mr. Hamlin. Yes, sir.

Mr. Tayler. And where did you understand she was married?

Mr. Hamlin. On the Pacific coast.

Mr. Tayler. By whom?

Mr. Hamlin. Well, our understanding was that President Joseph F. Smith married her (*Reed Smoot Case*, vol. 2, pp.67-68).

Mrs. Wilhelmina C. Ellis, who had been a plural wife of the Mormon Apostle Abraham H. Cannon, testified:

Mr. Tayler. How old were you when you married Abraham Cannon?

Mrs. Ellis. Nineteen.

Mr. Tayler. You were a plural wife?

Mrs. Ellis. Yes, sir.

. . . .

Mr. Tayler. When did he marry Lillian Hamlin?

Mrs. Ellis. I do not know the date.

Mr. Tayler. I do not care about the exact date.

Mrs. Ellis. After June 12 and before July 2.

Mr. Tayler. Of what year?

Mrs. Ellis. 1896.

Mr. Tayler. He was at that time an Apostle?

Mrs. Ellis. Yes, sir.

. . . .

Mr. Tayler. Did he say he was going away that day, or that evening, to California?

Mrs. Ellis. He told me to pack his grip or his satchel and told me he was going on this trip.

Mr. Tayler. What did he say about Miss Hamlin?

Mrs. Ellis. Of course I understood, in fact he said she was going with him and President Smith.

Mr. Tayler. And President Smith?

Mrs. Ellis. Yes, sir.

Mr. Tayler. And that they were going to be married?

Mrs. Ellis. Yes, sir.

. . . .

Mr. Tayler. . . . What did Mr. Cannon say to you shortly before his death about his having married Miss Hamlin?

Mrs. Ellis. He told me he had married her and asked my forgiveness.

MR. TAYLER. What else did he say about it?

MRS. ELLIS. He said he had never had a well day since he had married her. I think it killed him.

MR. TAYLER. You have stated, have you not, . . . that he also told you that Joseph F. Smith married him?

MRS. ELLIS. No, sir; I have never said that.

MR. TAYLER. You have never said that?

MRS. ELLIS. No, sir; not that he told me.

MR. TAYLER. You have stated frequently that Joseph F. Smith did marry them?

MRS. ELLIS. Yes, sir.

. . . .

MR. TAYLER. Did you not know they were married on the high sea?

MRS. ELLIS. Only from reports.

MR. TAYLER. . . . It was an inference from the fact that your husband said he was going to marry her, and went away to California for that purpose, and that Joseph F. Smith went along with them. From that you inferred that Joseph F. Smith had married them?

MRS. ELLIS. Yes, sir (vol. 2, pp.141-44).

In his testimony, Joseph F. Smith denied that he performed the marriage ceremony, but he acknowledged that he did go on a trip with Lillian Hamlin and Apostle Cannon at the time when the marriage was supposed to have taken place:

MR. SMITH. . . . The first time I ever saw her [Lillian Hamlin], . . . was some time in June—I do not remember the date—1896. I was at that time president of the Sterling Mining and Milling Company. . . . I was asked by the board of directors to accompany Abraham H. Cannon to Los Angeles . . . I accompanied Abraham H. Cannon and his wife on that trip, and had one of my wives with me on that trip.

. . . .

MR. TAYLER. When did you first learn that Lillian Hamlin was his wife?

MR. SMITH. The first that I suspected anything of the kind was on that trip, because I never knew the lady before (vol. 1, p.111).

MR. TAYLER. Were you out in a boat from there [Los Angeles]?

MR. SMITH. Yes, sir.

. . . .

MR. SMITH. . . . no one ever mentioned to me that they were or were not married. I simply judged they were married because they were living together as husband and wife.

. . . .

MR. TAYLER. Did you say anything by way of criticism to Abraham Cannon?

MR. SMITH. No, sir.

MR. TAYLER. For going about with this wife?

MR. SMITH. No, sir; I did not (vol. 1, pp.127-28).

Joseph F. Smith went on to testify that the church was "very sensitive" about charges that plural marriages were performed after the Manifesto, but then he had to admit that he had let the Cannon affair pass without making any inquiry:

> MR. TAYLER. What inquiry did you make to find out whether Abraham H. Cannon, one of the twelve apostles of the church, had made a plural marriage?
> MR. SMITH. I made no inquiry at all.
> . . . .
> MR. TAYLER. Did you have any interest in finding out whether there had been—
> MR. SMITH. Not the least (vol. 1, pp.476-77).

The evidence we have presented seems to show that it was Joseph F. Smith himself who performed the marriage ceremony.

Abraham H. Cannon's widow, Mrs. Ellis, was questioned about his diary, but she had not seen it "since his death." Many diaries belonging to Apostle Cannon have recently come to light. Unfortunately, however, if Cannon kept a diary at the time of his marriage in 1896, it has not been made public. Even though we do not have Cannon's diary for June of 1896, Michael Marquardt has pointed out some references in his diary for 1894 which throw important light on this marriage and on the attitude of the Mormon leaders concerning polygamy after the Manifesto.

The reader will remember that Frank J. Cannon quoted his father George Q. Cannon as saying: ". . . President Smith obtained the acquiescence of President Woodruff, on the plea that it wasn't an ordinary case of polygamy but merely a fulfilment of the biblical instruction that a man should take his dead brother's wife. Lillian was betrothed to David, and had been sealed to him in eternity after his death. . . ."

According to the diary of Abraham H. Cannon, April 5, 1894, his father George Q. Cannon, a member of the First Presidency, lamented the fact that his sons could not raise up seed to David through polygamy: "My son David died without seed, and his brothers cannot do a work for him, in rearing children to bear his name because of the Manifesto."

From an entry in Apostle Cannon's diary for October 24, 1894, it would appear that the Mormon leaders had decided that a plural marriage could be performed in Mexico to raise up seed to David. Although the diary has been damaged at this point and a few words are missing, the remaining portion shows that the Mormon leaders did not take the Manifesto seriously:

> After meeting I went to the President's Office and ———Father [George Q. Cannon] about *taking a wife for David.* I told him David had taken Anni[e] ———cousin, through the vail in life, and suggested she might be a good pe——— sealed to him for eternity. The suggestion pleased Father very much, and ——— Angus was there, He spoke to him about it *in the presence of the Presidency.* ——— not object providing Annie is willing. The *Presidents Woodruff and Smith both sa[i]d they were willing for such a ceremony to occur,* if done in Mexico, and Pres. Woodruf[f] promised *the Lord's blessing* to follow such an act ("Daily Journal of Abraham H. Cannon," October 24, 1894, vol. 18, p.170).

We may never know if Annie was "willing" to enter into this plural marriage, but we do know that less than two years later Lillian Hamlin was married to Apostle Cannon. Mrs. Wilhelmina C. Ellis, who had been one of Cannon's plural wives testified:

> MRS. ELLIS. He said he could marry her out of the State—out of the United States.
>
> . . . .
>
> MR. TAYLER. What conversation did you have with him then about his going away and about his getting married again? What did he say first about going?
>
> MRS. ELLIS. He told me he was going to marry her for time, and that she would be David's wife for eternity (*The Reed Smoot Case*, vol. 2, pp.142-43).

Apostle Cannon's journal not only reveals that the Mormon leaders approved of polygamy after the Manifesto, but it shows they were considering the idea of a secret system of concubinage wherein men and women could live together without being actually married:

> Father [George Q. Cannon] now spoke of the unfortunate condition of the people at present in regard to marriage. . . . *I believe in concubinage, or some plan whereby men and women can live together under sacred ordinances and vows until they can be married.* . . . such a condition would have *to be kept secret,* untill the laws of our government change to permit the holy order of wedlock which God has revealed, which will undoubtedly occur at no distant day, in order to correct the social evil. . . . —Pres. Snow. "I have no doubt but *concubinage will yet be practiced in this church,* but I had not thought of it in this connection. When the nations are troubled good women will come here for safety and blessing, and men will accept them *as concubines.*"–Pres. Woodruff: ."*If men enter into some practice of this character* to raise a righteous posterity, *they will be justified in it* . . ." ("Daily Journal of Abraham H. Cannon," April 5, 1894, vol. 18, p.70).

As we have shown earlier in this book, Joseph Smith's revelation on polygamy also said that concubinage was justifiable in God's sight: "Abraham received *concubines* and they bore him children; and it was accounted unto him *for righteousness . . .*" (*Doctrine and Covenants* 132:37).

"Manifesto a Deception"

After their investigation the Committee on Privileges and Elections submitted a report in which the following was stated:

> A sufficient number of specific instances of the *taking of plural wives since the manifesto of 1890*, so called, have been shown by the testimony as having taken place *among officials of the Mormon Church* to demonstrate the fact that the leaders in this church, the first presidency and the twelve apostles, *connive at the practice of taking plural wives*, and have done so ever since the manifesto was issued . . . as late as 1896 one Lillian Hamlin became the plural wife of Abraham H. Cannon, who was then an apostle . . . it was generally reputed in the community and understood by the families . . . that they had been married on the high seas by Joseph F. Smith. Lillian Hamlin assumed the name of Cannon, and a child to which she afterwards gave birth bears the name of Cannon. . . .
>
> George Teasdale, another apostle of the Mormon Church, contracted a plural marriage with Marion Scholes since the manifesto of 1890. . . . Charles E. Merrill, a bishop . . . took a plural wife in 1891. . . . The ceremony . . . was performed by his father, . . . an apostle in the Mormon Church. It is also shown that John W. Taylor, another apostle of the Mormon Church, has been married to two plural wives since the issuing of the so-called manifesto.
>
> Matthias F. Cowley, another of the twelve apostles, has also taken one or more plural wives since the manifesto. . . . Apostles Taylor and Cowley, instead of appearing before the committee and denying the allegation, evade service of process issued by the committee for their appearance, and refuse to appear after being requested to do so. . . .
>
> It is also proved that about the year 1896 James Francis Johnson was married to a plural wife, . . . the ceremony in this instance being performed by an apostle. . . . To these cases must be added that of Marriner W. Merrill, another apostle; J. M. Tanner, superintendent of church schools; Benjamin Cluff, jr., president of Brigham Young University; Thomas Chamberlain, counselor to the president of a stake; Bishop Rathall, John Silver, Winslow Farr, Heber Benion, Samuel S. Newton, a man named Okey, who contracted a plural marriage with Ovena Jorgensen in the year 1897, and Morris Michelson about the year 1902. . . .

281

It is morally impossible that all these violations of the laws of the State of Utah by the contracting of plural marriages could have been committed without the knowledge of the first presidency and the twelve apostles of the Mormon Church. . . .

SUPPRESSION OF TESTIMONY BY MORMON LEADERS.

It is a fact of no little significance in itself, bearing on the question whether polygamous marriages have been recently contracted in Utah by the connivance of the first presidency and twelve apostles of the Mormon Church, that the authorities of said church have endeavored to suppress, and have succeeded in suppressing, a great deal of testimony by which the fact of plural marriages contracted by those who were high in the councils of the church might have been established beyond the shadow of a doubt. Before the investigation had begun it was well known in Salt Lake City that it was expected to show on the part of the protestants that Apostles George Teasdale, John W. Taylor, and M. F. Cowley, and also Prof. J. M. Tanner, Samuel Newton and others who were all high officials of the Mormon Church had recently taken plural wives, and that in 1896 Lillian Hamlin was sealed to Apostle Abraham H. Cannon. . . . All, or nearly all, of these persons except Abraham H. Cannon, who was deceased, were then within reach of service of process from the committee. But shortly before the investigation began all these witnesses went out of the country.

Subpoenas were issued for each one of the witnesses named, but in the case of Samuel Newton only could the process of the committee be served. Mr. Newton refused to obey the order of the committee . . . John W. Taylor was sent out of the country by Joseph F. Smith on a real or pretended mission for the church. . . .

It would be nothing short of self-stultification for one to believe that all these most important witnesses chanced to leave the United States at about the same time and without reference to the investigation. All the facts and circumstances surrounding the transaction point to the conclusion that every one of the witnesses named left the country at the instance [sic] of the rulers of the Mormon Church and to avoid testifying before the committee. . . . The reason why the said witnesses left the country and have refused to come before the committee is easy to understand, in view of the testimony showing the contracting of plural marriages by prominent officials of the Mormon Church within the past few years.

It was claimed by the protestants that the records kept in the Mormon temple at Salt Lake City and Logan would disclose the fact that plural marriages have been contracted in Utah since the manifesto with the sanction of the officials of the church. A witness who was required to bring the records in the temple at

Salt Lake City refused to do so after consulting with President Smith. . . .

The witness who was required to bring the records kept in the temple at Logan excused himself from attending on the plea of ill health. But the important part of the mandate of the committee—the production of the records—was not obeyed by sending the records, which could easily have been done.

In the case of other witnesses who were believed to have contracted plural marriages since the year 1890 all sorts of shifts, tricks, and evasions were resorted to in order to avoid service of a subpoena to appear before the committee and testify. . . .

Aside from this it was shown by the testimony, and in such a way that the fact could not possibly be controverted, that a majority of those who give the law to the Mormon Church are now, and have been for years, living in open, notorious, and shameless polygamous cohabitation. The list of those who are thus guilty of violating the laws of the State and the rules of public decency is headed by Joseph F. Smith, the first president, "prophet, seer, and revelator". . . .

The list also includes George Teasdale, an apostle; John Henry Smith, an apostle; Marriner W. Merrill, also an apostle; Heber J. Grant, an apostle; M. F. Cowley, an apostle; Charles W. Penrose, an apostle; and Francis M. Lyman, who is not only an apostle, but the probable successor of Joseph F. Smith as president of the church. Thus it appears that the first president and eight of the twelve apostles, a considerable majority of the ruling authorities of the Mormon Church, are noted polygamists. . . .

These facts abundantly justify the assertion made in the protest that "the supreme authorities in the church, . . . the first presidency and twelve apostles, not only connive at violation of, but protect and honor the violators of the laws against polygamy and polygamous cohabitation."

It will be seen by the foregoing that not only do the first presidency and twelve apostles encourage polygamy by precept and teaching, but that a majority of the members of that body of rulers of the Mormon people give the practice of polgyamy still further and greater encouragement by living the lives of polygamists, and this openly and in the sight of all their followers in the Mormon Church. . . .

And not only do the president and a majority of the twelve apostles of the Mormon Church practice polygamy, but in the case of each and every one guilty of this crime who testified before the committee, the determination was expressed openly and defiantly to continue the commission of this crime without regard to the mandates of the law or the prohibition contained in the

manifesto. . . . those who are in authority in the Mormon
Church, of whom Mr. Smoot is one, are encouraging the practice
of polygamy among the members of that church, and that
polygamy is being practiced to such an extent as to call for the
severest condemnation in all legitimate ways (*Reed Smoot Case*,
vol. 4, pp.476-82).

Finally, some sixteen years after the Manifesto was issued,
President Joseph F. Smith was brought to trial for unlawful
cohabitation. The following appeared in the *Deseret News*: ". . .
President Smith appeared forthwith and entered *a plea of
guilty* and was fined three hundred dollars. The fine was
promptly paid and the defendant discharged" (*Deseret Evening
News*, November 23, 1906).

Heber J. Grant, who served as the seventh president of the
Mormon church from 1918 until 1945, was also convicted of
unlawful cohabitation after the Manifesto was issued. This occurred in 1899, some nine years after Woodruff issued the Manifesto (see the *Daily Tribune*, September 9, 1899). In 1903 *Heber
J. Grant fled the country to avoid being arrested again.* Charles
Mostyn Owen testified as follows:

> THE CHAIRMAN. Where did you say Grant was?
> MR. OWEN. Grant is in England.
> THE CHAIRMAN. When did he go to England?
> MR. OWEN. He left suddenly on the night of the 10th of November
> last year—1903.
> . . . .
> MR. OWEN. . . . he made a statement before the students of the
> State university at Salt Lake City, in which he held out in a very
> objectionable manner his association with two women as his
> wives. . . . I went before the county attorney and swore to an
> information for him, and a warrant was issued on that informa-
> tion. Before Mr. Grant was served, however, he left the country.
> . . . .
> THE CHAIRMAN. Has he returned since that time?
> MR. OWEN. No, sir.
> SENATOR PETTUS. Is he still an apostle?
> MR. OWEN. Yes, sir (*Reed Smoot Case*, vol. 2, pp.401-2).

Because of the insincerity of the Mormon leaders after the
Manifesto thousands of people in Utah are still living in
polygamy today. Mormon author John J. Stewart wrote the following regarding current polygamist groups:

> Secondly, Satan is exploiting the doctrine and history of plural
> marriage in our Church by persuading many men and women to
> rebel against current Church policy on the matter, and thus for-
> feit their membership in the Church and Kingdom of God. More

than seventy years after the first Manifesto was issued, as a step in suspending the practice of plural marriage, apostate sects are mushrooming throughout Mormondom in greater numbers than ever before, with the basic doctrine that plural marriage must be lived regardless of what the Church policy is (*Brigham Young and His Wives*, p.15).

On November 21, 1955, *Newsweek* magazine reported that "Utah polygamists may well number 20,000." Ten years later Wallace Turner said that "one expert estimates that *as many as 30,000 men, women and children* live in families in which polygamy is practiced" (*New York Times*, December 27, 1965). The Mormon writer Leonard J. Arrington felt that this was a "far-fetched estimate." Ben Merson, on the other hand, seems to feel that more than 30,000 people are involved:

In Utah . . . the practice of polygamy has never ceased. It is more widespread than ever. And increasing year by year.

In metropolitan Salt Lake City alone, *10,000 are living in plural marriage*. . . .

"Today in Utah," declares William M. Rogers, former special assistant to the State Attorney General, "there are more polygamous families than in the days of Brigham Young. *At least 30,000* men, women and children in this state are now living in plural households—and the number is rapidly increasing." *Thousands* more live in the adjoining states of Idaho, Nevada, Wyoming, Colorado, New Mexico and Arizona—plus sizable populations in Oregon, California, Canada and Mexico.

The majority live in Utah. And, says Rogers, neither the state law, . . . nor the Mormon church, which prohibits it on pain of excommunication, has been able to stem the rising tide of plural marriage.

Strangely, it also remains the chief obstacle to law enforcement. For 72 percent of Utah's 900,000 citizens are Mormon. And while most practice monogamy, they are aware of their polygamous heritage. . . . "This, coupled with the Mormon history of persecution," says Rogers, "makes them sympathetic toward the Fundamentalists. They feel that prison—and excommunication—is too harsh a penalty. And they refuse to testify against their polygamous neighbors."

So do the non-Mormons, who are referred to as Gentiles (*Ladies Home Journal*, June 1967, p.78).

Those who believe in practicing polygamy today are usually known as "fundamentalists," because they claim to go back to the fundamental doctrines of Mormonism.

The Dilemma

The Mormon leaders find themselves in a rather strange situation. On the one hand, they have to uphold polygamy as a righteous principle, but on the other, they have to discourage the members of the church from actually entering into its practice. If they repudiated the doctrine of polygamy they would be admitting that Joseph Smith was a deceiver, and that the church was founded on fraud. If, however, they openly preached and defended the doctrine, many people would probably enter into the practice and bring disgrace upon the church. Their position is about the same as a person saying, "My church believes in water baptism, but we are not allowed to practice it." Because of this peculiar dilemma, church leaders prefer that there is not much discussion of polygamy. Mormon writer Klaus J. Hansen depicted the sentiment in these words:

> Admittedly, descendants of polygamous families still proudly acknowledge their heritage; but many Mormons clearly wish it had never happened. A leading historian at the leading state university in Utah for years avoided any mention of the subject; references to it in graduate theses were eradicated with the remark, "Too controversial!" Preston Nibley, it will be remembered, wrote an entire book on Brigham Young without mentioning the dread word once (*Dialogue: A Journal of Mormon Thought*, Summer 1966, p.107).

To show the confusion of the Mormon leaders in regard to polygamy we have only to quote from a statement made by Apostle Bruce R. McConkie. In the same statement he says that millions of people have gained eternal exaltation by the practice of polygamy, that Joseph Smith and other Mormon leaders entered the practice in virtue and purity of heart, that polygamy will be practiced after the second coming of Christ; yet he states that anyone who enters polygamy today is living in adultery, has sold his soul to Satan and will be damned in eternity:

> ... the Lord frequently did command his ancient saints to practice plural marriage ... the whole history of ancient Israel was one in which plurality of wives was the divinely accepted and approved order of matrimony. Millions of those who entered this order have, in and through it, gained for themselves eternal exaltation in the highest heaven of the celesital world ... the Prophet and leading brethren were commanded to enter into the practice, which they did in all virtue and purity of heart ... plural marriage was openly taught and practiced until the year 1890. At that time conditions were such that the Lord by revelation with-

drew the command to continue the practice. . . . Obviously the holy practice will commence again after the Second Coming of the Son of Man and the ushering in of the millennium. . . .

Any who pretend or assume to engage in plural marriage in this day, when the one holding the keys has withdrawn the power by which they are performed, are guilty of gross wickedness. They are living in adultery, have already sold their souls to Satan, and (whether their acts are based on ignorance or lust or both) they will be damned in eternity (Mormon Doctrine, 1958, pp.522-23).

Is it any wonder that many Mormon people are confused over the practice of polygamy? They are taught that Joseph Smith entered polygamy in "virtue and purity of heart," yet they are taught that if they follow his example they are living in "adultery."

The Mormon people are taught that plural marriage is still practiced in heaven and will be practiced in the millennium. John J. Stewart stated: ". . . the restoration of the Church and Gospel of Jesus Christ, is to prepare for the second coming of the Savior, which is nigh at hand; to help usher in His great millennial reign, when the Gospel in its fulness *including plural marriage*, will be lived by worthy members of the Church" (*Brigham Young and His Wives*, p.73).

Apostle Orson Pratt once stated: "Does not everything that is consistent and reasonable, and everything that agrees with the Bible show that *plurality of wives must exist after the resurrection? It does* . . ." (*Journal of Discourses*, vol. 14, pp.244-45).

Since the Mormon people are taught that polygamy was right in Joseph Smith's time and that it will be practiced in heaven, is it any wonder that many of them are entering into the practice today? As long as the Mormon leaders continue to publish Joseph Smith's revelation on polygamy (*Doctrine and Covenants*, 132), there will, no doubt, be many people who will enter into the practice. They cannot completely repudiate this revelation, however, without repudiating their doctrine concerning temple marriage as the two doctrines are found in the same revelation.

Although the Mormon leaders will not give up the idea that this revelation is from God, they have already repudiated many of the teachings of the earlier leaders with regard to polygamy. For instance, Brigham Young taught: "*The only men who become Gods, even the Sons of God, are those who enter into polygamy*" (*Journal of Discourses*, vol. 11, p.269). The *Millennial Star* (vol. 15, p.226), contained this statement: "The order of plurality of wives is an everlasting and ceaseless order, de-live according to the word that is given to them; and if their husbands are good men, and they are obedient to them, they are entitled to certain blessings, and they will have the privilege of receiving certain blessings that they cannot receive unless they are sealed to men who will be exalted. Now, where a man in this church says, "I don't want but one wife, I will live my religion with one," he will perhaps be saved in the celestial kingdom; but when he gets there he will not find himself in possession of any wife at all. He has had a talent that he has hid up. He will come forward and say, "Here is that which thou gavest me, I have not wasted it, and here is the one talent," and he will not enjoy it, but it will be taken and given to those who have improved the talents they received, and he will find himself without any wife, and he will remain single for ever and ever. But if the woman is determined not to enter into a plural marriage, that woman when she comes forth will have the privilege of living in single blessedness through all eternity. Well, that is very good, a very nice place to be a minister to the wants of others. I recollect a sister conversing with Joseph Smith on this subject. She told him: "Now don't talk to me; when I get into the celestial kingdom, if I ever do get there, I shall request the privilege of being a ministering angel; that is the labor that I wish to perform. I don't want any companion in that world; and if the Lord will make me a ministering angel, it is all I want." Joseph said, "Sister, you talk very foolishly, you do not know what you will want." He then said to me: "Here, Brother Brigham, you seal this lady to me." I sealed her to him. This was my own sister according to the flesh. Now, sisters, do not say, "I do not want a husband when I get up in the resurrection." You do not know what you will want. I tell this so that you can get the idea. If in the resurrection you really want to be single and alone, and live so for ever and ever, and be made servants, while others receive the highest order of intelligence and are bringing worlds into existence, you can have the privilege. They who will be exalted cannot perform all the labor, they must have servants and you can be servants to them.

There was a certain woman brought to Father Adam whose name was Eve, because she was the first woman, and she was given to him to be his wife; I am not disposed to give any farther knowledge concerning her at present. There is no doubt but that he left many companions. The great and glorious doctrine that pertains to this I have not time to dwell upon; neither should I at present if I had time. He understood this whole machinery or system before he came to this earth; and I hope my brethren and sisters will profit by what I have told them.

Now we have been administering the sacrament here to the people, the bread and the water. It is to refresh our minds and bring to our understanding the death and sufferings of our Saviour. Is there any commandment with regard to this matter? Yes, there are laws concerning it. You take this book [the Book of Doctrine and Covenants] and you will read here that the Saints are to meet together on the Sabbath day. It is what we call the first day of the week. No matter whether it is the Jewish Sabbath or not. I do not think there is anybody who can bring facts to prove which is the seventh day, or when Adam was put in the garden, or the day about which the Lord spoke to Moses. This matter is not very well known, so we call the day on which we rest and worship God, the first day of the week. This people called Latter-day Saints are required by the revelations that the Lord has given, to assemble themselves together on this day. How many go riding or visiting, or go anywhere but to meeting, on the Sabbath day. It is probably not so here, but in Salt Lake City, as a general thing, Sunday is made a holiday for riding and visiting, etc. In this commandment we are required to come together and repent of our sins and confess our sins and partake of the bread and of the wine or water in commemoration of the death and sufferings of our Lord and Savior. I will ask the Latter-day Saints if you are entitled to these blessings unless you keep the Sabbath day. Now, what do you say? Why, every Latter-day Saint would answer we are not entitled to the blessing of partaking of the emblems or symbols of the body and the blood of Christ unless we observe his law. All the Latter-day

"Do you want ther wife sealed "Where is your w has left me." W are so full of the d not live with you will give a certifie another. They baptized for their d they have not p I do not want to but I do not think If the Lord will r If the Lord will c hers, and will hon and say that the their dead friends the heavens and it by his angel, and resurrection it sh unto them for th willing, I have n against it.

Now, then, w these ordinances, Lord has revealed of the dead; tho have received for men and women, you a great deal time; but there is and I want to s bring your mind present condition. Doctrine and Co gard to the buildi dom of God, the &c. I am anxiou to get the Latter gin where the Lo to begin when h build up this ki that we are to su the direction of ou who shall be appo dictate them in th ing to life, so that means in the hand accomplishing the quires at our han my mind to ask slow, tardy people; to see the order de ced. If I had the p legal, the legal have had some of t sisters organized to with bonds that ca but I cannot do th we desire to comm foundation that ca up and destroyed. Brethren, if you and operate togeth making cheese, ii and cattle and eve work, and get a fac co-operative store

A photograph of the Deseret News, Sept. 17, 1873. Brigham Young maintained that a man with just one wife will have her taken from him and given to a polygamist in heaven.

signed to exalt the choicest men and women to the most super-lative excellence, dominion, and glory."

Today, however, Mormon leaders teach that polygamy is not essential for exaltation. Bruce R. McConkie flatly stated: "Plural marriage is *not essential* to salvation or exaltation" (*Mormon Doctrine*, 1958, p.523).

Brigham Young once became so zealous to establish polygamy that he declared a man who would not enter into polygamy would have his wife taken from him in the resurrection and given to another:

> Now, where a man in this church says, "I don't want but one wife, I will live my religion with one." He will perhaps be saved in the Celestial kingdom; but when he gets there *he will not find himself in possession of any wife at all.* He has had a talent that he has hid up. He will come forward and say, "Here is that which thou gavest me, I have not wasted it, and here is the one talent," and he will not enjoy it, but it will be taken and given to those who have improved the talents they received, and he will find himself *without any wife,* and he will *remain single forever and ever.* . . . I recollect a sister conversing with Joseph Smith on this subject. She told him: "Now don't talk to me; when I get into the celestial kingdom, . . . I don't want any companion in that world; and if the Lord will make me a ministering angel, it is all I want." Joseph said, "Sister, you talk very foolishly, you do not know what you will want." He then said to me: "Here brother Brigham, you seal this lady to me." I sealed her to him. This was my own sister according to the flesh (*Deseret News*, September 17, 1873).

Mormon leaders today would not think of teaching that a man with only one wife would have her taken from him and given to a man who had taken more. Bruce R. McConkie states: "In our day, the Lord summarized by revelation the whole doctrine of exaltation and predicated it upon the marriage of one man to one woman" (*Mormon Doctrine*, p.523).

Although Mormon leaders have changed many of the teachings concerning polygamy, they still teach that it was a righteous practice in Joseph Smith's time. John J. Stewart makes it very clear that it is still an "integral part of LDS scripture":

> . . . the Church's strictness in excommunicating those advocating and practicing plural marriage today has apparently been misconstrued by not a few loyal Church members as an acknowledgement that the evil falsehoods . . . and other misconceptions about plural marriage, are true, and that the Church's near silence on the doctrine today is further evidence that it regrets and is embarrassed by the whole matter of plural marriage. Such an

inference is, of course, unjustified and unrealistic. The Church has never, and certainly will never, renounce this doctrine. The revelation on plural marriage is still an integral part of LDS scripture, and always will be. If a woman, sealed to her husband for time and eternity, precedes her husband in death, it is his privilege to marry another also for time and eternity, providing that he is worthy of doing so (*Brigham Young and His Wives*, pp.13-14).

CHANGING THE
ANTI-BLACK DOCTRINE

Chapter 10

On June 9, 1978, Mormon church leaders announced a very important change in their doctrine concerning blacks. They stated that blacks would now be given "all of the privileges and blessings which the gospel affords" (*Deseret News*, June 9, 1978). Prior to that time blacks of African lineage were not allowed to hold the Priesthood nor go through the temple even though they lived exemplary lives. The Mormon position concerning blacks was clearly stated in a letter written by the First Presidency on July 17, 1947: "From the days of the Prophet Joseph even until now, it has been the *doctrine of the Church*, never questioned by any of the Church leaders, that the *Negroes are not entitled to the full blessings of the Gospel*" (Letter from the First Presidency, quoted in *Mormonism and the Negro*, by John J. Stewart and William E. Berrett, pp.46-47).

Bruce R. McConkie, who now serves as an apostle in the Mormon church, wrote the following in a book published in 1958:

> Negroes in this life are denied the priesthood; under no circumstances can they hold this delegation of authority from the Almighty. The gospel message of salvation is not carried affirmatively to them. . . . Negroes are not equal with other races where the receipt of certain spiritual blessings are concerned . . . (*Mormon Doctrine*, 1958, p.477).

Black Skin and the Pre-Existence

As we have previously brought out, in Mormon theology "*a black skin is a mark of the curse of heaven* placed upon some portions of mankind" (*Juvenile Instructor*, vol. 3, p.157). This idea comes directly from Joseph Smith's *Book of Mormon* which says that the skins of the Indians became "*dark*, according to the mark which was set upon their fathers, which was *a curse* upon them because of their transgression . . ." (*Book of Mormon*, Alma 3:6).

Although Mormon theology has taught that anyone born

with a dark skin was inferior, blacks of African lineage were placed at the bottom of the scale. President Joseph Fielding Smith explained the LDS view concerning blacks:

> Not only was Cain called upon to suffer, but because of his wickedness he became the father of *an inferior race. A curse* was placed upon him and that curse has been continued through his lineage and must do so while time endures. Millions of souls have come into this world *cursed with a black skin* and have been denied the privilege of Priesthood and the fulness of the blessings of the Gospel. These are the descendants of Cain. Moreover, they have been made to feel *their inferiority* and have been separated from the rest of mankind from the beginning. . . .

> But what a contrast! The sons of Seth, Enoch and Noah honored by the blessings and rights of Priesthood! . . . And the sons of Cain, denied the Priesthood; not privileged to receive the covenants of glory in the kingdom of God! . . . we will also hope that blessings may eventually be given to our Negro brethren, for they are our brethren—children of God—notwithstanding their *black covering emblematical of eternal darkness*" (*The Way to Perfection*, Salt Lake City, 1935, pp.101-2).

In a book published in 1966, Wallace Turner, a correspondent for the *New York Times*, set forth the limitations blacks were confronted with in the Mormon Church:

> The Negro Mormon can hold no office whatsoever in a church which offers some office to every one of its male members at some time in his life. A gray-haired Negro Mormon who may have spent his adult life in the careful practice of all the complicated and demanding rules set down by the LDS church stands disenfranchised before the altar where a youth whose beard is just beginning to fuzz may preside. A twelve-year-old boy may become a member of the Aaronic priesthood, more than this Negro man has been able to achieve through a lifetime of devotion. To hold any church office, a Mormon must be a member of the priesthood (*The Mormon Establishment*, pp.243-44).

Some Mormons who questioned this doctrine found themselves in serious trouble with the Church. For example, Grant Syphers related:

> "In all humility I must say that God has not inspired me to feel good about the Church's practices regarding Negroes. . . . when my wife and I went to San Francisco Ward's bishop to renew our temple recommends, he told us that anyone who could not accept the Church's stand on Negroes as divine doctrine was not supporting the General Authorities and *could not go to the temple.* Later, in an interview with the stake president we were told the same thing: if you express doubts about the divinity of this

"doctrine" you cannot go to the temple (*Dialogue: A Journal of Mormon Thought*, Winter 1967, p.6).

To understand the Mormon attitude concerning blacks, a person must first understand the doctrine of pre-existence. One of the basic doctrines of the Mormon church is that the spirit of man existed before the world was created. Joseph Smith once stated:

> . . . the soul, the mind of man, the immortal spirit. All men say God created it in the beginning. *The very idea lessens man in my estimation;* I do not believe the doctrine, I know better . . . I am going to tell of things more noble. . . .
>
> The mind of man *is as immortal as God himself* . . . *God never did have power to create the spirit* of man at all (*Times and Seasons*, vol. 5, p.615, reprinted in *History of the Church*, vol. 6, pp.310-11).

From this doctrine of the pre-existence of the soul, came the idea of some spirits being more noble than others. Joseph Smith's Book of Abraham talks of "the noble and great ones" (*Pearl of Great Price*, Book of Abraham 3:22). The Mormon leaders taught that the "more noble" or choice spirits are born as Mormons. Blacks, on the other hand, were considered to have been more unfaithful in the pre-existence than any of the spirits who were allowed to take bodies. Apostle McConkie maintained that "those who were less valiant in pre-existence and who thereby had certain spiritual restrictions imposed upon them during mortality are known to us as the Negroes. Such spirits are sent to earth through the lineage of Cain, the mark put upon him for his rebellion against God and his murder of Abel being *a black skin* (*Mormon Doctrine*, pp.476-77).

Mormon historian B. H. Roberts asserted that in the pre-existence the Negroes "through their indifference or lack of integrity to righteousness, rendered themselves unworthy of the Priesthood and its powers, and hence it is withheld from them to this day (*The Contributor*, vol. 6, pp.296-97).

Apostle Mark E. Petersen presented the Mormon thinking concerning the doctrine of pre-existence:

> Is there reason then why the type of birth we receive in this life is not a reflection of our worthiness or lack of it in the pre-existent life? . . . can we account in any other way for the birth of some of the children of God in darkest Africa, or in flood-ridden China, or among the starving hordes of India, while some of the rest of us are born here in the United States? We cannot escape the conclusion that because of performance in our pre-existence some of us are born as Chinese, some as Japanese, some as

Latter-day Saints. These are rewards and punishments, fully in harmony with His established policy in dealing with sinners and saints, rewarding all according to their deeds. . . .

Let us consider the great mercy of God for a moment. A Chinese, born in China *with a dark skin*, and with all the handicaps of that race seems to have little opportunity. But think of the mercy of God to Chinese people who are willing to accept the gospel. In spite of *whatever they might have done in the pre-existence to justify being born over there as Chinamen*, if they now, in this life, accept the gospel and live it the rest of their lives they can have the Priesthood, go to the temple and receive endowments and sealings, and that means they can have exaltation. Isn't the mercy of God marvelous?

"Think of the Negro, cursed as to the priesthood. . . . This Negro, who, in the pre-existence lived the type of life which justified the Lord in sending him to the earth in the lineage of Cain with a black skin, and possibly being born in darkest Africa—if that Negro is willing when he hears the gospel to accept it, he may have many of the blessings of the gospel. *In spite of all he did in the pre-existent life*, the Lord is willing, if the Negro accepts the gospel with real, sincere faith, and is really converted, to give him the blessings of baptism and the gift of the Holy Ghost. If that Negro is faithful all his days, he can and will enter the celestial kingdom. *He will go there as a servant*, but he will get celestial glory (*Race Problems—As They Affect The Church,* Address by Mark E. Petersen at the Convention of Teachers of Religion on the College Level, delivered at Brigham Young University, Provo, Utah, August 27, 1954).

Descendants of Cain Through the Flood

In Joseph Smith's *History of the Church,* we read that "the negroes" are the "sons of Cain" (vol. 4, p.501). Apostle Bruce R. McConkie explains the curse put on Cain as follows:

Though he was a rebel and an associate of Lucifer in pre-existence, and though he was a liar from the beginning whose name was Perdition, Cain managed to attain the privilege of mortal birth. . . . he came out in open rebellion, fought God, worshiped Lucifer, and slew Abel. . . .

As a result of his rebellion, *Cain was cursed with a dark skin; he became the father of the Negroes,* and those spirits who are not worthy to receive the priesthood are born through his lineage. He became the first mortal to be cursed as a son of perdition. As a result of his mortal birth he is assured of a tangible body of flesh and bones in eternity, a fact which will enable him to rule over Satan (*Mormon Doctrine,* 1958, p.102).

In the "Book of Moses," a revelation given to Joseph Smith in

December 1830, it is stated that the "children of Canaan" were black: "For behold, the Lord shall curse the land with much heat, and the barrenness thereof shall go forth forever; and there was *a blackness* came upon all the children of Canaan, that they were despised among all people" (*Pearl of Great Price*, Book of Moses 7:8).

Brigham Young declared that the flat nose and black skin were part of the mark put upon the descendants of Cain: "Cain slew his brother. . . . and the Lord put a mark upon him, which is *the flat nose and black skin* . . ." (*Journal of Discourses*, vol. 7, p.290).

Mormon leaders taught that it was Ham's descendants who were "cursed as to the priesthood" after the flood. They claimed that Ham married a black woman named Egyptus, and that the curse was continued "through Ham's wife." Bruce R. McConkie said that "Noah's son Ham married Egyptus, a descendant of Cain, thus preserving the Negro lineage through the flood" (*Mormon Doctrine*, 1958, p.477).

John Taylor, the third president of the church, likewise maintained: "And after the flood we are told that the curse that had been pronounced upon Cain was continued through Ham's wife, as he had married a wife of that seed. And why did it pass through the flood? because it was necessary that *the devil should have a representation upon the earth* as well as God . . ." (*Journal of Discourses*, vol. 22, p.304).

In the "Book of Abraham" (a part of the *Pearl of Great Price*, one of the four standard works) the following appears:

> Now this king of Egypt was a descendant from the loins of Ham, and was a partaker of the blood of the Canaanites by birth.
>
> From this descent sprang all the Egyptians, and thus the blood of the Canaanites was preserved in the land.
>
> The land of Egypt being first discovered by a woman, who was the daughter of Ham, and the daughter of Egyptus, which in the Chaldean signifies Egypt, which signifies that which is forbidden.
>
> When this woman discovered the land it was under water, who afterward settled her sons in it; and thus, from Ham, sprang that race which preserved the curse in the land.
>
> Now the first government of Egypt was established by Pharaoh, the eldest son of Egyptus, the daughter of Ham. . . .
>
> Pharaoh, being a righteous man, . . . seeking earnestly to imitate that order established by the fathers . . . even in the reign of Adam, and also of Noah, his father, who blessed him with the blessings of the earth, and with the blessings of wisdom, but

cursed him as pertaining to the Priesthood (*Pearl of Great Price*, Book of Abraham 1:21-26).

Mormon writer Arthur M. Richardson made this statement concerning blacks: "Referring to Elder Hyde's statement we find, then, that those assigned to *a dishonorable body* on this earth came through the accursed lineage of Canaan through Ham's wife who was a descendant of the first murderer Cain . . ." (*That Ye May Not Be Deceived*, pp.6-7).

Briefly stated, then, the Mormon doctrine concerning blacks was this: In the "pre-existence" the blacks "lent an influence to the devil." Because of their "unfaithfulness in the spirit world," they were "assigned to a dishonorable body on this earth." They came through the "accursed lineage of Canaan," and were "marked" with a "flat nose" and a "black covering" which is "emblematic of eternal darkness." They were an "inferior" race. In fact, they were a "representation" of the "devil" upon the earth. They were "not equal with other races where the receipt of certain spiritual blessings are concerned," and they were "not entitled to the full blessings of the Gospel." They were "denied the priesthood," and they could not be married in a Mormon temple. But, "in spite" of all they "did in the pre-existence," they could be baptized and receive the Holy Ghost. If a black man was faithful all his life he could enter the celestial kingdom.

One Drop Disqualifies

Because of their doctrine Mormon leaders have been strongly opposed to intermarriage with blacks. The following appeared in the *Juvenile Instructor,* volume 3, page 165: "In fact we believe it to be a great sin in the eyes of our Heavenly Father for a white person to marry a black one. And further, that it is a proof of the mercy of God that no such race appear able to continue for many generations."

Brigham Young stated that if a person who belongs to the chosen seed mixes his blood with a black the penalty is *death on the spot*: "Shall I tell you the law of God in regard to the African race? If the white man who belongs to the chosen seed mixes his blood with the seed of Cain, the penalty, under the law of God, is death on the spot. This will always be so" (*Journal of Discourses*, vol. 10, p.110).

One reason the Mormon leaders were so opposed to intermarriage was that they taught "one drop of Negro blood" would prevent a person from holding the priesthood. Apostle Mark E. Petersen explained as follows:

were destroyed by the Indians That unfortunate affair has been laid to the charge of the whites. A certain judge that was then in this Territory wanted the whole army to accompany him to Iron county to try the whites for the murder of that company of emigrants. I told Governor Cumming that if he would take an unprejudiced judge into the district where that horrid affair occurred, I would pledge myself that every man in the regions round about should be forthcoming when called for, to be condemned or acquitted as an impartial, unprejudiced judge and jury should decide; and I pledged him that the court should be protected from any violence or hindrance in the prosecution of the laws; and if any were guilty of the blood of those who suffered in the Mountain Meadow massacre, let them suffer the penalty of the law; but to this day they have not touched the matter, for fear the Mormons would be acquitted from the charge of having any hand in it, and our enemies would thus be deprived of a favorite topic to talk about, when urging hostility against us. "The Mountain Meadow massacre! Only think of the Mountain Meadow massacre!!" is their cry from one end of the land to the other. "Come, let us make war on the Mormons, for they burnt government property." And what was the government doing there with their property? They were coming to destroy the Mormons, in violation of every right principle of law and justice. A little of their property was destroyed, and they were left to gnaw, not a file, but dead cattle's bones. I was informed that one man brought five blood hounds to hunt the Mormons in the mountains, and that the poor devil had to kill them and eat them before spring to save himself from starving to death, and that he was fool enough to acknowledge it

afterwards in this city. This is the kind of outside pressure we have to meet with. Who wanted the army of 1857 here? Who sent for them? Liars, thieves, murderers, gamblers, whoremasters, and speculators in the rights and blood of the Mormon people cried to government, and government opened its ears, long and broad, saying, "I hear you, my children, lie on, my faithful sons Brocchus, Drummond and Co.," and so they did lie on until the parent sent an army to use up the Mormons. Now I say, for the consolation of all my brethren and sisters, they cannot do it; and that is worse to them than all the rest; they cannot do it.

The rank, rabid abolitionists, whom I call black-hearted Republicans, have set the whole national fabric on fire. Do you know this, Democrats? They have kindled the fire that is raging now from the north to the south, and from the south to the north. I am no abolitionist. neither am I a pro-slavery man; I hate some of their principles and especially some of their conduct, as I do the gates of hell. The Southerners make the negroes, and the Northerners worship them; this is all the difference between slaveholders and abolitionists. I would like the President of the United States and all the world to hear this.

Shall I tell you the law of God in regard to the African race? If the white man who belongs to the chosen seed mixes his blood with the seed of Cain, the penalty, under the law of God, is death on the spot. This will always be so. The nations of the earth have transgressed every law that God has given, they have changed the ordinances and broken every covenant made with the fathers, and they are like a hungry man that dreameth that he eateth, and he awaketh and behold he is empty.

The following saying of the prophet is fulfilled: "Now also many nations

A photograph of the *Journal of Discourses*, vol. 10, page 110. Brigham Young claimed that marriage to an African should be punished by death on the spot.

> Now what is our policy in regard to inter-marriage? As to the Negro, of course, there is only one possible answer. We must not inter-marry with the Negro. Why? If I were to marry a Negro woman and have children by her, *my children would all be cursed as to the priesthood.* Do I want my children cursed as to the priesthood? If there is *one drop of Negro blood* in my children, as I have read to you, *they receive the curse.* There isn't any argument, therefore, as to inter-marriage with the Negro, is there? There are 50 million Negroes in the United States. If they were to achieve complete absorption with the white race, think what that would do. With 50 million Negroes inter-married with us, where would the priesthood be? Who could hold it, in all America? Think what that would do to the work of the Church! (*Race Problems—As They Affect The Church*, Address by Mark E. Petersen at the Convention of Teachers of Religion on the College Level, Brigham Young University, Provo, Utah, August 27, 1954).

Outwardly the Mormon doctrine concerning blacks seemed to be firm and absolute. "One drop of Negro blood," the Mormon leaders declared, would prevent a man from holding the Priesthood. The truth is, however, that some people with much more than a "drop of Negro blood" were being ordained to the Priesthood. In the *Salt Lake City Messenger* for November, 1965, we demonstrated that a black man by the name of Elijah Abel was ordained to the Priesthood in the days of Joseph Smith, and that both his son and grandson were later ordained. Many of Abel's descendants pass as whites and although the Mormon leaders were aware of the situation, nothing was done to take the Priesthood from them. The hypocrisy of this whole matter was made plain in a letter from Joseph E. Taylor to President John Taylor.

> Now comes a case of a young girl residing in the Eighteenth Ward of the City by the name of Laura Berry whose mother was a white woman but whose father was a very light mullatto. It appears she has fallen in love with brother Barons Son and it is reciprocated.

> But the question of jeopardizing his future by such an alliance has caused a halt. She now desires to press *her claim to privileges that others who are tainted with that blood have received.* For example, the Meads family in the Eleventh Ward Mrs. Jones Elder Sister; (the former now resides in Logan) I am cognizant of all these having received their endowments here.

> Brother Meads is a white man he married his wife many years ago; she was a quadroon and died some three years ago their children (the oldest a girl, are married to a white man) are all very dark.

The question I desire to ask is: Can you give this girl any privileges of a like character? The girl is very pretty and quite white and *would not be suspected as having tainted blood* in her veins unless her parentage was known . . . (Letter from Joseph E. Taylor to President John Taylor, September 5, 1885, LDS church historical department, John Taylor Letter file, b1346, Box 20, file #3, typed copy).

Mormon writer Lester Bush claims that President David O. McKay allowed the church rule to be broken in some cases: "With the concurrence of President McKay, a young man of known *Negro ancestry was ordained to the priesthood* after receiving a patriarchal blessing which did not assign him to a "cursed" lineage. In another case, President McKay authorized two children with *Negro ancestry to be sealed in the temple* to the white couple who had adopted them (*Dialogue: A Journal of Mormon Thought*, Spring 1973, p.45).

The Mormon leaders certainly had a double standard concerning this matter. While the Abels and others were allowed to hold the priesthood, Lester Bush says that on August 28, 1947, "the Quorum upheld a decision by John Widtsoe denying a temple recommend to a 'sister having *one thirty-second of negro blood* in her veins' . . ." (*Ibid.*, p.66, n.184).

Objections to Doctrine

Many objections to the anti-black doctrine have been pointed out. One of the most important is that it is not in harmony with the Bible. In Acts 10:34 we read: "Then Peter opened his mouth, and said, Of a truth I perceive that God is no respecter of persons: but in every nation he that feareth him, and worketh righteousness, is accepted with him." In Acts 10:28 Peter said: ". . . God hath showed me that I should not call any man common or unclean." William E. Berrett admits that the Bible does not really lend support to the idea that blacks should be forbidden any rights in the church: "While the Bible contains no account of a Negro bearing the Priesthood of God, one would find rather scant materials upon which to base any policy limiting the rights and participation of the Negro in God's Church" (*Mormonism and the Negro*, part 2, p.3).

Although the *Book of Mormon* states that the Indians were cursed with a dark skin, it does not say anything concerning blacks. It states, in fact, that "all men are privileged the one like unto the other and none are forbidden" (*Book of Mormon*, 2 Nephi 26:28). In 2 Nephi 26:33 this statement appears:". . . he inviteth them all to come unto him and partake of his goodness; and he denieth none that come unto him, *black* and white, bond and free, male and female; and he remembereth the heathen; and *all are alike unto God*, both Jew and Gentile."

Ninth President David O. McKay conceded: "I know of *no scriptural basis* for denying the Priesthood to Negroes other than *one verse in the Book of Abraham* (1:26); however, I believe, as you suggest that the real reason dates back to our pre-existant life" (*Mormonism and the Negro*, part 2, p.19).

Tenth President Joseph Fielding Smith admitted that he could not find any scriptural basis for not allowing blacks to hold the Priesthood other than the statement in the "Book of Abraham," which is part of the *Pearl of Great Price*: "It is true that the negro race is barred from holding the Priesthood, and this has always been the case. The Prophet Joseph Smith taught this doctrine, and it was made known to him, although *we know of no such statement in any revelation in the Doctrine and Covenants, Book of Mormon, or the Bible*" (The Improvement Era, vol. 27, p.565).

Blacks and the Gospel

The Bible teaches that the gospel is to be carried to all people. Jesus is recorded as saying: ". . . go ye into all the world, and preach the gospel to every creature" (Mark 16:15). Jesus also said: "Go ye therefore, and teach all nations, baptizing them in the name of the Father, and of the Son, and of the Holy Ghost" (Matt. 28:19). Philip was actually commanded to preach the gospel to an Ethiopian (see Acts 8:26-39). An Ethiopian is defined in the dictionary as a Negro. Jeremiah asks, "Can the Ethiopian change his skin" (Jer. 13:23). Acts 8:38 tells us that Philip baptized the Ethiopian.

Although the Bible teaches that the gospel is to be carried to all people, including blacks, the Mormon church tried to avoid doing missionary work among the black people. Apostle Bruce R. McConkie stated: "The *gospel message of salvation is not carried affirmatively to them* . . ." (*Mormon Doctrine*, p.477). William E. Berrett said that "*no direct efforts have been made to proselyte* among them" (*Mormonism and the Negro*, part 2, p.5). The Mormon writer Arthur M. Richardson very bluntly stated: ". . . The Church of Jesus Christ of Latter-day Saints, has *no call to carry the gospel to the Negro, and it does not do so*" (*That Ye May Not Be Deceived*, p.13).

The *Pearl of Great Price*, considered Scripture by Latter-day Saints, was used to justify not taking the gospel to blacks. In the "Book of Moses," which is part of the *Pearl of Great Price*, we read: ". . . and there was a blackness came upon all the children of Canaan, that they were despised among all people.

... And it came to pass that Enoch continued to call upon all people, *save it were the people of Canaan*, to repent" (*Pearl of Great Price*, Book of Moses 7:8, 12).

Joseph Fielding Smith claimed that "the Canaanites before the flood preserved the curse in the land; the Gospel was not taken to them, and no other people would associate with them" (*The Way to Perfection*, p.108).

Apostle Mark E. Petersen concluded: "When he told Enoch *not to preach the gospel to the descendants of Cain* who were black, *the Lord engaged in segregation*" (*Race Problems as They Affect the Church*, Address by Mark E. Petersen, August 27, 1954).

Arthur M. Richardson in the same vein declared:

> Also, the gospel was *not carried to this segregated black group* ... the Negroes tread the earth with black dishonorable bodies as a judgment of God because at the time of decision in the pre-existence they were faint-hearted and exhibited an infirmity of purpose—they were not valiant in the cause of the Lord Jesus Christ. Therefore, they were entitled to no better earthly lineage than that of the first earthly murderer, Cain. They were to be the "servant of servants." They were to be segregated. *No effort was made to carry the gospel to them* as a people (*That Ye May Not Be Deceived*, pp.9-10).

Rooted in Prejudice

An examination of early Mormon history plainly reveals that the doctrine concerning blacks grew out of prejudice. At the time the Mormon leaders were formulating their doctrine concerning blacks, slavery was an accepted practice in the southern part of the United States and other parts of the world. In many places blacks were treated like animals. Some people thought they were "without souls and made only to serve the white man."

The Mormons, of course, would not want us to believe that their leaders were influenced by the prejudice of their time. John J. Stewart in defense of Joseph Smith wrote: "To suppose that he would curry the favor of the world by manifesting a prejudice against the Negro is an affront to this courageous man, and to the known facts of history" (*Mormonism and the Negro*, part 1, p.15).

Actually, the truth of the matter is that Joseph Smith and other early leaders of the Mormon church did show prejudice against blacks and were influenced by the views of their time.

It would appear that at first the Mormon church had no real doctrine concerning blacks. By the year 1833, however, some members of the church began to compromise with regard to blacks to appease their slave-holding neighbors. In the Mormon paper, *The Evening and the Morning Star,* July 16, 1833, the following appeared: "Having learned with extreme regret, that an article entitled, 'Free People of Color,' in the last number of the *Star,* has been misunderstood, we feel in duty bound to state, in this Extra, that our intention was not only to stop free people of color from emigrating to this state, but to prevent them from being admitted as members of the Church" (Reprinted in *History of the Church,* vol. 1, pp.378-79).

By 1836 Joseph Smith himself was endorsing the idea of slavery. He wrote a letter for the *Messenger and Advocate* (later reprinted in the *History of the Church*) in which he attacked abolitionists and showed he favored the practice of slavery:

> DEAR SIR:—This place [Kirtland] having recently been visited by a gentleman who advocated the principles or doctrines of those who are called Abolitionists, . . . I fear that the sound might go out, that "an Abolitionist" had held forth several times to this community, . . . all, except a very few, attended to their own vocations, and left the gentleman to hold forth his own arguments to nearly naked walls. I am aware that many, who profess to preach the Gospel, complain against their brethren of the same faith, who reside in the South, and are ready to withdraw the hand of fellowship, because they will not renounce the principle of slavery, and raise their voice against everything of the kind. This must be a tender point, and one which should call forth the candid reflections of all men, and more especially before they advance in an opposition calculated to lay waste the fair states of the South, and let loose upon the world a community of people, who might, peradventure, overrun our country, and violate the most sacred principles of human society, chastity and virtue. . . . *I do not believe that the people of the North have any more right to say that the South shall not hold slaves, than the South have to say the North shall.*
>
> How any community can ever be excited with the chatter of such persons, boys and others, who are too indolent to obtain their living by honest industry, and are incapable of pursuing any occupation of a professional nature, is unaccountable to me; and when I see persons in the free states, signing documents against slavery, it is no less, in my mind, than an army of influence, and a declaration of hostilities, against the people of the South. What course can sooner divide our union? . . . I do not doubt, but those who have been forward in raising their voices against the South, will cry out against me as being uncharitable, unfeeling, unkind, and wholly unacquainted with the Gospel of Christ . . . *the first mention we have of slavery is found in the Holy Bible.* . . . And so far from that prediction being averse to the mind of God, *it remains as a lasting monument of the decree of Jehovah, to the*

shame and confusion of all who have cried out against the South, in consequence of their holding the sons of Ham in servitude. . . . I can say, *the curse is not yet taken off from the sons of Canaan*, neither will be until it is affected by as great a power as caused it to come; and the people who interfere the least with the purpose of God in this matter, will come under the least condemnation before him; and those who are determined to pursue a course, which shows an opposition, and a feverish restlessness *against the decrees of the Lord*, will learn, when perhaps it is too late for their own good, that God can do his own work, without the aid of those who are not dictated by His counsel (*History of the Church*, by Joseph Smith, vol. 2, pp.436-38).

In 1838 Joseph Smith answered the questions "which were frequently" asked him. Question number thirteen was concerning slavery:

"Thirteenth—'Are the Mormons abolitionists?'

"No, unless delivering the people from priestcraft, and the priests from the power of Satan, should be considered abolition. But we do not believe in setting the Negroes free" (*History of the Church*, vol. 3, p.29).

Toward the end of his life Joseph Smith seemed to change his mind somewhat concerning blacks and even spoke against slavery. Under the date of January 2, 1843, Joseph Smith was supposed to have said the following: "Had I anything to do with the negro, I would confine them by strict law to their own species, and put them on a national equalization" (*History of the Church*, vol. 5, p.218).

While Joseph Smith may have mentioned setting the slaves free toward the end of his life, he was basically a racist. Marvin Hill, who teaches history at Brigham Young University, agrees in this interesting comment:

> Even Joseph's "calling for the end of slavery by 1850" in his Presidential campaign is not so liberal as Brodie supposes. . . , Joseph Smith was, therefore, to some degree *a racist, a segregationist*, a colonizer, and only incidentally a supporter of abolition. He had some elements of liberalism in his thinking, but these had definite limits. His record . . . is marked by ambiguity (*Dialogue: A Journal of Mormon Thought*, Autumn 1970, p.99).

Slavery in Utah

Because the Mormon leaders believed blacks were an "inferior race" it was easy for them to accept the idea that they should be slaves. Slavery, therefore, became an accepted practice in the territory of Utah. The following appeared in the *Millennial Star* in 1851: "We feel it to be our duty to define our position in relation to the subject of Slavery. There are several men in the Valley of the Salt Lake from the Southern States, *who have their slaves with them"* (*Millennial Star*, 1851, p.63).

In 1855 Brigham Young said: "You must not think, from what I say, that I am opposed to slavery. *No! The negro is damned, and is to serve his master till God chooses to remove the curse of Ham . . ."* (*New York Herald*, May 4, 1855, as cited in *Dialogue*, Spring 1973, p.56).

In his Master's thesis, James Boyd Christensen observed: "In 1850 *Utah was the only western territory which had Negro slaves. . . .* In short, they countenanced slavery of Negroes among them . . ." ("A Social Survey of the Negro Population of Salt Lake City, Utah," Master's thesis, University of Utah, pp.11-12).

Brigham Young taught that slavery was a "divine institution" and therefore the Civil War could not free the slaves:

> Ham will continue to be servant of servants, as the Lord decreed, until the curse is removed. *Will the present struggle free the slave? No;* but they are now wasting away the black race by thousands. . . .
>
> Treat the slaves kindly and let them live, for Ham must be the servant of servants until the curse is removed. Can you destroy the decrees of the Almighty? *You cannot.* Yet our Christian brethren think that they are going to overthrow the sentence of the Almighty upon the seed of Ham. They cannot do that, though they may kill them by thousands and tens of thousands (*Millennial Star*, vol. 25, p.787; also in *Journal of Discourses*, vol. 10, p.250).

In his book *History of Utah*, page 618, A. L. Neff gives us a further affirmation concerning Brigham Young's views on slavery:

> The Mormon viewpoint with reference to the peculiar institution of the South was admirably set forth in the famous interview between abolitionist Horace Greeley, . . . and President Brigham Young, at Salt Lake City, July 13, 1859:
>
> "H. G.—What is the position of your church with respect to slavery?
>
> "B. Y.—We consider it of divine institution, and not to be abolished until the curse pronounced on Ham shall have been removed from his descendants.
>
> "H. G.—Are any slaves now held in this territory?
>
> "B. Y.—There are.
>
> "H. G.—Do your territorial laws uphold slavery?

"B. Y.—Those laws are printed—you can read for yourself. If slaves are brought here by those who owned them in the states, we do not favor their escape from the service of those owners."

The Territory of Utah gave up the practice of slavery along with the slave-holding states; however, the fact that they countenanced it when it was being practiced shows how insensitive they were to the feelings of black people. Even after the slaves were set free the Mormons continued to talk against blacks. In the year 1884, Angus M. Cannon said that "a colored man . . . is not capable of receiving the Priesthood, and can never reach the highest Celestial glory of the Kingdom of God" (*The Salt Lake Tribune*, October 5, 1884).

The idea that blacks were inferior and should only be servants to the whites persisted in Mormon theology. In fact, Mormon leaders seemed to feel that blacks would still be servants in heaven. On August 26, 1908, President Joseph F. Smith related that a black woman was sealed as a servant to Joseph Smith:

> The same efforts he said had been made by Aunt Jane to receive her endowments and be sealed to her husband and have her children sealed to their parents and her appeal was made to all the Presidents from President Young down to the present First Presidency. But President Cannon conceived the idea that, under the circumstances, it would be proper to permit her to go *to the temple to be adopted to the Prophet Joseph Smith as his servant and this was done.* This seemed to ease her mind for a little while but did not satisfy her, and she still pleaded for her endowments ("Excerpts From The Weekly Council Meetings Of The Quorum Of The Twelve Apostles . . ." as printed in *Mormonism–Shadow or Reality?* p.584).

The idea that a black is only worthy of the position of a servant has deep roots in Mormon theology. Mark E. Petersen, who is now serving as an Apostle in the church, once said that if a "Negro is faithful all his days, he can and will enter the celestial kingdom. He will go there as a servant, but he will get celestial glory" (*Race Problems–As They Affect The Church*, a speech delivered at Brigham Young University, August 27, 1954).

Civil Rights

The Mormon church has been very slow in allowing blacks equal rights. In the *First Year Book in the Seventy's Course in Theology*, written by the Mormon historian B. H. Roberts, and published in 1931, the idea of integration and social equality for blacks is condemned. Mr. Roberts declared:

Perhaps the most convincing book in justification of the south in denying to the Negro race social equality with the white race is the one written by William Benjamin Smith, entitled *The Color Line, . . .* from which the following is a quotation:

"Here, then, is laid bare the news of the whole matter: Is the south justified in this absolute denial of social equality to the Negro, no matter what his (personal) virtues or abilities or accomplishments?

"*We affirm, then that the south is entirely right* in thus keeping open at all times, at all hazards, and at all sacrifices *an impassible social chasm* between black and white. This she must do in behalf of her blood, her essence, of the stock of her Caucasian race. . . . The moment the bar of absolute separation is thrown down in the south, that moment the bloom of her spirit is blighted forever. . . . That *the negro is markedly inferior* to the Caucasian is proved both craniologically and by six thousand years of planet-wide experimentation; and that the commingling of inferior with superior must lower the higher is just as certain as that the half-sum of two and six is only four. . . ." (*First Year Book in the Seventy's Course in Theology,* pp.231-33).

Mark E. Petersen, a present-day Apostle in the Mormon church, defended segregation in 1954:

The discussion on civil rights, . . . *has blinded the thinking* of some of our own people, I believe. . . . We who teach in the Church certainly must have our feet on the ground and not be led astray by the philosophies of men. . . .

I think I have read enough to give you an idea of what the negro is after. He is not just seeking the opportunity of sitting down in a cafe where white people eat . . . it appears that the negro seeks absorption with the white race. He will not be satisfied until he achieves it by intermarriage. That is his objective and we must face it. We must not allow our feeling to carry us away, nor must we feel so sorry for negroes that we will open our arms and embrace them with everything we have. Remember the little statement that we used to say about sin, "First we pity, then endure, then embrace." . . .

Now let's talk segregation again for a few moments. Was segregation a wrong principle? When the Lord chose the nations to which the spirits were to come, determining that some would be Japanese and some would be Chinese and some Negroes and some Americans, *He engaged in an act of segregation.* . . . When he told Enoch not to preach the gospel to the descendants of Cain who were black, *the Lord engaged in segregation.* When He cursed the descendants of Cain as to the Priesthood, *He engaged in segregation.* . . .

Who placed the Negroes originally in darkest Africa? Was it some man, or was it God? And when He placed them there, *He segregated them*. . . . The Lord segregated the people both as to blood and place of residence. At least in the cases of the Lamanites and the Negroes we have the definite word of the Lord Himself that *He placed a dark skin upon them as a curse*—as a punishment and as a sign to all others. He forbade intermarriage with them under threat of extension of the curse. (2 Nephi 5:21) And *he certainly segregated the descendants of Cain when He cursed the Negro as to the Priesthood*, and drew an absolute line. You may even say He dropped an Iron curtain there. . . .

Now we are generous with the negro. We are willing that the Negro have the highest kind of education. I would be willing to let every Negro drive a cadillac if they could afford it. I would be willing that they have all the advantages they can get out of life in the world. But let them enjoy these things among themselves. *I think the Lord segregated the Negro* and who is man to change that segregation? It reminds me of the scripture on marriage, "what God hath joined together, let not man put asunder." Only here we have the reverse of the thing—*what God hath separated, let not man bring together again* (*Race Problems—As They Affect The Church*, an address delivered by Apostle Mark E. Petersen at Brigham Young University, August 27, 1954).

With regard to this speech it is important to note that Apostle Petersen is now second in line to be president of the Mormon church.

In his book *Mormon Doctrine* (1958, pp.107-8), Apostle Bruce R. McConkie reasons:

Certainly the caste systems in communist countries and in India, for instance, are man made and are not based on true principles.

However, in a broad sense, *caste systems have their root and origin in the gospel itself*, and when they operate according to the divine decree, the resultant *restrictions and segregation are right and proper* and have the approval of the Lord. To illustrate: Cain, Ham, and the whole negro race have been cursed with a black skin, the mark of Cain, so they can be identified as a caste apart, a people with whom the other descendants of Adam should not intermarry.

Since 1968 the Mormon-owned Brigham Young University has received a great deal of criticism for its racist policies. Many of the schools where BYU's athletic teams played have had demonstrations against these policies. On November 13, 1969, the *Salt Lake Tribune* announced that Stanford University said "it will schedule no new athletic or other competitions with Brigham Young University because of alleged racial discrimination by the Mormon Church." Obert C. Tanner, professor of philosophy at the University of Utah, called Stanford's action "easily the sharpest criticism of the Mormon religion in this century" (*Ibid.*, January 7, 1970).

Mormon leaders made a number of concessions to avoid trouble with the black people. For instance, on November 15, 1969, the *Denver Post* reported: "The Church of the Black Cross, . . . is calling for: Boycott of Mormon goods, such as record albums of the Mormon Tabernacle Choir."

Shortly after this article appeared, Mormon leaders decided to bring blacks into the choir. Wallace Turner reported: "Recently the Mormon Tabernacle Choir took in two Negro women as second sopranos, and reportedly, is about to welcome a Negro tenor" (*New York Times*, January 25, 1970).

That many members of the Mormon church were dissatisfied over the anti-black doctrine became very evident. Mormon defender John J. Stewart said that "there are at least two points of doctrine and history of this Church about which many LDS themselves—to say nothing of many non-Mormons—feel ill at ease or critical. One of these is its doctrine regarding the Negro" (*Mormonism and the Negro*, part I, p.7).

Wallace Turner observed: "A ferment is working in the Mormon community over the Negro question, particularly among the intellectual element. The mistreatment of Negroes by the LDS church is the reason given by many intellectuals who candidly admit that they have become silent, concealed apostates. Even among many who cling tenaciously to their belief, there is a swelling opinion that the church is dead wrong on this issue" (*The Mormon Establishment*, p.246).

The New "Revelation"

The *Los Angeles Times* for August 27, 1967, carried an article which reported: "The deeply rooted Mormon attitude apparently discriminating against Negroes because of their race is becoming a burning issue in that church—and beyond the church. . . . The increasing heat of racial pressure in the country has brought it into focus as one of the few uncracked fortresses of discrimination."

For eleven years after the *Los Angeles Times* published this criticism the Latter-day Saints continued to cling tenaciously to a policy of discrimination. Church leaders claimed that the doctrine could only be changed by revelation from God. Finally, on June 9, 1978 the Mormon church's *Deseret News* carried a startling announcement by the First Presidency which said that a new revelation had been given and that blacks would be allowed to hold the priesthood:

> . . . we have pleaded long and earnestly in behalf of these, our faithful brethren, spending many hours in the upper room of the Temple supplicating the Lord for divine guidance.
>
> He has heard our prayers, and by revelation has confirmed that the long-promised day has come when every faithful, worthy man in the church may receive the holy priesthood, with power to exercise its divine authority, and enjoy with his loved ones every blessing that flows therefrom, including the blessings of the temple. Accordingly, all worthy male members of the church may be ordained to the priesthood without regard for race or color (*Deseret News*, June 9, 1978, page 1A).

Since we probably printed more material critical of the Mormon anti-black doctrine than any other publisher, the new "revelation" seemed to be a vindication of our work. We printed our first criticism of this doctrine in 1959, and this was certainly not a popular cause to espouse in those days. In 1967 the original papyrus from which Joseph Smith "translated" the "Book of Abraham" was rediscovered. Immediately after the papyrus came to light we began publishing material which showed that Joseph Smith was completely mistaken in his purported translation. The papyrus was in reality a copy of the Egyptian Book of Breathings, a pagan text that had absolutely nothing to do with Abraham or his religion. Since the "Book of Abraham" was the real source of the church's teaching that blacks could not hold the priesthood, we called upon the Mormon leaders to "repudiate the Book of Abraham and renounce the anti-Negro doctrine contained in its pages" (*Salt Lake City Messenger*, March 1968). For a complete treatment of this subject see chapter 11 of this book.

The translation of the papyrus by noted Egyptologists caused many of the intellectual Mormons to lose faith in Joseph Smith's work and consequently the church's anti-black doctrine began to be more openly criticized by members of the church. Some were even excommunicated because of their opposition to the church's position.

Those of us who have criticized the Mormon church for its racial teaching have been ridiculed for attempting to change the doctrine. Mormon apologist Armand L. Mauss wrote: "My plea, then to the civil rights organizations and to all the critics of the Mormon Church is: get off our backs! . . . agitation over the 'Negro issue' by non-Mormon groups, or even by Mormon liberals, is likely simply to increase the resistance to change" 309

(*Dialogue: A Journal of Mormon Thought*, Winter 1967, pp.38-39).

John L. Lund said that "Those who believe that the Church 'gave in' on the polygamy issue and subsequently should give in on the Negro question are not only misinformed about Church History, but are apparently unaware of Church doctrine. . . . Therefore, those who hope that pressure will bring about a revelation need to take a closer look at Mormon history and the order of heaven" (*The Church and the Negro*, 1967, pp.104-5). On page 109 of the same book, Mr. Lund emphasized that "those who would try to pressure the Prophet to give the Negroes the Priesthood do not understand the plan of God nor the order of heaven. Revelation is the expressed will of God to man. Revelation is not man's will expressed to God. All the social, political, and governmental pressure in the world is not going to change what God has decreed to be."

When Stewart Udall, a noted Mormon, came out against the church's anti-black doctrine, Paul C. Richards responded:

> The Church is either true or it isn't. If it changes its stand on the strength of the "great stream of modern religious and social thought," it will be proven untrue. If that happens, the more serious members would do well to join the Cub Scouts. It's cheaper and there is less work and less criticism. . . .
>
> If the Church is true, it will hold to its beliefs in spite of its members. If it is false, more power to the easy-way-out philosophers who claim to know the "imperious truths of the contemporary world" (*Dialogue: A Journal of Mormon Thought*, Autumn 1967, p.6).

In the *Salt Lake City Messenger* for March 1970, we commented: "The Lord plainly reveals to us, as he did to Peter many years ago, that 'GOD IS NO RESPECTER OF PERSONS' (Acts 10:34). To accept the anti-Negro doctrine is to deny the spirit of revelation. If we allow others to do our thinking on this vital issue it could lead to violence or bloodshed. Because we felt that it was not right to put our trust in man, we separated ourselves from the Mormon Church."

As early as 1963 we printed a sheet entitled, "Will There Be a Revelation Regarding the Negro?" At the bottom of this sheet we predicted: "If the pressure continues to increase on the Negro question, the leaders of the Mormon Church will probably have another revelation which will allow the Negro to hold the priesthood." In other writings we pointed out that if the church should change its policy and allow blacks to hold the priesthood, it would not be the first time that Mormon doctrine was revised to fit a changing world. We showed, for instance, that twenty-five years before the Mormon church gave up the practice of polygamy it was declaring that no such change could be made. In the *Millennial Star*, October 28, 1865, the following appeared: "We have shown that in requiring the relinquishment of polygamy, they ask the renunciation of the entire faith of this people. . . . There is no half way house. The childish babble about another revelation is only an evidence how half informed men can talk." As the pressure increased against polygamy, Wilford Woodruff issued the Manifesto (now claimed to be a revelation) which suspended the practice of plural marriage.

Brigham Young Misrepresented

We feel that the Mormon church's change on the doctrine concerning blacks is a very good move because it will undoubtedly help blacks obtain equality in Utah and will probably prevent much bloodshed and trouble. Nevertheless, we must point out that Brigham Young and other leaders have been misrepresented in order to make the change palatable to the Mormon people. For instance, the church's *Deseret News* would have us believe that the change was a fulfillment of a prophecy uttered by Brigham Young: "The announcement Friday fulfilled statements made by most LDS Church presidents since Joseph Smith that blacks would one day obtain the full blessings of the church, including the priesthood. Speaking against slavery, Brigham Young once told the Utah Legislature, '. . . the day will come when all that race (blacks) will be redeemed and possess all the blessings which we now have' " (*Deseret News*, June 10, 1978, p.1A).

While it is true that Brigham Young believed that blacks would eventually receive the priesthood, he made it clear that this was not to happen until *after* the resurrection. The context of the speech which the *Deseret News* cites reveals that Brigham Young believed it would be a sin for the church to give blacks the priesthood before the "last of the posterity of Able [*sic*]" had received it. He went on to say that if the church gave "all the blessings of God" to the blacks prematurely, the priesthood would be taken away and the church would go to destruction. This address is preserved in the church historical department. Michael Marquardt has provided a typed copy (which retains the spelling errors of the original). We extract the following from Brigham Young's speech:

What is that mark? you will see it on the countenance of every African you ever did see upon the face of the earth, . . . the Lord told Cain that he should not receive the blessings of the priesthood nor his seed, until the last of the posterity of Able [sic] had received the priesthood, until the redemtion of the earth. If there never was a prophet, or apostle of Jesus Christ spoke it before, I tell you, this people that are commonly called negroes are the children of old Cain . . . they cannot bear rule in the priesthood, for the curse on them was to remain upon them, until the resedue of the posterity of Michal and his wife receive the blessings, . . . until the times of the restitution shall come . . . Then Cain's seed will be had in remembrance, and the time come when that curse should be wiped off. . . .

I am as much opposed to the principle of slavery as any man in the present acceptation or usage of the term, it is abused. I am opposed to abuseing that which God has decreed, to take a blessing, and make a curse of it. It is a great blessing to the seed of Adam to have the seed of Cain for servants. . . . Let this Church which is called the kingdom of God on the earth; we will sommons the first presidency, the twelve, the high counsel, the Bishoprick, and all the elders of Isreal, suppose we summons them to appear here, and here declare that it is right to mingle our seed, with the black race of Cain, that they shall come in with with us and be pertakers with us of all the blessings God has given to us. On that very day, and hour we should do so, the priesthood is taken from this Church and kingdom and God leaves us to our fate. The moment we consent to mingle with the seed of Cain the Church must go to desstruction,—we should receive the curse which has been placed upon the seed of Cain, and never more be numbered with the children of Adam who are heirs to the priesthood untill that curse be removed (Brigham Young Addresses, Ms d 1234, Box 48, folder 3, dated February 5, 1852, located in the LDS church historical dept.).

The Mormon people are now faced with a serious dilemma; if they really believe Brigham Young was a prophet, then it follows from his statement that the church has lost the priesthood, been put under "the curse" and is going to destruction! In spite of Brigham Young's emphatic warning against giving blacks "all the blessings God has given us," the present leaders have announced that blacks will now receive "all of the privileges and blessings which the gospel affords" (Deseret News, June 9, 1978).

After the First Presidency made their statement, many people became confused over the church's position on interracial marriage. It soon became apparent, however, that the church's ban on marriage to blacks had been lifted. Joseph

Freeman, the first black man ordained to the priesthood after the change, indicated that he wanted to be sealed in the temple to his wife who was not of African descent. Church spokesman Don LeFevre said that such a marriage would be possible and that although the church did not encourage interracial marriage, there was no longer a ban on whites marrying blacks: "That is entirely possible, said Mr. LeFevre. . . . 'So there is no ban on interracial marriage. If a black partner contemplating marriage is worthy of going to the Temple, nobody's going to stop him—if he's marrying a white, an Oriental . . . if he's ready to go to the Temple, obviously he may go with the blessings of the church' " (*Salt Lake Tribune*, June 14, 1978).

On June 24, 1978 the *Tribune* announced that "Joseph Freeman, 26, the first black man to gain the priesthood in the Church of Jesus Christ of Latter-day Saints, Friday went in the Salt Lake Temple with his wife and sons for sacred ordinances . . . Thomas S. Monson, member of the church's Quorum of Twelve Apostles, conducted the marriage and sealing cerenonies [sic]."

In allowing temple marriage between whites and blacks, the church is completely disregarding what President Young referred to as "the law of God in regard to the African race." The reader will remember that President Young taught that the "penalty" for interracial marriage "under the law of God, is death on the spot. This will always be so" (*Journal of Discourses*, vol. 10, p.110). Since Brigham Young taught that this "law of God" could never be changed, the new policy will present a serious problem for some Mormons. As late as 1967 the Mormon writer John L. Lund wrote:

> Brigham Young made a very strong statement on this matter when he said, ". . . Shall I tell you the law of God in regard to the African race? If the white man who belongs to the CHOSEN SEED mixes his blood with the seed of Cain, the penalty under the law of God, is death on the spot. This will always be so." God has commanded Israel not to intermarry. To go against this commandment of God would be to sin. Those who willfully sin with their eyes open to this wrong will not be surprised to find that they will be separated from the presence of God in the world to come. This is spiritual death. . . . It does not matter if they are one-sixth Negro or one-one hundred and sixth, the curse of no Priesthood is still the same. . . . To intermarry with a Negro is to forfeit a "Nation of Priesthood holders" (*The Church and the Negro*, 1967, pp.54-55).

Although we have no way of knowing exactly how many interracial temple marriages have been performed since the change in policy, there is reason to believe that several have taken place. As early as June 9, 1978 Brigham Young University's newspaper, *The Universe*, reported that "Debbie Hall, an elementary education staff member from Seattle, Wash., said a good friend of hers, who is black, is a member of the church and married a white girl. 'It's going to be neat to see them go through the temple,' she said." In the same issue we find the following: "Mrs. Frazier, and her five children are all black but her husband John is white and an Elder in the church. . . . One event that Mrs. Frazier said she has long yearned for is temple marriage and the chance to see her children be able to pass the sacrament."

On page 4 of the same issue of *The Universe*, we find that a black Mormon by the name of Robert L. Stevenson "married Susan V. Bevan about six weeks ago. She is white and also LDS." The paper quoted Stevenson as saying: "We are already planning our temple marriage."

At any rate, the Church Section of the *Deseret News* for June 17, 1978 says that "former presidents of the Church have spoken of the day when the blessings of the priesthood would come to the blacks." A quotation from a sermon by Brigham Young which appeared in the *Journal of Discourses*, volume 7, is cited, but when we go to the original book we find that it has been taken out of context. In this sermon Brigham Young plainly taught that blacks could not receive the priesthood until all of Adam's other children receive it:

> Cain slew his brother . . . and the Lord put a mark upon him, which is the flat nose and black skin. . . . How long is that race to endure the dreadful curse that is upon them? That curse will remain upon them, and they never can hold the Priesthood or share in it until all the other descendants of Adam have received the promises and enjoyed the blessings of the Priesthood and the keys thereof. Until the last ones of the residue of Adam's children are brought up to that favourable position, the children of Cain cannot receive the first ordinances of the Priesthood. They were the first that were cursed, and they will be the last from whom the curse will be removed. When the residue of the family of Adam come up and receive their blessings, then the curse will be removed from the seed of Cain, and they will receive blessings in like proportion (*Journal of Discourses*, vol. 7, pp.290-91).

Brigham Young also taught this doctrine in other published sermons:

> When all the other children of Adam have had the privilege of receiving the Priesthood, and of coming into the kingdom of God, and of being redeemed from the four quarters of the earth,

possess the kingdom, and to have the whole of it under his own control, and not allow any body else the right to say one word, what did he do? He killed his brother. The Lord put a mark on him; and there are some of his children in this room. When all the other children of Adam have had the privilege of receiving the Priesthood, and of coming into the kingdom of God, and of being redeemed from the four quarters of the earth, and have received their resurrection from the dead, then it will be time enough to remove the curse from Cain and his posterity. He deprived his brother of the privilege of pursuing his journey through life, and of extending his kingdom by multiplying upon the earth; and because he did this, he is the last to share the joys of the kingdom of God.

Here are the Lamanites, another example. Their wickedness was not so great as those who slew the Son of God. Jesus revealed himself to them after he was slain, preached to them the Gospel. But in the fourth generation the Priesthood was driven from their midst, and after that, the laws, ordinances, and power of the Gospel ceased to be with them. Is their curse as great as that of those in Palestine? No, it is light, in comparison. They began to thirst for each other's blood, and massacred each other, from generation to generation, until they sunk into wickedness, and evil principles the most degrading, and have become loathsome and vile. Still, the curse will be removed from them before it will be removed from the children of Judah; and they will become "a white and delightsome people."

Brother Ballantyne, and many of our brethren in distant lands write, "O, how we would rejoice to have the privilege of visiting our mountain home!" I would rather undertake to convert five thousand Lamanites, than

to convert one of those poor miserable creatures whose fathers killed the Savior, and who say, "Amen to the deed," to this day. Yea, I would rather undertake to convert the devil himself, if it were possible.

Then I say to the Elders in those regions, be not astonished if you have to see hard times. And if I had a voice that would reach the ears of all those Elders, I would say, LEAVE THEM, AND COME HOME, THE LORD DOES NOT REQUIRE YOU TO STAY THERE, FOR THEY MUST SUFFER AND BE DAMNED.

Now, sisters, write to your husbands who are in regions where the Gospel has been preached anciently, to come home; and I say to all the Elders who are in lands where the Gospel has been preached previous to our day, come away from that people, and leave them to live and die in their sins and ignorance. For the sins of their fathers are a sweet morsel to them, and they take pleasure in their wickedness; therefore, *let them alone*, and come home, and preach to the Lamanites.

There are many in this city who can bear witness to an incident I will now relate. Last spring, when we visited Walker, the Indian chief, he was dull and sulky, and lay in his tent, and would not come out to meet me. I went into his tent, and the first thing he said was, "Brother Brigham, lay your hands upon me, for my spirit has gone away from me, and I want it to come back again." He was full of anger, for his people had been fighting, and he did not know whether to turn on to the side of peace or of war.

We laid hands upon him, and he felt better. At his request, we sung some "Mormon" hymns, and, as we left his tent, he was full of the good Spirit, and would not injure this people, no, not one particle. He was full of kindness, and love to God, and to all His works. He travelled with us

A photograph of the *Journal of Discourses*, vol. 2, page 143. Brigham Young maintained the curse should not be removed from the blacks until after the resurrection.

and have received their resurrection from the dead, then it will be time enough to remove the curse from Cain and his posterity . . . he is the last to share the joys of the kingdom of God (*Journal of Discourses*, vol. 2, p.143).

They will go down to death. And when all the rest of the children have received their blessings in the Holy Priesthood, then that curse will be removed from the seed of Cain, and they will then come up and possess the priesthood, and receive all the blessings which we now are entitled to (*Ibid.*, vol.11, p.272).

In 1949 the First Presidency of the Mormon church issued a statement in which they cited Brigham Young's teaching that blacks cannot receive the priesthood until after the resurrection (see *Mormonism and the Negro*, by John J. Stewart and William E. Berrett, 1960, part 2, p.16). Joseph Fielding Smith, who served as the tenth president of the Mormon Church in the early 1970s, taught that blacks would never hold the priesthood as long as "time endures":

Not only was Cain called upon to suffer, but because of his wickedness he became the father of an inferior race. A curse was placed upon him and that curse has been continued through his lineage and must do so while time endures. Millions of souls have come into this world cursed with a black skin and have been denied the privilege of Priesthood and the fullness of the blessings of the Gospel. . . . they have been made to feel their inferiority and have been separated from the rest of mankind from the beginning (*The Way To Perfection*, 1935, p.101).

In a meeting held in Barratt Hall on October 11, 1958, Joseph Fielding Smith commented that "the Lord will, in due time, remove the restrictions. Not in this world but the time will come. . . ." N. Eldon Tanner, a member of the First Presidency who finally signed the statement granting blacks the priesthood, was completely opposed to the idea in 1967: " 'The church has no intention of changing its doctrine on the Negro,' N. Eldon Tanner, counselor to the First Presidency told SEATTLE during his recent visit here. 'Throughout the history of the original Christian church, the Negro never held the priesthood. There's really nothing we can do to change this. It's a law of God' " (*Seattle Magazine*, December 1967, p.60).

Mormon writer John L. Lund claimed that if the president of the Mormon church gave a revelation that blacks were to hold the priesthood, members of the church would accept it, but he emphasized that such a revelation would not be forthcoming because the "present prophets are in complete agreement with Brigham Young and other past leaders on the question of the Negro and the Priesthood":

Brigham Young revealed that the Negroes will not receive the Priesthood until a great while after the second advent of Jesus Christ, whose coming will usher in a millennium of peace. . . .

In view of what President Young and others have said, it would be foolish indeed to give anyone the false idea that a new revelation is immediately forthcoming on the issue of the Negroes receiving the Priesthood. . . . our present prophets are in complete agreement with Brigham Young and other past leaders on the question of the Negro and the Priesthood. President McKay was asked by a news reporter at the dedication of the Oakland Temple, "When will the Negroes receive the Priesthood?" He responded to the question over a national television network saying, "Not in my lifetime, young man, nor yours." . . .

Social pressure and even government sanctions cannot be expected to bring forth a new revelation . . . all the social pressure in the world will not change what the Lord has decreed to be. . . .

The prophets have declared that there are at least two major stipulations that have to be met before the Negroes will be allowed to possess the Priesthood. The first requirement relates to time. The Negroes will not be allowed to hold the Priesthood during mortality, in fact, not until after the resurrection of all of Adam's children. The other stipulation requires that Abel's seed receive the first opportunity of having the Priesthood. . . . Negroes must first pass through mortality before they may possess the Priesthood ("they will go down to death"). Reference is also made to the condition that the Negroes will have to wait until after the resurrection of all of Adam's children before receiving the Priesthood . . . the last of Adam's children will not be resurrected until the end of the millennium. Therefore, the Negroes will not receive the Priesthood until after that time . . . this will not happen until after the thousand years of Christ's reign on earth. . . .

The second major stipulation that needs to be met . . . is the requirement that Abel's seed receive the opportunity of holding the Priesthood first. . . .

The obvious question is, "When will Abel's seed be redeemed?" It will first of all be necessary that Abel marry, and then be resurrected, and ultimately exalted in the highest degree of the Celestial Kingdom so that he can have a continuation of his seed. It will then be necessary for Abel to create an earth for his spirit children to come to and experience mortality. These children will have to be "redeemed" or resurrected. After the resurrection or redemption of Abel's seed, Cain's descendants, the Negroes, will then be allowed to possess the Priesthood (*The Church and the Negro*, 1967, pp.45-49).

On pages 109-10 of the same book, John L. Lund reiterates: **317**

"First, all of Adam's children will have to resurrect and secondly, the seed of Abel must have an opportunity to possess the Priesthood. These events will not occur until sometime after the end of the millennium."

As late as 1974 Apostle Bruce R. McConkie questioned the spirituality of church members who believed it was time for a new revelation on the blacks. In a conference message delivered October 4, 1974, Apostle McConkie said:

> Am I valiant in the testimony of Jesus if my chief interest and concern in life is laying up in store the treasures of the earth, rather than the building up of the kingdom? . . .

> Am I valiant if I am deeply concerned about the Church's stand on who can or who cannot receive the priesthood and think it is time for a new revelation on this doctrine? . . .

> Am I valiant if I engage in gambling, play cards, go to pornographic movies . . . (*The Ensign*, November 1974, p.35).*

Even though most Mormons claim they are happy with the doctrinal change with regard to blacks, there is evidence that the "revelation" came as a real shock. A class at Brigham Young University which conducted a "random telephone survey" of Utah County residents found that 79 percent of those interviewed did not expect a change at this time. Furthermore, many people compared the news to an announcement of some kind of disaster or death:

> Some 45 percent of those who heard of the doctrine from personal sources expressed doubt that the news was true. This compares with only 25 percent of those who learned from media sources. Sixty-two percent of the former group expressed shock, compared with 52 percent of the latter. . . .

---

*After the revelation was given Apostle Bruce R. McConkie actually gave a speech in which he chastised those "disbelieving people" who were reluctant to accept the new revelation because it contradicted things taught in the past: "There are statements in our literature by the early brethren which we have interpreted to mean that the Negroes would not receive the priesthood in mortality. I have said the same things, and people write me letters and say, 'You said such and such, and how is it now that we do such and such?' And all I can say to that is that it is time disbelieving people repented and got in line and believed in a living, modern prophet. Forget everything that I have said, or what President Brigham Young or President George Q. Cannon or whomsover has said in days past that is contrary to the present revelation. We spoke with a limited understanding and without the light and knowledge that now has come into the world. . . . We have now had added a new flood of intelligence and light on this particular subject, and it erases all the darkness. . . . It doesn't make a particle of difference what anybody ever said about the Negro matter before the first day of June of this year (1978)." ("*All Are Alike Unto God,*" by Elder Bruce R. McConkie of the Council of the Twelve, pages 1-2)

Those surveyed appeared surprised by the announcement, Haroldsen said. Thirty-nine percent said they did not think "it would ever happen"—that the priesthood would ever be given to blacks.

Another 40 percent expected it years in the future, after Christ's return, during the Millenium, or "not in my lifetime." . . .

In trying to explain how they reacted to the news, 14 persons compared its impact with that of the assassination of President John F. Kennedy. Another 13 compared it to the news of the death of an LDS Church president. Eight compared it to a natural disaster, especially the Teton dam break.

Others compared the news with the death of a family member or friend, with a declaration of war, or other major political event (*The Daily Universe*, June 22, 1978).

After the "revelation" was announced a number of Mormons who could not accept the new teaching left the church. A full-page advertisement attacking the change was published in the *Salt Lake Tribune* on July 23, 1978 by a group calling themselves "Concerned Latter-day Saints." From this article it would appear that members of this group are also disturbed because of the earlier doctrinal change relating to plural marriage.

Better Late Than Never

Writing in the *New York Times*, June 11, 1978, Mario S. De-Pillis observed: "For Mormonism's anti-black policy a revelation was the only way out, and many students of Mormonism were puzzled only at the lateness of the hour." That the Mormon church was forced into the revelation is obvious to anyone who seriously examines the evidence. We have already pointed out that athletic teams from the church's Brigham Young University were the target of very serious protests and that in 1969 Stanford University announced it would "schedule no new athletic or other competitions with Brigham Young University." Immediately following the announcement of the new "revelation," Gary Cavalli, athletic director for Stanford University, said, "I think the ban will be lifted" (*Salt Lake Tribune*, June 21, 1978).

In 1974 the Mormon doctrine of discrimination against blacks brought the Boy Scouts into a serious confrontation with the NAACP. The Boy Scouts of America do not discriminate because of religion or race, but Mormon-sponsored troops did have a policy of discrimination. On July 18, 1974, the *Salt Lake Tribune* reported: "A 12-year-old boy scout has been denied a senior patrol leadership in his troop because he is black, Don L. Cope, black ombudsman for the state, said Wednesday. . . . Mormon 'troop policy is that in order for a scout to become a patrol leader, he must be a deacon's quorum president in the LDS Church. Since the boy cannot hold the priesthood, he cannot become a patrol leader.' "

Mormon leaders apparently realized that they could never prevail in this matter and a compromise was worked out:

> Shortly before Boy Scout officials were to appear in Federal Court Friday morning on charges of discrimination, the Church of Jesus Christ of Latter-day Saints issued a policy change which will allow black youths to be senior patrol leaders, a position formerly reserved for white LDS youths in troops sponsored by the church. . . . An LDS Church spokesman said Friday under the "guidelines set forth in the statement, a young man other than president of the deacons quorum could (now) become the senior patrol leader if he is better qualified" (*Salt Lake Tribune*, August 3, 1974).

Since 1976 the Mormon church was repeatedly embarrassed by one of its own members who became alienated over the anti-black doctrine and decided to take matters into his own hands. On April 3, 1976 the *Salt Lake Tribune* reported that Douglas A. Wallace "ordained a black into the priesthood Friday, saying he did so in an attempt to force a revision in Mormon doctrine about the Negro race. . . . Wallace said he has long been bothered by the Mormon Church's bias against blacks, and he feels the time has come to challenge it. He said often all that is required to change a policy is for someone to break out of tradition . . . he hopes there are no recriminations against him for his action, such as excommunication."

On April 13, 1976 the *Salt Lake Tribune* revealed that "Douglas A. Wallace was excommunicated from the Church of Jesus Christ of Latter-day Saints Sunday for ordaining a black man into the church's priesthood." After a confrontation with church personnel at an April conference session, Mr. Wallace was ejected from the Tabernacle. Later he was served with "a court order barring him from attending conference" (*Ibid.*, October 4, 1976).

Although we did not agree with some of Mr. Wallace's ideas on religion, we did not consider him to be dangerous and we were rather surprised to notice the close surveillance the police kept him under when he walked along the public sidewalk outside of Temple Square. The fear of the threat Mr. Wallace presented to the church seems to have led to a tragic incident where a policeman was accidentally shot and permanently paralyzed. This occurred at the time of the church's conference held in April, 1977. The Salt Lake City police had placed a stakeout around a home where Wallace was staying and at 4:20 A.M. on a Sunday morning one of the policemen accidentally shot his partner. At first the police "denied" that they had Mr. Wallace under surveillance (see *Salt Lake Tribune*, April 5, 1977), but when Wallace pressed for an investigation the police were forced to admit the truth about the matter: "Salt Lake City police officers admitted Thursday that the accidental wounding of an undercover officer occurred during surveillance of Mormon dissident Douglas A. Wallace. . . . Reports released Thursday by both the county sheriff's office and the county attorney show that six officers were on stakeout around the John W. Fitzgerald home . . . where Mr. Wallace was staying" (*Salt Lake Tribune*, April 8, 1977).

Douglas Wallace claimed that the Mormon church "was behind April police surveillance . . . that led to the accidental shooting of a Salt Lake City police officer" (*Ibid.*, September 17, 1977). Finally, David Olson, the disabled police officer, took exception to a press release issued by the church. In a letter to the editor of the *Salt Lake Tribune*, January 18, 1978, Mr. Olson attacked President "Spencer W Kimball for his incorrect press release concerning the police involvement combined with the LDS church's efforts to restrict Douglas A. Wallace from the temple grounds, specifically the Tabernacle, on April 3, 1977. His denial of these actions is wrong. Any man who can take such actions and still call himself a prophet deserves more than I to be confined to this wheelchair."

Douglas Wallace filed lawsuits amounting to millions of dollars against the Mormon church, and although he was not able to prevail against the church in the courts, the publicity surrounding the suits caused the church no end of trouble. We feel that his actions and the embarrassment they caused the church played a part in bringing about the decision to have a new "revelation."

Another Mormon who put a great deal of pressure on the church is Byron Marchant. Mr. Marchant took a very strong stand against racism in the church. The *Dallas Morning News* for October 20,1977 reported: "The man who cast the first vote in modern history against a leader of the Church of Jesus Christ of Latter-day Saints has been excommunicated and fired as chapel janitor." When Mr. Marchant tried to distribute literature at Temple Square at the next conference he was arrested "on charges of trespassing" (*Salt Lake Tribune*, April 3, 1978). Mr. Marchant published a sheet in which he called for a dem-

onstration against the church's policy: "Next October Conference (1978) I will join all interested in a march on Temple
Square in Salt Lake City. . . . every person and/or group concerned about Utah Racism is encouraged to speak out and attend the October protest." Mr. Marchant's threat of a demonstration at the next conference may have caused Mormon leaders to think more seriously about having a new revelation. We
feel that the church was wise to change its policy before the
demonstration because the issue was so explosive that the
slightest incident could have touched off a riot where innocent
people could have been injured.

However this may be, when the Mormon church yielded, Mr.
Marchant dropped a civil suit filed "against Church President
Spencer W. Kimball" (*Salt Lake Tribune*, June 10, 1978).
Another article in the same issue of the *Tribune* observed that
"the last three years have also seen repeated attempts by church
dissidents to subpoena Mormon leaders into court proceedings, with the central issue often related to the church's belief
about blacks."

Problem in Brazil

Besides all the problems the church was having with dissidents, it was faced with an impossible situation in Brazil. Even
the church's own *Deseret News* admitted that "a major problem
the church has faced with its policy regarding blacks was in
Brazil, where the church is building a temple. Many people
there are miied [mixed?] racially, and it is often impossible to
determine whether church members have black ancestry"
(*Deseret News*, June 10, 1978).

Mormon leaders have been aware of this problem for some
time. Lester E. Bush, Jr., gave this revealing information in an
article published in *Dialogue: A Journal of Mormon Thought*,
Spring 1973, page 41:

> The decision to deny the priesthood to anyone with Negro an-
> cestry ("no matter how remote"), had resolved the theoretical
> problem of priesthood eligibility, but did not help with the prac-
> tical problem of identifying the "blood of Cain" in those not
> already known to have Negro ancestry. . . .
>
> The growth of the international Church was clearly bringing
> new problems. Brazil was particularly difficult. . . . J. Reuben
> Clark, First Counselor to George Albert Smith, reported that the
> Church was entering "into a situation in doing missionary work
> . . . where it is very difficult if not impossible to tell who has
> negro blood and who has not. He said that if we are baptizing
> Brazilians, we are almost certainly baptizing people of negro

blood, and that if the Priesthood is conferred upon them, which no doubt it is, we are facing a very serious problem."

The hypocrisy of the situation in South America was pointed out in 1966 by Wallace Turner: "A different thing is going on in South America where Mormon missionaries are pushing ahead full throttle. There the former careful selection to keep out "white Negroes" has been allowed to slide a little. . . . 'There is no question but that in Brazil they have been ordaining priests who are part Negro,' said one careful observer" (*The Mormon Establishment,* 1966, p.261).

With the opening of the new temple in Brazil, the situation would have turned into a real nightmare. Actually, the Mormon church has the same problem in the United States. Patriarch Eldred G. Smith remarked: "I had a young lady who was blonde, a[n]d no sign or indications visibly of the Negro line at all, but yet she was deprived of going to the Temple. . . . We have these conditions by the thousands in the United States today and are getting more of them. If they have any blood of the Negro at all in their line, in their veins at all, they are not entitled to the blessings of the Priesthood. . . . No limit as to how far back so far as I know" (*Patriarchal Blessings,* Institute of Religion, January 17, 1964, p.8).

Time Magazine for June 30, 1958, page 47, pointed out Dr. Robert P. Stuckert reached the conclusion that of 135 million Americans classified as white in 1950, about 28 million (21 percent) had some African ancestry. The church's stress on genealogical research placed many members of the church in a very embarrassing position. Many members of the church discovered they had black ancestors and attempted to cover it up. This situation has caused a great deal of unnecessary guilt among members of the church who have diligently followed the teaching concerning the necessity of genealogical research.

New "Revelation" Evades the Real Issues

O. Kendall White, Jr., made these interesting observations six years before the revelation was given:

> Since they believe in "continuing revelation," Mormons have a mechanism that enables them to reverse previous positions without repudiating the past. . . . That the church will invoke such a mechanism to resolve the racial issue is not too unlikely . . . this approach has a serious drawback. It is the tendency not to acknowledge the errors of the past. While revelation could be used to legitimate a new racial policy and to redefine Mormon relations with black people, Mormons might still be unwilling to condemn the racism involved in their history. They might be

323

inclined to argue that Mormons in earlier periods were under a different mandate than the one binding them. This obviously implies that the church is never wrong. Thus, change may come through the notion of continuing revelation, but the racist aspects of Mormon history will not necessarily be condemned (*The Journal of Religious Thought*, Autumn-Winter, 1973, pp.57-58).

It would appear that church leaders have done exactly what Mr. White warned against, they have used revelation as a means of side-stepping the real issues involved. Mario S. DePillis pointed out that "the revelation leaves unsolved other racist implications of the Book of Mormon and the Pearl of Great Price—scriptures that are both cornerstones and contradictions" (*New York Times*, June 11, 1978).

One issue that Mormon leaders now seem to be dodging is that concerning skin color. As we pointed out earlier, Mormon theology has always taught that "a black skin is a mark of the curse of heaven placed upon some portions of mankind" (*Juvenile Instructor*, vol. 3, p.157). The *Book of Mormon* itself is filled with the teaching that people with dark skins are cursed (see our discussion of this matter on pp. 208-15). President Spencer W. Kimball, who gave the new "revelation" which allows blacks to hold the priesthood, actually believes that God is changing the Indians "to whiteness and to delightsomeness" (*Improvement Era*, December 1960, pp.922-23). He feels, however, that this has to be done by the power of God and has suppressed Joseph Smith's 1831 revelation which commanded the Mormons to take "wives of the Lamanites and Nephites, that their posterity may become white, delightsome and just." We seriously doubt that President Kimball will ever allow this revelation to be canonized in the *Doctrine and Covenants* since he has in the past discouraged intermarriage with the Indians. In 1958 he gave an address which touched on this subject. President Kimball's statement was reprinted in the Church Section of the *Deseret News* on June 17, 1978: ". . . there is one thing that I must mention, and that is interracial marriages. When I said you must teach your young people to overcome their prejudices and accept the Indians, I did not mean that you would encourage intermarriage."

Although the Mormon church is now opening the door to temple marriages between blacks and whites, President Kimball is probably not too enthused about the matter. An endorsement of Joseph Smith's 1831 revelation encouraging intermarriage with Indians could now lead white members to seek marriages with blacks. Since blacks are no longer cursed as to the priesthood, the revelation might just as logically be interpreted that Mormons should "take unto you wives" of the Ethiopians or Nigerians "that their posterity may become white, delightsome and just."

Another matter which the new revelation allowing blacks to hold the priesthood does not resolve is the teaching concerning pre-existence. In the past Mormon leaders have stressed that blacks were cursed as to the priesthood because of "unfaithfulness in the spirit—or pre-existence." Should a faithful Mormon continue to believe that blacks were unrighteous in a pre-existent state? It will be especially interesting to see how church leaders explain this matter to blacks in the church. Monroe Fleming, for instance, was converted to the church over twenty-five years ago. President Joseph Fielding Smith explained to him why he could not hold the priesthood, but since the new "revelation" he is being encouraged to be ordained. Now, was Mr. Fleming really unfaithful in a pre-existent state or did church leaders just make a mistake in the past when they said he could not hold the priesthood? Church leaders should explain if they believe black babies born after the new "revelation" were inferior spirits in a pre-existent state.

Now that they have abandoned the idea that blacks cannot hold the priesthood, they should explain if they are giving up some of their teachings on the pre-existence. They should also explain if they are repudiating the *Book of Mormon* teaching that a dark skin is given by God as a "curse." By giving a "revelation" on the blacks without explaining its implications, the Mormon leaders are leaving their people in a dense doctrinal fog. If the church continues to hide behind a purported revelation on the blacks and fails to come to grips with its racist doctrines, thousands of people are going to continue believing these doctrines and the church will be plagued with racism for many years to come.

Does the Revelation Really Exist?

One thing that should be noted about the new "revelation" is that the church has failed to produce a copy of it. All we have is a statement by the First Presidency which says a revelation was received. Joseph Smith, the first Mormon prophet, printed many of his revelations in the *Doctrine and Covenants* and other church publications, and the early Mormon church even mocked the Catholics because they did not allow the revelations given by their popes to enter the "sacred canon." In refusing to canonize or even make public the new "revelation" on blacks, the Mormon leaders are now practicing the very thing

325

the Catholics were accused of doing. The *Salt Lake Tribune* for June 13, 1978 reported: "Kimball refused to discuss the revelation that changed the church's 148-year-old policy against ordination of blacks, saying it was a 'personal thing.' . . . Kimball said the revelation came at this time because conditions and people have changed. 'It's a different world than it was 20 or 25 years ago. The world is ready for it,' he said."

We seriously doubt that President Kimball will ever put forth a written revelation on the bestowal of priesthood on blacks. We doubt, in fact, that any such document exists. What probably happened was that the leaders of the church finally realized that they could no longer retain the anti-black doctrine without doing irreparable damage to the church. Under these circumstances they were impressed with the fact that the doctrine had to be changed and this impression was referred to as a revelation from God. In a letter to the Editor of the *Salt Lake Tribune*, June 24, 1978, Eugene Wagner observed:

> . . . was this change of doctrine really a revelation from the Lord, or did the church leaders act on their own? Why don't they publish that revelation and let the Lord speak in his own words? All we saw was a statement of the First Presidency, and that is not how a revelation looks.
>
> When God speaks the revelation starts with the words: "Thus sayeth the Lord . . ." It seems when the Lord decides to change a doctrine of such great importance he will talk himself to the people of his church. If such a revelation cannot be presented to the members it is obvious that the first presidency acted on its own, most likely under fear of public pressure to avoid problems of serious consequences and to maintain peace and popularity with the world.

At the 148th Semiannual Conference of the Mormon church, members of the church were asked to "accept this revelation as the word and will of the Lord," but the only document presented to the people was the letter of the First Presidency, dated June 8, 1978 (see *The Ensign*, November 1978, p.16).

Some Mormons have put forth the rumor that the power of God was manifested as on the day of Pentecost when President Kimball gave the "revelation." Kimball himself seems to be trying to dispel this idea. The following statement about the "revelation" appeared in *Time* on August 7, 1978, p.55: "In other renditions it came complete with a visitation from Joseph Smith. . . . In an interview, his first since the announcement, Kimball described it much more matter of factly to *Time* staff writer Richard Ostling: 'I spent a good deal of time in the temple alone, praying for guidance, and there was a gradual and general development of the whole program, in connection with the Apostles.' "

For some time after the anti-black doctrine was changed, Mormon leaders were reluctant to inform their own people of the details surrounding the giving of the "revelation." Finally, six months after the event, the church news staff asked President Kimball if he would "care to share with the readers of the Church News any more of the circumstances under which that was given?" President Kimball's answer is very revealing. He makes no reference to a voice or any written revelation. In fact, his statement gives the impression that it was only a feeling or an assurance that he received:

> It went on for some time as I was searching for this, because I wanted to be sure. We held a meeting of the Council of the Twelve in the temple on the regular day. We considered this very seriously and thoughtfully and prayerfully.
>
> I asked the Twelve not to go home when the time came. I said, "Now would you be willing to remain in the temple with us?" And they were. I offered the final prayer and I told the Lord if it wasn't right, if He didn't want this change to come in the Church that I would be true to it all the rest of my life, and I'd fight the world against it if that's what He wanted.
>
> We had this special prayer circle, then I knew that the time had come. I had a great deal to fight, of course, myself largely, because I had grown up with this thought that Negroes should not have the priesthood and I was prepared to go all the rest of my life till my death and fight for it and defend it as it was. But this revelation and assurance came to me so clearly that there was no question about it (*Deseret News,* Church Section, January 6, 1979, p.4).*

---

*In his speech *"All Are Alike Unto God,"* pages 2-3, Apostle Bruce R. McConkie told how the "revelation" was received. His description indicates that there was no spoken or written revelation—only a very good "feeling": "The result was that President Kimball knew, and each one of us knew, independent of any other person, by direct and personal revelation to us, that the time had now come to extend the gospel . . . to . . . the black race. . . . The Lord could have sent messengers from the other side to deliver it, but he did not. He gave the revelation by the power of the Holy Ghost. Latter-day Saints have a complex: many of them desire to magnify and build upon what has occurred, and they delight to think of miraculous things. And maybe some of them would like to believe that the Lord himself was there, or that the Prophet Joseph Smith came to deliver the revelation . . . which was one of the possibilities. Well, these things did not happen. The stories that go around to the contrary are not factual or realistic or true, . . . I cannot describe in words what happened; I can only say that it happened and that it can be known and understood only by the feeling that can come into the heart of man. You cannot describe a testimony to someone."

In putting forth his new "revelation" on blacks, President Kimball will not admit to any wrongdoing on the part of the church: "There are members of the Church who had brought to President David O. McKay their reasons why it should be changed. Others had gone to Joseph Fielding Smith and Harold B. Lee and to all the former presidents and it had not been accepted because the time had not come for it" (*Ibid.*, p.15). We feel that it is wrong to attribute such a "revelation" to God. It makes it appear that God has been a racist for thousands of years, and that Mormon leaders by "pleading long and earnestly in behalf of these, our faithful brethren, spending many hours in the upper room of the Temple" have finally persuaded God to give blacks the priesthood. The truth of the matter, however, is that "God is no respecter of persons: but in every nation he that feareth him, and worketh righteousness, is accepted with him" (Acts 10:34-35). It is the Mormon leaders who have kept blacks under a curse. They have continually and stubbornly opposed the advancement of black people, threatening and excommunicating those who differed with them on the matter. Finally, when their backs were to the wall, the Mormon leaders were forced to change their position.

Impact of Revelation

Some people believe the Mormon church is not sincere in opening priesthood advancement to blacks. We feel, however, that even though the Mormon leaders have failed to face some important issues, they have made a major concession which will gradually weaken racism throughout the church. The *Deseret News*, Church Section, January 6, 1979, reported that "Brother (Helecio) Martins (a black member) is now a member of the stake presidency."

We feel that one of the important reasons the church decided to confer priesthood on blacks was that the anti-black doctrine was hurting missionary work. With a change in this policy, we anticipate that the church will make many more converts. On the other hand, many members of the church have become disillusioned because of the church's handling of the racial issue, and the new "revelation" has tended to confirm in their minds that the Lord had nothing to do with the whole matter. For those Christians working with Mormons, this may really prove to be an opening for effective witnessing.

FALL OF THE BOOK OF ABRAHAM

Chapter 11

The Book of Abraham was supposed to have been written on papyrus by Abraham about 4,000 years ago. According to Mormon writers, this same papyrus fell into Joseph Smith's hands in 1835. He translated the papyrus and published it under the title, "The Book of Abraham." The Book of Abraham was accepted by the Mormon church as Scripture and is now published as part of the *Pearl of Great Price*—one of the four standard works of the church.

If the papyrus were really written by Abraham, as the Mormons claim, its discovery was probably one of the most important finds in the history of the world. To say that the papyrus would be worth a million dollars would be greatly underestimating its value, for it would be older than any portion of the Bible. Dr. Sidney B. Sperry, of Brigham Young University, observed: "If a manuscript were to be found in the sands of Egypt written in Egyptian characters with the title of 'The Book of Abraham,' it would cause a sensation in the scholarly world. Our people do profess to have such a scripture containing but five chapters which was written by Abraham . . ." (*Ancient Records Testify in Papyrus and Stone*, 1938, p.39).

On page 83 of the same book, Dr. Sperry boasts:

> . . . the Book of Abraham will some day be reckoned as one of the most remarkable documents in existence . . . the author or editors of the book we call Genesis lived after the events recorded therein took place. Our text of Genesis can therefore not be dated earlier than the latest event mentioned by it. It is evident that the writings of Abraham . . . must of necessity be *older* than the original text of Genesis. I say this in passing because some of our brethren have exhibited surprise when told that the text of the Book of Abraham is *older than that of Genesis*.

From this it is plain to see that if the "Book of Abraham" is an authentic record of Abraham its value to the world could not be estimated. If, on the other hand, the papyrus was not really written by Abraham, then Joseph Smith was guilty of misrepresentation, and serious doubt is cast upon the *Book of Mormon* and other writings which he claimed were Scripture.

The Papyri Rediscovered

For many years Joseph Smith's collection of papyri was lost, but on November 27, 1967, the Mormon-owned *Deseret News* announced:

> NEW YORK—A collection of pa[p]yrus manuscripts, long believed to have been destroyed in the Chicago fire of 1871, was presented to The Church of Jesus Christ of Latter-day Saints here Monday by the Metropolitan Museum of Art. . . .
>
> Included in the papyri is a manuscript identified as the original document from which Joseph Smith had copied the drawing which he called "Facsimile No. 1" and published with the Book of Abraham.

The importance of this find cannot be overemphasized, for now Joseph Smith's ability as a translator of ancient Egyptian writing can be put to an absolute test.

In February, 1968, the *Improvement Era*, a Mormon publication, announced that there was an "unprecedented interest generated throughout the Church by the recovery of 11 pieces of papyrus that were once the property of the Prophet Joseph Smith." Many members of the church felt that Joseph Smith's work had been vindicated. Dr. Sidney B. Sperry, however, warned his people to be cautious (see *Mormonism—Shadow or Reality?* p.294). Dr. Hugh Nibley, who is supposed to be the Mormon church's top authority on the Egyptian language, warned his people that there was trouble ahead. On December 1, 1967, the *Daily Universe*, published at Brigham Young University, reported these statements by Dr. Nibley:

> "The papyri scripts given to the Church do not prove the Book of Abraham is true," Dr. Hugh Nibley said . . . Wednesday night. "LDS scholars are *caught flat footed* by this discovery," he went on to say.
>
> According to Dr. Nibley, Mormon scholars should have been doing added research on the Pearl of Great Price years ago. Non-Mormon scholars will bring in questions regarding the manuscripts which will be hard to answer because of lack of scholarly knowledge on the subject. . . . Dr. Nibley said worldly discoveries are going to "bury the Church in criticism" if members of the Church don't take it upon themselves to become a people of learning.

On another occasion Dr. Nibley discussed the papyri and

commented that "in the moment of truth the Mormons have to face the world *unprepared*, after having been given a hundred years' fair warning" (*BYU Studies*, Winter 1968, pp.171-72).

Although these are strange words to be coming from the man whom Mormon leaders have chosen to defend the "Book of Abraham," they are certainly the truth.

In order to understand the problems involved it is necessary to give a brief history of the papyri. Joseph Smith's *History of the Church* contains the following account of the discovery of the papyri: "The records were obtained from one of the catacombs of Egypt, . . . by the celebrated French traveler, Antonio Sebolo, . . . he made a will of the whole, to Mr. Michael H. Chandler. . . . On opening the coffins, he discovered . . . two rolls of papyrus . . ." (*History of the Church*, vol. 2, pp.348-49).

After receiving some mummies along with the papyri, Mr. Chandler traveled about exhibiting them. He arrived in Kirtland, Ohio in 1835. Joseph Smith became interested in the papyri, and the Mormons purchased both the papyri and the mummies from Mr. Chandler. Joseph Smith examined the papyri and declared that they were the writings of Abraham and Joseph of Egypt: ". . . I commenced the translation of some of the characters or hieroglyphics, and much to our joy found that one of the rolls contained the writings of Abraham, another the writings of Joseph of Egypt, etc. . . ." (*History of the Church*, vol. 2, p.236).

In 1842 Joseph Smith published his translation of the "Book of Abraham" in the *Times and Seasons*. Three drawings from the "Book of Abraham" were included in this work.

During the time that Joseph Smith possessed the papyri many people were allowed to see them. Josiah Quincy, who met with Joseph Smith at Nauvoo, gave the following account of his visit:

> The prophet referred to his miraculous gift of understanding all languages. . . . "And now come with me," said the prophet, "and I will show you the curiosities." . . . "These are mummies," said the exhibitor. "I want you to look at that little runt of a fellow over there. He was a great man in his day. Why, that was Pharaoh Necho, King of Egypt!" Some parchments inscribed with hieroglyphics were then offered us. . . . "That is *the handwriting of Abraham*, the Father of the Faithful," said the prophet. "This is the autograph of Moses, and these lines were written by his brother Aaron. Here we have the earliest account of the Creation, from which Moses composed the First Book of Genesis." . . . We were further assured that the prophet was the only mortal who could translate these mysterious writings, and that his power

was given by direct inspiration (*Among the Mormons*, pp.136-37).

In Joseph Smith's time the science of Egyptology was in its infancy. Therefore, Joseph Smith's work as a translator could not be adequately tested. The knowledge of hieroglyphic, hieratic and demotic Egyptian writing had been lost many centuries before, and it was not until the beginning of the nineteenth century that there appeared much hope of deciphering these strange writings. Just before the turn of the century (1799) some French soldiers found a stone with Greek, demotic and hieroglyphic writings upon it. This is known as the Rosetta Stone. Since the Greek writing recorded the same information as the Egyptian, it was used as a key to decipher Egyptian writings.

At the time Joseph Smith received the papyri there were only a very limited number of scholars who understood anything about the Egyptian language. In his book, An *Egyptian Hieroglyphic Dictionary* (vol. 1, p.xvii), E. A. Wallis Budge stated: "In 1837, . . . Birch . . . decided to attempt to publish a 'Hieroglyphical Dictionary.' . . . publishers were not eager to spend their money on a dictionary of a language of which scarcely a dozen people in the whole world had any real knowledge."

From this information it is plain to see that there was little chance of Joseph Smith's work coming into conflict with the science of Egyptology during his lifetime. Joseph Smith was murdered in 1844, and within a few years the Mormons came out West. Smith's mother as well as his widow refused to go West, and therefore the Mormon church lost control of the collection of papyri. Nevertheless, Joseph Smith had included three drawings in his "Book of Abraham," and also gave an interpretation of much of the material which appeared in these drawings.

By the year 1860 the science of Egyptology had advanced to the point where some people felt that it could be used to test Joseph Smith's ability as a translator. The printed facsimiles from the "Book of Abraham" were submitted to Egyptologist M. Theodule Deveria. Deveria not only accused Joseph Smith of making a false translation but also of altering the scenes shown in the facsimiles. Deveria's work on the "Book of Abraham" seemed to have little influence on the Mormons.

In 1912, however, another attack was made on the "Book of Abraham." Mormon historian B. H. Roberts explained: "In 1912 a wide-spread interest was awakened in the Book of Abraham by the publication of a brochure, by Rt. Rev. F. S. Spalding. . . . The bishop submitted the facsimiles of some of the parchment pages from which the Book of Abraham had been translated . . . to a number of the foremost of present day Egyptian scholars" (*A Comprehensive History of the Church*, vol. 2, p.138).

On page 23 of *Joseph Smith, Jr., As A Translator*, F. S. Spalding reproduced a letter from Dr. A. H. Sayce of Oxford, England, which said: "It is difficult to deal seriously with Joseph Smith's impudent fraud. . . . Smith has turned the Goddess into a king and Osiris into Abraham."

James H. Breasted, Ph.D., Haskell Oriental Museum, University of Chicago, stated: ". . . these three facsimiles of Egyptian documents in the 'Pearl of Great Price' depict the most common objects in the mortuary religion of Egypt. Joseph Smith's interpretations of them as part of a unique revelation through Abraham, therefore, very clearly demonstrates that he was totally unacquainted with the significance of these documents and absolutely ignorant of the simplest facts of Egyptian writing and civilization" (pp.26-27).

The other Egyptologists whom Spalding contacted rendered a similar verdict—i.e., the "Book of Abraham" was a work of Joseph Smith's imagination and had no basis in fact. The Mormon leaders did not know how to deal with Spalding's pamphlet. Mormon historian B. H. Roberts admitted that there "were no Egyptian scholars in the church of the Latter-day Saints who could make an effective answer to the conclusions of the eight scholars who in various ways pronounced against the correctness of Joseph Smith's translation . . ." (*A Comprehensive History of the Church*, vol. 2, p.139).

The Mormons, however, did receive help from a writer who called himself "Robert C. Webb, Ph.D." Fawn M. Brodie claimed that Robert C. Webb's real name was "J. E. Homans," and that he was "neither an Egyptologist nor a Ph.D." (*No Man Knows My History*, 1957, p.175). From this it is rather obvious that the Mormon leaders were guilty of deception. Strange as it may seem, Dr. Sidney B. Sperry, of Brigham Young University, confirmed the fact that Robert C. Webb was no Ph.D: "He wrote a wonderful book, . . . under the name of Robert C. Webb, Ph.D. I regret that the brethren let him put down Robert C. Webb, Ph.D., because *he was no Ph.D.*" (*Pearl of Great Price Conference*, December 10, 1960, 1964 ed., p.9). On page 6 of the same publication, Dr. Sperry stated that Dr. Webb's "real name was J. C. Homans."

At any rate, the Mormon church was able to survive Spalding's attack on the "Book of Abraham" with very little injury because church members felt that "Dr. Webb" had answered the critics. Writing in the *Improvement Era*, April 1913, N. L. Nelson stated: "Dr. Webb has, indeed, vindicated the prophet better than he knew himself."

After the excitement over Spalding's pamphlet died down, the Mormons took little interest in the science of Egyptology. Then, in 1967, the church announced the rediscovery of the Joseph Smith Papyri and Dr. Nibley had to admit that "LDS scholars are caught flat footed by this discovery."

In *Mormonism—Shadow or Reality?* (pp.302-6), we show that the circumstances surrounding the rediscovery of the Joseph Smith Papyri are very suspicious. We show, in fact, that a Mormon scholar, Walter Whipple, knew that the papyri were in the Metropolitan Museum as early as 1962, five years before the rediscovery was announced.

Another interesting development is the fact that the Mormon church has an actual piece of papyrus from Joseph Smith's collection which they suppressed for 130 years. In 1966 we printed *Joseph Smith's Egyptian Alphabet and Grammar,* which included a photograph of this fragment. Grant Heward identified it as an actual fragment of papyrus, and we published this fact in the *Salt Lake City Messenger* for April 1966. Finally, after the rediscovery of the papyri in the Metropolitan Museum was announced, the church leaders admitted that they had this fragment of papyrus. Their admission was published in the *Improvement Era* in February 1968, page 40-H.

Mormon writer Jay M. Todd now admits that Dr. James R. Clark, of Brigham Young University, knew about this fragment for thirty years but was told to suppress this information: "Outside of a few associates, Dr. Clark had kept the fragment a matter of confidence, under instructions from the Historian's Office, for over 30 years" (*The Saga of the Book of Abraham,* p.364).

No Gift to Translate

After receiving the papyri from the Metropolitan Museum, Mormon leaders turned them over "to Dr. Hugh Nibley, scholar, linguist at Brigham Young University, . . . for further research and study" (*Improvement Era,* February 1968, p.13). This turned out to be a very serious mistake. To begin with, the fact that the papyri were turned over to Dr. Nibley is almost an admission that church leaders are not guided by revelation as they claim. The Mormon church is led by a man who is sustained by the people as "Prophet, Seer, and Revelator." The *Book of Mormon* says that a "seer" can "translate all records that are of ancient date" (Mosiah 8:13). Apostle John A. Widtsoe stated that if "records appear needing translation, the President of the Church may at any time be called, through revelation, to the special labor of translation" (*Evidences and Reconciliations*, vol. 1, p.203).

Since the church claims to have the "seer stone" and is supposed to be led by a "Prophet, Seer, and Revelator," we might expect a translation by this means. Instead, however, the papyri were sent to Dr. Nibley to be translated by "the wisdom of the world." Thus, it appears that the prophet does not have the gift to translate languages as has been previously claimed.

Since Mormon leaders did not seem to have the gift to translate the papyri themselves, they should have turned the job over to qualified Egyptologists. Instead of doing this, however, they gave the task to Dr. Hugh Nibley. Now there is little doubt that Dr. Nibley is a brilliant man and that he knows several different languages, but this did not qualify him to deal with the Egyptian language. Egyptian is very difficult and it takes many years of experience for a person to become skilled in working with it. Dr. Nibley had taken some classes in the Egyptian language, but this was not sufficient to qualify him for the job of translating the papyri. He admitted that he was not an Egyptologist in a letter to Dee Jay Nelson, dated June 27, 1967 (see *Mormonism—Shadow or Reality?* p.308, for a photograph of this letter): "I don't consider myself an Egyptologist at all, and don't intend to get involved in the P.G.P. business unless I am forced into it. . . ."

When Dr. Nibley speaks of the "P.G.P." he is referring to the *Pearl of Great Price* that, of course, contains the "Book of Abraham." Even though Dr. Nibley claimed that he was not an Egyptologist and that he did not intend to get involved in the argument concerning the authenticity of the "Book of Abraham," he allowed himself to become more deeply involved defending the "Book of Abraham" than anyone else in the church. He has written articles for the *Improvement Era*, *Brigham Young University Studies*, and *Dialogue: A Journal of Mormon Thought*.

Dr. Nibley began a series of articles for the *Improvement Era* in January, 1968. This series ran for over two years, and was finally brought to a conclusion with the issue published May, 1970. Although Dr. Nibley was supposed to unfold "the meaning of the hieroglyphics" in this series of articles, no translation of the Joseph Smith Papyri ever appeared in this series. It would appear that Dr. Nibley's main objective in this series was to blind the eyes of his fellow church members so that they could not see the real issues involved in this matter. Although he used almost 2,000 footnotes, he never did deal with the main problem.

Dr. Nibley gave this excuse for not translating the papyri in an article published in *Brigham Young University Studies*, (Spring 1968, p.251): "We have often been asked during the past months why we did not proceed with all haste to produce a translation of the papyri the moment they came into our possession. Well, for one thing others are far better equipped to do the job than we are, and some of those early expressed a willingness to undertake it. But, more important, it is doubtful whether any translation could do as much good as harm."

In the *Salt Lake Tribune* for November 11, 1973, we criticized Dr. Nibley for not producing a translation of the papyri. He replied that he had prepared a book which "is 800 pages long, but that is not enough to account for keeping the impatient Tanners waiting for six years. What took up all that time was having to find out about a lot of things" (*Salt Lake Tribune,* November 25, 1973). This book, which many people believed would answer the objections of the critics and save the "Book of Abraham," was finally published by the church's Deseret Book Company in 1975 under the title, *The Message of the Joseph Smith Papyri: An Egyptian Endowment.* Although the First Presidency of the church assigned Dr. Nibley to work on the papyri, they were reluctant to give his work any real official endorsement. When John L. Smith asked about Nibley's new book, Francis M. Gibbs, secretary to the First Presidency, sent him a reply in which he stated: ". . . the writings of Dr. Hugh Nibley concerning the papyri scrolls have been done entirely on his own responsibility and do not have the official approval and sanction of the Church" (Letter dated August 22, 1975).

Although Dr. Nibley's book is nicely printed and bound, the contents are very disappointing. Of the eleven fragments of papyrus which were discovered, ten of them contain significant Egyptian messages which can be translated. We would expect that any book about the papyri would at least have a translation of all these pieces. Dr. Nibley's book, however, only contains a translation of two fragments! Among the fragments which Dr. Nibley has not translated is the original of "Facsimile No. 1" in the "Book of Abraham." This fragment contains a number of lines of hieroglyphs which relate to the meaning of the drawing. The reason Dr. Nibley has not translated these lines seems obvious: they show that "Facsimile No. 1" is not a picture of "Abraham fastened upon an altar" as Joseph Smith proclaimed, but rather a picture of an Egyptian by the name of Hor being prepared for burial. We will have more to say about this later.

Those of us who have purchased Dr. Nibley's writings in the *Improvement Era,* the *BYU Studies* and now his new book, which sells for $14.95, have spent at least $30.00. What do we have to show for this investment? We have hundreds of pages of material with thousands of footnotes, but we have a translation of only two of the fragments of papyrus and no answer to the main problems about the "Book of Abraham." To say the least, Dr. Nibley's book contains some very serious errors (see the *Salt Lake City Messenger*, April 1976). Michael Marquardt has prepared a good rebuttal entitled, *The Book of Abraham Papyrus Found: An Answer to Dr. Hugh Nibley's Book 'The Message of the Joseph Smith Papyri: An Egyptian Endowment'*.

The Mormon leaders evidently did not want non-Mormon Egyptologists to translate the papyri. They could have sent the original papyri to the University of Chicago so that Dr. Wilson could have worked with them, but instead they brought them to the Brigham Young University. In a letter written December 4, 1967, Henry G. Fischer, of the Metropolitan Museum, stated: "We have not been commissioned to translate the papyri, nor do I know of anyone else who has been asked to do so."

The translations of the papyri by John A. Wilson, Richard A. Parker and Klaus Baer were not requested by the Mormon leaders, but rather by the editors of *Dialogue: A Journal of Mormon Thought*—a publication not controlled by the LDS church.

Nelson's Work

Although Dr. Nibley was not able to translate the papyri at the time it came to light, there was an elder in the church who was qualified—Dee Jay Nelson. Mr. Nelson is a nationally-known explorer naturalist. He is a member of the Adventurers Club and has lectured on the Dead Sea Scrolls. In 1957 he was invited by Prime Minister David Ben-Gurion to make the first motion picture of the Dead Sea Scrolls. He has studied the Egyptian language and religion for about thirty years and has participated in archeological excavations in Egypt. Mr. Nelson made the first translation of "The Egyptian Book of Life." (For more information about him see *Montana Arts*, vol. 20, no. 1, p.21.)

When Dr. Nibley learned of Dee Jay Nelson's ability as an Egyptologist, he wanted him to help defend the church. In a letter dated June 27, 1967, he told Nelson that he could "see no reason in the world why you should not be taken into the confidence of the Brethren if this thing ever comes out into the open; in fact, you should be enormously useful to the Church ... there are parties in Salt Lake who are howling for a showdown on the P.G.P.; if they have their way we may have to get together."

On January 4, 1968, Dee Jay Nelson visited with Dr. Nibley at Brigham Young University and examined the original papyri. Dr. Nibley agreed that Nelson should translate the papyri, and he sent a note to N. Eldon Tanner, a member of the First Presidency, stating that "it would be a good idea to let Prof. Dee J. Nelson have copies" of the papyri. This was before the Mormon leaders allowed photographs of all the papyri to be published. Mr. Nelson translated the papyri, but he was unable to find any mention of Abraham or his religion in any portion of the papyri. He found the names of many pagan gods who were worshiped by the Egyptians but nothing concerning the God of Abraham.

After completing his translation, Mr. Nelson contacted us and asked if we wanted to print it. Since the translation proved unfavorable to the church, it was obvious that the church would not print it. He stated that Dr. Nibley seemed to be stalling, and he felt that his people should know the truth about the papyri. Therefore, he decided to let us publish his findings. When we completed the publication of Nelson's work we tried to advertise it in the *Deseret News* but church leaders would not allow the ad to be run. The editor of the *Deseret News* told us that he did not believe Nelson's work was accurate. He claimed that he had had a conversation with Dr. Nibley concerning Nelson's work, and that Nibley told him that he did not believe that the translation was correct.

Now, if Dr. Nibley made the statements that the editor of the Deseret News attributed to him, he seems to have changed his mind, for he wrote the following for the *Brigham Young University Studies* (Spring, 1968, pp.245, 247):

> The publication of the Joseph Smith Egyptian Papyri has now begun to bear fruit. Two efforts at translation and commentary have already appeared, the one an example of pitfalls to be avoided, the other a conscientious piece of work for which the Latter-day Saints owe a debt of gratitude to Mr. Dee Jay Nelson. ... *This is a conscientious and courageous piece of work.* . . . Nelson ... has taken the first step in a serious study of the Facsimiles of the Pearl of Great Price, supplying students with a *usable and reliable translation* of the available papyri that once belonged to Joseph Smith.

Dr. Nibley's statements concerning Nelson's work probably came as a great shock to the editor of the *Deseret News*. Notice that Nibley claims that Nelson's work is a "reliable translation" and that the Mormons owe him a "debt of gratitude." It would appear, then, that the leaders of the church deliberately suppressed knowledge of Nelson's work because they did not want their people to have a "reliable translation" of the papyri. Actually, we were rather surprised that Hugh Nibley would publicly endorse Nelson's work after Mormon leaders had sup-

338

pressed the ad in the *Deseret News.*

At any rate, Dee Jay Nelson feels that Joseph Smith's "Book of Abraham" is a false translation and that the church must give it up. Because of the church's stubborn refusal to face the truth with regard to the "Book of Abraham," Dee Jay Nelson and his family have finally withdrawn their membership from the church. In a letter to the First Presidency, dated December 8, 1975, Mr. Nelson wrote:

> This letter is to inform you that it is our considered desire that my own name and those of my wife and daughter be removed from the membership rolls of the Latter Day Saint Church. . . . Following my translation (the first to be published) of the bulk of the hieratic and hieroglyphic Egyptian texts upon the Metropolitan-Joseph Smith Papyri Fragments three of the most eminent Egyptologists now living published corroborating translations. These amply prove the fraudulent nature of the Book of Abraham. . . .

Source of the Book of Abraham

As we stated before, when the papyri were located many members of the Mormon church felt that Joseph Smith's work had been vindicated. We quoted Dr. Hugh Nibley, however, as stating that the papyri "do not prove the Book of Abraham is true" and that LDS scholars are "caught flat footed" by the discovery. While Dr. Nibley and a few others may have realized that the papyri could not be used to prove Joseph Smith's work true, they evidently were not aware of the devastating blow that the papyri were about to deal to the "Book of Abraham." Within six months from the time the Metropolitan Museum gave the papyri to the church, the "Book of Abraham" had been proven untrue!

The fall of the "Book of Abraham" has been brought about by the identification of the actual fragment of papyrus from which Joseph Smith "translated" the book. On page 341 of this book the reader will find a photograph of the right side of this fragment of papyrus.

The identification of this fragment as the original from which Joseph Smith translated the "Book of Abraham" has been made possible by a comparison with *Joseph Smith's Egyptian Alphabet and Grammar*—handwritten documents we photographically reproduced in 1966. Dr. James R. Clark, of Brigham Young University, gives this information:

> . . . there are in existence today in the Church Historian's Office what seem to be two separate manuscripts of Joseph Smith's translations from the papyrus rolls, presumably in the hand writ-

ing of Joseph Smith and Oliver Cowdery. . . . One manuscript is the Alphabet and Grammar. . . . Within this Alphabet and Grammar there is a copy of the characters, together with their translation of Abraham 1:4-28 only. The second and separate of the two manuscripts contains none of the Alphabet and Grammar but is a manuscript of the text of the Book of Abraham as published in the first installment of the *Times and Seasons* March 1, 1842 (*The Story of the Pearl of Great Price,* 1962, pp.172-73).

Mormon leaders were either not aware of the fact that the gift of papyri included the very fragment which was the basis for the text of the "Book of Abraham," or they hoped no one else would notice it. The following statement appeared in the Mormon paper, *Deseret News:* "As far as has yet been determined, the papyri do not contain any of the original material translated as the Book of Abraham itself" (*Deseret News,* November 28, 1967).

When the Mormon magazine, *Improvement Era,* printed sepia photographs of the papyri, the fragments of papyrus from which Joseph Smith translated the "Book of Abraham" was printed as the very last photograph. It is found on page 41 of the February 1968 issue, and is labeled: "XI. Small 'Sensen' text (unillustrated)."

All of the first two rows of characters on the papyrus fragment can be found in the manuscript of the "Book of Abraham" that is published in *Joseph Smith's Egyptian Alphabet and Grammar.* On page 341 of this book is a photograph of the original fragment of papyrus from which Joseph Smith was supposed to have translated the Book of Abraham. Just below it is a photograph of the original manuscript of the "Book of Abraham" as it appears in *Joseph Smith's Egyptian Alphabet and Grammar.* We have numbered some of the characters on the first line of the fragment of papyrus so that the reader can compare them with the characters found in the handwritten manuscript.

The reader will probably be startled at the large number of English words which Joseph Smith "translated" from each Egyptian character. We will have more to say about this later.

As James R. Clark indicated, there is another copy of the "Book of Abraham" manuscript in the church historical department. Dr. Clark stated about this manuscript:

I have in my possession a photostatic copy of the manuscript of the Prophet Joseph Smith's translation of Abraham 1:1 to 2:18. This manuscript was bought by Wilford Wood in 1945 from Charles Bidamon, son of the man who married Emma after the death of the Prophet. The original of this manuscript is in the

At the top is a photograph of the right side of the original fragment of papyrus from which Joseph Smith was supposed to have translated the Book of Abraham.

Below is a photograph of the original manuscript of the Book of Abraham as it appears in *Joseph Smith's Egyptian Alphabet and Grammar*.

Church Historian's Office in Salt Lake City. *The characters from which our present book of Abraham was translated are down the left-hand column and Joseph Smith's translation opposite*, so we know approximately how much material was translated from each character (*Pearl of Great Price Conference*, December 10, 1960, 1964 ed., pp.60-61).

The Brigham Young University had photographs of this manuscript which Mr. Grant Heward was able to examine. This manuscript goes further than the one in the *Alphabet and Grammar*, and Mr. Heward found that the characters on this manuscript continue in consecutive order into the fourth line of the papyrus. This brings the text to Abraham 2:18. This is very interesting because when Joseph Smith printed the first installment of the "Book of Abraham" in the *Times and Seasons* he ended it at this point. We have been able to obtain photographs of this manuscript and can confirm Grant Heward's statements concerning it. (For a photographic reproduction of four pages of this manuscript and a comparison of the characters on it with those found on the papyrus see *Mormonism–Shadow or Reality?* pp.312-13.) A careful examination of this manuscript reveals that Joseph Smith used less than four lines from the papyrus to make forty-nine verses in the "Book of Abraham." These forty-nine verses are composed of more than 2,000 English words! In his book, *Ancient Records Testify in Papyrus and Stone*, page 79, Dr. Sperry informs us that there are "5,470 words" contained in the text of the "Book of Abraham." If Joseph Smith continued to translate the same number of English words from each Egyptian character, then the text for the entire "Book of Abraham" is probably contained on this one fragment of papyrus.

Egyptologist Dee Jay Nelson confirmed the fact that the small "Sensen" fragment was the piece of papyrus which Joseph Smith used as the basis for his "Book of Abraham":

What do the newly discovered "Metropolitan Papyri" have to do with the Book of Abraham? The original ancient text from which Joseph Smith 'translated' the Book of Abraham has been found! A substantial part of it can be seen in column 1 (right hand) on the smaller Hor Sensen Papyrus Fragment (unillustrated). . . .

How do we know that Joseph Smith "translated" the Book of Abraham from column 1 of the Hor Sensen Fragment No. 1? Joseph Smith tells us that it is so in the most positive way by supplying a list of the ancient characters and attaching to it the "translation." This list of characters, though crudely copied, precisely matches the first two lines of hieratic characters in column 1 on the Hor Papyrus Fragment No. 1. Joseph Smith's character list and the attached "translation" is found in the notebook entitled *Grammar and Alphabet of the Egyptian Language*. . . . Grant Heward . . . pointed out to me that the characters drawn by Joseph Smith in the left hand margin of the Grammar and Alphabet were the same as in the original Hor Sensen text. The fact is indisputable.

The "translation" starts on page J of the Grammar and Alphabet and almost exactly matches the published version of the Book of Abraham beginning with Chapter 1, verse 4 and ending with Chapter 2, verse 5. We can be absolutely sure that Joseph Smith intended the "translation" to match the characters written down the left margin because beginning on page S (there is some inconsistency in his page numbering) he again lists the characters in the margin and repeats the "translation" almost word-for-word. The groups of marginal characters are in each instance represented by the same "translations." If the characters were irrelevant and independent of the "translation," as some have suggested, they would not have been so meticulously placed and identically oriented in each of the two "translations." This fact proves without a doubt that the "translation" relates to the marginal characters and to no others (*The Joseph Smith Papyri*, part 2, 1968, pp.13-14).

Klaus Baer, an Egyptologist at the University of Chicago, also concluded concerning the "Sensen" fragment: "Joseph Smith thought that this papyrus contained the Book of Abraham" (*Dialogue: A Journal of Mormon Thought*, Autumn 1968, p.111). In footnote 11 of the same article, Klaus Baer states that "This identification is now certain."

Mormon scholar Richley Crapo likewise observed:

In December of 1967, I was able to examine the original papyri in the vaults of the BYU library and obtain one of the first released sets of photographic copies. . . . A more careful examination of these revealed the startling fact that one of the papyri of the Church collection, known as the Small Sen-Sen Papyrus, contained the same series of heiratic symbols, which had been copied, in the same order, into the Book of Abraham manuscript next to verses of that book! In other words, there was every indication that the collection of papyri in the hands of the Church *contained the source which led to a production of the Book of Abraham*. It was naturally this document which I immediately began to translate (*Book of Abraham Symposium*, LDS Institute of Religion, Salt Lake City, April 3, 1970, p.27).

Although Dr. Hugh Nibley later reversed his position in an attempt to save the "Book of Abraham," in 1968 he frankly admitted that the papyrus which Joseph Smith used for the text of the "Book of Abraham" had been located. He wrote the following for the *Improvement Era*, May, 1968, page 54: ". . . the presence on the scene of some of the original papyri, including those *used by the Prophet in preparing the text of the Book of Abraham* and the Facsimiles with their commentaries, has not raised a single new question, though, as we shall see, it has solved some old ones."

Dr. Nibley made this admission in *Dialogue: A Journal of Mormon Thought*, Summer, 1968, page 102: "But after all, what do the papyri tell us? That Joseph Smith had them, and that the smallest and most insignificant-looking of them is *connected in some mysterious way to the Pearl of Great Price*."

At a meeting held at the University of Utah, Dr. Nibley stated:

> Within a week of the publication of the papyri students began calling my attention, in fact, within a day or two, I think it was Witorf [?], called my attention to the fact that, the *very definite fact that, one of the fragments seemed to supply all of the symbols for the Book of Abraham.* This was the little "Sensen" scroll. Here are the symbols. The symbols are arranged here, and *the interpretation goes along here and this interpretation turns out to be the Book of Abraham.* Well, what about that? Here is the little "Sensen," because that name occurs frequently in it, the papyrus, in which *a handful of Egyptian symbols was apparently expanded in translation to the whole Book of Abraham.* This raises a lot of questions. It doesn't answer any questions, unless we're mind readers (Speech given by Hugh Nibley, University of Utah, May 20, 1968).

Only the Book of Breathings

In the *Salt Lake City Messenger* for March, 1968, we stated that Grant Heward felt that the fragment of papyrus Joseph Smith used as the basis for his "Book of Abraham" was in reality a part of the Egyptian "Book of Breathings." This identification has been confirmed by several prominent Egyptologists.

In order to understand what the "Book of Breathings" is about we must have some understanding of the Egyptian "Book of the Dead." E. A. Wallis Budge, who was keeper of the Egyptian and Assyrian antiquities in the British Museum, explained:

> . . . the Book of the Dead cannot be regarded as the work of any one man or body of men, . . . the beliefs of many people and periods are gathered together in it. As a whole, the Book of the Dead was regarded as the work of the god Thoth, the scribe of the gods . . . in the Book of Breathings, in an address to the deceased it is said, "Thoth, the most mighty god, the lord of Khemennu (Hermopolis), cometh to thee, and he writeth for thee the Book of Breathings with his own fingers." Copies of the

Book of the Dead, and works of a similar nature, were placed either in the coffin with the deceased, or in some part of the hall of the tomb, or of the mummy chamber, generally in a niche which was cut for the purpose (*The Book of the Dead, An English Translation of the Chapters, Hymns, Etc., Of The Theban Recension, With Introduction, Notes, Etc.*, London, 1901, vol. 1, pp.50-51 of intro.).

Egyptologist James Henry Breasted said that the "Book of the Dead" "was dominated by magic; by this all-powerful means the dead might effect all that he desired" (*A History of Egypt*, 1967, pp.205-6). In his book, *Development of Religion and Thought in Ancient Egypt*, (pp.293-96), Breasted comments:

There were sumptuous and splendid rolls, sixty to eighty feet long and containing from seventy-five to as many as a hundred and twenty-five or thirty chapters. . . . the Book of the Dead . . . is but a far-reaching and complex illustration of the increasing dependence on magic in the hereafter. . . . Besides many charms which enabled the dead to reach the world of the hereafter, there were those which prevented him from losing his mouth, his head, his heart, others which enabled him to remember his name, to breathe, eat, drink, avoid eating his own foulness, to prevent his drinking-water from turning into flame, to turn darkness into light, to ward off all serpents and other hostile monsters, and many others. The desirable transformations, too, had now increased, and a short chapter might in each case enable the dead man to assume the form of a falcon of gold, a divine falcon, a lily, a Phoenix, a heron, a swallow, a serpent called "son of earth," a crocodile, a god, and, best of all, there was a chapter so potent that by its use a man might assume any form that he desired. . . . To call it the Bible of the Egyptians, then, is quite to mistake the function and content of these rolls.

On page 308, Breasted tells us that the "Book of the Dead is chiefly a book of magical charms." Those who have studied the "Book of the Dead" know that it was written by a very superstitious people, and is quite different from the religion taught in the Bible.

The "Book of Breathings" is an outgrowth of the Egyptian "Book of the Dead." It did not appear until the later stages of Egyptian history—just a few centuries before the time of Christ. E. A. Wallis Budge supplies this information about it:

The "Book of Breathings" is one of a number of short funeral works, . . . it was addressed to the deceased by the chief priest conducting the funeral service. . . . The "Book of Breathings" represents the attempt to include all essential elements of belief in a future life in a work shorter and more simple than the Book of the Dead. . . . To give the work an enhanced value it was

345

declared to be the production of Thoth, the scribe of the gods (*The Book of the Dead, Facsimiles of the Papyri of Hunefer, Anhai, Kerasher and Netchemet*, by E. A. Wallis Budge, London, 1899, p.33).

Speaking of the fragment of papyrus Joseph Smith used as the basis for his Book of Abraham, the Egyptologist Dee Jay Nelson explains:

> This piece . . . is a part of the Ptolemaic text known as the Shait en Sensen or Book of Breathings. This fact is established by the appearance of the name of the book in column 1, line 4. . . .
>
> 1. This papyrus is a traditional copy of the Shait en Sensen, Book of Breathings and is of a late origin. It most probably was written in the Ptolemaic Period (after 332 B.C.) (*The Joseph Smith Papyri*, pp.40-41).

Egyptologist Richard A. Parker also confirmed the fact that what Joseph Smith claimed was the "Book of Abraham" was in reality the "Book of Breathings." The editors of *Dialogue* stated:

> Richard A. Parker is the Wilbour Professor of Egyptology and Chairman of the Department of Egyptology at Brown University. . . . He remarks that the Book of Breathings is a late (Ptolemaic and Roman periods) and greatly reduced version of the Book of the Dead. . . . He would provisionally date the two Book of Breathings fragments in the Church's possession to the last century before or the first century of the Christian era . . . (*Dialogue: A Journal of Mormon Thought*, Summer 1968, p.86).

Three Witnesses Against the Book of Abraham

In the *Book of Mormon* we find this statement: "And in the mouth of three witnesses shall these things be established . . ." (Ether 5:4). Joseph Smith's witnesses to the *Book of Mormon* were not trained in the science of Egyptology, and therefore could not possibly know whether Joseph Smith's "gold plates" were authentic or whether he translated them correctly. In the case of the "Book of Abraham," however, we have a different story. Three men who have been trained in the science of Egyptology have examined the text Joseph Smith used as a basis for the "Book of Abraham" and have declared that it is in reality the instructions for wrapping up the "Book of Breathings" with the mummy, and that it has nothing at all to do with Abraham or his religion. These three men have translated the text and their renditions have been published.

The first witness against the authenticity of the "Book of Abraham" is Dee Jay Nelson. Mr. Nelson had more than twenty years experience with the Egyptian language at the time he began working with the Joseph Smith Papyri. He was an elder in the Mormon church but his research forced him to reject Joseph Smith's work. Mormon scholar John Tvedtnes classified Dee Jay Nelson as a "serious, unbiased scholar," and said that his competence in the Egyptian language is "unquestioned" (*Book of Abraham Symposium*, April 3, 1970, p.70). Dee Jay Nelson's translation of the papyrus Joseph Smith used for his "Book of Abraham" was published in *The Joseph Smith Papyri*, Part 2, 1968, page 21.

The second witness is Klaus Baer. *Dialogue: A Journal of Mormon Thought* gave this information concerning him: "Klaus Baer is Associate Professor of Egyptology at the University of Chicago's Oriental Institute, and was one of Professor Hugh Nibley's primary tutors in the art of reading Egyptian characters" (*Dialogue*, Autumn 1968, p.109). Klaus Baer's translation appears on pages 119-20 of the same issue.

The third witness against the "Book of Abraham" is Professor Richard A. Parker, chairman of the department of Egyptology at Brown University. Dr. Hugh Nibley had a copy of Richard Parker's translation of the "Sensen" text before it appeared in *Dialogue*, and in a speech delivered at the University of Utah on May 20, 1968, he stated: ". . . Professor Parker has translated that controversial little thing called the 'Sensen' papyrus, the little section, that text that matches up with some of the Book of Abraham." Instead of attacking Professor Parker's translation, as we might have expected him to do, Dr. Nibley praised it: ". . . here is Parker's translation of the 'Sensen' papyrus. . . . Parker being the best man in America for this particular period and style of writing. And Parker agreed to do it and he's done it. So it's nice. . . . it will be available . . . in the next issue of the *Dialogue*."

In *Mormonism–Shadow or Reality?* page 317, we reproduced all three translations of the papyrus Joseph Smith used as the basis for his "Book of Abraham." To save space here we will only include Professor Parker's translation:

1. [. . . . . .] this great pool of Khonsu
2. [Osiris Hor, justified], born of Taykhebyt, a man likewise.
3. After (his) two arms are [fast]ened to his breast, one wraps the Book of Breathings, which is
4. with writing both inside and outside of it, with royal linen, it being placed (at) his left arm
5. near his heart, this having been done at his
6. wrapping and outside it. If this book be recited for him, then
7. he will breath like the soul[s of the gods] for ever and

8. ever (*Dialogue: A Journal of Mormon Thought*, Summer 1968, p.98).

Except for a few minor variations, the other two renditions of the text are essentially in agreement with Professor Parker's. The "Book of Abraham," therefore, has been proven to be a spurious work. The Egyptologists find no mention of Abraham or his religion in this text. The average number of words that the three Egyptologists used to convey the message in this text is ninety-two, whereas Joseph Smith's rendition contains thousands of words. It is impossible to escape the conclusion that the "Book of Abraham" is a false translation.

After the publication of the papyri it became very obvious that Dr. Nibley was unprepared to deal with the problems related to the translation of the "Book of Abraham" and that he had no real answers to give his people. In an article published in *Dialogue: A Journal of Mormon Thought*, Summer, 1968, page 101, he queried:

> Since the Sen-Sen business makes very little sense to anybody, while the Book of Abraham makes very good sense, one might suppose that Smith could have produced the latter without any reference to the former . . . why on earth would he fasten on this particularly ugly little piece and completely by-pass the whole collection of handsome illustrated documents at his disposal? Did he really think he was translating? If so he was acting in good faith. But *was he really translating?* If so, it was by a process which quite *escapes the understanding of the specialists* and lies in the realm of the imponderable. . . .
>
> Today nobody claims that Joseph Smith got his information through ordinary scholary channels. In that case one wonders how any amount of checking along ordinary scholarly channels is going to get us very far.

When Dr. Nibley spoke at the University of Utah on May 20, 1968, he admitted that if Joseph Smith was "really translating the papyri" he did it in a way that is unknown to Egyptologists:

> By what process could the Book of Abraham have been squeezed out of a few dozen brief signs? Nobody has told us yet. Was Joseph Smith really translating the papyri? If so, *it was not in any way known to Egyptology.* . . . Did he really need these symbols? This is a funny thing. Are they actually the source upon which he depended? Well, if he really depended on them, he must really have been translating them. But, you say, he couldn't possibly have been translating. Could he have used this as a source at all? These questions arise. If he was merely faking, of course, pretending to be translating them, well, he wouldn't need the Egyptian text at all. Yet he used one, and he used it

secretly. . . . Why does he ignore the wealth of handsome illustrated texts at his disposal to concentrate only on the shortest and ugliest and most poorly written of the lot? . . . Well, all sorts of questions arise.

At one point Dr. Nibley became so desperate to save the "Book of Abraham" that he suggested that the "Sensen" text may have a second meaning unknown to Egyptologists: ". . . you very often have texts of double meaning . . . it's quite possible, say, that this 'Sensen' papyrus, telling a straight forward innocent little story or something like that, should contain also *a totally different text concealed within it.* . . . they [the Egyptians] know what they're doing, but we don't. We don't have the key" (Speech by Hugh Nibley, University of Utah, May 20, 1968).

Writing in the *Brigham Young University Studies*, Spring 1968, page 249, Dr. Nibley stated that Joseph Smith treated the characters as super-cryptograms—that is, writing with a hidden meaning: "It has long been known that the characters 'interpreted' by Joseph Smith in his Egyptian Alphabet and Grammar are treated by him as super-cryptograms; and now it is apparent that the source of those characters is the unillustrated fragment on which the word Sen-sen appears repeatedly. This identifies it as possibly belonging to those writings known as The Book of Breathings. . . ."

When Marvin Cowan asked Professor Richard Parker if the papyri could have a second meaning, he replied that he knew of "no Egyptologist who would support such a claim" (Letter dated January 9, 1968). Egyptologist Dee Jay Nelson said that such an idea "is not even remotely possible," and that "it is mathematically impossible to express the total complexities of Joseph Smith's 'translation' with the characters involved" (*The Joseph Smith Papyri*, part 2, p.14).

Although Dr. Nibley gave some support to the theory that the papyrus might have a second or hidden meaning, he seems to have come to his senses and now realizes that such an idea cannot be successfully maintained. Unfortunately, however, he has come up with another theory which is as fantastic as the first: that the "Sensen" papyrus has no relationship to the "Book of Abraham." It is, in fact, "the directions for wrapping up the Joseph Smith papyri with the mummy" (*The Message of the Joseph Smith Papyri: An Egyptian Endowment*, p.6). According to Dr. Nibley's theory, Joseph Smith's scribes mistakenly copied the characters from the "Sensen" papyrus into the three handwritten manuscripts of the "Book of Abraham:"

> Is the Book of Abraham a correct translation of Joseph Smith Papyri X and XI? No, the Book of Breathings is not the Book of Abraham! . . . Doesn't the text of the Book of Abraham appear in a number of manuscripts in columns running parallel with characters from the Book of Breathings? Yes, the brethren at Kirtland were invited to try their skill at translation; in 1835 the Prophet's associates, . . . made determined efforts to match up the finished text of the Book of Abraham with characters from the J. S. Papyrus No. XI . . . (p.2).

Dr. Nibley's suggestion that Joseph Smith's scribes added the wrong characters in the translation manuscripts is absolutely preposterous. That Joseph Smith would allow his scribes to copy the characters from the wrong papyrus into three different manuscripts of the "Book of Abraham" is really beyond belief. A person might almost as reasonably conclude that the "Book of Abraham" itself was made up by Joseph Smith's scribes. Dr. Nibley's attempt to separate the "Sensen" papyrus from the "Book of Abraham" cannot be accepted by anyone who honestly examines the evidence. The reader should remember that Dr. Nibley himself originally accepted the "Sensen" text as the source of the "Book of Abraham."

For more evidence to show that Dr. Nibley is making a grave error in trying to separate the "Book of Abraham" from the "Sensen" papyrus the reader should see our article in *The Salt Lake City Messenger*, April 1976, and Michael Marquardt's pamphlet *The Book of Abraham Papyrus Found: An Answer to Dr. Hugh Nibley's Book* . . .

Since the original papyrus has been located, some Mormon apologists have suggested that Joseph Smith may have obtained the "Book of Abraham" by way of direct revelation and not from the papyrus. The person who tries to use this escape will find himself trapped by the words of Joseph Smith himself. At the beginning of the handwritten manuscript Joseph Smith stated that it was a "Translation of the Book of Abraham written by his own hand upon papyrus and found in the catacombs of Egypt." The introduction to the "Book of Abraham" still maintains that it was "Translated From The Papyrus, By Joseph Smith" (*Pearl of Great Price*, p.29). Joseph Smith not only claimed that he translated it from the papyrus, but according to the *History of the Church*, volume 2, page 351, he said it was "a correct translation."

In *Mormonism—Shadow or Reality?* pages 322-24, we examine the Egyptian words which appeared in the handwritten manuscripts of the "Book of Abraham" and show how Joseph Smith mistranslated them. In one case we show that

Joseph Smith "translated" 177 words out of the word "Khons"—the name of an Egyptian moon-god. The fact that Smith would make 177 English words from one Egyptian word is absolutely astounding! It shows very clearly that he did not understand the Egyptian language and that the "Book of Abraham" is a work of his own imagination.

Destroys Basis for Anti-Black Doctrine

As we have already shown, until June 9, 1978 the Mormon church taught that blacks were cursed and therefore could not hold the priesthood or receive equal treatment in the church. The basis for this anti-black doctrine is found in the pages of the "Book of Abraham." Chapter 1, verses 21-27 all seem to relate to this doctrine, but verse 26 is the most important. President David O. McKay stated that the "Book of Abraham" contained the only "scriptural basis" for denying blacks the priesthood.

In *Mormonism—Shadow or Reality?* pages 324-25 we demonstrate that Joseph Smith could not have obtained the anti-black doctrine from Egyptian characters on the "Sensen" papyrus. The loss of confidence in the "Book of Abraham" by intellectuals in the church undoubtedly played a part in convincing Mormon leaders it was time for a new revelation which would allow blacks to hold the priesthood.

Complete Confusion

Egyptologist Dee Jay Nelson informs us concerning the "Sensen" text:

> Biblical experts believe that Abraham lived sometime around 1800 B.C., but the calligraphy, spelling and contents of the Hor Sensen Papyrus give every indication that it was not written until nearly the time of Christ (possibly shortly after) . . . one is faced with the unmistakable fact that this ancient document deals with pagan gods and pagan beliefs without mentioning Abraham or anything even remotely associated with him . . . religious meanings of the Book of Breathings (Sensen) are as pagan as can be and flaunt religious practices which were most abhorrent to Abraham (*Joseph Smith's "Eye of Ra,"* p.25).

The names of at least fifteen Egyptian gods or goddesses are mentioned on the "Sensen" papyri which Joseph Smith had in his possession, but not a word about Abraham. Mormon apologists have not been able to explain how Joseph Smith derived the "Book of Abraham" from this pagan text. The fact that they are in a real dilemma over this matter is very evident from their writings. Jay M. Todd stated:

> The scroll, according to Dr. Baer, was made for a priest named Hor, for his death and mummification ceremonies.
>
> Obviously, if this report by Dr. Baer is accurate, it suggests more than ever that either the papyrus "translated" by the Prophet is still unavailable or that the seer stone provided the actual text of which only a shadow and much corrupted version might have been on the papyri fragments. . . . the relationship—if any—between the Egyptian symbols on some of the handwritten copies of parts of the Book of Abraham and the text of the Book of Abraham and the appearance of these same Egyptian symbols on one of the papyrus fragments found in New York City is a most intriguing concern. Indeed, some critics of the Church are attempting to discredit the Book of Abraham . . . Dr. Nibley has suggested, however, that if there is no relationship between the symbols and the text, then Joseph Smith would have seen none either, nor, from our knowledge of the Prophet's character and personality, would he have attempted to deceive anyone by suggesting a relationship where he knew none existed. Indeed, Dr. Nibley has intimated that there still could be a relationship between the symbols and the English text of the Book of Abraham. Obviously, the matter of identifying the actual source of the Book of Abraham is still unresolved . . . (*The Saga of the Book of Abraham*, pp.377-80).

At the Book of Abraham Symposium, Mormon scholar Dr. Henry Eyring confessed:

> Now, the Lord didn't need the Book of Abraham—those scrolls. He was pretty well clear on everything without that. . . . the essential ingredient in the Book of Abraham is whatever the Prophet was inspired to write down. . . . I also wouldn't look into the matter to find out whether I thought Joseph Smith was a Prophet, . . . it seems to me evident that he was much more than that. . . . it wouldn't make a bit of difference to me if the scholars, studying the scrolls that led the Prophet to think about the problem of Abraham and write about it—*it wouldn't make a bit of difference to me if they discovered that it was a bill of lading for wheat in the Lower Nile.* You see, some people don't feel that way about it. But I think the Lord actually inspired Joseph (*Book of Abraham Symposium*, April 3, 1970, p.3).

The Mormon scholars John Tvedtnes and Richley H. Crapo have gone so far as to suggest that the "Sensen" text might have been a "memory device":

> In two different sections of the "Alphabet and Grammar," hieratic symbols taken in order from the "Small Sen-Sen Fragment" . . . have been juxtaposed to English symbols (i.e. words) com-

prising the text of the Book of Abraham. . . . This correlation was pointed out by certain non-members of the Church. . . . These same persons believed that the juxtaposition of small groups of hieratic symbols with English symbols in the "Alphabet and Grammar" implies a relationship of translation. . . .

This led to an objection on the part of the non-members: the size of the English text as opposed to that of the Egyptian text (i.e. the 25:1 ratio of the words) seems unbelievably high. Recently, Dee Jay Nelson, a member of the Church and a philologist of the Egyptian language, has accepted this view.

We should therefore reply to these objections if we wish to continue to maintain that the Book of Abraham is scripture, the more so because some respected members of the Church are beginning to accept the rationale behind the argument presented.

If the Book of Abraham is to be presented as authentic, there are two possible directions which can be taken:

A. We can simply discount the objection to the ratio of English to Egyptian symbols, which implies proving that the Book of Abraham text does indeed come from the Sen-Sen text.

B. We can show that there is a relationship between the juxtaposed symbols other than that of translation; we must find some other reason why Joseph Smith put them in juxtaposition.

As previously indicated, assumption "A" seems to be the more desirable, especially in the apparent absence of a reasonable substitute explanation for the juxtaposition. But this possibility appears to have been ruled out by the scholarly translations of the Sen-Sen text by Mr. Nelson, Dr. Richard A. Parker, and Dr. Klaus Baer, showing it to be a normal Egyptian funerary document.

Dr. Nibley, however, still seems to agree with us that possibility "A," a relationship of translation, is the more desirable explanation, for in recent articles he places emphasis on the possibility of a "supercryptogram," i.e. a deeper level of hidden translation. But no one has yet suggested what such a supercryptogram might be. . . . we recognized some months ago certain cases in which the hieratic words are found in the corresponding English text. . . . We theorized that perhaps each set of Egyptian symbols represented merely a "key-word" which would bring to mind a certain memorized set of phrases, which was part of a longer oral tradition. . . .

We propose, therefore, as a working hypothesis: either (1) that the Sen-Sen Papyrus was used as a memory device by Abraham (and perhaps by his descendants), each symbol or group of symbols bringing to mind a set number of memorized phrases relating to Abraham's account of his life, or (2) that the hieratic words in the "Alphabet and Grammar" are simply related to core-concepts in the corresponding English story of Abraham. Either hypothesis requires that Joseph Smith had a working knowledge of the hieratic words on the papyrus. In the second case, much of the English text may have been supplied by Joseph Smith as an inspired commentary on the hieratic words.

Viewed in this light, the Book of Abraham seems not to be a direct translation of the Egyptian text appearing on the Sen-Sen papyrus. Indeed, since the oral tradition itself would have long since disappeared with the death of Abraham or the last of his descendants acquainted with the story, the Book of Abraham would have had to be revealed to Joseph Smith, perhaps in connection with the use of the Egyptian symbols, inasmuch as the Prophet does relate long English passages to single Egyptian words or short phrases (*Newletter and Proceedings of the Society for Early Historic Archaeology*, Brigham Young University, October 25, 1968, pp.1-4).

In *Mormonism—Shadow or Reality?* page 329, we show that the idea that the "Sensen" papyrus was a "memory device" is completely unrealistic. Nevertheless, even Dr. Hugh Nibley has been influenced by this idea. In *Brigham Young University Studies*, Autumn 1968, pages 101-2, he made this statement about the relationship between the "Sensen" text and the Book of Abraham:

We still suspect that there is a relationship between the two documents, but we don't know what it is. . . . R. Crapo and J. A. Tvednes [sic], presented an interesting hypothesis to explain the relationship between the Breathing Certificate and the Book of Abraham. . . . This would make the "Sen-sen" papyrus a sort of prompter's sheet. . . .

Far-fetched as it may seem, there are many ancient examples of this sort of thing, the best-known of which is the alphabet itself. . . . In a preliminary statement in *Dialogue* it was suggested that the hieratic symbols placed over against the long sections of the Book of Abraham might be viewed not as texts but as topic headings. We still don't know what the connection is, but one thing is certain—that the relationship between the two texts was never meant to be that of a direct translation.

Mormon scholar Benjamin Urrutia tried his hand in an attempt to explain why Joseph Smith's translation differs from that given by Egyptologists:

In this essay my main objectives shall be to prove that the two titles that have been ascribed to PJS ("The Breathing Permit of Hor" and "The Book of Abraham") are both correct, and that the two translations . . . are both good and acceptable translations, each in its own way. . . .

The reasons that make the scholars "rage" and "imagine a vain thing" are that: a) Joseph's translations of PJS is very different from their own; and b) the Book of Abraham is disproportionately long. . . .

Abraham, . . . wrote the book that bears his name. This document was brought back to Egypt . . . when "there arose up a new king over Egypt who knew not Joseph" (Ex. 1:8), what became of the sacred book? . . .

The best way to save the book would have been to camouflage it to look like an Egyptian document instead of a Semitic one. Most likely it was already written in Egyptian characters, but that wasn't enough.

An enterprising Hebrew, whom we shall call X, conceived a code in which every character of a Mizraite funerary inscription, with only a few minor (though significant) changes, was the equivalent of two verses, more or less, of the book he was trying to save, the original of which no longer exists. . . . the Book of Abraham plus X's manipulations equals the Papyrus Joseph Smith.

But once the BA was rendered into code, what chance was there of ever decoding it again? X being dead, the secret was lost, and not a convention of all the world's cryptographist could find it again. The book was in all appearance, and even in reality, "The Breathing Permit of Hor." What was there to be done? What was the key to the lost code? The answer: the Urim and Thummim . . . this "translation" was not a translation in the usual sense of the word (as that of the Inspired Version was not, either), and that no man, no matter how wise or imaginative, could have done it by any normal means. . . . Therefore, my friends, cease raging, cease imagining vain things. Joseph was a prophet, not a linguist. Dr. Baer is a linguist, not a prophet. Each of these men did what he could do, and admirably well, but he could not have done the same kind of translation the other did (even from the same document) (*Dialogue: A Journal of Mormon Thought*, Summer 1969, pp.130, 131, 134).

The statements we have quoted clearly demonstrate the great lengths Mormon writers will go in their attempt to save the "Book of Abraham." It seems that they will propose almost any fantastic thesis rather than accept the simple truth that the "Book of Abraham" is a spurious work. These new theories certainly are not in harmony with Joseph Smith's statements concerning the papyrus and the translation. Joseph Smith never mentioned anything about a "memory device" or "supercryptograms"; instead, he clearly stated ". . . I commenced the translation of some of the characters or hieroglyphics, and much to our joy found that one of the rolls contained the writing of Abraham . . ." (*History of the Church,* vol. 2, p.236). If the "Book of Abraham" is not an actual translation of the papyrus then the introduction to it that appears in the *Pearl of Great Price* is a misrepresentation.

Our observations lead us to believe that there are a growing number of Mormons who are rejecting the "Book of Abraham." Grant Heward was one of the first openly to attack its authenticity, and for this offense he was excommunicated from the church. The fact that Mr. Heward was excommunicated did not stop Egyptologist Dee Jay Nelson from doing his work. In fact, Mr. Nelson finally came to the point that he felt he must withdraw his name from the church. Naomi Woodbury, another Mormon who has studied Egyptology, has also come out against the divinity of the "Book of Abraham." In a letter published in *Dialogue: A Journal of Mormon Thought,* Autumn 1968, page 8, she made these comments:

> I myself studied Egyptian hieroglyphics at UCLA several years ago in the hope of resolving some of the problems connected with the "Book of Abraham" in Joseph Smith's favor. Unfortunately, as soon as I had learned the language well enough to use a dictionary I was forced to conclude that Joseph Smith's translation was mistaken, however sincere it might have been. Facsimile No. 2 in the Pearl of Great Price contained enough readable writing to convince me that it had purely Egyptian significance. This was a disappointment to me. . . .
>
> After the appearance of the photographs of the papyri . . . I made some attempt to translate the "Book of Breathing(s)" text. . . . It belongs to a kind of literature which is alien to Christianity and to our Church. . . .
>
> Let us not lose sight of what I think is the primary importance of this papyri find. It can free us from our dilemma about excluding Negroes from the Priesthood. Perhaps our Father in Heaven intended the papyri to come to light now for just this purpose.

The rediscovery of the papyri was probably one of the most important factors in causing Thomas Stuart Ferguson to lose his faith in Joseph Smith's work (see *Mormonism—Shadow or Reality?* pp.332-33).

The Facsimiles

Although the translation of Papyus XI provides the greatest evidence against the "Book of Abraham," we feel that a very good case can be made against the book on the basis of the facsimiles printed in its pages. Facsimile No. 1, for instance,

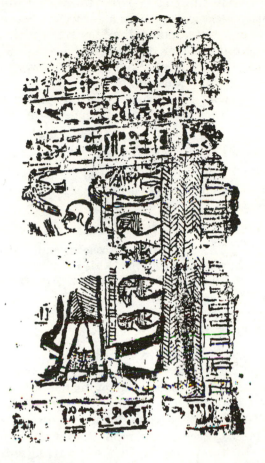

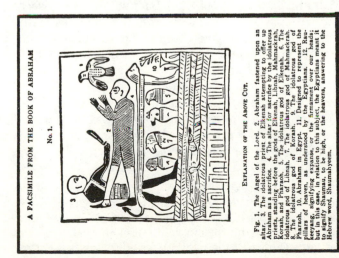

To the right is a photograph of the original papyrus from which Facsimile No. 1 was taken. To the left is a copy of Facsimile No. 1 as it appears in the *Pearl of Great Price* together with Joseph Smith's interpretation.

has now been identified as a part of the same scroll from which the "Sensen" text was taken. In other words, Facsimile No. 1 is in reality an illustration for the "Book of Breathings." Fortunately, the original papyrus from which Facsimile No. 1 was copied is among the eleven fragments which were rediscovered at the Metropolitan Museum of Art (see photograph on page 357 of this book). Egyptologist Dee Jay Nelson supplies this information in his first booklet on the papyri:

> "This scene of Anubis embalming Osiris is often seen in copies of the Shait en Sensen, Book of Breathings. . . .
>
> 1. This fragment bears the original illustration from which the cut for Facsimile No. 1 Pearl of Great Price, Book of Abraham was made. . . .
>
> 2. The fragment is badly damaged.
>
> 3. This vignette is typical of scenes from the Shait en Sensen, Book of Breathings, showing Osiris lying dead upon his funeral bier in the process of being embalmed by the jackal-headed god, Anubis.
>
> 4. The illustration is of the type popular in the Ptolemaic Period after 332 B.C. (*The Joseph Smith Papyri*, pp.42, 44).

Klaus Baer, of the University of Chicago, has now proved beyond all doubt that this is part of the same scroll which contained the small "Sensen" papyrus that Joseph Smith used as the basis for the text of the "Book of Abraham." He has shown that when the two fragments are placed together they match perfectly (see photograph in *Mormonism—Shadow or Reality?* p.333). Writing in *Dialogue: A Journal of Mormon Thought* (Autumn 1968, p.112), Klaus Baer states: "They seem to have been cut apart after being mounted. The edges match exactly in the photograph, and the pattern of vertical lines drawn on the backing about 2 cm. apart continues evenly from P.JS XI onto the left end of P.JS I when the two are placed in contact."

Just before his article was printed in *Dialogue*, Klaus Baer went to Brigham Young University and examined the original papyrus fragments. His work with the original manuscripts confirmed the research he had done with photographs of the papyri. In an addendum to his article he stated:

> The reverse of the backings of both P.JS I contain parts of the plan mentioned in n.117, and they clearly adjoin as proposed in n.15; matching upper and lower parts of handwriting are on the two pieces of paper with the cut going through the letters. The fiber patterns show that the papyri were adjoining parts of the

same scroll and not simply mounted on adjoining pieces of paper. Papyrus fibers are always irregular and can be used (much like fingerprints) to check whether fragments come from the same sheet; in this case, the horizontal fibers on the left and right edges of P.JS I and XI, respectively, match exactly (*Dialogue: A Journal of Mormon Thought*, Autumn 1968, pp.133-34).

Even Dr. Hugh Nibley has to admit that before the papyrus was cut Papyrus XI followed immediately after Facsimile No. 1 on the roll: "It can be easily shown by matching up the cut edges and fibers of the papyri that the text of the Joseph Smith 'Breathing' Papyrus (No. XI) was written on the same strip of material as Facsimile No. 1 and immediately adjoining it" (*The Message of the Joseph Smith Papyri*, p.13).

Writing in *BYU Studies*, Winter 1971, pages 160-61, Dr. Nibley stated:

> Of particular interest to us is the close association of the Book of Breathing with the Facsimiles of the Book of Abraham. It can be easily shown by matching up the fibers of the papyri that the text of Joseph Smith Pap. No. XI was written on the same strip of material as Facsimile Number 1, . . . our "Sensen" Papyrus is closely bound to all three facsimiles by physical contact, putting us under moral obligation to search out possible relationships between the content of the four documents.

The text of the "Book of Abraham" itself shows that the drawing shown as Facsimile No. 1 was supposed to be at the beginning of the scroll. In Abraham 1:12 we read: "And it came to pass that the priests laid violence upon me, that they might slay me also, as they did those virgins upon this altar; and that you may have a knowledge of this altar, I will refer you to *the representation at the commencement of this record.*"

As we have already shown, Joseph Smith was "translating" from the small "Sensen" text. Since he was working from right to left, the drawing would have to appear on the right side of the scroll to be at the "commencement of this record." The illustration shown in *Mormonism—Shadow or Reality?* page 333, proves that the drawing was found on the right side of the "Sensen" text, which is consistent with the statement found in Abraham 1:12. It is also consistent with a statement in Abraham 1:14 which speaks of Facsimile No. 1 as being "*at the beginning*" of the record.

The reader will notice that the original papyrus fragment from which Facsimile No. 1 was copied has several rows of hieroglyphs which were not included in the printed facsimile. This writing becomes very significant when we try to determine what the drawing is about. In the photograph on page 357 of this book the reader will see the hieroglyphs which appear on the two sides of the drawing. There is another row just above the arm of the standing figure, but most of it has broken off.

Dr. Hugh Nibley has implied that this writing contains some "extraordinary" message, but he has never had the courage to provide a translation of the text. A person would certainly expect to find a translation of this text in his new book, *The Message of the Joseph Smith Papyri*, but no translation can be found anywhere in the book. Fortunately, Klaus Baer, an Egyptologist from the University of Chicago, has provided a translation of this fragment:

> Lines 1-3 give the titles, name, and parentage of the man for whose benefit the *Breathing Permit* was written:
>
> . . . the prophet of Amonrasonter, prophet [?] of Min Bull-of-his-Mother, prophet [?] of Khons the Governor . . . Hor, justified son the holder of the same titles, master of secrets, and purifier of the gods Osorwer, justified [?] . . . Tikhebyt, justified. May your ba live among them, and may you be buried in the West. . . .
>
> Too little is left of line 4 to permit even a guess at what it said. Insofar as I can make it out, line 5 reads:
>
> May you give him a good, splendid burial on the West of Thebes just like . . . (*Dialogue: A Journal of Mormon Thought*, Autumn 1968, pp.116-17).

The reader will notice that Klaus Baer reads the names Hor and Tikhebyt on this fragment. These are the very names that appear in the text of the "Sensen" fragments. This establishes beyond all doubt that the fragment is part of the pagan funeral text known as the "Book of Breathings." The names of Egyptian gods are written on the fragment, and the word *burial* appears twice on this piece of papyrus. It is interesting to note that Klaus Baer translates the word *Thebes* from the fifth line of the fragment. Dr. Hugh Nibley states that the mummies were "found in Thebes" (*Improvement Era*, February 1968, p.21), and Klaus Baer states that "all the known copies" of the "Book of Breathings" "seem to come" from Thebes. Furthermore, the gods mentioned in the text are the very gods that were worshiped at Thebes. All evidence, therefore, points to the unescapable conclusion that this is a pagan document and that it could not have been written by Abraham. No wonder Dr. Nibley refused to provide a translation of this important text.

Dr. Nibley would have us believe that the fragment of papyrus from which Joseph Smith copied Facsimile No. 1 is a unique document. Egyptologist Dee Jay Nelson, however, has studied many similar scenes:

This scene is intimately familiar to me. I have seen it many times. As a matter of fact, in one temple alone, located at Denderah, thirty seven miles north of Luxor are twenty nine wall bas-reliefs representing Osiris lying upon a lion-headed bier which exactly resembles the one on this papyrus fragment. Five of these even show him with one leg raised above the bed. Two of them also show a jackal-headed god standing near the foot of the bier (behind it) facing the head. One of these has the following similarities. I should say, precise equivalents:

1. The bier has a lions head and an upturned tail.
2. A person is lying on the bier, face up.
3. The hands of the reclining person are held above his face, palms downward (the sign of grief).
4. The reclining figure has his right leg somewhat elevated.
5. A dark figure stands near the foot of the bier facing the head of the couch.
6. A hawk-headed (ba) hovers over the reclining figure (*The Joseph Smith Papyri*, p.42).

Egyptologists who have examined the papyrus fragment from which Facsimile No. 1 was copied feel that Joseph Smith's interpretation of it is totally incorrect. What Joseph Smith called "Abraham fastened upon an altar" is in reality Osiris lying upon his bier. The "idolatrous priest of Elkenah" is the god "Anubis" ministering to Osiris.

The Egyptians believed that Osiris was killed by his brother Set. The body was found by Isis, and he was embalmed by Anubis. Osiris was resurrected and became the god of the dead.

The four jars which appear below the bier in Facsimile No. 1 prove that it is a funerary scene. These canopic jars were used to hold the soft parts of the body which were removed during the embalming process. Joseph Smith's statement that they are the gods of Elkenah, Libnah, Mahmackrah, and Korash is completely wrong (see *The Joseph Smith Papyri*, p.42).

Egyptologists have always claimed that the Mormons altered the scene shown in Facsimile No. 1. They claim that the standing figure (Anubis) should have a jackal's head instead of a human head. Some Egyptologists claim that the knife in Anubis' hand has been added and that the bird should have a human head. Mormon apologists ridiculed Egyptologists for making these charges, but now that the original papyrus has been located the entire picture has changed. The Mormon position has been considerably weakened because the portions of the papyrus which have been in question—the parts that would have contained the head of Anubis, the head of the bird, and the knife—are missing!

In *Mormonism—Shadow or Reality?*, we present a thorough study of all three of the facsimiles published in the "Book of Abraham." We show that Joseph Smith and his successors made drastic alterations in Facsimile No. 2. One of the scenes shown in Facsimile No. 2 was actually a pornographic representation of an ithyphallic god.

The Moment of Truth

In a letter dated September 15, 1968, Mormon Egyptologist Dee Jay Nelson wrote: "Does it not impress you that the facts against the Book of Abraham are coming one on the heels of another? I believe that God has decided that the time is right that these untruths (The Book of Abraham) be unmasked (in this decade). Do you not also think that God is blessing us greatly by giving us this chance to serve His purposes!" As we have already shown, Dee Jay Nelson finally left the Mormon church over the issue of the Book of Abraham.

The Reorganized Church of Jesus Christ of Latter Day Saints, the largest of the groups that broke off from the Mormons, seems to have accepted the truth about the "Book of Abraham." Richard P. Howard, RLDS church historian says that "it may be helpful to suggest that the 'Book of Abraham' represents simply the product of Joseph Smith Jr.'s imagination, wrought out in the midst of what to him must have been a very crucial and demanding complex set of circumstances" (*The New York Times*, May 3, 1970).

Although the RLDS church seems to have come to grips with this important issue, the Utah Mormon leaders will not face the truth concerning this matter. In an article in the *Salt Lake Tribune*, May 4, 1970, we read:

> "The First Presidency of the Church of Jesus Christ of Latter-day Saints accepts the 'Book of Abraham' as 'scripture given to us through the Prophet (Joseph Smith)," President N. Eldon Tanner said Sunday night.
>
> President Tanner, second counselor in the church's First Presidency, made the statement in response to an article saying the translation of the "Book of Abraham" was the product of Joseph Smith Jr.'s "imagination."

That the Utah Mormon leaders would continue to endorse the "Book of Abraham" in the face of the evidence that has been presented is almost beyond belief.

We feel that if any person will honestly examine this matter he will see that the evidence to disprove the "Book of Abraham" is conclusive. We have shown that the original papyrus fragment Joseph Smith used as the basis for the "Book of Abraham" has been identified and that this fragment is in reality a part of the Egyptian "Book of Breathings." It is a pagan text and contains absolutely nothing concerning Abraham or his religion.

Perhaps one reason the Mormon leaders refuse to face the facts concerning the "Book of Abraham" is that to do so would cast a serious shadow of doubt upon the authenticity of the *Book of Mormon.* Samuel A. B. Mercer concluded: ". . . both books were translated from the same Egyptian language, and if the translator failed in the translation of the one book, our faith in his translation of the other must necessarily be impaired . . ." (*The Utah Survey*, September 1913, p.5).

The Mormon leaders cannot repudiate the "Book of Abraham" without seriously discrediting the validity of the *Book of Mormon.*

Dr. Hugh Nibley has stated: ". . . a few faded and tattered little scraps of papyrus may serve to remind the Latter-day Saints of how sadly they have neglected serious education. . . . Not only has our image suffered by such tragic neglect, but now in the moment of truth the Mormons have to face the world unprepared, after having been given a hundred years' fair warning" (*Brigham Young University Studies*, Winter 1968, pp.171-72).

Truly, this is the moment of truth for the Mormon people. The "Book of Abraham" has been proven untrue, and even Dr. Nibley is unprepared to face the situation. For a number of years we have been calling upon the Mormon leaders to repudiate the "Book of Abraham" and the anti-black doctrine contained in its pages. They have finally yielded to pressure and allowed blacks to hold the priesthood. We feel, however, they should go one step further and admit the "Book of Abraham" is a work of Joseph Smith's imagination.

MORMON SCRIPTURES AND THE BIBLE

Chapter 12

The Mormon church accepts the Bible as one of its four standard works. The *Book of Mormon* quotes large portions of the King James Version of the Bible, and Joseph Smith's other revelations are filled with material from the Bible. Since the King James Version was printed about 200 years before Joseph Smith was even born, it is in no way dependent upon Mormon Scriptures. Joseph Smith's works, on the other hand, could not stand if the Bible were proven false, for many of his revelations are built upon the historical accuracy of the Bible, even though they may differ in doctrinal content. Nevertheless, many Mormons, seemingly ignorant of the fact that they are undermining the whole foundation of their own church, have made some vicious attacks on the Bible. Most of these attacks are not based upon sound historical evidence or methods. In fact, they reveal a lack of knowledge concerning Bible history and problems. Heber C. Snell, a former LDS institute director, has observed regarding the status of the Bible in the Mormon church:

> In 1830, when the Church was organized, it had two sacred books, the Bible and the Book of Mormon. . . .
>
> From occupying the status of the first of two books of scripture in the Church the Bible became, in the course of about two decades, one of four. There are indications that it has now declined to the position of third or even fourth place among the Church's sacred books. . . .
>
> This change of status of the Bible seems to be well attested by the relatively little attention given it by Church speakers and writers. . . . An examination of the *Improvement Era* Master Index, . . . gave thirty-six titles under Bible, or 137 pages as compared with 124 titles and 725 pages under Book of Mormon. . . . My work, as a teacher of the Bible in L.D.S. collegiate institutions over a period of a quarter of a century, has failed to convince me that our people have made much advancement in biblical knowledge

(*Dialogue: A Journal of Mormon Thought,* Spring 1967, pp.56-57).

Paine's Influence

Davis Bitton, who is now an assistant church historian, had this to say concerning Mormonism of the nineteenth century:

> For the Mormons the Bible was only one among several scriptures; its message was often discribed as applicable to a certain time and place in the past, with modern problems requiring new revelation; it was seen as having been corrupted, distorted, and inaccurately translated. . . . The Mormons could scarcely be charged with Bibliolatry, and it is perhaps understandable that Protestant ministers saw Mormon criticism of the Bible to be essentially the same as that of the rationalists (*Dialogue: A Journal of Mormon Thought,* Autumn 1966, p.113).

In a footnote on the same page, Davis Bitton states: "J. B. Turner, . . . argues rather convincingly that Mormons were so convinced of the inadequacy of the Bible and the apostate condition of Christianity that, if they ever abandoned Mormonism, they were almost inevitably agnostic toward all religion." Although Davis Bitton does not feel that Mormons were as radical in their criticism of the Bible as some others, he does feel that "rationalists such as Thomas Paine had furnished valuable ammunition" for the Mormon attack on the accuracy of the Bible.

Thomas Paine's book *The Age of Reason,* undoubtedly had an influence on Mormon thinking. This book, written in the 1790s, caused a great deal of controversy and was therefore well known in Joseph Smith's time. In fact, a copy has been traced to Joseph Smith's father. While Paine was a brilliant man and raised a number of important questions in his book, he wrote with such sarcasm that his work was very offensive to a Christian. In one place he talks of "the stupid Bible of the church, that teacheth man nothing" (*The Age of Reason,* reprinted by the Thomas Paine Foundation, New York, p.189).

Thomas Paine felt that the Bible could not be trusted as "the word of God" because of the problems involved in translation: ". . . as to translations, every man who knows anything of languages knows that it is impossible to translate from one language to another, not only without losing a great part of the original, but frequently of mistaking the sense . . ." (*The Age of Reason,* p.32).

It is interesting to note that Joseph Smith also cast doubt upon the translation of the Bible, for in "The Articles of Faith," he wrote: "8. We believe the Bible to be *the word of God as far as it is translated correctly*; we also believe the Book of Mormon to be the word of God" (*Pearl of Great Price*, p.59).

In his pamphlet, "Spiritual Gifts," Apostle Orson Pratt used arguments which resemble the ideas of Thomas Paine:

> God gave many revelations to Hebrew Prophets, in the Hebrew language. . . . The same revelations have been translated many times by different authors: . . . These clashing translations are circulated among the people, as the words of God, when, in reality they are the words of translators; . . . the Bible in . . . all the languages of the earth, except the original in which it was given, is *not the word of God, but the word of uninspired translators* . . . so far as the uninspired translators and the people are concerned, no part of the Bible can, with certainty, be known by them to be the word of God.
>
> 23. — The Hebrew and Greek manuscripts of the Bible from which translations have been made, are evidently very much corrupted, . . . the learned are under the necessity of translating from such mutilated, imperfect, and, in very many instances, contradictory copies as still exist. This uncertainty, combined with the imperfections of uninspired translators, *renders the Bibles of all languages, at the present day, emphatically the words of men, instead of the pure word of God* (*Pamphlets by Orson Pratt*, pp. 70-71).

In a pamphlet published in the 1850's, Apostle Pratt further commented:

> Many Protestants say they take the Bible as their only rule of faith . . . What evidence have they that the book of Matthew was inspired of God, or any other of the books of the New Testament? The only evidence they have is tradition. . . . If it could be demonstrated by tradition, that every part of each book of the Old and New Testament, was, in its original, actually written by inspiration, still it cannot be determined that there is one single true copy of those originals now in existence. . . . What shall we say then, concerning the Bible's being a sufficient guide? Can we rely upon it in its present known corrupted state, as being a faithful record of God's word? We all know that but a few of the inspired writings have descended to our times, which few quote the names of some twenty other books which are lost, . . . What few have come down to our day, have been *mutilated, changed, and corrupted*, in such a shameful manner that no two manuscripts agree. Verses and even whole chapters have been added by unknown persons; and even we do not know the authors of some whole books; and we are not certain that all those which we do know, were wrote by inspiration. Add all this imperfection to the uncertainty of the translation, and *who, in his right mind, could, for one moment, suppose the Bible in its present*

form to be a perfect guide? Who knows that *even one verse of the whole Bible has escaped pollution,* so as to convey the same sense now that it did in the original? . . . There can be no certainty as to the contents of the inspired writings until God shall inspire some one to rewrite all those books over again. . . . No reflecting man can deny the necessity of such a new revelation (*Orson Pratt's Works,* "The Bible Alone An Insufficient Guide," pp.44-47).

While we would expect an open enemy of Christianity like Thomas Paine to make the statements he did about the Bible, it is quite shocking to find a man who professed to be a Christian making such an attack upon the Bible. Even Brigham Young felt that Apostle Pratt went too far in his attack on the Bible (see *Journal of Discourses,* vol.3, p.116). Apostle Pratt's statement that the Bible may have been changed so much that we can't even rely upon one verse sounds very strange in light of the fact that the *Book of Mormon* quotes hundred of verses from the Bible. In almost all cases these verses carry the same meaning as they do in the Bible. This alone should be sufficient evidence to show Mormons that Orson Pratt was wrong in implying that we don't know "that even one verse of the whole Bible has escaped pollution, so as to convey the same sense now" as it did in the original. Thus it is plain to see that the·Bible cannot be discredited without casting doubt on the *Book of Mormon* also. If the Bible is all wrong, then the *Book of Mormon* is also.

Mormon Apostle Mark E. Petersen is more tactful than Pratt in his criticism of the Bible. Although he claims that portions were removed from the Bible, the identical wording of Scriptures found in the King James Version and the *Book of Mormon* has forced him to believe that "the Lord did have a hand in the translation of the King James version": "The Book of Mormon gives many detailed quotations from the records of Laban, incidentally, giving irrefutable evidence of the accuracy of the King James version, even though much of the scripture as given originally is now missing" (*As Translated Correctly,* 1966, p.45).

Apostle Petersen feels that the quotations from Isaiah found in the *Book of Mormon* are "no doubt the only truly accurate quotations in existence today" (p.54). He even goes so far as to judge the text of the Bible by the text found in the *Book of Mormon:*

A direct reference to baptism was plainly deleted from Isaiah 48:1.

In the Old Testament this reference reads:

"Hear ye this, O house of Jacob, which are called by the name of Israel, and are come forth out of the waters of Judah, which sware by the name of the Lord. . . ."

And now note this same passage from the brass plates [the Book of Mormon]: "Hearken and hear this, O house of Jacob, who are called by the name of Israel, and are come forth out of the waters of Judah, OR OUT OF THE WATERS OF BAPTISM, who sware by the name of the Lord. . . . " (1 Nephi 20:1).

How many similar deletions were made, no one knows, because we have only fragments from the brass plates.

But the Bible as we know it is a different volume from what it was—and would have been—had it not been changed so much by those with selfish interests (*As Translated Correctly*, p.67).

Apostle Petersen certainly picked a poor example to try to prove his charge, for there is definite proof that the change was made in the text of the *Book of Mormon* rather than in the text of the Bible. The text of the original 1830 printing of the *Book of Mormon* did *not* have the phrase concerning baptism in it. It followed the text of the Bible: "Hearken and hear this, O house of Jacob, which are called by the name of Israel, and are come forth out of the waters of Judah, which swear by the name of the Lord, . . ." (*Book of Mormon*, 1830 ed. p.52).

The phrase "or out of the waters of baptism" was added in later editions. It did not appear in the original handwritten manuscript, and even Dr. Nibley has to admit that it is an interpolation: "It is said that *Parley P. Pratt suggested the phrase*, . . . Isaiah did *not* have to tell his ancient hearers that he had the waters of baptism in mind, but it is necessary to tell it to the modern reader . . ." (*Since Cumorah*, p.151).

Apostle Petersen made a serious mistake when he tried to condemn the text of the Bible on the basis of this verse from the *Book of Mormon*.

Evidence Compared

Orson Pratt once claimed: "This generation have *more than one thousand times* the amount of evidence to demonstrate and for ever establish the Divine Authenticity of the Book of Mormon than they have in favor of the Bible!" In a discourse delivered in the Tabernacle on January 2, 1859, Orson Pratt expanded his comments:

. . . I will endeavor to bring forth some few of the evidences which establish the Divine authenticity of the Book of Mormon.

I shall compare this evidence with the evidence for the Divine authenticity of the Bible. . . .

The oldest manuscripts of any of the books of the Old Testament at the present day date from the twelfth century of the Christian era. . . . The oldest manuscripts of the New Testament which this age are in possession of are supposed to date from the sixth century of the Christian era. . . . We have five manuscripts in existence that were supposed to have been written as early as the sixth or seventh century after Christ. . . .

The Book of Mormon . . . was translated from the original plates themselves. . . . We defy the world to produce a true copy of the original of any book of the Bible. . . . Where is there a man who has heard the voice of God testifying concerning the truth of King James' translation? . . . the testimony establishing the truth of the Book of Mormon is far superior to that establishing the Bible in its present form . . . any person who will carefully examine this subject will be obliged in their own hearts to say there is a hundredfold more evidence to prove the Divine authenticity of the Book of Mormon than what we have to prove the Palestine records (*Journal of Discourses*, vol. 7, pp.23,26,29,30,36,37).

Apostle Pratt's statement that there is "more than one thousand times" the amount of evidence to prove the *Book of Mormon* than to prove the Bible is certainly a misrepresentation. We have already shown that the only evidence for the *Book of Mormon* is the testimony of the witnesses and that this testimony cannot be relied upon.

As far as historical and manuscript evidence is concerned Joseph Smith's scriptures have absolutely no foundation. The "records of the Nephites," for instance, were never cited by any ancient writer, nor are there any known manuscripts or even fragments of manuscripts in existence older than the ones dictated by Joseph Smith in the late 1820s.

Joseph Smith's "Book of Moses" is likewise without documentary support. The only handwritten manuscripts for the "Book of Moses" are those dictated by Joseph Smith in the early 1830s.

Since Joseph Smith's revelations in the *Doctrine and Covenants* do not purport to be translations of ancient records, we would not expect to find any ancient manuscript evidence concerning them. There is one revelation, however, which purports to be a translation of a "record made on parchment by John and hidden up by himself." This revelation, found in the *Doctrine and Covenants* as Section 7, has no documentary support for its claims.

The "Book of Abraham" purports to be a translation of an ancient Egyptian papyrus. However, the original papyrus is in reality the Egyptian "Book of Breathings" and has nothing to do with Abraham or his religion. Therefore, we have no evidence for the "Book of Abraham" prior to the handwritten manuscripts dictated by Joseph Smith in the 1830s. It would appear, then, that there is no documentary evidence for any of Joseph Smith's works that dates back prior to the late 1820s.

When we turn to the Bible, however, we find a great deal of historical evidence—some of which dates back more than 2,000 years—showing that the Bible was known and used in early times. While this in itself does not prove that the Bible is divinely inspired, it does give a person a basis for faith.

Dead Sea Scrolls

The reader will remember that Apostle Orson Pratt stated that the "oldest manuscripts of any of the books of the Old Testament at the present day date from the twelfth century of the Christian Era." While this statement may have been true in Orson Pratt's time, the discovery of the Dead Sea Scrolls has changed the entire picture. We now have some manuscripts that date back prior to the time of Christ.

The Dead Sea Scrolls were discovered in 1947 when a boy threw a rock into a cave near the Dead Sea. He was startled by the sound of something breaking and later came back to find jars with ancient manuscripts in them. This was only the beginning, for further search by a number of people led to the discovery of many important manuscripts. In *Compton's Encyclopedia*, we read: "The Biblical manuscripts known as the Dead Sea Scrolls have been called by scholars 'the greatest manuscript discovery of modern times.' They include Old Testament books and non-Biblical texts dating from 100 B.C. to A.D. 68" (vol. 6, p.41a).

In his book, *The Ancient Library of Qumran*, Frank Moore Cross, Jr., describes the scrolls:

> A sketch of the contents of Cave IV may be helpful. . . . At the end of four years' labor 382 manuscripts have been identified from this cave. . . . Of the manuscripts identified thus far, about one hundred, slightly more than one fourth of the total, are biblical. All of the books of the Hebrew canon are now extant, with the exception of the Book of Esther. . . .

> Three very old documents have been found in Cave IV. . . .They include an old copy of Samuel, preserved in only a handful of fragments; a patched and worn section of Jeremiah, . . . and a copy of Exodus . . . of which only a column and a few tatters are extant. . . .

The archaic Samuel scroll can date scarcely later than 200 B.C. A date in the last quarter of the third century is preferable. The Jeremiah is probably slightly later. The archaic Exodus . . . appears to be no later than the old Samuel fragments and probably is earlier.

One copy of Daniel is inscribed in the script of the late second century B.C. . . .

The biblical scrolls from Qumran span in date about three centuries. A few archaic specimens carry us back to the end of the third century, as we have seen. The heavy majority, however, date in the first century B.C. and in the first Christian century . . . (*The Ancient Library of Qumran*, by Frank Moore Cross, Jr., New York, 1961, pp.39,40,42,43).

Mormon scholars accept the authenticity of the Dead Sea Scrolls, although they have not come to grips with the serious problems that these manuscripts create for the *Book of Mormon* and Joseph Smith's *Inspired Version of the Bible*.

Werner Keller summarized the situation concerning the Isaiah scroll:

The text of Isaiah from the cave at Qumran had actually been copied about 100 B.C., as Professor Albright had been first to recognize . . . with the discovery of the Dead Sea scroll of Isaiah we have a Hebrew text of the Bible. . . . And the remarkable and wonderful fact is that ancient scroll of Isaiah, just like the book of the prophet in any printed Bible, whether in Hebrew, Greek, Latin, German, or any other language, . . . agrees with our present-day text.

Seventeen sheets of leather sewn together into a length of almost twenty-three feet—this must have been what the roll of the prophet looked like as it was handed to Jesus in the synagogue at Nazareth so that he might read from it to the congregation. "And there was delivered unto him the book of the prophet Esaias [Isaiah]." (Luke 4:16,17) "Every movement of Jesus' hands is brought closer to us," writes Professor Andre Parrot, "for we can still see on the reverse side of the leather the marks of the readers' fingers" (*The Bible as History*, by Werner Keller, William Neil, trans., New York, 1957, pp.423-24).

Dr. Gleason L. Archer points out about the Isaiah scrolls that "even though the two copies of Isaiah discovered in Qumran Cave 1 near the Dead Sea in 1947 were a thousand years earlier than the oldest dated manuscript previously known (A.D. 980), they proved to be word for word identical with our standard Hebrew Bible in more than 95 per cent of the text. The 5 per cent of variation consisted chiefly of obvious slips of the pen and variations in spelling" (*A Survey of Old Testament Introduction*, p.19).

Bible scholars have reason to rejoice over the discovery of manuscripts of Isaiah dating back to ancient times. Mormon scholars, however, are faced with a dilemma, for although these manuscripts support the text of the Bible, they could turn out to be one of the strongest evidences against Joseph Smith's "inspired revision" of the Bible and his "translation" of the text of Isaiah found in the *Book of Mormon*. For years Mormon scholars have labored to prove that the text of Isaiah in the *Book of Mormon* is actually a translation of an ancient copy of Isaiah and is therefore superior to the translation found in the Bible. They have attempted to show parallels between the text of Isaiah found in the *Book of Mormon* and that found in some ancient manuscripts. We have shown, however, that these parallels are of little value because the manuscripts were known and studied in Joseph Smith's time (See *Mormon Scriptures and the Bible*, pp.9-10).

If Mormon scholars could find similarities between the text of the *Book of Mormon* and documents that were not known in Joseph Smith's day, this type of evidence would be impressive. The Dead Sea Scrolls, for instance, should provide a great deal of evidence for the *Book of Mormon* if it is really an ancient record. The Isaiah scroll found at Qumran Cave 1 should have caused a great deal of joy among Mormon scholars, for here is a manuscript of Isaiah which is hundreds of years older than any manuscript previously known. Surely, if the *Book of Mormon* were true, this manuscript would be filled with evidence to support the text of Isaiah in the *Book of Mormon* and thus prove that Joseph Smith was a prophet of God. Instead of proving the *Book of Mormon*, however, it has turned out to be a great disappointment to Mormon scholars.

Lewis M. Rogers, who was assistant professor of religion at Brigham Young University, wrote a paper entitled, "The Significance of the Scrolls and a Word of Caution." In this article he stated:

> Latter-day Saints have cause to rejoice with other Christians and Jews for the new light and fresh perspective brought to them by the Dead Sea Scrolls, but occasionally they need to be reminded that their hopes and emotions make them vulnerable. It is quite possible that claims for the Book of Mormon and for L.D.S. theology will *not* be greatly advanced as a consequence of this discovery (*Progress in Archaeology*, Brigham Young University, 1963, pp.46-47).

Wayne Ham wrote his M.A. thesis for the department of biblical languages at Brigham Young University in 1961. His thesis compared the Isaiah scroll with the *Book of Mormon* and is titled, "A Textual Comparison of the Isaiah Passages in the Book of Mormon with the Same Passages in the St. Mark's Isaiah Scroll of the Dead Sea Community." After making this study, Mr. Ham was forced to the conclusion that the Isaiah scroll does not support the text in the *Book of Mormon*. In an article published in *Courage* in 1970, he stated:

> Latter Day Saints were hopeful that these Isaiah scrolls would bring some supportive evidence for the Book of Mormon. The Dead Sea Isaiah scroll, which dates probably from the second century B.C., predates by one thousand years what was previously considered to be the oldest surviving text of the Old Testament.
>
> After a thorough investigation of the matter, . . . this writer *found no noteworthy instances of support for the Book of Mormon claims (Courage, vol. 1, no. 1, September 1970, p.20).*

Mormon apologist Dr. Sidney B. Sperry, of Brigham Young University, had to admit that the Dead Sea Scrolls do not help the case for the *Book of Mormon*:

> After reading the Scrolls very carefully, I come to the conclusion that *there is not a line in them that suggests that their writers knew the Gospel as understood by Latter-day Saints.* In fact, there are a few passages that seem *to prove the contrary. . . .*
>
> We should be especially interested in the light the Isaiah scroll throws on the problem of the Isaiah text in the Book of Mormon. I have compared in some detail the text of the scroll with its parallels in the Book of Mormon text. This tedious task has revealed that *the scroll seldom agrees with the departures of the Book of Mormon text* from that of the conventional Masoretic text of Isaiah and consequently the Authorized Version. . . . The Isaiah scroll *is of relatively little use to Latter-day Saints as showing the antiquity of the text of Isaiah in the Book of Mormon. . . .* The Scrolls undoubtedly contribute much to the history of Judaism and Christianity, and specialists of the Old and New Testaments are properly much concerned with them. . . .
>
> But aside from their technical value to scholars, I believe that the importance of the Scrolls in a religious sense has been highly overrated by certain scholars. Their practical importance to Latter-day Saints *is relatively small (Progress in Archaeology,* pp.52-54).

Evidence for New Testament

The reader will remember that in his attack upon the Bible, Apostle Orson Pratt stated that the "oldest manuscripts of the New Testament which this age are in possession of are supposed to date from the sixth century of the Christian era." He mentions both the Codex Vaticanus and the Codex Alexandrinus. Scholars now feel that the Codex Vaticanus "was written about the middle of the fourth century and contained both Testaments as well as the books of the Apocrypha..." (*The Text of the New Testament: Its Transmission, Corruption, and Restoration*, by Bruce M. Metzger [New York: Oxford University Press, Inc., 1964] p.47).

Dr. Gleason L. Archer regards the Codex Vaticanus as "a magnificent" manuscript and states that it was written about "A.D. 325-350" (*A Survey of Old Testament Introduction*, Chicago: Moody Press, 1973, p.40).

The Codex Alexandrinus was probably written in the fifth century. Bruce M. Metzger states: "This handsome codex, dating from about the fifth century, contains the Old Testament, except for several mutilations, and most of the New Testament. ... Today it rests along with codex Sinaiticus in one of the prominent showcases in the Department of Manuscripts of the British Museum" (*The Text of the New Testament*, p.46).

The same year (1859) that Orson Pratt was making one of his most vicious attacks on the Bible, Constantinus Tischendorf discovered the Codex Sinaiticus, which has turned out to be one of the most important manuscripts of the Bible. Scholars feel that this manuscript was written in the fourth century. George E. Ladd briefly reviews the information concerning this manuscript: "After the Russian revolution, the U.S.S.R. sold the manuscript to the British Museum in London for $500,000—a sale which attracted world-wide attention. This manuscript, called Codex Sinaiticus, dates from the early fourth century, and has proved to be one of the best texts we possess of the New Testament" (*New Testament and Criticism* [Grand Rapids: Wm. B. Eerdmans Publishing Co., 1967], p.62).

These three ancient manuscripts are very important as far as the text of the New Testament is concerned. Even some of the most zealous enemies of Christianity concede that they are authentic.

F. F. Bruce, a Christian writer from the University of Manchester and a New Testament authority, surveys the documentary evidence for the New Testament:

> The evidence for our New Testament writings is ever so much greater than the evidence for many writings of classical authors, the authenticity of which no-one dreams of questioning. ...

> There are in existence about 4,000 Greek manuscripts of the New Testament in whole or in part. The best and most important of these go back to somewhere about AD 350. ...

Perhaps we can appreciate how wealthy the New Testament is in manuscript attestation if we compare the textual material for other ancient historical works. For Caesar's Gallic War (composed between 58 and 50 BC) there are several extant MSS, but only nine or ten are good, and the oldest is some 900 years later than Caesar's day. Of the 142 books of the Roman history of Livy (59 BC—AD 17) only thirty-five survive; these are known to us from not more than twenty MSS of any consequence, only one of which, and that containing fragments of Books iii-vi, is as old as the fourth century. Of the fourteen books of the Histories of Tacitus (c. AD 100) only four and a half survive; of the sixteen books of his Annals, ten survive in full and two in part. The text of these extant portions of his two great historical works depends entirely on two MSS, one of the ninth century and one of the eleventh. The extant MSS of his minor works (Dialogus de Oratoribus, Agricola, Germania) all descend from a codex of the tenth century. The History of Thucydides (c. 460-400 BC) is known to us from eight MSS, the earliest belonging to c. AD 900, and a few papyrus scraps, belonging to about the beginning of the Christian era. The same is true of the History of Herodotus (c. 480-425 BC). Yet no classical scholar would listen to an argument that the authenticity of Herodotus or Thucydides is in doubt because the earliest MSS of their works which are of any use are over 1,300 years later than the originals.

But how different is the situation of the New Testament in this respect! In addition to the two excellent MSS of the fourth century mentioned above, which are the earliest of some thousands known to us, considerable fragments remain of papyrus copies of books of the New Testament dated from 100 to 200 years earlier still (*The New Testament Documents: Are They Reliable?* Grand Rapids: Eerdmans, 1967 (Leicester: Inter-Varsity Press, 1960) pp.15-17, used by permission).

Floyd V. Filson provides further details concerning the papyrus manuscripts:

> ... it is in Egypt that the overwhelming majority of papyri have survived. . . . it is the papyri which give us manuscripts that go further back than the fourth century. However, papyrus suffers from a serious drawback. It is fragile, and decays easily or becomes brittle and breaks in pieces; and so up to this time we have found only very limited fragments of papyrus manuscripts of New Testament books. Papyrus Bodmer II is outstanding in that so much of John is preserved in full page form (*The Biblical Archaeologist*, September 1957, p.55).

In *Mormonism—Shadow or Reality?* (p.379), we included a photograph from *The Biblical Archaeologist*, September 1957, p.61. This photograph shows "Rylands Greek Papyrus 457, dated about 125-130 A.D., the oldest known fragment of a New

Testament manuscript. It contains John 18:31-33 on one side and 18:37-38 on the other." J. A. Thompson writes concerning the Rylands Fragment of John:

> The style of writing enabled it to be assigned to the first half of the second century. . . . the fact that it was not only written in Egypt but that it had been used in a provincial town in Egypt at this early date points to the fact that John's Gospel, far from being a late second-century production as some had maintained, was in fact far earlier, and more likely to have been written in the first century, or at least very early in the second (*The Bible and Archaeology*, p.437).

F. F. Bruce adds this interesting information about the papyrus manuscripts:

> In addition to the two excellent MSS of the fourth century mentioned above, which are the earliest of some thousands known to us, considerable fragments remain of papyrus copies of books of the new Testament dated 100 to 200 years earlier still. The Chester Beatty Biblical Papyri, . . . consists of portions of eleven papyrus codices, three of which contained most of the New Testament writings. One of these, containing the four Gospels with Acts, belongs to the first half of the third century; another, containing Paul's letters to churches and the Epistle to the Hebrews, was copied at the beginning of the third century; the third, containing Revelation, belongs to the second half of the same century. . . .
>
> Earlier still is a fragment of a papyrus codex containing John xviii. 31-33, 37f., now in the John Rylands Library, Manchester, dated on palaeographical grounds around AD 130. . . .
>
> A more recently discovered papyrus manuscript of the same Gospel, while not so early as the Rylands papyrus, is incomparably better preserved; this is the Papyrus Bodmer II, whose discovery was announced by the Bodmer Library of Geneva in 1956; it was written about AD 200, and contains the first fourteen chapters of the Gospel of John with one lacuna (of twenty-two verses), and considerable portions of the last seven chapters (*The New Testament Documents: Are They Reliable?* pp.17-18).

Besides the thousands of Greek manuscripts, there is additional evidence for the text of the New Testament found in early translations into other languages and in quotations found in the writings of early Christians.

"130,000 Different Readings"

Orson Pratt proclaimed in a discourse delivered in 1859: "All the most ancient manuscripts of the New Testament known to the world differ from each other in almost every verse. . . . The learned admit that in the manuscripts of the New Testament alone there are no less than *one hundred and thirty thousand different readings* . . . . No one can tell whether even one verse of either the Old or New Testament conveys the ideas of the original author. Just think, 130,000 different readings in the New Testament alone!" (*Journal of Discourses*, vol. 7, pp.27-28).

In his book *The World and the Prophets*, page 188, Mormon apologist Dr. Hugh Nibley charges that "there are more than 8,000 ancient manuscripts of the New Testament, no two of which read exactly alike!" Now, while it is true that there are many different readings in manuscript copies of the New Testament, Mormon writers have greatly exaggerated the importance of this matter. Gleason L. Archer, remarks:

> But what about the text of the Bible as we now possess it? Is that text necessarily free from all mistakes of every kind? Not when it comes to copyists' errors, for we certainly do find discrepancies among the handwritten copies that have been preserved to us, even those which come from the earliest centuries. Some slips of the pen doubtless crept into the first copies made from the original manuscripts, and additional errors of a transmissional type found their way into the copies of copies. It is almost unavoidable that this should have been the case. No man alive can sit down and copy out the text of an entire book without a mistake of any kind (*A Survey of Old Testament Introduction*, p.18).

F. F. Bruce further clarifies the matter:

> It is easily proved by experiment that it is difficult to copy out a passage of any considerable length without making one or two slips at least. When we have documents like our New Testament writings copied and recopied thousands of times, the scope for copyists' errors is so enormously increased that it is surprising there are no more than there actually are. Fortunately, if the number of MSS increases the number of scribal errors, it increases proportionately the means of correcting such errors, so that the margin of doubt left in the process of recovering the exact original wording is not so large as might be feared; it is in truth remarkably small (*The New Testament Documents: Are They Reliable?* p.19).

In a footnote on page 55 of the book, *Our Bible and the Ancient Manuscripts*, we find this illuminating comment:

> Dr. Hort, whose authority on the point is quite incontestable, estimates the proportion of words about which there is some doubt [in the New Testament] at about one-eighth of the whole; but by far the greater part of these consists merely of differences in order and other unimportant variations, and "the amount of

what can in any sense be called substantial variation . . . can hardly form more than a thousandth part of the entire text" (*Introduction to The New Testament in the Original Greek*, p.2).

Mormon leaders claim that the Catholics conspired to alter the Bible. In the *Book of Mormon* we read:

. . . thou seest the foundation of a great and abominable church, which is most abominable above all other churches; for behold, they have taken away from the gospel of the Lamb many parts which are plain and most precious; and also many covenants of the Lord have they taken away.

And all this have they done that they might pervert the right ways of the Lord, that they might blind the eyes and harden the hearts of the children of men.

Wherefore, thou seeth that *after the book hath gone forth through the hands of the great and abominable church*, that there are *many plain and precious things taken away from the book*, which is the book of the Lamb of God.

. . . because of these things which are taken away out of the gospel of the Lamb, an exceeding great many do stumble, yea, insomuch that Satan hath great power over them (*Book of Mormon*, I Nephi 13:26-29).

Joseph Fielding Smith, Jr., son of the tenth president of the church, said that "The early 'Apostate Fathers' did not think it was wrong to tamper with inspired scripture. If any scripture seemed to endanger their viewpoint, it was altered, transplanted or completely removed from the Biblical text" (*Religious Truths Defined*, p.175).

Apostle Mark E. Peterson casts doubt on the reliability of the Bible: "Many insertions were made, some of them 'slanted' for selfish purposes, while at times *deliberate falsifications and fabrications* were perpetrated" (*As Translated Correctly*, p.4). "It is evident then that many of the 'plain and precious' things were omitted from the Bible by failure to choose all of the authentic books for inclusion, and by *deliberate changes, deletions and forgeries* . . ." (p.14).

While it is true that there are various readings in the original handwritten manuscripts of the Bible, the *Book of Mormon's* charge that the Catholics deliberately conspired to remove "many plain and precious things" out of the Bible is proven false by the Dead Sea Scrolls and other important manuscripts which have been discovered.

Anthony A. Hoekema observes:

The Mormon contention that "after the book [the Bible] hath gone forth through the hands of the great and abominable church . . . there are many plain and precious things taken away from the book. . ." (I Nephi 13:28), is completely contrary to fact. The many copies of Old Testament manuscripts which we now possess do vary in minor matters—the spelling of words, the omission of a phrase here and there—but there is no evidence whatsoever that any major sections of Old Testament books have been lost. The manuscripts found among the Dead Sea Scrolls, generally dated from about 200 to 50 B.C., include portions of every Old Testament book except Esther; studies have revealed that these documents—older by a thousand years than previously discovered Old Testament manuscripts—are substantially identical to the text of the Old Testament which had been previously handed down. As far as New Testament manuscripts are concerned, the oldest of which go back to the second century A.D., the situation is substantially the same. The variations that are found in these manuscripts . . . are of a relatively minor nature. There is no indication whatever that any large sections of material found in the originals have been lost. Most of the manuscript variations concern matters of spelling, word order, tense, and the like; no single doctrine is affected by them in any way (*The Four Major Cults*, [Grand Rapids: Wm. B. Eerdmans Publishing Co., 1963], pp.30-31).

The *Book of Mormon* plainly states that the changes in the Bible were made *after* the time of Christ and *after* the formation of the Catholic Church:

The book . . . is a record of the Jews . . . when it proceeded forth from the mouth of a Jew it contained the plainness of the gospel of the Lord . . . these things go forth *from the Jews in purity* unto the Gentiles . . . thou seest the foundation of a great and abominable church . . . they have taken away from the gospel of the Lamb . . . after the book hath gone forth through the hands of the great and abominable church . . . there are many plain and precious things taken away from the book . . . (*Book of Mormon*, I Nephi 13:23-28).

In 1832 the Mormon publication *The Evening and the Morning Star* (vol. 1, No. 1, p.3), said that the changes in the Bible were made "by the Mother of Harlots while it was confined in that Church,—say, from the year A.D. *460 to 1400.*"

The "great Isaiah scroll" found at Qumran provides important evidence to show that the Catholics did not take away "many plain and precious things" from the Bible. This scroll is dated at *about 100 B.C.,* and therefore *could not have been touched by the Catholics.* Also it should be remembered that this scroll is a Jewish production, and the *Book of Mormon* claims that the Jews had the Scriptures in their "purity." Why, then, does this scroll fail to support the text of Isaiah as found in the *Book of Mormon* or Joseph Smith's "inspired revision" of the Bible?

The Catholic Church certainly was not in existence prior to the time of Christ, and even President Joseph Fielding Smith, had to admit that the Catholics did not become the "ruling power in religion" until after "the beginning of the fourth century" (*Essentials in Church History*, p. 10).

In 1887 Rev. M. T. Lamb queried:

> Have a great many of the best things in the New Testament been taken out of it by a great and abominable church since the Apostles' day, as the Book of Mormon tells us? . . .

> Such a piracy of Holy Scripture could not have occurred later than 350 A.D., because there are now in existence copies of the Bible that are between fifteen and sixteen hundred years old, copies written out by hand not later than 350 years after Christ—250 years after the death of the Apostle John (*The Golden Bible*, p. 329).

At the time M. T. Lamb wrote the above statement there was still a substantial gap between the original manuscripts and the earliest copies known to scholars. Consequently, Mormons would not accept these fourth-century manuscripts as evidence against Joseph Smith's works. Since the turn of the century, however, the situation has entirely changed, for papyrus fragments have been found which virtually close the gap and prove that the Scriptures have not been rewritten by a "great and abominable church."

Floyd V. Filson says that "the text of the Gospels previously known from manuscripts of the fourth century and later agrees substantially with the text which we find in these third and second century fragments (second century fragments are admittedly rare and small)" (*The Biblical Archaeologist*, February 1961, p. 3).

Sir Fredric Kenyon, who was the director of the British Museum and a well known authority on Bible manuscripts, concludes that "The interval then between the dates of original composition and earliest extant evidence becomes so small as to be in fact negligible, and the last foundation for any doubt that the Scriptures have come down to us substantially as they were written has now been removed. Both the authenticity and the general integrity of the books of the New Testament may be regarded as finally established" (*The Bible and Archaeology*, 1940, p.288, as quoted in *The New Testament Documents: Are They Reliable?* p.20).

Because of recent discoveries of papyrus manuscripts Mormon writers are faced with a serious dilemma. It is no longer possible to maintain Joseph Smith's teaching that the Catholics conspired to change the Bible in light of these discoveries. Dr. Richard L. Anderson, of Brigham Young University, is undoubtedly one of the top authorities on Bible manuscripts in the Mormon church. In a paper read at the "Fourteenth Annual Symposium on the Archaeology of the Scriptures," Dr. Anderson seemed to be warning his people against the idea that the New Testament has been drastically altered:

> In studying a particular author in antiquity, the classical scholar typically works with a few principal manuscripts, together with a few more extensive fragments or portions of manuscripts. The New Testament scholar, however, faces the wonderful but impossible prospect of attempting to comprehend a text preserved in about 3,000 manuscripts. . . . Nor is sheer quantity most impressive, for the antiquity of his manuscripts should be the envy of all ancient studies. . . .
>
> This process of uncovering the major papyrus manuscripts of the New Testament has largely taken place not only in our own century, but in our own generation. . . . Almost the whole New Testament is represented in the papyrus fragments. The only two exceptions now are I and II Timothy. The real achievement, then, is that the antiquity of the text has now been pushed back almost another century. . . . the gap now separating the time of the writing of the New Testament and the oldest preserved manuscripts is now generally no more than 200 years, and as we shall soon see in the case of the letters of Paul and two Gospels, that gap has been narrowed by at least another fifty years. To underline the extent of the findings, let us stress that some part of every book of the New Testament is represented by papyrus dated as early as the third century with the present exception of Philemon, I Timothy, II Timothy, I, II, and III John. . . . the Rylands fragment, . . . shows that the Gospel of John had been written and also had been disseminated in Egypt before the middle of the second century. . . . a copy of the Gospel of John made not very many years after the writing of that Gospel, is a dramatic confirmation of the essential claim of Christianity, as it relates in fragmentary but clear form the question of Pilate, "Are you a king?"—and Jesus' affirmation, "To this end was I born, and for this cause came I into the world, that I should bear witness unto the truth. Every one that is of the truth heareth my voice." . . . the most impressive of the Beatty papyri are the extensive portions of what originally was a collection of Paul's letters, . . . thought by leading papyrologists to be no later than 200 A.D. This means that the oldest collection of Paul's letters now dates from a maximum of 150 years after Paul wrote. With such an early collection, the question naturally arises how the

381

text is different from the traditional one. Differences lie in numerous details, but the outstanding conclusion is that there is *little, if any, significant change.* . . .

Only within the last decade have come what are in many ways the most important papyrus discoveries yet for New Testament study. . . .

Among the Bodmer Papyri, the greatest treasures are the copies of the Gospels dating back to the end of the second century. The original publication took place in 1956 of a manuscript enumerated P[66]. It is a practically complete copy of the Gospel of John, which the editor dates about 200 A.D. . . . the most impressive contribution of the new manuscripts of Luke and John is not the few differences, but the extent of their agreement with the life and teachings of Christ as preserved in other manuscripts.

It is easy to get lost in debate on details and fail to see the overwhelming agreement of all manuscripts to the historical record of the New Testament. . . . For a book to undergo progressive uncovering of its manuscript history and come out with so little debatable in its text is a great tribute to its essential authenticity. . . . no new manuscript discovery has produced serious differences in the essential story. This survey has disclosed the leading textual controversies, and together they would be well within one percent of the text. Stated differently, *all manuscripts agree on the essential correctness of 99% of the verses in the New Testament.* . . .There is more reason today, then, to agree with him [Sir Frederic Kenyon] that we possess the New Testament "in substantial integrity" and to underline that "the variations of text are so entirely questions of detail, not of essential substance."

It is true that the Latter-day Saints have taken the position that the present Bible is much changed from its original form. However, greatest changes would logically have occurred in writings more remote than the New Testament. The textural history of the New Testament gives every reason to assume a fairly stable transmission of the documents we possess. . . .

Joseph Smith said that 'many important points touching the salvation of man, had been taken from the Bible, or lost before it was compiled.' (Documentary History of the Church, I, 245, 1832.) Major losses might occur by elimination of whole books rather than alterations of those admitted as canonical. Nor do subsequent changes have to be based on open changes of the writings. The forces of evil are more effective at changing the meaning of true terms and concepts than removing them (*Fourteenth Annual Symposium of the Archaeology of the Scriptures*, Brigham Young University, 1963, pp.52-59).

382   These statements will probably come as a surprise to Mormon

writers who claim that the Catholics conspired to change the Bible, especially since they come from the pen of one of their most noted scholars.

Before Mormon writers accuse Christians of altering the Bible they should take a serious look at some of their own revelations published in the *Doctrine and Covenants*. If the churches that preserved the Bible these many centuries had altered it at the same rate that Joseph Smith changed his revelations, we would be lucky to have anything the same as it was originally written.

"Inspired Revision"

Mormon writer William E. Berrett admits: "In the spring of 1831, Joseph Smith began what has come to be known as 'The Inspired Translation of the Bible.' It was in large part not a translation at all. It was rather a revision of the King James Bible" (*The Restored Church*, 1956, p.134).

Bruce R. McConkie claims:

> ... at the command of the Lord and while acting under the spirit of revelation, the Prophet corrected, revised, altered, added to, and deleted from the King James Version of the Bible to form what is now commonly referred to as the Inspired Version of the Bible. ... the marvelous flood of light and knowledge revealed through the Inspired Version of the Bible is one of the great evidences of the divine mission of Joseph Smith (*Mormon Doctrine*, 1958, pp. 351-52).

Actually, the *Inspired Version* of the Bible has been the source of much embarrassment for Mormon church leaders. It was never published during Joseph Smith's lifetime. Joseph Smith's wife Emma retained the manuscript and would not give it to Willard Richards, who was sent by Brigham Young to obtain it. In 1866 Emma gave the manuscript to the Reorganized Church of Jesus Christ of Latter Day Saints and it was published the following year by that church. Since Brigham Young was unable to obtain the manuscript from Emma, he tried to play down the importance of Joseph Smith's inspired translation: "That made us very anxious, in the days of Joseph, to get the new translation; but *the Bible is good enough just as it is*, it will answer my purpose . . ." (*Journal of Discourses*, vol. 3, p.116).

This statement by Brigham Young seems to throw in question the revelations given by Joseph Smith, for Smith claimed that he was commanded by God to make this revision of the Scriptures. In a revelation given January 10, 1832, we read: "Now, verily I say unto you my servants, Joseph Smith, Jun., and Sidney Rigdon, saith the Lord, it is expedient to translate again;

"And, inasmuch as it is practicable, to preach in the regions round about until conference; and after that it is expedient to *continue the work of translation until it be finished"* (*Doctrine and Covenants,* 73:3-4).

Mormon scholar Reed C. Durham, Jr., informs us concerning this matter:

> . . . God had commanded him to make that Revision. The command from God was reason enough, the knowledge gained from the above revelation conditioned his soul to better understand that command.
>
> There are eighteen sections in the Doctrine and Covenants wherein the Lord gives commands and specific instructions relating to the Revision ("A History of Joseph Smith's Revision of the Bible," Ph.D. dissertation, Brigham Young University, 1965, pp.23-24).
>
> To the early Church members this work was considered to be an important and an essential part of the restoration work, whereas, in the present day, the Revision work is too often thought to be a lesser work not essential to the work of the Lord (p.72).
>
> Though it was clear to the Church that it was the Lord's will that the Revision should be published, the lack of sufficient time and money, prevented its publication during Joseph Smith's lifetime (p.83).

When the Reorganized Church printed the "inspired revision" in 1867, Brigham Young was very much opposed to the idea of members of his church receiving it from an "apostate" organization. Apostle Orson Pratt, on the other hand, wanted to accept it and this caused some conflict between the two men.

Although the Mormon church has never printed the *Inspired Version,* the Reorganized Church's printing is now available at the Mormon-owned Deseret Book Store, and Mormon scholars use it freely in their writings.

Apostle John A. Widtsoe affirms:

> Joseph Smith accepted the Bible as far as it was translated correctly but felt that many errors which should be corrected had crept into the work of the copyist and translators. . . . he endeavored through inspiration from on high to correct those many departures from the original text. This was not fully completed when he died, but his manuscript exists in the original and in copies, and has been published by the Reorganized Church of Jesus Christ of Latter Day Saints. It is a remarkable evidence of the prophetic power of Joseph Smith. Hundreds of changes make clear many a disputed text (*Joseph Smith — Seeker After Truth,* p.251).

Dr. Truman G. Madsen, of the Brigham Young University, has assured that "the recent 1944 New Corrected Edition of the Reorganized Church, which book many interested Latter-day Saints have acquired, is faithful to the original manuscript and a most accurate printing. . . . this edition is worthy of trust" (*Improvement Era*, March 1970, p.70).

Before Joseph Fielding Smith became president of the church he claimed that he wanted the church to publish its own edition of the "inspired revision." He finally became president in 1970, but the church still did not make any move toward publishing Joseph Smith's "inspired revision." On November 20, 1974, the Mormon church obtained microfilm copies of the original manuscripts of the "inspired revision" from the Reorganized Church. We do not feel, however, that any president of the church will allow this book to be printed because it would tend to embarrass the church and to show that Joseph Smith was not a prophet of God.

The Mormon church is faced with a peculiar dilemma with regard to Joseph Smith's "inspired revision." They cannot reject it entirely without admitting that he was a deceiver. On the other hand, if they were to print the revision and fully endorse it, they would be faced with equally unsurmountable problems. The contents of the "inspired revision" actually contradict doctrines that are now taught in the Mormon church. Therefore, the Mormon church can neither fully accept nor fully reject the *Inspired Version* of the Bible. They claim that Joseph Smith was inspired to translate, and then turn right around and use the King James Version. Joseph Fielding Smith stated: "The Church uses the King James Version of the Bible because it is the best version translated by the power of man" (*Doctrines of Salvation*, vol. 3, p.191).

Since the Mormon leaders cannot come right out and say that Joseph Smith made mistakes in his *Inspired Version*, they have devised another excuse to keep from fully endorsing it. They claim that Joseph Smith never finished the translation. Joseph Fielding Smith wrote:

> The revision of the Bible which was done by Joseph Smith at the command of the Lord was not a complete revision of the Bible. There are many parts of the Bible in which the Prophet did not change the meaning where it is incorrect. He revised as far as the Lord permitted him at the time, and it was his intention to do more, but because of persecution this was not accomplished (*Doctrines of Salvation*, vol. 3, p.191).

Reed Durham says that "the Revision was incomplete be-

385

cause after it was finished it still contained errors and contradictions" ("A History of Joseph Smith's Revision of the Bible," p.128). While we certainly agree that Joseph Smith's "inspired revision" still contains "errors and contradictions,"
there is evidence to show that at one time the early Mormons
considered it to have been complete. In fact, in the *Doctrine and
Covenants* 73:4, Joseph Smith was commanded to "continue
the work of translation until it be finished."

In the *History of the Church*, under the date of February 2,
1833, we find this statement by Joseph Smith: "I completed the
translation and review of the New Testament, on the 2nd of
February, 1833, and sealed it up, no more to be opened till it
arrived in Zion" (*History of the Church*, vol. 1, p.324).

In the *Church Chronology*, by Andrew Jenson, we find the
following under the date of February 2, 1833: "Joseph Smith,
jun., completed the translation of the New Testament." Under
the date of July 2, 1833, this statement appears: "Joseph the
Prophet finished the translation of the Bible." In a letter dated
July 2, 1833, signed by Joseph Smith, Sidney Rigdon, and F. G.
Williams, the following statement is found: "We this day
finished the translation of the Scriptures, for which we return
gratitude to our Heavenly Father . . ." (*History of the Church*,
vol. 1, p.368).

Mormon writer Arch S. Reynolds says that "the scriptures at
that time were considered finished. This is proved by revelation
from the Lord commanding the printing and publishing the
same . . . the Lord felt that the Bible contained his word and
also was given *in fulness*" ("A Study of Joseph Smith's Bible
Revision," typed copy, p.17).

In the *Doctrine and Covenants*, Joseph Smith was definitely
commanded to print the *Inspired Version*:

> . . . I have commanded you to organize yourselves, even to
> shinelah [print] my words, the fulness of my scriptures . . .
> (Doctrine and Covenants, 104:58).

> . . . the second lot . . . shall be dedicated unto me for the building
> of a house unto me, for the work of the *printing of the translation
> of my scriptures* . . . (94:10).

> . . . let him [William Law] from henceforth hearken to the coun-
> sel of my servant Joseph, . . . and *publish the new translation* of
> my holy word unto the inhabitants of the earth (124:89).

These commandments were never obeyed. Arch Reynolds
confesses: "Why the Bible was not published is still an enigma;
of course the Saints were unsettled: they were persecuted, but

Phelps is conducting the *Star* at present, we hope he will seek to render it more and more interesting. In relation to the size of Bishoprics: When Zion is once properly regulated there will be a Bishop to each square of the size of the one we send you with this; but at present it must be done according to wisdom. It is needful, brethren, that you should be all of one heart, and of one mind, in doing the will of the Lord.

There should exist the greatest freedom and familiarity among the rulers in Zion.

We were exceedingly sorry to hear the complaint that was made in Brother Edward Partridge's letter, that the letters attending the Olive Leaf had been kept from him, as it is meet that he should know all things in relation to Zion, as the Lord has appointed him to be a judge in Zion. We hope, dear brethren, that the like occurrence will not take place again. When we direct letters to Zion to any of the High Priests, which pertain to the regulation of her affairs, we always design that they should be laid before the Bishop, so as to enable him to perform his duty. We say so much, hoping it will be received in kindness, and our brethren will be careful of one anothers' feelings, and walk in love, honoring one another more than themselves, as is required by the Lord.   Yours as ever,   J. S.,
                                                                 S. R.,
                                                                 F. G. W.

A SECOND COMMUNICATION TO THE BRETHREN IN ZION.

KIRTLAND, July 2nd, 1833.

To the Brethren in Zion:

We received your letters of June 7th: one from Brothers William W. Phelps and Oliver Cowdery; one from Brother David Whitmer; and one from Brother Sidney Gilbert, for which we are thankful to our Heavenly Father, as also to hear of your welfare, and the prosperity of Zion. Having received your letters in the mail of today, we hasten to answer, in order that our reply may go with tomorrow's mail.

We are exceedingly fatigued, owing to a great press of business. We this day finished the translating of the Scriptures, for which we returned gratitude to our Heavenly Father, and sat immediately down to answer your letters. We rejoiced greatly to hear of the safe arrival of Sister Vienna Jaques and Brother William Hobert, and thank our Heavenly Father that their lives have been spared them till their arrival. The health of the brethren and sisters in Kirtland is good at present; no case of sickness known to us. Brother Joseph C. Kings-

A photograph of the *History of the Church*, vol. 1, page 368. Joseph Smith says he finished the translation of the Bible on July 2, 1833.

many other works were published so why not the Holy Scriptures? . . . The Lord gave Joseph a commandment to publish the Bible to the world, and the Lord prepared the way to accomplish this but it *was not fulfilled*" ("A Study of Joseph Smith's Bible Revision," p.32).

Even with all the money the Mormon church has today, it still has not obeyed the command to publish the *Inspired Version* of the Bible to the world.

Perhaps the strangest thing of all concerning the *Inspired Version* of the Bible is the fact that Joseph Smith himself did not take it seriously. For instance, he ignored his own "inspired" renderings concerning the Godhead. Mr. Reynolds remarked:

> At times Joseph Smith *ignored his own renderings* of the Inspired Bible and quoted the King James version in his letters, sermons, etc. . . .
>
> In twenty-six different quotations to different parties in and out of the Church . . . in the first six volumes of the *History of the Church*, they are like the King James Bible although he had given previous varied renderings in the Inspired Bible. These passages are pertaining to all the principles of the gospel. . . . The above various renderings as given by Joseph differing in essential parts from both the King James and his previous revision show that he had grown in doctrine and had broadened in learning German, Greek, and Hebrew ("A Study of Joseph Smith's Bible Revision," typed copy, pp.20, 21, 25).

While it took many scholars, who were authorities in Greek and Hebrew, years to complete the King James Version of the Bible, Joseph Smith began his work without any knowledge of these languages and completed it in three years. Arch S. Reynolds clarified the matter:

> We know that Joseph Smith was not at that time familiar with either the Greek or Hebrew language; therefore it would be impossible for him to have translated the Bible from the original tongues. Later, however, the need of the knowledge of these languages was seen by him, so he studied those languages and became quite proficient in reading the holy scriptures in those tongues. But in 1830, he was unlearned in those ancient languages. So, technically speaking, he did not translate the scriptures in his Inspired Bible ("A Study of Joseph Smith's Bible Revision," p.61).

Although some Mormon scholars now hesitate to call Joseph Smith's *Inspired Version* a translation, Robert J. Matthews points out that "every reference to it in the Doctrine and Covenants and the History of the Church calls it a translation" (BYU Studies, Autumn 1968, p.3).

R. C. Evans registered this comment about Joseph's *Inspired Version*:

> Those who wish to read this marvellous work, the new Bible translated by Joseph Smith, by direct revelation, will discover that he has not translated a single word, that he had no manuscript of any kind, that he was an ignorant young man, is admitted. There is no evidence that he compared any originals with each other, nor could he have done so if the originals were before him. The claim is that it was all done by direct inspiration from the Almighty, but to call it a translation is the height of impudence and nonsense. . . .
>
> Here is the secret of Smith's power to translate. He read the Bible, thought that such and such a change should be made, either by adding a few verses, or taking away a few verses. If he had the burning sensation in his bosom it was right, and so he cut and slashed away at the Word of God to his heart's content, and the result is the Mormon Bible (*Forty Years in the Mormon Church—Why I Left It!* Toronto, Canada, 1920, pp.111-12).

Joseph Smith not only made many unnecessary changes in the Bible, but he also failed to see the places where the text of the Bible really needed correction. There is one statement in the King James Version, 1 John 5:7 and 8, which scholars are certain is an interpolation. In modern versions of the Bible this statement has been removed to conform with the ancient Greek manuscripts. Following is a comparison of the text in the King James Version and that found in the *Revised Standard Version*:

King James Version: 1 John 5:6-8: "6. This is he that came by water and blood, even Jesus Christ; not by water only, but by water and blood. And it is the Spirit that beareth witness, because the Spirit is truth. 7. *For there are three that bear record in heaven, the Father, the Word, and the Holy Ghost: and these three are one. 8. And there are three that bear witness in earth,* the Spirit, and the water, and the blood: and these three agree in one."

Revised Standard Version: 1 John 5:6-8: "6. This is he who came by water and blood, Jesus Christ, not with the water only but with the water and the blood. 7. And the Spirit is the witness, because the Spirit is the truth. 8. There are three witnesses, the Spirit, the water, and the blood; and these three agree."

In *Our Bible and the Ancient Manuscripts*, page 258, we learn that "the text is found in no Greek MSS. except a few of very late date in which it has been inserted from the Latin. It is a purely Latin interpolation of African origin, which, beginning as a gloss, first found its way into the text of Spain, where it appears in the Freising Fragments, and later in the Vulgate codices Cavensis and Toletanus. Thence it spread over Europe as an unequivocal Scripture 'proof' of the doctrine of the Trinity."

Even in Joseph Smith's time this portion of 1 John was rejected by many scholars. Adam Clarke wrote: "Though a conscientious advocate for the sacred doctrine contained in the disputed text, and which I think expressly enough revealed in several other parts of the sacred writings, I must own the passage in question stands on a most dubious foundation" (*Clarke's Commentary*, vol. 6, p.929).

An examination of the writings of Mormon scholars reveals that they also question the authenticity of this verse. Arch S. Reynolds stated: "The extraneous matter added in the Authorized Version is clearly an interpolation . . ." ("A Study of Joseph Smith's Bible Revision," p.169).

Richard L. Anderson, of Brigham Young University, agrees: "One of the few major additions that seem apparent is I John 5:7. . . . The text of the fifth century did *not* speak of the heavenly Trinity, and the fact that very few Greek manuscripts add the heavenly Trinity makes it probable that this comment was not an original part of John's letter" (*Fourteenth Annual Symposium on the Archaeology of the Scriptures*, BYU, 1963, p.53).

Now, if Joseph Smith was inspired at all in his work on the Scriptures we would expect to find this interpolation removed in his "inspired revision." Instead, however, we find that it appears exactly as written in the King James Version:

"For there are three that bear record in heaven, the Father, the Word, and the Holy Ghost; and these three are one.

"And there are three that bear witness in earth, the Spirit, and the water, and the blood; and these three agree in one" (*Inspired Version*, by Joseph Smith, 1 John 5:7-8).

In our book *Mormon Scriptures and the Bible* we presented more evidence to show that Joseph Smith relied so heavily upon the King James Version of the Bible that he failed to see some of the real textual problems found in the Bible. While this is certainly a serious defect in Joseph Smith's work, even more objectionable is the fact that he made changes which cannot be supported by any evidence. For instance, John 1:1 in the King

James Version reads: "In the beginning was the Word, and the Word was with God, and the Word was God."

Joseph Smith, however, changed this verse to read: "In the beginning was the gospel preached through the Son. And the gospel was the word, and the word was with the Son, and the Son was with God, and the Son was of God" (*Inspired Version,* John 1:1).

To our knowledge Joseph Smith's rendition of this verse is not supported by any evidence. In fact, in *Mormonism— Shadow or Reality?* p.384, we show that "Papyrus Bodmer II," dated about 200 A.D., reads exactly like the King James Version.

Mormon writer Robert J. Matthews admits that "in the main the passages revised by Joseph Smith are not supported by the three great parchment manuscripts that now enjoy popularity, nor by the thousands of papyrus manuscripts and fragments, nor by the Dead Sea Scrolls. In some few passages there is a type of similarity but these are the exception rather than the rule" ("Joseph Smith's Revision of the Bible," by Robert J. Matthews, 1968, typed copy, p.17).

Dr. Sperry, of Brigham Young University, made a similar admission with regard to the text of the Sermon on the Mount found in the *Book of Mormon:*

> The divergent readings of the Nephite text are all interesting and thought-provoking, but lack the confirmation of practically all ancient Greek manuscripts of the New Testament. Nor do the ancient versions lend much support, a fact which might well be expected. . . .
>
> The remainder of 3 Nephi 12 differs in a marked degree from the parallel readings in Matthew 5. . . . We point out here also that the Greek manuscripts of the Gospels, as well as other ancient versions offer little support to the divergent Nephite readings (*The Problems of the Book of Mormon,* 1964, pp.105-6).

The best Dr. Sperry can offer his people is a hope that some day supporting evidence in the Greek manuscripts will be found: "A Latter-day Saint textual critic would be thrilled to find Greek manuscripts of the New Testament with readings like some of those in the Book of Mormon. And who knows but someday some will be found!" (*Book of Mormon Institute,* BYU, December 5, 1959, p.7).

In his "inspired revision" Joseph Smith even indicated that the book of Genesis originally contained a prophecy concerning the *Book of Mormon* and that his own name was mentioned there. Over 800 words were added into Genesis 50:24. In this

391

large interpolation we find the following: "And that seer will I bless, and they that seek to destroy him shall be confounded; for this promise I give unto you; for I will remember you from generation to generation; and his name shall be called Joseph, and it shall be after the name of his father. . . ."

The reader will notice that the "choice seer" was to be "called Joseph, . . . after the name of his father." Joseph Smith was obviously referring to himself, for his father's name was Joseph. Apostle Mark E. Petersen claimed that "one of the most interesting parts of the Old Testament as it should have been, . . . were the predictions pertaining to Joseph Smith, through the writings of Joseph who was sold into Egypt" (*As Translated Correctly,* p.64).

The Septuagint—a Greek version of the Old Testament said to have been translated from the Hebrew before the time of Christ—offers no support for Joseph Smith's "inspired revision" of Genesis 50:24, but instead is almost identical with the King James Version.

It is almost impossible to believe that this prophecy could have been dropped from both the Greek and Hebrew manuscripts without being detected. Mormon writer Merrill Y. Van Wagoner admits the difficulty but suggests that such changes were planned by the "Spirit of Darkness" (see *The Inspired Revision of the Bible,* pp.33-34).

Besides adding his own name to the Bible, Joseph Smith added many of his own views. For instance, his bias against Blacks is apparent in several interpolations he made in the book of Genesis. In the "inspired revision," Genesis 7:10, 14 and 29 we read: "And there was *a blackness* came upon all the children of Cainan, that they were despised among all people. . . . Enoch continued to call upon all the people, save it were the people of Cainan, to repent. . . . the seed of Cain *were black, and had not place among them.*"

In the King James Version, Genesis 9:26 reads: "And he said, Blessed be the Lord God of Shem; and Canaan shall be his servant." In his *Inspired Version,* Joseph Smith changed this to indicate that a "veil of darkness" came upon Canaan: "And he said, Blessed be the Lord God of Shem; and Canaan shall be his servant, and a *veil of darkness shall cover him,* that he shall be known among all men" (*Inspired Version,* Gen.9:30).

Joseph Smith's rendition of this verse is not supported by the Septuagint.

One of the most unusual things concerning Joseph Smith's "inspired revision" is that he put New Testament quotations and practices into the Old Testament. For instance, the "inspired revision" indicates that Adam was baptized and received the Holy Ghost:

> And he called upon our father Adam . . . he also said unto him, If thou wilt, turn unto me and hearken unto my voice, and believe, and repent of all thy transgressions, and be baptized, even in water, in the name of mine Only Begotten Son, who is full of grace and truth, which is Jesus Christ, the only name which shall be given under heaven, whereby salvation shall come unto the children of men; and ye shall receive the gift of the Holy Ghost, asking all things in his name, and whatsoever ye shall ask it shall be given you (*Inspired Version*, Genesis 6:52-53).

Mormon leaders have always had a great deal to say about apocryphal books and claim that many books were removed from the Bible. Since Joseph Smith was supposed to have been "inspired" in his work on the Bible, we would expect to find the missing books restored in his *Inspired Version*. While he did make some interpolations in the Bible, he did not restore any of the "lost" books. Robert J. Matthews admits: "Apparently he attempted to make an ammended or amplified version rather than a literal translation. Nor did he attempt to restore any of the so-called 'lost books' of the Bible" (*Joseph Smith's Revision of the Bible*, p. 18).

Dr. Matthews refers us to the *History of the Church*, (vol. 1, p.363). This is a letter written by Joseph Smith and his counselors, in which was stated: "We have not found the Book of Jasher, nor any other of the lost books mentioned in the Bible as yet; nor will we obtain them at present."

Instead of restoring the "lost books," Joseph Smith actually in the end had one less book than we have in the King James Version. He claimed that "The Songs of Solomon are not inspired writings" and removed this book from his Bible (see "A History of Joseph Smith's Revision of the Bible," pp.64-65).

Robert J. Matthews, director of academic research for the department of seminaries and institutes in the Mormon church, has done a great deal of research on Joseph Smith's *Inspired Version*. In an article published in *Brigham Young University Studies*, Dr. Matthews admits the possibility that Joseph Smith may have added material which was never contained in the original manuscripts of the Bible:

> The question might be raised whether the Prophet actually restored the text as Matthew wrote it, or whether, being the seer that he was, he went beyond Matthew's text and recorded an event that actually took place during the delivery of the Sermon, but which Matthew did not include. This cannot be determined with certainty; . . . it is unlikely that he would "add or take

393

from" unless he did it by the authority of divine revelation. . . .
The how of the Prophet's revision of the Sermon on the Mount
calls for an expression of inspiration and could represent either a
restoration of material that was once in Matthew's account of the
Sermon, or could go beyond Matthew and reiterate an event immediately behind the text which took place during the Sermon
but which Matthew did not record.

Another example of direct discourse found only in the Inspired
Version is Matthew 9:18-21 which tells of a confrontation between Jesus and the Pharisees and relates an exchange of information about the subject of baptism that is not recorded in the
King James Version. . . . As with the earlier example the question
may again be asked whether this encounter between Jesus and
the Pharisees actually took place as recorded in the Inspired
Version. It is either historical or it is not. If not historical then it
would simply be a literary device used by the Prophet to convey
a doctrine; but since the Prophet is not known to use devices of
this kind . . . there is considerable reason to believe that the
Prophet regarded this passage as a statement of historical fact. It
seems reasonable to conclude that the Inspired Version at this
point represents either a restoration of Matthew's original record
or an addition of an event that took place in the ministry of Jesus
which Matthew did not record but which is, nevertheless, ger-
maine to the discussion in Matthew's account. . . . It is probable
that the Inspired Version is many things, and that only portions
of it represent restorations while other portions may be explanations, interpolations, enlargements, clarifications and the like.

The science of textual criticism offers an objection to the Inspired Version being a restoration of the original text on the basis
that the Prophet's work is not extensively supported by the many
ancient manuscripts and fragments of the Bible that are now in
common use by scholars. However, this may possibly be accounted for in two ways. First, no original manuscripts of the
Bible are available, and even the earliest available documents are
removed from the originals by many decades. Corruption of the
texts could have taken place in the intervening years. Second,
many of the passages in the Inspired Version may be reiterations
of events which were either not recorded by the Biblical writers
or were lost before the Bible was compiled, in which case even
the original Bible manuscripts would not contain the information. . . .

My analysis leads me to conclude that the Inspired Version is
many things. There are passages that are strongly persuasive of
being restorations of the original text, or even of *historical events
beyond the text*. There are other passages that may be *inspired
explanations*, but not necessarily restorations (*BYU Studies*,
Winter 1969, pp.170-74).

Mormon scholar Dr. Hugh Nibley has stated that "Whatever translation comes by the gift and power of God is certainly no translation in the ordinary sense. . . . In every case in which he has produced a translation, Joseph Smith has made it clear that his inspiration is by no means bound to any ancient text, but is free to take wings at any time" (*BYU Studies*, Autumn 1969, p.71).

Dr. Nibley and other Mormon scholars would, no doubt, like to prove that Joseph Smith carefully followed the ancient texts which he claimed to translate, but since the evidence is so clearly against such an idea, they are forced to say that Joseph Smith's inspiration went beyond the written texts. We feel that this is an extremely compromised position and comes very close to rejecting Joseph Smith's entire work. The question comes to mind: Where do you draw the line between "inspiration" and "imagination"?

"Drastically Changed"

While the Mormon church has not printed the *Inspired Version* in its entirety, a few chapters are printed in the *Pearl of Great Price* under the title, "Book of Moses." Joseph Smith's "inspired revision" of Matthew, chapter 24, is also included in the *Pearl of Great Price*. The Mormon church accepts the *Pearl of Great Price* as Scripture, and it is one of the four standard works of the LDS church.

When we compare the text of the "Book of Moses" as it was first printed in 1851 with the way it reads today we find that some serious changes have been made. James R. Harris, who was a student at Brigham Young University, wrote a thesis in which he stated:

> Orson Pratt was the Editor of the first American edition of the Pearl of Great Price. This publication became available to the public about the 21st of June 1878.

> The American edition was more drastically changed than any previous publication by a member of the Church ("A Study of the Changes in the Contents of the Book of Moses From the Earliest Available Sources to the Current Edition," M.A. thesis, Brigham Young University, 1958, typed copy, p.226).

> From the standpoint of omissions and additions of words, the American Edition is the most spectacular rendition. . . . There were 147 words omitted in the American edition, 113 of those omissions are sustained in our current edition. Some of the words added to the American edition had impressive doctrinal implications (pp.224-25).

Although Dr. Harris admits that changes were made in the *Pearl of Great Price*, he feels that Joseph Smith himself made the changes in manuscripts before his death. In other words, he feels that when the Mormon leaders changed the text of the *Pearl of Great Price* in 1878, they were bringing it into conformity with changes Joseph Smith made in the manuscripts during his lifetime. Richard P. Howard, church historian for the Reorganized Church, has recently released new information which gives some support to Dr. Harris' idea. He shows that there were a number of different manuscripts involved in the production of the inspired revision and that Joseph Smith often revised his own revisions and left the manuscripts in a very confused state:

> Many texts reveal that the process was not some kind of automatic verbal or visual revelatory experience on the part of Joseph Smith. He often caused a text to be written in one form and later reworded his initial revision. The manuscripts in some cases show a considerable time lapse between such reconsiderations. . . .

> A considerable number of places in NT #2 [as Mr. Howard now numbers the manuscripts] show that initially Joseph Smith considered certain texts in the King James Version to be either correct or in need of slight revision, but that on latter consideration he decided to amend them further. Since the manuscript pages were already written and filled to the extent that the later corrections could not be included, the problem was solved by writing the text out on a scrap of paper and pinning or sewing it to the appropriate manuscript page (*Restoration Scriptures*, pp. 93, 96).

> . . . OT #3 represents a third draft manuscript of Section 22 and Genesis 1-7, a second draft manuscript of Genesis 8-24:42a, and a first draft manuscript of the remainder of the Old Testament, although revised considerably by interpolations written in later years between the lines and on separate scraps of paper pinned to the manuscript pages (p. 106).

> When one turns to nearly any page of OT #3 containing substantial initial revision of the King James Version, different colors of ink appear, showing later revisions, written between the lines or on separate scraps of paper and pinned to the manuscript pages (p. 122).

> . . . the manuscripts indicate rather clearly that Joseph Smith, Jr., by his continued practice of *rerevising his earlier texts* (occasionally *as many as three times*), demonstrated that he did not believe that at any of those points of rerevision he had dictated a perfectly inerrant text by the power or voice of God. . . . It is thus unnecessary and could be misleading to appear to claim 'direct'

revelation in the determination of the entire text of the Inspired
Version as the preface written for the 1867 edition apparently
implied (p.151).

Richard P. Howard's admission that Joseph Smith rerevised
his earlier texts "occasionally as many as three times" is certainly a serious indictment against Joseph Smith's work and
plainly shows that his "inspired revision" is anything but "inspired." The fact that he could not make up his mind shows
that he was tampering with the Scriptures according to his own
imagination rather than receiving revelation from God. Mormon writer Truman G. Madsen admitted that Joseph Smith "often revised a passage, later added to or amended it, and then, in
a third attempt, clarified it further" (*Improvement Era*, March
1970, p. 70).

The many changes in the "inspired" renderings tend to
undermine confidence in Joseph Smith's work on the Bible.
Earlier in this chapter we quoted Apostle John A. Widtsoe as
saying that the "inspired revision" is "a remarkable evidence of
the prophetic power of Joseph Smith." We cannot accept this
statement, for a careful examination of his work reveals unmistakable evidence that it is merely a human production and contains many serious errors.

Mormon writer Milton R. Hunter made a fantastic claim concerning Joseph Smith's works: "The Prophet Joseph Smith
produced for the world three new volumes of holy scriptures,
. . . and, in addition, he revised the Bible. No prophet who has
ever lived has accomplished such a tremendous feat. There are
only 177 pages in the Old Testament attributed to Moses, while
Joseph Smith either translated through the gift and power of
God or received as direct revelation from Jehovah 835" (*Deseret
News*, Church Section, July 18, 1970, p.14).

While we must agree that Joseph Smith produced a great deal
of material that purports to be Scripture, it does not appear that
this material bears any evidence of divine inspiration.

CHANGES IN JOSEPH SMITH'S HISTORY

Chapter 13

In 1838 Joseph Smith started writing the account of his life
which is now published by the church. Smith began publishing this history in the *Times and Seasons* in 1842. It was published in installments, and therefore only part of the history
appeared in print before Joseph Smith's death. The church continued to publish the history in the *Times and Seasons* after his
death until the Mormons were driven from Nauvoo. The remainder of the history was published in the *Millennial Star* and
also in the *Deseret News*. After the turn of the century the
History of the Church was reprinted in seven volumes. It has
been republished several times since then.

Mormon leaders have claimed that Joseph Smith's *History of
the Church* is the most accurate history in the world and that it
has never been changed or falsified in any way. President
Joseph Fielding Smith boasted: "The most important history in
the world is the history of our Church, and it is the *most accurate history in all the world*, it must be so" (*Doctrines of Salvation*, vol. 2, p.199).

Apostle John A. Widtsoe claimed that "the *History of the
Church* and the utterances therein contain, if read properly, a
continued evidence that Joseph Smith told the truth. . . . There
is in them *no attempt to 'cover up' any act* of his life. . . .
Mormon history and doctrine have been carefully preserved in
the published records of the Church—and all has been published" (*Joseph Smith—Seeker After Truth*, 1951, pp.256-57).

Apostle Widtsoe also maintained that "The History of Joseph
Smith, published by the Church, as to events and dates, may be
accepted as an unusually accurate historical document. . . . The
history is trustworthy. No flaws have been found in it" (p.297).

In the preface to volume 1 of Joseph Smith's *History of the
Church*, we find the claim that "no historical or doctrinal
statement has been changed" (*History of the Church*, vol. 1,
p.vi).

The material which follows will prove beyond all doubt that the statements quoted above are completely false. Actually, Mormon historians have broken almost all the rules of honesty in their publication of Joseph Smith's *History of the Church*. It is a well known fact that when an omission is made in a document it should be indicated by ellipses points. Mormon historians have almost completely ignored this rule; in many cases they have deleted thousands of words without any indication. They have also added thousands of words without any indication. They have changed spelling, grammar, punctuation, and rearranged the words. There can be no doubt that the changes were deliberate, although there may have been a few typographical errors. For instance, we have already shown that three important changes were made to cover up the fact that Joseph Smith broke the "Word of Wisdom" (see p.387). Certainly, no one would argue that these changes happened by accident, for they bear unmistakable evidence of falsification.

Mormon historians have also changed some of Joseph Smith's prophecies that did not come to pass. Many exaggerated and contradictory statements were either changed or deleted without indication. Crude or indecent statements were also deleted. Joseph Smith quoted the enemies of the church as using the name of the Lord in vain many times in the history, but much of this profanity has been removed by Mormon leaders. In the first printed version of Joseph Smith's history he cursed his enemies, condemned other churches and beliefs, and called the President of the United States a fool. Many of these extreme statements were omitted or changed. Mormon leaders did not dare let their people see the real Joseph Smith. They would rather falsify the *History of the Church* than allow Joseph Smith's true character to be known. Mormon leaders have not only changed the *History of the Church*, but they have further deceived their people by making the claim that no historical or doctrinal statement has been changed.

Not only has the *History of the Church* been changed since it was first printed, but there is also evidence to prove that changes were made before it was first published. In other words, there is evidence that even the first printed version of the history is inaccurate. It does not agree with the handwritten manuscript.

When the history was first printed church historians George A. Smith and Wilford Woodruff (who later became president of the church) stated that "a history more correct in its details than this was never published," and that it was "one of the most authentic histories ever written" (*History of the Church*,

399

vol. 1, Preface v-vi). There is an abundance of evidence to show that this statement is absolutely false. Charles Wesley Wandell, who worked in the church historians's office after the death of Joseph Smith, must have been one of the first to accuse the leaders of the Mormon church of falsifying the history. When he saw the way that they were printing it in 1855, he commented in his journal:

> I notice the interpolations because having been employed (myself) in the Historian's office at Nauvoo by Doctor Richards, and employed, too, in 1845, in compiling this very autobiography, I know that after Joseph's death his memoir was 'doctored' to suit the new order of things, and this, too, by the direct order of Brigham Young to Doctor Richards and systematically by Richards (Statement from the journal of Charles Wesley Wandell, as printed in the Reorganized Church's *Journal of History*, vol. 8, p.76).

Written by Joseph Smith?

In 1965 we published a book entitled *Changes in Joseph Smith's History*. In this book we showed that thousands of words were added, deleted, or changed since Joseph Smith's *History of the Church* was first published. In this book we also cast serious doubt on the claim that Joseph Smith was really the author of such a large work:

> On the title page to Vol. 1 of the *History of the Church*, this statement appears: "History of Joseph Smith, the Prophet *BY HIMSELF*"; this study, however, reveals that much of the history was not written by Joseph Smith. Only a small part of the history was printed during Joseph Smith's lifetime, and we are very suspicious that Joseph Smith did not finish writing the history before his death. Joseph Smith probably kept a journal which the historians used to write part of the history. The entries in the *History of the Church* for 1835 sound very much like a day-to-day journal. The Church Historians, no doubt, used Joseph Smith's journals, but they also interpolated material of their own and tried to make it appear that Joseph Smith had written it. An example is found in the *Millennial Star*, v. 19, p.7:
>
> ". . . on this evening *JOSEPH THE SEER* commenced giving instructions to the scribe concerning writing the proclamation to the kings of the earth. . . ."
>
> It is very obvious that Joseph Smith did not write this; when this was reprinted in the *History of the Church*, the words "*JOSEPH THE SEER*" were changed to the word "*I.*" In the *Millennial Star*, v. 19, p.630, Joseph Smith was referred to in the third person four different times, but when this was reprinted in the *History of the Church* it [was] changed to the first person to

make it appear that Joseph Smith was writing the history. . . .
The account of the "Kirtland Camp" was probably not written by
Joseph Smith, but rather by someone who was with the camp. . . .

In the *Millennial Star,* v. 23, pp.737-739, the Mormon Historians
included an article which was found in the *Times and Seasons.*
Joseph Smith could not have included this article in the history
as it was not published in the *Times and Seasons* until after his
death. Later Mormon Historians evidently became aware of this
and deleted it from the history . . . in the year 1840 there seems
. . . to be an abundance of information concerning England but
very little concerning incidents that were happening in Nauvoo
(where Joseph Smith was). The interesting thing about this is
that Brigham Young, George A. Smith and Heber C. Kimball (the
men who 'revised' Joseph Smith's history after his death) were
in England at this time. Could it be that they wrote this part of
the history after Joseph Smith's death? See especially the *History of the Church,* v. 6, pp.233-239. . . .

The Mormon Historians evidently feel that more converts can be
won to the church with a bogus history than with a true factual
one. It is apparently felt that the truth will not bear its own
weight and that a little forgery here and there is not wrong as
long as it helps win converts to the Church. . . . Perhaps some
day the members of the Church will demand an honest history
and that the "secret manuscripts" be made available (*Changes in
Joseph Smith's History,* pp.7-9).

New Discoveries

Since we published our book, *Changes in Joseph Smith's
History,* a great deal of information has come to light that supports our conclusions concerning the falsification of Joseph
Smith's history. For instance, a microfilm copy of the original
handwritten manuscript of Joseph Smith's History, Book A-1
and part of B-1, was given to us. This manuscript is the basis for
the *History of the Church* up to the year 1835. Mormon leaders
were very upset about this matter because this film provided
devasting evidence against Joseph Smith's history. Recently, we
became aware of the fact that the Reorganized Church of Jesus
Christ of Latter Day Saints had traded microfilm copies of documents with the Mormon church and that they had films of all
of the original handwritten manuscripts of Joseph Smith's history. Although we live within two miles of the historical department of the Mormon church, its restrictive policy forced us
to travel to Independence, Missouri, the location of the headquarters of the RLDS church, to see the Joseph Smith collection. We had only a few days to examine the documents, but a
preliminary examination clearly reveals the duplicity of the   **401**

early Mormon historians. Now that we have had a brief look at the entire manuscript of Joseph Smith's History—i.e., books A-1 through F-1—we must conclude that the history is in a deplorable state. Thousands of words—sometimes entire pages—have been crossed out so that they could be deleted from the printed version. On the other hand, the films show that many pages of material were interpolated after Joseph Smith's death.

In *Mormonism—Shadow or Reality?* pages 128 and 131, we tell how we were fortunate enough to obtain a microfilm of the newspaper published in Nauvoo by the Mormons. This newspaper was originally called *The Wasp*, but the name was later changed to *The Nauvoo Neighbor*. At any rate, the microfilm not only proves that the changes made in Joseph Smith's history were deliberate falsifications, but it provides evidence to show that Joseph Smith did not finish the *History of the Church* and that it was actually written after his death. In our study of the film we found articles that were slightly reworked and inserted in the *History of the Church* as if they were the very words of Joseph Smith himself. For example, in the *Wasp* for August 13, 1842, the following was written concerning Joseph Smith:

> . . . *Joseph Smith* was arrested upon a requisition of Gov. Carlin, . . . Mr. Rockwell was arrested at the same time as principal. . . . these officers . . . left them in care of the Marshal, without the original writ by which *they* were arrested, and by which only *they* could be retained, and returned back to Gov. Carlin for further instruction,—and *Messrs. Smith* and Rockwell went about *their* business. . . .
>
> As to Mr. Smith, *we* have yet to learn by what rule of right *he* was arrested to be transported to Missouri for a trial of the kind stated (*The Wasp*, August 13, 1842).

The reader will notice that this same material was changed to the first person and inserted in the *History of the Church* as if it were part of Joseph Smith's personal narrative:

> . . . I was arrested . . . on a warrant issued by Governor Carlin, . . . Brother Rockwell was arrested at the same time as principal. . . . these officers . . . left us in the care of the marshal, without the original writ by which *we* were arrested, and by which only *we* could be retained, and returned to Governor Carlin for further instructions, and *myself* and Rockwell went about *our* business.
>
> I have yet to learn by what rule of right I was arrested to be transported to Missouri for a trial of the kind stated (*History of the Church*, vol. 5, pp.86-87).

Over Sixty Percent After Joseph Smith's Death

As we did more research with regard to the *History of the Church* we saw that all evidence pointed to the unmistakable conclusion that Joseph Smith never finished his history. As early as 1965 we printed the evidence we had on this subject, but we were very skeptical as to whether Mormon writers would receive it because of the heavy blow it would deal to the foundation of the Mormon church. For a number of years there was complete silence, but in 1971 Dean C. Jessee, of the LDS church historian's office, published an article that contained some very startling admissions. We were very pleased that this article verified our contention that Joseph Smith did not finish his *History of the Church* and that it was actually completed after his death. Mr. Jessee stated:

> Not until Willard Richards was appointed secretary to Joseph Smith in December 1842 was any significant progress made on the History. At the time he began writing, not more than 157 pages had been completed, covering events up to November 1, 1831. By May 8, 1843, he had written 114 pages beyond W. W. Phelps' last entry. *At the time of Joseph Smith's death, the narrative was written to August 5, 1838. . . .*

> By February 4, 1846, the day the books were packed for the journey west, the History had been completed to March 1, 1843. . . . resumption of work on the History occurred on "Dec. 1, 1853 [when] Dr. Willard Richards wrote one line of History being sick at the time — and was never able to do any more." . . .

> The remainder of Joseph Smith's History of the Church from March 1, 1843 to August 8, 1844, was completed under the direction of George A. Smith. . . .

> The Joseph Smith History *was finished in August 1856, seventeen years after it was begun* (Brigham Young University Studies, Summer 1971, pp.466, 469, 470, 472).

Dean C. Jessee frankly admits that the manuscript was only completed to page 812 at the time of Joseph Smith's death (*Ibid.*, p.457). Since there were almost 2,200 pages, this would mean that *over sixty percent of Joseph Smith's history was not compiled during his lifetime!*

As we had suspected, Willard Richards played a prominent part in making up this bogus history after Joseph Smith's death in June, 1844. Dean C. Jessee said that "Bullock became the chief scribe under Willard Richards when work resumed on the Joseph Smith History in 1845" (*Ibid.*, p.456).

In his diary Thomas Bullock admitted that he helped Willard Richards in "preparing Church History." In 1845 he made these interesting entries in his diary: "March 15. . . . finished the year 1839—wrote 56 pages last week. . . . May 3 Saturday Office—writing history finished July 1842 being the end of Vol. 3" (Thomas Bullock Diary, February 11, 1844—August 5, 1845, as cited in *Brigham Young University Studies,* Summer 1971, p.467).

Dean C. Jessee cites a letter from the Mormon historian George A. Smith which shows that he was still writing the last part of Joseph Smith's history many years after Smith's death:

> On the 10th April 1854, I commenced to perform the duties of Historian by taking up the History of Joseph Smith where Dr. Willard Richards had left it when driven from Nauvoo on the 4th day of February 1846. I had to revise and compare two years of back history which he had compiled, filling up numerous spaces which had been marked as omissions on memoranda by Dr. Richards.
>
> I commenced compiling the History of Joseph Smith from April 1st 1840 to his death on June 27th 1844. I have filled up all the reports of sermons by Prest. Joseph Smith and others from minutes of sketches taken at the time in long hand . . . which was an immense labor, requiring the deepest thought and the closest application, as there were mostly only two or three words (about half written) to a sentence. . . . The severe application of thought to the principles of the History, the exercise of memory &c., have caused me to suffer much from a nervous headache or inflamation [sic] of the brain; and my application of mind being in exercise both day and night, deprived me of a great portion of necessary sleep (Letter from George A. Smith to Woodruff, April 21, 1856, as cited in *Brigham Young University Studies,* Summer 1971, pp.470-72).

This letter certainly provides irrefutable evidence against the authenticity of "Joseph Smith's history."

Rocky Mountain Prophecy

Important evidence concerning Joseph Smith's prophecy that the Mormons would come to the Rocky Mountains has recently come to light. This prophecy was reported to have been given in 1842 in Illinois. Joseph Smith himself was supposed to have said:

> While the Deputy Grand-Master was engaged in giving the requisite instructions to the Master-elect, I had a conversation with a number of brethren in the shade of the building on the subject of our persecutions in Missouri and the constant annoyance which has followed us since we were driven from that state. I

prophesied that the Saints would continue to suffer much affliction and would be driven to the Rocky Mountains, many would apostatize, others would be put to death by our persecutors or lose their lives in consequence of exposure or disease, and some of you will live to go and assist in making settlements and build cities and see the Saints become a mighty people in the midst of the Rocky Mountains (*History of the Church*, vol. 5, p.85).

In our book *Falsification of Joseph Smith's History*, page 10, we stated concerning this prophecy:

> There is some evidence that Joseph Smith considered going west to build his kingdom, but since we now know that the Mormon Historians actually compiled Joseph Smith's History after his death and that they drew from many sources, we cannot help being suspicious of the authorship of this prophecy. An examination of the original handwritten manuscript would probably help solve this problem, but the Mormon leaders are still suppressing this portion of the manuscript.

Just after we wrote this statement the situation changed and we were able to make this statement in the Appendix to the same book: "We are now happy to announce that a photograph of the portion of the original handwritten manuscript containing this 'prophecy' has been located at the Visitor Center in Nauvoo, Illinois. Wesley P. Walters of Marissa, Illinois, has sent us a photograph of this page. . . . This photograph is taken from 'Joseph Smith's Manuscript History,' Book D-1, page 1362."

An examination of the photograph revealed that the part concerning the Mormons becoming "a mighty people in the midst of the Rocky Mountains" was crammed in between the lines of the text in a much smaller handwriting. This indicated that the famous prophecy had been added to the manuscript sometime after this page had originally been written. When we published an enlarged edition of *Mormonism—Shadow or Reality?* we stated that "Dean C. Jessee's study proves that this prophecy could not have been written in 'Joseph Smith's Manuscript History' until at least a year after Joseph Smith's death. He shows that page 1362 of the Manuscript History—the page containing the prophecy—was not even written until July 4, 1845!"

We reasoned that if the page was not written until July 4, 1845, then it was likely that the interpolation containing the prophecy was not added until after the Mormons came to Utah. We have recently found new evidence which further undermines the authenticity of this prophecy. Fortunately, in 1845 Brigham Young had ordered the scribes to make a "duplicate handwritten copy of the History" (*Brigham Young University*

Studies, Summer 1971, p.469). We examined this second manuscript, Book D-2, p.2, and found that the "Rocky Mountain
Prophecy" was written in very small handwriting between the
lines. In other words, it was obviously added at a later time to
this manuscript.

The situation, then, boils down to the following: we have two
handwritten manuscripts, books D-1 and D-2. Neither of these
books were even started until *after* Joseph Smith's death. In
both cases the prophecy concerning the Mormons coming to
the Rocky Mountains was interpolated in a smaller handwriting. From this evidence we can reach only one conclusion: the
famous "Rocky Mountain Prophecy" is not authentic. The
church historical department has Joseph Smith's diary for
1842-43, but the first entry does not appear until December
21—some four months after the prophecy was supposed to
have been given. Mormon scholars have been unable to come
up with anything to support the authenticity of this prophecy.
Davis Bitton, an assistant church historian, has written almost
five pages concerning this matter. He frankly states that "there
is *no such prophecy in the handwriting of Joseph Smith or
published during the Prophet's lifetime,* but it was referred to
in general terms in 1846 during the trek west. After the arrival
in the Salt Lake Valley the prophecy was frequently cited and
became *more specific as time went on*" ("Joseph Smith in the
Mormon Folk Memory," The John Whitmer address, delivered
at the Second Annual Meeting of the John Whitmer Historical
Association, Lamoni, Iowa, September 28, 1974, unpublished
manuscript, p.16).

Davis Bitton goes on to state that "The manuscript history
covering this period was written *in 1845. . . .*" This is, of course,
a year after Joseph Smith's death. Mr. Bitton then admits that
the prophecy is *an "insertion" which was added into the manuscript as "an afterthought"* (p.18). Although Davis Bitton cannot find any real evidence that Joseph Smith made the famous
"Rocky Mountain Prophecy," he does feel that there was "a
time when something like this might have been said by Joseph
Smith with considerable plausibility. Anytime during the last
four years of his life, . . . the Prophet had good reason to consider possibilities for relocation. It can be demonstrated that he
considered the possibility of settling in Oregon (or on Vancouver Island). He was attempting to negotiate some kind of
colonization venture in Texas . . ." (p.17).

Mr. Bitton admits that other changes were made in Joseph
Smith's documents to support the idea that he knew the Mormons would come to the Rocky Mountains:

And in February 1844 the Prophet was organizing an exploring expedition to go to the West. There are some interesting changes in the way the description of this expedition was written by Willard Richards, secretary of Joseph Smith at the time, and the later revisions. The original, handwritten version reads: "Met with the Twelve in the assembly room concerning the Oregon Expedition." This has been modified to read "the Oregon *and California Exploring* Expedition." Continuing, the Richards manuscript reads, "I told them I wanted an exposition of all that country,"—which has been changed to "exploration of all that *mountain* country." There are other such changes that make one suspect that the *later compilers* of the history, notably George A. Smith and his assistants in the 1850s, were *determined to have Joseph Smith contemplating the precise location where the Saints had by then settled.* Oregon would not do; Oregon and California as then defined at least included the Rocky Mountains. If the Prophet could be made to say "mountain country" instead of just "country," it would appear that he clearly had in mind the future history of his followers (pp.17-18).

Although some Mormons would like us to believe that Brigham Young knew all along that he was going to lead the Mormons to "the midst of the Rocky Mountains," there is evidence to show that he was somewhat confused about the matter. In a letter dated December 17, 1845, Young stated: ". . . we expect to emigrate West of the mountains next season. If we should eventually settle on Vancouver's Island, according to our calculation we shall greatly desire to have a mail route, . . . if Oregon should be annexed to the United States, . . . and Vancouver's Island incorporated in the same by our promptly paying the national revenue, and taxes, we can live in peace with all men" (Photograph of letter in *Prologue*, Spring 1972, p.29).

There is another important change in Joseph Smith's history that seems to be related to this matter. In the History as it was first published in the *Millennial Star*, volume 23, page 280, the following words were attributed to Joseph Smith: "The Lord had an established law in relation to the matter: there must be a particular spot for the salvation of our dead. I verily believe *this* will be *the* place. . . ."

In the *History of the Church*, volume 6, page 319, this has been changed to read: "The Lord has an established law in relation to the matter: there must be a particular spot for the salvation of our dead. I verily believe *there* will be *a* place. . . ."

The reason for this change in wording is obvious: the Mormons were driven from Nauvoo in 1846, just two years after Joseph Smith was supposed to have said "this will be the place." It is reported that when Brigham Young looked over the valley where Salt Lake City now stands he stated: "This is the place." A temple has been built at Salt Lake City and work for the dead is performed in this temple. The change in the location of the headquarters of the church seemed to make it necessary to change Joseph Smith's history.

Selected Changes

Although we deal with some of the most important changes in Joseph Smith's history in other chapters, we will cite a few examples at this point.

One of the most interesting changes in the history is concerned with the name of the angel who was supposed to have appeared in Joseph Smith's room and told him about the *Book of Mormon* plates. In the history, as it was first published by Joseph Smith, we learn that the angel's name was Nephi: "He called me by name and said . . . that his name was *Nephi*" (*Times and Seasons*, vol. 3, p.753).

In modern printings of the *History of the Church*, this has been changed to read "Moroni": "He called me by name, and said . . . that his name was *Moroni* . . ." (*History of the Church*, vol. 1, p.11).

The original handwritten manuscript shows that the name was originally written as "Nephi," but that someone at a later date wrote the word "Moroni" above the line (see photograph in *Mormonism—Shadow or Reality?* p.136). In our book *Falsification of Joseph Smith's History*, page 13, we showed that this change was made after Joseph Smith's death. An examination of the duplicate copy of the handwritten manuscript, Book A-2, provides additional evidence that the change was not made during Joseph Smith's lifetime. This manuscript was not even started until about a year after Smith's death. Like the other manuscript (Book A-1), it has the name "Nephi" with the name "Moroni" interpolated above the line.

It is interesting to note that Joseph Smith lived for two years after the name "Nephi" was printed in *Times and Seasons* and he never published a retraction. In August, 1842, the *Millennial Star*, printed in England, also published Joseph Smith's story stating that the angel's name was "Nephi" (see *Millennial Star*, vol. 3, p.53). On page 71 of the same volume we read that the "message of the angel *Nephi* . . . opened a new dispensation to man. . . ."

The name was also published in the 1851 edition of the *Pearl of Great Price* as "Nephi." Walter L. Whipple, in his thesis written at BYU, stated that Orson Pratt "published *The Pearl of*

the day. While this was progressing great numbers were being baptized in the font.

Those who wish for further information concerning the scenes of the Sabbath in Nauvoo, or any other day in the week would do well to "come and see." W. WOODRUFF.

HISTORY OF JOSEPH SMITH.
(Continued.)

While I was thus in the act of calling upon God I discovered a light appearing in the room which continued to increase until the room was lighter than at noonday, when immediately a personage appeared at my bedside standing in the air for his feet did not touch the floor. He had on a loose robe of most exquisite whiteness. It was a whiteness beyond any thing earthly I had ever seen; nor do I believe that any earthly thing could be made to appear so exceedingly white and brilliant, his hands were naked and his arms also a little above the wrist. So also were his feet naked, as were his legs a little above the ankles. His head and neck were also bare. I could discover that he had no other clothing on but this robe, as it was open so that I could see into his bosom. Not only was his robe exceedingly white but his whole person was glorious beyond description, and his countenance truly like lightning. The room was exceedingly light, but not so very bright as immediately around his person. When I first looked upon him I was afraid, but the fear soon left me. He called me by name, and said unto me that he was a messenger sent from the presence of God to me, and that his name was Nephi. That God had a work for me to do, and that my name should be had for good and evil, among all nations, kindreds, and tongues; or that it should be both good and evil spoken of among all people. He said there was a book deposited written upon gold plates, giving an account of the former inhabitants of this continent, and the source from whence they sprang. He also said that the fullness of the everlasting gospel was contained in it, as delivered by the Saviour to the ancient inhabitants. Also that there were two stones in silver bows, and these stones fastened to a breastplate constituted what is called the Urim and Thummim, deposited with the plates, and the possession and use of these stones was what constituted seers in ancient or former times, and that God had prepared them for the purpose of translating the book. After telling me these things he commenced quoting the prophecies of the Old Testament, he first quoted part of the third chapter of Malachi; and he quoted also the fourth or last chapter of the same prophecy though with a little variation from the way it reads in our Bibles. Instead of quoting the first verse as reads in our books he quoted it thus; "For behold the day cometh that shall burn as an oven, and all the proud yea and all that do wickedly shall burn as stubble, for they that cometh shall burn them saith the Lord of hosts, that it shall leave them neither root nor branch," and again he quoted the fifth verse thus, "Behold I will reveal unto you the Priesthood by the hand of Elijah the prophet before the coming of the great and dreadful day of the Lord." He also quoted the next verse differently, "And he shall plant in the hearts of the children the promises made to the fathers, and the hearts of the children shall turn to their fathers, if it were not so the whole earth would be utterly wasted at his coming." In addition to these he quoted the eleventh chapter of Isaiah saying that it was about to be fulfilled. He quoted also the third chapter of Acts, twenty second and twenty third verses precisely as they stand in our New Testament. He said that that prophet was Christ, but the day had not yet come when "they who would not hear his voice should be cut off from among the people," but soon would come.

He also quoted the second chapter of Joel from the twenty eighth to the last verse. He also said that this was not yet fulfilled but was soon to be. And he further stated the fulness of the gentiles was soon to come in. He quoted many other passages of scripture and offered many explanations which cannot be mentioned here. Again he told me that when I got those plates of which he had spoken (for the time that they should be obtained was not yet fulfilled) I should not show them to any person, neither the breastplate with the Urim and Thummim only to those to whom I should be commanded to show them, if I did I should be destroyed. While he was conversing with me about the plates the vision was opened to my mind that I could see the place where the plates were deposited and that so clearly and distinctly that I knew the place again when I visited it.

A photograph of the *Times and Seasons*, vol. 3, page 753. Joseph Smith says that it was "Nephi" who appeared to him. This was changed to "Moroni" in later printings of the *History of the Church*.

Great Price in 1878, and *removed the name of Nephi* from the text entirely and *inserted the name Moroni* in its place" ("Textual Changes in the Pearl of Great Price," typed copy, p.125).

At the bottom of page 120 of volume 1 of the *History of the Church,* there is nothing to indicate that a deletion has been made, but approximately 3,400 words which were printed in the *Times and Seasons* have been deleted. These words were very complimentary to Sidney Rigdon. Since Rigdon was excommunicated after Joseph Smith's death, it was apparently felt best to remove Joseph Smith's praise concerning him. An examination of the original handwritten manuscript reveals that these words have been crossed out, which proves that this was an intentional deletion. If Rigdon had remained faithful to the church, the Mormon historians would probably have left these 3,400 words concerning him in the *History of the Church.*

At another point in the history, speaking of a member of a mob who assaulted him, Joseph Smith stated: ". . . the fellow that I kicked came to me and thrust his hand into my face, all covered with blood, (for I hit him on the nose,) and with an exulting horse laugh, muttered . . ." (*Times and Seasons,* vol. 5, p. 611).

When this was reprinted in the *History of the Church* the words *"for I hit him on the nose"* were deleted without any indication: ". . . the fellow that I kicked came to me and thrust his hand, all covered with blood, into my face and with an exulting hoarse laugh, muttered . . ." (*History of the Church,* vol. 1, p.262).

The original handwritten manuscript of Joseph Smith's history bears witness against the modern edition of the *History of the Church,* since it contains the words "for I hit him on the nose."

In the *History of the Church,* volume 1, pages 295-97, seventy-four words are added which were not in the *Times and Seasons* (see vol. 5, p.673). This interpolation reads as follows: "About the 8th of November I received a visit from Elders Joseph Young, Brigham Young, and Heber C. Kimball of Mendon, Monroe county, New York. They spent four or five days at Kirtland, during which we had many interesting moments. At one of our interviews *Brother Brigham Young and John P. Greene spoke in tongues,* which was the first time I had heard this gift among the brethren; others also spoke, and I received the gift myself."

This interpolation was made after Joseph Smith's death in an obvious attempt to glorify Brigham Young. The interpolation was too large to be inserted into the handwritten manuscript at its proper place ("Manuscript History," Book A-1, p.240), therefore it was written in the "Addenda" which follows page 553. (The addenda contains a great deal of material which was to be inserted into Joseph Smith's history and was obviously written after his death.) In *Mormonism—Shadow or Reality?* page 138, we have a photograph from the addenda showing the words concerning Brigham Young which were to be added to the *History of the Church*. A close examination of this photograph reveals that although Mormon leaders added most of this interpolation into Joseph Smith's history in its printed form, they omitted two lines. These lines contain some very important information: "Brother Joseph Young is a great man, but Brigham is a greater, and the time will come when he will preside over the whole church."

Although Mormon historians added the part about Brigham Young speaking in tongues, they have never dared to add the rest, i.e., the prophecy about Brigham Young becoming the leader of the church. We must remember that many people questioned the leadership of Brigham Young. In fact, Apostle William Smith, Joseph Smith's brother, left the church and stated that he once heard Joseph say that if Brigham Young ever led the church "he would certainly lead it to destruction" (*Warsaw Signal*, October 29, 1845). However this may be, Mormon historians never dared to add in the "prophecy" found in the "Addenda." They probably realized that the dissenters would question such a statement in Joseph Smith's history and ask for proof. An examination of the original manuscript, however, would soon reveal that the prophecy is a forgery made after Brigham Young had become the leader of the church.

In the *History of the Church*, volume 5, page 67, 1,179 words have been deleted without any indication. These words are found in the *Millennial Star*, volume 19, pages 598-600. The words deleted contain the Phrenological Charts of Brigham Young and Heber C. Kimball. Phrenology is defined as "the theory that one's mental powers are indicated by the shape of the skull" (*The American College Dictionary*). A phrenologist had examined the heads of several prominent Mormons in Nauvoo, and his findings were originally a part of the history.

In the *History of the Church*, volume 5, page 212, nineteen words have been deleted which were printed in the *Millennial Star*, volume 20, page 263. These words are concerning Joseph Smith's cure for the cholera: "Salt, vinegar, and pepper, given internally, and plunging into the river when the paroxysms begin, will cure the cholera." Few Mormons today would recommend this "cure."

Some very important changes concerning Apostle Orson Pratt have been made in Joseph Smith's history. According to the way the *History of the Church* was first printed, Orson Pratt should have become the third president of the church. John Taylor, however, became president and the history was falsified to cover up this change in seniority. (For details concerning this matter see *Mormonism—Shadow or Reality?* p.139.)

Joseph Smith's Diaries Discredit History

Since we now know that more than sixty percent of Joseph Smith's *History of the Church* was not compiled until after his death, the question arises as to what sources Mormon historians used to create the purported history. We know that they used newspapers and journals of other Mormon leaders and that much of the material came only from memory. It was, of course, written in the first person to make it appear that Joseph Smith was the author. We have always felt that Joseph Smith's private diaries were used in preparing the history, but we were denied access to them. Finally, in August, 1976, we were able to examine microfilm copies of these diaries; therefore, we are able to make some preliminary observations concerning them.

The first thing we notice is that there are large periods of Joseph Smith's life that are not covered by extant diaries— unless the Mormon leaders are still suppressing some of his diaries. According to the information furnished in the *Register of the Joseph Smith Collection in the Church Archives, The Church of Jesus Christ of Latter-day Saints,* only a small percentage of Joseph Smith's thirty-eight years are covered by his diaries. As we indicated earlier, at the time of Joseph Smith's death, his *History of the Church* had only been completed to August 5, 1838. Since Smith died in June, 1844, this left a period of almost six years which the Mormon historians had to fill in from Joseph Smith's diaries and other sources. Now, there are a few brief diaries from 1838 and 1839, but for the next three years there are no extant diaries. The last period of Joseph Smith's life, December 21, 1842 — June 22, 1844, is covered by four diaries. If there were other diaries they were either lost, destroyed or suppressed. However this may be, only three of the last six years of Joseph Smith's lifetime as it appears in the *History of the Church* can be checked against his diaries.

Unfortunately, these diaries do not contain the important information that we would expect to find about Joseph Smith's life. Many pages are left blank or only contain information on the weather or other trivial matters. The value of the diaries decreases even more when we learn that a large part of the entries were not written in the first person, but rather by Joseph Smith's scribe Willard Richards. For instance, under the date October 20, 1843, we read this entry in Joseph Smith's diary: "heard that Joseph went to Ramus yesterday has not returned." In the *Register of the Joseph Smith Collection*, page 4, Jeffery O. Johnson admitted that "Joseph Smith himself kept very little in his own hand. Under Joseph's direction, for example, Willard Richards wrote many of the daily entries in the prophet's journal, relating experiences they both shared in many cases, but this was done in the words as well as in the hand of the clerk."

Our brief examination of the diaries reveals that although they were used as one source for Joseph Smith's history, there was no attempt to follow them faithfully. Mormon leaders chose only the portions of the journals which served their purposes. For instance, in his diary Joseph Smith related a dream and its interpretation which tended to discredit his famous prophecy about the Civil War. This material was simply omitted in Joseph Smith's history. We will have more to say about this matter in the chapter on false prophecy.

Another portion Mormon leaders omitted was the passage where Joseph Smith boasted of his great strength. Under the date of January 1, 1843, the following appears in Joseph Smith's diary:

> . . . while supper was preparing Joseph related an anecdote while young his father had a fine large watch dog. which bit off an ear from David Stafford hog, which Stafford had turned into Smiths corn field. Stafford shot the dog, & with six other fellows pitched upon him unawares & Joseph *whipped the whole of them*, & escaped unhurt. which they swore to as recorded in Hurlburt or Howes Book

> While in Kirtland a Baptist Priest came in my house & abused my family—I turned him out of doors. he raised his cane to strike me & continued to abuse me. *I whipped him till he begged.*—he threatened to prosecute me—I sent Luke Johnson the constable after him & he run him out of the county into Mentor (Joseph Smith's Diary, January 1, 1843, pp.34-35).

This portion was entirely omitted in Joseph Smith's history (see vol. 5, p.216).

The early Mormon historians were not too sensitive about Joseph Smith's inability to observe the Word of Wisdom (see chapter 18). For example, in the first printing they included his statement about having "a glass of beer at Moessers." (As we have shown, it was later Mormon historians who deleted this from the *History of the Church*). Nevertheless, some material which related to Joseph Smith's attitude toward the Word of

Wisdom never made it into the printed text. Under the date of January 20, 1843, the following was recorded in Joseph Smith's diary:

"Elder Hyde told of the excellent *white wine* he drank in the east. *Joseph prophesied in the name of the Lord—that he would drink wine with him in that country.*" These words were never placed in the printed *History of the Church.*

Under the date of March 11, 1843, the following is recorded in Joseph Smith's Diary: ". . . in the office Joseph said he had *tea* with his breakfast. his wife asked him if [it] was good. he said *if it was a little stronger he should like* it better. when Mother Granger remarked, 'It is so strong, and good, I should think it would answer Both for drink and food.' " This was entirely omitted in the *History of the Church* (see vol. 5, p.302).

The following statement appears in Joseph Smith's diary under the date of May 19, 1844: "eve I talked *a long time in the bar Room* . . ." In the *History of the Church*, volume 6, page 398, this has been changed to read: "In the evening I talked *to the brethren at my house* . . ."

Our preliminary study of the diaries of Joseph Smith leads us to the conclusion that they were used as a source for the *History of the Church.* Unfortunately, however, there was no attempt to accurately follow the text of the diaries. Mormon leaders used only the parts that suited their purposes. Where a portion did not say what they wanted, they altered it or ignored it completely, sometimes using an entirely different source. The diaries of Joseph Smith, then, tend only to deal another heavy blow to the credibility of Joseph Smith's *History of the Church.* No wonder Mormon leaders suppressed these diaries for so long.

Conclusion

We do not have room to go into a detailed study of the changes that the Mormon leaders have made in Joseph Smith's history. Some of the more important ones are discussed in other chapters of this book. In the book *Changes in Joseph Smith's History,* we show that "more than 62,000 words" were either added or deleted. A thorough examination of the original handwritten manuscript would undoubtedly reveal thousands of changes which we have not discovered in our brief examination of the manuscripts. More important than this, however, is the evidence we uncovered that *Joseph Smith did not finish his work.* Dean C. Jessee, of the church historical department, admits that *the greater part* of the history was not written until after Joseph Smith's death. This portion therefore stands on a very shaky foundation.

The Mormon leaders must face the serious implications of this whole matter. Less than forty percent of the history attributed to Joseph Smith was written during his lifetime, and this portion has had serious changes made in it. The remaining portion—*more than sixty percent of the history—was not even compiled until after Joseph Smith's death*. Since it was compiled by men who believed in falsification and deceit, it cannot be trusted as a reliable history of Joseph Smith.

The evidence concerning Joseph Smith's history is beginning to have an effect on some of the Mormon scholars. Davis Bitton, who now serves as an assistant church historian, frankly admitted that the *History of the Church* "does not come off well" when measured against a standard like "the monumental edition of Jefferson papers" (*Dialogue: A Journal of Mormon Thought*, Winter 1968, page 31). Dr. Bitton states that the "basic text" of Joseph Smith's history has "not been treated with proper respect," and goes on to concede that "hundreds of changes have been made." On page thirty-two of the same article, he makes the astonishing statement that "for researchers in early Mormon history Rule Number One is 'Do not reply on the DHC [the documentary *History of the Church*]; never use a quotation from it without comparing the earlier versions.' "

We were going to include a lengthy extract from this article, but Dr. Bitton refused to give his permission. Those who are interested in pursuing the matter further will have to consult *Dialogue: A Journal of Mormon Thought*, Winter 1968, pages 30-32.

Marvin S. Hill, of the Brigham Young University history department, has now admitted that "large portions" of Joseph Smith's history were not written by him:

> One reason that Brodie concluded that Joseph had veiled his personality behind a "perpetual flow of words" in his history may be that she assumed he had actually dictated most of it. We now know that *large portions of that history were not dictated but were written by scribes and later transferred into the first person to read as though the words were Joseph's*. That fact makes what few things Joseph Smith wrote himself of great significance (*Dialogue: A Journal of Mormon Thought*, Winter 1972, p.76).

Mormon scholar Paul R. Cheesman has a very revealing notation concerning Joseph Smith's *History of the Church*. It is found in an unpublished manuscript at the Brigham Young University Library and reads as follows:

As of now, the original source of Joseph Smith's statement, under the date of May 1, 1843, concerning the Kinderhook Plate, *cannot be found.* Much of Volume V of the Documentary History of the Church was recorded by Leo Hawkins in 1853, *after* the saints were in Utah, and was collected by Willard Richards from journals. (Dean Jesse, Church Historian's office, Appendix #2) *Liberty was taken by historians of those days to put the narrative in the first person, even though the source was not as such.* Verification of the authenticity of Joseph Smith's statement is still under study. In examining the diary of Willard Richards, the compiler of Volume V, the Kinderhook story is not found there. Our research has taken us through numerous diaries and letters written at this particular time, and the Kinderhook story is not mentioned ("An Analysis Of The Kinderhook Plates," by Paul R. Cheesman, March, 1970, Brigham Young University Library).

Now that Mormon writers are willing to admit that Joseph Smith's history was not finished until after his death and that many sources not written by Joseph were put in "the first person" to make it appear that they were written by Smith, they will have to face the serious implications of this whole matter. Mormon scholar Hugh Nibley says that "a forgery is defined by specialists in ancient documents as 'any document which was not produced in the time, place, and manner claimed by it or its publishers" (*Since Cumorah, p.160*). Under this definition the *History of the Church* must be classed as a forgery. While it does contain some very important information about Joseph Smith, most of it "was not produced in the time, place, and manner claimed by it or its publishers."

FALSE PROPHECY

Chapter 14

Mormon writers state that Joseph Smith's claim to be a prophet is established by the fulfillment of his prophecies. Actually, a careful examination of the evidence seems to prove just the opposite.

The Canadian Revelation

David Whitmer, one of the three witnesses to the *Book of Mormon*, tells of a false revelation that Joseph Smith gave when the *Book of Mormon* was in the hands of the printer:

> When the Book of Mormon was in the hands of the printer, more money was needed to finish the printing of it. We were waiting on Martin Harris who was doing his best to sell a part of his farm, in order to raise the necessary funds. After a time Hyrum Smith and others began to get impatient, thinking that Martin Harris was too slow and under transgression for not selling his land at once, even if at a great sacrifice. Brother Hyrum thought they should not wait any longer on Martin Harris, and that the money should be raised in some other way. Brother Hyrum was vexed with Brother Martin, and thought they should get the money by some means outside of him, and not let him have anything to do with the publication of the Book, or receiving any of the profits thereof if any profits should accrue. . . . Brother Hyrum said it had been suggested to him that some of the brethren might go to Toronto Canada, and sell the copy-right of the Book of Mormon for considerable money: and he persuaded Joseph to inquire of the Lord about it. Joseph concluded to do so. He had not yet given up the stone. Joseph looked into the hat in which he placed the stone, and *received a revelation that some of the brethren should go to Toronto, Canada, and that they would sell the copy-right of the Book of Mormon.* Hiram Page and Oliver Cowdery went to Toronto on this mission, but they *failed entirely* to sell the copyright, returning without any money. Joseph was at my father's house when they returned. I was there also, and am an eye witness to these facts. . . . Well, we

were all in great trouble, and we asked Joseph how it was that he had received a revelation from the Lord for some brethren to go to Toronto and sell the copy-right, and the brethren had utterly failed in their undertaking. Joseph did not know how it was, so he enquired of the Lord about it, and behold the following revelation came through the stone: "*Some revelations are of God: some revelations are of man: and some revelations are of the devil.*" So we see that the revelation to go to Toronto and sell the copy-right was not of God, but was of the devil or the heart of man (*An Address To All Believers In Christ*, 1887, pp.30-31).

Mormon historian B. H. Roberts commented concerning this false revelation:

> . . . May this Toronto incident and the Prophet's explanation be accepted and faith still be maintained in him as an inspired man, a Prophet of God? I answer unhesitatingly in the affirmative. *The revelation respecting the Toronto journey was not of God*, surely; else it would not have failed; but the Prophet, overwrought in his deep anxiety for the progress of the work, *saw reflected in the 'Seer Stone' his own thought*, or that suggested to him by his brother Hyrum, rather than the thought of God . . . *in this instance of the Toronto journey, Joseph was evidently not directed by the inspiration of the Lord* (A Comprehensive History of the Church, vol. 1, p.165).

David Whitmer states that there were "other false revelations that came through Brother Joseph as mouthpiece. . . . Many of Brother Joseph's revelations were never printed. The revelation to go to Canada was written down on paper, but was never printed" (*An Address To All Believers in Christ*, p.31).

Joseph Fielding Smith admits that "not all the revelations given to Joseph the Seer were placed in the *Doctrine and Covenants* in his day. . . . Some of them were for the Church and not for the world, and therefore are given only to the saints" (*Doctrines of Salvation*, vol. 1, p.280).

The Mormon church leaders complain that the Catholics withheld the Scriptures from the common people, and yet they have hid some of Joseph Smith's revelations from their own people.

The Lord's Coming

In 1835 Joseph Smith prophesied that the coming of the Lord was near and that fifty-six years should wind up the scene. In the *History of the Church*, volume 2, page 182, we read as follows: "President Smith then stated . . . it was the will of God that those who went to Zion, with a determination to lay down their lives, if necessary, should be ordained to the ministry, and go forth to prune the vineyard for the last time, or the *coming of the Lord*, which was nigh—even *fifty-six years should wind up the scene*."

Joseph Smith later said that a voice once told him the following: " 'My son, if thou livest until thou art eighty-five years of age, thou shalt see the face of the Son of Man.' I was left to draw my own conclusions concerning this; and I took the liberty to conclude that if I did live to that time, He would make His appearance. But I do not say whether He will make his appearance or I shall go where He is" (*History of the Church*, vol. 5, p.336).

On the same page Joseph Smith said: "There are those of the rising generation who shall not taste death till Christ comes." Joseph Smith then proceded to make a prophesy about the coming of Christ. Since the last six words have been deleted in the *History of the Church* (under the date of April 6, 1843) we cite the original source—i.e., Joseph Smith's diary, March 10, 1843—July 14, 1843: ". . . I prophecy in the name of the Lord God—& let it be written: that the Son of Man will not come in the heavens till I am 85 years old *48 years hence or about 1890*. . . ."

Klaus J. Hansen says that "in 1890 there was a widespread belief among church members that Joseph Smith's prediction of 1835, that fifty-six years would 'wind up the scene,' would be fulfilled" (*Dialogue: A Journal of Mormon Thought*, Autumn 1966, p.76).

On October 14, 1886, Abraham H. Cannon recorded the following in his journal:

> *Thursday, Oct. 14th:*—The following are words spoken by *Apostel* [sic] *Moses Thatcher*, at Lewiston, . . .

> "It is my belief, that the time of our deliverance will be *within five years*; the time indicated *being February 14th, 1891*. . . . And that the man raised up will be no other than the Prophet Joseph Smith in his resurrected body. . . . *the government will pass into the hands of the Saints*, and *that within five years*. There will not be a city in the Union that will not be in danger of disruption by the Knights of Labor, who are becoming a formidable power in the land. . . ." (A servant of God, holding the power and keys of the Holy Apostleship does not speak in this manner for mere pastime. There is more in these utterances than we are apt to attach to them, unless we are aided by the Spirit of God.) ("Daily Journal of Abraham H. Cannon," October 14, 1886, BYU Library).

Under the date of January 23, 1833, Joseph Smith recorded the following in his *History of the Church*, volume 1, page 323:

". . . my father presented himself, . . . I asked of him a father's blessing, which he granted by laying his hands upon my head, in the name of Jesus Christ, and declaring that I should continue in the Priest's office until Christ comes."

When the Twelve Apostles were first ordained in the Mormon church some of them also received the promise that they would live until Christ came: "The blessing of Lyman E. Johnson was, . . . that he shall live until the gathering is accomplished, . . . and he shall see the Savior come and stand upon the earth with power and great glory" (*History of the Church*, vol. 2, p.188).

William Smith's blessing stated: "He shall be preserved and remain on the earth, until Christ shall come to take vengeance on the wicked" (*Ibid.*, vol. 2, p.191).

Heber C Kimball and Orson Hyde received similar blessings, although Hyde's blessing has been falsified somewhat in modern printings of the *History of the Church* (see *Mormonism— Shadow or Reality?* p.188).

Of course none of the Mormon Apostles lived to see the Lord come, and Joseph Smith's statement that "fifty-six years should wind up the scene" did not come to pass.

Writing in 1838, Apostle Parley P. Pratt said the following: "Now, Mr. Sunderland, . . . I will state as a prophesy, that there will not be an unbelieving Gentile upon this continent 50 years hence; and if they are not greatly scourged, and in a great measure overthrown, within five or ten years from this date, then the Book of Mormon will have proved itself false" (*Mormonism Unveiled—Truth Vindicated*, by Parley P. Pratt, p.15; copied from a microfilm of the original at the Mormon church historian's library).

This tract was reprinted in the book *Writings of Parley P. Pratt*, but this entire prophecy was deleted without any indication.

A Temple in Zion

In a revelation given by Joseph Smith September 22 and 23, 1832, the following statements appear:

> Yea, the word of the Lord concerning his church, established in the last days for the restoration of his people, . . . for the gathering of his saints to stand upon Mount Zion, which shall be the city of New Jerusalem.

> Which city shall be built, beginning at the temple lot, which is appointed by the finger of the Lord, in the western boundaries of the State of Missouri, and dedicated by the hand of Joseph Smith, Jun., and others . . .

> Verily this is the word of the Lord, that the city New Jerusalem shall be built by the gathering of the saints, beginning at this place, even the place of the temple, which temple shall be reared in this generation.
>
> For verily this generation shall not all pass away until an house shall be built unto the Lord, and a cloud shall rest upon it. . . .
>
> Therefore, as I said concerning the sons of Moses—for the sons of Moses and also the sons of Aaron shall offer an acceptable offering and sacrifice in the house of the Lord, which house shall be built unto the Lord in this generation, upon the consecrated spot as I have appointed (*Doctrine and Covenants* 84:2-5, 31).

Notice that this revelation, given in 1832, plainly states that a temple would be built in the *western boundaries of the state of Missouri* (that is, in Independence, Missouri) before all of those that *were then living passed away*. The leaders of the Mormon church understood this revelation to mean exactly what it said. Although the Mormons were driven from Independence (Jackson County, Missouri) they expected to return and fulfill the prophecy.

On March 10, 1861, Apostle George A. Smith stated: "Who is there that is prepared for this move back to the centre stake of Zion, . . . let me remind you that it is predicted that this generation shall not pass away till a temple shall be built, and the glory of the Lord rest upon it, according to the promises" (*Journal of Discourses*, vol. 10, p.344).

In the 1870s Apostle Orson Pratt still maintained that the temple would be built in his generation. The following statements are taken from his discourses:

> We have . . . confidence in returning to Jackson county. . . . There are many . . . still living, whose faith in returning to Jackson County, and the things that are coming, is as firm and fixed as the throne of the Almighty (*Journal of Discourses*, vol. 13, p.138).
>
> . . . God promised in the year 1832 that we should, *before the generation then living had passed away*, return and build up the City of Zion in Jackson County. . . .
>
> We believe in these promises as much as we believe in any promise ever uttered by the mouth of Jehovah. The Latter-day Saints just as much expect to receive a fulfillment of that promise during the generation that was in existence in 1832 as they expect that the sun will rise and set to-morrow. Why? Because *God cannot lie*. He will fulfil all His promises. He has spoken, it must come to pass. This is our faith (vol. 13, p.362).

... a temple will be reared on the spot that has been selected, and the corner-stone of which has been laid, *in the generation when this revelation was given*; we just as much expect this as we expect the sun to rise in the morning and set in the evening. .... But says the objector, "thirty-nine years have passed away." What of that? The generation has not passed away; all the people that were living thirty-nine years ago have not passed away; but *before they do pass away this will be fulfilled* (vol. 14, p.275).

God said, in the year 1832, before we were driven out of Jackson County, in a revelation ... that before that generation should all pass away, a house of the Lord should be built in that county. ...

This was given forty-two years ago. The generation then living was not only to commence a house of God in Jackson County, Missouri, but was actually to complete the same, . . . if you believe in these revelations you just as much expect the fulfillment of the revelation as of any one that God has ever given in these latter times, . . . we Latter-day Saints expect to return to Jackson County and to build a Temple there before the generation that was living forty-two years ago has all passed away. Well, then, the time must be pretty near when we shall begin the work (vol. 17, p.111).

By February 7, 1875, Orson Pratt was teaching that only a few of those who were driven from Jackson County would return to receive their inheritances: "There will be some that will live to behold that day, and will return ... according to the promise" (vol. 17, p.292).

Klaus J. Hansen shows that as late as 1900 Lorenzo Snow, the fifth president of the church, was still hoping that the prophecy would be fulfilled: "In 1900, Woodruff's successor, Lorenzo Snow, affirmed at a special priesthood meeting in the Salt Lake Temple that 'there are many here now under the sound of my voice, probably a majority, who will live to go back to Jackson County and assist in building that temple'" (*Dialogue: A Journal of Mormon Thought*, Autumn 1966, p.74).

The 1890 edition of the *Doctrine and Covenants* carried a footnote which read: "a generation does not all pass away in one hundred years"(*Doctrine and Covenants*, 1890 ed. section 84, p.289). This footnote has been deleted in more recent editions.

As late as 1935 Joseph Fielding Smith, who later became president of the church, maintained that the revelation would be fulfilled: "I firmly believe that there *will be some of that generation who were living when this revelation was given who shall be living when this temple is reared*. ... I have full confidence in the word of the Lord and that it shall not fail" (*The*

Most High God, we have not fulfilled his law; we have disobeyed the word which he gave through his servant Joseph, and hence the Lord has suffered us to be smitten and afflicted under the hands of our enemies.

Shall we ever return to the law of God? Yes. When? Why, when we will. We are agents; we can abide his law or reject it, just as long as we please, for God has not taken away your agency nor mine. But I will try to give you some information in regard to the time. God said, in the year 1832, before we were driven out of Jackson County, in a revelation which you will find here in this book, that before that generation should all pass away, a house of the Lord should be built in that county, (Jackson County), "upon the consecrated spot, as I have appointed; and the glory of God, even a cloud by day and a pillar of flaming fire by night shall rest upon the same." In another place, in the same revelation, speaking of the priesthood, he says that the sons of Moses and the sons of Aaron, those who had received the two priesthoods, should be filled with the glory of God upon Mount Zion, in the Lord's house, and should receive a renewing of their bodies, and the blessings of the Most High should be poured out upon them in great abundance.

This was given forty-two years ago. The generation then living was not only to commence a house of God in Jackson County, Missouri, but was actually to complete the same, and when it is completed the glory of God should rest upon it.

Now, do you Latter-day Saints believe that? I do, and if you believe in these revelations you just as much expect the fulfillment of that revelation as of any one that God has ever given in these latter times, or in former ages. We look, just as much

for this to take place, according to the word of the Lord, as the Jews look to return to Palestine, and to re-build Jerusalem upon the place where it formerly stood. They expect to build a Temple there, and that the glory of God will enter into it; so likewise do we Latter-day Saints expect to return to Jackson County and to build a Temple there before the generation that was living forty-two years ago has all passed away. Well, then, the time must be pretty near when we shall begin that work. Now, can we be permitted to return and build up the waste places of Zion, establish the great central city of Zion in Jackson County, Mo., and build a Temple on which the glory of God will abide by day and by night, unless we return, not to the "new order," but to that law which was given in the beginning of this work? Let me answer the question by quoting one of these revelations again, a revelation given in 1834. The Lord, speaking of the return of his people, and referring to those who were driven from Jackson County, says—"They that remain shall return, they and their children with them to receive their inheritances in the land of Zion, with songs of everlasting joy upon their heads." There will be a few that the Lord will spare to go back there, because they were not all transgressors. There were only two that the Lord spared among Israel during their forty years travel—Caleb and Joshua. They were all that were spared, out of some twenty-five hundred thousand people, from twenty years old and upwards, to go into the land of promise. There may be three in our day, or a half dozen or a dozen spared that were once on that land who will be permitted to return with their children, grand-children and great-grand-children unto the waste places of Zion and build them

A photograph of the *Journal of Discourses*, vol. 17, page 111. The Apostle Orson Pratt maintained the temple would be built in Jackson county before the generation living in 1832 passed away.

Way to Perfection, 1935, p.270).

In a more recent book, however, Joseph Fielding Smith stated: "It is also reasonable to believe that *no soul living in 1832, is still living* in mortality on the earth" (*Answers to Gospel Questions*, vol. 4, p.112). It has now been 147 years since Joseph Smith gave the prophecy that the temple would be built in that generation. Since the Mormons have not even begun work on this temple, it appears that there is no way possible for Joseph Smith's prophecy to be fulfilled.

The Civil War

On December 25, 1832, Joseph Smith gave his famous revelation concerning the Civil War. In this revelation we find the following:

> 1. Verily, thus saith the Lord concerning the wars that will shortly come to pass, beginning at the rebellion of South Carolina, which will eventually terminate in the death and misery of many souls;
> 2. And the time will come that war will be poured out upon all nations, beginning at this place.
> 3. For behold, the Southern States shall be divided against the Northern States, and the Southern States will call on other nations, even the nation of Great Britain, as it is called, and they shall also call upon other nations, in order to defend themselves against other nations; and then war shall be poured out upon all nations.
> 4. And it shall come to pass, after many days, slaves shall rise up against their masters, who shall be marshalled and disciplined for war.
> 5. And it shall come to pass also that the remnants who are left of the land will marshal themselves, and shall become exceedingly angry, and shall vex the Gentiles with a sore vexation (*Doctrine and Covenants*, 87:1-5).

The Mormon people believe that this revelation proves Joseph Smith was a prophet. Larry Jonas, on the other hand, shows that Joseph Smith could easily have received the idea for this revelation from the views of his time:

> On July 14, 1832, Congress passed a tariff act which South Carolina thought was so bad, she declared the tariff null and void. President Andrew Jackson alerted the nation's troops. At the time Smith made his prophecy, the nation expected a war between North and South to begin at the rebellion of South Carolina. This can be confirmed in a U.S. history book. Better yet, let me confirm it from a Latter-day Saints Church publication, *Evening and Morning Star*, . . . the issue which came out for January 1833. The news of South Carolina's rebellion was

known before January 1833. It was known before December 25, 1832 but it was not available in time for the December issue. It takes quite a while for news to be set up even today in our dailies. We would expect it to wait for a month to come out in a monthly. The example contains the information available to the church before the paper hit the street. The example and the prophecy are strangely similar. . . . Both consider the pending war a sign of the end—which it was not. In fact, the war expected in 1832 did not come to pass. . . .

Far from being evidences of Smith's divine calling, the most famous prophecies which he made are evidences that he can copy views of his time (*Mormon Claims Examined*, by Larry S. Jonas, p.52).

One further fact that supports the argument that Joseph Smith borrowed from the "views of his time" is that there is another article printed in the January 1833 issue of the original paper, *The Evening and the Morning Star*, which has the title "Rebellion in South Carolina." Interestingly enough, Joseph Smith's revelation has the words "beginning at the *rebellion of South Carolina*" in the first verse. In this article we read as follows: "In addition to the above tribulations, *South Carolina has rebelled* . . . Gen. Jackson has ordered several companies of Artillery to Charleston, and issued a Proclamation, urging submission and declaring such moves as that of S. Carolina Treason" (*The Evening and the Morning Star*, vol. 1, issue 8).

Joseph Smith was familiar with the fact that South Carolina had rebelled at the time he gave the revelation. Just before the revelation concerning the Civil War is recorded in Joseph Smith's history, the following statement is attributed to him: ". . . the United States, amid all her pomp and greatness, was threatened with dissolution. The people of South Carolina, in convention assembled (in November), passed ordinances, declaring their state a free and independent nation . . ." (*History of the Church*, vol. 1, p.301).

Thus we see that the statement in Joseph Smith's revelation that the wars would begin at the rebellion of South Carolina was undoubtedly inspired by the fact that South Carolina had already rebelled before the revelation was given. This rebellion did not end in war, but the Civil War did start some years later over trouble in South Carolina.

The fact that Joseph Smith predicted a civil war is not too remarkable. Many people believed there would be a civil war before it actually took place. The December 1840 issue of the *Millennial Star*, volume 1, page 216, quoted an article from the *New York Herald*. In this article a civil war was predicted: "We

begin to fear this unhappy country is on the eve of a bloody
civil war, a final dismemberment of the Union. . . ."

It is interesting to note that verse 3 of Joseph Smith's revelation concerning the Civil War did not come to pass. In verse 3
we read: ". . . the Southern States will call on other nations,
even the nation of Great Britain, as it is called, and *they shall
call upon other nations in order to defend themselves against
other nations; and then war shall be poured out upon all nations.*" War was certainly not poured out on *all nations* at that
time as Joseph Smith predicted.

Brigham Young prophesied that the Civil War would continue until the land was emptied so that the Mormons could
return to Missouri:

> . . . they have begun to empty the earth, to cleanse the land, and
> prepare the way for the return of the Latter-day Saints to the
> centre Stake of Zion. . . . I expect to go back. . . . Many of the
> Saints will return to Missouri, and there receive an inheritance.
> . . . The earth will also be emptied upon natural principles: . . .
> will it be over in six months or in three years? No; it will take
> years and years, and will *never cease until the work is ac-
> complished.* There may be seasons that the fire will appear to be
> extinguished, and the first you know it will break out in another
> portion, and all is on fire again, and *it will spread and continue
> until the land is emptied (Journal of Discourses,* vol. 9, pp.142-
> 43).

Brigham Young also predicted that the Civil War could not
free the slaves: "Will the present struggle free the slave? No; . . .
they cannot do that, . . ." (*Millennial Star,* vol. 25, p.787; also
Journal of Discourses, vol. 10, p.250).

Verse 5 of Joseph Smith's prophecy concerning the Civil War
is rather unclear: "And it shall come to pass also that the remnants who are left of the land will marshal themselves, and
shall become exceedingly angry, and shall vex the Gentiles
with a sore vexation." Apostle Orson Pratt explained that the
"remnants" mentioned are the Indians:

> To add to the sufferings and great calamities of the nation, they
> will be greatly distressed *by the aborigines,* who "will marshal
> themselves and become exceeding angry" and vex them "with a
> sore vexation." We are inclined to believe that this will not take
> place until millions of the nation have already perished in their
> own revolutionary battles. To what extent the Indians will have
> power over the nation is not stated in this revelation . . . (*The
> Seer,* p.242).

The fact that Joseph Smith believed the wicked of his genera-

What is the cause of all this waste of life and treasure? . To tell it in a plain, truthful way, one portion of the country wish to raise their negroes or black slaves, and the other portion wish to free them, and, apparently, to almost worship them. Well, raise and worship them, who cares? I should never fight one moment about it, for the cause of human improvement is not in the least advanced by the dreadful war which now convulses our unhappy country.

Ham will continue to be the servant of servants, as the Lord has decreed, until the curse is removed. Will the present struggle free the slave? No; but they are now wasting away the black race by thousands. Many of the blacks are treated worse than we treat our dumb brutes; and men will be called to judgment for the way they have treated the negro, and they will receive the condemnation of a guilty conscience, by the just Judge whose attributes are justice and truth.

Treat the slaves kindly and let them live, for Ham must be the servant of servants until the curse is removed. Can you destroy the decrees of the Almighty? You cannot. Yet our Christian brethren think that they are going to overthrow the sentence of the Almighty upon the seed of Ham. They cannot do that, though they may kill them by thousands and tens of thousands.

According to accounts, in all probability not less than one million men, from twenty to forty years of age, have gone to the silent grave in this useless war, in a little over two years, and all to gratify the caprice of a few,—I do not think I have a suitable name for them, shall we call them abolitionists, slaveholders, religious bigots, or political aspirants? Call them what you will, they are wasting away each other, and it seems as though they will not be satisfied until they have brought universal destruction and desolation upon the whole country. It appears as though they would destroy every person; perhaps they will, but I think they will not.

God rules. Do you know it? It is the kingdom of God or nothing for the Latter-day Saints.

Do you know that it is the eleventh hour of the reign of Satan on the earth? Jesus is coming to reign, and all you who fear and tremble because of your enemies, cease to fear them, and learn to fear to offend God, fear to trangress his laws, fear to do any evil to your brother, or to any being upon the earth, and do not fear Satan and his power, nor those who have only power to slay the body, for God will preserve his people.

We are constantly gathering new clay into the mill. How many of the new comers I have heard say, "Oh that I had been with you when you had your trials." We have promised them all the trials that are necessary, if they would be patient.

Are you going to be patient and trust in God, and receive every trial with thanksgiving, acknowledging the hand of the Lord in it? You will have all the trial you can bear. The least thing tries some people. Brother Heber and myself going to the island in Great Salt Lake, a week ago last Friday, created numerous surmisings and misgivings with some. I have thought that it might, perhaps, be well to notify you regularly, through the *Deseret News*, of my outgoings and in-comings; and I may as well now notify you that it is my intention to visit Sanpete, and, perhaps, our southern settlements this fall. If I should do so, I hope that my brethren and sisters will feel satisfied, for I shall go, come, stay and act as I feel dictated by the Spirit of God God being my helper, asking no odds of any person.—Amen.

A photograph of the *Journal of Discourses*, vol. 10, page 250. Brigham Young predicted the civil war would not free the slaves.

tion would be completely destroyed is obvious from a letter he wrote N. E. Seaton, on January 4, 1833. In this letter he stated:

> And now I am prepared to say by the authority of Jesus Christ, that not many years shall pass away before the United States shall present such a scene of bloodshed as has not a parallel in the history of our nation; pestilence, hail, famine, and earthquake will sweep the wicked of this generation from off the face of the land, to open and prepare the way for the return of the lost tribes of Israel from the north country . . . flee to Zion, before the overflowing scourge overtake you, for there are those now living upon the earth whose eyes shall not be closed in death until they see all these things, which I have spoken, fulfilled (History of the Church, vol. 1, pp.315-16).

Both Joseph Smith and Brigham Young predicted that the U.S. government would be broken up.

Suppressed Material on Civil War

Joseph Smith's revelation concerning the Civil War was never published during his lifetime, and although it is included in the handwritten manuscript of the History of the Church, it was suppressed the first two times that Joseph Smith's history was printed (see Times and Seasons, vol. 5, p.688; also Millennial Star, vol. 14, pp.296, 305). It is obvious that this was a deliberate omission on the part of the Mormon historians, for over 300 words were deleted without any indication!

Mormon historian B. H. Roberts informs us that the revelation was not printed until 1851 (seven years after Joseph Smith's death). Brigham Young and other Mormon leaders apparently did not have much confidence in this revelation at first because they waited nineteen years before they published it.

In the History of the Church, volume 5, page 324, we find another reference to the 1832 prophecy attributed to Joseph Smith: "I prophesy, in the name of the Lord God, that the commencement of the difficulties which will cause much bloodshed previous to the coming of the Son of Man will be in South Carolina. It may probably arise through the slave question. This a voice declared to me while I was praying earnestly on the subject, December 25th, 1832."

In our research in the diary of Joseph Smith we found that this statement does appear under the date of April 2, 1843, although there have been a few changes in wording. A careful examination of this portion of Joseph Smith's diary, however, reveals that some very important material has been suppressed. Before we can understand the significance of this matter we must turn back in Joseph Smith's diary to the date of March 11,

1843, where we find the following:

> *A dream*, then related, Night before last I dreamed that an old man came to me and said there was a mob force coming upon him, and he was likely to loose his life, that I was Leut General and had the command of a large force, and I was also a patriot and disposed to protect the innocent & —— [word unclear] finding & wanted I should assist him. I told him I wanted some written documents to show the facts that they are the aggressors, & I would raise a force sufficient for his protection, that I would call out the Legion. He turned to go from me, but turned again and said to me. "I have any amount of men at my command and will put them under your command."

This dream, with some modifications, appears in the *History of the Church*, volume 5, page 301.

Now, when we move ahead to the date of April 2, 1843, in the diary of Joseph Smith, we find that just before Joseph Smith gives his second account of the prophecy concerning South Carolina, there is an interpretation of the dream which reads as follows: "Related the dream written on page 3—Book B Interpretation by O. Hyde—old man.—government of these United States, who will be invaded by a foriegn [sic] foe, probably England. U. S. Government will call on Gen. Smith to defend probably all this western territory and offer him any amount of men he shall desire & put them under his command."

This important interpretation of the dream should appear in the *History of the Church*, volume 5, page 324, just before the words "I prophesy." The reader will find, however, that the interpretation has been completely omitted. The reason that it was suppressed is obvious: Joseph Smith was dead by the time the Civil War started, and therefore the interpretation could not be fulfilled. In his first account of the prophecy on the Civil War, *Doctrine and Covenants* 87:3, Joseph Smith had predicted that England would come into the war and that the war would spread until it "shall be poured out upon all nations." The war did not spread to "all nations" as Smith had predicted, and the U.S. government certainly did not call upon Joseph Smith to protect it from England or any other country. As we shall show later, Joseph Smith was lieutenant general of the Nauvoo Legion, and he did ask the U. S. Government for "100,000 men to extend protection to persons wishing to settle Oregon and other portions of the territory" (*History of the Church*, vol. 6, p.282). This request, however, was denied.

We feel that the interpretation of the dream that was suppressed undermines the prophecy on the Civil War. It should be noted also that the part omitted should have appeared in the middle of a portion of Joseph Smith's history (vol. 5, pp.323-24) which was later canonized as a revelation in the *Doctrine and Covenants*, section 130. In other words, section 130 contains the abbreviated material from the *History of the Church*. The portion that was suppressed should appear between verses 11 and 12.

Conclusion

The prophecy concerning the Mormons being driven to the Rocky Mountains and the one concerning the Civil War are considered Joseph Smith's most important prophecies. These are used to try to prove that he was a prophet of God. In the chapter dealing with changes in Joseph's history we demonstrate that the prophecy concerning the Rocky Mountains is a forgery which was written after Joseph Smith's death. In this chapter we have shown that the prophecy about the Civil War came because of the rebellion of South Carolina in 1832, and that it contains inaccuracies which tend to invalidate it. In addition to this, the Mormon leaders have suppressed part of Joseph Smith's diary which tended to discredit the revelation.

THE ARM OF FLESH

Chapter 15

In Jeremiah 17:5 we read: "Thus saith the Lord; Cursed be the man that trusteth in man, and maketh flesh his arm. . . ." This Scripture means that we are not to put our trust in any man, but that we are to rely only upon God and put our trust in Him. Men can lead us into error, but God leads us only into truth and righteousness.

The Mormon church condemns the Catholics for teaching that the Pope is infallible, yet it teaches essentially the same thing. Brigham Young boasted: "The Lord Almighty leads this Church, and he will never suffer you to be led astray if you are found doing your duty. You may go home and *sleep as sweetly as a babe in its mother's arms*, as to any danger of your leaders leading you astray . . ." (*Journal of Discourses*, vol. 9, p.289).

Since Brigham Young's death, Mormon leaders have continued to teach that the Lord will "never permit" the president of the church to lead anyone astray. Mormons are encouraged to put all their trust in the church authorities and not try to do their own thinking. The ward teacher's message for June, 1945, contained this admonition:

> Any Latter-day Saint who denounces or opposes, whether actively or otherwise, any plan or doctrine advocated by the "prophets, seers, and revelators" of the Church is cultivating the spirit of apostasy. . . . Lucifer . . . wins a great victory when he can get members of the Church to speak against their leaders and to "*do their own thinking*.". . .
>
> *When our leaders speak, the thinking has been done.* When they propose a plan—it is God's plan. When they point the way, there is no other which is safe. When they give direction, it should mark the end of controversy (*Improvement Era*, June 1945, p.354).

Heber C. Kimball, First Councilor to Brigham Young, exhorted the Mormon people to ". . . learn to do as you are told,

. . . if you are told by your leader to do a thing, do it, *none of your business whether it is right or wrong"* (*Journal of Discourses,* vol. 6, p.32).

"If you do things according to counsel and they are wrong, the consequences will fall on the heads of those who counseled you, so don't be troubled" (*William Clayton's Journal,* p.334).

Joseph Smith gave a revelation in which the Mormons were told to "give heed unto all his words and commandments which he shall give unto you . . . his word ye shall receive, *as if from mine own mouth,* in all patience and faith" (*Doctrine and Covenants* 21:4-5).

Apostle Orson Pratt asked:

> Have we not a right to make up our minds in relation to the things recorded in the word of God, and speak about them, whether the living oracles believe our views or not? We have not the right. . . .
>
> God placed Joseph Smith at the head of this Church; God has likewise placed Brigham Young at the head of this Church. . . . We are commanded to give heed to their words in all things, and receive their words as from the mouth of God, in all patience and faith (*Journal of Discourses,* vol. 7, pp.374-75).

Joseph Smith himself once boasted: "God made Aaron to be the mouthpiece for the children of Israel, and He will make me to be *god to you* in His stead, and the Elders to be mouth for me; and *if you don't like it, you must lump it"* (*Teachings of the Prophet Joseph Smith,* by Joseph Fielding Smith, p.363; also *History of the Church,* vol. 6, pp.319-20).

No New Revelation

On April 3, 1976, the Church Section of the *Deseret News* announced that "Two revelations received by former Presidents of the Church, were accepted as scripture Saturday afternoon, April 3, by vote of Church membership."

This was certainly a surprising move for the Mormon leaders to make. Since one of the revelations which was canonized was given by Joseph F. Smith, we feel that it is possible this move was made to counter some statements which we printed in *Mormonism—Shadow or Reality?* We cite the following from that book:

> Although the Mormon Church claims to be led by revelation, Joseph F. Smith, the sixth President of the Mormon Church, testified as follows in the Reed Smoot Investigation:
>
> Senator Dubois.—*Have you received any revelations from God, which has been submitted by you and the apostles to the body of*

the church in their semiannual conference, which revelation has been sustained by that conference, through the upholding of their hands?

Mr. Smith.—Since when?

Senator Dubois.—Since you became President of the Church.

Mr. Smith.—*No, sir; none whatever.*

Senator Dubois.—Have you received any individual revelations yourself, since you became President of the church under your own definition, even, of a revelation?

Mr. Smith.—*I cannot say that I have.*

Senator Dubois.—Can you say that you have not?

Mr. Smith.—No; I cannot say that I have not.

Senator Dubois.—Then you do not know whether you have received any such revelation as you have described or whether you have not?

Mr. Smith.—Well, I can say this: That if I live as I should in the line of my duties, I am susceptible, I think, of the impressions of the Spirit of the Lord upon my mind at any time, *just as any good Methodist* or any other good church member might be. And so far as that is concerned, I say yes; I have had impressions of the Spirit upon my mind very frequently, but they are *not in the sense of revelations.* (*Reed Smoot Case*, Vol. 1, pages 483-484)

On page 99 of the same volume Joseph F. Smith stated: "*I have never pretended to nor do I profess to have received revelations.*" From this it is plain to see that just because a man is ordained a "Prophet, Seer, and Revelator," it does not necessarily mean that he is. If Joseph F. Smith was only susceptible to the impressions of the Spirit of the Lord as "any good Methodist," then why should his word be trusted above that of a good Methodist?

Although the Mormon Church is supposed to be led by revelation, the evidence of this revelation is very hard to find. The Manifesto of 1890 is the last revelation, if it can be termed a revelation, that has been added to the *Doctrine and Covenants.* So we see that the last revelation that was added to the *Doctrine and Covenants* is eighty years old. Bruce R. McConkie, of the First Council of Seventy, admits that there is not much written revelation in the church today, but he still maintains that the church leaders are receiving "daily revelation":

"It is true that not many revelations containing doctrinal principles are now being written, because all we are as yet capable and worthy to receive has already been written. But the Spirit is giving direct and daily revelation to the presiding Brethren in the administration of the affairs of the Church. . . .

"The presence of revelation in the Church is positive proof that it is the kingdom of God on earth" (*Mormon Doctrine*, Salt Lake City, 1966, page 650).

The Reorganized LDS Church has continued to add new revelations to their Doctrine and Covenants, but the Utah Mormon Church has not added a new revelation since they added the Manifesto of 1890. It is interesting to note that during the last century, when new revelations were being added to the Doctrine and Covenants, the Mormon leaders were condemning the Catholics for not adding new revelations to their "sacred canon." The Mormon Apostle Orson Pratt stated:

"That the Romanists have continued in their apostacy until the present day is demonstrated from the fact that they have not added one single book to their canon since they first formed it. Now, if there had been any prophet or apostle among them, during the last seventeen centuries, they certainly would have canonized his epistles, revelations, and prophecies, as being equally sacred with those of the first century. As they have not done this, it shows most clearly, that even they, themselves, do not consider that they have had apostles, prophets, and revelators among them, during that long period of time. . . . Upwards of 250 Popes pretend to have successively filled the chair of Peter. . . . Why then has the church showed such great partiality? Why has she placed Pope St. Peter's writings in the sacred canon, and left all the writings of the other Popes out?. . . Here, indeed, is a strange inconsistency! Even the Catholic church herself, evidently places no confidence in the popes and bishops, the pretended successors of St. Peter and the rest of the apostles; if she did, she would have canonized their revelations along with the rest of the revelations of the New Testament. . . . Well might the revelator John, . . . call her 'THE MOTHER OF HARLOTS AND ABOMINATIONS OF THE EARTH!' " (*Orson Pratt's Works*, "The Bible Alone An Insufficient Guide," pp.38-39).

The very words used by Orson Pratt concerning the Catholics could now be applied to the Mormon Church, for "*if there had been any prophet or apostle among them,*" during the past eighty years, "*they certainly would have canonized his epistles, revelations, and prophecies. . . .*" The Church "*evidently places no confidence*" in the last six Presidents; "*if she did, she would have canonized their revelations along with the rest of the revelations*" in the Doctrine and Covenants (*Mormonism–Shadow or Reality?* p.184).

It is difficult to resist the idea that the Mormon leaders decided to canonize two "new" revelations to offset the criticism found in *Mormonism–Shadow or Reality?* That they would choose a revelation given to Joseph F. Smith is especially interesting. This purported revelation was given less than two months before Joseph F. Smith's death in 1918. He had served as "Prophet, Seer and Revelator" for some seventeen years before receiving this revelation. The reader will remember that Joseph F. Smith had previously admitted he had served as "Prophet, Seer, and Revelator" for some time without receiving any revelation: "I have never pretended to nor do I profess to have received revelations."

The other revelation which the Mormons canonized was given to Joseph Smith on January 21, 1836. We have previously shown that this revelation was falsified before publication to avoid a major contradiction.

Joseph F. Smith once stated that any new revelations would be added to the *Doctrine and Covenants*, but Mormon leaders have decided that these two revelations should be added to the *Pearl of Great Price* instead (*Deseret News*, Church Section, April 3, 1976).

At any rate, these two revelations can hardly be considered as "new" revelations. The one given to Joseph F. Smith is sixty-one years old, and the revelation given to the Prophet Joseph Smith is 143 years old. On September 20, 1976, the *Salt Lake Tribune* reported: "President Kimball said the church is based on 'revelations of God.' He declined to say if he has had any in his three years as president and prophet."

On June 9, 1978 President Kimball claimed he had a revelation that blacks could receive the priesthood. We have noted, however, that the church has failed to produce a copy of it. All we have is a statement by the First Presidency which says a revelation was received. Furthermore, Kimball himself made a statement that gives the impression that it was only a feeling or assurance that he received. The reader will remember that President Joseph F. Smith admitted that "any good Methodist or any other church member" is susceptible to "impressions of the Spirit of the Lord." If the Mormon leaders really believe they are led by revelation, why don't they canonize a revelation by Spencer W. Kimball which begins with the words, "Thus saith the Lord your God. . . ."?

In any case, the church has now had twelve presidents. Only four of the first six presidents have received revelations that have been canonized in the "four standard works." None of the last six presidents have received revelations which have been canonized. Where, then, is the evidence of present-day revelation? We are told that revelation is found in the Conferences of the Church, when the leaders of the church speak under the inspiration of the Lord, but how can we know when they are

is no matter if the whole world is against us, God is for us. Could not they kill you? Yes, if it be the Lord's will. If it be the will of the Lord for the people to live, they will live. If it had been the will of the Lord that Joseph and Hyrum should have lived, they would have lived. It was necessary for Joseph to seal his testimony with his blood. Had he been destined to live he would have lived. The Lord suffered his death to bring justice on the nation. The debt is contracted and they have it to pay. The nations of the earth are in the Lord's hands; and if we serve Him we shall reap the reward of so doing. If we neglect to obey His laws and ordinances, we shall have to suffer the consequences.

Well, brethren and sisters, try and be Saints. I will try; I have tried many years to live according to the law which the Lord reveals unto me. I know just as well what to teach this people and just what to say to them and what to do in order to bring them into the celestial kingdom, as I know

the road to my office. It is just as plain and easy. The Lord is in our midst. He teaches the people continually. I have never yet preached a sermon and sent it out to the children of men, that they may not call Scripture. Let me have the privilege of correcting a sermon, and it is as good Scripture as they deserve. The people have the oracles of God continually. In the days of Joseph, revelation was given and written, and the people were driven from city to city and place to place, until we were led into these mountains. Let this go to the people with "Thus saith the Lord," and if they do not obey it, you will see the chastening hand of the Lord upon them. But if they are plead with, and led along like children, we may come to understand the will of the Lord and He may preserve us as we desire.

Let us, then, you and me and all who profess to be Latter-day Saints, try to be Saints indeed. God bless you, Amen.

DISCOURSE BY ELDER GEORGE Q. CANNON,

DELIVERED IN THE NEW TABERNACLE, SALT LAKE CITY, APRIL 6, 1869.

(Reported by David W. Evans.)

THE ORDER OF ENOCH—SOCIALISTIC EXPERIMENTS—THE SOCIAL PROBLEM.

I look upon this Conference as one of the most important, in many respects, that we have ever had the privilege of participating in, for, to my view, there are more interesting and important events connected with the work of God at the present time than have ever been developed before in our history. We are undergoing a great change, a great revolution is

A photograph of the *Journal of Discourses*, vol. 13, page 95. Brigham Young claimed that his sermons were to be received as scripture.

speaking under the Spirit of the Lord? Obviously, much of what has been said at the conferences of the church down through the years was not spoken under the inspiration of the Lord. If a leader of the church were to stand up in conference today and say the same things that Brigham Young said, he would stand the chance of being excommunicated from the church; yet it was Brigham Young himself who stated: "I have never yet preached *a sermon* and sent it out to the children of men, that *they may not call scripture"* (*Journal of Discourses*, vol. 13, p.95). In a letter to Morris L. Reynolds, dated May 16, 1966, Mormon Apostle LeGrand Richards takes a different position: "Your next question: 'Can the *Journal of Discourses* be used as doctrine if the man speaking says, 'Thus saith the Lord' I cannot answer that question because I don't know what part of the *Journal of Discourses* you have in mind. I would have to know just what you were referring to."

Conclusion

The search for revelation, that is, present-day revelation, in Mormonism is really in vain. As we have pointed out, no new revelations have been added to the *Doctrine and Covenants* since the "Manifesto" of 1890, and even the Manifesto is only an "official statement" which does not contain the words, "Thus saith the Lord your God. . . ." The two revelations which have been added to the *Pearl of Great Price* are certainly not from the present time—one is sixty-one years old and the other 143 years old.* The sermons given in conference may be con-

---

*Just as this book was about to go to press the Mormon Church announced plans to add three new items to the *Doctrine and Covenants:* "The extension of the Mormon priesthood to blacks is one of three changes to be made in the *Doctrine and Covenants* . . . Mr. LeFevre said the announcement . . . includes the June 1978 declaration on blacks and two portions of the *Pearl of Great Price.* . . . Church founder Joseph Smith's 'Vision of the Celestial Kingdom' and former church president Joseph F. Smith's 'Vision of the Redemption of the Dead' will be the first additions since the 1890 manifesto on polygamy, Mr. LeFevre said" (*Salt Lake Tribune,* June 3, 1979). This announcement is apparently another attempt to offset criticism that the Church does not have any present-day revelation. The reader will remember that the "June 1978 declaration on blacks" is only a statement written by the First Presidency, not a revelation beginning with the words: "Thus saith the Lord your God. . . ." The addition of the other two revelations to the *Doctrine and Covenants* only tends to emphasize that the Church is led by fallible men rather than by direct revelation from God. The Church Section of the *Deseret News* for April 3, 1976 had announced that these revelations "will be arranged in verses as part of the *Pearl of Great Price."* As we pointed out earlier in this chapter, "Joseph F. Smith once stated that any new revelations would be added to the *Doctrine and Covenants."* The Mormon authorities apparently realized that they had made a mistake when they put the revelations in the *Pearl of Great Price,* and therefore they have now decided to print them as part of the *Doctrine and Covenants.*

schisms such might not have been the case. I have taken the liberty of telling the Latter-day Saints in this and other places something with regard to the Apostles in this our day. It is true that we have a greater assurance of the Kingdom and the power of God being upon the earth than was possessed by the Apostles anciently, and yet right here in the Quorum of the Twelve, if you ask one of its members what he believes with regard to the Deity, he will tell you that he believes in those great and holy principles which seem to be exhibited to man for his perfection and enjoyment in time and in eternity. But do you believe in the existence of a personage called God? "No, I do not," says this Apostle. So you see there are schisms in our day. Do you think there was any in the days of the Apostles? Yes, worse than this. They were a great deal more tenacious than we are.

We have another one in the Quorum of the Twelve who believes that infants actually have the spirits of some who have formerly lived on the earth, and that this is their resurrection, which is a doctrine so absurd and foolish that I cannot find language to express my sentiments in relation to it. It is as ridiculous as to say that God—the Being whom we worship—is principle without personage. I worship a person. I believe in the resurrection, and I believe the resurrection was exhibited to perfection in the person of the Savior, who rose on the third day after his burial. This is not all. we have another one of these Apostles, right in this Quorum of the Twelve, who, I understand, for fifteen years, has been preaching on the sly in the chimney corner to the brethren and sisters with whom he has had influence, that the Savior was nothing more than a good man, and that his death had nothing to do with your salvation or mine. The question might arise, if the ancient Apostles believed doctrines as absurd as these, why were they not handed down to after generations that they might avoid the dilemma, the vortex, the whirlpool of destruction and folly? We will not say what they did or did not believe and teach, but they did differ one from another, and they would not visit each other. This was not through the perfection of the gospel, but through the weakness of man.

The principles of the gospel are perfect, but are the Apostles who teach it perfect? No, they are not. Now, bringing the two together, what they taught is not for me to say, but it is enough to say this, that through the weaknesses in the lives of the Apostles many were caused to err. Our historians and ministers tell us that the church went into the wilderness, but they were in the wilderness all the time. They had the way marked out to get out of the wilderness and go straightforward into the Kingdom of God, but they took various paths, and the two substantial churches that remain—a remnant from the apostles, that divided, are now called the Holy Catholic Church and the Greek Church. You recollect reading in the Revelations of John what the angel said to John, when he was on the Isle of Patmos, about the Seven Churches. What was the matter with those Churches? They were not living according to the light that had been exhibited. Do the Latter-day Saints live according to the light that has been exhibited to them? No, they do not. Did the ancient saints live according to the revelations given through the Savior and written by the Apostles, and the revelations given through the Apostles, and left

A photograph of the *Journal of Discourses*, vol. 12, page 66. Brigham Young frankly admitted that some of the Mormon Apostles disagreed about God and reincarnation.

sidered as revelation today, but fifty years from now they may be rejected as many of Brigham Young's sermons are today.

Even though the leaders of the church are supposed to be led by revelation, it is evident that they are not always in harmony as to which doctrines are from the Lord. Brigham Young once stated that there were apostles in the Mormon church who taught that there was no personage called God, that Jesus was not the Saviour and that the spirits of some who lived formerly have been reincarnated:

> ... and yet right here in the Quorum of the Twelve, if you ask one of its members what he believes with regard to the Deity, he will tell you that he believes in those great and holy principles which seem to be exhibited to man for his perfection and enjoyment in time and in eternity. But do you believe in the existence of a *personage called God? "No, I do not,"* says this *Apostle.* So you see there are schisms in our day. . . .

> We have another one in the Quorum of the Twelve who believes that infants actually *have the spirits of some who have formerly lived on the earth,* and that this is their resurrection. . . . This is not all. we [sic] have another one of these Apostles, right in this Quorum of the Twelve, who, I understand, for fifteen years, has been preaching on the sly in the chimney corner to the brethren and sisters with whom he has had influence, that the Savior was *nothing more than a good man, and* that his death had nothing to do with your salvation or mine (*Journal of Discourses,* vol. 12, p.66).

During the past few years Mormon leaders have been faced with some serious problems. Their response to these problems plainly shows that they are not led by revelation. Serveral of these problems appear to be complicated by the fact that some of the Mormon leaders are very old. David O. McKay, the ninth president of the church, lived to be ninety-six years old. But he was in very poor health toward the end of his life and was hardly in any condition to function as prophet, seer and revelator for the church. Instead of appointing a younger man after McKay's death, church leaders chose Joseph Fielding Smith who was ninety-three years old. Smith lived to be ninety-five, and the leadership of the church passed to Harold B. Lee who was seventy-three years old. Lee lived for less than two years and Spencer W. Kimball became president. President Kimball is now in his eighties. The way the Mormon hierarchy is structured there seems to be little hope of a younger leader, and apparently less hope for any new revelation. The claim of being led by a "living Prophet" has for a long time appeared to be just an idle boast.

439

THE PRIESTHOOD

Chapter 16

The Mormon church has no paid ministry other than those referred to as "General Authorities." Apostle Hugh B. Brown explains:

> The presiding authority of the Church is the First Presidency, consisting of three high priests, a president and his two counselors. Associated with them and next in authority are twelve apostles . . . also a Patriarch to the Church. . . .
>
> Also numbered among the General Authorities of the Church is the First Council of The Seventy. . . . Next in order is the Presiding Bishopric, three high priests. . . .
>
> These presiding quorums in the Church are made up of men from various walks of life. . . . When men are called into this ministry they give up their other activities and devote themselves exclusively to Church work . . . (Mormonism, tract by Hugh B. Brown, 1963, p.13, Deseret News Press).

Apostle Brown goes on to explain the Mormon priesthood, with its two divisions of Melchizedek and Aaronic priesthoods, as follows:

> All the affairs of the Church, (general, stake, ward and mission) are directed by men who hold the Melchizedek Priesthood, with the office of high priest, seventy, or elder, in descending order. . . . There is also the Aaronic Priesthood with priest, teachers, and deacons. . . Every male member over 12 years of age, if he lives worthily, has the privilege of being ordained to some office in the priesthood.

A bishop presides over a congregation known as a ward. He continues to work at his regular employment, performing his duties as bishop in his free time. The many responsibilities attached to directing a ward are shared by the members.

The Mormon leaders claim that those who hold the priesthood in the Mormon church are the only ones who have the authority to administer the ordinances of the gospel. This con-

L.D.S. Church Organization

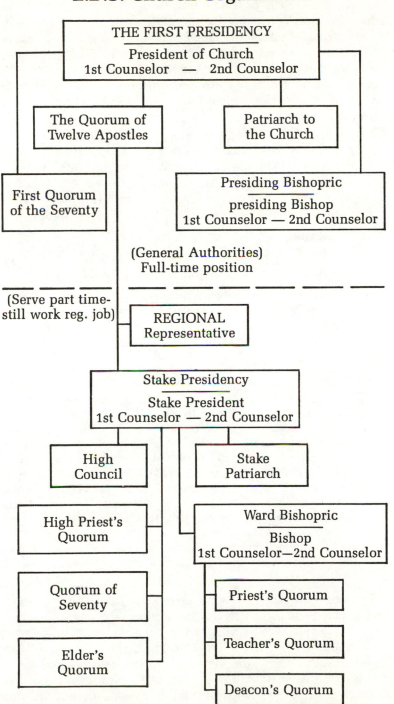

THE FIRST PRESIDENCY

President of Church
1st Counselor — 2nd Counselor

The Quorum of
Twelve Apostles

Patriarch to
the Church

First Quorum
of the Seventy

Presiding Bishopric

presiding Bishop
1st Counselor — 2nd Counselor

(General Authorities)
Full-time position

(Serve part time-
still work reg. job)

REGIONAL
Representative

Stake Presidency

Stake President
1st Counselor — 2nd Counselor

High
Council

Stake
Patriarch

High Priest's
Quorum

Ward Bishopric

Bishop
1st Counselor—2nd Counselor

Quorum of
Seventy

Priest's Quorum

Teacher's Quorum

Elder's
Quorum

Deacon's Quorum

cept leads members of the church to believe that the work of other churches is in vain. In the missionary manual Mormon missionaries are instructed to tell reluctant contacts that "many priests and ministers are good, sincere individuals. However, being good or sincere does not qualify a person to represent the Lord. . . . a person cannot simply decide on his own initiative to represent the Lord, but must be chosen and must receive the authority to preach his gospel and administer his ordinances" (*The Uniform System For Teaching Families*, p.F-26).

In the Bible we read that Jesus once rebuked John for holding a similar belief: "And John answered and said, Master, we saw one casting out devils in thy name; and we forbad him, because he followed not with us. And Jesus said unto him, forbid him not: for he that is not against us is for us" (Luke 9:49-50).

Added Later

David Whitmer, one of the three witnesses to the *Book of Mormon*, related the following concerning the priesthood:

> This matter of "priesthood," since the days of Sydney Rigdon, has been the great hobby and stumbling-block of the Latter Day Saints. Priesthood means authority; and authority is the word we should use. I do not think the word priesthood is mentioned in the New Covenant of the Book of Mormon. Authority is the word we used for the first two years in the church—until Sydney Rigdon's days in Ohio. This matter of two orders of priesthood in the Church of Christ, and lineal priesthood of the old law being in the church, all originated in the mind of Sydney Rigdon. He explained these things to Brother Joseph in his way, out of the old Scriptures, and got Brother Joseph to inquire, etc. He would inquire, and as mouthpiece speak out the revelations just as they had it fixed in their hearts. As I have said before, according to the desires of the heart, the inspiration comes, but it may be the spirit of man that gives it. . . . This is the way the High Priests and the "priesthood" as you have it, was introduced into the Church of Christ almost two years after its beginning—and after we had baptized and confirmed about two thousand souls into the church (*An Address To All Believers In Christ*, by David Whitmer, p.64).

The question might well be asked, If what David Whitmer says is true, how can section 27 and other sections of the *Doctrine and Covenants* be accounted for? It does seem as if there is a contradiction here. Section 27 tells of the bestowal of the lesser priesthood and the visitation of Peter, James and John, and is dated August 1830, whereas David Whitmer stated that the idea of two orders of priesthood, lineal priesthood, etc., did not come into the church until Sidney Rigdon's days in Ohio.

Actually, these revelations have been changed from the way they originally read when they were first printed in the *Book of Commandments*. David Whitmer claimed:

> You have *changed the revelations* from the way they were first given and as they are today in the Book of Commandments, to support the error of Brother Joseph in taking upon himself the office of Seer to the church. You have *changed the revelations to support the error of high priests*. You have changed the revelations to support the error of a President of the high priesthood, high counselors, etc. You have *altered the revelations* to support you in going beyond the plain teachings of Christ in the new covenant part of the Book of Mormon (*An Address To All Believers In Christ*, p.49).

LaMar Petersen, in speaking about the changes concerning priesthood which have been made in Joseph Smith's revelations, notes:

> The important details that are missing from the "full history" of 1834 are likewise missing from the *Book of Commandments* in 1833. The student would expect to find all the particulars of the Restoration in this first treasured set of 65 revelations, the dates of which encompassed the bestowals of the two Priesthoods, but they are conspicuously absent. . . . The *notable revelations on Priesthood* in the *Doctrine and Covenants* before referred to, Sections 2 and 13, *are missing*, and Chapter 28 gives no hint of the Restoration which, if actual, had been known for four years. *More than four hundred words were added* to this revelation of August 1829 in Section 27 of the *Doctrine and Covenants*, the additions made to include the names of heavenly visitors and two separate ordinations. The *Book of Commandments* gives the duties of Elders, Priests, Teachers, and Deacons and refers to Joseph's apostolic calling but there is no mention of Melchizedek Priesthood, High Priesthood, Seventies, High Priests, nor High Councilors. *These words were later inserted into the revelation on Church organization and government* of April, 1830, making it appear that they were known at that date, but they do not appear in the original, Chapter 24 of the Book of Commandments three years later. Similar interpolations were made in the revelations known as Sections 42 and 68 (*Problems In Mormon Text*, by LaMar Petersen, pp.7-8).

At this point the reader may be interested in taking a closer look at the photographs showing the changes made in Joseph Smith's revelations which we presented in chapter 3 (see CHANGES E, I, K, M, N, O, P, and Q).

Aaronic Priesthood

The Mormon church claims to have the Aaronic Priesthood;   **443** whereas the Bible makes it clear that it was fulfilled and abolished at the death of Christ. In Hebrews 7:11-14 we read:

> If therefore perfection were by the Levitical priesthood, (for under it the people received the law,) what further need was there that another priest should rise after the order of Melchisedec, and not be called after the order of Aaron? For *the priesthood being changed*, there is made of necessity a change also of the law. For he of whom these things are spoken pertaineth to another tribe, of which no man gave attendance at the altar. For it is evident that our Lord sprang out of Juda; of which tribe Moses spake nothing concerning priesthood.

Members of the early Christian church were not ordained to the Aaronic Priesthood; neither is there any mention of the Aaronic Priesthood in the *Book of Mormon*. Apostle Parley P. Pratt admitted that "the Aaronic Priesthood is no where pretended to in the Book of Mormon" (*Writings of Parley Parker Pratt*, p.209).

The Mormon church claims that on May 15, 1829, John the Baptist conferred the Aaronic Priesthood on Joseph Smith and Oliver Cowdery. Section 13 of the *Doctrine and Covenants* is cited as evidence that the Aaronic Priesthood was conferred on Smith and Cowdery. We must remember, however, that this section did not appear in the revelations as they were originally printed in the *Book of Commandments*. It was published in the *Times and Seasons* on August 1, 1842, but it was not added to the *Doctrine and Covenants* until 1876.

Section 27 of the *Doctrine and Covenants* might lead one to believe that in 1830 the ordination of Joseph Smith and Oliver Cowdery to the Aaronic Priesthood by John the Baptist was common knowledge in the church. In verse 8 we read: "Which John I have sent unto you, my servants, Joseph Smith, Jun., and Oliver Cowdery, to ordain you unto the first priesthood which you have received, that you might be called and ordained even as Aaron."

Since the introduction to this revelation states that it was given in 1830, Mormon writers use it in their attempt to prove the restoration of the priesthood. A careful examination of this revelation, however, reveals that it has been falsified. Verse 8 was *not* in the revelation as it was originally published in the *Book of Commandments*. It was added to the *Doctrine and Covenants* in 1835 (see Change K).

Melchizedek Priesthood

It is claimed by the Mormon leaders that before the church

was organized Peter, James, and John restored the Melchizedek Priesthood. Apostle LeGrand Richards admits that the exact date of this ordination is not known: "While we are a record-keeping people, as the Lord commanded, nevertheless our records are not complete. . . . we do *not* have the date that Peter, James and John conferred the Melchizedek Priesthood upon them" (Letter from LeGrand Richards, dated September 26, 1960).

The *Doctrine and Covenants* 27:12 is cited as proof that the Melchizedek Priesthood was conferred at a very early date: "And also with Peter, and James, and John, whom I have sent unto you, by whom I have ordained you and confirmed you to be apostles. . . ."

This verse, however, did *not* appear in the revelation when it was published in the *Book of Commandments* in 1833. It was added into the *Doctrine and Covenants*, and therefore cannot be cited as proof that the Melchizedek Priesthood was in the church at the time the revelation was given (see Change K).

It is claimed that an elder is an office in the Melchizedek Priesthood, but neither the Bible nor the *Book of Mormon* support this idea. In the *Doctrine and Covenants* 107:7 we read: "The office of an elder comes under the priesthood of Melchizedek." There is evidence, however, that in the beginning the elders of the Mormon church did *not* have the Melchizedek Priesthood. Joseph Smith himself made this statement concerning a conference held in June, 1831: ". . . the authority of the Melchizedek Priesthood was manifested and conferred for the first time upon several of the Elders" (*History of the Church*, vol. 1, pp.175-76).

John Whitmer, who was church historian, confirmed the fact that the Elders were ordained to the High Priesthood on June 3, 1831: "June 3, 1831. A general conference was called . . . the Lord manifest to Joseph that it was necessary that such of the elders as were considered worthy, should be ordained to the high priesthood" (*John Whitmer's History*, chap. 7).

If the Melchizedek Priesthood is really necessary it is certainly odd that the elders were able to function from the organization of the church until June, 1831, without it. All evidence points to the fact that the Melchizedek Priesthood did not come from the hands of Peter, James, and John in 1829, but rather from the mind of Sidney Rigdon in Ohio in 1831. Mormon historian B. H. Roberts admitted concerning the restoration of the Melchizedek Priesthood: ". . . there is *no definite account* of the event in the history of the Prophet Joseph, or, for matter of that, in any of our annals . . ." (*History of the Church*,

vol. 1, p.40, footnote). In trying to prove that there was a restoration of the Melchizedek Priesthood, Roberts cites two statements by Oliver Cowdery. These statements are of little value,
however, since they were not made until the late 1840s and
were not published until some time later.

High Priests

David Whitmer, one of the three witnesses to the *Book of
Mormon*, also wrote concerning the ordination of high priests
in the Mormon church:

> The next grievous error which crept into the church was in or-
> daining high priests in June, 1831. This error was introduced at
> the instigation of Sydney Rigdon. The office of high priests was
> never spoken of, and never thought of being established in the
> church until Rigdon came in. Remember that we had been
> preaching from August 1829, until June, 1831—almost two
> years—and had baptized about 2,000 members into the Church
> of Christ, and had not one high priest. During 1829, several times
> we were told by Brother Joseph that an elder was the highest
> office in the church. . . . In Kirkland, Ohio, in 1831, Rigdon
> would expound the Old Testament scriptures of the Bible and
> Book of Mormon (in his way) to Joseph, concerning the priest-
> hood, high priests, etc., and would persuade Brother Joseph to
> inquire of the Lord about this doctrine, and of course a revelation
> would always come just as they desired it. Rigdon finally per-
> suaded Brother Joseph to believe that the high priests which had
> such great power in ancient times, should be in the Church of
> Christ to-day. He had Brother Joseph inquire of the Lord about it,
> and they received an answer according to their erring desires
> (*An Address To All Believers In Christ*, p.35).

> High Priests were only in the church before Christ; and to have
> this office in the "Church of Christ" is not according to the
> teachings of Christ in either of the sacred books: Christ himself is
> our great and last High Priest. Brethren—I will tell you one thing
> which alone should settle this matter in your minds; it is this:
> you cannot find in the New Testament part of the Bible or Book
> of Mormon where one single high priest was ever in the Church
> of Christ. It is a grievous sin to have such an office in the church.
> As well might you add to the teachings of Christ—
> circumcision—offering up the sacrifice of animals—or break the
> ordinances of Christ in any other way by going back to the old
> law of Moses (*Ibid.*, pp.62-63).

> In Kirtland, Ohio, in June, 1831, . . . the first High Priests were
> ordained. . . . When they were ordained, right there at the time,
> the devil caught and bound Harvey Whitlock so he could not
> speak, his face twisted into demon-like shape. Also John Mur-

dock and others were caught by the devil in a similar manner. Now brethren, do you not see that the displeasure of the Lord was upon their proceedings, in ordaining High Priests? Of course it was (*Ibid.*, pp.64-65).

Hiram Page, one of the eight witnesses to the *Book of Mormon*, also said that "the office of High Priest does *not* belong to the church of Christ under the gospel dispensation" (*The Olive Branch*, Springfield, Ill., August 1849, p.28).

Without their alleged priesthood, the Mormon's claim of authority vanishes.

In this chapter we have covered some of the problems one encounters when studying the Mormon priesthood. There are many other problems and inconsistencies which we cannot cover for lack of space, but we highly recommend LaMar Petersen's *Problems in Mormon Text* to those interested in pursuing the matter further. Hal Hougey's *Latter-Day Saints – Where Did You Get Your Authority?* and *The Bible and Mormon Doctrine* by Sandra Tanner contain important information on this subject.

JOSEPH SMITH

Chapter 17

The importance of Joseph Smith in Mormon theology cannot be overemphasized. Brigham Young, the church's second president, boasted:

> Well, now, examine the character *of the Savior*, and examine the characters of those who have written the Old and New Testament; and then *compare them with the character of Joseph Smith*, the founder of this work . . . and you will find that *his character stands as fair as that of any man's mentioned* in the Bible. We can find *no person* who presents a better character to the world when the facts are known *than Joseph Smith, Jun.*, the prophet, and his brother, Hyrum Smith, who was murdered with him (*Journal of Discourses*, vol. 14, p.203).

> . . . no man or woman in this dispensation will ever enter into the celestial kingdom of God *without the consent of Joseph Smith*. . . . Every man and woman must have the certificate of Joseph Smith, junior, as a passport to their entrance into the mansion where God and Christ are . . . I cannot go there without his consent. . . . He reigns there as *supreme a being* in his sphere, capacity, and calling, *as God does in heaven* (vol. 7, p.289).

> . . . I am *an Apostle of Joseph Smith*. . . . all who reject my testimony will go to hell, so sure as there is one, no matter whether it be hot or cold . . . (vol. 3, p.212).

> I will now give my scripture—"*Whosoever confesseth that Joseph Smith was sent of God . . . that spirit is of God*; and every spirit that does not confess that God has sent Joseph Smith, and revealed the everlasting Gospel to and through him, is *of Antichrist* . . . (vol. 8, p.176).

Heber C. Kimball, a member of the first Presidency under Brigham Young, said that the time would come when people would "prize brother Joseph Smith as the Prophet of the Living God, and look upon him as a God, and also upon Brigham Young, our Governor in the Territory of Deseret" (*Journal of Discourses*, vol. 5, p.88).

and be prepared to receive glory, immortality, and eternal life, that when they go into the spirit-world, their work will far surpass that of any other man or being that has not been blessed with the keys of the Priesthood here.

Joseph Smith holds the keys of this last dispensation, and is now engaged behind the vail in the great work of the last days. I can tell our beloved brother Christians who have slain the Prophets and butchered and otherwise caused the death of thousands of Latter-day Saints, the priests who have thanked God in their prayers and thanksgiving from the pulpit that we have been plundered, driven, and slain, and the deacons under the pulpit, and their brethren and sisters in their closets, who have thanked God, thinking that the Latter-day Saints were wasted away, something that no doubt will mortify them— something that, to say the least, is a matter of deep regret to them—namely, that no man or woman in this dispensation will ever enter into the celestial kingdom of God without the consent of Joseph Smith. From the day that the Priesthood was taken from the earth to the winding-up scene of all things, every man and woman must have the certificate of Joseph Smith, junior, as a passport to their entrance into the mansion where God and Christ are—I with you and you with me. I cannot go there without his consent. He holds the keys of that kingdom for the last dispensation— the keys to rule in the spirit-world; and he rules there triumphantly, for he gained full power and a glorious victory over the power of Satan while he was yet in the flesh, and was a martyr to his religion and to the name of Christ, which gives him a most perfect victory in the spirit-world. He reigns there as supreme a being in his sphere, capacity, and calling, as God does in heaven. Many will ex-

claim—"Oh, that is very disagreeable! It is preposterous! We cannot bear the thought!" But it is true.

I will now tell you something that ought to comfort every man and woman on the face of the earth. Joseph Smith, junior, will again be on this earth dictating plans and calling forth his brethren to be baptized for the very characters who wish this was not so, in order to bring them into a kingdom to enjoy, perhaps, the presence of angels or the spirits of good men, if they cannot endure the presence of the Father and the Son; and he will never cease his operations, under the directions of the Son of God, until the last ones of the children of men are saved that can be, from Adam till now.

Should not this thought comfort all people? They will, by-and-by, be a thousand times more thankful for such a man as Joseph Smith, junior, than it is possible for them to be for any earthly good whatever. It is his mission to see that all the children of men in this last dispensation are saved, that can be, through the redemption. You will be thankful, every one of you, that Joseph Smith, junior, was ordained to this great calling before the worlds were. I told you that the doctrine of election and reprobation is a true doctrine. It was decreed in the counsels of eternity, long before the foundations of the earth were laid, that he should be the man, in the last dispensation of this world, to bring forth the word of God to the people, and receive the fulness of the keys and power of the Priesthood of the Son of God. The Lord had his eye upon him, and upon his father, and upon his father's father, and upon their progenitors clear back to Abraham, and from Abraham to the flood, from the flood to Enoch, and from Enoch to Adam. He has watched that family and that blood as it has circulated from its fountain to the

A photograph of the *Journal of Discourses*, vol. 7, page 289. Brigham Young claimed that no one would enter the celestial kingdom without the consent of Joseph Smith.

In the Bible we read that when Stephen was stoned, he died "calling upon God, and saying, Lord Jesus, receive my spirit" (Acts 7:59). When Brigham Young died, however, his last words which were distinctly understood were: "Joseph, Joseph, Joseph!" (*A Comprehensive History of the Church*, vol. 5, p.509).

Mormons tend to elevate Joseph Smith almost to the same level as Jesus Christ. Mormon writer John J. Stewart surmised that Joseph Smith was "perhaps the most Christ-like man to live upon the earth since Jesus himself" (*Joseph Smith—The Mormon Prophet*, p.1). It is interesting, however, to compare this with a statement attributed to Joseph Smith in the *History of the Church*, volume 5, page 335: "I am not so much a 'Christian' as many suppose I am. When a man undertakes to ride me for a horse, I feel disposed to kick up and throw him off, and ride him."

The following appeared in *Tiffany's Monthly* in 1859, p.170:

> People sometimes wonder that the Mormon can revere Joseph Smith. That they can by any means make a Saint of him. But they must remember, that the Joseph Smith preached in England, and the one shot at Carthage, Ill., are not the same. The ideal prophet differs widely from the real person. To one, ignorant of his character, he may be idealized and be made the impersonation of every virtue. He may be associated in the mind with all that is pure, true, lovely and divine. Art may make him, indeed, an object of religious veneration. But remember, the Joseph Smith thus venerated, is not the real, actual Joseph Smith. . .but one that art has created.

A Fighting Prophet

Joseph Smith was a man of great physical strength. He enjoyed wrestling and other sports where he could display his strength. Under the date of March 11, 1843, we find this entry in the *History of the Church*, (vol. 5, p.302). "In the evening, when pulling sticks, I pulled up Justus A. Morse, *the strongest man* in Ramus, *with one hand*." Two days later we find this statement: "Monday, 13.—I wrestled with William Wall, *the most expert wrestler in Ramus*, and threw him" (p.302). On June 30, 1843, Joseph Smith gave a speech in Nauvoo in which he was supposed to have stated: "I feel as strong as a giant. I pulled sticks with the men coming along, and I pulled up *with one hand the strongest man that could be found.* Then two men tried, but they could not pull me up . . ." (p.466).

Mrs. Mary Ettie V. Smith reports in her book *Mormonism: Its Rise, Progress, And Present Condition*: "It appears the Prophet Joseph had one day broken the leg of my brother Howard, while wrestling . . . by an unlucky pass, Howard fell with a broken leg. It was immediately set by the 'Prophet,' . . . Howard to this day claims he experienced no pain of any amount, and believes yet that Joseph healed it" (p.52).

John D. Lee related that one day Joseph Smith and some of his men were wrestling. Because it was "the Sabbath day" Sidney Rigdon tried to break it up. Joseph Smith "dragged him from the ring, bareheaded, and tore Rigdon's fine pulpit coat from the collar to the waist; then he turned to the men and said: 'Go in, boys, and have your fun" (*Confessions of John D. Lee,* pp.76-78).

Jedediah M. Grant, a member of the First Presidency under Brigham Young, recounted a humorous incident:

> I am aware that a great many have so much piety in them, that they are like the Baptist priest who came to see Joseph Smith. . . . and folding his arms said, "Is it possible that I now flash my optics upon a man who has conversed with my Savior?" "Yes," says the Prophet, "I don't know but you do; *would not you like to wrestle with me?*" That, you see, brought the priest right on to the thrashing floor, and he turned a summerset right straight. After he had whirled round a few times, like a duck shot in the head, he concluded that his piety had been awfully shocked, even to the centre, and went to the Prophet to learn why he had so shocked his piety (*Journal of Discourses,* vol. 3, pp.66-67).

Benjamin F. Johnson recalled how Joseph Smith sometimes lost his temper and resorted to physical violence:

> And yet, although so social and even convival [sic] at times, he would allow no arrogance or undue liberties. Criticisms, even by his associates, were rarely acceptable. Contradictions would arouse in him the lion at once. By no one of his fellows would he be superceded. In the early days at Kirtland, and elsewhere, one or another of his associates were more than once, for their impudence, helped from the congregation *by his foot.* . . . He soundly *thrashed his brother* William. . . . While with him in such fraternal, social and sometimes convivial moods, we could not then so fully realize the greatness and majesty of his calling. But since his martyrdom, it has continued to magnify in our view as the glories of this last dispensation have more fully unfolded to our comprehension (Letter by Benjamin F. Johnson, 1903, as printed in *Testimony of Joseph Smith's Best Friend,* pp.4-5).

Calvin Stoddard once testified that "Smith then came up and *knocked him in the forehead* with his flat hand—the blow knocked him down, when *Smith repeated the blow four or five times, very hard*—made him blind—that Smith afterwards came to him and asked his forgiveness . . ." (*Conflict at Kirtland,* p.132).

Mormon writer Max Parkin quotes Luke Johnson as saying that when a minister insulted Joseph Smith at Kirtland, Ohio, Smith "boxed his ears with both hands, and turning his face towards the door, *kicked him into the street* . . ." (*Ibid.*, p.268).

In Joseph Smith's history for the year 1843, we read of two fights which he had in Nauvoo: "Josiah Butterfield came to my house and insulted me so outrageously that I *kicked him* out of the house, across the yard, and into the street" (*History of the Church*, vol. 5, p.316).

"Bagby called me a liar, and picked up a stone to throw at me, which so enraged me that I followed him a few steps, and *struck him two or three times*. Esquire Daniel H. Wells stepped between us . . . I told the Esquire to assess the fine for the assault, and I was willing to pay it. He not doing it, I rode down to Alderman Whitney, stated the circumstances, and he imposed a fine which I paid . . ." (*Ibid.*, p.524).

According to the *History of the Church*, Joseph Smith admitted that he had tried to choke Walter Bagby: "I met him, and he gave me some abusive language, taking up a stone to throw at me: *I seized him by the throat to choke him off*" (*Ibid.*, p.531).

The reader will remember also that some material appears in Joseph Smith's diary that has been suppressed in the *History of the Church*. Under the dates January 1 and 2, 1843, Joseph Smith related that he had "whipped" seven men at once and on another occasion had "whipped" a Baptist minister "till he begged."

Brigham Young once made this evaluation of Joseph Smith: "Some may think that I am rather too severe; but if you had the Prophet Joseph to deal with, you would think that I am quite mild. . . . He would not bear the usage I have borne, and would appear as though he would tear down all the houses in the city, and tear up trees by the roots, if men conducted to him in the way they have to me" (*Journal of Discourses*, vol. 8, pp.317-18).

General Smith

Joseph Smith's interest in military matters is reflected in the *Book of Mormon*, for it is filled with accounts of wars and bloodshed. Dr. Hugh Nibley claims there are "170 pages of wars and alarms" in the *Book of Mormon*.

Only four years after Joseph Smith published the *Book of Mormon*, he organized an army and marched "to Missouri to 'redeem Zion.' " This project was a complete failure (see *Mormonism — Shadow or Reality?* pp.192-93). In 1838 Smith had the Mormons organized into an army at Far West, Missouri, but he ended up surrendering to the militia.

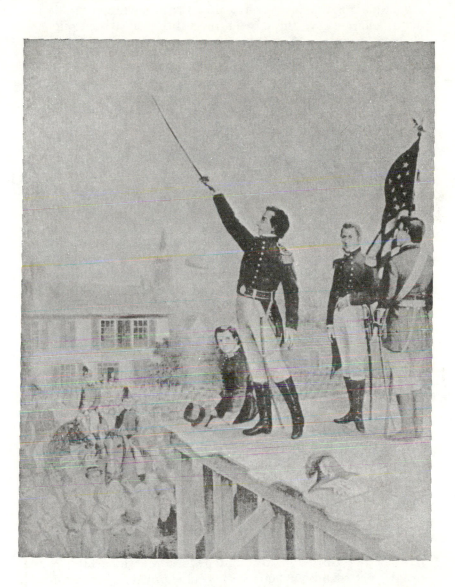

A drawing of "Lieutenant-General Joseph Smith" with sword drawn.

At Nauvoo, Illinois, the Mormons organized the Nauvoo Legion. Robert Bruce Flanders explains: "The crowning provision of the charter gave the city its own little army, the famous Nauvoo Legion. . . . The Legion was therefore independent of and not subject to the military laws of Illinois" *(Nauvoo: Kingdom On The Mississippi,* p.100).

> ". . . Colonel," "Captain," or "General" came to replace "Brother," "Elder," or "President" in the address of the Saints. Military trappings were for them a particular symbol of status, prestige, and reassurance. . . . The record clearly reveals that Lieutenant General (he preferred the full title) Smith set great store by his military role. . . .
>
> As the city grew, so did the Legion, exciting apprehension among gentiles in the vicinity concerning the nature and intent of the Mormon kingdom *(Ibid.,* pp.112-13).

Mormon writer Hyrum L. Andrus recorded: "Of the Prophet's appearance as a Lieutenant General at the head of the Nauvoo Legion, Lyman L. Woods recalled, 'I have seen him on a white horse wearing the uniform of a general. . . . He was leading a parade of the Legion and *looked like a god*' " *(Joseph Smith, The Man And The Seer,* p.5).

Joseph Smith was very proud of his position as head of the Nauvoo Legion and liked to be referred to as "Lieutenant-General Joseph Smith" (see *History of the Church,* vol. 4, p.382). Actually, this title did not amount to anything outside of Nauvoo.

Joseph Smith seems to have loved military displays. Under the date of May 7, 1842, we find this statement in the *History of the Church*: "The Nauvoo Legion . . . was reviewed by Lieutenant-General Joseph Smith, who commanded through the day. . . . At the close of the parade, Lieutenant-General Joseph Smith . . . remarked 'that his soul was never better satisfied than on this occasion' " (vol.5, p.3).

Joseph Smith seems to have desired to lead a large army, for he prepared a "Petition to the Senate and House of Representatives of the United States, dated 26th March, asking the privilege of raising 100,000 men to extend protection to persons wishing to settle Oregon and other portions of the territory of the United States, and extend protection to the people in Texas" *(History of the Church,* vol. 6, p.282). In this document we read:

> Section 1. Be it ordained . . . that Joseph Smith, . . . is hereby authorized and empowered to raise a company of one hundred thousand armed volunteers . . .
>
> Sec. 2. And be it further ordained that if any person or persons

454

shall hinder or attempt to hinder or molest the said Joseph Smith from executing his designs in raising said volunteers, . . . he, or they so hindering molesting, or offending, shall be punished by a fine not exceeding one thousand dollars . . . or by hard labor on some public work not exceeding two years, or both, . . .

See. [sic] 3. And be it further ordained, . . . the said Joseph Smith is hereby constituted a member of the army of these United States, . . . (*History of the Church*, vol. 6, p.277).

There was, of course, hardly any chance that Joseph Smith's petition would be accepted. On April 25, 1844, Orson Hyde wrote a letter from Washington in which he stated: "Mr. Semple said that Mr. Smith could not constitutionally be constituted a member of the army by law; and this, if nothing else, would prevent its passage" (*Ibid.*, vol. 6, p.372).

Joseph Smith's military plans and maneuvers were very disturbing to the non-Mormons who lived around Nauvoo. On July 21, 1841, the anti-Mormon paper, *Warsaw Signal* reported: "How military these people are becoming! Everything they say or do seems to breathe the spirit of military tactics. Their prophet appears, on all occasions, in his sp[l]endid regimental dress   signs his name Lieut. General, and more titles are to be found in the Nauvoo Legion, than any one book on military tactics can produce; . . . Truly fighting must, be a part of the creed of these Saints!"

Joseph Smith seems to have envisioned himself as a great military leader. The reader may remember the dream and interpretation in Joseph Smith's diary which indicated that the U.S. government would plead with Smith for his help against a foreign foe.

"The Greatest Egotist"

In 1843 Charlotte Haven wrote some letters from Nauvoo which contain some candid observations about Joseph Smith:

Joseph Smith . . . is evidently a great egotist and boaster, for he frequently remarked that at every place he stopped going to and from Springfield people crowded around him, and expressed surprise that he was so "handsome and good looking" (*Overland Monthly*, December 1890, p.621).

He talked incessantly about himself, what he had done and could do more than other mortals, and remarked that he was "a giant, physically and mentally." In fact, he seemed to forget that he was a man. . . . They say he is very kindhearted, and always ready to give shelter and help to the needy (p.623).

I rushed out with the umbrella to shield Mrs. Smith, the others followed, . . . Mrs. Smith was pleasant and social, more so than we had ever seen her before, . . . while her husband is the greatest egotist I ever met (p.631).

Josiah Quincy related: "In a tone half-way between jest and earnest, and which might have been taken for either at the option of the hearer, the prophet put this inquiry: 'Is not here one greater than Solomon, who built a Temple with the treasures of his father David and with the assistance of Huram [*sic*], King of Tyre? Joseph Smith has built his Temple with no one to aid him in the work' " (*Figures of the Past*, as cited in *Among the Mormons*, p.138).

A reporter who visited Joseph Smith wrote in 1843:

> We spent about an hour conversing on various subjects, the prophet himself, with amazing volubility, occupying the most of the time, and his whole theme was himself. Let us give what turn we would to the conversation, he would adroitly bring it back to himself. . . . he said: 'The world persecutes me, it has always persecuted me. . . . When I have proved that I am right, and get all the world subdued under me. I think I shall deserve something (*The New York Spectator*, September 23, 1843).

Smith Ordained King

Toward the end of his life Joseph Smith seems to have become obsessed with a desire for power and fame. He set up a secret "Council of Fifty" and had himself ordained to be a king. In 1853 William Marks, who had been a member of the Council of Fifty, revealed: "I was also witness of the introduction (secretly,) of a kingly form of government, in which *Joseph suffered himself to be ordained a king*, to reign over the house of Israel forever; which I could not conceive to be in accordance with the laws of the church, but I did not oppose this move, thinking it none of my business" (*Zion's Harbinger and Baneemy's Organ*, St. Louis, July, 1853, p.53).

In his master's thesis, Klaus J. Hansen tells that George Miller, who had been a member of the Council of Fifty, admitted that Joseph Smith was ordained to be a king: "Rumors implying that the Prophet assumed royal pretensions are somewhat substantiated by George Miller who stated on one occasion that 'In this council *we ordained Joseph Smith as King on earth*' " ("The Theory and Practice of the Political Kingdom of God in Mormon History, 1829-1890," master's thesis, BYU, 1959, typed copy, p.114).

In *Dialogue: A Journal of Mormon Thought*, Summer 1966, page 104, Mr. Hansen frankly admitted that "Joseph Smith did start a political kingdom of God and a Council of Fifty; he was made king over that organization. . . ."

When Fawn Brodie stated that Joseph Smith was anointed king, Dr. Nibley claimed that there was not enough evidence to support this accusation. Since that time a great deal of new evidence has come to light, and now many Mormon scholars are willing to concede that Joseph Smith was made king. For instance, Kenneth W. Godfrey, who was director of the LDS Institute at Stanford University, admitted that Joseph Smith was "ordained 'King over the Immediate House of Isreal' by the Council of Fifty" (*Brigham Young University Studies*, Winter 1968, pp.212-13). Among other things, Dr. Godfrey's footnote refers us to the "Diary of George A. Smith, May 9, 1844," which is in the "Library of the Church Historian." In a dissertation written at Brigham Young University, Dr. Godfrey observed:

> Davidson states that Joseph Smith had himself annointed King and Priest . . . in a revelation dated 1886 given to President John Taylor, mention is made of Joseph Smith being crowned a king in Nauvoo. Not only was he ordained a king but the leading members of the Church were assigned governmental responsibilities. Brigham Young was to be president, John Taylor vice president, members of the Church were assigned to represent different states in the house and senate of the United States, and a full cabinet was appointed ("Causes of Mormon Non-Mormon Conflict in Hancock County, Illinois, 1839-1846," Ph.D. dissertation, BYU, 1967, pp.63-65).

Joseph Smith for President

In 1844 the Council of Fifty decided to run Joseph Smith for the presidency of the United States. Klaus J. Hansen said that "the Council of Fifty, while seriously contemplating the possibility of emigration, also considered a rather spectacular alternative, namely, to run its leader for the presidency of the United States in the campaign of 1844. . . . Smith and the Council of Fifty seems to have taken the election quite seriously, much more so, indeed, than both Mormons and anti-Mormons have heretofore suspected" (*Quest for Empire*, p.74).

The elders of the church were actually called to electioneer for Joseph Smith. At a special meeting of the elders on April 9, 1844, Brigham Young declared: "It is now time to have a President of the United States. Elders will be sent to preach the Gospel and electioneer" (*History of the Church*, vol. 6, p.322). At the same meeting Heber C. Kimball affirmed: ". . . we design to send Elders to all the different States to get up meetings and protracted meetings, and electioneer for Joseph to be the next

President" (*Ibid.*, p.325). Mormon writer John J. Stewart refers to those who were sent to campaign as a "vast force of political missionaries" (*Joseph Smith the Mormon Prophet*, p.209).

Under the date of January 29, 1844, this statement is attributed to Joseph Smith in the *History of the Church*, "If you attempt to accomplish this, you must send every man in the city who is able to speak in public throughout the land to electioneer. . . . There is oratory enough in the Church to carry me into the presidential chair the first slide" (vol. 6, p.188).

On March 7, 1844, Joseph Smith was reported to have said: "When I get hold of the Eastern papers, and see how popular I am, I am afraid myself that I shall be elected . . ." (*History of the Church*, vol. 6, p.243).

The fact that Joseph Smith would allow himself to be crowned king shows that he was driven by the idea of gaining power. It is very possible that Smith seriously believed that he would become president and that he would rule as king over the people of the United States. The attempt by Joseph Smith to become president seems to have been a treasonous plot to bring the United States Government under the rule of the priesthood. Klaus J. Hansen observed: "But what if, through a bold stroke, he could capture the United States for the Kingdom? The Council of Fifty thought there might be a chance and nominated the Mormon prophet for the Presidency of the United States" (*Dialogue: A Journal of Mormon Thought*, Autumn 1966, p.67).

George Miller, who had been a member of the Council of Fifty, recorded in a letter dated June 28, 1855:

> It was further determined in Council that all the elders should set out on missions to all the States to get up an electorial [sic] ticket, and do everything in our power to have Joseph elected president. If we succeeded in making a majority of the voters converts to our faith, and elected Joseph president, in such an event the dominion of the Kingdom would be forever established in the United States; and if not successful, we could fall back on Texas, and be a kingdom notwithstanding (Letter by George Miller, as quoted in *Joseph Smith and World Government*, by Hyrum Andrus, 1963, p.54).

Instead of going to Texas the Mormons settled in the Great Salt Lake valley. Hyrum Andrus admits that Smith had even "considered the alternative of establishing the Saints in the capacity of an independent nation, should all other alternatives fail" (*Ibid.*, p.60).

Before the election Joseph Smith was assassinated. Thus he was unable to establish the kingdom he had planned.

of Adam. A large majority of the whole have stood by me. Neither Paul, John, Peter, nor Jesus ever did it. I boast that no man ever did such a work as I. The followers of Jesus ran away from Him; but the Latter-day Saints never ran away from me yet. You know my daily walk and conversation. I am in the bosom of a virtuous and good people. How I do love to hear the wolves howl! When they can get rid of me, the devil will also go. For the last three years I have a record of all my acts and proceedings, for I have kept several good, faithful, and efficient clerks in constant employ: they have accompanied me everywhere, and carefully kept my history, and they have written down what I have done, where I have been, and what I have said; therefore my enemies cannot charge me with any day, time, or place, but what I have written testimony to prove my actions; and my enemies cannot prove anything against me. They have got wonderful things in the land of Ham. I think the grand jury have strained at a gnat and swallowed the camel.

A man named Simpson says I made an affidavit against him, &c. Mr. Simpson says I arrested him. I never arrested Mr. Simpson in my life. He says I made an affidavit against him. I never made an affidavit against him in my life. I will prove it in court. I will tell you how it was: Last winter I got ready with my children to go to the farm to kill hogs. Orrin P. Rockwell was going to drive. An Englishman came in and wanted a private conversation with me. I told him I did not want any private conversations. "I demand one of you!" Such a one I am bound to obey anyhow. Said he—"I want a warrant against the man who stabbed Brother Badham. He said it was a man who boarded at Davis'. He said it was Mr. Simpson—it answered his description. I said I had no jurisdiction out of the city. He said—"The man must be arrested, or else he will go away." I told him—"You must go to Squire Wells, Johnson, or Foster." Mr. Lytle stepped up and said—"I am a policeman." I jumped into my carriage, and away I went.

When I came back I met Mr. Jackson. He said—"You did wrong in arresting Mr. Simpson." I told him I did not do it. I went over and sat down, and related the circumstances. He turned round and said—"Mr. Smith, I have nothing against you; I am satisfied." He went and supped with me. He declared in the presence of witnesses, that he had nothing against me. I then said—"I will go over to Esquire Johnson, and testify what the Englishman told me." I told him not to make out that I believe he is the man, but that I believe he is innocent. I don't want to swear that he is the man. Messrs. Coolidge, Rockwell, Hatfield, and Hawes were present.

Mr. Johnson made one [a complaint] out in due form: and as I sat down in a bustle the same as I do when one of the clerks brings a deed for

A photograph of the *History of the Church*, vol. 6, page 409. Joseph Smith boasted that "no man ever did such a work as I."

Greater than Jesus?

The *History of the Church* contains some statements which show that Joseph Smith felt he was almost equal with God:

> I am a lawyer; I am a big lawyer and comprehend heaven, earth and hell, to bring forth knowledge that shall cover up all lawyers, doctors and other big bodies (vol. 5, p.289).

> Don't employ lawyers, or pay them for their knowledge, for I have learned that they don't know anything. I know more than they all (vol. 5, p.467).

> I combat the errors of ages; I meet the violence of mobs; I cope with illegal proceedings from executive authority; I cut the gordian knot of powers, and I solve mathematical problems of universities, with truth-diamond truth; and God is my "right hand man" (vol. 6, p.78).

> If they want a beardless boy to whip all the world, I will get on the top of a mountain and crow like a rooster: I shall always beat them. . . . *I have more to boast of than ever any man had.* I am the *only man* that has ever been able to keep *a whole church together* since the days of Adam. A large majority of the whole have stood by me. Neither Paul, John, Peter, nor *Jesus ever did it.* I boast that *no man ever did such a work as I. The followers of Jesus ran away from Him,* but the Latter-day Saints *never ran away from me yet* (vol. 6, pp.408-9).

Destruction of Expositor

One of the most important factors leading to Joseph Smith's death was his interference in politics. On July 15, 1842, this statement appeared in the *Sangamo Journal,* published at Springfield, Illinois: "We received the Mormons into this state as we did every other sect. Disclosures have shown that the head of that church acts not under the influence of that pure religion which Jesus Christ established upon the earth; and that his vaulting ambition would secure to himself the control of our State elections" (*Sangamo Journal,* July 15, 1842).

Thomas Ford, governor of Illinois from 1842-1846, similarly explained:

> But the great cause of popular fury was, that the Mormons at several preceding elections had cast their vote as a unit, thereby making the fact apparent that no one could aspire to the honors or offices of the country, within the sphere of their influence, without their approbation and votes. . . . It is indeed unfortunate for their peace that they do not divide in elections, according to their individual preferences or political principles, like other people.

This one principle and practice of theirs arrayed against them in deadly hostility all aspirants for office who were not sure of their support, all who have been unsuccessful in elections, and all who were too proud to court their influence, with all their friends and connections (*History of Illinois,* as quoted in *History of the Church,* vol. 7, pp.2-3).

Joseph Smith admitted that the Mormons were united in their politics but claimed they "were driven to union in their elections by persecution" (*History of the Church,* vol. 5, p.232). Although it is true that the Mormons were persecuted, evidence shows that much of this persecution was the result of Joseph Smith's intemperate speech and actions (see *Mormonism – Shadow or Reality?* p.256).

Anti-Mormons accused Joseph Smith and his brother Hyrum of mixing politics and revelation. That there was a great deal of truth to this charge is verified by the *History of the Church.* Under the date of August 6, 1843, these words are attributed to Joseph Smith: "Brother Hyrum tells me this morning that he has had a testimony to the effect it would be better for the people to vote for Hoge; and I never knew Hyrum to say he ever had a revelation and it failed. Let God speak and all men hold their peace" (*History of the Church,* vol. 5, p.526).

Mormon writer Kenneth W. Godfrey in discussing factors that stirred the conflict in Illinois wrote:

Antagonism toward the Mormon Prophet was further incited when it was correctly rumored, that he had been ordained 'King over the Immediate House of Israel' by the Council of Fifty. . . . newspapers and tracts repeatedly charged that the Prophet conducted himself like a dictator and that his actions were not only treasonable but a violation of the constitutional principle that church and state should be disassociated. Thus, his kingly ordination only incensed the populace, and his untimely death became even more inevitable.

The Prophet's mayoral order, with the consent of the city council, to destroy the *Nauvoo Expositor* became the immediate excuse to stamp out his life. . . .

Perhaps in retrospect both Mormons and Gentiles were partly to blame for conflict which developed between them (*Brigham Young University Studies,* Winter 1968, pp.212-14).

The *Nauvoo Expositor,* spoken of by Kenneth Godfrey, was to be printed in Nauvoo by a number of people who opposed Joseph Smith's political ambitions and the practice of polygamy. Mormon writer John J. Stewart summarized the problem: "They attempted to set up their own church with

William Law as President. They bought a press and published a newspaper entitled the *Nauvoo Expositor*, . . .Joseph Smith as mayor ordered the *Expositor* press destroyed" (*Brigham Young and His Wives*, p.34).

Mormon writers often refer to the *Nauvoo Expositor* as a scandalous and vile publication, but in reality it advocated high morals and obedience to the law. This newspaper was strongly opposed to Joseph Smith's "political schemes." The thing that really disturbed the Mormon leaders, however, was that the *Nauvoo Expositor* exposed Joseph Smith's secret teaching on polygamy. In an affidavit published in the *Nauvoo Expositor*, June 7, 1844, Austin Cowles charged:

> In the latter part of the summer, 1843, the Patriarch, Hyrum Smith, did in the High Council, of which I was a member, introduce what he said was a revelation given through the Prophet; . . . according to his reading there was contained the following doctrines; 1st, the sealing up of persons to eternal life, against all sins, save that of shedding innocent blood or of consenting thereto; 2nd, the doctrine of a plurality of wives, or marrying virgins; that "David and Solomon had many wives, yet in this they sinned not save in the matter of Uriah."

The Mormon leaders claimed that Austin Cowles had lied, but eight years after Joseph Smith's death they published the revelation on polygamy. This revelation proves beyond all doubt that the statements in the *Expositor* were true. Thus it is clear that the *Expositor* was condemned on the basis of false testimony given by Joseph Smith and his brother Hyrum.

In a synopsis of the proceedings of the Nauvoo City Council we find the following:

> Mayor [Joseph Smith] said, if he had a City Council who felt as he did, the establishment (referring to the Nauvoo Expositor) would be declared a nuisance before night. . . .

> Councilor Stiles said . . . he would go in for suppressing all further publications of the kind.

> Councilor Hyrum Smith believed the best way was to smash the press and pi the type (*History of the Church*, vol. 6, pp.441,445).

The Nauvoo City Council ordered the press to be destroyed. The following is recorded in Joseph Smith's history under the date of June 10, 1844: "The Council passed an ordinance declaring the *Nauvoo Expositor* a nuisance, and also issued an order to me to abate the said nuisance. I immediately ordered the Marshal to destroy it without delay. . . . About 8 p.m., the Marshal returned and reported that he had removed the press, type, printed paper, and fixtures into the street, and destroyed them" (*History of the Church*, vol. 6, p.432).

Mormon historian B. H. Roberts concedes concerning the destruction of the *Expositor* that, "the legality of the action of the Mayor and City Council was, of course, questionable, though some sought to defend it on legal grounds; but it must be conceded that neither proof nor argument for legality are convincing. On the grounds of expediency or necessity the action is more defensible" (*History of the Church*, vol. 6, p.xxxviii).

Mormon writer John J. Stewart reports that after the *Expositor* was destroyed, "The apostate publishers dashed away to Carthage, squealing like stuck pigs, and before Justice of the Peace Thomas Morrison, a notorious Mormon hater, sued out a writ for the arrest of Joseph and seventeen other Church and city officials, on a charge of riot" (*Joseph Smith the Mormon Prophet*, p.220).

Charles A. Foster, one of the publishers of the *Expositor*, wrote the following in a letter dated June 11, 1844:

> ...a company consisting of some 200 men, armed and equipped, with muskets, swords, pistols, bowie knives, sledge-hammers, &c, assisted by a crowd of several hundred minions, who volunteered their services on the occasion, marched to the building, and breaking open the doors with a sledge-hammer, commenced the work of destruction. . . .

> They tumbled the press and materials into the street, and set fire to them, and demolished the machinery with a sledge hammer, and injured the building very materially (*Warsaw Signal*, June 12, 1844).

Charles A. Foster's description of the destruction of the *Expositor* sounds more like a mob scene than a legal act. Vilate Kimball, the wife of Heber C. Kimball and a faithful Mormon, in her description wrote: "June 11th. Nauvoo was a scene of excit[e]ment last night. Some hundreds of the brethren turned out and *burned the press of the opposite party* (Letter by Vilate Kimball, as published in *Life of Heber C. Kimball*, p.350).

Mormon author William E. Berrett said:

> The destruction of the *Nauvoo Expositor* June 10, 1844, proved to be the spark which ignited all the smoldering fires of opposition into one great flame. It offered the occasion for which the apostates from the Church were waiting, a legal excuse to get the Prophet and other leaders into their hands. The cry that the "freedom of the press" was being violated, united the factions seeking the overthrow of the Saints as perhaps nothing else would have done (*The Restored Church*, p.255).

463

Like a Lamb?

Edward Bonney spoke of the excitement in his book, *Banditti of the Prairies*:

> This outrage upon the public press helped to fan the flame already kindled . . . and plainly foreshadowed the storm that was to burst with startling fury.
>
> The dissenting Mormons at once united with those opposed to that sect, and various meetings were called, and all parties urged to arm and prepare themselves to resist any further aggression: . . . Warrants were issued against the Smiths, and other leaders, in the destruction of the printing office of the *Expositor*, and though served by the proper officers, they refused to obey the mandates of the law, and laughed at its power!
>
> As in all former cases, the writ of habeas corpus was resorted to, and all the arrested at once set at liberty . . . defeating the ends of justice, and compelling the officer to return to Carthage without a single prisioner!
>
> This mock administration of law, added new fuel to the flame. The public . . . became enraged, and determined to rise in their might and enforce the law, even though it should be at the point of the bayonet or sabre. . . .
>
> The city of Nauvoo was declared under martial law, and all necessary preparations were made to sustain the edicts of the Prophet . . . Gov. Ford, instructing the officer having the writs from which the Mormons had discharged themselves, to proceed to Nauvoo and demand the surrender of the Smiths and others. . . .
>
> Morning came, and the hour of their departure arrived, but the Prophet could not be found, having crossed the Mississippi River during the night with his brother Hiram and secreted themselves in Iowa. . . .
>
> During the day, several dispatches crossed the river to and from the Prophet, some advising him to seek safety in flight, and others urging him to return and save the city. Thus urged, the Prophet and his companion in flight, recrossed the river about sunset, and on the following morning started for Carthage. . . .
>
> On arriving there, the prisoners were examined on the charge of riot in destroying the printing press, and held to bail for their appearance at the next term of the Hancock Circuit Court. Joseph and Hiram Smith were arrested on charge of treason, and committed to await examination.
>
> All being tranquil, and Governor Ford thinking an armed force no longer necessary, disbanded his troops on the morning of the

27th, leaving but a small force to guard the jail, and proceeded with his suite to Nauvoo. . . .

After the troops were disbanded, the most hostile of them believing the Smiths eventually would be acquitted on the charge of treason, . . . continued to fan the flame of revenge that had heretofore been burning but too brightly. Urged on by the Mormon dissenters, who were thirsting for blood, they collected, to the number of about 140, armed and disguised, and proceeded to the jail about five o'clock in the afternoon of the 27th. Having dispersed the guard, they attacked the jail, and Joseph and Hiram Smith in an effort to escape were both shot dead. Four balls pierced each of them, and any one of the wounds would have proved fatal. Having accomplished this cold-blooded murder (for surely no other name will apply to it) and glutted their appetite for blood, the mob instantly dispersed (*Banditti of the Prairies* [Norman, OK: University of Oklahoma Press, 1963] pp.20-24).

It is interesting to compare the death of Joseph Smith with that of Jesus. In Isaiah 53:7 we read: "He was oppressed, and he was afflicted, yet he opened not his mouth: he is brought as a lamb to the slaughter, and as a sheep before her shearers is dumb, so he openeth not his mouth." In the New Testament it is claimed that Christ fulfilled this prophecy (see Acts 8:32). He died without resistance. In 1 Peter 2:23 we read: "Who, when he was reviled, reviled not again; when he suffered, he threatened not; but committed himself to him that judgeth righteously."

When Peter tried to defend Jesus with the sword, Jesus told him to "put up thy sword into the sheath: the cup which my Father hath given me, shall I not drink it?" (John 18:11).

It is claimed that before Joseph Smith was murdered in the Carthage jail he stated: "I am going like a lamb to the slaughter" . . . (*Doctrine and Covenants*, 135:4).

Most Mormons believe that Joseph Smith died without putting up a struggle, but the actual truth is that he died in a gunfight. In the *History of the Church* the following account is given concerning Joseph Smith's death:

Immediately there was a little rustling at the outer door of the jail, and a cry of surrender, and also a discharge of three or four firearms followed instantly. . . . *Joseph* sprang to his coat for his *six-shooter*, Hyrum for his single barrel. . . .

When Hyrum fell, Joseph exclaimed, "Oh dear, brother Hyrum!" and opening the door a few inches he *discharged his six shooter* in the stairway (as stated before), two or three barrels of which missed fire.

Joseph, seeing there was no safety in the room, and no doubt

> thinking that it would save the lives of his brethren in the room
> if he could get out, turned calmly from the door, dropped *his
> pistol* on the floor, and sprang into the window . . . and he fell
> outward into the hands of his murderers . . . (*History of the
> Church*, vol. 6, pp.617-18).

In the introduction to volume 6 of the *History of the Church*,
page XLI, Joseph Smith is praised for his part in the gunfight: ".
. . the Prophet turned from the prostrate form of his murdered
brother to face death-dealing guns and bravely returned the fire
of his assailants, '*bringing his man down everytime*,' and com-
pelling even John Hay, who but reluctantly accords the Prophet
any quality of virtue, to confess that he 'made a handsome
fight.' . . ."

John Taylor, who became the third president of the church,
testified concerning the death of Joseph Smith:

> He, however, instantly arose, and with a firm, quick step, and a
> determined expression of countenance, approached the door,
> and pulling the six-shooter left by Brother Whellock from his
> pocket, opened the door slightly, and snapped the pistol six
> successive times; only three of the barrels, however, were dis-
> charged. I afterwards understood that two or three were
> wounded by these discharges, two of whom, I am informed died
> (*History of the Church*, vol. 7, pp.102-3).

From the preceding information it can be seen that the death
of Joseph Smith can in no way be compared to the death of
Jesus. Jesus did go like a "lamb to the slaughter," but Joseph
Smith died like a raging lion.

Today the Joseph Smith of Mormon adoration is a highly
romanticized version of the real Joseph Smith. While possessing natural abilities and talents, his personal character was far
from the saintly image his followers mold him into. His strong
egotism and drive for power, together with his deceptive practices led ultimately to his destruction.

THE WORD OF WISDOM

Chapter 18

On February 27, 1833, Joseph Smith gave the revelation known as the "Word of Wisdom" which appears as section 89 of the *Doctrine and Covenants*. In this revelation we read:

1. A Word of Wisdom, for the benefit of the council of high priests, assembled in Kirtland, and the church, and also the saints in Zion—

2. To be sent greeting; not by commandment or constraint, but by revelation and the word of wisdom, showing forth the order and will of God in the temporal salvation of all saints in the last days—

3. Given for a principle with promise, adapted to the capacity of the weak and the weakest of all saints, who are or can be called saints.

. . . . . .

5. That inasmuch as any man drinketh wine or strong drink among you, behold it is not good, neither meet in the sight of your Father, only in assembling yourselves together to offer up your sacraments before him.

. . . .

7. And, again, strong drinks are not for the belly, but for the washing of your bodies.

8. And again, tobacco is not for the body, neither for the belly, and is not good for man, but is an herb for bruises and all sick cattle, to be used with judgment and skill.

9. And again, hot drinks are not for the body or belly.

. . . .

12. Yea, flesh also of beasts and of the fowls of the air, I, the Lord, have ordained for the use of man with thanksgiving; nevertheless they are to be used sparingly;

13. And it is pleasing unto me that they should not be used, only in times of winter, or of cold, or famine.

....

(Doctrine and Covenants, 89).

Notice that the Word of Wisdom forbids the use of hot drinks, strong drinks, and tobacco. The Mormon church today interprets hot drinks to mean tea and coffee, although there is evidence that in the early history of the church all hot drinks were forbidden.

Although some portions of Joseph Smith's Word of Wisdom are stressed by the Mormon leaders, other portions are almost completely ignored. Mormon writer John J. Stewart observed: "The admonition to eat little meat is largely ignored, as are some other points of the revelation" (Joseph Smith the Mormon Prophet, p.90).

Origin of the Revelation

Brigham Young left us an interesting account concerning conditions that led to the giving of the Word of Wisdom:

> The first school of the prophets was held in a small room situated over the Prophet Joseph's kitchen. . . .When they assembled together in this room after breakfast, the first they did was to light their pipes, and, while smoking, talk about the great things of the kingdom, and spit all over the room, and as soon as the pipe was out of their mouths a large chew of tobacco would then be taken. Often when the Prophet entered the room to give the school instructions he would find himself in a cloud of tobacco smoke. This, and the complaints of his wife at having to clean so filthy a floor, made the Prophet think upon the matter, and he inquired of the Lord relating to the conduct of the Elders in using tobacco, and the revelation known as the Word of Wisdom was the result of his inquiry (Journal of Discourses, vol. 12, p.158).

It has been suggested that the temperance movement led to Joseph Smith's "Word of Wisdom." Leonard J. Arrington, who has since become church historian, provides this enlightening information:

> In recent years a number of scholars have contended that the revelation is an outgrowth of the temperance movement of the early nineteenth century. According to Dean D. McBrien, . . .the Word of Wisdom was a remarkable distillation of the prevailing thought of frontier America in the early 1830's. Each provision in the revelation, he claimed, pertained to an item which had formed the basis of widespread popular agitation in the early 1830's:

"A survey of the situation existing at Kirtland when the revelation came forth is a sufficient explanation for it. The temperance wave had for some time been engulfing the West. . . . In 1826 Marcus Morton had founded the American Temperance Society. . . . In June, 1830, the *Millenial Harbinger* quoted . . . an article from the *Philadelphia 'Journal of Health,'* . . . which article most strongly condemned the use of alcohol, tobacco, the eating intemperately of meats. . . . Temperance Societies were organized in great numbers during the early thirties, six thousand being formed in one year. . . . On October 6, 1830, the Kirtland Temperance Society was organized with two hundred thirty nine members. . . . This society at Kirtland was a most active one. . . . it revolutionized the social customs of the neighborhood."

McBrien then goes ahead to point out that the Temperance Society succeeded in eliminating a distillery in Kirtland on February 1, 1833, just twenty-seven days before the Latter-day Saint revelation counseling abstinence was announced, and that the distillery at Mentor, near Kirtland, was also closed at the same time (*Brigham Young University Studies*, Winter 1959, pp.39-40).

In his book *The Burned-Over District*, pages 211-12, Whitney R. Cross points out that "the temperance movement. . .began much earlier. . . . During the 1830's it attained national scope. . . . Further, if alcohol was evil because it frustrated the Lord's design for the human body, other drugs like tea, coffee, and tobacco must be equally wrong . . . Josiah Bissell, . . . had even before the 1831 revival 'got beyond Temperance to the Cold Water Society—no tea, coffee or any other slops.' "

Joseph's Example

The Word of Wisdom is considered to be one of the most important revelations in the Mormon church. A Mormon who continues to break the Word of Wisdom is considered to be weak in the faith. Breaking the Word of Wisdom is considered a sin which can bar a person from the Temple. Joseph Fielding Smith claimed that the habit of drinking tea can "bar" a person from the "celestial kingdom of God":

SALVATION AND A CUP OF TEA. . . . my brethren, if you drink coffee or tea, or take tobacco are you letting a cup of tea or a little tobacco stand in the road and bar you from the celestial kingdom of God, where you might otherwise have received a fulness of glory? . . . There is not anything that is little in this world in the aggregate. One cup of tea, then it is another cup of tea and another cup of tea, and when you get them all together, they are not so little (*Doctrines of Salvation*, vol. 2, p.16).

Mormon writer John J. Stewart claims that Joseph Smith "carefully observed the Word of Wisdom, and insisted upon its observance by other men in high Church positions . . ." (*Joseph Smith the Mormon Prophet*, p.90). Mr. Stewart also states that "no one can hold high office in the Church, on even the stake or ward level, nor participate in temple work, who is a known user of tea, coffee, liquor or tobacco."

Although most members of the church feel that Joseph Smith, the founder of the Mormon church, "carefully observed the Word of Wisdom," research reveals just the opposite. In fact, Joseph Smith, the man who introduced the temple ceremony into the Mormon church, would not be able to go through the Temple if he were living today because of his frequent use of alcoholic beverages.

Dr. Hugh Nibley wants to know where the evidence is that Joseph Smith drank. We would answer by saying that this evidence is found throughout Smith's own *History of the Church*. For example, under the date of May 2, 1843, the following statement is recorded in Joseph Smith's History: "Wednesday, 3.—Called at the office and *drank a glass of wine* with Sister Jenetta Richards, made by her mother in England, and reviewed a portion of the conference minutes" (*History of the Church*, vol. 5, p.380).

The following entries were made for January, 1836:

> We then partook of some refreshments, and our hearts were made glad with the fruit of the vine (*History of the Church*, vol. 2, p.369).

> Elders Orson Hyde, Luke S. Johnson, and Warren Parrish, then presented the Presidency with three servers of glasses filled with *wine* to bless. And it fell to my lot to attend to this duty, which I cheerfully discharged. It was then passed round in order, then the cake in the same order; and suffice it to say, our hearts were made glad while partaking of the bounty of earth which was presented, until we had taken our fill . . . (*History of the Church*, vol. 2, p.378).

Joseph continued to disobey the Word of Wisdom until the day of his death. The *History of the Church* records the following incident in Carthage jail: . . . "The guard wanted some wine. *Joseph* gave Dr. Richards two dollars to give the guard; . . . The guard immediately sent for a *bottle of wine, pipes,* and two small *papers of tobacco;* . . . Dr. Richards uncorked the bottle, and presented a *glass to Joseph,* who tasted, as brother Taylor and the doctor, and the bottle was then given to the guard, who turned to go out" (*History of the Church*, vol. 6, p.616).

We do not know how often Joseph Smith used tobacco, but we do know that at one time "he rode through the streets of Nauvoo smoking a cigar" ("Joseph Smith As An Administrator," M.A. thesis, Brigham Young University, May 1969, p.161).

As we have already shown, Mormon leaders have made three important changes concerning the Word of Wisdom in Joseph Smith's *History of the Church.*

In one instance, Joseph Smith asked "Brother Markam" to get "a pipe and some tobacco" for Apostle Willard Richards. These words have been replaced with the word "medicine" in recent printings of the *History of the Church.*

At another time Joseph Smith related that he gave some of the "brethren" a "couple of dollars, with directions to replenish" their supply of "whisky." In modern editions of the *History of the Church,* twenty-three words have been deleted from this reference to cover up the fact that Joseph Smith encouraged the "brethren" to disobey the Word of Wisdom.

In the third instance, Joseph Smith frankly admitted that he "drank a glass of beer at Moessers." These words have been omitted in recent printings of the *History of the Church.*

The reader may remember that there were two interesting entries in Joseph Smith's diary that were omitted when the *History of the Church* was compiled. In the first instance (March 11, 1843) Joseph Smith told of having "tea with his breakfast." When his wife asked him how he liked it, he replied that "if it was a little stronger he should like it better." In the second reference "Joseph prophesied in the name of the Lord that he would drink wine" with Orson Hyde "in the east" (Joseph Smith Diary, January 20, 1843).

Mormon apologist F. L. Stewart tries to defend Joseph Smith's practice of drinking wine: "The 'Word of Wisdom' actually states that wine should be taken 'only in assembling yourselves together, to offer up your sacraments before him.' . . . Since both weddings and baptisms were considered to be sacraments, Joseph was not breaching this revelation when he drank wine at weddings . . ." (*Exploding the Myth About Joseph Smith, The Mormon Prophet,* p.55). Mrs. Stewart goes on to point out that "this custom is no longer practiced at baptism and weddings, and water is now used in the place of wine for the sacrament of the Lord's Supper."

Mrs. Stewart's attempt to explain away Joseph Smith's disregard for the Word of Wisdom cannot be taken seriously. Joseph Smith's "glass of wine" with Jenetta Richards had nothing to do with a "sacrament," nor can his "beer at Moessers" be explained in this manner. When Joseph Smith and his friends drank wine in the jail at Carthage, it was certainly not taken as a sacrament. John Taylor made this point very clear in the *His-*

tory *of the Church:* "Sometime after dinner we sent for some wine. It has been reported by some that this was taken as a sacrament. *It was no such thing:* our spirits were generally dull and heavy, and it was sent for to revive us. . . . I believe we all drank of the wine . . ." (*History of the Church*, vol. 7, p.101).

It is interesting to note that Apostle John Taylor continued to use alcoholic beverages after Joseph Smith's death. Hosea Stout recorded the following in his diary on June 3, 1847: "While I was explaining this Prests O. Hyde, P. P. Pratt and John Taylor also came in. . . . Says I. 'I hope you will all conform to the rules of the police then.' 'Certainly' says Taylor 'Bring on the jug' says I at which they were presented with a *large jug of whiskey.* . . . they *all* paid due respect to the jug . . ." (*On The Mormon Frontier, The Diary of Hosea Stout;* vol. 1, p.259).

All of the early Mormon apostles seem to have used alcoholic beverages after the Word of Wisdom was given. This account of an incident in 1840 is found in Joseph Smith's *History of the Church,* (vol. 4, p.120): "April 17.—This day the twelve blessed and drank a bottle of wine at Penworthan, made by Mother Moon forty years before." Under the date of July 1, 1845, Hosea Stout recorded in his diary: "This day there was a grand concert . . . we had also the 12 and other authorities with us, and was also provided with as much beer, wine, cakes &c as we could eat and drink" (*On The Mormon Frontier, The Diary Of Hosea Stout,* vol. 1, p.50).

Since Joseph Smith and other Mormon leaders did not observe the Word of Wisdom, members of the church became confused over the matter. George A. Smith related: ". . . a certain family, . . . arrived in Kirtland, and the Prophet asked them to stop with him . . . Sister Emma, in the mean time, asked the old lady if she would have a cup of tea . . . or a cup of coffee. This whole family apostatized because they were invited to take a cup of tea or coffee, after the Word of Wisdom was given" (*Journal of Discourses*, vol. 2, p.214).

Because of the fact that Joseph Smith did not keep the Word of Wisdom, Almon W. Babbitt felt that he had a right to break it. On August 19, 1835, Mr. Babbitt was brought to trial, one of the charges being "that he was not keeping the Word of Wisdom." In hid own defence Babbitt "said that he had taken the liberty to break the Word of Wisdom, from the example of President Joseph Smith Jun., and others, but acknowledged that it was wrong . . ." (*History of the Church*, vol. 2, p.252).

Joseph Smith's Bar

In Nauvoo Joseph Smith sold liquor. The following ordinance

relating to this matter was passed in 1843, *Joseph Smith being mayor of Nauvoo at the time:*

Ordinance on the Personal Sale of Liquors.

Section 1. Be it ordained by the City Council of Nauvoo, that the Mayor of the city be and is hereby authorized *to sell or give spirits of any quantity* as he in his wisdom shall judge to be for the health and comfort or convenience of such travelers or other persons as shall visit his house from time to time.
Passed December 12, 1843.

Joseph Smith, Mayor.

Willard Richards, Recorder. (*History of the Church,* vol. 6, p.111).

Joseph Smith's own son related the following:

About 1842, a new and larger house was built for us . . . and a sign was put out giving it the dignified name of "The Nauvoo Mansion" . . . Mother was to be installed as landlady, and soon made a trip to Saint Louis. . . .

When she returned Mother found installed in the keeping-room of the hotel—that is to say, the main room where the guests assembled and where they were received upon arrival—*a bar,* with counter, shelves, bottles, glasses and other paraphernalia customary for a fully-equipped tavern bar, and Porter Rockwell in charge as tender.

She was very much surprised and disturbed over this arrangement. . . . "Joseph," she asked, "*What is the meaning of that bar in this house?* . . . How does it look," she asked, "for the spiritual head of a religious body to be keeping a hotel in which is a room fitted out as a liquor-selling establishment?"

He reminded her that all taverns had their bars at which liquor was sold or dispensed. . . .

Mother's reply came emphatically clear, though uttered quietly: "Well, Joseph, . . . I will take my children and go across to the old house and stay there, for I will not have them raised up under such conditions as this arrangement imposes upon us, nor have them mingle with the kind of men who frequent such a place. You are at liberty to make your choice; *either that bar goes out of the house,* or we will!"

It did not take Father long to make the choice, for he replied immediately, "Very well, Emma; I will have it removed at once"—and he did (*The Saints' Herald,* January 22, 1935, p.110).

Oliver Boardman Huntington recorded the following incident in his journal:

Robert Thompson was a faithful just clerk for Joseph Smith the Prophet in Nauvoo and had been in his office steady near or quite 2 years. Joseph said to brother Thompson one day. "Robert I want you to go and get on a buss [bust?] go and get drunk and have a good spree, If you don't you will die."

Robert did not do it. He was very pious exemplary man and never guilty of such an impropriety as he thought that to be. In less than 2 weeks he was dead and buried (Journal of Oliver B. Huntington, typed copy at Utah State Historical Society, vol. 2, p.166).

Brigham Young's Distillery

Brigham Young spoke a great deal about the Word of Wisdom, but he seemed to have a difficult struggle applying it to his own life. According to Hosea Stout's diary (*On The Mormon Frontier*, vol. 1, p.75). Brigham Young declared on September 27, 1845: ". . . I am and ever intend to be the Master of my passions . . . some may say that I am in the habits of *taking snuff and tea* yet I am no slave to these passions and can leave these off if they make my brother affronted. . . ." In 1854 Brigham Young drank coffee on a regular basis (see *Mormonism – Shadow or Reality?* p.408). On April 7, 1867, Brigham Young acknowledged in the Tabernacle that he had chewed tobacco for many years: ". . . it is not my privilege to drink liquor, neither is it my privilege to eat tobacco. Well, bro. Brigham, have you not done it? Yes, for many years, but I ceased its habitual practice. I used it for toothache; now I am free from that pain, and my mouth is never stained with tobacco" (*Journal of Discourses*, vol. 12, p.404).

On the way to Utah, Brigham Young counseled the Mormons to "make beer as a drink" (*John D. Lee*, p.116). Historian Hurbert Howe Bancroft says that "the first bar-room in S.L. City, and the only one for years, was in the Salt Lake House, owned by President Young and Feramorz Little" (*History of Utah*, p.540, footnote 44).

Stanley P. Hirshon writes:

> In Utah the church dominated the liquor trade. In 1856 Caleb Green freighted six tons of tobacco, rum, whiskey, brandy, tea, and coffee across the plains for Young, and two years later *The New York Times* reported that the "principal drinking-saloon and gambling-room are in Salt Lake House, a building under the control of the Church and the immediate superintendency of Heber C. Kimball." . . . Young tried his best to rid himself of rival brewers (*The Lion of the Lord*, p.285).

On June 7, 1863, Brigham Young acknowledged publicly that

he had built a distillery:

"When there was no whisky to be had here, and we needed it for rational purposes, I built a house to make it in. When the distillery was almost completed and in good working order, an army was heard of in our vicinity and I shut up the works; I did not make a gallon of whisky at my works, because it came here in great quantities, more than was needed" (*Journal of Discourses*, vol. 10, p.206).

Hubert Howe Bancroft records: "Peter K. Dotson, . . .came to Salt Lake City in 1851, and was first employed by Brigham as manager of a distillery, afterwards becoming express and mail agent" (*History of Utah*, p.573, footnote 2). Josiah F. Gibbs provided further information concerning Brigham Young's distillery:

> During forty years the Mormon prophets absolutely controlled the city council and police force of Salt Lake. . . .
>
> Instead, however, of bringing their unappealable dictum to bear on the side of temperance and decent morals, the Prophet Brigham became a distiller of whiskey and other intoxicants, and high priests were the wholesale and retail distributors. . . .
>
> On July 2, 1861, the special committee, to whom was referred the subject of the manufacture and sale of liquor, presented a report reading as follows:
>
> "To the Honorable Mayor of Salt Lake City: —
>
> "Your committee, to whom was referred the subject of the manufacture and sale of spirituous liquor, would report that they visited several distilleries in and near the city and would respectfully recommend that the City Council purchase or rent the distillery erected by Brigham Young near the Mouth of Parley's canyon, and put the same in immediate operation, employing such persons as shall be deemed necessary to manufacture a sufficient quantity to answer the public demand; controlling the sale of the same, and that the profits accruing therefrom be paid into the City Treasury.
>
> > (Signed)
> >
> > Alderman Clinton,
> >
> > Alderman Sheets,
> >
> > Councilman Felt"

(*Lights and Shadows of Mormonism*, 1909, pp.248-49).

On July 26, 1890, Judge Orlando W. Powers gave a speech in which he charged:

> It will please you to know that notwithstanding the fact that the

city had gone into the whisky business on its own hook, on August 19, 1862, it granted Brigham Young a license to distill peaches into brandy. August 11, 1865, Mr. Young and George Q. Cannon addressed the Council on the liquor question. Mr. Young said:

"This community needs vinegar and will require spirituous liquor for washing and for health, and it will be right and proper for the city to continue its sale as it has done and make a profit.

... Brigham Young kept an open account on the city books, and this account shows that from 1862 to 1872 there were 235 different charges for liquor purchased by him amounting in the aggregate to $9316.66, or an average of $846.97 per year. ...

"An examination of the official records of the United States shows that from 1862, when the tax on distilled spirits was first levied, until the coming of the Union Pacific railroad in 1869, which was the beginning of the Gentile era in Utah, thirty-seven distilleries existed in this Territory. ... These facts, taken from public records, dispose of the charge that the Gentiles invaded a temperance community" (*The Salt Lake Tribune*, July 14, 1908).

According to John D. Lee, Brigham Young kept a large supply of liquor. Under the date of May 14 [15th], 1867, Lee recorded in his journal: "About 5 P.M. Prest. B. Young & suite arrived ... On the following day I went to see him ... He had a decanter of splendid wine brought in of his own make & said, I want to treat Bro. Lee to as Good an article, I think, as can be bought in Dixie. The wine indeed was a Superiour article. He said that he had some 300 gallons & treated about 2000$ worth of liquers yearly & continued that we [he] wish[e]d that some one would take his wine at 5$ per gallon & sell it, where upon Pres. D. H. Wells said that he would take 200 gals. at 6$ a gallon &c." (*A Mormon Chronicle, The Diaries of John D. Lee*, vol. 2, pp.71-72).

Leonard J. Arrington, now church historian, observed concerning the Word of Wisdom:

The strong and increased emphasis on the Word of Wisdom which characterized the official Mormon attitude throughout the remainder of the century appears to have begun in 1867. ...

The explanation for these rules and the widespread resolves to obey the Word of Wisdom seems to lie in the conditions of the Mormon economy ... it was necessary for the Latter-day Saints to develop and maintain a self-sufficient economy in their Rocky Mountain retreat. ... There must be no waste of liquid assets on imported consumers' goods. ... Saints who used their cash to purchase imported Bull Durham, Battle-Axe plugs, tea, coffee, and similar "wasteful" (because not productive) products were taking an action which was opposed to the economic interests of the territory. In view of this situation, President Young came to be unalterably opposed to the expenditure of money by the Saints on imported tea, coffee, and tobacco. It was consistent with the economics of the time that he should have had no great objection to tobacco chewing if the tobacco was grown locally. It was also consistent that he should have successfully developed a locally-produced "Mormon" tea to take the place of the imported article (*Brigham Young University Studies*, Winter 1959, pp.43-44).

Dr. Arrington quotes Brigham Young as saying:

> I know of no better climate and soil than are here for the successful culture of tobacco. Instead of buying it in a foreign market and importing it over a thousand miles, why not raise it in our own country or do without it? . . .

> Tea is in great demand in Utah, and anything under that name sells readily at an extravagant price. . . . Tea can be produced in this Territory in sufficient quantities for home consumption, and if we raise it ourselves we know that we have the pure article. If we do not raise it, I would suggest that we do without it (*Ibid.*, p.45).

In his sermons Brigham Young occasionally discussed the idea of Mormons producing their own tea, coffee, tobacco and whiskey:

> You know that we all profess to believe the "Word of Wisdom." There has been a great deal said about it. . . . We as Latter-day Saints, care but little about tobacco: but as "Mormons" we use a great deal. . . . The traders and passing emigration have sold tons of tobacco, besides what is sold here regularly. I say that $60,000 annually is the smallest figure I can estimate the sales at. Tobacco can be raised here as well as it can be raised in any other place. It wants attention and care. If we use it, let us raise it here. I recommend for *some man to go to raising tobacco*. . . . go to and make a business of raising tobacco and stop sending money out of the territory for that article. . . . We annually expend only $60,000 to break the "Word of Wisdom," and we can save the money and still break it, if we will break it (*Journal of Discourses*, vol. 9, p.35).

> It is true that we do not raise our own tobacco: we might raise it if we would. We do not raise our tea; but we might raise it if we would, for tea-raising, this is as good a country as China; and the coffee bean can be raised a short distance south of us. . . . We can sustain ourselves; and as for such so-called luxuries as tea, coffee, tobacco and whiskey, we can produce them or do without them (*Ibid.*, vol. 11, pp.113-14).

Brigham Young also recommended that the Mormons make wine. Angus M. Woodbury stated: "A circular was sent out to the various orders of the stake by Brigham Young and George A. Smith suggesting policies of operation. In brief, it suggested that fruit be canned or dried fit for any market; that wine be made at [a] few places under expert direction for exportation; . . ." (*The Mormon United Order in Utah*, p.9).

Leonard J. Arrington informs us that Brigham Young wanted most of the wine to be sold to the gentiles:

> The attempts of the latter-day Saints in southern Utah and elsewhere to make wine are all illustrative of the dominating philosophy of economic self-sufficiency. One function of these enterprises, of course, was to provide wine for the sacrament of the Lord's Supper. . . . Wine was used in the sacrament of the church as late as 1897. A more important function of wine-making, however, was to provide much-needed income for the poverty-striken pioneers in Utah's Dixie. The intention was to sell most of the wine in mining communities in southern Utah and Nevada. Brigham Young instructed as follows: "First, by lightly pressing make *a white wine*. Then give a heavier pressing and make *a colored wine*. Then barrel up this wine, and if my counsel is taken, this wine will not be drunk here, but will be exported, and thus increase the fund." More of the Dixie wine was consumed in the Mormon settlements than church officials had hoped, however, and the enterprise was discontinued before 1900 (*Brigham Young University Studies*, Winter 1959, pp.46-47).

In his book *Desert Saints* (Chicago: University of Chicago Press, 1966. Copyright © 1942, 1966 by The University of Chicago. Quotations used by permission.), Nels Anderson discusses the problems resulting from the church's involvement in making wine:

> Wine-making was another Mormon enterprise that came to the same end as the cotton, iron, and silk missions. The St. George Tithing Office reported on March, 1887, a supply of 6,610 gallons of wine, valued at 50 cents per gallon. . . . The tithing office at St. George received wine of many grades. It met the problem by setting up standards. The tithing clerk issued these instructions on September 20, 1879:
>
> "In order to obtain a more uniform grade of wine than we are able to obtain by mixing together the tithes of small pressings in the hands of sundry individuals; it is suggested that those having but small quantities of grapes to make up into wine, deliver their tithes in grapes at this office. . . ."

478   Thus *the church found itself the chief single producer of wine* in

the Dixie area. . . . Because the tithing offices held the largest amount of wine for the market at any time, it was in a position to name the price. Church interest is evidenced in a letter sent by the St. George Tithing Office August 12, 1880. This letter was a bill sent to the managers in charge of building the Manti Temple, to whom had been sent a quantity of wine—4 barrels, or 158 gallons. It was not sold, but tithing credit was asked as follows: $187.50 for the wine; $20.00 for the barrels; for hauling the wine to Manti, $16.00; total $233.50. This was given in pay to the builders of the temple.

In 1889 Edward H. Snow, clerk of the St. George Tithing Office, wrote the presiding bishop at Salt Lake City regarding wine: "Our sales during the year do not amount to half of what we are obliged to make up from the grapes that are brought in. . . . We have made at this office alone over 600 gallons this year. We cannot refuse the grapes or the wine, and I see no way to get rid of it." Snow wanted the presiding bishop to take the surplus. Later the tithing office sent men with loads of wine to the northern settlements, where they traded Dixie's liquid wealth for wheat and flour or took it to the mining camps. . . .

Dixie brethren did not follow Brother Brigham's counsel. They drank so much of the wine that *by 1890 drunkenness* was a worry to the church leaders. The tithing office discontinued accepting wine for tithes and abandoned its own presses (pp.373-74).

Since the St. George Tithing Office, as a practical measure, had originally joined with the farmers in making wine, the church authorities were much embarrassed in pushing their drive against wine-drinkers. About 1887 the tithing office discontinued making wine. The passing of Silver Reef as a market left the producers with quantities of wine on hand. The tithing office managed, as well as it could, to get rid of the more than six thousand gallons on hand.

From the moral angle, church leaders were forced to recognize that their people could not be makers of liquor without being drinkers of it, too. There were too many drinkers of wine and too few moderate drinkers among them (p.436).

Wine and Visions

One anti-Mormon writer claimed that the witnesses to the *Book of Mormon* were drunk at the time they received their vision concerning the plates. We have been unable to find any evidence to support this accusation. There is, however, evidence to show that wine was used to excess in the Kirtland Temple at the very time the Mormons were claiming to receive important revelations. William Harris made this report in 1841:

In the evening, they met for the endowment. The fast was then broken by eating light wheat bread, and drinking as much wine as they saw proper. Smith knew well how to infuse the spirit which they expected to receive; so he encouraged the brethren to drink freely, telling them that the wine was consecrated, and would not make them drunk . . . they began to prophecy, pronouncing blessings upon their friends, and curses upon their enemies. If I should be so unhappy as to go to the regions of the damned, I never expect to hear language more awful, or more becoming the infernal pit, than was uttered that night (*Mormonism Portrayed*, pp.31-32).

Charles L. Walker, a faithful Mormon, recorded the following in his diary:

Sun., Nov. 21, 1880. . . . Bro. Milo Andress . . . Spoke of blessings and power of God manifested in the Kirtland Temple. Said he once asked the Prophet who [why?] he (Milo) did not feel that power that was spoken of as the power which was felt on the day of Pentecost? . . . when we had fasted for 24 hours and partaken of the Lord's supper, namely a piece of bread as big as your double fist and *half a pint of wine* in the temple, I was there and saw the Holy Ghost descend upon the heads of those present like cloven tongues of fire ("Diary of Charles L. Walker," 1855-1902, excerpts typed, 1969, p.35).

The statement by Mormon Apostle George A. Smith would also lead a person to believe that wine was used to excess: ". . . after the people had fasted all day, they sent out and got wine and bread, . . . they ate and drank, . . . some of the High Counsel of Missouri stepped into the stand, and, as righteous Noah did when he awoke *from his wine*, commenced to curse their enemies (*Journal of Discourses*, vol. 2, p.216).

In a statement dated February 27, 1885, Mrs. Alfred Morley charged: "I have heard many Mormons who attended the dedication, or endowment of the Temple, say that very many became drunk. . . . The Mormon leaders would stand up to prophesy and were so drunk they said they could not get it out, and would call for another drink. Over a barrel of liquor was used at the service" (*Naked Truths About Mormonism*, Oakland, Calif., April, 1888, p.2). Isaac Aldrich said that his brother "Hazen Aldrich, who was president of the Seventies, told me when the Temple was dedicated a barrel of wine was used and they had a drunken 'pow-wow' " (*Ibid.* , p.3). Stephen H. Hart said that a Mormon by the name of McWhithey told him that "they passed the wine in pails several times to the audience, and each person drank as much as he chose from a cup. He said it was mixed liquor, and he believed the Mormon leaders intended to get the audience under the influence of the mixed liquor, so they would believe it was the Lord's doings. . . . When the liquor was repassed Mr. McWhithey told them he had endowment enough . . ." (*Ibid.*, p.3).

The reader will remember that David Whitmer, one of the three witnesses to the *Book of Mormon*, called the endowment "a trumped up yarn" and said that "*there was no visitation*" (*The Des Moines Daily News*, October 16, 1886). William E. McLellin, who had served as an Apostle in the Mormon church, commented: "As to the endowment in Kirtland, I state positively, it was *no endowment from God*. Not only myself was not endowed, but no other man of the five hundred who was present—*except it was with wine*" (*True Latter-Day Saints' Herald*, XIX, 437, as cited in *Hearts Made Glad*, p.137).

The fact that the Mormons fasted for some time and then drank an excessive amount of wine probably led many of them to curse their enemies and to believe they had seen visions.

LaMar Petersen has detailed the problems relating to the Kirtland Temple and the Word of Wisdom in his book, *Hearts Made Glad—The Charges of Intemperance Against Joseph Smith the Mormon Prophet*.

Hypocrisy

Orson Pratt once quipped: "I do not wonder that the world say that the Latter-day Saints do not believe their own revelations. Why? Because we do not practice them" (*Journal of Discourses*, vol. 17, p.104).

We have shown that Joseph Smith, the founder of the Mormon church, did not keep the Word of Wisdom, yet, according to Joseph Fielding Smith, the Prophet Joseph Smith taught that a member of the church could not hold an office unless he observed it: ". . . Joseph Smith, who presided, gave his decision as follows: 'No official member in this Church *is worthy to hold an office* after having the word of wisdom properly taught him; and he, the official member, neglecting to comply with or obey it.' This decision was confirmed by unanimous vote" (*Essentials in Church History*, p.169).

It is certainly perplexing that Joseph Smith could break the Word of Wisdom and yet retain his position as president of the church. The thing that makes this especially strange is that when a member of the church did not observe the Word of Wisdom, this was sometimes used against him if he was tried for his fellowship. Leonard J. Arrington stated: "Moreover, when a council at Far West tried a high church official (David Whitmer) for his fellowship, the first of the five charges against

him was that he did not observe the Word of Wisdom"
(*Brigham Young University Studies*, Winter 1959, p.40). As we
have already shown, when Almon W. Babbitt was charged with
not observing the Word of Wisdom, his only defense was that
he "had taken the liberty to break the Word of Wisdom, from
the example of President Joseph Smith, Jun., and others." We
have also shown that after Joseph Smith's death, Brigham
Young and other church leaders did not observe the Word of
Wisdom.

Heber C. Kimball, who was a member of the First Presidency,
once claimed that "virtuous Saints, . . . will not sell whiskey,
and stick up grogeries, and establish distilleries" (*Journal of
Discourses*, vol. 2, p.161). This statement seems very strange
when we learn that Joseph Smith sold whiskey in Nauvoo, and
that Brigham Young built a distillery and sold alcoholic beverages in Utah. Even the Mormon-owned Zions Cooperative Mer-
cantile Institution (now known as ZCMI) sold the items forbidden in the Word of Wisdom. On October 7, 1873, George A.
Smith, a member of the First Presidency, admitted: "We are
doing a great business in tea, coffee, and tobacco in the
Cooperative Store" (*Journal of Discourses*, vol. 16, p.238).

In 1908 the *Salt Lake Tribune* accused the Mormon leaders of
trying to monopolize the liquor business in Utah: ". . . the
Mormon priesthood . . . resisted to the utmost the establishment of liquor houses by Gentiles here for a good while, not
because they were liquor houses, but because the Gentiles were
getting the trade. . . . This fierce effort to retain the liquor traffic
here as a monopoly of the church was quite in accord with the
present status of affairs here where *the church is running the
biggest liquor businesss in the State*, through its Z.C.M.I. drug
store and also through the big liquor business done by Apostle
Smoot in his drug store at Provo" (*Salt Lake Tribune*, July 14,
1908).

Although the Word of Wisdom contains some good precepts,
it is obviously a product of the thinking of Joseph Smith's time.
Alcoholic beverages were condemned by the temperance
movement years before Joseph Smith gave his "revelation." Although Smith was correct in stating that tobacco is harmful, we
do not feel that this proves his "revelation" is divinely inspired. The *Wayne Sentinel*—a newspaper printed in the
neighborhood where Joseph Smith grew up—published these
statements concerning tobacco three years before Joseph Smith
gave the Word of Wisdom:

"It is really surprising that a single individual could be
found, who, after experiencing the distressing sensations al-

most invariably produced by the first use of tobacco, would be willing to risk their recurrence a second time: . . . Tobacco is, in fact, an absolute poison . . ." (*Wayne Sentinel*, November 6, 1829).

While Mormons presently make much of abstinence from tobacco and alcoholic beverages, little is said about the Word of Wisdom cautioning against the use of meat except "in times of winter, or of cold or famine." With the exception of tea and coffee, "hot drinks" are freely used.

OLD TESTAMENT PRACTICES

Chapter 19

There are several Old Testament practices that have found their way into Mormonism; one of these is the practice of cursing ones enemies. Both the Bible and the *Book of Mormon* state that this practice was to cease with the coming of Christ. Now that Christ has come, we are supposed to rely upon Him and let Him take all hate out of our hearts. If we have no hate in our hearts, we will have no desire to curse our enemies or wish any evil upon them. The words which Jesus spoke in the Sermon on the Mount are also recorded in the *Book of Mormon:*

"And behold it is written also, that thou shalt love thy neighbor and hate thine enemy; But behold I say unto you, love your enemies, bless them that curse you, do good to them that hate you, and pray for them who despitefully use you and persecute you" (3 Nephi 12:43-44).

In the Bible, Romans 12:14, we are counseled: "Bless them which persecute you; bless, and curse not."

In spite of these clear teachings in both the Bible and the *Book of Mormon,* Joseph Smith gave a revelation which sanctioned the cursing of ones enemies:

"And inasmuch as mine enemies come against you . . . ye shall curse them; And whomsoever ye curse, I will curse, and ye shall avenge me of mine enemies" (*Doctrine and Covenants,* 103:24-25).

Wine and Curses

The cursing of enemies was actually carried out in the Kirtland Temple. Apostle George A. Smith left us this account:

> Now I will illustrate this still further. The Lord did actually reveal one principle to us there, and that one principle was apparently so simple, and so foolish in their eyes, that a great many apostatized over it, because it was so contrary to their notions and views. It was this, after the people had fasted all day, they sent out and got wine and bread, . . . and they ate and drank, and

484

prophesied, and bore testimony, and continued so to do until some of the High Council of Missouri stepped into the stand, and, as righteous Noah did when he awoke from his wine, commenced *to curse their enemies.* You never felt such a shock go through any house or company in the world as went through that. There was almost a rebellion because men would get up and curse their enemies. . . . Some of the brethren thought it was best to apostatize. . . . The Lord dared not then reveal anything more; He had given us all we could swallow . . . (*Journal of Discourses*, vol. 2, p.216).

William Harris, in a statement we quoted in the previous chapter, said concerning the cursing:

After this they began to prophecy, pronouncing blessings upon their friends, and curses upon their enemies. If I should be so unhappy as to go to the regions of the damned, *I never expect to hear language more awful,* or more becoming the infernal pit, than was uttered that night. The curses were pronounced principally upon the clergy of the present day, and upon the Jackson county mob in Missouri. After spending the night in alternate blessings and cursings, the meeting adjourned (*Mormonism Portrayed*, pp.31-32).

When Joseph Smith wrote this portion of the *History of the Church,* he told of the cursing in the Kirtland Temple; however, his words have been censored in modern printings. In the *Millennial Star,* Joseph Smith's words are given as follows: "The brethren began to prophesy upon each other's heads, and cursings upon the enemies of Christ, who inhabit Jackson county, Missouri . . ." (vol. 15, p.727).

In the *History of the Church* (vol. 2, p.431), Joseph Smith's words have been censored to read: "The brethren began to prophesy upon each other's heads, and upon the enemies of Christ, who inhabited Jackson county, Missouri. . . ." Notice that the word "cursings" has been entirely removed.

In his letter written in 1903, Benjamin F. Johnson admitted that "In Missouri we were taught to 'pray for our enemies, that *God would damn them, and give us power to kill them.*'" Apostle George A. Smith said: ". . . we were then very pious, and we prayed the Lord to kill the mob" (*Journal of Discourses*, vol. 5, p.107).

John Taylor emphatically proclaimed in a sermon delivered in the Tabernacle in 1858: ". . . they were so damnable, mean, and cowardly as to make war on the sick and infirm that could not leave. The poor, miserable, cursed, damned scoundrels, *I pray that they may go to hell.* [The whole congregation shouted 'Amen.']" (*Journal of Discourses*, vol. 7, p.122).

Heber C. Kimball, first councilor to Brigham Young, often cursed his enemies from the pulpit. He even went so far as to curse the President of the United States. Below are some extracts from his sermons:

> There are men and women in this congregation of that stamp. I wish I had some stones; I want to pelt your cursed heads, for you lie like hell. . . .

> There is a poor curse who has written the bigger part of those lies which have been printed in the States; and *I curse him*, in the name of Israel's God, and by the Priesthood and authority of Jesus Christ; and the disease that is in him shall sap and dry up the fountain of life and eat him up. Some of you may think that he has not the disease I allude to; but he is full of pox from the crown of his head to the point of its beginning. That is the curse of that man; it shall be so, and all Israel shall say, Amen. [The vast congregation of Saints said, "Amen."] . . . May God Almighty curse such men, . . . and every damned thing there is upon the earth that opposes this people. I tell you I feel to curse them to-day (*Journal of Discourses*, vol. 5, p.32).

> Will *the President* that sits in the chair of state be tipped from his seat? Yes, he will die an untimely death, and God Almighty *will curse him*; and He will also *curse his successor*, if he takes the same stand; . . . God Almighty will curse them, and *I curse them in the name of the Lord Jesus Christ*, according to my calling; and if there is any virtue in my calling, they shall be cursed, every man that lifts his heel against us from this day forth. [Voices: "Amen."] (p.133).

> And may God Almighty curse our enemies. [Voices: "Amen."] I feel to *curse my enemies*: and when God won't bless them, I do not think he will ask me to bless them. If I did, it would be to put *the poor curses to death* who have brought death and destruction on me and my brethren. . . . Poor rotten curses! And the *President* of the United States, inasmuch as he has turned against us . . . he *shall be cursed, in the name of Israel's God*, and he shall not rule over this nation, . . . and *I curse him* and all his coadjutors [sic] in his cursed deeds, *in the name of Jesus and by the authority of the Holy Priesthood*; and all Israel shall say amen (p.95).

> . . . I feel, in the name and by the authority of Jesus Christ and my calling, to curse that man that lifts his heel against my God. . . . The President of the United States and his coadjutors [sic] that have caused this thing shall never rest again, for they shall go to hell (vol. 6, p.38).

In Romans 12:20 we read: "Therefore if thine enemy hunger, feed him. . . ." According to Charles L. Walker, Brigham Young

and we will bring about the restitution of the house of Israel.

I do not care if we die in twenty minutes,—as true as there is a resurrection, or ever was, Brigham Young, Heber C. Kimball, and Joseph, and thousands of others will be redeemed and get their resurrection; and I will see you as I see you to-day, and we will save all that we can, and the rest will have to go to hell.

I believe in annihilation in one degree. Men will sin so that they will be damned spiritually and temporally. There will be a dissolution of the natural body and of the spirit, and they will go back into their native element, the same as the chemist can go to work and dissolve a five-dollar gold piece, and throw it into a liquid. Does not that show there can be a dissolution of the natural body and of the spirit? This is what is called the second death.

May the Almighty bless you! May the peace of God be with you, and upon your children, and your children's children, for ever and ever! And may God Almighty curse our enemies. [Voices: "Amen."] I feel to curse my enemies: and when God won't bless them, I do not think he will ask me to bless them. If I did, it would be to put the poor curses to death who have brought death and destruction on me and my brethren—upon my wives and my children that I buried on the road between the States and this place.

Did I ever wrong them, a man or woman of them, out of a dime? No; but I have fed thousands where I never received a dime. Poor rotten curses! And the President of the United States, inasmuch as he has turned against us and will take a course to persist in pleasing the ungodly curses that are howling around him for the destruction of this people, he shall be cursed, in the name of Israel's God, and he shall not rule over this nation, because they are my brethren; but they have cast me out and cast you out; and I curse him and all his coadjutors in his cursed deeds, in the name of Jesus Christ and by the authority of the Holy Priesthood; and all Israel shall say amen.

Send 2,500 troops here, our brethren, to make a desolation of this people! God Almighty helping me, I will fight until there is not a drop of blood in my veins. Good God! I have wives enough to whip out the United States; for they will whip themselves. Amen.

A photograph of the *Journal of Discourses*, vol. 5, page 95. Heber C. Kimball, First Councilor to Brigham Young, cursed the President of the United States and other enemies.

taught just the opposite: "Sun., Apr. 28. Went up to the Tabernacle . . . Bro. Brigham . . . said that those who sell their provisions to feed our enemies either man or woman should be cursed, and said he, *I curse them* in the name of the Lord Jesus Christ and the congregation shouted, Amen" ("Diary of Charles L. Walker," 1853-1902, excerpts typed, p.13).

Jesus said, "Love your enemies," but Apostle George A. Smith remarked: "You must know that I love my friends, and God Almighty knows that I do *hate my enemies*" (*Journal of Discourses*, vol. 5, p.110).

Jesus said that we should pray for our enemies. Heber C. Kimball prayed for his enemies in the following manner: "Pray for them? Yes, I pray that God Almighty would send them to hell. Some say across lots; but I would like to have them take a round about road, and be as long as they can be in going there" (*Ibid.*, p.89).

Animal Sacrifice After Christ

Animal sacrifice after the death of Christ is another Old Testament practice that has found a place in Mormon beliefs. It was Joseph Smith himself who taught this doctrine:

> . . . it is generally supposed that sacrifice was entirely done away when the Great Sacrifice . . . was offered up, and that there will be no necessity for the ordinance of sacrifice in [the] future: but those who assert this are certainly not aquainted with the duties, privileges and authority of the priesthood, or with the Prophets. . . .
>
> These *sacrifices*, as well as every ordinance belonging to the Priesthood, will, when the Temple of the Lord shall be built, . . . be *fully restored* and attended to in all their powers, ramifications, and blessings (*History of the Church*, vol. 4, p.211).

In the Journal of Wandle Mace the following is recorded: "*Joseph* told them to go to Kirtland, and cleanse and purify a certain room in the Temple, that they must *kill a lamb and offer a sacrifice* unto the Lord which should prepare them to ordain Willard Richards a member of the Quorum of the Twelve Apostles" ("Journal of Wandle Mace," p.32, microfilmed copy at Brigham Young University Library).

Joseph Fielding Smith said that "the law of sacrifice will have to be restored. . . . Sacrifice by the shedding of blood was instituted in the days of Adam and of necessity will have to be restored" (*Doctrines of Salvation*, vol. 3, p.94).

It is interesting to note that even though the Mormon church teaches animal sacrifice after the death of Christ, they cannot find any support for this doctrine in the *Book of Mormon*. In fact, the *Book of Mormon* condemns it in the strongest terms. In 3 Nephi 9:19 Jesus was supposed to have said: "And ye shall offer up unto me no more the shedding of blood; yea, your sacrifices and your burnt offerings shall be done away, for I will accept none of your sacrifices and your burnt offerings."

There are many other Old Testament practices in Mormonism. This should be sufficient, however, to convince the reader that the Mormon church leaders have sometimes followed Old Testament practices in preference to the clear teachings of Christ.

BLOOD ATONEMENT

Chapter 20

In a manuscript written in 1839, Reed Peck said that Joseph
Smith claimed he had a revelation in which Apostle Peter told
him that he had killed Judas: "He [Joseph Smith] talked of
dissenters and cited us to the case of Judas, saying that Peter
told him in a conversation a few days ago that himself *hung
Judas for betraying Christ . . ."* (*The Reed Peck Manuscript*,
p.13).

Although this doctrine was kept secret at first, when the
Mormons were settled in Utah they began to teach it openly. On
December 13, 1857, Heber C. Kimball, a member of the First
Presidency, preached in the Tabernacle that

> Judas lost that saving principle, and *they took him and killed
> him*. It is said in the Bible that his bowels gushed out; but they
> actually *kicked him until his bowels came out*. . . . Judas was like
> salt that had lost its saving principles—good for nothing but to
> be cast out and trodden under foot of men. . . . It is so with you,
> ye Elders of Israel, when you forfeit your covenants. . . . I know
> the day is right at hand when men will forfeit their Priesthood
> and turn against us and against the covenants they have made,
> and they will be *destroyed as Judas was* (*Journal of Discourses*,
> vol. 6, pp.125-26).

President Brigham Young, who at first denied the doctrine of
blood atonement, became one of its greatest advocates:

> There are sins that men commit for which they cannot receive
> forgiveness in this world, or in that which is to come, and if they
> had their eyes open to see their true condition, they would be
> perfectly willing *to have their blood spilt upon the ground*, that
> the smoke thereof might ascend to heaven as an offering for their
> sins; and the smoking incense *would atone for their sins*,
> whereas, if such is not the case, they will stick to them and
> remain upon them in the spirit world.
>
> I know, when you hear my brethren telling about *cutting people
> off from the earth*, that you consider it is strong doctrine, but *it is
> to save them*, not to destroy them. . . . I know there are transgres-

sors, who, if they knew themselves, and the only condition upon which they can obtain forgiveness, would beg of their brethren *to shed their blood*, that the smoke thereof might ascend to God as an offering to appease the wrath that is kindled against them, and that the law might have its course. I will say further; I have had men come to me and *offer their lives to atone for their sins.*

It is true that the blood of the Son of God was shed for sins through the fall and those committed by men, yet men can commit *sins which it can never remit.* As it was in ancient days, so it is in our day. . . . There are sins that can be atoned for by an offering upon an altar, as in ancient days, and there are sins that the blood of a lamb, of a calf, or of turtle doves, cannot remit, but they must be *atoned for by the blood of the man.* That is the reason why men talk to you as they do from this stand; they understand the doctrine and throw out a few words about it. You have been taught that doctrine, but you do not understand it (Sermon by Brigham Young, *Journal of Discourses*, vol. 4, pp.53-54; also published in the *Deseret News*, October 1, 1856, p.235).

Since this sermon was published in the official organ of the Mormon church there can be no doubt that blood atonement was a doctrine of the church.

J. M. Grant, who was a member of the First Presidency under Brigham Young, made some very strong statements concerning blood atonement:

Some have received the Priesthood and a knowledge of the things of God, and still they dishonor the cause of truth, commit adultery, and every other abomination beneath the heavens, . . . they will seek unto wizards that peep, . . . get drunk and wallow in the mire and filth, and yet they call themselves Saints, . . . there are men and women that I would advise to go to the President immediately, and ask him to appoint a committee to attend to their case; and then let a place be selected, and *let that committee shed their blood.*

We have those amongst us that are full of all manner of abominations, those who need to have their blood shed, for water will not do, their sins are of too deep a dye.

You may think that I am not teaching you Bible doctrine, but what says the apostle Paul? I would ask how many covenant breakers there are in this city and in this kingdom. I believe that there are a great many; and if they are covenant breakers we need a place designated, where we can shed their blood (*Journal of Discourses*, vol. 4, pp.49-50; also published in *Deseret News*, Oct. 1, 1856).

offer their lives to atone for their sins.

It is true that the blood of the Son of God was shed for sins through the fall and those committed by men, yet men can commit sins which it can never remit. As it was in ancient days, so it is in our day; and though the principles are taught publicly from this stand, still the people do not understand them; yet the law is precisely the same. There are sins that can be atoned for by an offering upon an altar, as in ancient days; and there are sins that the blood of a lamb, of a calf, or of turtle doves, cannot remit, but they must be atoned for by the blood of the man. That is the reason why men talk to you as they do from this stand; they understand the doctrine and throw out a few words about it. You have been taught that doctrine, but you do not understand it.

It is our desire to be prepared for a celestial seat with our Father in heaven. It was observed by brother Grant that we have not seen God, that we cannot converse with Him; and it is true that men in their sins do not know much about God. When you hear a man pour out eternal things, how well you feel, to what a nearness you seem to be brought with God. What a delight it was to hear brother Joseph talk upon the great principles of eternity; he would bring them down to the capacity of a child, and he would unite heaven with earth, this is the beauty of our religion.

When it was mentioned this morning about seeing God, about what kind of a being He was, and how we could see and measurably understand Him, I thought I would tell you. If we could see our heavenly Father, we should see a being similar to our earthly parent, with this difference, our Father in heaven is exalted and glorified. He has received His thrones, His principalities and powers, and He sits as a governor, as a monarch, and overrules kingdoms, thrones, and dominions that have been bequeathed to Him, and such as we anticipate receiving. While He was in the flesh, as we are, He was as we are. But it is now written of Him that our God is as a consuming fire, that He dwells in everlasting burnings, and this is why sin cannot be where He is.

There are principles that will endure through all eternity, and no fire can obliterate them from existence. They are those principles that are pure, and fire is made typical use of to show the glory and purity of the gods, and of all perfect beings. God is the Father of our spirits; He begat them, and has sent them here to receive tabernacles, and to prove whether we will honour them. If we do, then our tabernacles will be exalted; but if we do not, we shall be destroyed; one of the two—dissolution or life. The second death will decompose all tabernacles over whom it gains the ascendancy; and this is the effect of the second death, the tabernacles go back to their native element.

We are of the earth, earthy; and our Father is heavenly and pure. But we will be glorified and purified, if we obey our brethren and the teachings which are given.

When you see celestial beings, you will see men and women, but you will see those beings clothed upon with robes of celestial purity. We cannot bear the presence of our Father now; and we are placed at a distance to prove whether we will honor these tabernacles, whether we will be obedient and prepare ourselves to live in the glory of the light, privileges, and blessings of celestial beings. We could not have the glory and the light without first knowing the contrast. Do you comprehend that we could have no exaltation, without first learning by contrast?

When you are prepared to see our

A photograph of the *Journal of Discourses*, vol. 4, page 54. Brigham Young teaches the doctrine of "Blood Atonement."

Crimes Worthy of Death

When we look into the early Mormon publications we find that there were many crimes that the Mormon church leaders taught were worthy of death. The following is a list of those crimes:

Murder. Joseph Smith has been quoted as saying: "In debate, George A. Smith said imprisonment was better than hanging. I replied, I was opposed to hanging, even if a man kill another, I will shoot him, or cut off his head, spill his blood on the ground, and let the smoke thereof ascend up to God; and if ever I have the privilege of making a law on that subject, I will have it so" (*History of the Church*, vol. 5, p.296).

The early Mormons believed in beheading and incorporated this into their laws in Utah: "In accordance with the law of Utah, the doomed man was given his choice of three methods of execution—hanging, shooting or beheading" (*A Mormon Chronicle, The Diaries of John D. Lee*, p.xix).

In footnote 143 on page 129 of the same book, we read: "Even the law of territorial Utah, as we have explained in the Introduction, allowed John D. Lee, or any other man condemned to death, to elect to be beheaded as a means of saving his immortal soul by the shedding of his blood."

Although we do not hear of murderers having their heads cut off in Utah today, the law still allows the murderer to be shot so that his blood can flow and atone for his sin. Joseph Fielding Smith stated:

> ... the founders of Utah incorporated in the laws of the Territory provisions for the capital punishment of those who wilfully shed the blood of their fellow men. This law, which is now the law of the State, granted unto the condemned murderer the privilege of choosing for himself whether he die by hanging, or whether he be *shot* and thus have his *blood shed in harmony with the law of God; and thus atone,* so far as it is in his power to atone, for the death of his victim. Almost without exception the condemned party chooses the latter death (*Doctrines of Salvation*, vol. 1, p.136).

Apostle Bruce R. McConkie once explained: "As a mode of capital punishment, hanging or execution on a gallows *does not comply with the law of blood atonement, for the blood is not shed*" (*Mormon Doctrine*, 1958, p.314).

The *Salt Lake Tribune* for January 28, 1968, reported: "Japanese District and Family Court Judge Hiroshige Takasawa, after more than a year of research studies of Utah's 'unique' form of capital punishment, has found 'evidence that *present laws stem* from early Mormon philosophy of *blood atonement.*' "

As long as the Mormon church teaches the doctrine of blood atonement there is probably little chance of Utah using a gas chamber or electric chair for the condemned murderer.

Adultery and Immorality. Apostle Bruce R. McConkie once lamented: "Modern governments *do not take the life of the adulterer,* and some of them have done away with the supreme penalty where murder is involved—all of which is further evidence of the direful apostasy that prevails among the peoples who call themselves Christians" (*Mormon Doctrine*, 1958, p.104).

Brigham Young proclaimed:

> Let me suppose a case. Suppose you found your brother in bed with your wife, and *put a javelin through both of them,* you would be justified, and they would *atone for their sins,* and be received into the kingdom of God. I would at once do so in such a case; and under such circumstances, I have no wife whom I love so well that I would not *put a javelin through her heart,* and I would do it with clean hands. . . .

> There is not a man or woman, who violates the covenants made with their God, that will not be required to pay the debt. *The blood of Christ will never wipe that out, your own blood must atone for it . . .* (*Journal of Discourses*, vol. 3, p.247).

Heber C. Kimball, who was a member of the First Presidency, reflected:

> These are my views, and the Lord knows that I believe in the principles of sanctification; and when I am guilty of seducing any man's wife, or any woman in God's world, I say, sever my head from my body (*Journal of Discourses*, vol. 7, p.20).

> But they cannot whore it here; for, gentlemen, if there is anything of that kind, we will slay both men and women. We will do it, as the Lord liveth—we will slay such characters. Now, which would be the most worthy to be slain—the woman that had had her endowments and made certain covenants before God, or the man that knew nothing about it? The woman, of course (*Ibid.,* vol. 6, p.38).

> . . . our females . . . are not unclean, for we wipe all unclean ones from our midst: we not only wipe them from our streets, but we wipe them out of existence . . . so help me God, while I live, I will lend my hand to wipe such persons out: and I know this people will (*Millennial Star*, vol. 16, p.739; also printed in the *Journal of Discourses*, vol. 7, p.19).

494   Apostle George A. Smith adds: "The principle, the only one

A few of the men and women who go into the house of the Lord, and receive their endowments, and in the most sacred manner make covenants before the Almighty, go and violate those covenants. Do I have compassion on them? Yes, I do have mercy on them, for there is something in their organization which they do not understand; and there are but few in this congregation who do understand it.

You say, "That man ought to die for transgressing the law of God." Let me suppose a case. Suppose you found your brother in bed with your wife, and put a javelin through both of them, you would be justified, and they would atone for their sins, and be received into the kingdom of God. I would at once do so in such a case; and under such circumstances, I have no wife whom I love so well that I would not put a javelin through her heart, and I would do it with clean hands. But you who trifle with your covenants, be careful lest in judging you will be judged.

Every man and women has got to have clean hands and a pure heart, to execute judgment, else they had better let the matter alone.

Again, suppose the parties are not caught in their iniquity, and it passes along unnoticed, shall I have compassion on them? Yes, I will have compassion on them, for transgressions of the nature already named, or for those of any other description. If the Lord so order it that they are not caught in the act of their iniquity, it is pretty good proof that He is willing for them to live; and I say let them live and suffer in the flesh for their sins, for they will have it to do.

There is not a man or woman, who violates the covenants made with their God, that will not be required to pay the debt. The blood of Christ will never wipe that out, your own blood must atone for it; and the judgments

of the Almighty will come, sooner or later, and every man and woman will have to atone for breaking their covenants. To what degree? Will they have to go to hell? They are in hell enough now. I do not wish them in a greater hell, when their consciences condemn them all the time. Let compassion reign in our bosoms. Try to comprehend how weak we are, how we are organized, how the spirit and the flesh are continually at war.

I told you here, some time ago, that the devil who tempted Eve, got possession of the earth, and reigns triumphant, has nothing to do with influencing our spirits, only through the flesh; that is a true doctrine. Inasmuch as our spirits are inseparably connected with the flesh, and, inasmuch as the whole tabernacle is filled with the spirit which God gave, if the body is afflicted, the spirit also suffers, for there is a warfare between the flesh and the spirit, and if the flesh overcomes, the spirit is brought into bondage, and if the spirit overcomes, the body is made free, and then we are free indeed, for we are made free by the Son of God. Watch yourselves, and think. As I heard observed, on the evening of the 14th, at the Social Hall, "think, brethren, think," but do not think so far that you cannot think back again. I then wanted to tell a little anecdote, but I will tell it now.

In the eastern country there was a man who used to go crazy, at times, and then come to his senses again. One of his neighbors asked him what made him go crazy; he replied, "I get to thinking, and thinking, until finally I think so far that I am not always able to think back again." Can you think too much for the spirit which is put in the tabernacle? You can, and this is a subject which I wish the brethren instructed upon, and the people to understand. The spirit is the intelligent part of man,

A photograph of the *Journal of Discourses*, vol. 3, page 247. Brigham Young claims that the blood of Christ cannot atone for certain sins and therefore those who commit these sins must have their own blood shed.

that beats and throbs through the heart of the entire inhabitants of this Territory, is simply this: The man who seduces his neighbors wife must die, and her nearest relative must kill him!" (*Journal of Discourses*, vol. 1, p.97).

Stealing. The following statement appeared in the Mormon publication *Times and Seasons*: "President Joseph Smith said, . . . I want the elders to make honorable proclamation abroad concerning what the feelings of the first presidency is, for stealing has never been tolerated by them. I despise a thief above ground" (*Times and Seasons*, vol. 4, pp.183-84).

Brigham Young taught that thieves should have their throats cut:

> President Young then spoke against thieving, . . . said he, I should be perfectly willing to see thieves have their throats cut; some of you may say, if that is your feelings Brigham, we'll lay you aside sometime, well, do it if you can; I would rather die by the hands of the meanest of all men, false brethren, than to live among thieves (*History of the Church*, vol. 7, p.597).

> If you want to know what to do with a thief that you may find stealing, I say kill him on the spot, and never suffer him to commit another iniquity. . . . if I caught a man stealing on my premises I should be very apt to send him straight home, and that is what I wish every man to do, . . . this appears hard, and throws a cold chill over our revered traditions . . . but I have trained myself to measure things by the line of justice. . . . If you will cause all those whom you know to be thieves, to be placed in a line before the mouth of one of our largest cannon, well loaded with chain shot, I will prove by my works whether I can mete out justice to such persons, or not. I would consider it just as much my duty to do that, as to baptize a man for the remission of his sins (*Journal of Discourses*, vol. 1, pp.108-9).

Apostle Orson Hyde said: "It would have a tendency to place a terror on those who leave these parts, that may prove their salvation when they see the heads of thieves taken off, or shot down before the public . . . I believe it to be pleasing in the sight of heaven to sanctify ourselves and put these things from our midst" (*Journal of Discourses*, vol. 1, p.73).

Using the Name of the Lord in Vain. In the journal of Hosea Stout, Brigham Young is recorded as saying: ". . . I tell you the time is coming when that man uses the name of the Lord is used the penalty will be affixed and immediately be executed on the spot . . ." (Journal of Hosea Stout, vol. 2, p.71; p.56 of the typed copy at Utah State Historical Society).

For Not Receiving the Gospel. Brigham Young once proclaimed: "The time is coming when justice will be laid to the line and righteousness to the plummet; when we shall ask, 'Are you for God?' and if you are not heartily on the Lord's side, you will be hewn down" (*Journal of Discourses*, vol. 3, p.226).

For Marriage to an African. Brigham Young said: "Shall I tell you the law of God in regard to the African race? If the white man who belongs to the chosen seed mixes his blood with the seed of Cain, the penalty, under *the law of God is death on the spot.* This will always be so" (*Journal of Discourses*, vol. 10, p.110).

Wilford Woodruff, who became the fourth president of the Mormon church, recorded in his journal an address delivered by President Brigham Young in 1852. In this address we find the following: "And if any man mingle his seed with the seed of Cane [sic] the ownly [sic] way he could get rid of it or have salvation would be to come forward and have *his head cut off* & spill his Blood upon the ground it would also *take the life of his children* . . ." ("Wilford Woodruff's Journal," January 16, 1852, typed copy; original located in LDS church archives).

Mormon writer Lester E. Bush, Jr., admits that in this address Brigham Young taught that "miscegenation required blood atonement (offspring included) for salvation . . ." (*Dialogue: A Journal of Mormon Thought*, Spring 1973, p.26).

According to the "Excerpts From The Weekly Council Meetings Of The Quorum Of The Twelve Apostles," this doctrine was still being taught in 1897. In the report for December 15, 1897, we read:

> President Cannon said he had understood President Taylor to say that a man who had the priesthood who would marry a woman of the accursed seed, that if the law of the Lord were administered upon him, he would *be killed, and his offspring,* for the reason that the Lord had determined that the seed of Cain should not receive the priesthood in the flesh . . . ("Excerpts From The Weekly Council Meetings Of The Quorum Of The Twelve Apostles, Dealing With The Rights Of Negroes In The Church, 1849-1940," as published in *Mormonism – Shadow or Reality?* p.582).

On August 22, 1895, in this same source, George Q. Cannon taught the same doctrine: "President Cannon remarked that the Prophet Joseph taught this doctrine: That the seed of Cain could not receive the Priesthood . . . and that any white man who mingled his seed with that of Cain *should be killed*, and thus prevent any of the seed of Cain's coming into possession of the priesthood."

For Covenant Breaking. Jedediah M. Grant, who was second counselor to Brigham Young, preached:

> I say, that there are men and women that I would advise to go to the President immediately, and ask him to appoint a committee to attend to their case; and then let a place be selected, and *let that committee shed their blood.*

> We have those amongst us that are full of all manner of abominations, those who need to have their blood shed . . . I would ask how many covenant breakers there are in this city and in this kingdom. I believe that there are a great many; and if they are covenant breakers we need a place designated, where we can shed their blood. . . . I go for letting the sword of the Almighty be unsheathed, not only in word, but in deed . . . you who have committed sins that cannot be forgiven through baptism, let your blood be shed, and let the smoke ascend, that the incense thereof may come up before God as an atonement for your sins, and that the sinners in Zion may be afraid (*Deseret News*, October 1, 1856, p.235; also *Journal of Discourses*, vol. 4, pp.49-51).

On another occasion Jedediah M. Grant exclaimed:

> What disposition ought the people of God to make of covenant breakers . . . What does the Apostle say? He says they are worthy of death. . . . Putting to death transgressors would exhibit the law of God, no difference by whom it was done; that is my opinion. . . . people will look into books of theology, and argue that the people of God have a right to try people for fellowship, but they have no right to try them on property or life. That makes the devil laugh, saying, I have got them on a hook now; . . . has not the people of God a right to carry out that part of his law as well as any other portion of it? It is their right to baptize a sinner to save him, and it is also their right *to kill a sinner to save him,* when he commits those crimes that can only be atoned for by shedding his blood. . . . We would not kill a man, of course, unless we killed him to save him. . . .

> Do you think it would be any sin to kill me if I were to break my covenants? . . . Do you believe you would kill me if I broke the covenants of God, and you had the Spirit of God? Yes; and the more Spirit of God I had, the more *I should strive to save your soul by spilling your blood,* when you had committed sin that could not be remitted by baptism (*Deseret News*, July 27, 1854).

Heber C. Kimball, the first counselor to Brigham Young, stated: ". . . if men turn traitors to God and His servants, their blood will surely be shed, or else they will be damned, and that too according to their covenants" (*Journal of Discourses*, vol. 4, p.375).

For Apostasy. Brigham Young threatened: "I say, rather than

498

that apostates should flourish here, I will unsheath my bowie knife and conquer or die. (Great commotion in the congregation, and a simultaneous burst of feeling, assenting to the declaration.) Now, you nasty apostates, clear out, or judgment will be put to the line, and righteousness to the plummet. (Voices, generally, 'go it, go it.') If you say it is right, raise your hands. (All hands up.) Let us call upon the Lord to assist us in this, and every good work" (*Journal of Discourses*, vol. 1, p.83)

On another occasion Brigham Young explained:

> Now take a person in this congregation who has knowledge with regard to being saved . . . and suppose that he is overtaken in a gross fault, that he has committed a sin that he knows will deprive him of that exaltation which he desires, and that he cannot attain to it without the shedding of his blood, and also knows that by having his blood shed he will atone for that sin, and be saved and exalted with the Gods, is there a man or woman in this house but what would say "shed my blood that I may be saved and exalted with the Gods?"

> All mankind love themselves, and let these principles be known by an individual, and he would be glad to have his blood shed. That would be loving themselves, even unto an eternal exaltation. Will you love your brothers and sisters likewise, *when they have committed a sin that cannot be atoned for without the shedding of their blood? Will you love that man or woman well enough to shed their blood?*

> I could refer you to plenty of instances where men have been *righteously slain, in order to atone for their sins.* I have seen scores and hundreds of people for whom there would have been a chance (in the last resurrection there will be) if their lives had been taken and their blood spilled on the ground as a smoking incense to the Almighty, but who are now angels to the devil. . .I have known a great many men who left this Church for whom there is no chance whatever for exaltation, but *if their blood had been spilled,* it would have been better for them, the wickedness and ignorance of the nations forbids this principle's being in full force, but the time will come when the law of God will be in full force.

> This is loving our neighbor as ourselves; if he needs help, help him; and if he wants salvation and it is necessary to spill his blood on the earth in order that he may be saved, *spill it.* Any of you who understand the principles of eternity, if you have sinned a sin requiring the shedding of blood, except the sin unto death, would not be satisfied nor rest until your blood should be spilled, that you might gain that salvation you desire. That is the *way to love mankind* (*Deseret News*, February 18, 1857; also reprinted in *Journal of Discourses*, vol. 4, pp.219-20).

Heber C. Kimball counseled: ". . . when it is necessary that blood should be shed, we should be as ready to do that as to eat an apple . . . we will let you know that the earth can swallow you up, as it did Korah with his host; and as brother Taylor says, you may dig your graves, and we will slay you, and you may crawl into them" (*Journal of Discourses*, vol. 6, pp.34-35).

Mrs. Brooks remarked that John D. Lee "had seen many cases, among them that of Nephi Stewart, wherein a man was ruined financially and his life endangered by a public announcement that he had been cut off the Church" (*John D. Lee*, p.293).

For Lying. Brigham Young made this statement in 1846: "I . . . warned those who lied and stole and followed Israel that they would have their heads cut off, for that was the law of God and it should be executed" ("Manuscript History of Brigham Young," December 20, 1846, typed copy; original in LDS church archives).

For Counterfeiting. On February 24, 1847, Brigham Young declared: "I swore by the Eternal Gods that if men in our midst would not stop this cursed work of stealing and counterfeiting their throats should be cut" ("Manuscript History of Brigham Young," February 24, 1847, typed copy).

For Condemning Joseph Smith or Consenting to his Death. Norton Jacob quoted Brigham Young as saying: "A man may live here with us and worship what God he pleases or none at all, but he must not blaspheme the God of Israel or damn old Joe Smith or his religion, for we will salt him down in the lake" (*Quest for Empire*, p.127).

Joseph F. Smith, the sixth president of the church, once admitted that he was about to stab a man with his pocket knife if he even expressed approval of the murder of Joseph Smith. Apostle Abraham H. Cannon recorded the following in his journal under the date of December 6, 1889:

> About 4:30 p.m. this meeting adjourned and was followed by a meeting of Presidents Woodruff, Cannon and Smith and Bros. Lyman and Grant. . . . Bro. *Joseph F. Smith* was traveling some years ago near Carthage when he met a man who said he had just arrived five minutes too late to see the Smiths killed. Instantly a dark cloud seemed to overshadow Bro. Smith and he asked how this man looked upon the deed. Bro. S. was oppressed by a most horrible feeling as he waited for a reply. After a brief pause the man answered, "Just as I have always looked upon it—that it was a d—d cold-blooded murder." The cloud immediately lifted from Bro. Smith and he found that he had *his open pocket knife grasped in his hand* in his pocket, and he believes that had this man given his approval to that murder of the prophets he *would have immediately struck him to the heart* ("Daily Journal of

Abraham H. Cannon," December 6, 1889, pp.205-6; see
Mormonism—Shadow or Reality? p.403, for an actual photograph from the journal).

Blood Atonement in Actual Practice

Although the doctrine of blood atonement was openly proclaimed and put into practice in the 1850s, so many gentiles
came to Utah that the church leaders found it impossible to
continue the practice. Mormon writer Klaus J. Hansen noted:

> In 1888, apostle Charles W. Penrose observed that "Because of
> the laws of the land and the prejudices of the nation, and the
> ignorance of the world, this law can not be carried out, but when
> the time comes that the law of God shall be in full force upon the
> earth, then this penalty will be inflicted for those crimes com-
> mitted by persons under covenant not to commit them." How-
> ever, shortly after the Mormons established the government of
> God in Utah on what they believed to be a permanent basis, they
> attempted to enforce the doctrine. Brigham Young insisted that
> there were "plenty of instances where men have been righ-
> teously slain in order to atone for their sins" (*Quest for Empire*,
> p.70).

Apostle Bruce R. McConkie claims that blood atonement was
not actually practiced but feels that it is a true principle: ". . .
under certain circumstances there are some serious sins for
which the cleansing of Christ does not operate, and the law of
God is that men must have their own blood shed to atone for
their sins . . ." (*Mormon Doctrine*, 1958, p.87).

As we have already shown, Joseph F. Smith was such a firm
believer in the doctrine of blood atonement that he almost
killed a man at Carthage. His son Joseph Fielding Smith taught
the doctrine, although he could not face the fact that it was
actually practiced in early Utah. In his book *Doctrines of Salvation* he stated:

> Just a word or two now, on the subject of blood atonement . . .
> man may commit certain grievous sins—according to his light
> and knowledge—that will place him *beyond the reach of the
> atoning blood of Christ*. If then he would be saved he must *make
> sacrifice of his own life to atone*—so far as in his power lies—for
> that sin, for the blood of Christ alone under certain circum-
> stances will not avail. . . . Joseph Smith taught that there were
> certain sins so grievous that man may commit, that they will
> place the transgressor beyond the power of the atonement of
> Christ. If these offenses are committed, then the blood of Christ
> will not cleanse them from their sins even though they repent.
> Therefore their only hope is to have *their own blood shed to
> atone*, as far as possible, in their behalf. . . . And men for certain

501

crimes have had to atone as far as they could for their sins wherein they have placed themselves beyond the redeeming power of the blood of Christ (*Doctrines of Salvation*, vol. 1, pp.133-36).

After expressing a belief in the doctrine of blood atonement, however, President Smith turned right around and said that it was never actually practiced by the Mormon church. This claim is certainly far from the truth. In our book *The Mormon Kingdom*, volume 2, we documented the fact that many people lost their lives in early Utah because of the doctrine of blood atonement. One example is found in the "Confessions of John D. Lee":

> . . . the sinful member was to be slain for the remission of his sins, it being taught by the leaders and believed by the people that the right thing to do with a sinner who did not repent and obey the Council, was to take the life of the offending party, and thus save his everlasting soul. This was called "Blood Atonement.". . .

The most deadly sin among the people was adultery, and many men were killed in Utah for that crime.

Rosmos Anderson was a Danish man. . . . He had married a widow lady somewhat older than himself, and she had a daughter that was fully grown at the time of the reformation. The girl was very anxious to be sealed to her stepfather, and Anderson was equally anxious to take her for a second wife, but as she was a fine-looking girl, Klingensmith desired her to marry him, and she refused. At one of the meetings during the reformation Anderson and his step-daughter confessed that they had committed adultery, believing when they did so that Brigham Young would allow them to marry when he learned the facts. Their confession being full, they were rebaptized and received into full membership. They were then placed under covenant that if they again committed adultery, Anderson should suffer death. Soon after this a charge was laid against Anderson before the Council, accusing him of adultery with his step-daughter. This Council was composed of Klingensmith and his two counselors; it was the Bishop's Council. Without giving Anderson any chance to defend himself or make a statement, the Council voted that Anderson must die for violating his covenants. Klingensmith went to Anderson and notified him that the orders were that he must die by having his throat cut, so that the running of his blood would atone for his sins. Anderson, being a firm believer in the doctrine and teachings of the Mormon Church, made no objections, but asked for half a day to prepare for death. His request was granted. His wife was ordered to prepare a suit of clean clothing, in which to have her husband buried, and was informed that he was to be killed for his sins, she being directed to tell those who should enquire after her husband that he had gone to California.

Klingensmith, James Haslem, Daniel McFarland and John M. Higbee dug a grave in the field near Cedar City, and that night, about 12 o'clock, went to Anderson's house and ordered him to make ready to obey the Council. Anderson got up, dressed himself, bid his family good-bye, and without a word of remonstrance accompanied those that he believed were carrying out the will of the "Almighty God." They went to the place where the grave was prepared; Anderson knelt down upon the side of the grave and prayed, Klingensmith and his company then cut Anderson's throat from ear to ear and held him so that his blood ran into the grave.

As soon as he was dead they dressed him in his clean clothes, threw him into the grave and buried him. They then carried his bloody clothing back to his family, and gave them to his wife to wash, when she was again instructed to say that her husband was in California. She obeyed their orders.

No move of that kind was made in Cedar City, unless it was done by order of the "Council" or of the "High Council." I was at once informed of Anderson's death. . . . The killing of Anderson was then considered a religious duty and a just act. It was justified by all the people, for they were bound by the same covenants, and the least word of objection to thus treating the man who had broken his covenant would have brought the same fate upon the person who was so foolish as to raise his voice against any act committed by order of the Church authorities (*Confessions of John D. Lee*, 1880, pp.282-83).

Gustive O. Larson, professor of church history at Brigham Young University, admits that blood atonement was actually practiced:

To whatever extent the preaching on blood atonement may have influenced action, it would have been in relation to Mormon disciplinary action among its own members. In point would be a verbally reported case of a Mr. Johnson in Cedar City who was found guilty of adultery with his step-daughter by a Bishop's Court and sentenced to death for atonement of his sin. According to the report of reputable eyewitnesses, judgment was executed with consent of the offender *who went to his unconsecrated grave in full confidence of salvation through the shedding of his blood.* Such a case, however primitive, is understandable within the meaning of the doctrine and the emotional extremes of the Reformation (*Utah Historical Quarterly*, January 1958, p.62, note 39).

Although many Mormons continue to believe in blood

atonement as a doctrine, it is not practiced by faithful Mormons today. Some of the polygamous cults which have broken off from the Mormon church still strongly advocate the doctrine of blood atonement. The *Deseret News* for September 29, 1977, reported that a "polygamist cult leader" by the name of Ervil LeBaron "has been linked to more than a dozen deaths and disappearances in the West. . . ."

As we indicated earlier, the idea that murderers should be shot so that their blood can flow to atone for their sins was an outgrowth of the blood atonement doctrine. A grim reminder of this doctrine was found in the *Salt Lake Tribune* on January 17, 1977: "UTAH STATE PRISON—A last-minute court decision cleared the way today for the execution of Gary Mark Gilmore, 36, and moments later the condemned killer was shot to death here by a firing squad."

THE HEREAFTER

Chapter 21

Because the Universalists were claiming that man would not receive eternal punishment for his sins, the question of justice and mercy was a burning issue during Joseph Smith's lifetime. Evangelist Charles G. Finney tells of an incident that took place in the 1820s:

> . . . a Universalist minister came in and began to promulge his objectionable doctrines. . . . there was a large number that seemed to be shaken in their minds, in regard to the commonly received views of the Bible. . . . The great effort of the Universalist was of course to show that sin did not deserve endless punishment. He inveighed against the doctrine of endless punishment as unjust, infinitely cruel and absurd. . . . how could a God of love punish men endlessly? . . .
>
> When the evening came for my lecture, the house was crowded. I took up the question of the justice of endless punishment, and discussed it through that and the next evening. There was general satisfaction with the presentation (*Charles G. Finney*, pp.48-49).

Like Charles G. Finney, Joseph Smith originally took a very strong stand against the doctrine of the Universalists. When we examine the *Book of Mormon* we see that it is filled with this controversy. In Alma 1:3 we read of a wicked man who "had gone about among the people, preaching to them that which he termed to be the word of God." In the fourth verse of the same chapter it becomes clear that this man was a Universalist in his doctrine: "And he also testified unto the people that *all mankind should be saved at the last day,* and that they need not fear nor tremble, but that they might lift up their heads and rejoice; for the Lord had created all men, and had also redeemed all men; and, in the end, *all men should have eternal life*" (Alma 1:4).

The reader will notice that this wicked man taught that "all mankind should be saved at the last day." In the Universalist publication, *Gospel Advocate*, we find many similar expressions: "The Universalists believe . . . *all men* will ultimately enjoy happiness . . ." (*Gospel Advocate*, Feb. 17, 1826, p.47). ". . . he both can and will *save all mankind* with an everlasting salvation . . ." (p.47). ". . . *all men will finally be saved*" (p.178).

The Universalists taught that "the devil is a nonentity, and an endless hell of brimstone a bug-bear. . ." (*Gospel Advocate*, August 25, 1826, p.245).

The *Book of Mormon*, on the other hand, warns against such a teaching: "And behold, others he *flattereth away, and telleth them there is no hell;* and he saith unto them: I am no devil, for there is none — and thus he whispereth in their ears, until he grasps them with his awful chains, . . .and all that have been seized therewith must. . .go into the place prepared for them, even a lake of fire and brimstone, which is endless torment" (2 Nephi 28:22-23).

Although Joseph Smith vigorously opposed the doctrine of the Universalists and supported the orthodox position concerning hell in his *Book of Mormon*, within a year he had completely changed his mind concerning this matter. In a revelation given to Martin Harris in March, 1830, Joseph Smith proclaimed: "Nevertheless, it is *not written that there shall be no end to this torment*, but it is written endless torment" (*Doctrine and Covenants* 19:6). Smith goes on to explain that "endless punishment" does not mean that the sinner will suffer the punishment eternally. B. H. Roberts explained: "Christians believed that to receive eternal punishment was to be punished eternally. This popular Christian error was corrected in a revelation to Martin Harris . . ." (*Outlines of Ecclesiastical History*, p.408).

Joseph Fielding Smith likewise stated: "We learn from the *Doctrine and Covenants* that eternal punishment, or everlasting punishment, does *not* mean that a man condemned will endure this punishment forever . . ." (*Doctrines of Salvation*, vol. 2, p.160).

When Joseph Smith became converted to the ideas of the Universalists he completely repudiated the teachings of the *Book of Mormon*. It would almost appear that he had completely forgotten what he had previously written. In his later theology he taught that eternal punishment would eventually come to an end, but in the *Book of Mormon* he stated that eternal punishment is as eternal as the life of the soul: "Now, repentence could not come unto men except there were a punishment, which also was *eternal as the life of the soul* should be, affixed opposite to the plan of happiness, which was as eternal also as the life of the soul" (Alma 42:16).

In Mosiah 3:38-39, we read that it is a final doom: "Therefore if that man repenteth not, and remaineth and dieth an enemy to God, . . . mercy hath no claim on that man; therefore his *final doom is to endure a never ending torment.*" In 3 Nephi 27:11 and 17, it is made clear that the wicked can never return: ". . . and by and by the end cometh, and they are hewn down and cast into the fire, from *whence there is no return.* . . . And he that endureth not unto the end, the same is he that is also hewn down and cast into the fire, from whence they can *no more return,* because of the justice of the Father."

Although at first it seems almost incredible that Joseph Smith completely reversed his position regarding eternal punishment, we must remember that he did this with regard to many other doctrines and practices. For instance, he condemned polygamy and secret societies in the *Book of Mormon,* yet he became a polygamist and a Mason before his death. Also, he originally taught monotheism but completely turned to polytheism. Joseph Smith may have changed his mind with regard to eternal punishment because of his friendship with Universalists. At one time Joseph Smith lived with Joseph Knight and his family who "were Universalists in their faith" (*Comprehensive History of the Church,* vol. 1, p.200). It has been discovered that even Joseph Smith's own father was a member of "a Universalist Society in 1797" (*The Ensign,* February 1971, p.16). It is reported also that Martin Harris, the man to whom Joseph Smith gave the revelation denying eternal punishment, was at one time a Universalist.

Although Joseph Smith took a great deal of space in the *Book of Mormon* to warn against an "awful hell," toward the end of his life he seemed to be indifferent and even flippant concerning this matter (see *Mormonism—Shadow or Reality?* p.198).

The fact that Joseph Smith completely changed his position concerning hell has led to a great deal of confusion among the Mormon people. Brigham Young taught that there would probably be no women in hell: "I doubt whether it can be found, from the revelations that are given and the facts as they exist, that there is a female in all the regions of hell" (*Journal of Discourses,* vol. 8, p.222).

Apostle John A. Widtsoe taught that "very few will be so condemned" as to become the "sons of perdition" because "very few have the knowledge required." Apostle Widtsoe went on to state: "All others, who are not classed as sons of perdition, will be 'redeemed in the due time of the Lord'; that is, they will all be saved. *The meanest sinner will find some place in the heavenly realm. . . .* In the Church of Jesus Christ of Latter-day Saints, *there is no hell.* All will find a measure of salvation. . . . The gospel of Jesus Christ has no hell in the old proverbial sense" (*Joseph Smith—Seeker After Truth,* pp.177-78).

It is interesting to note that the *Book of Mormon* claims it is the devil who will say there is no hell. In 2 Nephi 28:21,22 we read:

> And others will he pacify, and lull them away into carnal security, that they will say: All is well in Zion; yea, Zion prospereth, all is well—and thus the devil cheateth their souls, and leadeth them away carefully down to hell. And behold, others he flattereth away, and telleth them *there is no hell;* . . . and thus he whispereth in their ears, until he grasps them with his awful chains, from whence there is no deliverance.

It is certainly strange that Apostle Widtsoe would teach the very thing that the *Book of Mormon* so strongly condemns.

Mormon Purgatory

Milton V. Backman, assistant professor of church history at Brigham Young University, admitted: "Joseph Smith . . . accepted the Roman Catholic concept that there was an intermediate or preparatory stage between death and a final judgment" (*Seminar On The Prophet Joseph Smith,* BYU, February 18, 1961).

Joseph Fielding Smith taught that "It is the duty of men in this life to repent. Every man who hears the gospel message is under obligation to receive it. If he fails, then in the spirit world he will be called upon to receive it . . ." (*Doctrines of Salvation,* vol. 2, p.183).

On page 220 of the same book President Smith claimed: "*Even the wicked of the earth* . . . shall at last come forth from the prison house, repentant and willing to bow the knee and acknowledge Christ. . . ." President Smith also stated: "It is decreed that the unrighteous shall have to spend their time during this thousand years in *the prison house* prepared for them where they *can repent and cleanse themselves* through the things which they shall suffer" (*Doctrines of Salvation,* vol. 3, p.60).

Heber C. Kimball, who was a member of the First Presidency under Brigham Young, added:

> That is loving the wicked, to send them there to hell to be burnt out until they are purified. Yes, they shall go there and stay there

and be burnt, like an old pipe that stinks with long usage and corruption, until they are burnt out, and then their spirits may be saved in the day of God Almighty" (*Journal of Discourses*, vol. 4, p.223).

You have often heard me talk about my kindred. . . . they will be saved as I have told you many of this people will; they will first go to hell and remain there until the corruption with which they are impregnated is burnt out; and the day will yet come when they will come to me and acknowledge me as their savior, and I will redeem them and bring them forth from hell to where I live and make them my servants; and they will be quite willing to enter into my service (vol. 3, p.109).

In accepting the Roman Catholic concept of a purgatory or "preparatory stage between death and a final judgment," the Mormon church leaders have had to lay aside the teachings of the *Book of Mormon*. In Alma 34:32-35 it is made very clear that there is no chance for repentance after death:

For behold, this life is the time for men to prepare to meet God; yea, behold the day of this life is the day for men to perform their labors. . . . I beseech of you that ye do not procrastinate the day of your repentance until the end; for after this day of life, which is given us to prepare for eternity, behold, if we do not improve our time while in this life, then cometh the night of darkness wherein there can be no labor performed.

Ye cannot say, when ye are brought to that awful crisis, that I will repent, that I will return to my God. Nay, ye cannot say this; for that same spirit which doth possess your bodies at the time that ye go out of this life, that same spirit will have power to possess your body in that eternal world.

For behold, if ye have procrastinated the day of your repentance even until death, behold, ye have become subjected to the spirit of the devil, and he doth seal you his; therefore, the Spirit of the Lord hath withdrawn from you, and hath no place in you, and the devil hath all power over you; and this is the final state of the wicked.

Degrees of Glory

On February 16, 1832, Joseph Smith gave a revelation which states that there will be three different degrees of glory after the resurrection (see *Doctrine and Covenants*, section 76). In the *History of the Church*, it is taught: "Except a man be born again, he cannot see the Kingdom of God . . . A man may be saved, after the judgment, in the terrestrial kingdom, or in the telestial kingdom, but he can never see the celestial kingdom of God, without being born of water and the Spirit." (vol. 1, p.283).

Joseph Fielding Smith claimed that "Those who reject the gospel, but live honorable lives, shall also be heirs of salvation, but not in the celestial kingdom. The Lord has prepared a place for them in the terrestrial kingdom. Those who live lives of wickedness may also be heirs of salvation, that is, they too shall be redeemed from death and from hell eventually" (*Doctrines of Salvation*, vol. 2, p.133).

This doctrine of three degrees of glory is certainly not in harmony with the teachings of the *Book of Mormon*. In 1 Nephi 15:35 we read that there is only a heaven and a hell: "And there is a place prepared, yea, even that awful hell of which I have spoken, and the devil is the foundation of it; wherefore the final state of the souls of men is to dwell in the kingdom of God, or to be cast out because of that justice of which I have spoken."

In Alma 5:24, 25, and 39, we read that those who are cast out of the kingdom of heaven are of the kingdom of the devil:

> Behold, my brethren, do ye suppose that such an one can have a place to sit down in the kingdom of God. . . I say unto you, Nay; except ye make our Creator a liar from the beginning, . . . ye cannot suppose that such can have place in the kingdom of heaven; but they shall be cast out for they are the children of the kingdom of the devil (vv. 24-25). And now if ye are not the sheep of the good shepherd, of what fold are ye? Behold, I say unto you, that the devil is your shepherd, and ye are of his fold; and now, who can deny this? Behold, I say unto you, whosoever denieth this is a liar and a child of the devil (v. 39).

Apostle Orson Pratt had to admit that the Bible and *Book of Mormon* did not lend much support to the doctrine of three degrees of glory: "Then again, what could we learn from either the Bible or Book of Mormon in regard to three glories—the celestial, the terrestrial and the telestial glories? What did we know concerning those that should inhabit these various worlds of glory? Nothing at all" (*Journal of Discourses*, vol. 20, p.70).

The Mormon church uses the statement made by Paul in 1 Corinthians 15:40 to try to prove there are three degrees of glory: "There are also celestial bodies, and bodies terrestrial: but the glory of the celestial is one, and the glory of the terrestrial is another."

The first thing that should be noted about this verse is that it does not use the word "telestial"; this is a word that was made up by Joseph Smith. Bruce R. McConkie, who is now an Apostle, maintains that "The fact that some of these are telestial bodies has been lost from the King James Version of the Bible"

(*Mormon Doctrine*, 1966, p.777). Apostle McConkie and other Mormon writers are, of course, unable to furnish any evidence that this has been deleted from the Bible or even that "telestial" is an actual word.

The second thing that should be noted is the meaning of the words "celestial" and "terrestrial." The *American College Dictionary* tells us that the meaning of celestial is "pertaining to the spiritual or invisible heaven; *heavenly.* . ." The word terrestrial means "pertaining to, consisting of, or representing *the earth.* . . ." So we see that the word celestial simply means "heavenly" and the word terrestrial means "earthly." In *Young's Literal Translation of the Holy Bible*, the original Greek words are rendered as "heavenly" and "earthly" instead of "celestial" and "terrestrial": ". . . and there are *heavenly* bodies, and *earthly* bodies; but one is the glory of the heavenly and another that of the earthly. . . ."

The third thing that should be noted concerning this verse is the context it appears in. A careful examination of the context, verses 35-54, reveals that Paul was comparing our earthly body with the body we shall receive in the resurrection; he was not speaking of three kingdoms in heaven. All of us now have a terrestrial or earthly body, but in the resurrection we shall have a celestial or heavenly body. Verse 44 makes it clear that Paul was speaking of the difference between the body we now have and the body we shall receive in the resurrection: "It is sown a natural body; it is raised a spiritual body. There is a natural body, and there is a spiritual body."

Therefore, we see that the doctrine of three degrees of glory cannot be supported from the Bible, nor can it be supported from the *Book of Mormon.* Both books condemn this teaching.

The reader will find a chart on page 561 illustrating the Mormon plan of eternal progression.

TEMPLE WORK

Chapter 22

In order really to understand present-day Mormonism and the hold it has upon its people it is necessary to know about the work that goes on in Mormon temples. The ceremonies performed in these temples are secret, and only "worthy" members of the Mormon church may participate in them.

Baptism for the Dead

The Mormon doctrine of baptism for the dead was first practiced in Nauvoo, Illinois. Wilford Woodruff reported that "Joseph Smith himself . . . went into the Mississippi River one Sunday night after meeting, and baptized a hundred. I baptized another hundred. The next man, a few rods from me, baptized another hundred. We were strung up and down the Mississippi, baptizing for our dead. But there was no recorder, . . . the Lord told Joseph that he must have recorders present . . . Of course, we had to do the work over again. Nevertheless, that does not say the work was not of God" (*The Deseret Weekly*, vol. 42:554, as quoted in *Temples of the Most High*, by N. B. Lundwall, 1962, p.69).

On May 2, 1843, Charlotte Haven wrote a letter in which she told of watching the Mormon elders baptizing for the dead in the river which was "icy cold" at that time: "We drew a little nearer and heard several names repeated by the elders as the victims were douched, and you can imagine our surprise when the name *George Washington* was called. So after these fifty years he is out of purgatory and on his way to the 'celestial' heaven!" (*Overland Monthly*, December 1890).

The early Mormon leaders seem to have been very confused concerning baptism for the dead. Brigham Young once stated: "Hundreds and thousands, I suppose, were baptized before any record was kept at all, and they were baptized over, and a record kept . . . the Lord did not reveal everything at once; but I need not dwell on this any longer" (*Journal of Discourses*, vol. 18, p.241).

The Mormon leaders teach that the spirits of people who have died cannot enter the celestial kingdom of heaven until a Mormon is baptized for them by proxy—i.e., a living person is immersed on behalf of the dead person. This information about baptism for the dead is found in Joseph Smith's history:

> Chrysostum says that the Marchionites practiced baptism for their dead. "After a catechumen was dead, they had a living man under the bed of the deceased; then coming to the dead man, they asked him whether he would receive baptism, and he making no answer, the other answered for him, and said that he would be baptized in his stead; and so they baptized the living for the dead." The church of course at that time was degenerate, and the particular form might be incorrect, but the thing is sufficiently plain in the Scriptures, hence Paul, in speaking of the doctrine, says, "Else what shall they do which are baptized for the dead, if the dead rise not at all? Why are they then baptized for the dead?" (I Cor. xv:29) (*History of the Church*, vol. 4, p.599).

Bible scholars are divided as to the meaning of the verse which is cited above. Mormons, of course, believe that it applies to temple work, where a living person is baptized in behalf of someone that has died. Even if this verse did apply to a living person being baptized for someone else, as the Mormons maintain, this would not prove that faithful Christians were practicing it. Paul does not say that "we" are baptized for the dead, but rather that "they" are baptized for the dead. The use of the word "they" instead of the word "we" could make a great deal of difference in the meaning of the statement. If a Protestant made the statement, "Why do they then pray for the dead, if the dead rise not at all," it would not mean that he was endorsing the Catholic doctrine of prayers for the dead. If, however, a person made the statement, "Why do we then pray for the dead, if the dead rise not at all," we would assume that he believed in prayers for the dead.

A good discussion of 1 Corinthians 15:29 is found in the pamphlet *Baptism for the Dead*, by Charles R. Hield and Russell F. Ralston:

> A careful reading of this epistle shows that the Apostle Paul writes to the Corinthian Saints using the words "I," "we," "ye," "you," when referring to them and/or himself all the way through his message; but when he mentions baptism for the dead, he changes to "they." "What shall they do?" "Why are they then baptized for the dead?" In the verses following, he returns to the use of "we" and "you." Thus he seems to disassociate himself and the righteous Saints from the methods used

by those groups who at that time were practicing baptism for the dead.

The Apostle Paul did not urge his hearers to practice the principle, nor did he command it. He merely used the case as an illustration. Paul did not worship the "unknown God" of the pagans because he found an altar to the pagan unknown god (Acts 17:23). . . . There is no mention of baptism for the dead in the Bible up until Paul—and no mention afterward. Paul, as well as the other apostles, rather than endorsing baptism for the dead as then practiced, seems to have exercised a counteracting influence upon this ordinance, for it was perpetuated only among heretics.

The Bible contains no specific authorization of this doctrine. Christ does not mention it, nor do any of the apostles, save Paul; who makes only an indirect reference to it (Independence, Mo: Herald Publishing House, 1951, pp.23-24).

The fact that Christ never mentioned baptism for the dead is strong evidence that no such doctrine existed in the early Christian Church.

Orson Pratt admitted that the Bible does not contain any information as to how baptism for the dead should be performed. His excuse for the Bible not containing this information was that it was probably lost or taken out of the Bible. He claimed:

This doctrine of baptism for the dead must have been well understood by them. . . . Now when, and in what manner was this doctrine communicated to them? It *may have been* fully developed to them in the epistle which he says that he had previously written to them. This doctrine *may have been* as important as baptism to the living. Does the written or unwritten word of God with which Christendom are acquainted, inform them anything about how this ceremony is to be performed? Does it inform them who is to officiate? Who is the candidate in behalf of the dead? What classes of the dead are to be benefitted by it? Does scripture or tradition inform us in what particular baptism for the dead will affect them in the resurrection? Does it inform us whether baptism for the dead can be administered in all places, or only in a baptismal font, in a temple consecrated for that purpose? All these important questions *remain unanswered by scripture and tradition (Orson Pratt's Works, 1891, p.205).*

Although Joseph Smith performed baptism for the dead in the Mississippi River, it is now performed only in temples. The Mormon people are very zealous about this work for the dead, for they believe they are saving their ancestors. President John Taylor stated: ". . . we are the only people that know how to save our progenitors, . . . we in fact are *the saviours of the world*, if they ever are saved . . ." (*Journal of Discourses*, vol. 6, p.163). President Wilford Woodruff felt that he had saved John Wesley, Columbus, and all of the presidents of the United States except three:

> . . . two weeks before I left St. George, the *spirits of the dead gathered around me*, wanting to know why we did not redeem them. . . . These were the signers of the Declaration of Independence, and they waited on me for two days and two nights. . . . I straightway went into the baptismal font and called upon brother McCallister to *baptize me for the signers of the Declaration of Independence*, and fifty other eminent men, making one hundred in all, including John Wesley, Coumbus, and others; I then baptized him for every President of the United States, except three; and when their cause is just, somebody will do the work for them (*Journal of Discourses*, vol. 19, p.229).

The Mormons are spending millions of dollars doing genealogical research in order to find the names of those who have died so that they can do proxy baptism for them. Bruce R. McConkie wrote concerning this matter:

> Before vicarious ordinances of salvation and exaltation may be performed for those who have died . . . they must be accurately and properly identified. Hence, genealogical research is required. . . . the Church maintains in Salt Lake City one of the world's greatest genealogical societies. Much of the genealogical source material of various nations of the earth has been or is being microfilmed by this society; millions of dollars is being spent; and a reservior of hundreds of millions of names and other data about people who lived in past generations is available for study (*Mormon Doctrine*, 1966, pp.308-9).

Heber J. Grant, the seventh president of the church, told of employing "a sister who devotes *all her time* to the preparation of genealogical records. . . . pertaining to the families to which I belong in direct descent and through marriage." The Church Section of the *Deseret News* for April 23, 1966, tells of a woman who "searched 15 years" before she found the "names of four new ancestors" for whom she had been looking. Wallace Turner informs us:

> This microfilming of records is a tremendous work, growing in scope continually, operated entirely for the benefit of the ancestor tracing that leads to the vicarious Temple ceremonies. As of July 1, 1965, the microfilm division had a total of 406,682 rolls of microfilm of 100 feet each. . . . The total microfilm load included 579,679,800 pages of documents. There were *more than 5 billion names* in the files. . . .

The church puts about $4 million a year into the Genealogical Society. It has 575 employees and is run by a board which includes two apostles. The microfilm unit sends crews all over the world to locate and photograph records. . . . The negative microfilms are stored in a great vault system dug out of the rocks of Cottonwood Canyon . . . southeast of Salt Lake City. This underground storage system was produced by the church at a cost of $2.5 million. It has six vaults, which each hold a million rolls of film. . . . During 1964, the microfilming units worked in fourteen countries (*The Mormon Establishment*, pp.81-82).

Apostle LeGrand Richards predicted that "in the not too far distant future, the Church Genealogical Library will not only be the best in the world but will also be a repository of most all other genealogical libraries" (*A Marvelous Work and a Wonder*, p.192).

Many people wonder why the Mormon church spends so much time and money searching for the names of the dead when there are so many people starving to death. It would seem far better to spend this money and time on the living and let the Lord take care of the dead. The Mormon leaders admit that in spite of all they can do they will never be able to find all of the names until the Lord gives them during the millennium. Since the Mormons believe that the Lord will have to provide most of the names anyway, would it not be better to spend this time and money helping the living instead of searching for the names of the dead? Because of this emphasis on work for the dead, one Mormon has compared the church to the ancient Egyptians. The Egyptians, of course, spent a fantastic amount of time and money building pyramids and doing other work for their dead.

The *Book of Mormon* says that the false churches "rob the poor because of their fine sanctuaries" (2 Nephi 28:13), yet the Mormon church is spending millions of dollars building beautiful temples. The Salt Lake Temple, for instance, cost millions of dollars and took almost forty years to build. *The Salt Lake Tribune* for August 31, 1974, gave this information about the temple that the Mormons built in Washington, D.C.: ". . . it is indeed marble, 288 feet high, $15 *million worth*, and that makes the new Washington Temple of the Church of Jesus Christ of Latter-day Saints not only one of the most architecturally amazing but also *one of the most expensive church edifices to rise in recent years*. . . . It is the 16th temple to be built by the Church of Jesus Christ of Latter-day Saints. . . ."

The Mormon leaders are planning to build temples in a number of other countries in the near future. Most of the "endowments" performed in Mormon temples are for the dead;

therefore, when we add the millions of dollars spent for temples and their upkeep to the millions spent on genealogical research, we find that the Mormons are similar to the ancient Egyptians in their attitudes toward the dead. This obsession with the dead approaches very close to ancestral worship. Adney Y. Komatsu, a member of the First Quorum of Seventy in the Mormon church, stated in the 146th General Conference of the Church:

> May I share with you this afternoon an experience that happened to a young couple who were members of the Church in Japan. . . . the couple joined with others in seeking out their ancestors and in planning to have the temple work done for them. The girl searched diligently through shrines, cemeteries, and government record offices, and was able to gather seventy-seven names. . . . As this young couple joined their family members . . . they displayed their book of remembrance. . . . They discussed with those relatives assembled their ancestral lines and the importance of completing the genealogical research. *It was difficult for their nonmember families to understand the reasons for a Christian church teaching principles such as "ancestral worship," for this was a Buddhist teaching* and tradition. . . . Through genealogical research and through doing temple work for their progenitors, and especially with a temple now becoming available in Tokyo, members can so live that the gospel will yet be embraced by many more in the Orient (*The Ensign*, May 1976, p.102).

Joseph Fielding Smith proclaimed that the "greatest commandment given us, and made obligatory, is the temple work in our own behalf and in behalf of our dead" (*Doctrines of Salvation*, vol. 2, p.149).

On page 146 of the same book, we read: "The Prophet Joseph Smith declared, 'The greatest responsibility in this world that God has laid upon us is to seek after our dead.' "

Jesus certainly never taught anything about baptism for the dead or seeking after our dead. In fact, he said that "the first of all the commandments is, Hear, O Israel; The Lord our God is one Lord: And thou shalt love the Lord thy God with all thy heart, and with all thy soul, and with all thy mind, and with all thy strength: this is the first commandment. And the second is like, namely this, Thou shalt love thy neighbor as thyself. There is none other commandment greater than these" (Mark 12:29-31).

The Bible says nothing about doing extensive genealogical research to save the dead. On the contrary, Apostle Paul makes two statements which are often used against the practice: "Neither give heed to fables and *endless genealogies*, which minister questions, rather than godly edifying which is in faith: so do" (1 Tim. 1:4). "But avoid foolish questions, and *genealogies*, and contentions and strivings about the law; for they are unprofitable and vain" (Titus 3:9).

Perhaps the most embarrassing thing to the Mormon church concerning the doctrine of baptism for the dead is the *Book of Mormon* itself. The *Book of Mormon* is supposed to contain "the fullness of the everlasting Gospel" (see *Pearl of Great Price*, p.51, v.34). In the *Doctrine and Covenants* 42:12 we read: "And again, the elders, priests, and teachers of this church shall teach the principles of my gospel, which are in the Bible and the Book of Mormon, in the which is the fulness of the gospel."

Even though the *Book of Mormon* is supposed to contain the "fulness of the gospel," it never mentions the doctrine of baptism for the dead, *not even once!* The word "baptism" appears twenty-five times in the *Book of Mormon*. The word "baptize" appears twenty-eight times. The word "baptized" appears eighty-five times, and the word "baptizing" appears six times, but the doctrine of baptism for the dead is not mentioned at all!

The excuse that the doctrine of baptism for the dead was removed from the Bible certainly would not prove true in the case of the *Book of Mormon*. The Catholics never had the *Book of Mormon* and therefore they could not be charged with removing it.

Actually, the *Book of Mormon* condemns the very ideas that led to the practice of baptism for the dead. It plainly indicates that there is no chance for a person to repent after death if he has known the gospel and has rejected it (see our previous chapter on "The Hereafter").

Temple Marriage

The Mormon church teaches that it is necessary for a person to be married or sealed in the Temple so that he can obtain the highest exaltation in the hereafter. This work is done for both the living and the dead. The doctrine of Temple Marriage comes from Section 132 of the *Doctrine and Covenants*, which is a revelation given to Joseph Smith on July 12, 1843. Joseph Fielding Smith explains the need for Temple Marriage:

> If you want *salvation in the fullest*, that is exaltation in the kingdom of God, so that you may become his sons and his daughters, you have got to go *into the temple of the Lord and receive these holy ordinances* which belong to that house, which cannot be had elsewhere (*Doctrines of Salvation*, vol. 2, p.44).

It fills my heart with sadness when I see in the paper the name of a daughter or a son of members of this Church, and discover that she or he is going to have a ceremony and be married outside of the temple of the Lord, because I realize what it means, that *they are cutting themselves off from exaltation* in the kingdom of God.

SORROW IN RESURRECTION IF NO ETERNAL MARRIAGE. These young people who seem to be so happy now, when they rise in the resurrection—and find themselves in the condition in which they will find themselves—then there will be *weeping*, and *wailing*, and *gnashing of teeth*, and *bitterness of soul* . . . (*Ibid.*, p.60).

On page 61 of the same book, the following statement appears: "CIVIL MARRIAGE MAKES *SERVANTS* IN ETERNITY," and on page 62 we read: "CELESTIAL MARRIAGE MAKES *GODS* IN ETERNITY."

The Mormon leaders teach that those who marry in the temple will have the power to continually beget children in heaven. Apostle Bruce R. McConkie explains:

Those who gain eternal life (exaltation) also gain eternal lives, meaning that in the resurrection they have eternal "increase," "a continuation of the seeds," a "continuation of the lives." Their spirit progeny will "continue as innumerable as the stars; or, if ye were to count the sand upon the seashore ye could not number them." (D.&C. 131:1-4; 132:19-25, 30, 55).

"Except a man and his wife enter into an everlasting covenant and be married for eternity, while in this probation, by the power and authority of the holy priesthood," The Prophet says, "They will cease to increase when they die; that is, they will not have any children after the resurrection" (*Mormon Doctrine*, 1966, p.238).

Joseph Fielding Smith warned: "Restrictions will be placed upon those who enter the terrestial and telestial kingdoms, and even those in the celestial kingdom who do not get the exaltation; *changes will be made in their bodies* to suit their condition; and there will be no marrying or giving in marriage, nor living together of men and women, because of these restrictions" (*Doctrines of Salvation*, vol. 2, p.73).

Mormon theology teaches that even God Himself has a wife and that in the pre-existence we were spiritually born and lived as His sons and daughters. Milton R. Hunter claimed: "Jesus is man's spiritual brother. We dwelt with Him in the spirit world as members of that large society of eternal intelligences, which included our Heavenly Parents . . ." (*The Gospel Through the Ages*, 1958, p.21).

Mormon authorities teach that it is absolutely impossible for a person to receive the highest exaltation without temple marriage. Milton R. Hunter remarked: "Marriage is not only a righteous institution, but obedience to this law is absolutely necessary in order to obtain the highest exaltation in the Kingdom of God" (*Ibid.*, p.119).

If the Mormon doctrine of "sealing" were true we would expect to find evidence that Jesus was married in the temple. No such evidence has been found. The Bible never mentions the doctrine of eternal marriage. In fact, Jesus seems to have taught just the opposite: "And Jesus answering said unto them, The children of this world marry, and are given in marriage: But they which shall be *accounted worthy* to obtain that world, and the resurrection from the dead, *neither marry, nor are given in marriage*: Neither can they die any more: for they are equal unto the angels; and are the children of God, being the children of the resurrection" (Luke 20:34-36).

Apostle LeGrand Richards frankly admits that the "principle of eternal marriage did not come to the Prophet Joseph Smith by reading the Bible, but through the revelations of the Lord to him" (*A Marvelous Work and a Wonder*, p.195).

While Mormon apologists have a hard time explaining the fact that the Bible does not support the doctrine of temple marriage, they are faced with an even greater problem when they turn to the *Book of Mormon*. It is supposed to contain the "fulness of the gospel," yet it does *not contain even one passage to support the doctrine of temple marriage!*

Temple marriage or sealing, like many other doctrines, was not part of the original Mormon faith. The first edition of the *Doctrine and Covenants*, published in 1835, page 251, said that "all marriages in this church of Christ of Latter Day Saints, should be solemnized *in a public meeting*, or feast. . . . All legal contracts of marriage made before a person is baptized into this church, should be held *sacred and fulfilled*." This section on marriage was so diametrically opposed to the later teachings of the church, that it finally had to be completely removed from the *Doctrine and Covenants*. Joseph Fielding Smith frankly admitted that this section was removed because it contained "false teachings" (see *Mormonism—Shadow or Reality?*, p.456).

Connected with Polygamy

The revelation which contains the information concerning temple marriage is also the revelation which contains the teaching of polygamy—i.e., section 132 of the *Doctrine and Covenants*. Therefore, polygamy and temple marriage stand or

"No, sir, you have a wife, she is in her grave, she was married to you for time and all eternity, now I desire a husband for all eternity myself. Is there any provision made for me if I go in as the second wife?" Why, yes. The provision is that both may be sealed to him for time and all eternity and not violate the law of God.

All these principles that I have treated upon, pertaining to eternal marriage, the very moment that they are admitted to be true, it brings in plurality of marriage, and if plurality of marriage is not true or in other words, if a man has no divine right to marry two wives or more in this world, then marriage for eternity is not true. and your faith is all vain, and all the scaling ordinanecs and powers, pertaining to marriages for eternity are vain, worthless, good for nothing; for as sure as one is true the other also must be true. Amen.

DISCOURSE BY ELDER WILFORD WOODRUFF,

DELIVERED IN THE TABERNACLE, AT LOGAN, SUNDAY MORNING, AUGUST 1ST, 1880.

(Reported by Geo. F. Gibbs.)

REVELATION, PROPHESYING, PREDICTIONS OF THE SERVANTS OF GOD, ETC.

It is a common saying with us, that the Lord has set his hand to build up his kingdom; but, notwithstanding, it is a true and a very interesting one. Let us turn our minds which way we will, as men of God, as Elders in Israel, if we enjoy any portion of the Spirit of the Lord, we cannot help seeing the hand of the Lord in his works in these mountains and in the earth. It is a difficult matter, many times, for men of the world to understand the literal fulfilment of revelation; in fact, some of our leading men, men of wisdom, men who have enjoyed a good portion of the Spirit of the Lord—it has been difficult for them to understand the fulfilment of prophecy. In conversation with

A photograph of the *Journal of Discourses*, vol. 21, page 296. Apostle Orson Pratt maintains that if polygamy is not true, then marriage for eternity is also false.

fall together. Charles Penrose, who was later sustained as first councilor in the First Presidency, made this perfectly clear at a conference in Centerville, Utah: "Elder Charles W. Penrose . . . showed that the revelation . . . was [the] only one published on Celestial Marriage, and *if the doctrine of plural marriage was repudiated so must the glorious principle of marriage for eternity, the two being indissolubly interwoven with each other*" (*Millennial Star*, vol. 45, p.454).

Apostle Orson Pratt argued that "*if plurality of marriage is not true* or in other words, if a man has no divine right to marry two wives or more in this world, *then marriage for eternity is not true*, and your faith is all vain, and all the sealing ordinances and powers, pertaining to marriages for eternity are vain, worthless, good for nothing; for as sure as one is true the other also must be true" (*Journal of Discourses*, vol. 21, p.296).

While the Mormon people are no longer allowed to practice polygamy, they have not repudiated the doctrine. They still teach that polygamy is practiced in heaven. Mormon writer John J. Stewart explains:

> The Church has never, and certainly will never, renounce this doctrine. The revelation on plural marriage is still *an integral part of LDS scripture*, and always will be. If a woman, sealed to her husband for time and eternity, precedes her husband in death, it is his privilege to marry another also for time and eternity, providing that he is worthy of doing so. Consider, for instance, the case of President Joseph Fielding Smith of the Council of the Twelve, one of the greatest men upon the earth. . . . After the death of his first wife President Joseph Fielding Smith married another, and each of these good women are sealed to him for time and all eternity (*Brigham Young and His Wives*, 1961, p.14).

Joseph Fielding Smith confirmed Mr. Stewart's point when he said that if he was "faithful and worthy of an exaltation, . . . my wives will be mine in eternity." (*Doctrines of Salvation*, vol. 2, p.67).

Harold B. Lee, the eleventh president of the church, also remarried and was planning on living plural marriage in heaven. President Lee wrote a poem in which he reflected:

> My lovely Joan was sent to me;
> So Joan Joins Fern
> That three might be, more fitted for eternity.
> "O Heavenly Father, my thanks to thee" (*Deseret News 1974 Church Almanac*, p.17).

While Mormon men are allowed more than one wife in

heaven, a woman can have but one husband. President Joseph Fielding Smith explained:

> When a man and a woman are married in the temple for time and all eternity, and then the man dies and the woman marries another man, she can be married to him for time only.
>
> When a man marries a woman who was married previously to her husband in the temple but who has now died, he does so, or should, with his eyes open. If the children are born to this woman and her "time' husband, he has no claim upon those children. They go with the mother. This is the law. Certainly a man cannot in reason expect to take another man's wife, after that man is dead, and rear a family by her and then claim the children.
>
> If he wants a family of his own, then he should marry a wife that he can have in eternity (*Doctrines of Salvation*, vol. 2, pp.78-79).

Because the Mormons believe that a woman can have only one husband in heaven a problem has arisen for those doing work for the dead. In a newsletter published by Sandy First Ward we find the following:

> . . . Brother Christiansen talked about new rulings concerning sealings for the dead. It is now possible for a woman that was married more than once *to be sealed to ALL her husbands*, providing that in life she had not been sealed to any of her husbands.
>
> The First Presidency of the Church has ruled that rather than try to decide which husband a deceased woman should be sealed to, *she can be sealed to all of them. However, only one sealing will be valid* and accepted before God. God and the woman will decide which one of the sealings will be accepted on Judgment Day (*Tele-Ward*, Sandy First Ward, January 25, 1976, vol. V, no. 2, p.5).

However this may be, at one time Brigham Young became so zealous to establish polygamy that he declared that a man who would not enter into polygamy would have his wife taken from him in the resurrection and given to another:

> Now, where a man in this church says, "I don't want but *one wife*, I will live my religion with one," he will perhaps be saved in the Celestial kingdom; but *when he gets there he will not find himself in possession of any wife at all*. He has had a talent that he has hid up. He will come forward and say, "Here is that which thou gavest me, I have not wasted it, and here is the one talent," and he will not enjoy it but it will be *taken and given to those who have improved the talents they received*, and he will find himself *without any wife*, and *he will remain single forever and ever* (*Deseret News*, September 17, 1873).

A Secret Ceremony

While the revelation commanding temple marriage is printed in the *Doctrine and Covenants*, the ritual itself is supposed to be kept secret. Nevertheless, throughout the years numerous Mormons who became alienated from the church exposed the ceremony. Over two dozen of these accounts have been printed. Because the ritual is kept secret many false impressions and charges of gross immorality have been circulated. On February 18, 1846, the *Warsaw Signal* charged that those who participated in the ritual were "in a state of nudity" throughout the ceremony. In response to this article a woman who had been through the endowment wrote a letter to the editor in which she stated that the ceremony had been misrepresented:

> Mr. Sharp:—Dear Sir:—I discover by your paper, in what you have published in regard to the Mormon endowments, . . . that you have been wrongly informed. . . .
>
> I went into this pretended holy operation . . . We were first received past the Guard into a private room . . . this was the room of preparation or purification—We were divested of all our apparel, and in a state of perfect nudity we were washed from head to foot,—a blanket was then thrown about our persons, and then commencing at the head we were anointed from head to foot with sweet oil scented (I think) with lavender. We were then clothed in white robes. All this was done by sisters in the church—none others were present—it is false to say that men and women are admitted together in an indecent manner. We were then conducted into a room called the Garden of Eden . . . After a considerable ceremony, . . . a very dandy-like fellow appeared with a black cap[e] on, that had a long tail attached to it; he . . . induced some of our sisters to eat of the 'forbidden fruit.' . . . The Lord pronounces a curse upon him—he gets down upon his belly and crawls off. . . . We were then presented with aprons, . . . we passed into another room . . . This was called the Terrestrial Kingdom . . . After a considerable parade and ceremony, we passed into another room, or Celestial Kingdom. Here I saw . . . Brigham Young, with a white crown upon his head, and as I have since been told, representing God himself. We passed this room without much ceremony into another. . . . we took upon ourselves oaths and obligations not to reveal the secrets of the priesthood. . . . In one place I was presented with a new name, which I was not to reveal to any living creature, save the man to whom I should be sealed for eternity, . . . and from all that I can gather, all the females had the same name given them, but we are not allowed to reveal it to each other, . . . I have forgotten a part of the penalties (*Warsaw Signal*, April 15, 1846, p.2).

Increase McGee Van Dusen and his wife exposed the temple ritual in 1847. Their account was reprinted many times. On

February 12, 1906, the *Salt Lake Tribune* published the temple ceremony. In 1931 W. M. Paden published a pamphlet entitled, "Temple Mormonism—Its Evolution, Ritual and Meaning." While this was supposed to be one of the most accurate accounts of the ritual, Mormon leaders have made a number of important changes in the ceremony. Because of this fact we published an account in *Mormonism—Shadow or Reality?* (pp.462-73) which we felt was very accurate and up to date as of 1969.

Actually, we can get some idea of what goes on in the temple simply be searching through Mormon publications and journals. One of the most revealing statements by Brigham Young about the temple endowment was recorded in the diary of L. John Nuttall:

> When we got our washings and anointing under the hands of the Prophet Joseph at Nauvoo, we had only one room to work in, with the exception of a little side room or office where we were washed and anointed, had our garment placed upon us and received our new name; and after he had performed these ceremonies, he gave the key-words, signs, tokens, and penalties. Then after, we went into the large room over the store in Nauvoo, Joseph Smith divided up the room the best that he could, hung up the veil, marked it, gave us our instructions as we passed along from one department to another, giving us signs, tokens, penalties, with the key-words pertaining to those signs (Statement by Brigham Young, recorded in the "Diary of L. John Nuttall," February 7, 1877, as quoted in *God, Man, and the Universe*, p.334).

It should be noted that Brigham Young mentioned *washings, anointings, garments,* the *new name, key-words, signs, tokens* and *penalties.* He also stated that there was a "veil" with certain marks on it.

According to a "Price List Issued by The General Board of Relief Society" on June 1, 1968, men who desired to go through the temple must have the following "Articles for Temple Wear": robe, cap, apron, shield, garments (old style), shoes or heavy moccasins, trousers, shirt, tie, hose, and belt.

Those who have been through the temple are required to wear "garments" for the rest of their lives. William J. Whalen says:

> The devout Mormon who has received his "endowments" in the temple will wear sacred temple undergarments at all times. Resembling a union suit, now abbreviated at the knees, the undergarments are worn by both men and women, awake and sleeping. It is said that older Mormons refuse to take off these garments

completely even while taking a bath; they will hang one leg out of the tub so that they will never lose contact with the garments. Mystic signs are embroidered on them to remind the wearers of their temple obligations (*The Latter-day Saints in the Modern Day World*, 1964, pp.18-19).

On page 168 of the same book, Mr. Whalen says that "the garment was a long union suit of muslin or linen with the specified cabalistic marks. It has been abbreviated in recent years especially in the interests of feminine fashions."

The fact that the garments have been abbreviated is very interesting, for the early Mormon leaders taught that they could not be changed. President Joseph F. Smith declared before the changes were made:

> The Lord has given unto us garments of the holy priesthood, and you know what that means. And yet there are those of us who mutilate them, in order that we may follow the foolish, vain and (permit me to say) indecent practices of the world. In order that such people may imitate the fashions, they *will not hesitate to mutilate that which should be held by them the most sacred of all things in the world*, next to their own virtue, next to their own purity of life. They should hold these things that God has given unto them sacred, *unchanged and unaltered* from the very pattern in which God gave them. Let us have the moral courage to stand against the opinions of fashion, and especially where fashion compels us to break a covenant and so commit a grievous sin (*The Improvement Era*, vol. 9:813, as quoted in *Temples of the Most High*, p.276).

In 1918 the First Presidency of the church sent a message to the bishops in which the following appears:

> FIRST: The garments worn by those who receive endowments must be white, and of the approved pattern; they must not be altered or mutilated, and are to be worn as intended, down to the wrist and ankles, and around the neck.

> Please inform all to whom you issue recommends that these requirements are imperative . . . The Saints should know that the pattern of endowment garments was revealed from heaven, and that the blessings promised in connection with wearing them will not be realized if any unauthorized change is made in their form, or in the manner of wearing them (*Messages of the First Presidency*, by J. R. Clark, 1971, vol. 5, p.110).

Although the Mormon leaders vigorously maintained that the "garments" must be "worn as intended, down to the wrist and ankles, and around the neck," and that they could not be altered from "the very pattern in which God gave them," women's fashions caused the arms and legs to be shortened and the neck line to be lowered. Until 1975, however, the Mormon leaders still required that members of the church wear the "old style" garments when they were taking part in the temple ritual. After the temple ceremony was over, members of the church would replace these garments, which came down to the wrists and ankles, with the abbreviated type. In our book *Mormonism–Shadow or Reality?* p.463, we have included a photograph of the "old style" garments.

The major change in the length of the garments was made in 1923. On June 14 of that year the First Presidency of the church sent out a message to various church leaders which contained the following:

> For some time past the First Presidency and Council of Twelve have had under consideration the propriety of permitting *certain modifications in the temple garment*, with the following result
>
> After careful and prayerful consideration it was unanimously decided that the following modifications may be permitted, and a garment of the following style be worn by those Church members who wish to adopt it, namely:
> > (1) Sleve to elbow.
> > (2) Leg just below knee.
> > (3) Buttons instead of strings.
> > (4) Collar eliminated.
> > (5) Crotch closed.
> . . . It is the mind of the First Presidency and Council of Twelve that this *modified garment* may be used by those who desire to adopt it, without violating any covenant they make in the House of the Lord, and with a clear conscience. . . .
>
> It should be clearly understood that *this modified garment does not supercede the approved garment now in use,* . . . those using either will not be out of harmony with the order of the Church. . . .
>
> Will you kindly advise the Bishops of your Stake of these changes, being careful to give the matter no unnecessary publicity.
>
> This letter is not to pass from your hands, nor are copies to be furnished to any other person (Letter by the First Presidency of the Mormon church, dated June 14, 1923).

Such a change could not be made without the gentiles noticing it. *The Salt Lake Tribune* reported:

> Coming not as an order, nor as a rule to be rigidly enforced, but rather permissive in character, is a recent outgiving of the first presidency. . . . It concerns the garments. . . .

While minor modifications of the temple garment, it is said, have been made at various times during past years, the latest order in permission is regarded by younger members of the church as most liberal and acceptable. . . . Some of the pioneer stock look upon any deviation from the old order as a departure from what they had always regarded as an inviolable rule. . . .

In the old days the temple garment was made of plain, un-bleached cotton cloth. . . . No buttons were used on the garment. . . . But despite these imperfections, the old-style garment is faithfully adhered to by many of the older and sincerely devout members of the church. These regard the garment as *a safeguard against disease and bodily harm*, and they believe that to alter either the texture of cloth or style, or to abandon the garment altogether would bring evil upon them.

One good woman . . . hearing of the change that has recently come about, went to the church offices and uttered fervid objection. "I shall not alter my garments, even if President Grant has ordered me to do so. . . . The pattern was revealed to the Prophet Joseph and Brother Grant has no right to change it," she said.

Explanation was made that the first presidency had merely issued permission to those who so desired to make the modifying change . . . The change in style is permitted for various good reasons, chief among which are promotion of freedom of movement in the body and cleanliness. Formerly the sleeves were long, reaching to the wrists. While doing housework the women would roll up the sleeves. If sleeves were to be rolled up they might as well be made short in the first place for convenience, it was argued. Permission to abbreviate is now given, but it is not an order. . . .

Encasing the lower limbs the old-style garment reaches to the ankles and is looked upon by young members as baggy, uncomfortable and ungainly. The young of the gentler sex complained that to wear the old style with the new and finer hosiery gave the limbs a knotty appearance. It was embarrassing in view of the generally accepted sanitary shorter skirt. Permission is therefore granted by the first presidency to shorten the lower garment. Also buttons are permitted to take the place of the tie-strings (*The Salt Lake Tribune*, June 4, 1923).

Since 1923 the temple garment has been abbreviated even more. The sleeves no longer came down to the elbow, nor do the legs hang down over the knee. The Mormon leaders now seem to put more emphasis on the importance of the marks in the garment rather than the garment itself. On August 31, 1964, the First Presidency of the Mormon church sent a letter to presidents of stakes and bishops of wards in which the following appeared:

The calling of men into military training renders it desirable to reaffirm certain observations heretofore made in the matter of wearing the temple garment.

1. The covenants taken in the temple and attached to the wearing of garments contemplate that they will be worn at all times.
. . .

3. Where the military regulations are of a character that "hinders," that is, makes impossible the wearing of the regulation garments, . . . effort should be made to wear underclothing that will approach as near as may be the normal garment.

Where military regulations require the wearing of two-piece underwear, such underwear should be properly marked, as if the articles were of the normal pattern. If circumstances are such that different underwear may be turned back to the wearer from that which he sends to the laundry, then the marks should be placed on small pieces of cloth and sewed upon the underwear while being worn, then removed when the underwear is sent to the laundry, and resewed upon the underwear returned.

As we indicated earlier, until 1975 Mormon leaders required members of the church to wear the "old style" garments when they went through the endowment ceremony. On November 10 of that year a change was made that permitted members to wear the abbreviated garments in the temple. In a letter to "All Temple Presidents" the First Presidency of the church instructed:

In the future, while involved in temple ordinances, patrons will have the option of wearing either the "approved style" garment (short sleeve and knee length) or the garment with the long sleeve and long leg.

Patrons receiving their initiatory ordinances may be clothed in their own "approved style" garment.

It is suggested that temple presidents not purchase any more of the long-sleeve, long-leg garments for rental purposes.

This may be announced to all temple workers and posted on the bulletin boards in the locker rooms. Notice is going forward to Stake, Mission, and District Presidents suggesting that they notify Bishops, Branch Presidents and other priesthood leaders. No other announcement or publicity is desired.

The suggestion that "temple presidents not purchase any more of the long-sleeve, long-leg garments for rental purposes" leads to the conclusion that Mormon leaders are embarrassed by the "old style" garments and want to gradually phase them out.

Changes in the Temple Ceremony

We do not have room to include the temple ceremony in this book. Those who are interested in this ritual will find it printed in *Mormonism—Shadow or Reality?* pp.464-73. The account we published there was written by a man who had been through the ceremony about 120 times, and even active Mormons who are familiar with the ritual have admitted that it is an accurate account.

The fact that changes have been made in the Mormon temple ceremony can be demonstrated by comparing earlier accounts with the one published in *Mormonism—Shadow or Reality?* Some of these changes were made after the turn of the century.

Ebenezer Robinson, who had been the editor of the *Times and Seasons*, made this statement concerning the original endowment ritual: "Here was instituted, undoubtedly the order of things which represented the scenes in the Garden of Eden, which was called in Nauvoo, the 'Holy Order,' a secret organization. The terrible oaths and covenants taken by those who entered there were known only to those who took them, as one of the members said to me, 'I could tell you many things, but if I should, my life would pay the forfeiture' " (*The Return*, vol. 2, pp.346-48, typed copy, p.153).

These oaths have been greatly modified since Joseph Smith's time. The changes were probably made within the last sixty years. Below are comparisons of the oaths as they were published in *Temple Mormonism* in 1931 with the way they are given today. The first oath we will deal with was printed as follows in 1931:

"We, and each of us, covenant and promise that we will not reveal any of the secrets of this, the first token of the Aaronic priesthood, with its accompanying name, sign or penalty. Should we do so; *we agree that our throats be cut from ear to ear and our tongues torn out by their roots*" (*Temple Mormonism*, p.18).

This oath has been changed to:

"I, ——— (think of the new name) do covenant and promise that I will never reveal the First Token of the Aaronic Priesthood, together with its accompanying name, sign and penalty. Rather than do so *I would suffer my life to be taken*" (*Mormonism—Shadow or Reality?* p.468).

The second oath was printed as follows by Paden in 1931:

"We and each of us do covenant and promise that we will not reveal the secrets of this, the Second Token of the Aaronic

Priesthood, with its accompanying name, sign, grip or penalty. Should we do so, *we agree to have our breasts cut open and our hearts and vitals torn from our bodies and given to the birds of the air and the beasts of the field*" (*Temple Mormonism*, p.20).

This has been softened to:

"I, ———— (think of the first given name), do covenant and promise that I will never reveal the second token of the Aaronic Priesthood, together with its accompanying name, sign and penalty. Rather than do so *I would suffer my life to be taken*" (*Mormonism—Shadow or Reality?* p.470).

The third oath, as printed in *Temple Mormonism*, p.20, read:

"We and each of us do covenant and promise that we will not reveal any of the secrets of this, the First Token of the Melchizedek Priesthood, with its accompanying name, sign or penalty. Should we do so, *we agree that our bodies be cut asunder in the midst and all our bowels gush out.*"

This oath now states:

"I covenant in the name of the Son that I will never reveal the first token of the Melchizedek Priesthood or sign of the nail, with its accompanying name, sign or penalty. Rather than do so *I would suffer my life to be taken.*"

Although the oaths are no longer as crude as they used to be, Mormons who go through the temple still draw the thumb across the throat, stomach, etc., as they take these oaths and are told that "The representation of the penalties indicates *different ways in which life may be taken* (*Mormonism—Shadow or Reality?* p.468).

To the early Mormon people these oaths were a very serious matter. In a discourse delivered December 13, 1857, Heber C. Kimball, a member of the First Presidency, declared: "Judas lost that saving principle, and they *took him and killed him.* . . . *they actually kicked him until his bowels came out.*

" '*I will suffer my bowels to be taken out* before I will forfeit the covenant I have made with Him and my brethren.' Do you understand me? . . . I know the day is right at hand when men will forfeit their Priesthood and turn against the covenants they have made, and *they will be destroyed as Judas was*" (*Journal of Discourses*, vol. 6, pp.125-26).

A person can only begin to imagine how serious these oaths must have been to the Mormon people when the doctrine of "Blood Atonement" was practiced. Now that the oaths have been modified and the practice of "Blood Atonement" abandoned, the Mormon leaders do not have as much control over their people.

One of the oaths which was formerly taken in the temple ritual was the source of so much trouble that the Mormon leaders finally removed it entirely from the ceremony. This oath was printed in *Temple Mormonism*, page 21, as follows: "You and each of you do solemnly promise and vow that you will pray, and never cease to pray, and never cease to importune high heaven *to avenge the blood of the prophets on this nation*, and that you will teach this to your children and your children's children unto the third and fourth generation."

A great deal of testimony has been given concerning this oath, and although all of the witnesses did not agree as to its exact wording, there can be little doubt that such an oath was administered to the Mormon people after Joseph Smith's death. John D. Lee related that the following occurred after Joseph Smith's death:

> . . . Brigham raised his hand and said, "I swear by the eternal Heavens that I have unsheathed my sword, and I will never return it *until the blood of the Prophet Joseph and Hyrum*, and those who were slain in Missouri, *is avenged*. This whole nation is guilty of shedding their blood, by assenting to the deed, and holding its peace." . . . Furthermore, every one who had passed through their endowments, in the Temple, were placed under the most sacred obligations to avenge the blood of the Prophet, whenever an opportunity offered, and to teach their children to do the same, thus making the entire Mormon people sworn and avowed enemies of the American nation (*The Confessions of John D. Lee*, p.160).

Some Mormon apologists have maintained that there was no "oath of vengeance" in the temple ceremony, but the "Daily Journal of Abraham H. Cannon" makes it very plain that there was such an oath. Under the date of December 6, 1889, Apostle Cannon recorded the following in his diary:

> About 4:30 p.m. this meeting adjourned and was followed by a meeting of Presidents Woodruff, Cannon and Smith and Bros. Lyman and Grant. . . . In speaking of the recent examination before Judge Anderson Father said that he understood when he had his endowments in Nauvoo that *he took an oath against the murderers of the Prophet Joseph* as well as other prophets, and *if he had ever met any of those who had taken a hand in that massacre he would undoubtedly have attempted to avenge the blood of the martyrs* ("Daily Journal of Abraham H. Cannon," December 6, 1889, pp.205-206).

Apostle Cannon went on to relate that Joseph F. Smith was about to murder a man with his pocket knife if he even expressed approval of Joseph Smith's death.

The oath of vengeance probably had a great deal to do with the massacre at Mountain Meadows, in which about 120 men, women, and children were killed, and other murders which were committed in early Utah (see *Mormonism–Shadow or Reality?* pp.493-515, 545-59).

Just after the turn of the century the Mormon leaders found themselves in serious trouble because of the oath of vengeance. They were questioned at great length concerning this oath in the "Reed Smoot Case." The oath of vengeance remained in the temple ceremony, however, even after the "Reed Smoot Case" was printed, for Stanley S. Ivins told us that he took it in 1914. It must have been removed sometime between then and 1937, because in a lecture delivered on February 28, 1937, Francis M. Darter complained that "The Law and prayer of Retribution, or divine judgment, against those who persecute the Saints, *has been entirely removed* from Temple services. . . . The reason why it was taken out, says one Apostle, was because it was offensive to the young people" (*Celestial Marriage*, p.60).

In the books *Mormonism–Shadow or Reality?* and *The Mormon Kingdom*, volume 1, we discussed a number of other changes made in the temple ceremony. We also present a great deal of testimony showing that the oaths taken in the temple were originally very crude. We only have room for one example here—i.e., the testimony of J. H. Wallis, Sr., who had been through the temple about 20 times:

> Mr. Wallis. The obligations of priesthood were taken, the two with the Aaronic priesthood and two with the Melchisedec. . . .
> Mr. Tayler. Go on.
>
> . . . .
>
> Mr. Wallis. (standing). "You, and each of you, do solemnly promise and vow that I will not reveal this the first token of the Aaronic priesthood with its accompanying name, sign, and penalty. Should I do so"—this is the sign [indicating]—I agree that my throat be cut from ear to ear and my tongue torn out by its roots from my mouth. . . ."
>
> . . . .
>
> Mr. Tayler. That is called the Aaronic?
> Mr. Wallis. That is called the first token of the Aaronic priesthood. The second token of the Aaronic priesthood.—its sign is that [indicating], and the obligation commences the same, only that "I agree to have my breast cut asunder and my heart and vitals torn from my body."
>
> Then the first token of the Melchisedec priesthood is this [indicating]; is this square [indicating], and about the same

words, only that "I agree to have my body cut asunder in the midst and all my bowels gushed out." The second token of the Melchisedec priesthood there is no penalty to, but the sign is the crucifixion sign, and the words accompanying that are "Pale, hail, hail." I do not know what it means.

. . . .

Mr. Tayler. At any other stage of that ceremony is there an obligation?

Mr. Wallis. Yes, sir. . . . There are vows—the "vow of the sacrifices" is one—where we vow conjointly to give all our substance and all we might ever become possessed of to the support of the Church. . . .

. . . .

Mr. Tayler. What other vow?

Mr. Wallis. Another is called the "vow of chastity," by which we all vowed we would have no connection with any of the other sex unless they were given to us by the priesthood; and another vow was what we used to call the "oath of vengeance." . . .

Mr. Tayler. Stand up, if it will help you, and give us the words, if you can.

Mr. Wallis (standing up). "That you and each of you do promise and vow that you will never cease to importune high heaven to avenge the blood of the prophets upon the nations of the earth or the inhabitants of the earth" (*The Reed Smoot Case*, vol. 2, pp.77-79).

The next day Mr. Wallis corrected his testimony concerning the oath of vengeance:

Mr. Wallis. In repeating the obligation of vengeance I find I made a mistake; I was wrong. It should have been "upon this nation." I had it "upon the inhabitants of the earth." It was a mistake on my part (*Ibid.*, pp.148-49).

The Temple Ceremony and Masonry

Apostle Bruce R. McConkie says the ordinances performed in the temple "were given in modern times to the Prophet Joseph Smith by revelation, many things connected with them being translated by the prophet from the papyrus on which the Book of Abraham was recorded" (*Mormon Doctrine*, 1966, p.779).

We have already shown that the papyri have nothing to do with Abraham or his religion. Now that it is plain that these papyri are pagan documents, Mormons must look elsewhere for the origin of the temple ceremony. It seems clear that at least part of the temple ritual came from Freemasonry. In fact, the similarities between the temple ceremony and the ritual of the Masons are very striking.

Joseph Smith Becomes a Mason

Although Joseph Smith's early writings are filled with material that condemns secret societies, the presence of the Danite band among the Mormons indicates that by 1838 his attitude toward secret societies had changed. After Joseph Smith went to Nauvoo, he became a Mason, formed the Council of Fifty, and established the secret temple ceremony. Mormon Apostle John A. Widtsoe admitted:

> Many of the Saints were Masons, such as Joseph's brother Hyrum, Heber C. Kimball, Elijah Fordham, Newel K. Whitney, James Adams, and John C. Bennett. . . .
>
> With the acquiescence of the Prophet, members of the Church already Masons petitioned the Grand Master of Illinois for permission to set up a lodge in Nauvoo. In answer they were granted permission, in October, 1841, to hold lodge meetings; but it was March 15, 1842, before authority was given to set up a lodge in Nauvoo and to induct new members. *Joseph Smith became a member* (*Evidences and Reconciliations*, 1 vol., pp.357-58).

The following statement is recorded in Joseph Smith's *History of the Church*, volume 4, page 551, under the date of March 15, 1842: "In the evening I received the first degree in Free Masonry in the Nauvoo Lodge, assembled in my general business office." The record for the very next day reads: "I was with the Masonic Lodge and rose to the sublime degree" (vol. 4, p.552).

The Mormons who joined the Masonic Lodge soon found themselves in trouble with other members of the fraternity. They had inducted large numbers into the fraternity and had departed from some of the "ancient landmarks." Finally, the Masons refused to allow the Mormons to continue "a Masonic Lodge at Nauvoo" (*Mormonism and Masonry*, by S. H. Goodwin, p.34).

Although Joseph Smith found himself in trouble with the Masons, he is said to have given the Masonic signal of distress just before he was murdered. Mormon writer E. Cecil McGavin stated:

> When the enemy surrounded the jail, rushed up the stairway, and killed Hyrum Smith, Joseph stood at the open window, his martyr-cry being these words, "O Lord My God!" This was not the beginning of a prayer, because Joseph Smith did not pray in that manner. This brave, young man who knew that death was near, started to repeat the distress signal of the Masons, expecting thereby to gain the protection its members are pledged to give a brother in distress (*Mormonism and Masonry*, by E. Cecil McGavin, p.17).

On page 16 of the same book, Mr. McGavin quotes the following from the *Life of Heber C. Kimball*, p.26: "Joseph, leaping the fatal window, gave the Masonic signal of distress."

In Utah the Masons will not allow a Mormon to become a member of their fraternity because of the things that happened in Nauvoo. One of the most important reasons for this ban is that they feel Joseph Smith stole part of the Masonic ritual and included it in his temple ceremony.

Masonic Ritual in the Temple Ceremony

The relationship between the Mormon temple ceremony and Masonry is too close to be called a coincidence. The fact that both Mormons and Masons have a temple in which they administer secret ceremonies is striking, but when we compare the ritual and learn that Joseph Smith was a Mason, we are forced to the conclusion that he borrowed from Masonry in establishing his temple ceremony.

In our study we have had access to two books which give the Masonic ritual. They were reprinted by Ezra A. Cook Publications, Inc., Chicago, Illinois. The first is Capt. William Morgan's *Freemasonry Exposed*, which was first published in 1827. (It should be remembered that the author of this book disappeared and that this set off the great controversy concerning Masonry.) The second is *Richardson's Monitor of Free-Masonry*. This book was published some time after Morgan's expose, but it is important because it gives some of the "higher degrees" not mentioned by Morgan.

In our book *Mormonism—Shadow or Reality?* pages 486-89, we present twenty-seven parallels between the ritual of the Masons and the Mormon temple ceremony. We will include these parallels here, although we will not give the documentation to prove each parallel as we did in our larger work. Because some of the details of the temple ceremony have been changed in recent years, we are using the pamphlet *Temple Mormonism—Its Evolution, Ritual and Meaning*, New York, 1931, to make our comparison.

1. Both the Masons and the Mormons have what is called "the five points of fellowship."

MORMONS:

The five points of fellowship are given by putting the inside of the right foot to the inside of the Lord's, the inside of your knee to his, laying your breast close to his, your left hands on each other's backs, and each one putting his mouth to the other's ear, in which position the Lord whispers:

Lord—"This is the sign of the token:

"Health to the navel, marrow in the bones, . . ."
(*Temple Mormonism*, p.22)

MASONS:

He (the candidate) is raised on what is called the five points of fellowship . . . This is done by putting the inside of your right foot to the inside of the right foot of the person to whom you are going to give the word, the inside of your knee to his, laying your right breast against his, your left hands on the back of each other, and your mouths to each other's right ear (in which position alone you are permitted to give the word), and whisper the word Mahhah-bone . . . He is also told that Mahhah-bone signifies marrow in the bone (*Freemasonry Exposed*, pp.84-85).

2. When the candidate receives "The First Token of the Aaronic Priesthood" he makes a promise similar to the oath taken in the "First Degree" of the Masonic ritual.

MORMONS:

. . . we will not reveal any of the secrets of this, the first token of the Aaronic priesthood, with its accompanying name, sign or penalty. Should we do so, we agree that our throats be cut from ear to ear and our tongues torn out by their roots (*Temple Mormonism*, p.18).

MASONS:

. . . I will . . . never reveal any part or parts, art or arts, point or points of the secret arts and mysteries of ancient Freemasonry . . . binding myself under no less penalty than to have my throat cut across, my tongue torn out by the roots. . . . (*Freemasonry Exposed*, pp.21-22).

3. In both ceremonies the thumb is drawn across the throat to show the penalty.

4. Those who receive the "First Token of the Aaronic Priesthood" give a grip that is similar to that used by the Masons in the "First Degree" of their ritual.

5. Some of the wording concerning the "grip" is similar.

MORMONS:

(. . . Peter now takes Adam by the right hand and asks:)
Peter—"What is that?"
Adam—"The first token of the Aaronic Priesthood."
Peter—"Has it a name?"
Adam—"It has."
Peter—"Will you give it to me?"
Adam—"I can not, for it is connected with my new name, but this is the sign" (*Temple Mormonism*, p.20).

MASONS:

The Master and candidate holding each other by the grip, as

before described, the Master says, "What is this?"
Ans. "A grip."
"A grip of what?"
Ans. "The grip of an Entered Apprentice Mason."
"Has it a name?"
Ans. "It has."
"Will you give it to me?"
Ans. "I did not so receive it, neither can I so impart it."
(*Freemasonry Exposed*, pp.23-24).

6. The oath of the "Second Token of the Aaronic Priesthood" is similar to that taken in the second degree of Masonry.

MORMONS:

We and each of us do covenant and promise that we will not reveal the secrets of this, the Second Token of the Aaronic Priesthood, with its accompanying name, sign, grip or penalty. Should we do so, we agree to have our breasts cut open and our hearts and vitals torn from our bodies and given to the birds of the air and the beasts of the field (*Temple Mormonism*, p.20).

MASONS:

I, . . . most solemnly and sincerely promise and swear, . . . that I will not give the degree of a Fellow Craft Mason to any one of an inferior degree, nor to any other being in the known world, . . . binding myself under no less penalty than to have my left breast torn open and my heart and vitals taken from thence . . . to become a prey to the wild beasts of the field, and vulture of the air . . . (*Freemasonry Exposed*, p.52).

7. Both have a similar sign.

MORMONS:

The sign is made by placing the left arm on the square at the level of the shoulder, placing the right hand across the chest with the thumb extended and then drawing it rapidly from left to right and dropping it to the side (*Temple Mormonism*, p.20).

MASONS:

The sign is given by drawing your right hand flat, with the palm of it next to your breast, across your breast from the left to the right side with some quickness, and dropping it down by your side . . . (*Freemasonry Exposed*, p.53).

8. Both have a similar grip.
9. In both cases a "name" is used.
10. The promise made when receiving the "First Token of the Melchizedek Priesthood" resembles the oath given by the Masons in the third or "Master Mason's Degree."
11. The sign of the penalty is similar in both cases.
12. In both cases a "name" is used.

13. The conversation at the "veil" in the temple ceremony is very similar to that of the "Fellow Craft Mason" when he is questioned concerning the "grip."

MORMONS:
> Lord—"What is this?"
> Endowee—"The second token of the Melchizedek Priesthood—The Patriarchal Grip or Sure Sign of the Nail."
> Lord—"Has it a name?"
> Endowee—"It has."
> Lord—"Will you give it to me?"
> Endowee—"I can not for I have not yet received it."
> (*Temple Mormonism*, p.22)

MASONS:
> . . . "What is this?"
> Ans. "A grip."
> "A grip of what?"
> Ans. "The grip of a Fellow Craft Mason."
> "Has it a name?"
> Ans. "It has."
> "Will you give it to me?"
> Ans. "I did not so receive it, neither can I so impart it."
> (*Freemasonry Exposed*, p.54).

14. Both the Masons and the Mormons have a vow regarding "chastity."

15. The grip known as "The Sign of the Nail" seems to be similar to one given by Masons in one of their higher degrees.

16. The "Oath of Vengeance" which used to be found in the Mormon temple ceremony resembles an oath in one of the higher degrees of Masonry.

17. Both Mormons and Masons change clothing before going through their rituals.

18. Both Mormons and Masons use an apron.

19. In one of the higher degrees the Masons anoint the candidate. This is somewhat similar to the anointing ceremony in the Mormon temple ritual.

20. Both Mormons and Masons give what they call a "new name" to the candidate.

21. In the Mormon temple ceremony the candidate cannot pass through the veil until he has given certain signs and words. In the Royal Arch Degree the Masons use veils. The "Principal Soujourner" cannot enter the Third Veil except "By the words, sign, and word of exhortation of the Master of the Second Veil" (*Richardson's Monitor of Free-Masonry*, pp.76-77).

22. In the Mormon temple ceremony a man represents Adam.   539

The Masons also have a man who personates Adam in the degree of "Knight of the Sun."

23. In the Mormon temple ceremony a man represents God. In the Mason's Royal Arch Degree a man "personates the Deity."

24. Both the Mormons and the Masons consider the square and the compass to be extremely important. The marks of the square and the compass appear on the Mormon temple garments and on the veil.

MORMONS:

> We now have the veil explained to us. We are told that it represents the veil of the temple. The marks are the same as those on the garments—the compass on the left and the square on the right side (*Temple Mormonism*, p.22).

MASONS:

> " ... the three great lights in Masonry are the Holy Bible, Square and Compass . . . the Square, to square our actions, and the Compass to keep us in due bounds with all mankind . . . (*Freemasonry Exposed*, pp.22-23).

Even a Mormon writer, E. Cecil McGavin, is willing to admit that "Mormon temple clothing contain certain marks of the priesthood, including the square and compass" (*Mormonism and Masonry*, p.72).

25. In the Masonic ritual the point of the compass is pressed against the left breast of the candidate. The Mormon temple garment has the mark of the compass on the left breast.

MORMONS:

> "The marks are the same as those on the garments—the compass on the left . . . (*Temple Mormonism*, p.22).

MASONS:

> "The candidate then enters, the Senior Deacon at the same time pressing his naked left breast with the point of the compass ..." (*Freemasonry Exposed*, p.19).

26. The angle of the square is pressed against the right breast in the Masonic ritual. The mark of the square appears on the right breast of the Mormon temple garment.

MORMONS:

> " . . . the square on the right side . . ." (*Temple Mormonism*, p.22).

MASONS:

> "As he enters, the angle of the square is pressed hard against his naked right breast . . . " (*Freemasonry Exposed*, p.50).

27. A mallet is used by both the Masons and the Mormons in their ceremonies.

Other parallels between the Mormon temple ceremony and the Masonic ritual could be shown, but these should be sufficient to demonstrate to the reader that Joseph Smith borrowed from the Masons when he established the endowment ceremony.

Mormon writer E. Cecil McGavin is willing to admit that there are some similarities between Mormonism and Masonry:

> The Mormons, the American Indians, the ancient Essenes, and the early Druids are not the only ones who have "Masonic" symbols and practices in their rituals. . . . other fraternal orders have their secret signs, grips, tokens, and passwords. The Masons certainly have no monopoly on that vast field of ritual and symbolism . . . the Masonic ritual embraces a few features that resemble the rudimental ceremonies of the Temple endowment, yet these few points of similarity are largely restricted to the rituals pertaining to the Aaronic priesthood (*Mormonism and Masonry*, pp.196-97).

> Masons who visit the Temple Block in Salt Lake City are impressed by what they call the *Masonic emblems* displayed on the outside of the Mormon Temple.

> *Yes, the "Masonic emblems" are displayed on the walls of the Temple*—the sun, moon, and stars, "Holiness to the Lord," the two right hands clasped in fellowship, the All-seeing eye, Alpha and Omega, and the beehive. Masonic writers tell us the Mormon Temple ritual and their own are slightly similar in some respects.

> Without any apologies we frankly admit that there may be some truth in these statements.

> Yes, the public is entitled to an explanation of these mysteries and coincidences (*Ibid.*, Preface).

Mormon apologist Dr. Hugh Nibley has admitted concerning Mormonism and Masonry: "Among the first to engage in the Latter-day Temple work were many members of the Masons, . . . whose rites present unmistakable parallels to those of the temple" (*What Is A Temple?* BYU Press, 1968, p.247).

Since many members of the Mormon church were Masons and were familiar with its ritual, Joseph Smith must have realized that he would be accused of stealing the ceremonies from Masonry. In what was apparently a move to offset this criticism, Joseph Smith claimed that Masonry once had the true endowment and that it had become corrupted through the passage of time. E. Cecil McGavin explains: "In the diary of

Benjamin F. Johnson, an intimate friend and associate of Joseph Smith, it is recorded that 'Joseph told me that Freemasonry was the apostate endowment, as sectarian religion was the apostate religion.' Elder Heber C. Kimball, who had been a Mason for many years, related that after Joseph Smith became a Mason, he explained to his brethren that Masonry had been taken from the priesthood" (*Mormonism and Masonry*, p.199).

In trying to explain why their temple ritual resembles that of the Masons, some Mormons claim that the endowment was given in Solomon's Temple and that the Masons preserved part of the ceremony. Apostle Melvin J. Ballard has been quoted as saying the following:

> "Modern Masonry is a fragmentary presentation of the ancient order established by King Solomon. From whom it is said to have been handed down through the centuries.

> "Frequent assertion that some details of the Mormon Temple ordinances resemble Masonic rites, led him to refer to this subject," the speaker declared, and he added, "that he was not sorry there was such a similarity, because of the fact that the ordinances and rites revealed to Joseph Smith constituted a reintroduction upon the earth of the divine plan inaugurated in the Temple of Solomon in ancient days. . . .

> "Masonry is an apostasy from the ancient early order, just as so-called Christianity is an apostasy from the true Church of Christ" (*The Salt Lake Herald*, December 29, 1919, as cited in *Mormonism and Masonry*, by S. H. Goodwin, pp.49-50).

Mormon writer E. Cecil McGavin agrees:

> Yes, there may be some similarities in the rituals . . . In the light of the evidence supplied by Masonic historians, the conclusion is forced upon us that some of the features of the ritual once administered in Solomon's Temple have persisted in Masonry. . . .

> Since some of the Masonic ritual has descended from Solomon's time, altered and corrupted by the passing centuries, should one be surprised to find a few similarities when the Temple ritual is again established? . . .

> If the facts were available and the original sources extant, it would doubtless be apparent that everything in the ritual of the Mormons that the Masons say was taken from their ceremonies, dates back to Solomon's time (*Mormonism and Masonry*, pp.192-94).

William J. Whalen replied in rebuttal to McGavin's statements:

McGavin accepts the most fanciful claims to antiquity put forth by such discredited Masonic historians as Mackey, Anderson and Oliver. These early Masonic writers were wont to claim Solomon, Adam, and most of the upright men of the Old Testament as early lodge brothers. Modern Masonic historians date the origin of the lodge in the early eighteenth century and recognize that these pioneer speculative Masons simply adopted the story of the building of Solomon's temple as a dramatic background for their initiations. . . .

A few elements in modern Masonry here and there can be traced to the medieval guilds of working masons, but no one with a scholarly reputation would try to maintain that the degree system as it is worked now—and as it was worked in Nauvoo in 1842—could have possibly been derived from Solomonic rites (*The Latter-day Saints in the Modern Day World*, pp.203-4).

Historically there seems to be only one logical explanation for the many parallels between the temple ceremony and Masonry, and that is that Joseph Smith borrowed from the Masons. The reader should remember that it was on March 16, 1842, that Joseph Smith "was with the Masonic Lodge and rose to the sublime degree" (*History of the Church*, vol. 4, p.552). Less than two months later (May 4, 1842), Joseph Smith introduced the temple endowment ceremony. According to Joseph Smith's *History of the Church*, vol. 5, pp.1-2), it was in the same room "where the Masonic fraternity meet occasionally":

Wednesday, 4. —I spent the day in the upper part of the store, that is in my private office . . . and in my general business office, or lodge room (that is where the Masonic fraternity meet occasionally, for want of a better place) in council with General James Adams, . . . Brigham Young and Elders Heber C. Kimball and Willard Richards, instructing them in the principles and order of the Priesthood, attending to washings, anointings, endowments and the communication of keys pertaining to the Aaronic Priesthood, and so on to the highest order of the Melchisedek Priesthood. . . .

One woman who was questioned concerning the temple ceremony gave this testimony:

A.—. . . I said I received endowments in Nauvoo, in the Masonic Hall, . . . All the ceremony was performed in the Masonic Hall. The washing was done in the Masonic Hall, and the anointing with oil.

Q.—What furniture was in the Masonic Hall at the time the endowment was performed?

A.— . . . if you are expecting me to tell you all about the particulars of what was there in the way of furniture and what was done there, you must not expect me to do it any more than you would expect a Mason or an Odd Fellow or any other member of a secret society to reveal the secrets of their order . . . (*Temple Lot Case*, pp.353-54).

With this very close connection between Mormonism and Masonry, it is almost impossible to believe that Joseph Smith did not borrow from Masonry in establishing the temple ceremony.

The Mormon leaders find themselves faced with several embarrassing questions regarding the temple ritual and Masonry. Many members of the church wonder how they can believe in a secret temple ritual, when the *Book of Mormon* condemns all secret societies, bands and oaths. In fact, it plainly states that "the Lord worketh not in secret combinations" (Ether 8:19).

Further, there is the question of why Joseph Smith would become a Mason. Besides all of the statements in the *Book of Mormon* which condemn secret societies, Joseph Smith joined with four others in stating: "We further, caution our brethren, against the impropriety of the organization of bands or companies, by covenants, oaths, penalties, or secresies, . . . pure friendship, always becomes weakened, the very moment you undertake to make it stronger by penal oaths and secrecy" (*Times and Seasons*, vol. 1, p.133).

Benjamin F. Johnson claims that Joseph Smith told him that "Freemasonry was the apostate endowment." Why would Joseph Smith join an organization that he believed was in a state of apostasy?

Mormon leaders now claim that it is not right for members of the church to join the Masons or other secret societies. Anthony W. Ivins, who was a member of the First Presidency, counseled that "The Mormon Church . . . advises its members to refrain from identifying themselves with any secret, oath-bound society. . . . It is difficult to serve two masters and do justice to both" (*The Relationship of "Mormonism" and Freemasonry*, p.8).

Joseph F. Smith said that those who "are identified with these secret organizations" are "not fit to hold" important offices in the church (see *Mormonism—Shadow or Reality?* p.491).

John A. Widtsoe added: "The activities of the Church, in all departments are sacred, not secret. This point of view makes it difficult for Latter-day Saints to look with favor upon secret, oath-bound societies. . . . Sometimes they cause loss of interest in Church duties, for no one can serve two masters with equal interest. . . . Divided allegiance is always unsatisfactory and often dangerous" (*Evidences and Reconciliations*, vol. 1, pp.213-14).

It is interesting to note that the same Apostle who made these statements against secret societies had to reverse himself and write a chapter entitled, "Why Did Joseph Smith Become a Mason?" He claimed that Smith joined the Masons to win friends among "the prominent and influential men of the state" so that the church would not be persecuted, but he had to admit that "the attempt to win sufficient friends through Masonry to stop persecution failed" (*Ibid.*, vol. 3, pp.114-17).

Joseph Smith's own words about "the impropriety of the organization of bands or companies, by covenant or oaths, by penalties or secrecies" could certainly be used against the Mormon temple ceremony. Apostle Widtsoe, however, maintains that "the temple endowment is not secret. All who meet the requirements for entrance to the temple may enjoy it" (*Ibid.*, p. 24). John A. Widtsoe's reasoning with regard to this matter is very poor. All secret societies allow their own members to participate in their rituals. The Mormon temple ceremony is kept secret from outsiders, and, after all, isn't this what makes a secret society? Many members of the Mormon church maintain that the temple ceremonies are sacred and not secret. The Mormons, of course, have a right to believe that their ceremonies are sacred, but this does not change the fact that they are secret. They are just as secret as the ceremonies of any other secret society.

At any rate, the connection between Mormonism and Masonry can be briefly summarized as follows:

1. Both Mormonism and Masonry have secret ceremonies that are performed in secret temples.

2. The "Masonic emblems" are displayed on the walls of the Mormon temple.

3. The Mormon temple ritual is similar in many respects to that used by the Masons.

4. Joseph Smith and many of the most prominent members of the Mormon church were also members of the Masonic lodge.

5. Temple ceremonies were actually performed in the Masonic hall.

Reed Durham, who has served as president of the Mormon History Association, has carefully examined the parallels between Mormonism and Masonry. Although Dr. Durham still maintains that Joseph Smith was a prophet, he has to admit that Masonry had a definite influence upon Mormonism:

... I am convinced that *in the study of Masonry lies a pivotal key to further understanding Joseph Smith and the Church.* . . . Masonry in the Church had its origin prior to the time Joseph Smith became a Mason. . . . It commenced in Joseph's home when his older brother became a Mason. Hyrum received the first three degrees of Masonry in Mount Moriah Lodge No. 112 of Palmyra, New York, at about the same time that Joseph was being initiated into the presence of God . . . The many parallels found between early Mormonism and the Masonry of that day are substantial . . .

I have attempted thus far to demonstrate that Masonic influences upon Joseph in the early Church history, preceding his formal membership in Masonry, were significant. However, these same Masonic influences exerted a more dominant character as reflected in the further expansion of the Church subsequent to the Prophet's Masonic membership. In fact, I believe that there are *few significant developments in the Church, that occurred after March 15, 1842, which did not have some Masonic interdependence.* Let me comment on a few of these developments. There is absolutely no question in my mind that the Mormon ceremony which came to be known as *the Endowment,* introduced by Joseph Smith to Mormon Masons, had an *immediate inspiration from Masonry.* This is not to suggest that no other source of inspiration could have been involved, but the *similarities between the two ceremonies are so apparent and overwhelming that some dependent relationship cannot be denied.* They are so similar, in fact, that one writer was led to refer to the Endowment as Celestial Masonry.

It is also obvious that the Nauvoo Temple architecture was in part, at least, Masonically influenced. Indeed, it appears that there was an intentional attempt to utilize Masonic symbols and motifs. . . .

Another development in the Nauvoo Church, which has not been so obviously considered as Masonically inspired, was the establishment of the Female Relief Society. This organization was the Prophet's intentional attempt to expand Masonry to include the women of the Church. That *the Relief Society was organized in the Masonic Lodge room,* and only one day after Masonry was given to the men, was *not* happenstance. . . . included in the actual vocabulary of Joseph Smith's counsel and instructions to the sisters were such words as: ancient orders, examinations, degrees, candidates, secrets, lodges, rules, signs, tokens, order of the priesthood, and keys; all indicating that the Society's orientation possessed Masonic overtones.

It was true that in orthodox Masonry, . . . the inclusion of women was definitely prohibited and certainly unheard of.

The Joseph Smith Masonry was daily becoming less orthodox

and tended to follow more in the direction of some unorthodox Masonry which had been imported to America from France. In this type of Masonry, two different women's groups operated. . . .

The second type of unorthodox female Masonry was known as 'Adoptive' Masonry. . . . *The ceremonies for women in this order were quite similar to those later found within the endowment ceremony of the Mormons.* . . . I suggest that enough evidence presently exists to declare that the entire institution of the political kingdom of God, including the Council of Fifty, the living constitution, the proposed flag of the kingdom, and the anointing and coronation of the king, had its genesis in connection with Masonic thoughts and ceremonies. . . . it appears that the Prophet first embraced Masonry, and, then in the process, he modified, expanded, amplified, or glorified it. . . . I believe he accepted Masonry because he genuinely felt he recognized true Ancient Mysteries contained herein. . . . The Prophet believed that his mission was to restore all truth, and then to unify and weld it all together into one. This truth was referred to as "the Mysteries," and these Mysteries were inseparably connected with the Priesthood. . . . Can anyone deny that Masonic influence on Joseph Smith and the Church, either before or after his personal Masonic membership? The evidence demands comments . . .

There are many questions which still demand the answers. . . . if we, as Mormon historians, respond to these questions and myrids [sic] like them relative to Masonry in an ostrich-like fashion, with our heads buried in the traditional sand, then I submit: there never will be "any help for the widow's son" (*Mormon Miscellaneous*, October, 1975, pp.11-16).

Conclusion

Although Mormon apologists would have us believe that Joseph Smith received the temple ceremony by revelation from God, the evidence is against it and clearly shows that he borrowed heavily from Masonry.

After careful examination of the temple ceremony, we have come to the conclusion that it bears unmistakable evidence of being a man-made ritual. The fact that so many changes had to be made in it to try to make it acceptable shows plainly that it is not from God.

FACING REALITY

Chapter 23

Reality is sometimes very hard to face. For instance, on July 26, 1969, the *Salt Lake Tribune* reported that members of the International Flat Earth Research Society still do not believe that the earth is round. They feel that the moon landing was "part of a great deception by NASA" and that the "astronauts are hypnotized into believing they go into space." It is easy to look at this and smile, but we who are honest with ourselves must admit that we also sometimes have difficulty facing reality.

One of the most difficult encounters we ever had with reality was when we discovered that the *Book of Mormon* was untrue. We found it very difficult to tell our friends that we no longer believed it was translated from gold plates.

One man, who had taught at the church's Brigham Young University for many years, made an extensive study of Mormon church history, but after spending much time and money to make this study, he was afraid to release his findings. He told us that the reason he would not disclose his findings was that he feared too many people would apostatize from the Church.

James R. Harris, who wrote a thesis for the Brigham Young University on the changes in the "Book of Moses," commented concerning the inability of church members to face reality:

> During the writing of this thesis an occasional inquisitive friend would ask about the nature and extent of changes in the contents of the Book of Moses. Encouraged by their interest, a variety of examples were pointed out. The reaction varied in emotional intensity but always ended with a caustic question or prediction, such as: "Why did you pick such a subject?" or "This will disturb a lot of people." . . . Our well-meaning friends were so fearful of doing injury to the church that they would abandon the search for truth ("A Study of the Changes in the Contents of the Book of Moses From the Earliest Available Sources to the Current Edition," typed copy, p.237).

Jesus once stated: "And ye shall know the truth, and the truth will set you free" (John 8:32). Why is it, then, that we fear the truth if the truth will make us free? Why do we stop our ears when the truth is proclaimed? It is because we love the bondage of our own preconceived ideas. We do not like to admit that we have been wrong.

Exalts the Pride of Man

The Mormon church, which professes to teach the true way of salvation, teaches many things that are not compatible with the teachings of Christ. For instance, Christ taught that a man must be meek and lowly: ". . . Verily I say unto you, except ye be converted, and become as little children, ye shall not enter into the kingdom of heaven" (Matt. 18:3).

Jesus also said:

> And he spake this parable unto certain which trusted in themselves that they were righteous, and despised others: Two men went up into the temple to pray; the one a Pharisee, and the other a publican. The Pharisee stood and prayed thus with himself, God, I thank thee, that I am not as other men are, extortioners, unjust, adulterers, or even as this publican. I fast twice in the week, I give tithes of all that I possess. And the publican, standing afar off, would not lift up so much as his eyes unto heaven, but smote upon his breast, saying, God be merciful to me a sinner. I tell you, this man went down to his house justified rather than the other: for every one that exalteth himself shall be abased; and he that humbleth himself shall be exalted (Luke 18:9-14).

Mormonism, on the other hand, exalts the pride of man. Joseph H. Weston, who joined the Mormon church three days after completing his book, exclaimed:

"Mormons don't grovel before God, prating their unworthiness and imploring mercy. They are not slaves! They are men, made in the image of God! They proudly stand, hold their heads high, and put out their hands to shake that of God in greeting, as any worthy son would be expected to respectfully but proudly stand before a wise and good father" (*These Amazing Mormons!* p.82).

The reader should compare this with the following statement made by Jesus: "So likewise ye, when ye shall have done all those things which are commanded you, say, We are *unprofitable* servants: we have done that which was our duty to do" (Luke 17:10).

Speaking of a Mormon sacrament meeting, Mr. Weston remarked:

549

> The meeting opened with the ancient hymn, "How Firm a Foundation." . . . There was no group confession of sins. There was no groveling and humbling of the dignity of man, either mentally or physically. . . .
>
> Sitting erect in the pride and dignity of being a human being, each member took a piece of bread . . .
>
> The almost starting [startling?] effect, psychologically, of this ultra-simple communion service was to *completely obliterate the feeling of supplication and meekness engendered at such a time in many other churches.* A man didn't feel that he drew nigh—"Unworthy as to so much as gather up the crumbs from His table"—Not at all! He felt that *he sat as an equal* and guest at Jesus' table, and after he had eaten and drunk, he went away with a greater appreciation of his own table, his own body, his own life—all godlike if he would make and keep them so (*These Amazing Mormons!* p.21).

In his M.A. thesis at the University of Utah, "The Social Psychological Basis of Mormon New-Orthodoxy," Owen Kendall White, Jr., made these interesting observations concerning Mormon theology:

> This dual nature of Mormonism often obscures its liberalism so that many Mormons and nonMormons alike misunderstand its subtle implications. Because of a commitment to biblical literalism, Mormon theology is frequently regarded as another expression of conservative orthodox Christianity. This popular notion is fundamentally inaccurate, for it fails to recognize that *the basic liberal doctrines in Mormon theology oppose the central doctrines of orthodox Christianity.* . . . The basic Mormon doctrines of God, man, and salvation are *radical departures* from traditional Christian thought. . . .
>
> In contrast with the sovereign God of Christian orthodoxy and neo-orthodoxy, the Mormon God is finite. This is indicated in the fact that God is not the only reality with necessary existence. That is, He is not the Creator of all that is (pp.85-86).
>
> From the above description of God, it should be apparent that the Mormon God is a heretical departure from traditional Christianity, and the traditional Christian terminology of omnipotence and omniscience are not justifiably applied to the Mormon God. . . .
>
> The Mormon conception of man is an even more heretical departure from Christian orthodoxy than the doctrine of God. . . . this very claim that the human predicament is not really a predicament in the traditional sense, that man's natural state, present state, is really more good than bad, is a radical denial of traditional Christian theology. . . .

Mormonism rejects the notion that man's condition is best described by "depravity." Nowhere within Mormon theology is its optimism concerning man's natural condition more clearly apparent then in this denial of the Christian doctrine of original sin. . . . to the Mormon the fall *is a fall upward rather that downward.* . . . In the April session of the 1964 General Conference, Hugh B. Brown . . . summarized much of what has been said in this chapter. He spoke:

"Our doctrine of man is positive and life affirming. . . . *We refuse to believe,* with some churches of Christendom, that the biblical account of the fall of man records the corruption of human nature or to accept the doctrine of original sin. We *do not believe* that man is incapable of doing the will of God or is unable to merit the reward of Divine approval; that he is therefore totally estranged from God and that whatever salvation comes to him must come as a free and undeserved gift. . . . "

. . . the Mormon doctrine of salvation not only provides further evidence of Mormon optimism, but it also argues for a claim that Mormon theology, in opposition to traditional Christian theology, is *man-centered rather than God centered.* . . .

Nowhere is the man-centered character of Mormon theology more clearly evident than in the Mormon conception of salvation. For, Mormon doctrines of salvation are radically different from the doctrine of salvation by grace which permeates Christian orthodoxy. . . . There is an almost complete dearth of Pauline theology within Mormonism. Generally, Mormons only refer to Paul on the subject of the resurrection or in his ethical exhortations. Seldom do they quote him on the subject of salvation, and, when they do, they distort his concept of grace to mean man will be physically resurrected by the gracious act of God. Mormonism denies traditional doctrines of grace. . . . Because of this emphasis upon salvation by merit and the idea that man's destiny is Godhood, the Mormon doctrine of salvation, along with the doctrines of God and man, stand as rank heresy within the orthodox Christian world. . . . Mormon theology on the doctrines of God, man, and salvation is a radical departure from Christian orthodoxy.

While the God of Christian orthodoxy is absolute, the God of Mormonism is finite . . . the Mormon doctrine of salvation emphasizes merit instead of grace. Although the theology has a doctrine of grace in the notion that Christ overcame physical and spiritual death, it is not to be confused with orthodox Christian conceptions of grace. For exaltation, the real salvation of man, is dependent upon works. . . .

If the author were to describe the fundamental difference between Mormon theology and orthodox Christianity in one sen-

551

tence, he would suggest that while orthodox Christianity is God-centered, Mormon theology is man-centered. . . . Mormon theology is much more concerned with the similarities between God and man than the differences between them . . . it is the notion that God has a physical body that leads to Mormon claims that man is literally, not figuratively, the offspring of God. Through its entire history, Mormonism has employed its extremely anthropomorphic conception of God to illustrate the similarities rather than the differences between God and man (pp.95,96,98,100,101,103,107,108,110-112,118-120,122).

It is certainly strange that Mormon leaders have rejected so many of the basic doctrines of Christianity, for these same doctrines are found in the *Book of Mormon*. As an example, the *Book of Mormon* teaches that man of himself is an enemy to God: "For *the natural man is an enemy to God*, and has been from the fall of Adam, and will be, forever and ever, unless he yields to the enticings of the Holy Spirit, and putteth off the natural man and becometh a saint through the atonement of Christ the Lord . . ." (*Book of Mormon*, Mosiah 3:19).

President Brigham Young, on the other hand, taught that the natural man is a friend of God: "It is, however, universally received by professors of religion as a Scriptural doctrine that man is naturally opposed to God. This is not so. Paul says, in his Epistle to the Corinthians, 'But the natural man receiveth not the things of God,' but I say it is the unnatural 'man that receiveth not the things of God.' . . . *The natural man is of God*" (*Journal of Discourses*, vol. 9, p.305). John Taylor, who became the third president of the church, said that "it is *not natural* for men to be evil" (*Ibid.*, vol. 10, p.50).

As Owen Kendall White, Jr., indicated, present-day Mormonism rejects the doctrine that salvation is by grace. The *Book of Mormon*, however, teaches this doctrine. In 2 Nephi 10:24 we read: ". . . it is only in and through the grace of God that ye are saved." The fact that the *Book of Mormon* teaches salvation by grace has caused some division in the church, and there are a few Mormon writers who are going back to the teaching of the *Book of Mormon* on this subject. (For more information concerning grace and works see our book, *A Look at Christianity*, pp.8,17,18.)

When the Mormon leaders proclaim that man is naturally good, they not only reject the teachings of the Bible and the *Book of Mormon*, but they are simply refusing to face reality about the nature of man. Karl A. Menninger, one of the world's leading psychiatrists, made these very revealing observations:

But today, after a long digression, we have in a measure come back to the sinfulness theory. For, in repudiating this theological tenet, modern science had reverted to the philosophy that man is the hapless prey, the potential victim of solely external forces, which is the philosophy of man as well as the helpless child; whereas to conceive of disease as related to sin recognizes the partial responsibility of the individual for his own fate. Instead of referring all danger to the outside world, or to the devil, it acknowledges the presence of danger from within (*Love Against Hate*, p.199).

President Joseph Fielding Smith frankly said he believed that Mormons are "the best people in the world. . . . We are morally clean, in every way equal, and in many ways superior to any other people" (*Doctrines of Salvation*, vol. 1, p.236). Apostle LeGrand Richards maintained that "there is no people in this world that are evidencing their love of God by doing his will like the Latter-Day Saints are." Actually, the Mormons are very much like other people. Mormon writer John J. Stewart complained: ". . . Satan, the father of all lies, . . . is wrecking [sic] havoc among us in the sacred matter of marriage and morals, . . . the frequency of adultery, through unwarranted divorce and otherwise, and the number of illegitimate births, among teenagers and older adolescents as well, have reached an appalling figure" (*Brigham Young and His Wives*, p.12).

James L. Clayton admitted:

> . . . except for the distinctive personal habits prescribed by the Word of Wisdom (including an implied proscription against narcotics), there is really little quantitative evidence to distinguish Mormon behavior today from that of comparable groups. Distinctions are usually asserted, for example, between Mormons and non-Mormons in the areas of sexual morality, education, crime, patriotism, and sobriety. Statistical data, however, clearly shows that in 1960 Utah's rate of illegitimate births was higher than the rate of illegitimacy for the white population of Alabama, Mississippi, New Jersey, and Pennsylvania, and was comparable with the rate for the white population of South Carolina, South Dakota, and Kansas. Even in Provo the rate of illegitimacy is not much different than it is in Dubuque, Iowa. . . . Regarding crime, according to the most recent data, Chicago is safer than Salt Lake City (total 1966 crime index 2172 vs. 2349) . . . . In short, we are no longer so much a peculiar people as typical Americans with a peculiar history (*Dialogue: A Journal of Mormon Thought*, Autumn 1968, p.71).

The *Salt Lake Tribune* for February 22, 1976, reported that "Utah continues to outstrip the rest of the nation in divorces. . . . 5.1 per 1,000 population were filed, compared with an average of 4.8 per 1,000 nationally."

Harold T. Christensen observed:

> It probably will come as a surprise to most Latter-day Saints that Utah is above average in its divorce rate. . . .

> One would expect it to be otherwise. Of the fifty states, Utah is unique in at least two respects: It is the most churched, . . . and it is the most homogeneous in church membership, meaning that religious affiliation is more concentrated into one denomination. . . . Somewhere between two-thirds and three-fourths of Utah's entire population is Latter-day Saint. . . . the logical expectation would be for a *lower* than average divorce rate, rather than a higher one. . . .

> Now this is not to suggest that divorce is rampant among the Latter-day Saints . . . there is evidence that divorces following temple marriage are disproportionately few in number. For example, in a record-linkage study of Salt Lake and Utah Counties—with the divorce records search for about ten years following each marriage—I found the following divorce percentages: civil marriages, 13.4; Latter-day Saint non-temple marriages, 10.2; non-Mormon religious marriages, 5.5; and Latter-day Saint temple marriages, 1.8 percent divorced . . . while the temple marrying group showed up with substantially the lowest divorce percentage, the Latter-day Saint non-temple group showed up with a percentage nearly twice that of all other churches grouped together. . . .

> Not only does Utah, which is largely Mormon, have a higher-than-normal divorce rate, but average marriage duration is significantly shorter than in most states, and the proportion of divorces involving children is higher than in most states (*Dialogue: A Journal of Mormon Thought*, Winter 1972, pp.21-23).

Mormon President Spencer W. Kimball has recently admitted that ten percent of the temple marriages end in divorce:

"PROVO (AP)—President Spencer W. Kimball . . . said Tuesday the church recommends that members marry partners who have the same racial, economic, social, educational, and religious background. . . .

"He said 10 percent of the marriages in the church's temples end in divorce. This is below average, but the church is still 'chagrined that any temple marriage ends on [sic] divorce,' he said" (*Salt Lake Tribune*, September 8, 1976).

Church Not Lost

Mormon leaders have made the tragic mistake of pointing their people toward a church instead of toward the Saviour. They claim that their church is the only true church and that all

554

others are false and have no authority. This tends to make people more concerned about an organization than about their relationship with Christ.

Mormonism teaches that shortly after the death of Christ, the whole Christian world fell into a state of apostasy. In the Bible, however, Jesus said ". . . upon this rock I will build my church; and the gates of hell shall *not prevail* against it" (Matt. 16:18).

Orson Pratt did not seem to believe the words of Jesus for he claimed: "Jesus . . . established his kingdom on the earth. . . . the kingdoms of this world made war against the kingdom of God, established eighteen centuries ago, and *they prevailed against it*, and the kingdom ceased to exist" (*Journal of Discourses*, vol. 13, p.125). ". . . the former-day kingdom no where exists on the earth, but *has been prevailed against and overcome*, and nothing is left but man-made churches and governments . . ." (*Pamphlets by Orson Pratt*, p.116).

Apostle Pratt's words are in direct contradiction to Jesus' statement that "the gates of hell *shall not prevail*" against His Church. While it is true that there was a great apostasy throughout the Christian world, there is no evidence that there was ever a time when there were not true Christians upon the earth. In John 1:12 we read: "But as many as received him, to them gave he power to become the sons of God, even to them that believe on his name." We believe that in all ages some people have believed in Jesus and have "become the sons of God," and these people were members of His Church. Although at times the numbers may have been small, Jesus promised that "where two or three are gathered together in my name, there am I in the midst of them" (Matt. 18:20).

Our Own Testimony

Statement by Jerald Tanner. I was born and raised in the Mormon church, and before I was eight years old I felt that it was the only true church. I remember being told that a certain man who was excommunicated from the church was possessed with the devil. I can recall walking past this man's house and being afraid of him because I firmly believed that he was possessed of the devil. I believed that a person would almost have to be possessed of the devil to leave "the true church." My conviction was so strong that I was shocked to hear a boy in Sunday school say that he didn't know for certain that the church was true. I felt that it was strange indeed for a person to be a member of the Mormon church and yet not know it was the only true church.

I believed very strongly that Joseph Smith was a prophet of

God and that I belonged to the only true church. When I was about eighteen years old I had to face reality. I can remember that the first time I saw David Whitmer's pamphlet, *An Address to All Believers in Christ*, I threw it down in disgust. After throwing it down, however, I began to think that perhaps this was not the right way to face the problem. If David Whitmer was wrong in his criticism of Joseph Smith, surely I could prove him wrong. So I picked up the pamphlet and read it through. I found that I could not prove David Whitmer wrong, and that the revelations Joseph Smith gave had been changed. I later went to Independence, Missouri, and saw a copy of the original *Book of Commandments*, which confirmed David Whitmer's statement that the revelations had been changed.

Since that time I have found more and more proof that the church in which I was raised is in error. The most important thing that I found, however, was not that the church was in error, but that I myself was in error. I found that I was a sinner in need of a Saviour. The Mormon church had taught me good morals, but they had not taught me much concerning the power of Christ that could change my life. There was much talk about Joseph Smith, but very little talk about Christ. Consequently, I began to think I had the power within myself to overcome sin. I didn't see how much I needed the help of God to overcome it. So I turned from one sin to another until I was deeply in bondage to sin. I found no help in the Mormon church; they were too busy preaching about the glory of the church, Joseph Smith, etc. They were too busy singing "praise to the man who communed with Jehovah" and "We thank thee O God for a prophet" to tell me about the Saviour I needed so badly. They were too busy talking about missions, tithing, the welfare plan, etc., to talk about the Christ. Consequently, there was almost nothing in the services that could give life and peace to my dying soul. Perhaps I should mention, however, that there was one thing that really touched my heart, and that was when we sang the song, "Oh, It Is Wonderful!" by Charles H. Gabriel.

> I stand all amazed at the love Jesus offers me,
> Confused at the grace that so fully he proffers me;
> I tremble to know that for me He was crucified—
> That for me, a sinner, He suffered, He bled, and died.
>
> Oh, it is wonderful that He should care for me!
> Enough to die for me!
> Oh, it is wonderful, wonderful to me!
>
> I marvel that He would descend from His throne divine,
> To rescue a soul so rebellious and proud as mine;

That He should extend His great love unto such as I;
Sufficient to own, to redeem, and to justify.

When we sang this song my heart burned within me. I have
since learned, however, that even this song was borrowed from
the Protestant faith. But regardless of where it came from, it
touched me very deeply. It made me think of my Saviour and
the great debt I owed to Him. If there had been more songs like
this in the Mormon church and if Christ had been preached
instead of Joseph Smith, I would, perhaps, have received Christ
into my life in the Mormon church. As it was, however, I was
nineteen years old before I heard the true message of Christ
preached, and that was in another church. A short time later I
received Christ into my life and found peace, joy, and deliverance from sin. As the Apostle Paul expressed it: "Therefore if
any man be in Christ, he is a new creature; old things are passed
away; behold, all things are become new" (2 Cor. 5:17).

Jerald Tanner

Statement by Sandra Tanner. Since I was born and raised in
the Mormon church, and am a great-great-grandchild of
Brigham Young, I had very strong ties to the Mormon faith. I
was about seventeen before I ever attended another church. As a
teenager my life centered around the Mormon church. Because
I was active and paying my tithing I thought I was in pretty
good standing with God. I knew I sinned but I felt my activity
in church would somehow outweigh what I did wrong. I believed (as the Mormons teach) that I was inherently good. I had
no fear of God's judgment. Besides the things that were wrong
in my own life, I began to have doubts about my church. Could
it really be the *only* true church? Was polygamy really right?
Why couldn't the Negro hold the priesthood? Was temple marriage really so important? Why were its rites kept such a secret?
Did God actually command Mormons to wear special under-
garments? I had many questions going through my mind.

When I started college I enrolled in the Mormon Institute of
Religion class. I started asking questions in class, trying to find
answers to my doubts. But one day my institute teacher took me
aside and told me to *please stop* asking questions in class.
There was a girl attending the class who was thinking of joining the church and I was disturbing her with my questions.
What a surprise! I had hoped to find answers to the many
things that were bothering me and now I had been silenced.

Shortly after this I met Jerald and we began studying the
Bible and Mormonism together. As we studied I began to see
the contradictions between the Bible and the teachings of the

Mormon church.

I had grown up thinking that Brigham Young was one of the greatest men that ever lived. He was always presented to me as such a holy man—God's prophet, seer, and revelator. Then Jerald had me read some of Brigham Young's sermons in the *Journal of Discourses* on blood atonement. I was shocked! I knew what Brigham Young was saying was wrong but I couldn't reconcile these sermons with the things I had always been taught concerning him. I knew these were not the words of a prophet of God.

Jerald also showed me the changes that had been made in Joseph Smith's revelations. The thought kept coming to me that if God had actually given those revelations to Joseph Smith why would they need rewriting? Surely the Creator of the universe could say it right the first time!

As I studied I not only found errors in Mormonism, I also began to comprehend there was something wrong in my own life. As I studied God's Word I realized I was a sinful hypocrite. In spite of my sins I had thought I was right with God. Yet the Bible says: "For the wages of sin is death; but the gift of God is eternal life, through Jesus Christ our Lord" (Rom. 6:23).

After Jerald and I were married we started visiting the different Protestant churches. As I listened to the sermons I began to realize that God was not concerned with peoples' church affiliations, but with a personal relationship. Christ taught a way of love, not a religious system. He stated: "By this shall all men know that ye are my disciples, if ye have love one to another" (John 13:35). Paul taught that we should "walk in love, as Christ also hath loved us, and hath given himself for us . . ." (Eph. 5:2).

God reaches out to man, not because he deserves it, but because God loves him. John wrote: "Herein is love, not that we loved God, but that he loved us, and sent his Son to be the propitiation for our sins" (1 John 4:10). Paul wrote: "But God, who is rich in mercy, . . . even when we were dead in sins, hath quickened us together with Christ . . . For by grace are ye saved through faith; and that not of yourselves: it is the gift of God: not of works, lest any man should boast" (Eph. 2:4,5,8,9).

I now want to share with you the particular events of the day I surrendered my heart and life to Jesus Christ:

Early one morning (October 24, 1959) I decided to listen to the radio for a while. I turned to the Christian radio station and listened to a sermon. The minister was preaching on the great love of God and the mercy offered to us through Jesus Christ. Nothing ever struck me with such force. I opened my heart to God and accepted Christ as my own personal Saviour. The Holy

Spirit flooded my soul with such joy that I wept for over an hour. After the sermon the station played this song written by Elton M. Roth—

> I love the Christ who died on Calv'ry,
> For He washed my sins away;
> He put within my heart a melody,
> And I know it's there to stay.
>
> In my heart there rings a melody,
> There rings a melody with heaven's harmony;
> In my heart there rings a melody,
> There rings a melody of love.
>
> (Copyright 1924. Renewal 1951. Hope Publishing Co., owner. All rights reserved. Used by permission.

This song fully describes the way I felt. How glorious to know Christ died for my sins so I could have a new life in Him.

Our lives testify to all we meet whether or not we are truly Christians. Paul wrote: "But the fruit of the Spirit is love, joy, peace, long-suffering, gentleness, goodness, faith, meekness, temperance: against such there is no law" (Gal. 5:22-23).

Sandra Tanner

Mormonism a Shadow

Hal Hougey stated: "The LDS use the Bible to try to prove the Book of Mormon; then they leave the Bible behind, and urge the prospect to read the Book of Mormon. Does not the Bible tell anything about Christ's mission?" (*Review of Mormon Missionary Handbook*, p.66).

The Mormon church is certainly not built upon the teachings of the Bible. Mormon Apostle LeGrand Richards has alleged that "the 'everlasting gospel' *could not be discovered through reading the Bible alone* . . . this is the only Christian church in the world that did *not have to rely upon the Bible* for its organization and government . . ." (*A Marvelous Work And A Wonder*, p.41).

Although many Christians realize that Mormonism has left the Bible far behind, they are surprised to learn that it is not even based on the *Book of Mormon*. Mormon writer John Henry Evans said:

> . . . the Book of Mormon bears no more basic a relation to the work known as "Mormonism" than the other visions and revelations given in this dispensation. . . . If the Nephite record had not been revealed at all, in this dispensation, it is doubtful whether the body of "Mormon" belief would in any essential particular be different from what it is. I do not say this in disparagement of the Book of Mormon, . . . but I call attention to the fact as show-

ing how little the whole body of belief of the Latter-day Saints really depends on the revelation of the Nephite record (*Improvement Era*, vol. 16, pp.344-45).

Mormon writer Robert J. Matthews has observed that most of present-day Mormonism cannot be found in the writings of the earliest period of Mormonism:

> What did the faithful convert of the Church in 1830-1831 accept as essential "Mormonism"? Was he instructed concerning marriage for time and eternity? Of the three degrees of glory in the resurrection? Was he taught concerning the temple endowment, of baptism for the dead, of patriarchal blessings, or of the word of wisdom? Was he instructed in detail concerning the various offices and quorums in the priesthood from the deacons up through the teachers, priests, elders, seventies, and high priests? Was he taught concerning the quorums of the Presiding Bishopric, the First Council of Seventy, the Patriarch to the Church, the Council of the Twelve, and the First Presidency? To each of these questions the answer must be "no" for the simple reason that these matters had not yet been revealed in this dispensation and were known, if at all, only by the scant mention of some of them in the Bible and the Book of Mormon (*Brigham Young University Studies*, Summer 1971, p.401).

With the changes and additions that have come since those simple days, the understanding of the true message of Christ has long since vanished. Today converts are swarming into the Mormon church, but very few of them really know much about Mormonism. We feel safe in saying that many of them are converted to the social program of the church rather than to its doctrines. Those who were born in the church in many cases "know" it is true but don't know why it is true. Many Mormons will stand up in testimony meeting and dogmatically assert that Joseph Smith was a prophet and that they belong to "the only true church," but very few of them check to make sure that their faith is based on reality. Many members of the Mormon church prefer to let their leaders do their thinking ("when our leaders speak, the thinking has been done"); it is so easy to let someone else do our thinking. The Bible warns: "Thus saith the Lord; Cursed be the man that trusteth in man, and maketh flesh his arm, and whose heart departeth from the Lord" (Jer. 17:5).

We sincerely hope and pray that the Mormon people will begin to awaken to the true message of Christ, realizing that in Him, and Him alone, can we have salvation—salvation that brings genuine deliverance from sin and real fellowship with the God who loved us enough to die for us.

Mormon Plan of
Eternal Progression

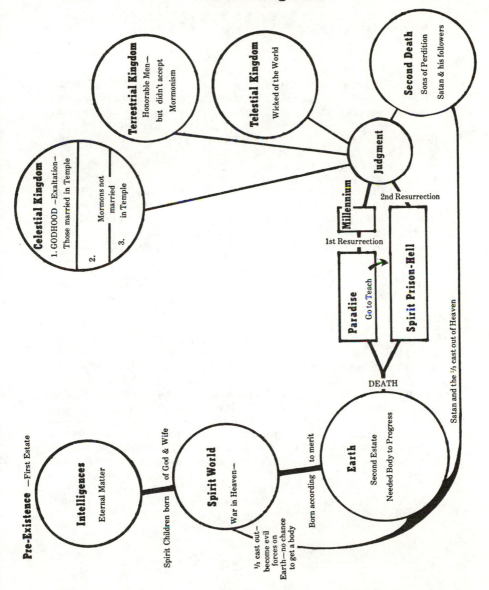

Pre-Existence —First Estate

Intelligences
Eternal Matter

Spirit World
War in Heaven—

Spirit Children born of God & Wife

⅓ cast out—become evil forces on Earth—no chance to get a body

Born according to merit

Earth
Second Estate
Needed Body to Progress

DEATH

Paradise
Go to Teach

Spirit Prison-Hell

1st Resurrection

Satan and the ⅓ cast out of Heaven

Millennium

2nd Resurrection

Judgment

Celestial Kingdom
1. GODHOOD —Exaltation— Those married in Temple
2.
3. Mormons not married in Temple

Terrestrial Kingdom
Honorable Men— but didn't accept Mormonism

Telestial Kingdom
Wicked of the World

Second Death
Sons of Perdition
Satan & his followers

561

THE NEW MORMON BIBLE

On page 385 of this book we pointed out that "The Mormon Church is faced with a peculiar dilemma with regard to Joseph Smith's 'inspired revision.' They cannot reject it entirely without admitting that he was a deceiver. On the other hand, if they were to print the revision and fully endorse it, they would be faced with unsurmountable problems. The contents of the 'inspired revision' actually contradict doctrines that are now taught in the Mormon Church. Therefore, the Mormon Church can neither fully accept nor fully reject the *Inspired Version* of the Bible." Just as this book was going to press, it was rumored that the Church was about to print the *Inspired Version*. As it turned out, however, the new Bible is only a printing of the King James text with "Excerpts from the Prophet Joseph Smith's translation ... Short excerpts are provided in the footnotes; longer excerpts are provided in the Appendix."

Two things should be noted about this Bible: One, the portions taken from Joseph Smith's "translation" have *not* been canonized. The shorter excerpts are merely footnotes to the King James text and the larger ones are separated from the Bible text by 793 pages of material, i.e., a "Topical Guide" and a "Bible Dictionary." Two, the book only contains "excerpts" from Smith's translation. In other words, the Mormon leaders have included only the portions which they deemed advisable. For instance, Joseph Smith's interpolation that Canaan would be made black ("...a veil of darkness shall cover him, that, he shall be known among all men.") is included in a footnote to Genesis 9:26 (page 14), but his revision of Matthew 5:40-41 is neither found in the footnotes nor in the longer excerpts. Joseph Smith had tried to destroy Jesus' teaching about going the extra mile in his *Inspired Revision,* but in doing this he had contradicted the translation he gave in the Book of Mormon (3 Nephi 12:40-41) which reads the same as the King James Version.

In any case, the fact that the Mormon leaders would print only "extracts" from Joseph Smith's translation and still use the King James version leads a person to believe they lack confidence in the work.

Bibliography

Works by Joseph Smith

A Book of Commandments, for the Government of the Church of Christ, Organized according to law, on the 6th of April, 1830. Independence, Mo.: 1833.

The Book of Mormon. Palmyra, N.Y.: 1830. The 1952 edition, which differs somewhat from the 1830 edition, has also been used.

Doctrine and Covenants of the Church of the Latter Day Saints: Carefully Selected from the Revelations of God. Kirtland, Ohio: 1835. The 1952 edition, which differs somewhat from the 1835 edition, has also been used.

History of the Church of Jesus Christ of Latter-Day Saints. Introduction and notes by B. H. Roberts. 6 vols. Salt Lake City: Deseret, 1951.

Inspired Version of the Holy Scriptures (A New Corrected Edition). Independence, Mo.: Reorganized Church of Jesus Christ of Latter Day Saints, 1965.

Joseph Smith's Egyptian Alphabet and Grammar. Photoreprint. Salt Lake City: Modern Microfilm Co., 1966. This publication is a photoreprint of a handwritten manuscript in the L.D.S. Historical Dept.

The Pearl of Great Price. Liverpool, England: 1851. The 1952 edition, which differs somewhat from the 1851 edition, has also been used.

L.D.S. Church Periodicals and Newspapers

(Listed chronologically by year of first issue)

The Evening and The Morning Star. Independence, Mo.: 1832-34.

Latter-Day Saints' Messenger and Advocate. 3 vols. Kirtland, Ohio:1834-37.

Elders' Journal. Kirtland, Ohio, and Far West, Mo.: 1837-38.

Times and Seasons. 6 vols. Nauvoo, Ill.: 1839-46.

L.D.S. Millennial Star. England:1840-1970.

The Wasp. Nauvoo, Ill.: 1842-43.

The Nauvoo Neighbor. Nauvoo, Ill.: 1843-45.

The Deseret News. Salt Lake City: 1850-Present.

Juvenile Instructor. Salt Lake City: 1866-1970.

The Young Woman's Journal. Salt Lake City: 1889-1928.

Improvement Era. Salt Lake City: 1897-1970.

Brigham Young University Studies. Provo, Utah: 1959-Present.

The Ensign. Salt Lake City: 1971-Present.

Books, Pamphlets, and Newspapers

Anderson, Nels. *Desert Saints—The Mormon Frontier in Utah.* Chicago: U. of Chicago Press, 1966.

Andrus, Hyrum L. *Doctrines of the Kingdom.* Salt Lake City: Bookcraft, 1973.

——. *God, Man, and the Universe.* Salt Lake City: Bookcraft, 1968.

——. *Joseph Smith and World Government.* Salt Lake City: Deseret, 1963.

——. *Joseph Smith, the Man and the Seer.* Salt Lake City: Deseret, 1965.

Arbaugh, George B. *Gods, Sex, and Saints—the Mormon Story.* Rock Island, Ill.: Augustana Press, 1957.

Archer, Gleason L., Jr. *A Survey of Old Testament Introduction.* Chicago: Moody, 1968.

Backman, Milton V. *Joseph Smith's First Vision.* Salt Lake City: Bookcraft, 1971.

Bancroft, Hurbert Howe. *History of Utah.* 1889. Reprint. Salt Lake City: Bookcraft, 1964.

Baskin, R.N. *Reminiscences of Early Utah.* Salt Lake City: 1914.

Berrett, La Mar C. *The Wilford C. Wood Collection.* Vol. 1. Salt Lake City: W.C. Wood Foundation, 1972.

Berrett, William E. *The Restored Church.* Salt Lake City: Deseret, 1956.

Biblical Archaeologist. Cambridge, Mass.: 1964.

Bonney, Edward. *Banditti of the Prairies.* Reprint. Norman, Okla.: U. of Okla. Press, 1963.

Book of Abraham Symposium—April 3, 1970. Salt Lake City: L.D.S. Institute of Religion, 1970.

Book of Mormon Institute—December 5, 1959. Provo, Utah: Brigham Young U., 1964 Edition.

Boudinot, Elias. *A Star in the West; or, A Humble Attempt to Discover the Long Lost Tribes of Israel.* Trenton, N.J.: 1816.

Braden, Clark, and Kelly, E. L. *Public Discussion of the Issues*

Between the Reorganized Church of Jesus Christ of Latter-day Saints and the Church of Christ, Disciples, Held in Kirtland, Ohio. Saint Louis: 1884.

Breasted, Henry James. *Development of Religion and Thought in Ancient Egypt.* New York: Harper and Row, 1959.

———. *A History of Egypt.* New York: Bantam, 1967.

Brodie, Fawn M. *No Man Knows My History—The Life of Joseph Smith.* New York: Knopf, 1957; enlarged edition 1971.

Brooks, Juanita, *John Doyle Lee—Zeolot—Pioneer Builder—Scapegoat.* Glendale, Calif.: A.H. Clark, 1962.

Bruce, F. F. *The New Testament Documents—Are They Reliable?* Grand Rapids: Eerdmans, 1967.

Budge, E. A. Wallis. *The Book of the Dead, an English Translation of the Chapters, Hymns, Etc., of the Theban Recension, with Introduction, Notes, Etc.* 3 vols. London: Kegan Paul, Trench, Truebner and Co., 1901.

———. *The Book of the Dead, Facsimiles of the Papyri of Hunefer, Anhai, Kerasher, and Netchemet.* London: 1899.

———. *An Egyptian Hieroglyphic Dictionary.* New York: Ungar, 1920.

Budvarson, Arthur. *The Book of Mormon Examined.* LaMesa, Calif.: Utah Christian Tract, 1959.

Campbell, Alexander. *Christian Baptist.* 7 vols. Buffaloe, Va.: 1827-29.

Clark, James R. *The Story of the Pearl of Great Price.* Salt Lake City: Bookcraft, 1962.

Clarke, Adam. *Clarke's Commentary.* New York: Abingdon.

Clayton, William. *William Clayton's Journal, a Daily Record of the Journey of the Original Company of "Mormon" Pioneers from Nauvoo, Illinois, to the Valley of the Great Salt Lake.* Salt Lake City: 1921.

Clemens, Samuel L. [Mark Twain]. *Roughing It.* New York: 1913.

Compton's Encyclopedia. Chicago: 1970 edition.

Confession of Faith: The Larger and Shorter Catechism. Philadelphia: W. W. Woodward, 1813. The Westminster Confession.

Cross, Frank Moore, Jr. *The Ancient Library of Qumran and Modern Biblical Studies.* New York: Anchor, 1961. Revised edition, Garden City, N.Y.: Doubleday.

Cross, Whitney R. *The Burned-Over District.* New York: Harper and Row, 1965.

Darter, Francis M. *Celestial Marriage.* Salt Lake City: 1937.

Deming, Arthur B. *Naked Truths About Mormonism.* Oakland, Calif.: January and April 1888.

Deseret News 1974 Church Almanac. Salt Lake City: Deseret, 1974.

Des Moines Daily News. Des Moines, Iowa: 1886.

Dialogue: A Journal of Mormon Thought. Arlington, Va.: 1966-present.

Ensign of Liberty. Kirtland, Ohio: 1847-48.

Evangelical Magazine and Gospel Advocate. Utica, N.Y.: 1831.

Evans, R.C. *Forty Years in the Mormon Church—Why I Left It!* Toronto, Canada: R.C. Evans, 1920.

Ferguson, Thomas Stuart. *One Fold and One Shepherd.* Salt Lake City: Olympus, 1962.

Finney, Charles G. *Charles G. Finney—An Autobiography.* Reprint. Westwood, N.J.: Revell, n.d.

Flanders, Robert Bruce. *Nauvoo: Kingdom on the Mississippi.* Urbana, Ill.: U. of Ill. Press, 1965.

Fourteenth Annual Symposium of the Archaeology of the Scriptures. Provo, Utah: Brigham Young U., April 13, 1963.

Fraser, Gordon H. *What Does the Book of Mormon Teach?* Chicago: Moody, 1964.

Frazer's Magazine. London: 1873.

Gentry, Leland H. "A History of the Latter-day Saints in Northern Missouri from 1836 to 1839." Ph.D. dissertation, Brigham Young U., 1965.

Gibbs, Josiah F. *Lights and Shadows of Mormonism.* Salt Lake City: Salt Lake Tribune, 1909.

Goodwin, S.H. *Mormonism and Masonry—A Utah point of View.* Utah: Grand Lodge, F. and A.M. of Utah, 1961.

Gospel Advocate. Buffalo, N.Y.: 1826.

Gospel Herald. Voree, Wisc.: 1848.

Hall, William. *The Abominations of Mormonism Exposed, Containing Many Facts and Doctrines Concerning That Singular People, During Seven Years' Membership with Them; from 1840 to 1847.* Cincinnati: I. Hart, 1852.

Hansen, Klaus J. *Quest for Empire—The Political Kingdom of God and the Council of Fifty in Mormon History,* with a new preface by the author. Lincoln, Nebr.: U. of Nebr., 1974. First edition, East Lansing, Mich.: Mich. State U., 1967.

Harris, William. *Mormonism Portrayed.* Warsaw, Ill.: 1841.

Hield, Charles R., and Ralston, Russell F. *Baptism for the Dead.* Independence, Mo.: Herald, 1951 ed.

Hinckley, Gordon B. *Truth Restored—A Short History of the Church of Jesus Christ of Latter Day Saints.* Salt Lake City: Deseret, 1969.

Hirshan, Stanley P. *The Lion of the Lord.* New York: Knopf, 1969.

Hoekema, Anthony A. *The Four Major Cults.* Grand Rapids: Eerdmans, 1963.

Holy, Sacred, and Divine Roll and Book; From the Lord God of Heaven to the Inhabitants of Earth. Canterbury, N.H.: 1843.

Hougey, Hal. *Archeology and the Book of Mormon.* Concord, Calif.: Pacific, 1976.

―――. *A Parallel—The Basis of the Book of Mormon.* Concord, Calif.: Pacific, 1963.

―――. *Review of Mormon Missionary Handbook.* Concord, Calif.: Pacific, 1969.

Howard, Richard P. *Restoration Scriptures—A Study of Their Textual Development.* Independence, Mo.: Herald, 1969.

Howe, E.D. *Mormonism Unveiled.* Painsville, Ohio: E.D. Howe, 1834.

Hunter, Milton R. *Gospel Through the Ages.* Salt Lake City: Deseret, 1958.

Hyde, John, Jr. *Mormonism: Its Leaders and Designs.* New York: W. P. Fetridge, 1857.

Jackson, Joseph H. *The Adventures and Experience of Joseph H. Jackson in Nauvoo, Disclosing the Depths of Mormon Villainy Practiced in Nauvoo.* Warsaw, Ill.: 1846.

Jenson, Andrew. *Church Chronology.* Salt Lake City: Deseret, 1899.

―――. *The Historical Record.* Vols. 5-9. Salt Lake City: 1886-90.

Johnson, Benjamin F. "Testimony of Joseph Smith's Best Friend." n.p.:n.d. Mimeographed.

Jonas, Larry. *Mormon Claims Examined.* Grand Rapids: Baker, 1961.

Jones, Wesley M. *A Critical Study of Book of Mormon Sources.* Detroit: Harlo, 1964.

Journal of Discourses, by Brigham Young, President of the Church of Jesus Christ of Latter-day Saints, His Two Counsellors, the Twelve Apostles, and Others. 26 vols. Liverpool: 1854-86. Photoreprint. Los Angeles, Calif.: General, 1961.

Journal of History. Vol. 18. Lamoni, Iowa: Reorganized L. D. S., 1908.

Keller, Werner. *The Bible As History.* Translated by William Neil, New York: Morrow, 1957.

Kenyon, Sir Frederick. *Our Bible and the Ancient Manuscripts.* Revised by A. W. Adams. New York: Harper and Row, 1965.

Kirkham, Francis W. *A New Witness for Christ in America.* Vols. 1-2. Independence, Mo.: Press of Zion, 1951. Vol. 2, enlarged edition, Salt Lake City: Utah Printing, 1959.

Ladd, George Eldon. *The New Testament and Criticism.* Grand

Rapids: Eerdmans, 1967.

Lamb, M. T. *The Golden Bible; or, The Book of Mormon, Is it from God?* New York: Ward and Drummond, 1887.

Lee, John D. *Confessions of John D. Lee.* 1880. Photoreprint of *Mormonism Unveiled; or, The Life and Confessions of Mormon Bishop John D. Lee.* Salt Lake City: Modern Microfilm.

————. *Journals of John D. Lee, 1846-47 and 1859.* Edited by Charles Kelly. Salt Lake City: 1938.

————. *A Mormon Chronicle, the Diaries of John D. Lee, 1848-1876.* Edited by Robert Glass Cleland and Junaita Brooks. San Marino, Calif.: Huntington Library, 1955.

Lund, John L. *The Church and the Negro.* John L. Lund, 1967.

Lundwall, N. B. *Temples of the Most High.* Salt Lake City: Bookcraft, 1962.

McConkie, Bruce R. *Mormon Doctrine—A Compendiom of the Gospel*, Revised and enlarged edition. Salt Lake City: Bookcraft, 1966. The 1958 edition, which differs somewhat from the 1966 edition, has also been used.

McGavin, E. Cecil. *Mormonism and Masonry.* Salt Lake City: Bookcraft, 1956.

Macgregor, Daniel. *Changing of the Revelations.* Independence, Mo.: Church of Christ—Temple Lot, n.d.

McKay, David O. *Gospel Ideals.* Salt Lake City: Improvement Era, 1953.

Marquardt, Michael. *The Book of Abraham Papyrus Found: An Answer to Dr. Hugh Nibley's Book "The Message of the Joseph Smith Papyri: An Egyptian Endowment."* Salt Lake City: Modern Microfilm, 1975.

————. *Strange Marriages of Sarah Ann Whitney to Joseph Smith the Mormon Prophet, Joseph C. Kingsbury, and Heber C. Kimball.* Salt Lake City: Modern Microfilm, 1973.

Matthews, Robert J. *Joseph Smith's Revision of the Bible.* Provo, Utah: Brigham Young U. Press, 1969.

Metzger, Bruce Manning. *The Text of the New Testament.* New York: Oxford U. Press, 1964.

Millennial Harbinger. Bethany, Va.: 1831.

Morgan, Capt. William. *Freemasonry Exposed.* 1827. Photoreprint. Chicago: Ezra A. Cook.

Mormon Miscellaneous. Edited by David Martin. Nauvoo, Ill.: 1975.

Nelson, Dee Jay. *The Joseph Smith Papyri.* Salt Lake City: Modern Microfilm, 1968.

————. *The Joseph Smith Papyri, Pt. 2.* Salt Lake City: Modern Microfilm, 1968.

————. *Joseph Smith's Eye of Ra.* Salt Lake City: Modern Microfilm, 1968.

The New Testament in Four Versions. Washington, D.C.: Christianity Today, 1966.

New York Spectator. New York: 1843.

Nibley, Hugh. *An Approach to the Book of Mormon.* Salt Lake City: Deseret, 1957.

————. *The Message of the Joseph Smith Papyri: An Egyptian Endowment.* Salt Lake City: Deseret, 1975.

————. *The Myth Makers.* Salt Lake City: Bookcraft, 1961.

————. *Since Cumorah.* Salt Lake City: Deseret, 1967.

————. *What Is a Temple?* Provo, Utah: Brigham Young U. Press, 1968.

————. *The World and the Prophets.* Salt Lake City: Deseret, 1954.

Nibley, Preston. *Joseph Smith the Prophet.* Salt Lake City: Deseret, 1944.

Noall, Claire. *Intimate Disiciple, a Portrait of Willard Richards.* Salt Lake City: U. of Utah Press, 1957.

Ohio Star. 1831.

The Olive Branch. Springfield, Ill.: 1849.

Overland Monthly. San Francisco: 1890.

Paine, Thomas. *The Age of Reason.* New York: Thomas Paine Foundation.

Palmyra Register. New York: 1819.

Parkin, Max. *Conflict at Kirtland—A Study of the Nature and Causes of External and Internal Conflict of the Mormons in Ohio Between 1830 and 1838.* Salt Lake City: Max Parkin, 1966. Originally a thesis, Brigham Young U., 1966.

Pearl of Great Price Conference. December 10, 1960. Provo, Utah: Brigham Young U., 1964.

Petersen, LaMar. *Hearts Made Glad—The Charges of Intemperance Against Joseph Smith the Mormon Prophet.* Salt Lake City: LaMar Petersen, 1975.

————. *Problems in Mormon Text.* Concord, Calif.: Pacific, 1957.

Petersen, Mark E. *As Translated Correctly.* Salt Lake City: Deseret, 1966.

Pfeiffer, Charles F., ed. *The Biblical World.* Grand Rapids: Baker. 1966.

Pratt, Orson. *Orson Pratt's Works.* Liverpool: 1851.

————. *Pamphlets by Orson Pratt.* n.p.:n.d.

————. *The Seer.* Washington, D.C.: 1853-54, Photoreprint. Salt Lake City: Eugene Wagner.

Pratt, Parley P. *Key to the Science of Theology.* Rev. ed. Salt

Lake City: Deseret, 1965. Originally, Liverpool: F.D. Richards, 1855.

———. *Mormonism Unveiled—Truth Vindicated*. New York: 1838.

———. *Writings of Parley P. Pratt*. Salt Lake City: Parker Pratt Robison, 1952.

Priest, Josiah. *The Wonders of Nature and Providence Displayed*. Albany, N.Y.: 1825.

Proceedings Before the Committee on Privileges and Elections of the United States Senate in the Matter of the Protests Against the Right of Honorable Reed Smoot, a Senator from the State of Utah, to Hold His Seat. Washington, D.C.: U.S. Government Printing Office, 1904. Referred to through out this work as the "Reed Smoot Case."

Progress in Archaeology—An Anthology. Edited by Ross T. Christensen. Provo, Utah: Brigham Young U., 1963.

Register of the Joseph Smith Collection in the Church Archives. Salt Lake City: L.D.S. Historical Dept., 1973.

The Return. Edited by Ebenezer Robinson. Davis City, Iowa: 1889.

Reynolds, Arch. *How Did Joseph Smith Translate?* Springville, Utah: 1952.

Reynolds, George. *A Complete Concordance of the Book of Mormon*. 1899. Reprint. Salt Lake City: Deseret, 1957.

———. *Myth of the "Manuscript Found."* Salt Lake City: Juvenile Instructor, 1883.

———, and Sjodahl, Janne M. *Commentary on the Book of Mormon*. Edited and arranged by Philip C. Reynolds. Vol. 1. Salt Lake City: Deseret, 1956.

Richards, LeGrand. *Marvelous Work and a Wonder*. Salt Lake City: Deseret, 1966.

Richardson, Arthur M. *That Ye May Not Be Deceived, a Discussion of the Racial Problem*. Salt Lake City: n.p., n.d.

Richardson's Monitor of Free-Masonry. Photoreprint, Chicago: Ezra A. Cook, 1968.

Roberts, B.H. *Comprehensive History of the Church*. 6 vols. Salt Lake City: Deseret, 1930.

———. *Life of John Taylor*. 1892. Reprint. Salt Lake City: Bookcraft, 1963.

———. *Outlines of Ecclesiastical History*. Salt Lake City: George Q. Cannon, 1895.

———, ed. *First Year Book in the Seventy's Course in Theology*. Salt Lake City: Deseret, 1907 and 1931.

Rocky Mountain Mason. Edited by George S. Sloan. Billings, Mont.: 1956.

Salt Lake Tribune. Salt Lake City: 1871-Present.

Sangamo Journal. Illinois: 1842.

Seminar on the Prophet Joseph Smith. Provo, Utah: Brigham Young U. Lecture Series, February 18, 1961.

Senate Document 189, 26th Congress, 2nd Session, 1841; The Testimony given before the judge of the fifth judicial circuit of the Sate of Missouri, on the trial of Joseph Smith Jr., and others, for high treason, and other crimes against that State.

Shook, Charles A. *True Origin of the Book of Mormon.* Cincinnati, Ohio: 1914.

Smith, Elias. *The Life, Conversion, Preaching, Travels, and Sufferings of Elias Smith.* Portsmouth, N.H.: 1816.

Smith, Ethan. *View of the Hebrews; or, The Tribes of Israel in America.* Poultney, Vt.: Smith and Shute, 1825.

Smith, Joseph Fielding. *Answers to Gospel Questions.* 3 vols. Salt Lake City: Deseret, 1957, 1958, 1960.

———. *Doctrines of Salvation.* 3 vols. Salt Lake City: Bookcraft, 1959.

———. *Essentials in Church History.* Salt Lake City: Deseret, 1942.

———. *Origin of the "Reorganized" Church and the Question of Succession.* Salt Lake City: Deseret, 1909.

———. *Teachings of the Prophet Joseph Smith.* Salt Lake City: Deseret, 1949.

———. *The Way to Perfection.* Salt Lake City: Genealogical Society of Utah, 1931.

Smith, Joseph Fielding, Jr. *Religious Truths Defined.* Salt Lake City: Bookcraft, 1959.

Smith, Lucy. *Biographical Sketches of Joseph Smith the Prophet.* Liverpool, London: Orson Pratt, 1853. Reprint under the title *History of Joseph Smith by His Mother.* Edited by Preston Nibley. Salt Lake City: Bookcraft, 1954.

Spalding, F. S. *Joseph Smith, Jr., as a Translator.* Salt Lake City: Arrow, 1912.

Sperry, Sidney B. *Ancient Records Testify in Papyrus and Stone.* 1938-39 Course of Study, Adult Department, M.I.A. Salt Lake City: 1938.

———. *The Problems of the Book of Mormon.* Salt Lake City: Bookcraft, 1964.

Stenhouse, Fanny (Mrs. T.B.H. Stenhouse). *Tell It All, the Story of a Life's Experience in Mormonism.* Hartford, Conn.: A. D. Worthington, 1874.

Stenhouse, T. B. H. *The Rocky Mountain Saints—A Full and Complete History of the Mormons. . . .* New York: D. Appleton, 1873.

Stewart, F. L. *Exploding the Myth About Joseph Smith, the Mormon Prophet.* New York: House of Stewart, 1967.

Stewart, John J. *Brigham Young and His Wives.* Salt Lake City: Mercury, 1961.

——. *Joseph Smith the Mormon Prophet.* Salt Lake City: Mercury, 1966.

——, and Berrett, William E. *Mormonism and the Negro.* Bookmark, 1960.

Stout, Hosea. *On the Mormon Frontier, the Diary of Hosea Stout.* Edited by Juanita Brooks. Salt Lake City: U. of Utah Press, 1964. Vol. 1, 1844-1848. Vol. 2, 1848-1861.

Susquehenna Register. Pennsylvania: 1834.

Tanner, Jerald, and Tanner, Sandra. *The Bible and Mormon Doctrine.* Salt Lake City: Modern Microfilm, 1971.

——. *Changes in Joseph Smith's History.* Salt Lake City: Modern Microfilm, 1965.

——. *Joseph Smith and Polygamy.* Salt Lake City: Modern Microfilm, 1966.

——. *Joseph Smith's Strange Account of the First Vision.* Salt Lake City: Modern Microfilm, 1965.

——. *A Look at Christianity.* Salt Lake City: Modern Microfilm, 1971.

——. *Mormonism like Watergate.* Salt Lake City: Modern Microfilm, 1974.

——. *Mormonism–Shadow or Reality?* Revised and enlarged ed. Salt Lake City: Modern Microfilm, 1972.

——. *The Mormon Kingdom.* Vols. 1-2, Salt Lake City: Modern Microfilm, 1969-1971.

——. *Mormon Scriptures and the Bible.* Salt Lake City: Modern Microfilm, 1970.

——. *3,913 Changes in the Book of Mormon.* Salt Lake City: Modern Microfilm, 1965.

Temple Lot Case. (In the Circuit Court of the United States Western District of Missouri. . . . The Reorganized Church of Jesus Christ of Latter Day Saints, Complainant vs The Church of Christ at Independence, Missouri . . . . Complainant's Abstract of Pleading and Evidence.) Lamoni, Iowa: Herald, 1893.

Thompson, J. A. *The Bible and Archaeology.* Grand Rapids: Eerdmans, 1962.

Todd, Jay M. *The Saga of the Book of Abraham.* Salt Lake City: Deseret, 1969.

True Latter Day Saint's Herald. Lamoni, Iowa: Reorganized Church of Jesus Christ of Latter Day Saints, 1860-76. Continued thereafter as *Saints Herald.*

Tullidge, Edward. *Women of Mormondom*. New York: 1877.

Turner, Wallace. *The Mormon Establishment*. Boston: Houghton Mifflin, 1966.

Uniform System for Teaching Families. Salt Lake City: Deseret, 1973. Copyright by Corp. of the President of the Church of Jesus Christ of Latter-day Saints.

Utah Holiday Magazine. Salt Lake City: 1976.

The Utah Survey. Social Service Commission of the Episcopal Church of Utah, 1913.

Van Wagoner, Merrill Y. *Inspired Revision of the Bible*. Revised ed. Salt Lake City: Deseret, 1963.

Walters, Wesley P. *New Light on Mormon Origins from the Palmyra (N.Y.) Revival*. LaMesa, Calif.: Utah Christian Tract, 1967.

Warsaw Signal. Illinois: 1845.

Washburn, J. N. *Contents, Structure, and Authorship of the Book of Mormon*. Salt Lake City: Bookcraft, 1954.

Wayne Sentinel. Palmyra, N.Y.: 1825.

Western Humanities Review. Salt Lake City: U. of Utah, 1959.

Weston, Joseph H. *These Amazing Mormons*. Salt Lake City: Western, 1961

Whalen, William J. *The Latter-day Saints in the Modern Day World*. New York: John Day, 1964.

Whitmer, David. *An Address to All Believers in Christ*. Richmond, Mo.: David Whitmer, 1887.

Whitmer, John. *John Whitmer's History*. Salt Lake City: Modern Microfilm. From typed copy of original at Reorganized Latter Day Saints Library.

Whitney, Orson F. *Life of Heber C. Kimball*. Salt Lake City: Kimball Family, 1888.

Widtsoe, John A. *Evidences and Reconciliations*. Arranged by G. Homer Durham. 3 vols. in 1. Salt Lake City: Bookcraft, 1960.

———. *Joseph Smith—Seeker After Truth*. Salt Lake City: Deseret, 1951.

Wilson, John A. *The Culture of Ancient Egypt*. Chicago: U. of Chicago Press, 1965.

Wyl, W. *Mormon Portraits*. Salt Lake City, 1886.

Young, Kimball. *Isn't One Wife Enough? The Story of Mormon Polygamy*. New York: Holt, 1954.

Zion's Harbinger and Baneemy's Organ. St. Louis: 1853.

INDEX

577

Smith, Joseph

accepts Unversalist doctrine of all being saved though Book of Mormon teaches endless punishment of wicked, 505-8

accepts Roman Catholic concept of a purgatory or preparatory stage after death, 508-9

accused of "affair" with Fanny Alger, 215-16

accuses *Book of Mormon* witnesses of wickedness, 96-99

adds to Genesis over 800 words containing his own name, 391-92

adds to Genesis words discrediting blacks, 392

advises Robert Thompson to get drunk, 474

alters revelations, 39, 55, 65-66

approves concubinage, 281

argues with wife over polygamy, 218, 230

asks for other men's wives, 236

asks United States to let him raise 100,000 men, 454-55

beats up a number of men, 451-52

becomes a Mason and incorporates Masonic ritual into temple ceremony, 534-47

begins writing *History of the Church*, 398

boasts that he did a better job of holding together the church than Jesus, 460

"Book of Breathings"—pagan funerary text from Egypt, 344, 346-47

Book of Moses "drastically changed," 395-96

breaks laws of land by living in polygamy, 219-20

changes his concept of Godhead, 162-63

changes text of *Book of Mormon*, 128-32

claims restoration of priesthood by John the Baptist and Peter, James, and John, 442-47

claims there is a Heavenly Mother, 178

claims to be a god to his people, 432

copies *Book of Mormon* characters for Harris to take to Anthon, 142

curses woman for telling Emma he went into a certain house, 230

declares God only an exalted man and that men can become Gods, 173

departs from *Book of Mormon's* teaching of only one God, 172-73

departs from *Book of Mormon's* teachings, 147

diaries suppressed because they discredit *History*, 412-14

dictates another contradictory account of first vision, 155-56

disobeys Word of Wisdom by drinking wine and beer and using tobacco, 470-72

earlier revelation commands Mormons to marry Indians to make them "white" and "delightsome," 207-8

encourages breaking Word of Wisdom, 33

encourages cursing of enemies, 484-85

engages in money-digging and "glass looking," 67-70

enjoys wrestling and other tests of strength, 450-51

entertains by describing ancient inhabitants before translating *Book of Mormon*, 125

establishes baptism for the dead, 512-14

establishes a secret temple ritual with washings, anointings, garments, signs, tokens, and penalties, 524-29

587